AF207890

Bretagne

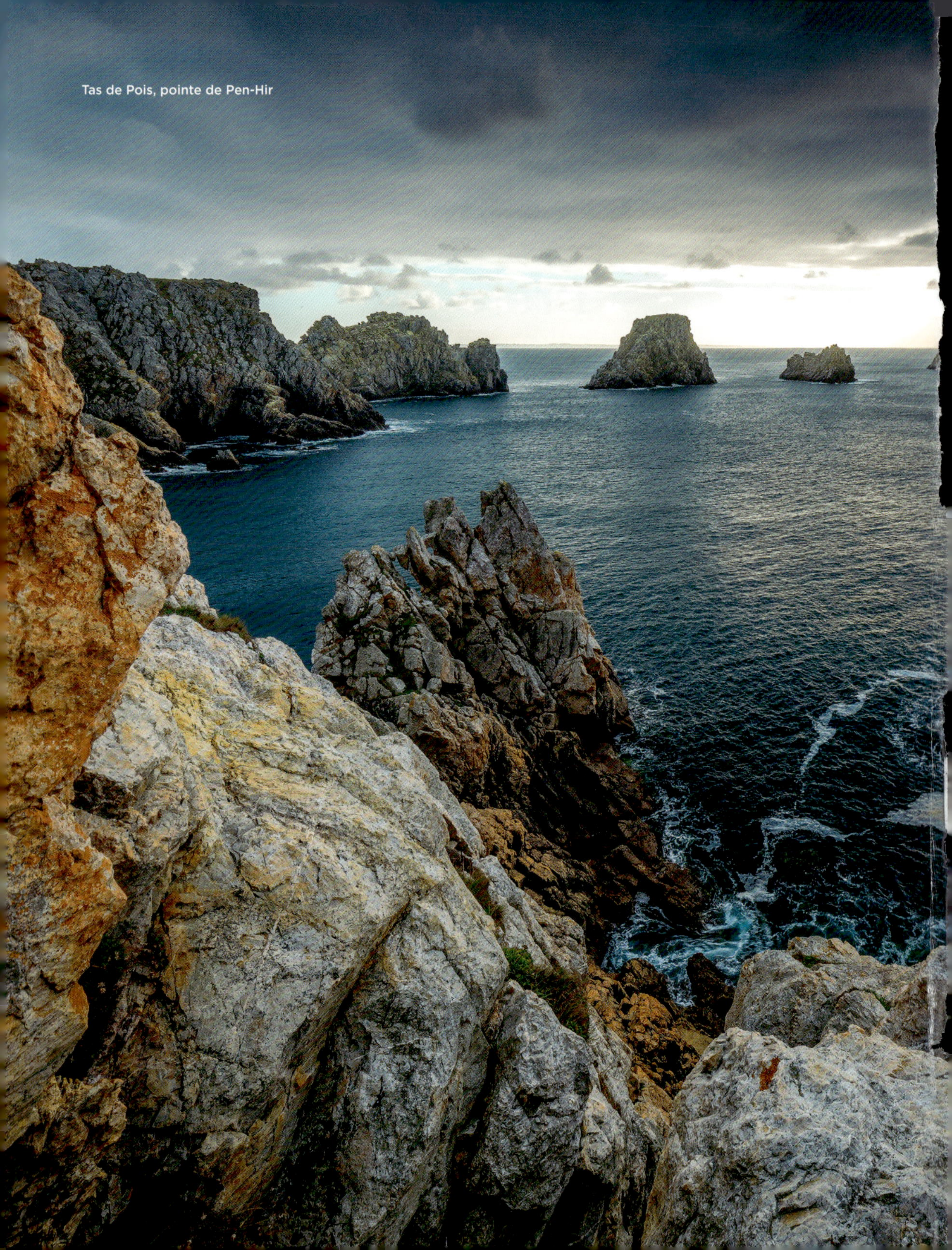

Tas de Pois, pointe de Pen-Hir

Bretagne

Catherine Laulhère

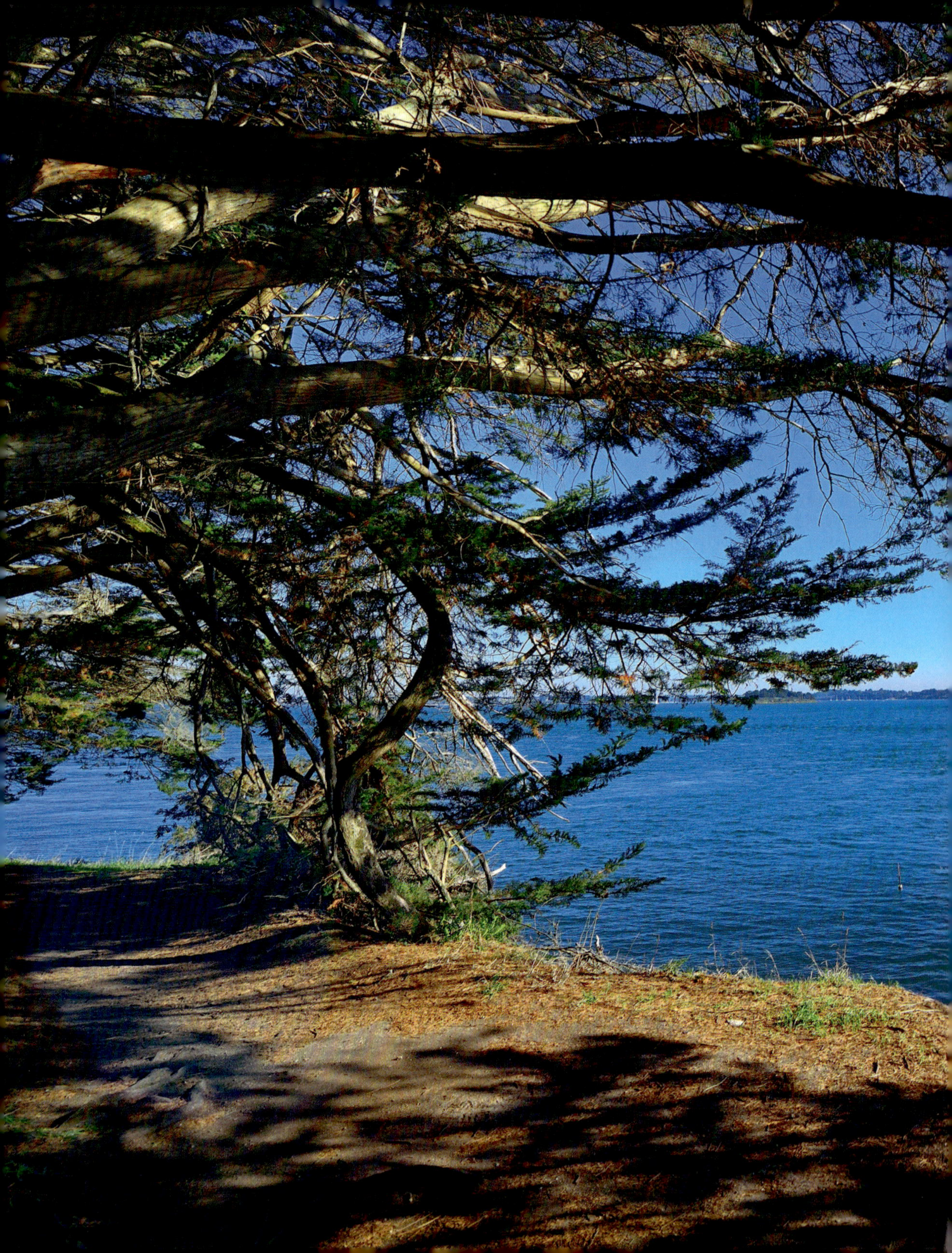

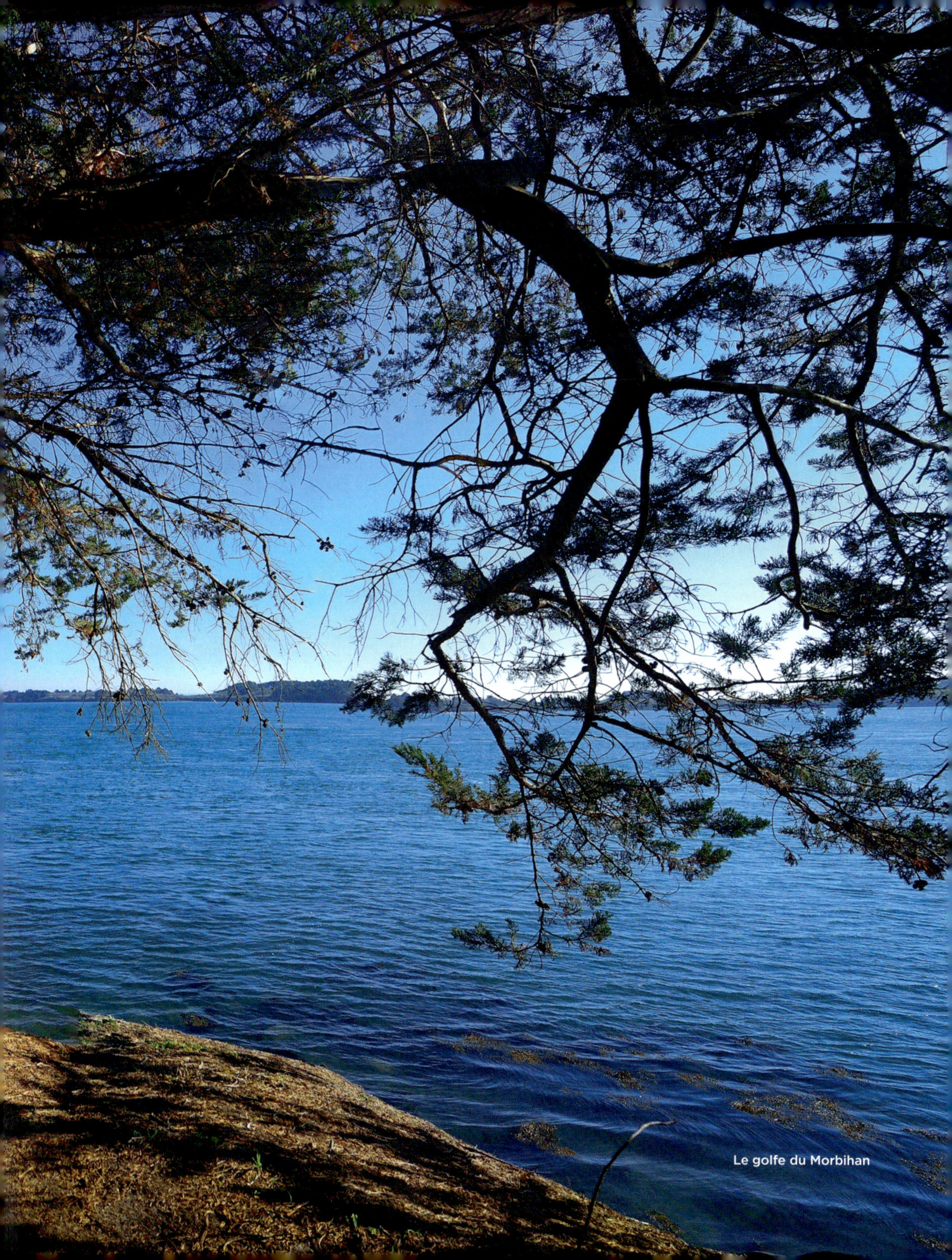

Le golfe du Morbihan

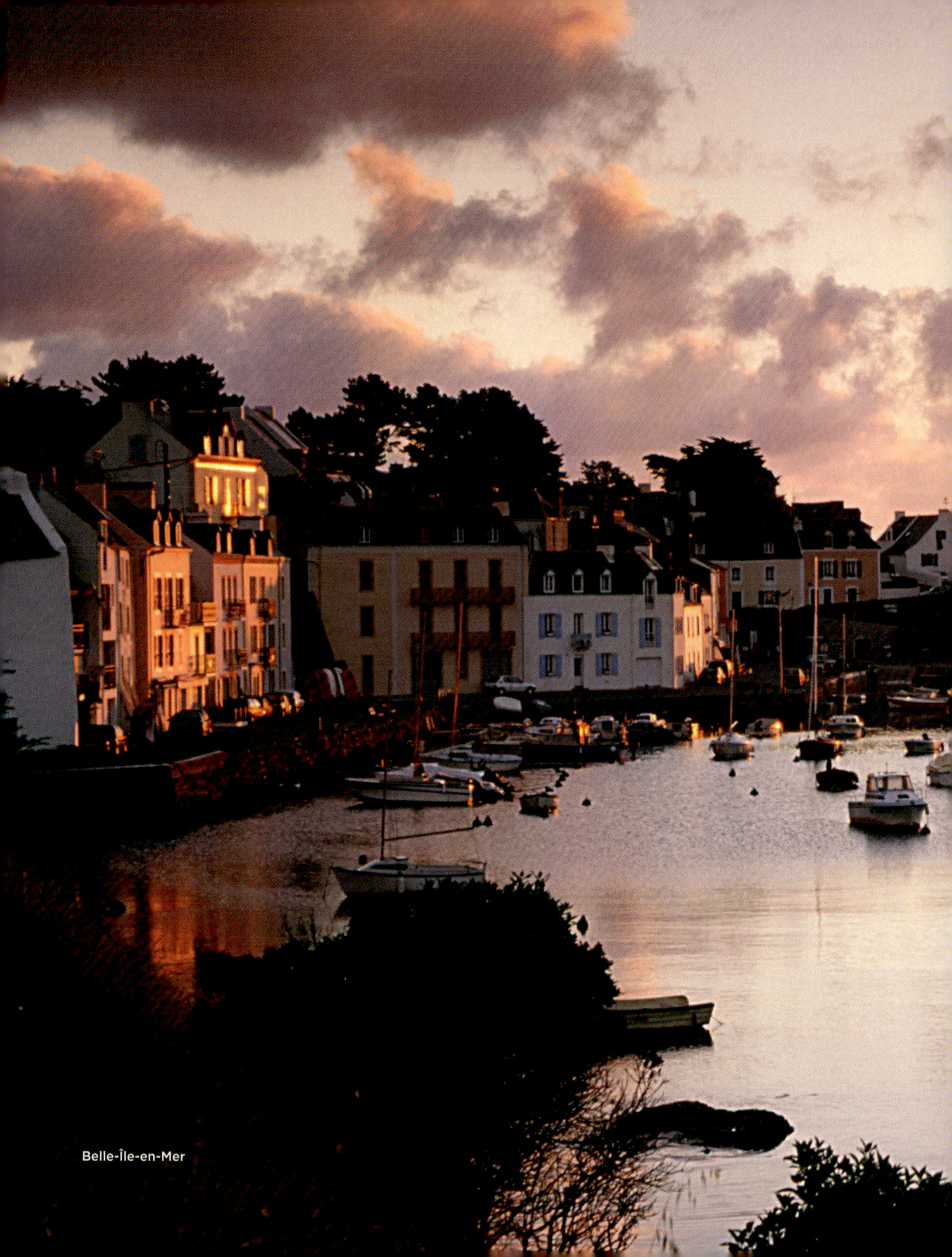
Belle-Île-en-Mer

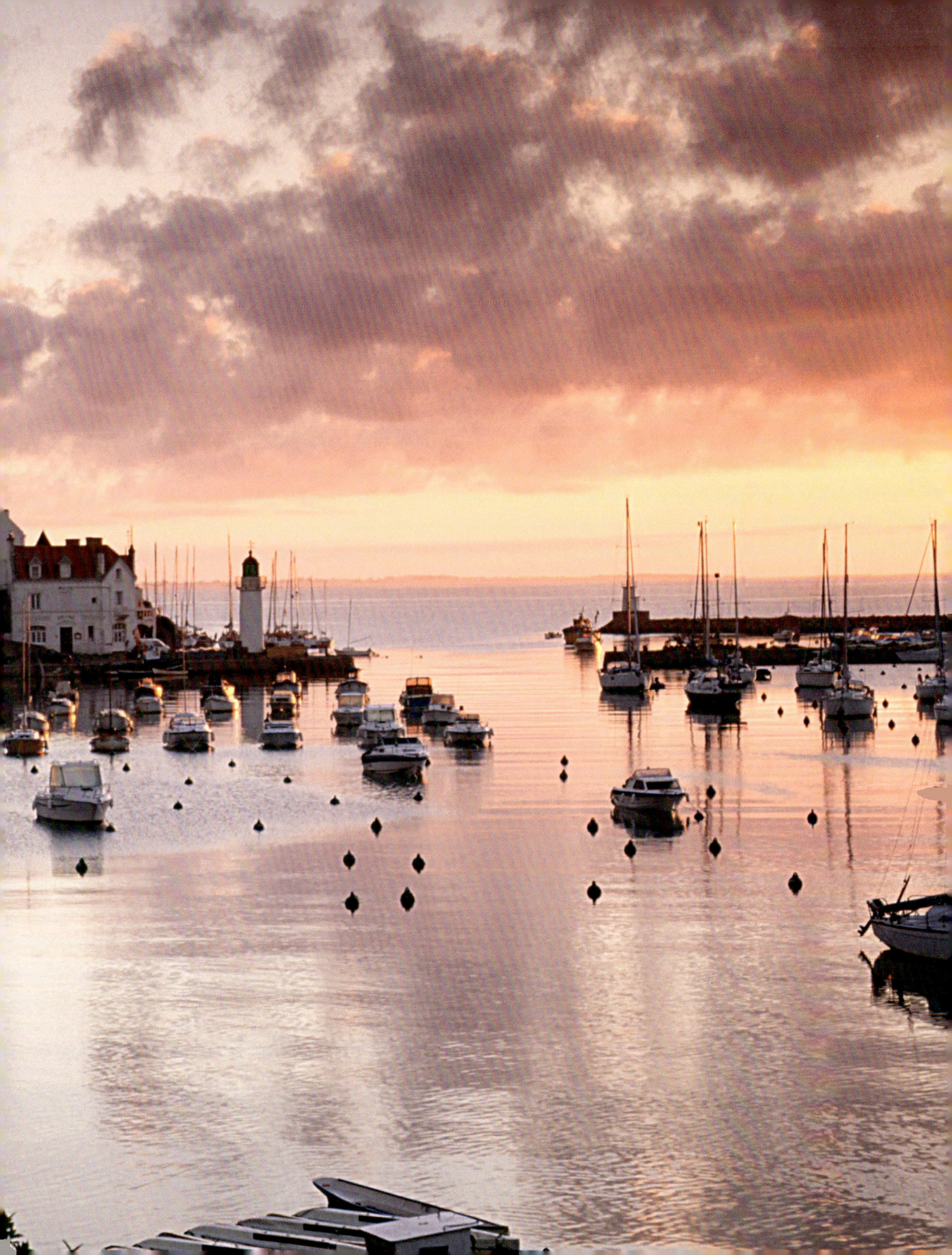

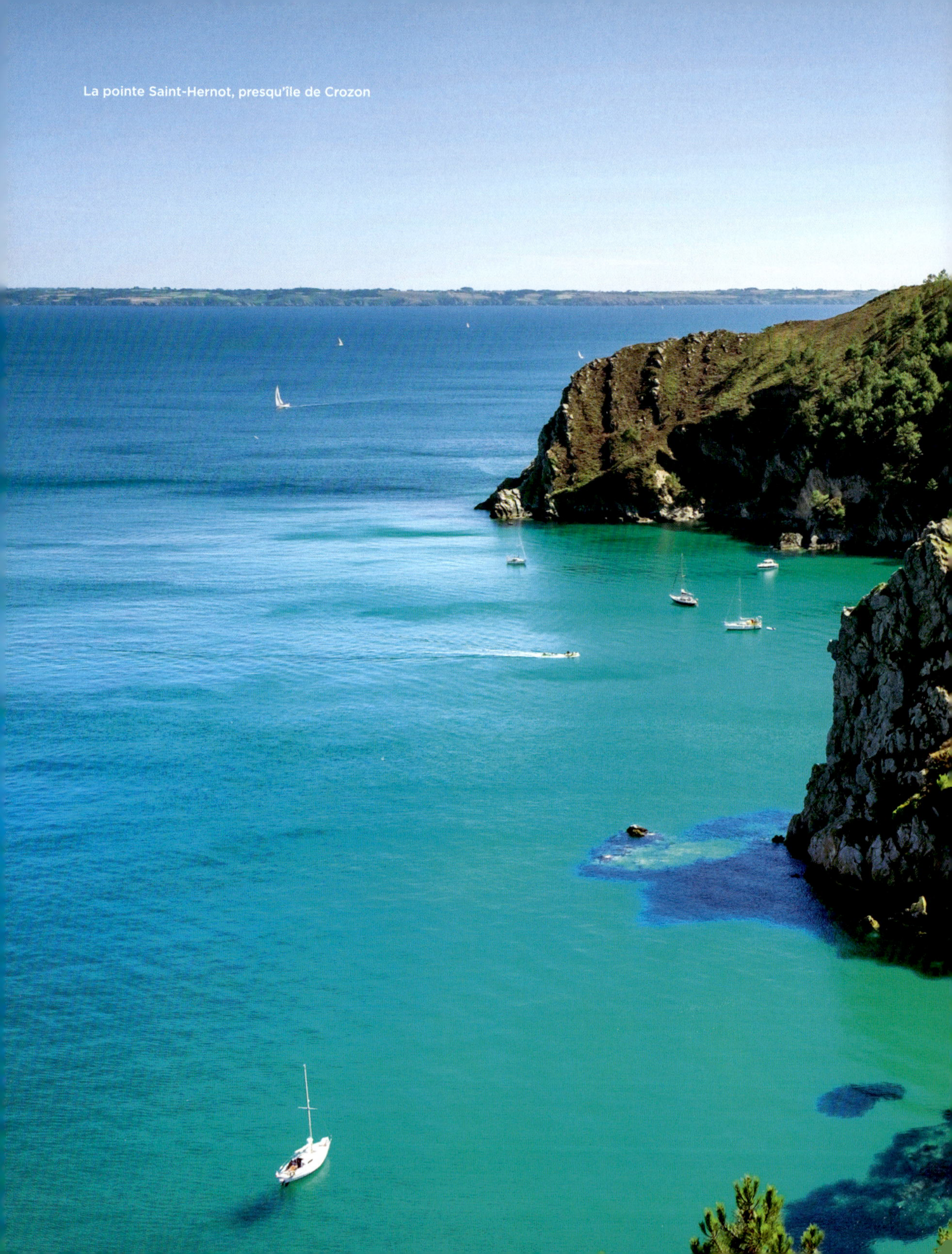

La pointe Saint-Hernot, presqu'île de Crozon

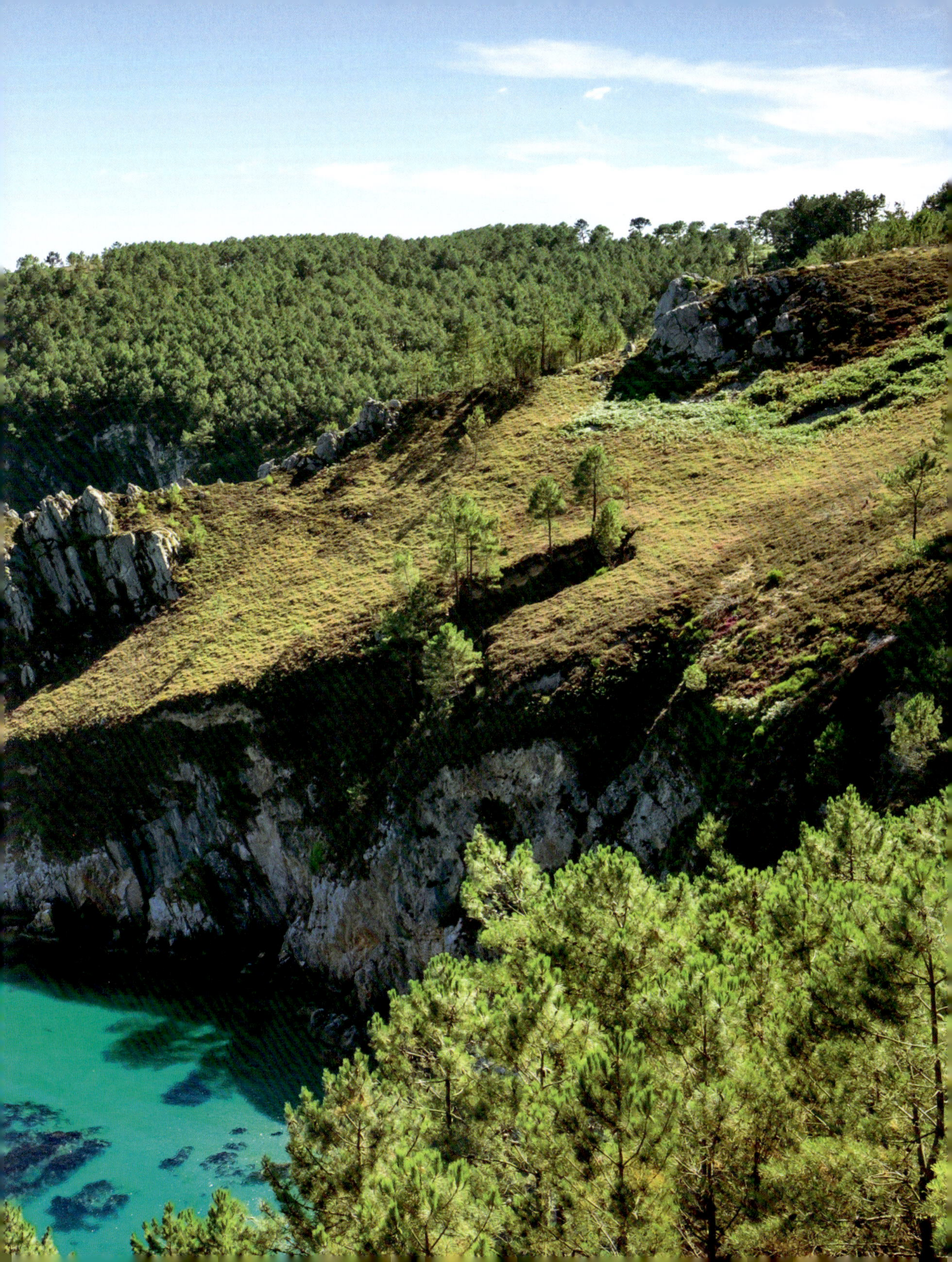

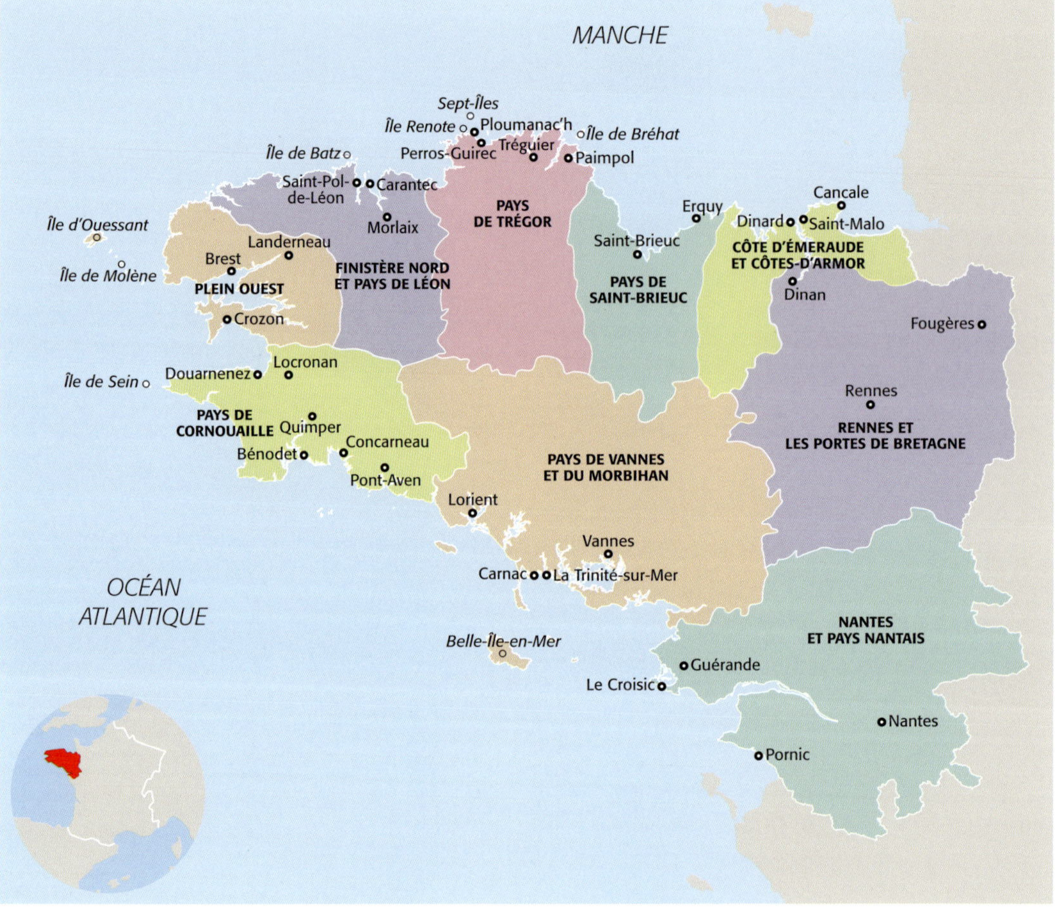

MANCHE
OCÉAN ATLANTIQUE
Île d'Ouessant
Île de Molène
Île de Sein
Sept-Îles
Île Renote
Ploumanac'h
Île de Bréhat
Perros-Guirec
Tréguier
Paimpol
Île de Batz
Saint-Pol-de-Léon
Carantec
Morlaix
PAYS DE TRÉGOR
Erquy
Cancale
Dinard
Saint-Malo
Saint-Brieuc
CÔTE D'ÉMERAUDE ET CÔTES-D'ARMOR
Landerneau
Brest
FINISTÈRE NORD ET PAYS DE LÉON
PAYS DE SAINT-BRIEUC
Dinan
PLEIN OUEST
Fougères
Crozon
Locronan
Douarnenez
Rennes
PAYS DE CORNOUAILLE
Quimper
Concarneau
RENNES ET LES PORTES DE BRETAGNE
Bénodet
Pont-Aven
PAYS DE VANNES ET DU MORBIHAN
Lorient
Vannes
Carnac
La Trinité-sur-Mer
Belle-Île-en-Mer
NANTES ET PAYS NANTAIS
Guérande
Le Croisic
Nantes
Pornic

Contents Sommaire Inhalt Índice Índice Inhoud

Introduction

Idyllic, maritime and rich in history - Brittany impresses with its diversity and authenticity! Immerse yourself in the colours of the countryside, become intoxicated by the sight of the sea and discover a unique cuisine. Brittany invites you to recharge your batteries between the emerald green sea, and the moors, cliffs, medieval towns, prehistoric sites, castles, rivers and floodgates. There are numerous nature reserves of exceptional beauty.

Brittany can be experienced by water, by land, on foot or by bicycle.

Like a trident, it extends over a length of 300 km with a diameter of 100 km into the Atlantic Ocean. The ancient kingdom, which first became a duchy and then a region of France, has fascinated visitors for centuries with its landscape full of headlands and rugged granite cliffs, deep inlets, rocky coves and sheltered beaches of sand and gravel. It is difficult to find a more rugged and unpredictable coast than that of Brittany, with its remarkable variety of landscapes.

Introduction

Bucolique, maritime et patrimoniale, la Bretagne s'offre dans sa plénitude et son authenticité! Il faut piocher dans sa palette de couleurs, s'enivrer d'embruns et goûter les saveurs de sa gastronomie… Expérience de tous nos sens, notre découverte de la Bretagne est prétexte à se ressourcer entre mer émeraude, landes, falaises, cités médiévales, vestiges de la Préhistoire, châteaux, rivières ou écluses. Les réserves naturelles sont nombreuses et les sites d'exception d'une rare beauté. La Bretagne se vit à la fois sur l'eau, sur terre, à pied ou à vélo.

Longue de 300 km environ, large de plus de 100 km, la Bretagne s'avance, tel un trident, dans l'océan Atlantique. Cet ancien royaume, devenu duché puis région, a changé de statut au fil des siècles, mais sa physionomie est restée la même, hérissée de caps et de falaises, découpée en pointes granitiques, en abers, en criques rocheuses, en baies abritées et en plages de sable et de galets. Difficile de trouver un rivage plus fracturé, plus imprévisible que le littoral breton et une variété de paysages aussi remarquable.

Einführung

Idyllisch, maritim und reich an Geschichte – die Bretagne besticht durch ihre Vielfalt und Authentizität! Tauchen Sie in die Farben der Landschaft ein, berauschen Sie sich am Anblick des Meeres und entdecken Sie eine einmalige Gastronomie. Die Bretagne lädt dazu ein, zwischen smaragdgrünem Meer, Mooren, Klippen, mittelalterlichen Städten, prähistorischen Orten, Burgen, Flüssen oder Schleusen neue Energie zu tanken. Es gibt zahlreiche Naturschutzgebiete, die von außergewöhnlicher Schönheit sind. Die Bretagne lässt sich zu Wasser, zu Lande, zu Fuß oder mit dem Fahrrad erleben.

Wie ein Dreizack reicht sie auf einer Länge von 300 km mit einem Durchmesser von 100 km in den Atlantik hinein. Das alte Königreich, das erst zu einem Herzogtum und anschließend zu einer Region Frankreichs wurde, fasziniert Besucher seit Jahrhunderten durch seine Landschaft voller Landspitzen und Klippen aus schroffen Granitfelsen, tief ins Landesinnere eindringende Meeresarme, felsige Buchten und geschützte Strände aus Sand und Kies. Es ist schwierig, eine zerklüftetere und unberechenbarere Küste zu finden als die bretonische und eine so bemerkenswerte Vielfalt an Landschaften.

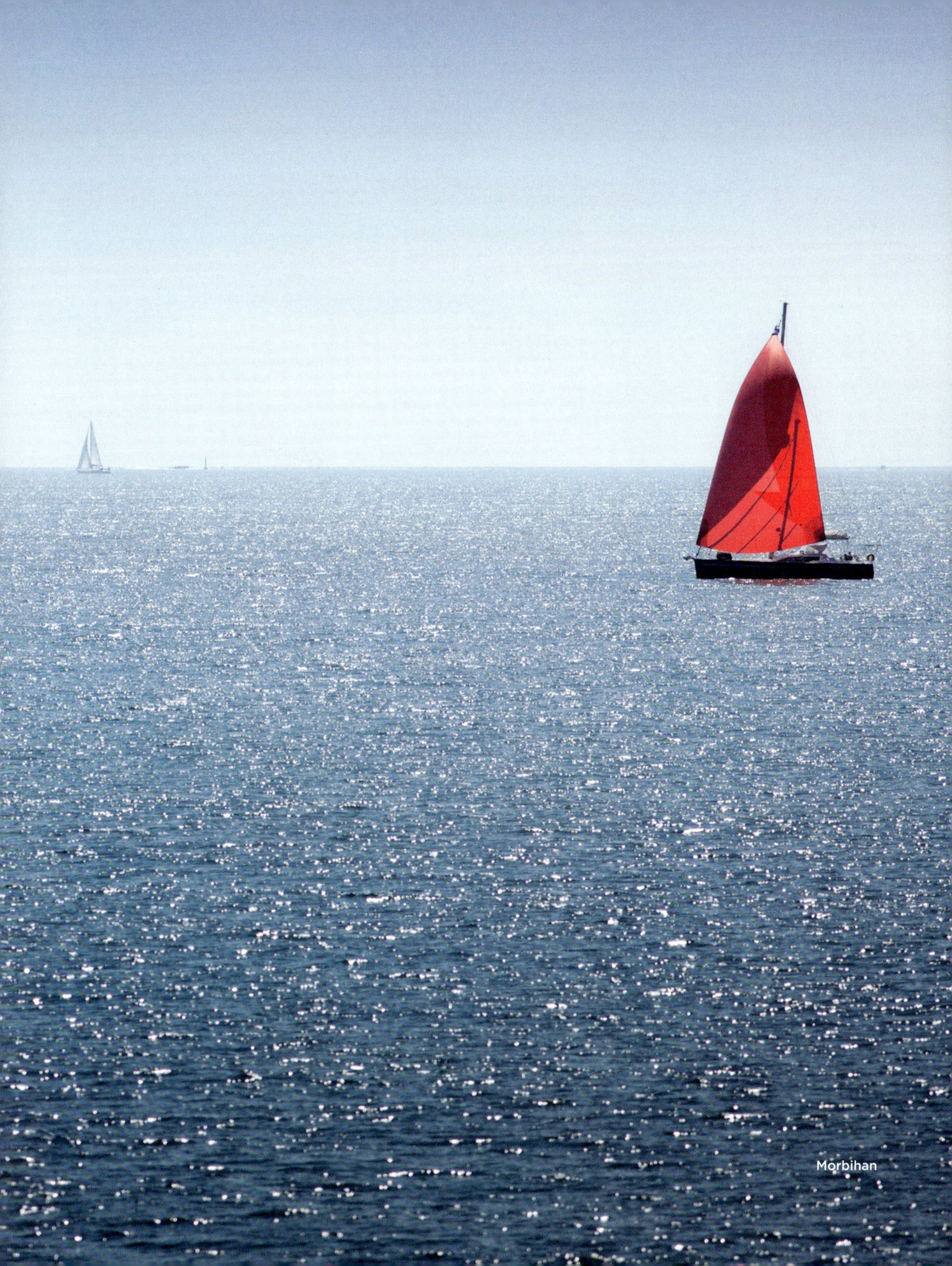

Morbihan

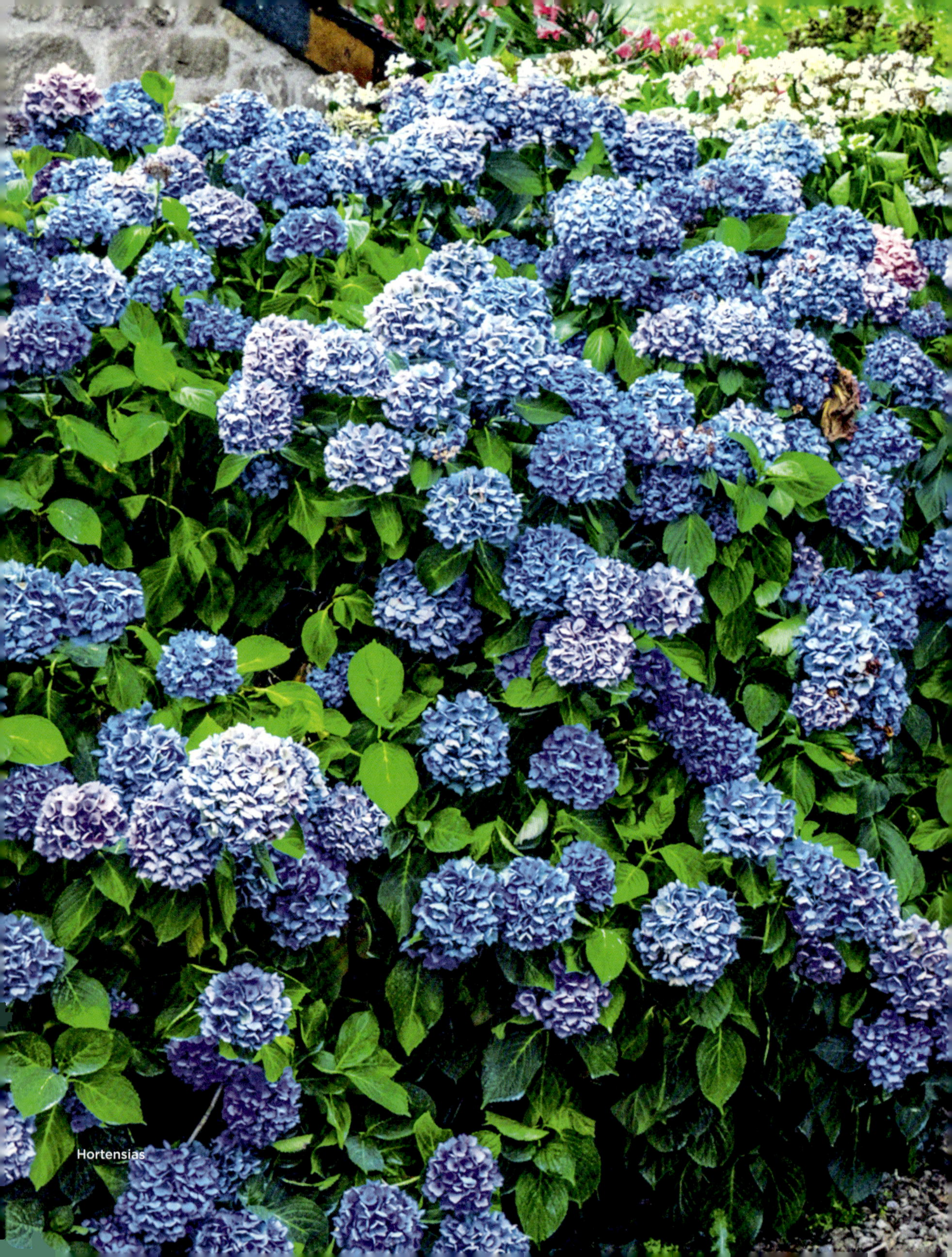
Hortensias

Introducción

Idílica, marítima y rica en historia, ¡Bretaña impresiona por su diversidad y autenticidad! Sumérjase en los colores del paisaje, déjese embriagar por la vista del mar y descubra una gastronomía única. Bretaña le invita a recargar las pilas entre el mar verde esmeralda, los páramos, los acantilados, las ciudades medievales, los sitios prehistóricos, los castillos, los ríos y las esclusas. Existen numerosas reservas naturales de excepcional belleza. Bretaña se puede vivir en el agua, en la tierra, a pie o en bicicleta. Como un tridente, se extiende sobre una longitud de 300 km con un diámetro de 100 km en el océano Atlántico. El antiguo reino, que primero se convirtió en ducado y luego en región de Francia, ha fascinado a los visitantes durante siglos con su paisaje lleno de cabos y acantilados de escarpadas rocas de granito, profundas sondas interiores, calas rocosas y playas protegidas de arena y grava. Es difícil encontrar una costa más escarpada e impredecible que la costa bretona y una variedad de paisajes tan notable.

Introdução

Idílica, marítima e rica em história - a Bretanha impressiona pela sua diversidade e autenticidade! Mergulhe nas cores da paisagem, deixe-se fascinar pela vista de mar e descubra uma gastronomia única. A Bretanha convida-o a recarregar energias por um mar verde-esmeralda, por pântanos, penhascos, cidades medievais, por sítios pré-históricos, castelos, rios e eclusas. Existem inúmeras reservas naturais de excepcional beleza. A Bretanha deixa-se desfrutar por água, por terra, a pé ou de bicicleta. Como um tridente, dominado pelo mar, estende-se por uma superfície de 300 km de comprimento e 100 km de diâmetro pelo Oceano Atlântico dentro. O antigo reino, que primeiro se tornou um ducado e, em seguida, uma região da França, tem fascinado os visitantes durante séculos com a sua paisagem cheia de cabos, pontas e falésias de granito escarpado, profundos braços de mar e baías, enseadas rochosas e praias abrigadas de areia e calhau. É difícil encontrar uma costa mais acidentada e imprevisível do que a costa bretã e uma variedade tão notável de paisagens.

Inleiding

Idyllisch, maritiem en rijk aan geschiedenis – Bretagne maakt indruk door zijn veelzijdigheid en authenticiteit! Onderga de kleuren van het landschap, raak in de ban van de zee en ontdek een unieke gastronomie. Bretagne nodigt u uit om tussen de smaragdgroene zee, heidevelden, klippen, middeleeuwse stadjes, prehistorische plaatsen, kastelen, rivieren en sluizen nieuwe energie op te doen. Er zijn talrijke beschermde natuurgebieden, die allemaal van uitzonderlijke schoonheid zijn.
Bretagne kan worden beleefd vanaf het water, over land, te voet of op de fiets.
Als een driehoek steekt Bretagne over een lengte van 300 km en met een diameter van 100 km de Atlantische Oceaan in. Het oude koninkrijk, dat eerst een hertogdom en daarna een regio van Frankrijk werd, fascineert bezoekers al eeuwenlang met zijn landschap vol met landpunten en klippen van ruig graniet, diep landinwaarts stekende zeearmen, rotsachtige baaien en beschutte stranden van zand en grind. Het is moeilijk kust met meer spleten en grotere onvoor-spelbaarheid te vinden dan de Bretonse of een even opmerkelijke verscheidenheid aan landschappen.

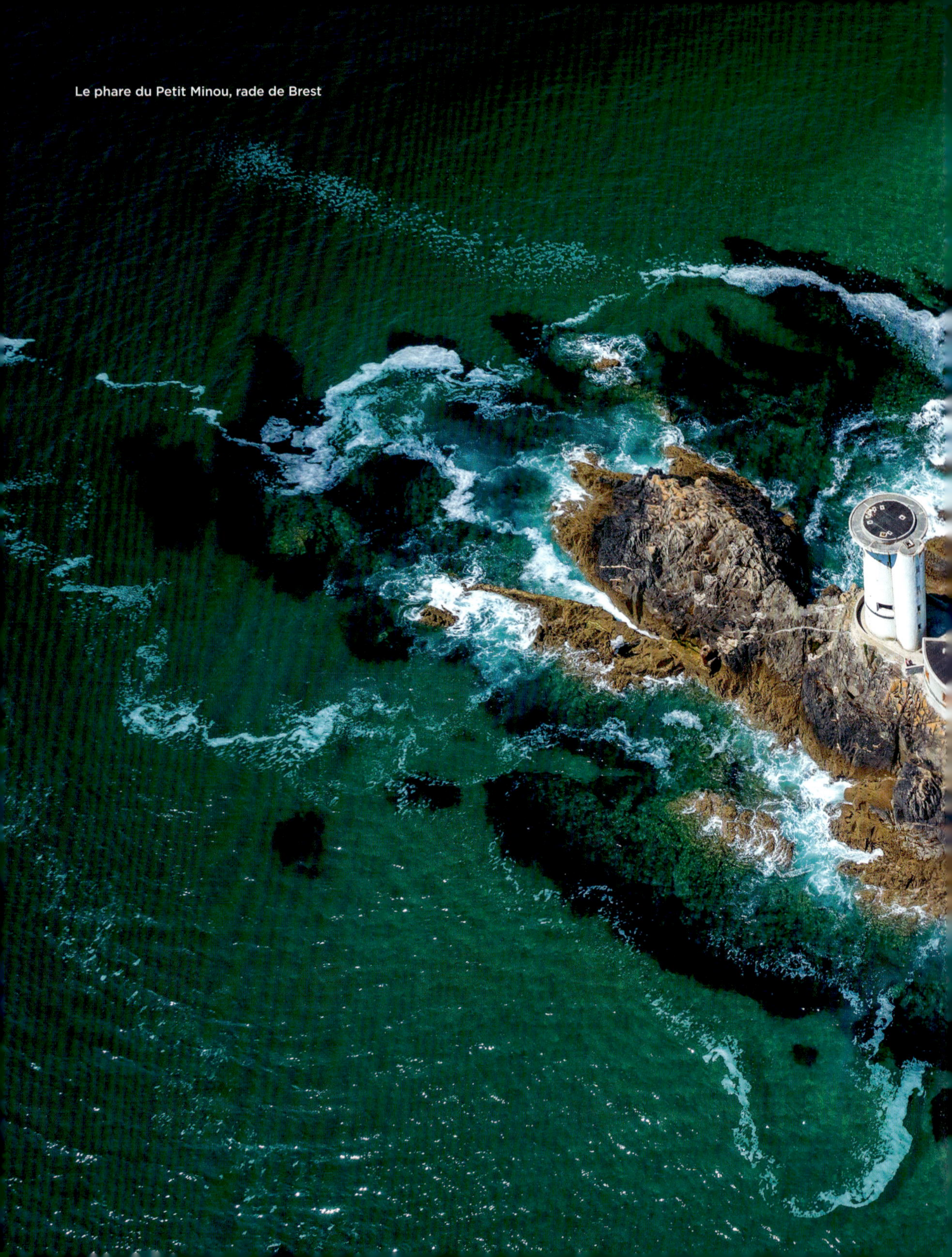
Le phare du Petit Minou, rade de Brest

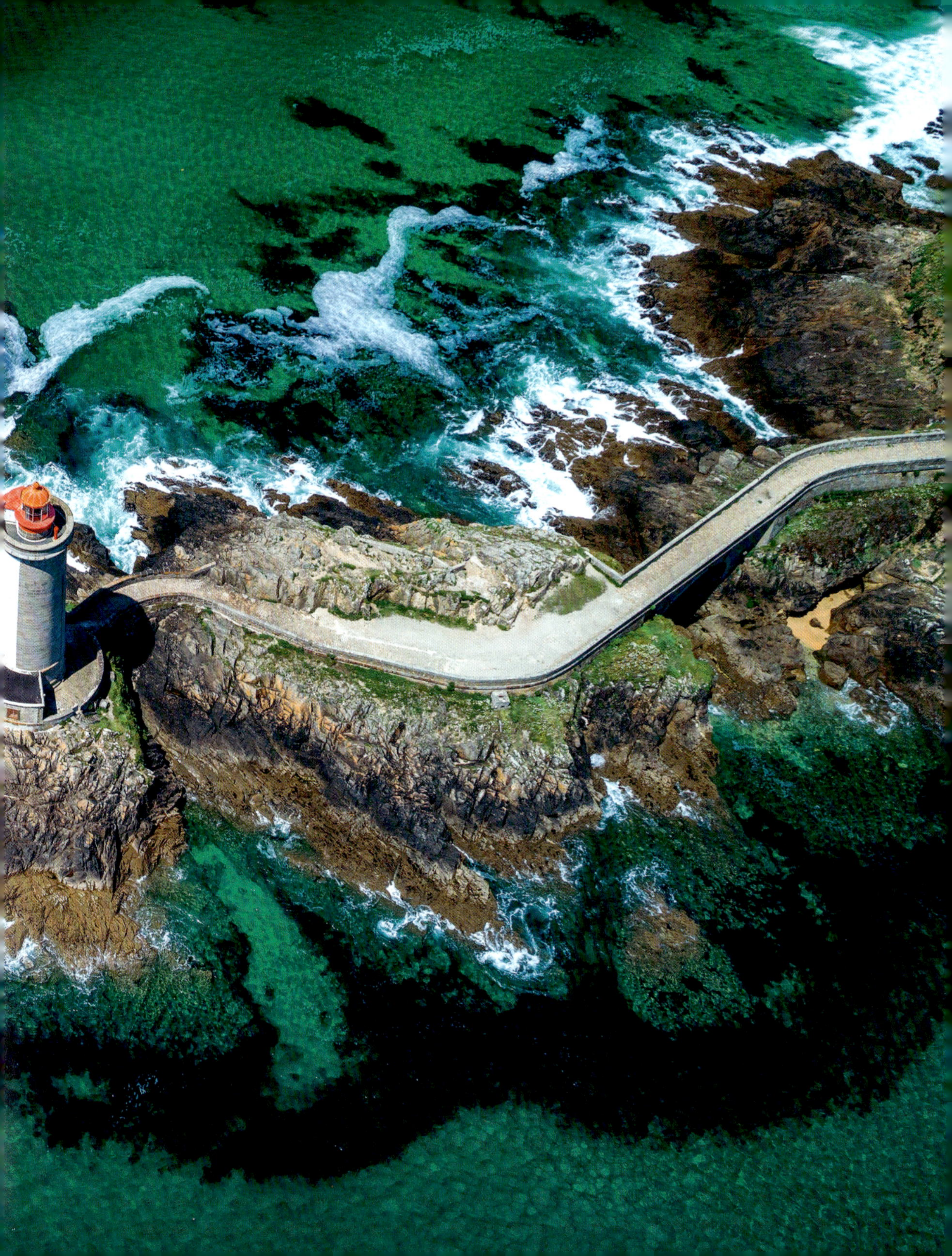

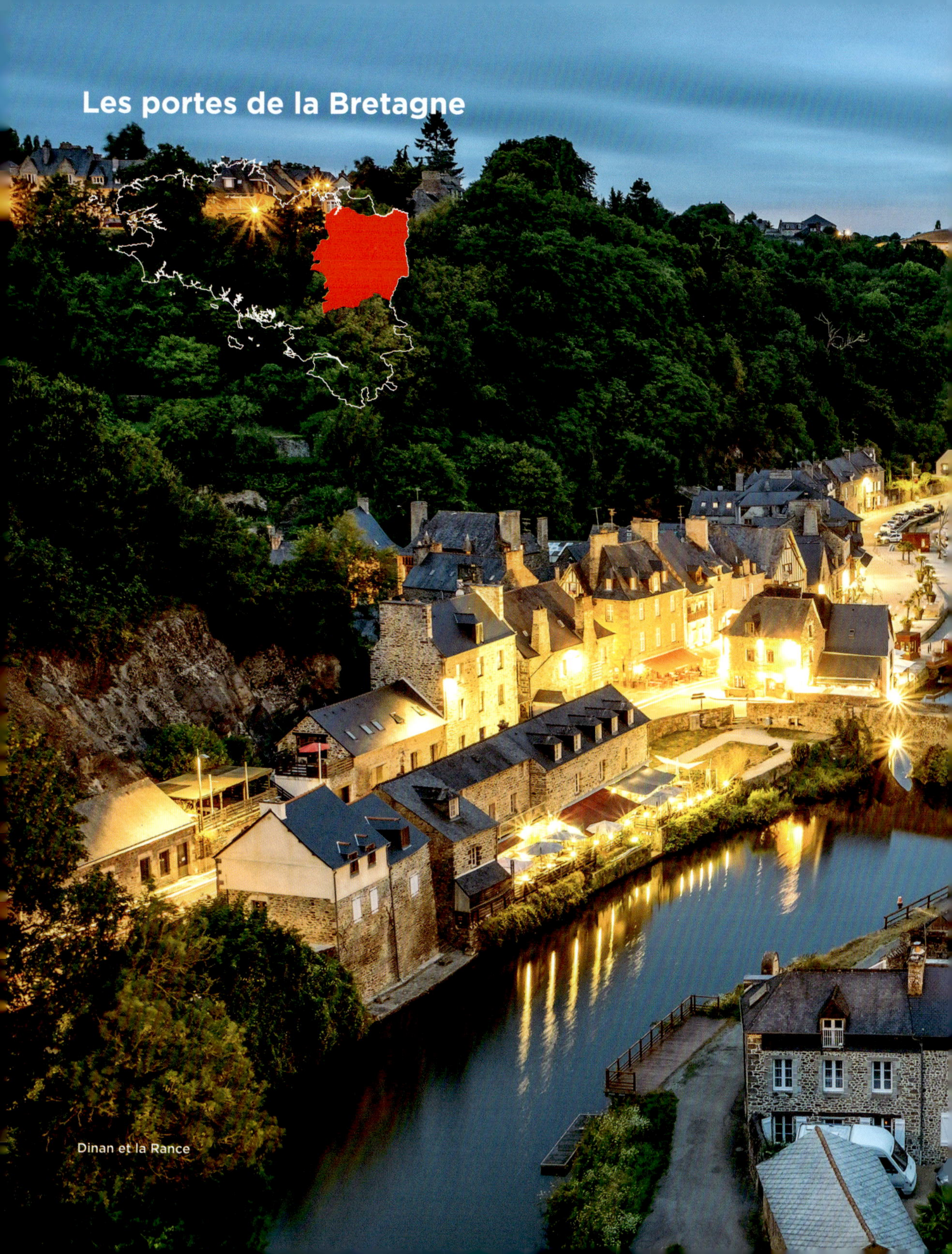
Les portes de la Bretagne
Dinan et la Rance

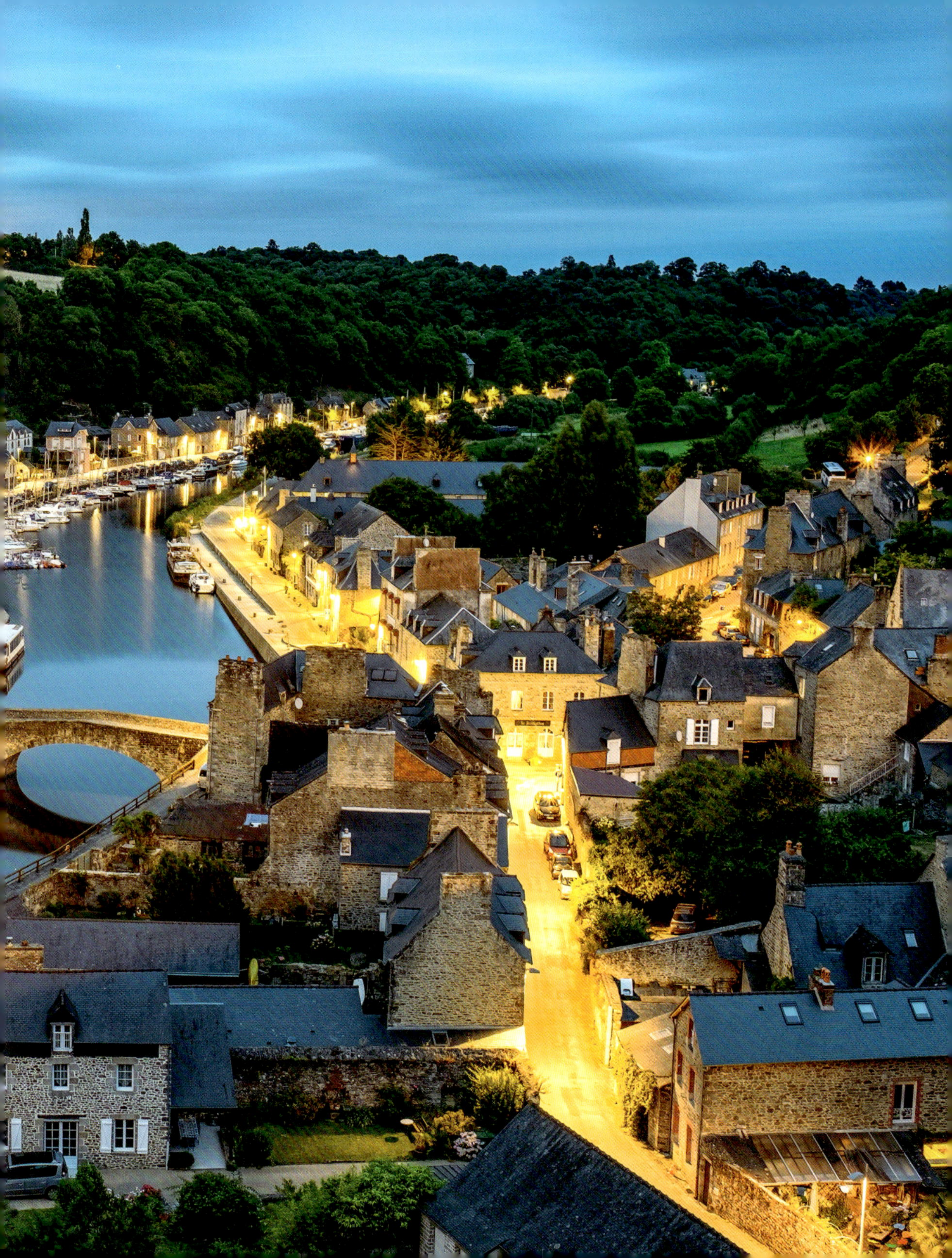

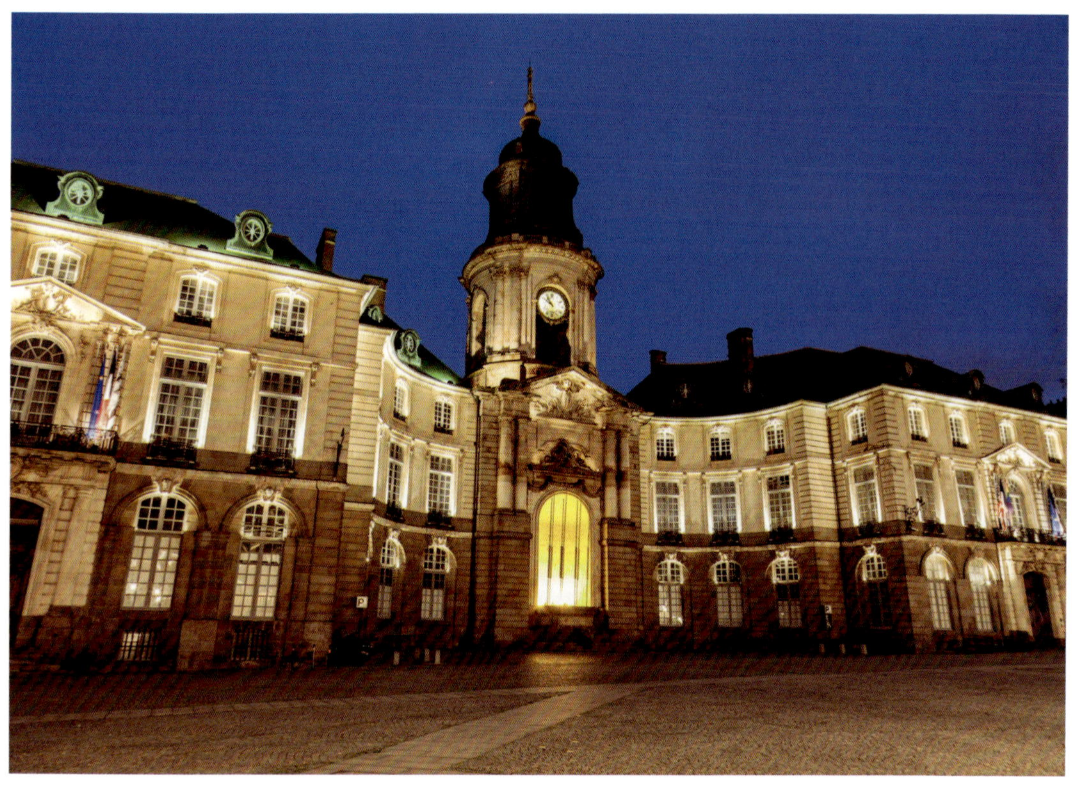

L'hôtel de ville, Rennes

Rennes: The gateway to Brittany

The origins of the capital of Brittany can be traced back to the Gallo-Roman period. In 2018 Rennes was voted by the magazine L'Express as the top of a list of cities with the highest quality of life in France. It is the only Breton city that has more than 25,000 inhabitants and that is not situated by the sea or at the mouth of a river.

Rennes : entrée en Bretagne

Première ville de la région Bretagne, l'histoire de Rennes remonte à l'époque gallo-romaine. Capitale du duché de Bretagne au Moyen Âge, elle est classée première en 2018 au «palmarès des villes de France où il fait bon vivre» selon le magazine *L'Express*. Elle est la seule ville bretonne de plus de 25 000 habitants qui ne soit pas située en bord de mer ou d'estuaire.

Rennes: Das Tor zur Bretagne

Die Ursprünge der Hauptstadt der Bretagne lassen sich bis in die galloromanische Zeit zurückverfolgen. Rennes wurde 2018 von dem Magazin L'Express an die Spitze der Liste der Städte mit der höchsten Lebensqualität Frankreichs gewählt. Sie ist die einzige bretonische Stadt, die mehr als 25.000 Einwohnern zählt und nicht am Meer oder an einer Flussmündung liegt.

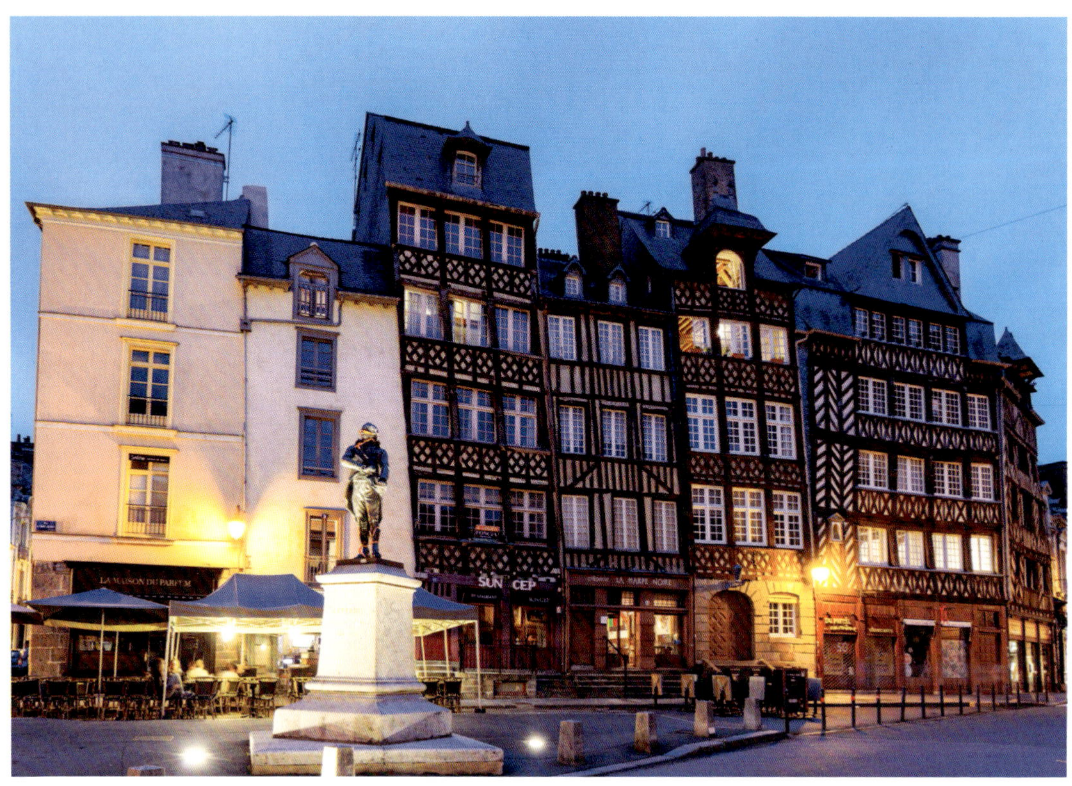

Rennes

Rennes: la puerta de entrada a Bretaña

Los orígenes de la capital de Bretaña se remontan a la época galorromana. Rennes fue situada en 2018 por la revista L'Express a la cabeza de la lista de ciudades con mayor calidad de vida en Francia. Es la única ciudad bretona con más de 25 000 habitantes y no está situada junto al mar ni en la desembocadura de un río.

Rennes: a entrada para a Bretanha

As origens da capital da Bretanha remontam ao período galo-romano. Rennes foi eleita, em 2018 pela revista L'Express, a cidade francesa com a qualidade de vida mais alta. É a única cidade bretã com mais de 25.000 habitantes que não está situada, nem à beira-mar, nem na foz de um rio.

Rennes: de poort naar Bretagne

De oorsprong van de hoofdstad van Bretagne gaat terug tot de Gallo-Romeinse periode. Rennes werd in 2018 door het tijdschrift L'Express verkozen tot de stad met de hoogste kwaliteit van leven in Frankrijk. Het is de enige stad in Bretagne met meer dan 25.000 inwoners en die niet aan zee of aan een riviermonding ligt.

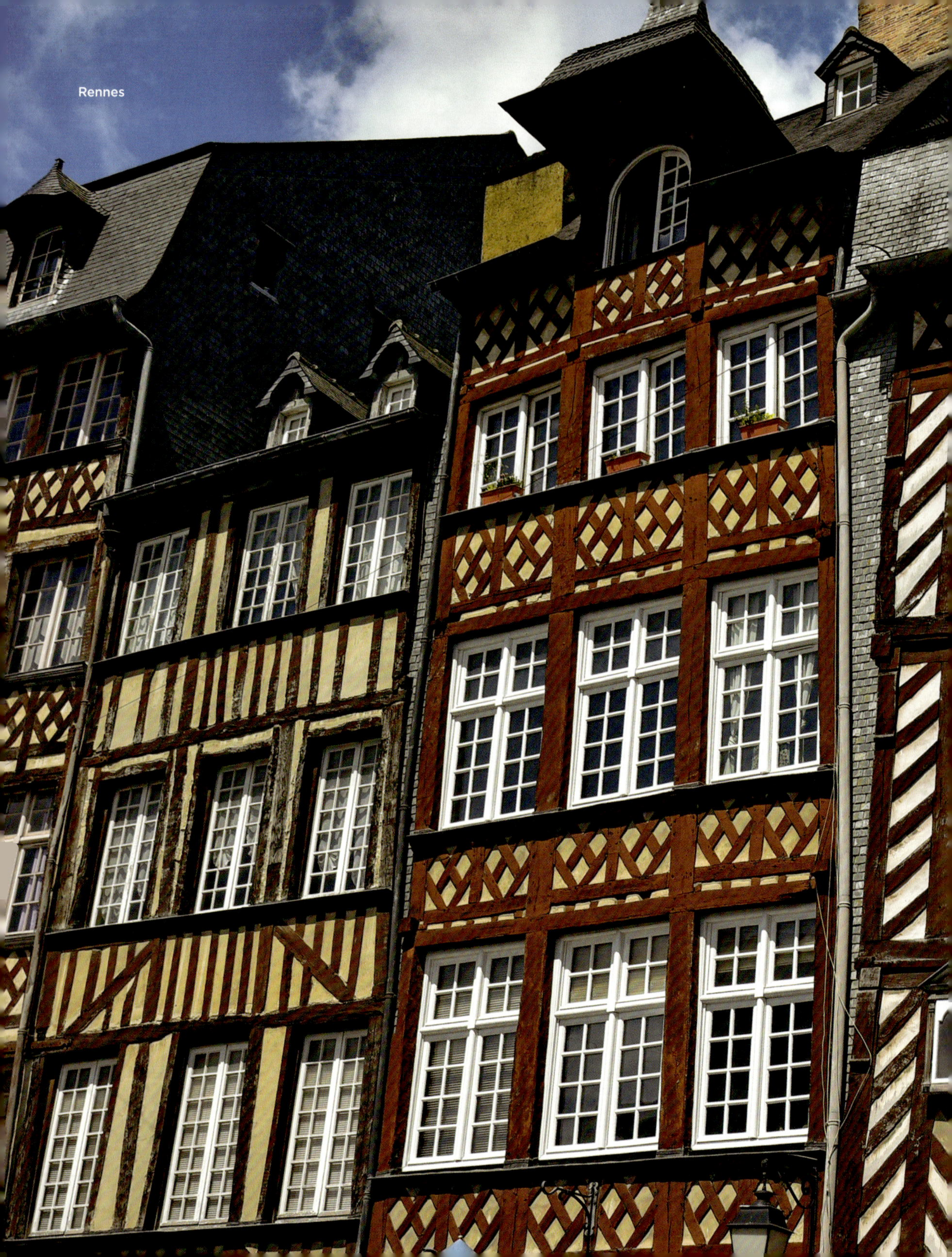
Rennes

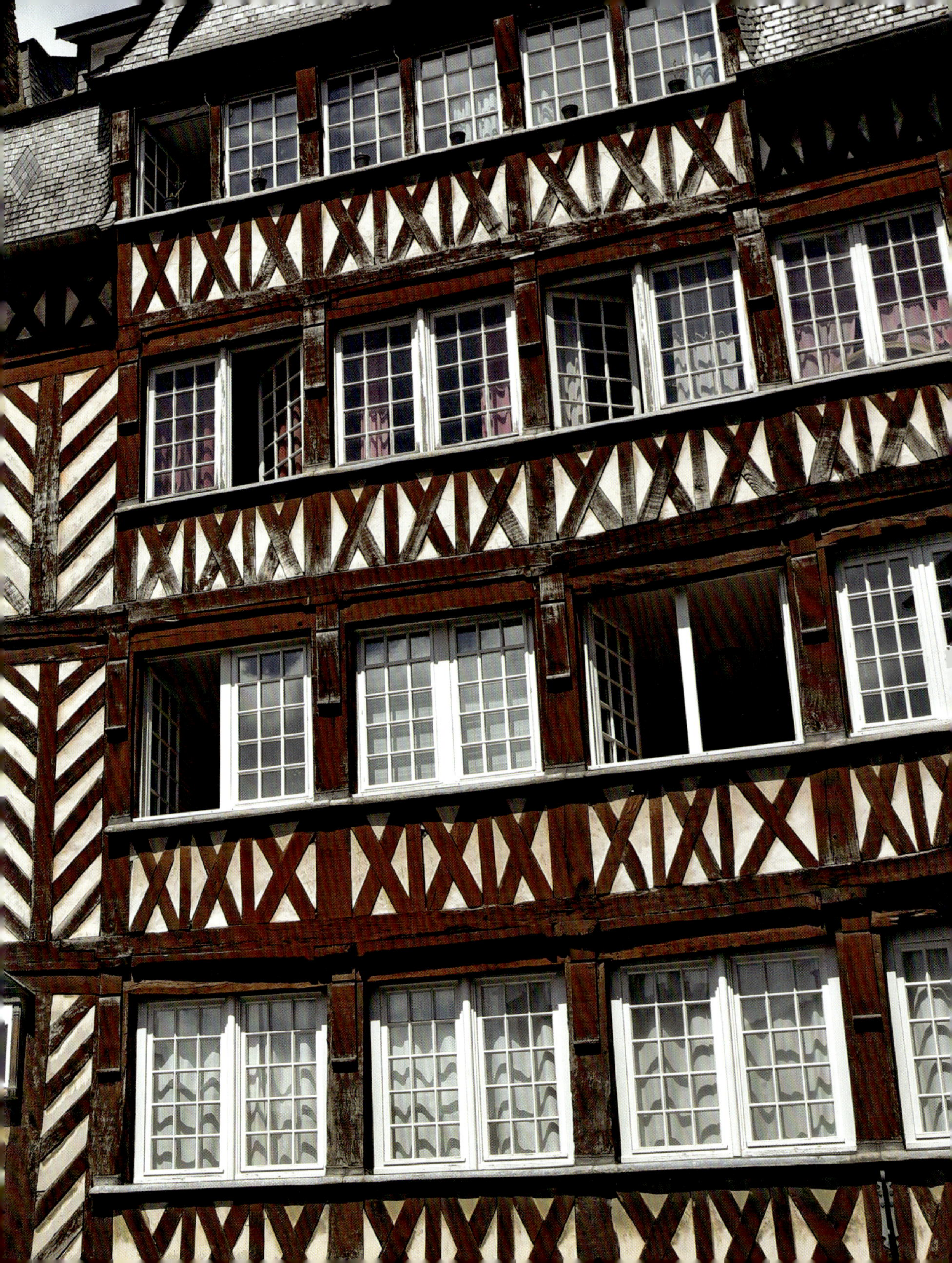

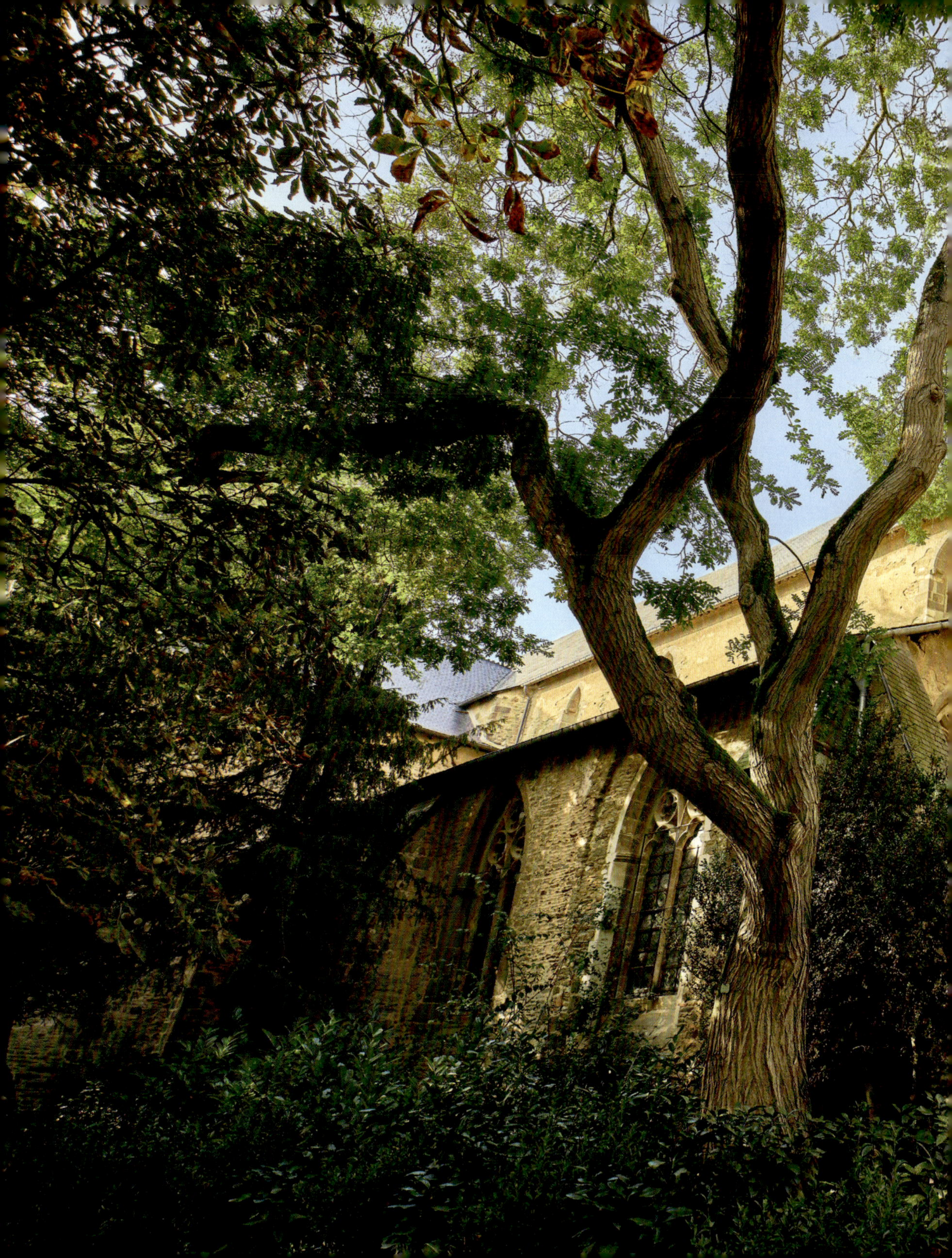

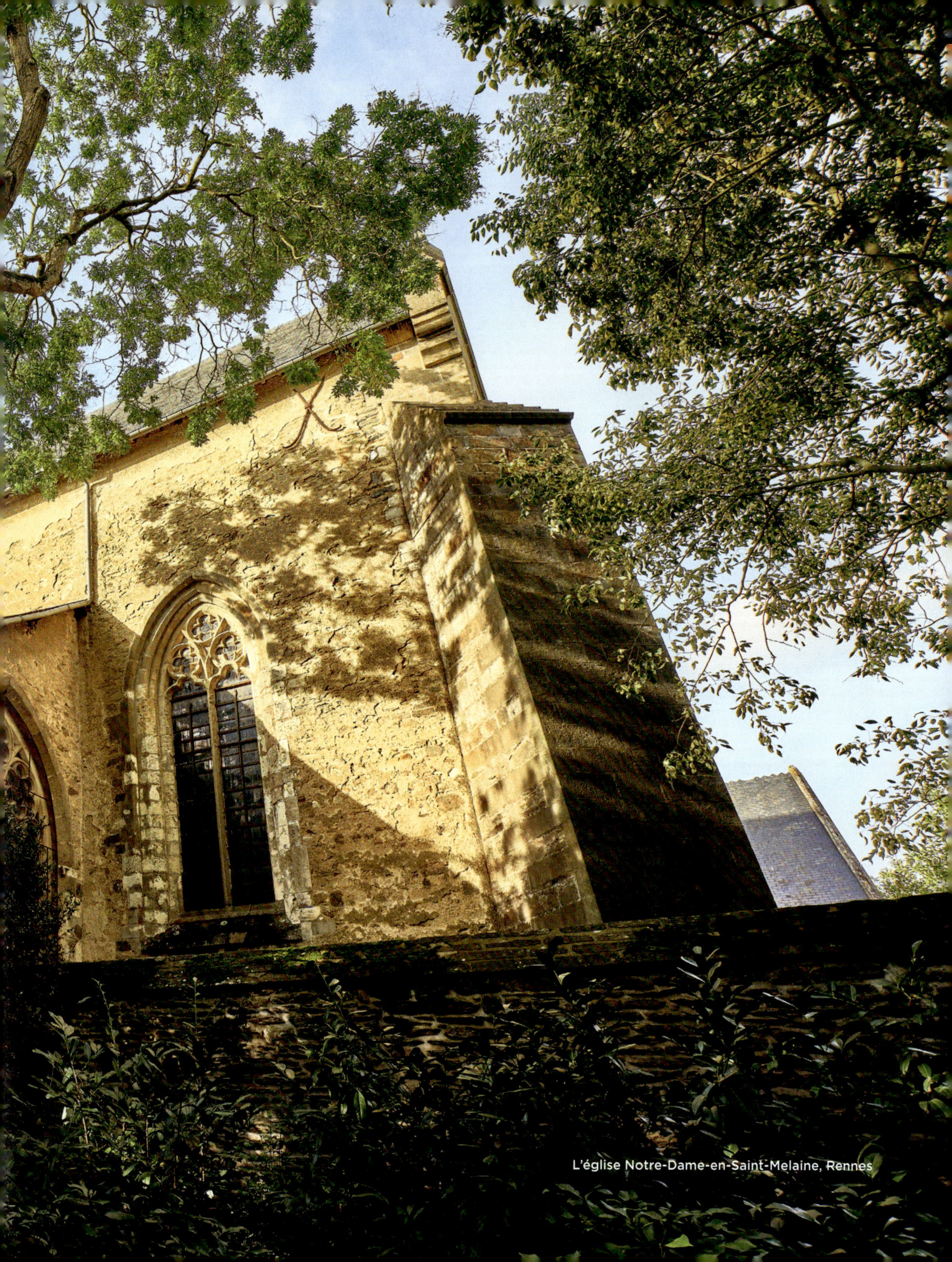

L'église Notre-Dame-en-Saint-Melaine, Rennes

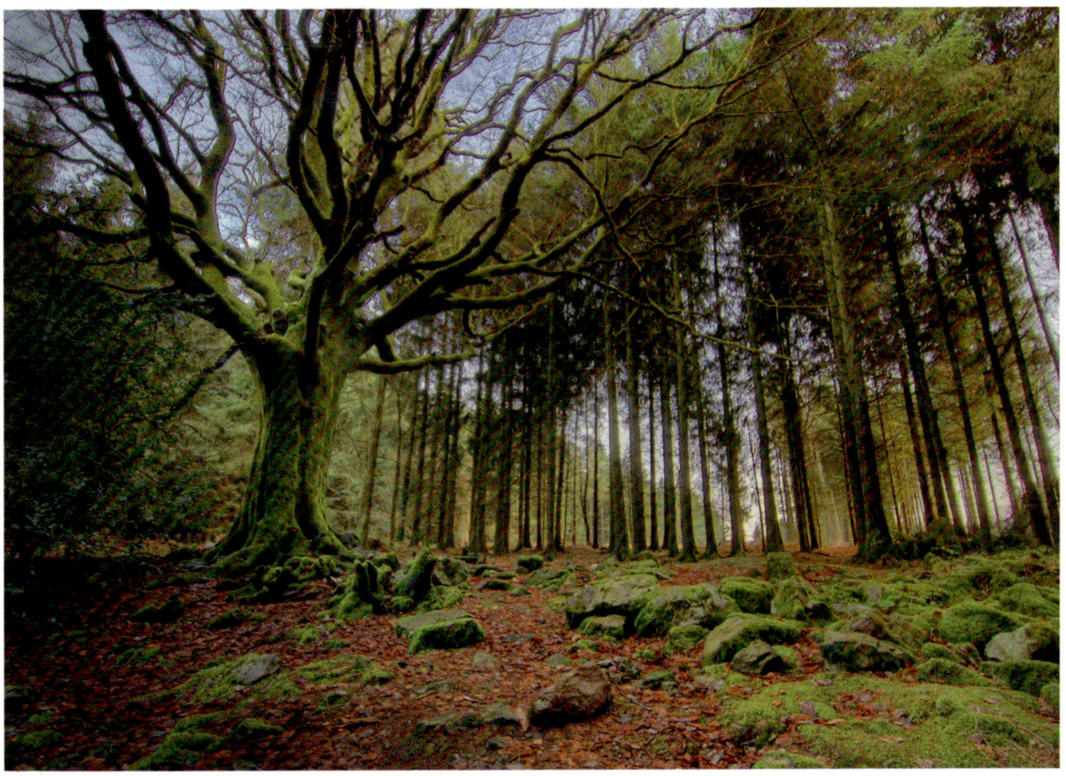

Forêt de hêtres, Brocéliande

The Forest of Brocéliande

The Forest of Brocéliande is entwined with numerous myths, mainly connected with the Arthurian legend. Covering more than 7,000 hectares, it is home to 14 ponds, several castles and a number of unique trees. The most spectacular of these is the Chêne à Guillotin (the guillotine oak), which is about a thousand years old and has a circumference of 9.65 metres.

La forêt de Brocéliande

La forêt de Brocéliande est mythique. Étendue sur plus de 7 000 hectares, riche de 14 étangs et de milliers de légendes, liées pour la plupart à la légende arthurienne, elle abrite plusieurs châteaux et des arbres remarquables. Le plus spectaculaire est le chêne à Guillotin, situé à Concoret, dont la circonférence est de 9,65 m, et qui est âgé d'environ mille ans.

Der Wald von Brocéliande

Um den Wald von Brocéliande ranken sich zahlreiche Mythen, die vor allem mit der Artussage verknüpft sind. Auf mehr als 7.000 ha beheimatet er 14 Teiche, mehrere Schlösser und eine Reihe von einzigartigen Bäumen. Der spektakulärste ist die etwa tausend Jahre alte Chêne à Guillotin (die Guillotine-Eiche), deren Umfang 9,65 m beträgt.

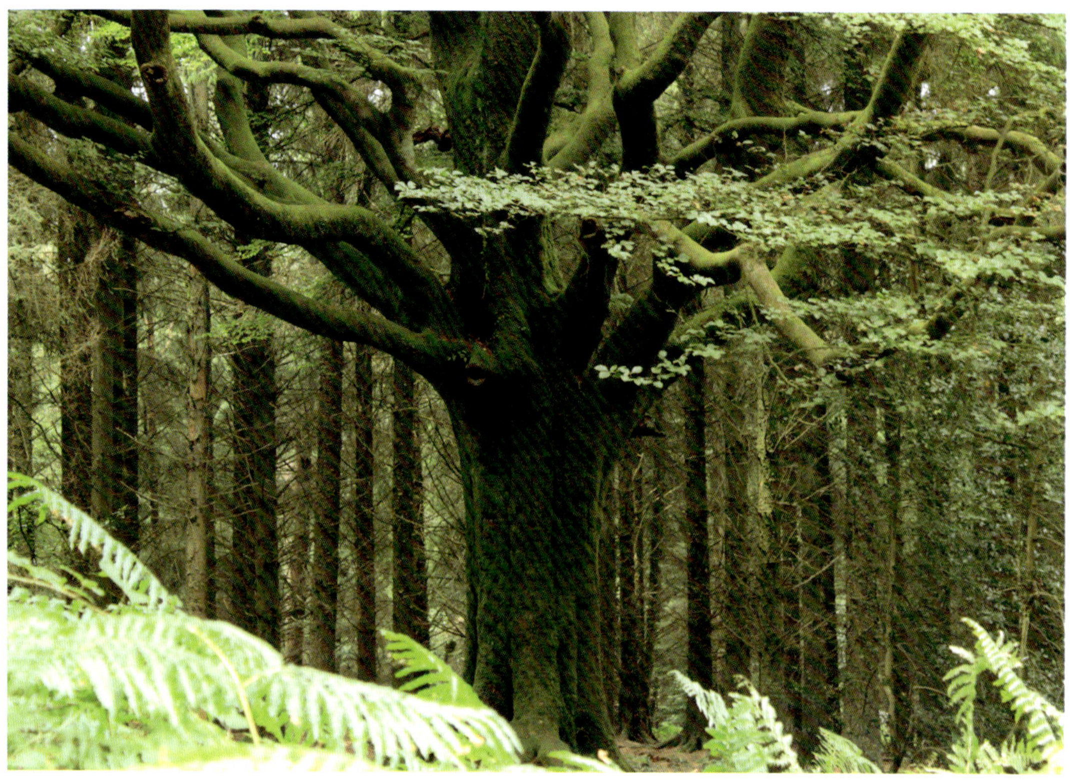

Brocéliande

El bosque de Brocelianda

El bosque de Brocelianda está entrelazado por numerosos mitos, principalmente relacionados con la leyenda de Arturo. En sus más de 7000 hectáreas, alberga 14 estanques, varios castillos y una serie de árboles únicos. La más espectacular es la Chêne à Guillotin (guillotina), que tiene unos mil años de antigüedad y una circunferencia de 9,65 metros.

A floresta de Brocéliande

São inúmeros os mitos ligados à floresta de Brocéliande, principalmente os relativos à lenda arturiana. Com mais de 7.000 hectares, abriga 14 lagoas, vários castelos e uma série de árvores únicas. A mais espectacular é a Chêne à Guillotin (carvalho guilhotina), aproximadamente com mil anos e um diâmetro de 9,65 metros.

Het bos van Brocéliande

Het bos van Brocéliande is verweven met tal van mythen, die vooral te maken hebben met de Arthur-legende. Op meer dan 7.000 hectare bevinden zich veertien poelen, diverse kastelen en een aantal unieke bomen. De spectaculairste is de chêne à Guillotin (de guillotine-eik), die zo'n duizend jaar oud is en een omtrek van 9,65 meter heeft.

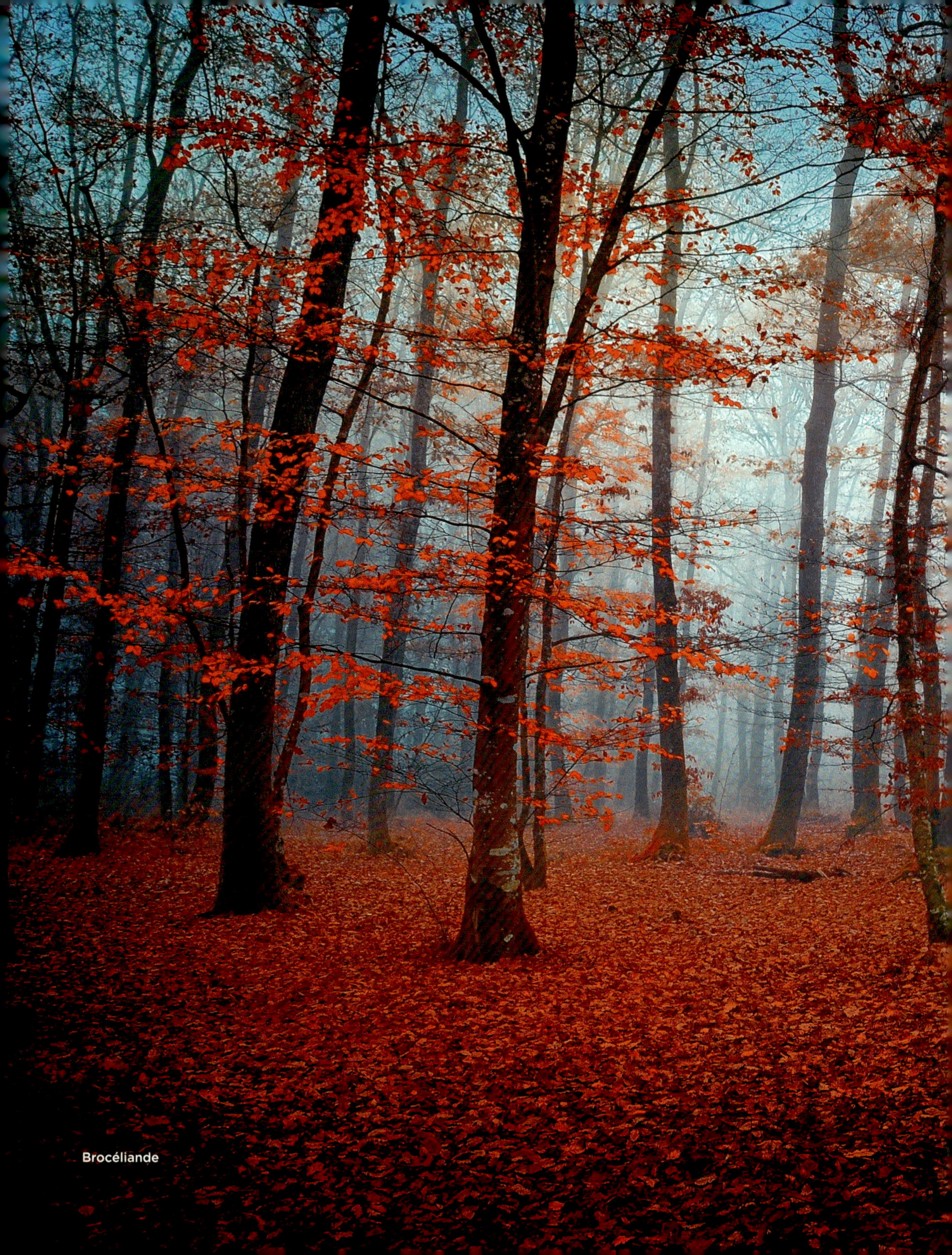

Brocéliande

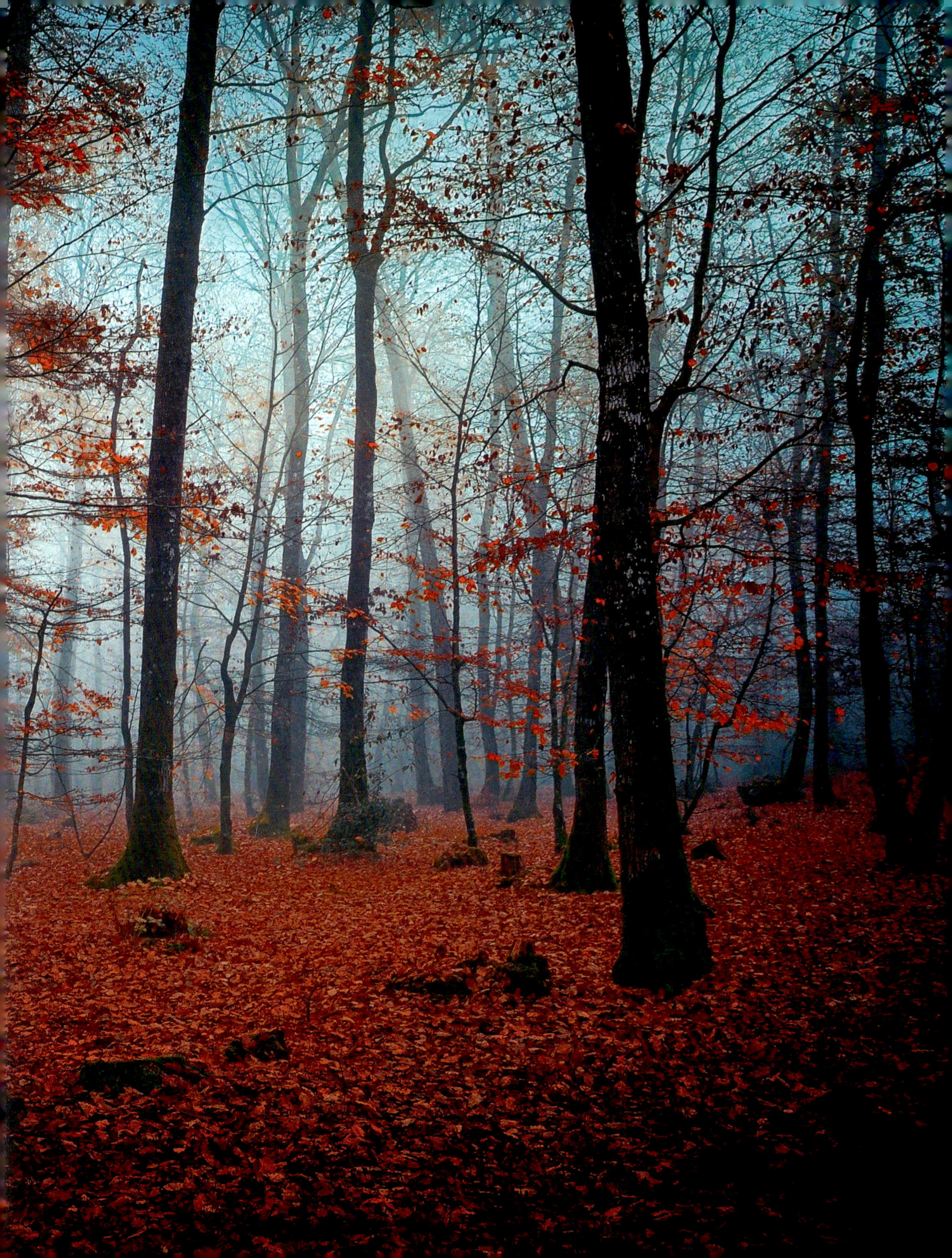

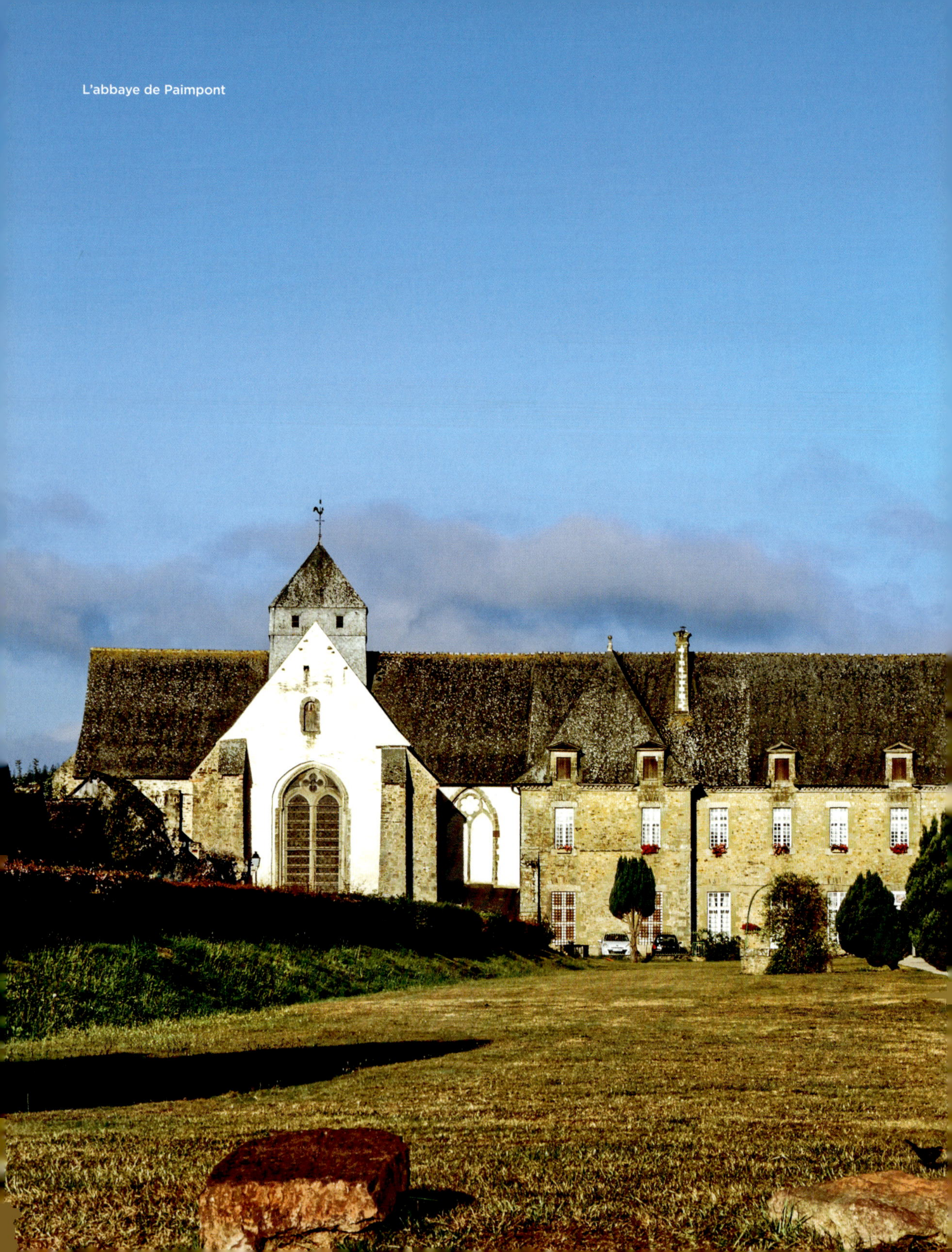

L'abbaye de Paimpont

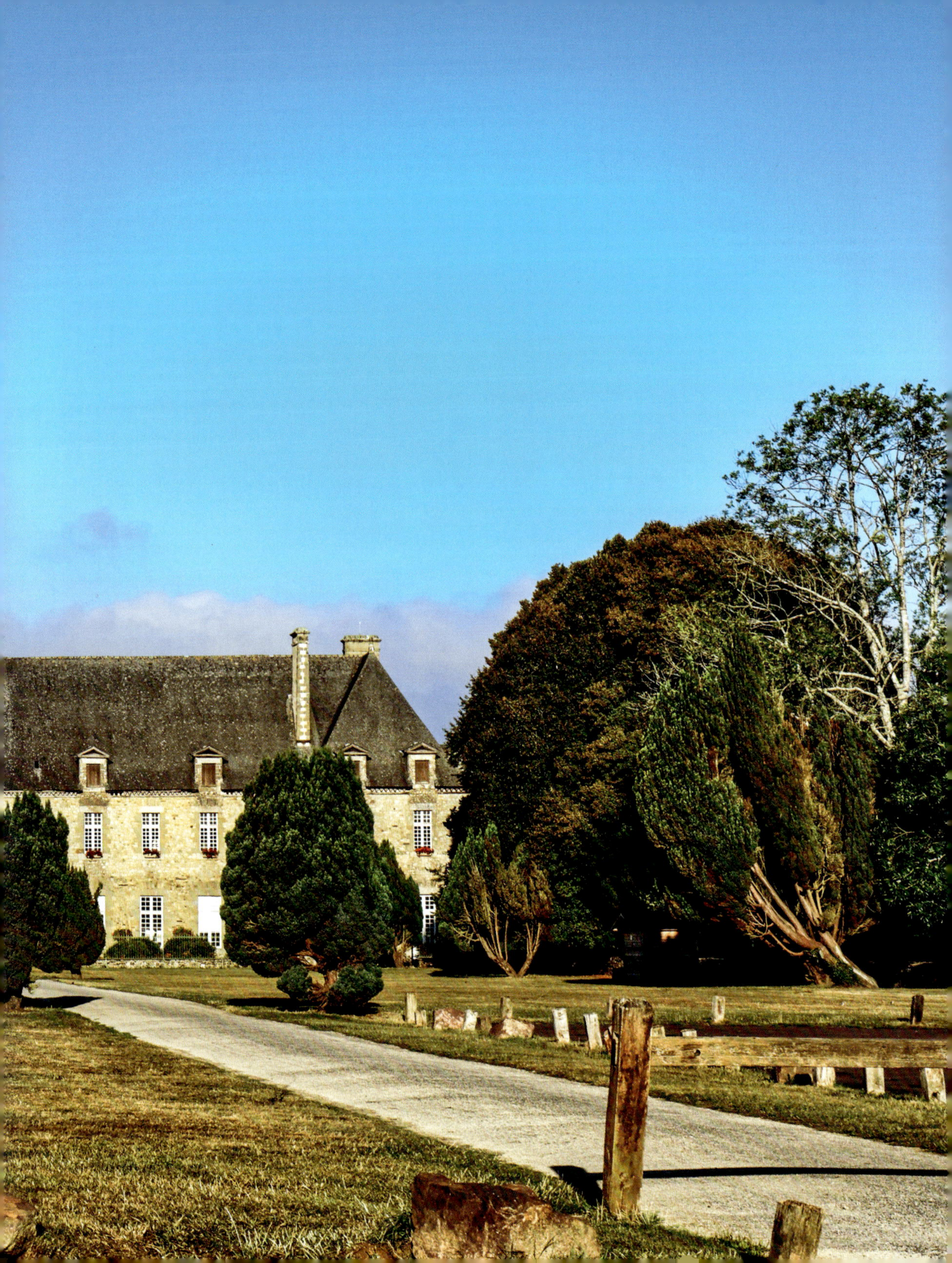

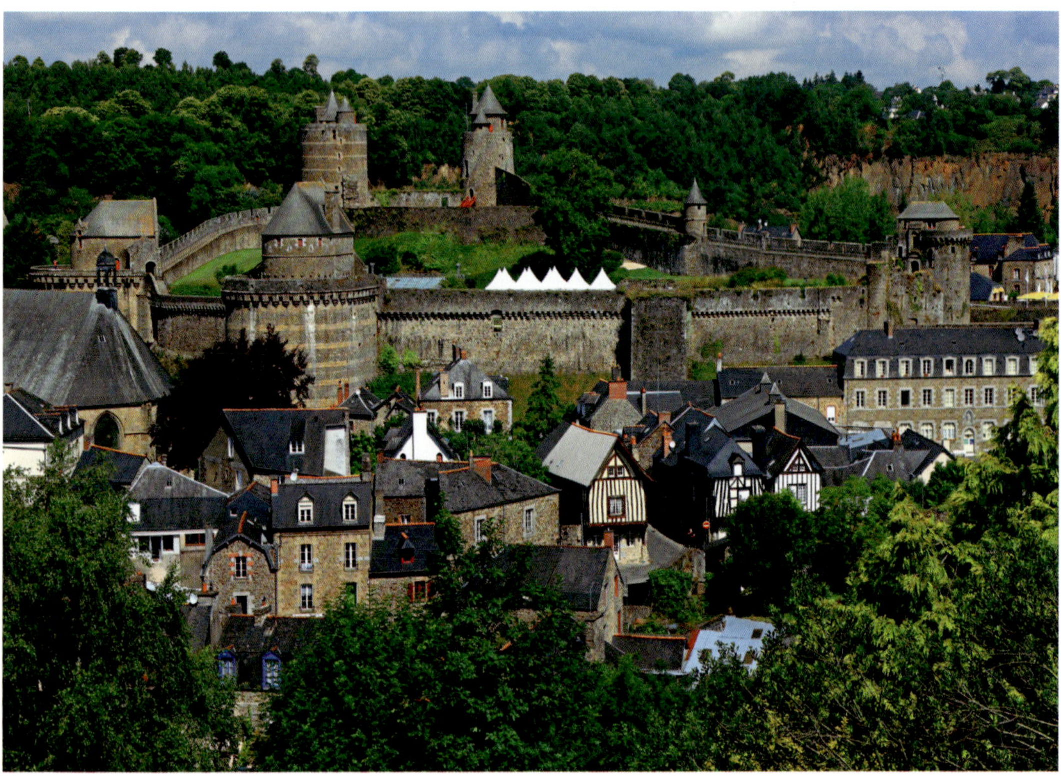

Fougères

Fougères

In 1836, Victor Hugo discovered his love for Fougères when he visited the village accompanied by his lover and muse Juliette Drouet, who was born there. At the centre is the castle, which was built more than a thousand years ago on a rocky promontory surrounded by water.

Fougères

Victor Hugo découvre Fougères en 1836, en compagnie de Juliette Drouet, son amante et sa muse, qui en est originaire. Le lieu central de Fougères est son château installé il y a plus de mille ans sur un éperon rocheux entouré des eaux de la rivière.

Fougères

Im Jahr 1836 entdeckt Victor Hugo seine Liebe für Fougères, als er den Ort in Begleitung seiner dort geborenen Geliebten und Muse Juliette Drouet besucht. Das Zentrum bildet die Burg, die vor mehr als tausend Jahren auf einem vom Wasser umgebenen Felsvorsprung erbaut wurde.

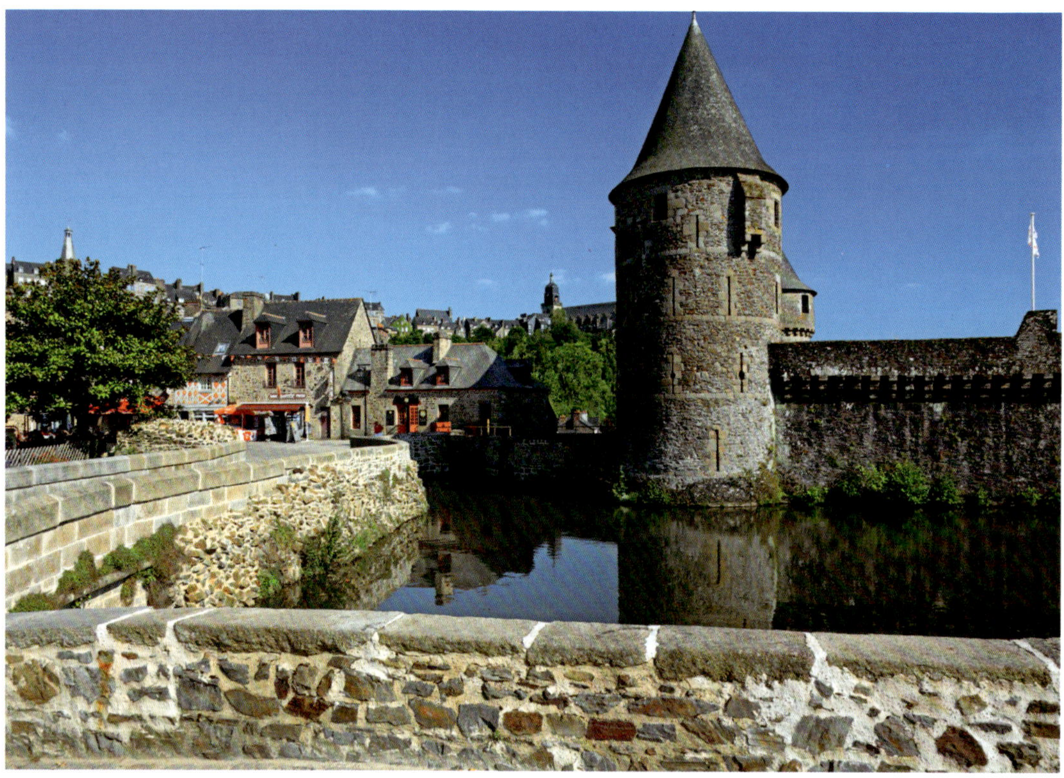

Les douves et la tour du château, Fougères

Fougères

En 1836, Victor Hugo descubrió su amor por Fougères cuando visitó el pueblo acompañado de su amante y musa Juliette Drouet, que nació allí. El centro es el castillo, que fue construido hace más de mil años sobre un promontorio rocoso rodeado de agua.

Fougères

Em 1836, Victor Hugo descobriu, pela primeira vez, o seu amor por Fougères quando visitou a aldeia acompanhado pela sua amada e musa Juliette Drouet, que ali tinha nascido. No centro da vila encontra-se o castelo, construído há mais de mil anos, sobre um rochedo saliente rodeado de água.

Fougères

In 1836 ontdekte Victor Hugo zijn liefde voor Fougères, toen hij het dorp bezocht met zijn geliefde en muze Juliette Drouet, die daar geboren was. Het kasteel, dat ruim duizend jaar geleden werd gebouwd op een uitstekende rots omringd door water, vormt het centrum.

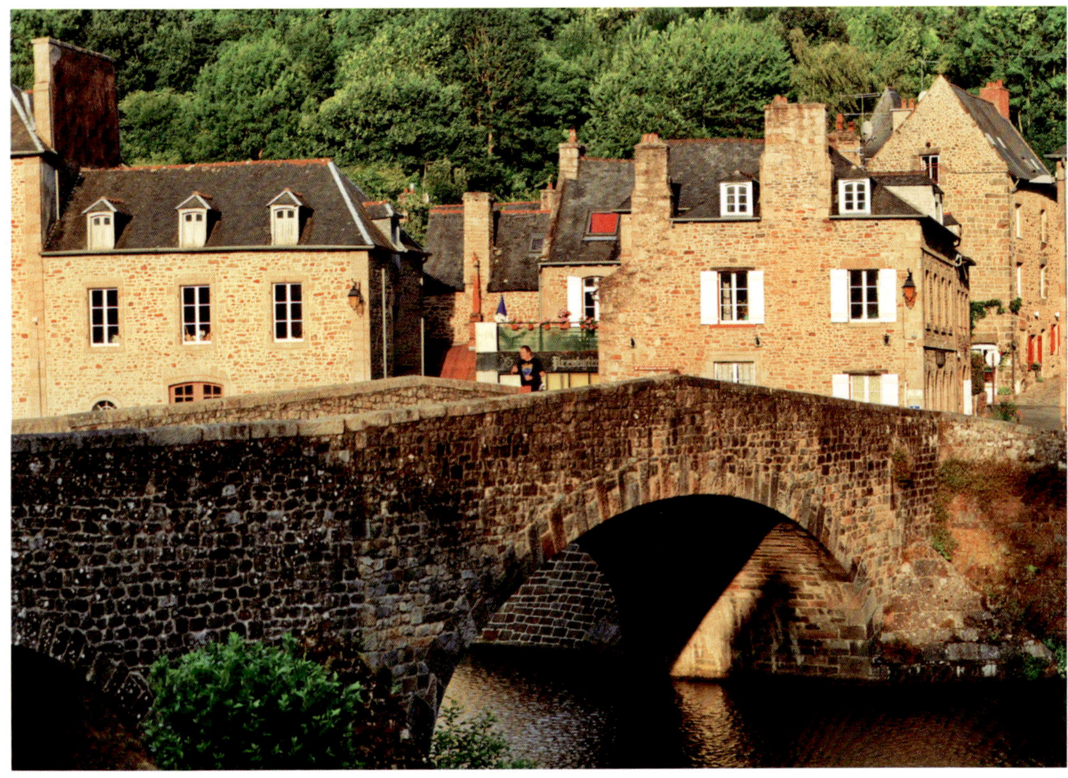

Dinan et la Rance

Interface between Land and Sea: Dinan

This historic and cultural city is surrounded by an almost 3 km long city wall. Its centre and the 14th century castle are enthroned high above the Rance, which leads to Dinard and Saint-Malo. The small marina is the starting point for excursions to the mouth of the river.

Entre terre et mer : Dinan

Ville d'art et d'histoire, entourée de près de 3 km de remparts, la ville de Dinan et son château du xive siècle surplombent la Rance qui coule jusqu'à Dinard et Saint-Malo. Son petit port de plaisance est le point de départ de belles balades le long de l'estuaire.

Schnittstelle zwischen Land und Meer: Dinan

Die historisch und kulturell sehenswerte Stadt wird von einer fast 3 km langen Stadtmauer umgeben. Ihr Zentrum und das Schloss aus dem 14. Jahrhundert thronen hoch über der Rance, die bis nach Dinard und Saint-Malo führt. Der kleine Jachthafen ist der Ausgangspunkt für Ausfahrten bis zur Mündung.

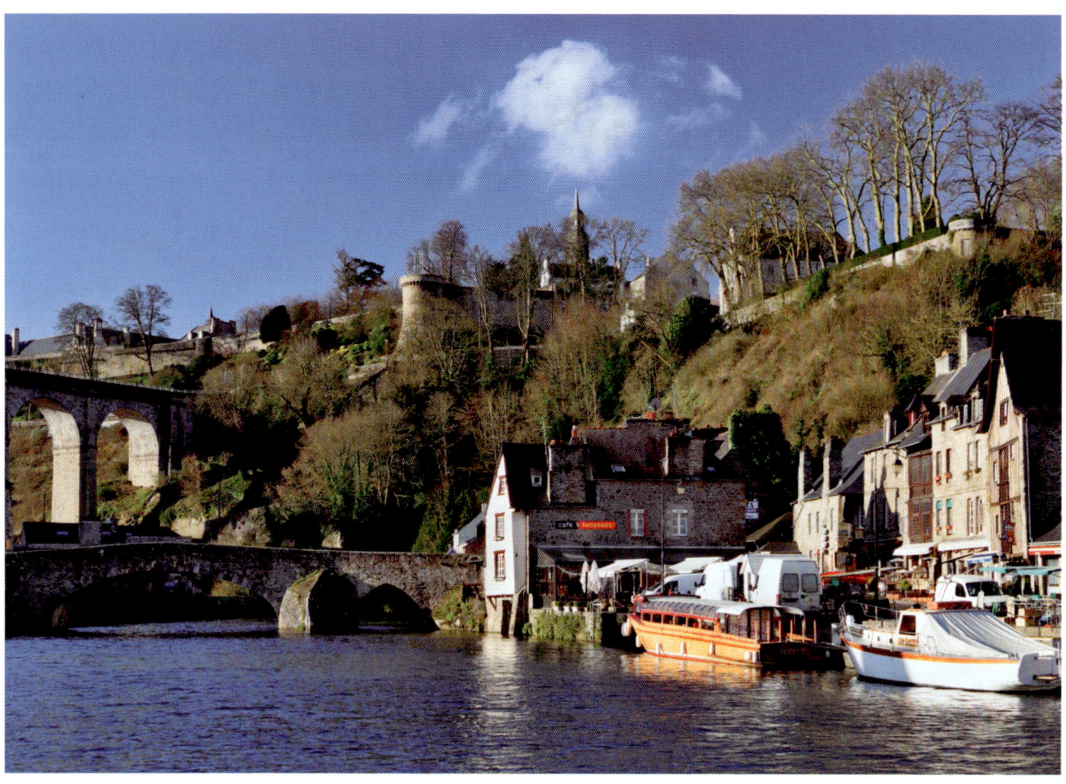

Dinan et la Rance

Interfaz entre tierra y mar: Dinan

La ciudad de interés histórico y cultural está rodeada por una muralla de casi 3 km de longitud. Su centro y el castillo del siglo XIV están en lo alto del Rance, que conduce a Dinard y Saint-Malo. El pequeño puerto deportivo es el punto de partida de las excursiones a la desembocadura del río.

Ponto de interceção entre a terra e o mar: Dinan

A notável cidade histórica e cultural é cercada por uma muralha com quase 3 km de extensão. O centro e o castelo do século XIV erguem-se no alto do rio Rance, que corre até Dinard e Saint-Malo. A pequena marina é o ponto de partida para excursões até à foz do rio.

Grens tussen land en zee: Dinan

De historische en qua cultuur bezienswaardige stad wordt omgeven door een bijna 3 km lange stadsmuur. Het centrum en het 14e-eeuwse kasteel liggen hoog boven de Rance, die naar Dinard en Saint-Malo stroomt. De kleine jachthaven is het vertrekpunt van excursies naar de riviermonding.

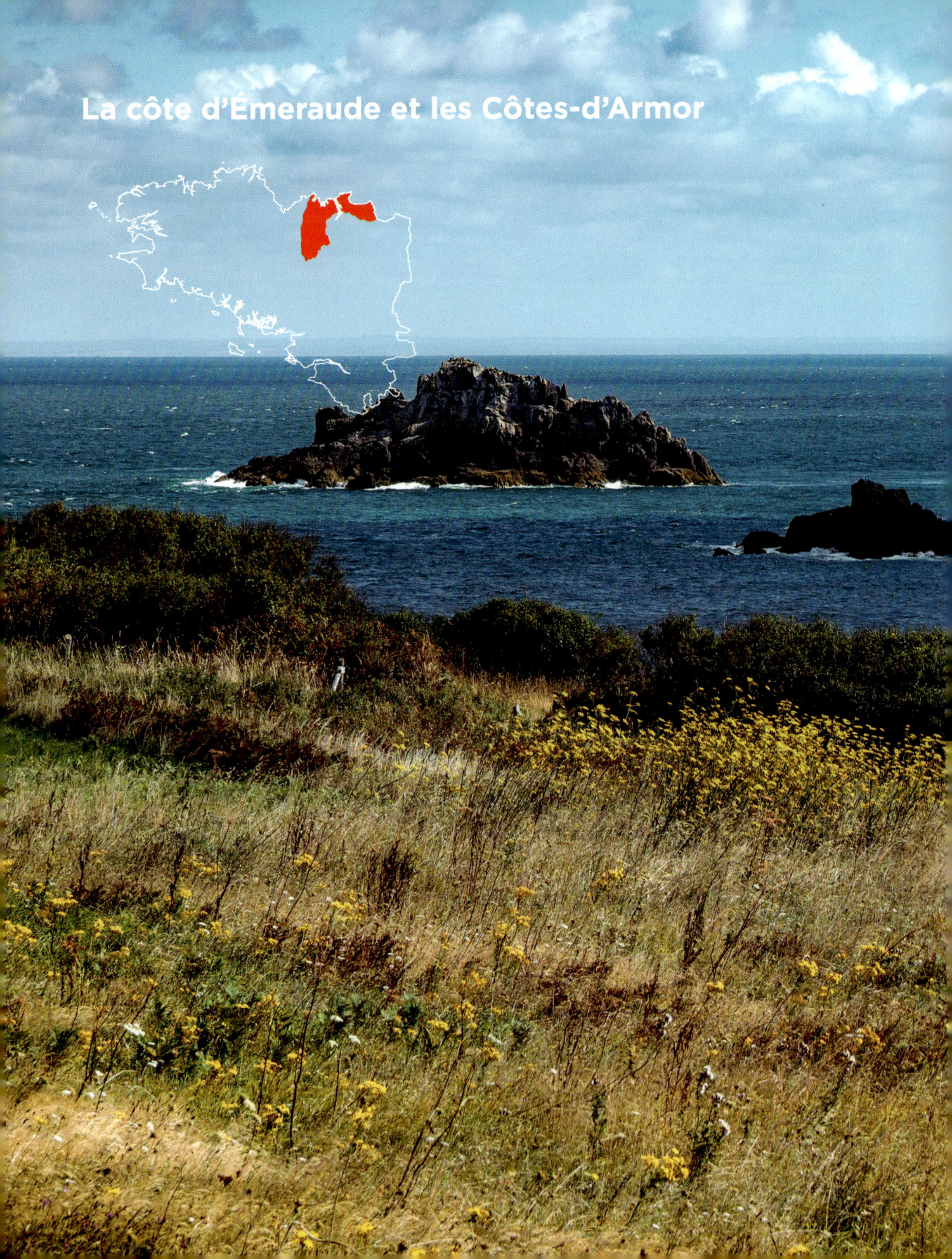

La côte d'Émeraude et les Côtes-d'Armor

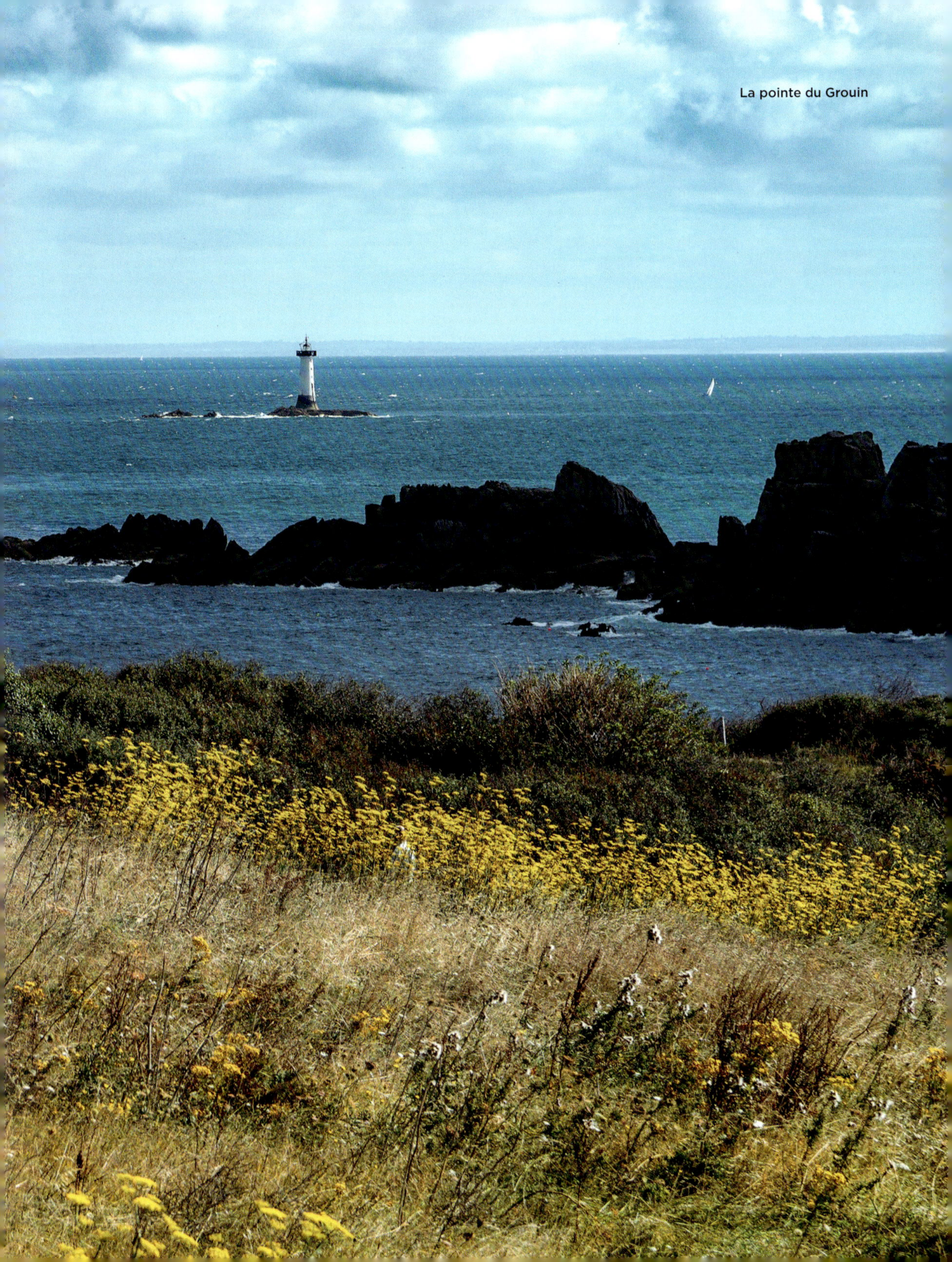

La pointe du Grouin

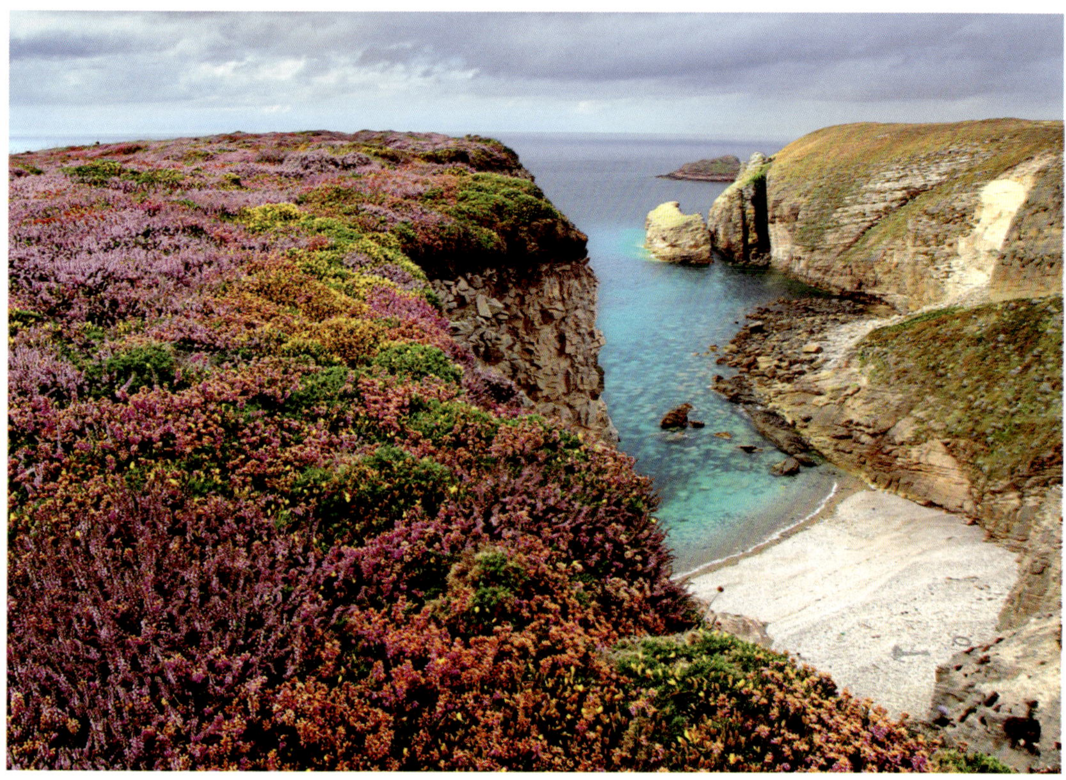

Le cap Fréhel

The Côte d'Émeraude

The name Côte d'Émeraude refers to the emerald green colour of the sea. It stretches between Cancale and the promontory of Cap Fréhel. The scenically unique coastal stretch offers 350 km of hiking trails, beautiful sandy beaches, small fishing ports, viewpoints to observe the wildlife, and a spectacular tidal range.

La côte d'Émeraude

La côte d'Émeraude est appelée ainsi en raison de la couleur vert émeraude de la mer à certains moments. Elle s'étend entre Cancale et le cap Fréhel. Cette magnifique partie littorale bretonne abrite 350 km de sentiers, de belles plages de sable fin, des petits ports de pêche, des points d'observation de la faune, et de grandes marées spectaculaires.

Die Côte d'Émeraude

Der Name der Côte d'Émeraude verweist auf die smaragdgrüne Farbe des Meeres. Sie erstreckt sich zwischen Cancale und der Landzunge Cap Fréhel. Der landschaftlich einmalige Küstenabschnitt bietet 350 km Wanderwege, wunderschöne Sandstrände, kleine Fischerhäfen, Aussichtspunkte, um die Tierwelt zu beobachten, und einen spektakulären Tidenhub.

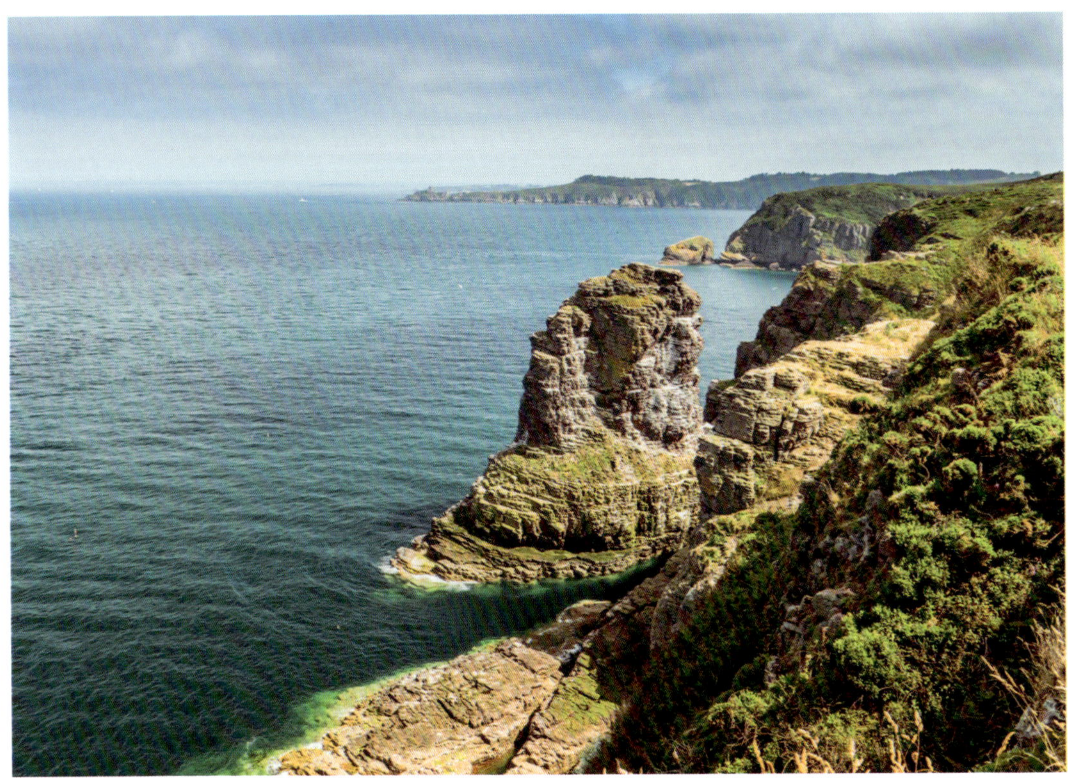

Le cap Fréhel

Côte d'Émeraude

El nombre de Côte d'Émeraude hace referencia al color verde esmeralda del mar. Se extiende entre Cancale y el promontorio de Cap Fréhel. El tramo costero, cuyo paisaje es único, ofrece 350 km de senderos, hermosas playas de arena, pequeños puertos pesqueros, miradores para observar la vida silvestre y una espectacular cordillera de mareas.

A Côte d'Émeraude/A Costa Esmeralda

O nome de Costa Esmeralda refere-se à cor verde esmeralda do mar. Estende-se entre Cancale e a língua de terra do Cap Fréhel. A costa, de beleza única, oferece 350 km de trilhos para caminhadas, praias com uma areia maravilhosa, pequenos portos de pesca, miradouros para observar a fauna e marés com amplitudes espantosas.

De Côte d'Émeraude

De naam 'Côte d'Émeraude' verwijst naar de smaragdgroene kleur van de zee. De kust strekt zich uit tussen Cancale en de landtong Cap Fréhel. De landschappelijk unieke kuststrook biedt 350 km aan wandelpaden, prachtige zandstranden, kleine vissershavens, uitkijkpunten ter observatie van de fauna en een spectaculair getijdeverschil.

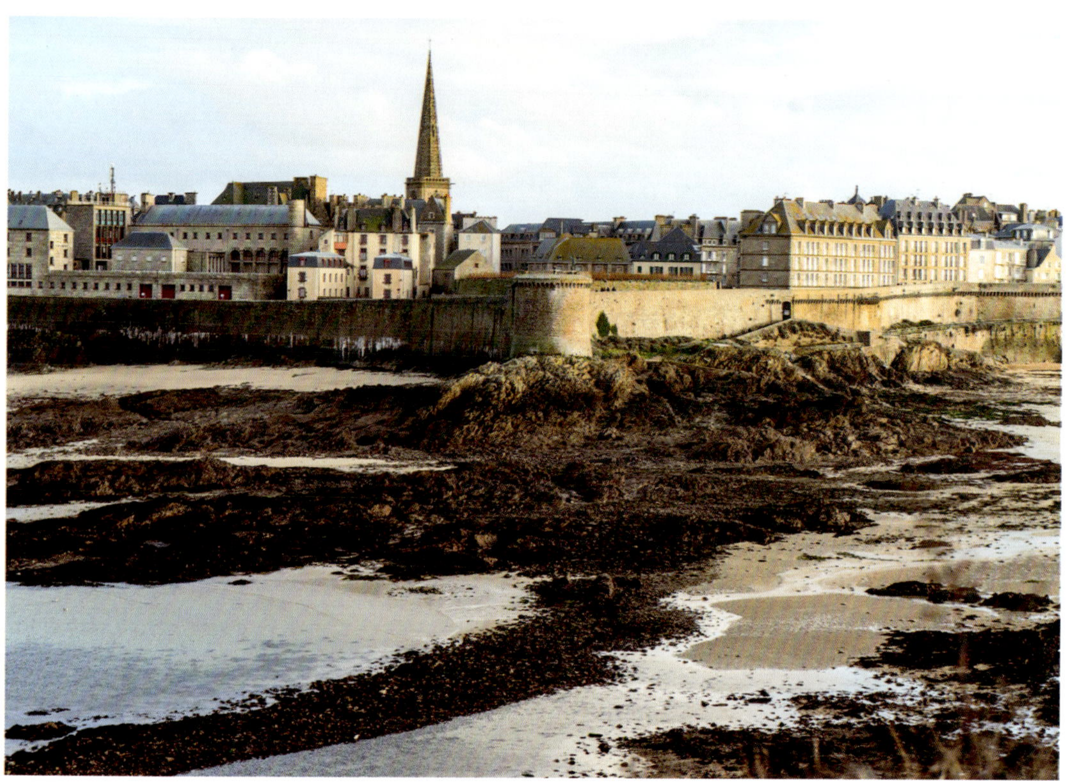

Saint-Malo intra-muros

Saint-Malo

Fortifications surround the old town, which was once a stronghold of buccaneers and pirates. The tomb of Chateaubriand lies directly by the sea. The beaches of Sillon - known for their breakwaters - connect Saint-Malo with Paramé. The Fort National, designed by Vauban and accessible at low tide, is located on an offshore island.

Saint-Malo

Des remparts entourent la vieille ville, qui fut autrefois un bastion pour les corsaires et les pirates. Le tombeau de Chateaubriand est face à la mer. Les plages du Sillon, connues pour leurs brise-lames, relient Saint-Malo à Paramé. Elles s'étendent face au Fort National, bastion conçu par Vauban, accessible à marée basse.

Saint-Malo

Festungsanlagen umgeben die Altstadt, die einst eine Hochburg der Freibeuter und Piraten war. Direkt am Meer liegt das Grab von Chateaubriand. Die Strände von Sillon – bekannt für ihre Wellenbrecher – verbinden Saint-Malo mit Paramé. Auf einer vorgelagerten Insel befindet sich das Fort National, das von Vauban entworfen wurde und bei Ebbe zugänglich ist.

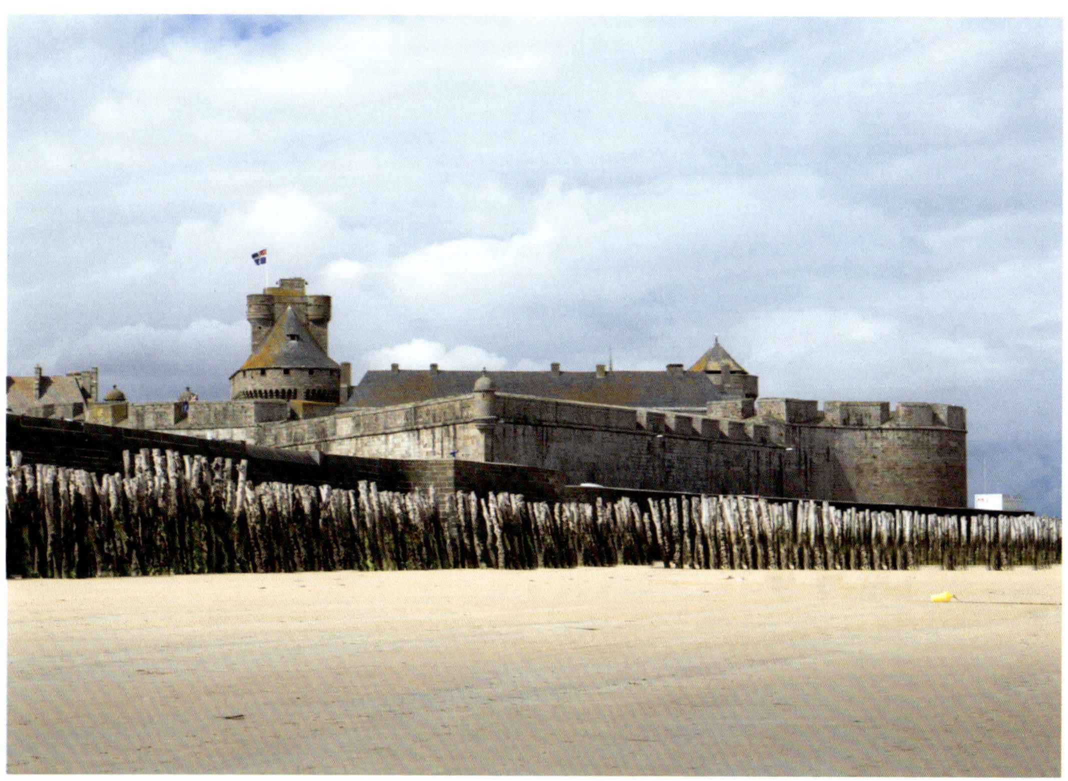

Plage du Sillon, Saint-Malo

Saint-Malo

Las fortificaciones rodean el casco antiguo, que en su día fue un bastión de bucaneros y piratas. La tumba de Chateaubriand se encuentra directamente junto al mar. Las playas de Sillon ,conocidas por sus espigones, conectan Saint-Malo con Paramé. En una isla costera se encuentra el Fuerte Nacional, diseñado por Vauban y accesible en marea baja.

Saint-Malo

As fortificações rodeiam a cidade velha, que, em tempos passados, foi um centro de corsários e piratas. O túmulo de Chateaubriand fica mesmo à beira-mar. As praias de Sillon - conhecidas pelos seus quebra-mares - ligam Saint-Malo a Paramé. Numa ilha em frente encontra-se o Fort National, projetado por Vauban e com acesso na maré baixa.

Saint-Malo

Vestingwerken omringen de oude stad, die ooit een bolwerk van zeerovers en piraten was. Het graf van Chateaubriand ligt direct aan zee. De stranden van Sillon – bekend om hun golfbrekers – verbinden Saint-Malo met Paramé. Op een eiland voor de kust staat het Fort National, dat door Vauban ontworpen en bij laag water toegankelijk is.

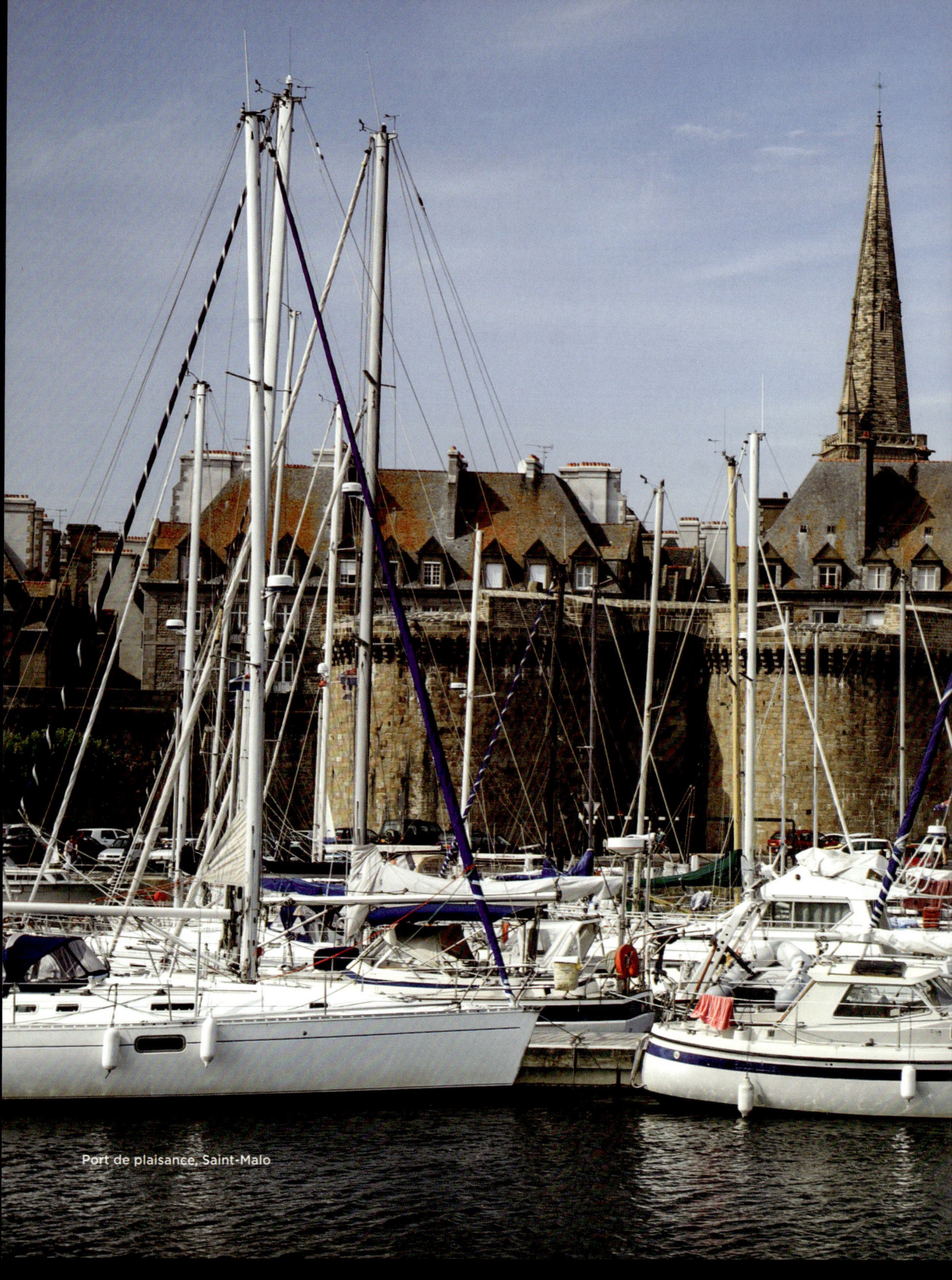

Port de plaisance, Saint-Malo

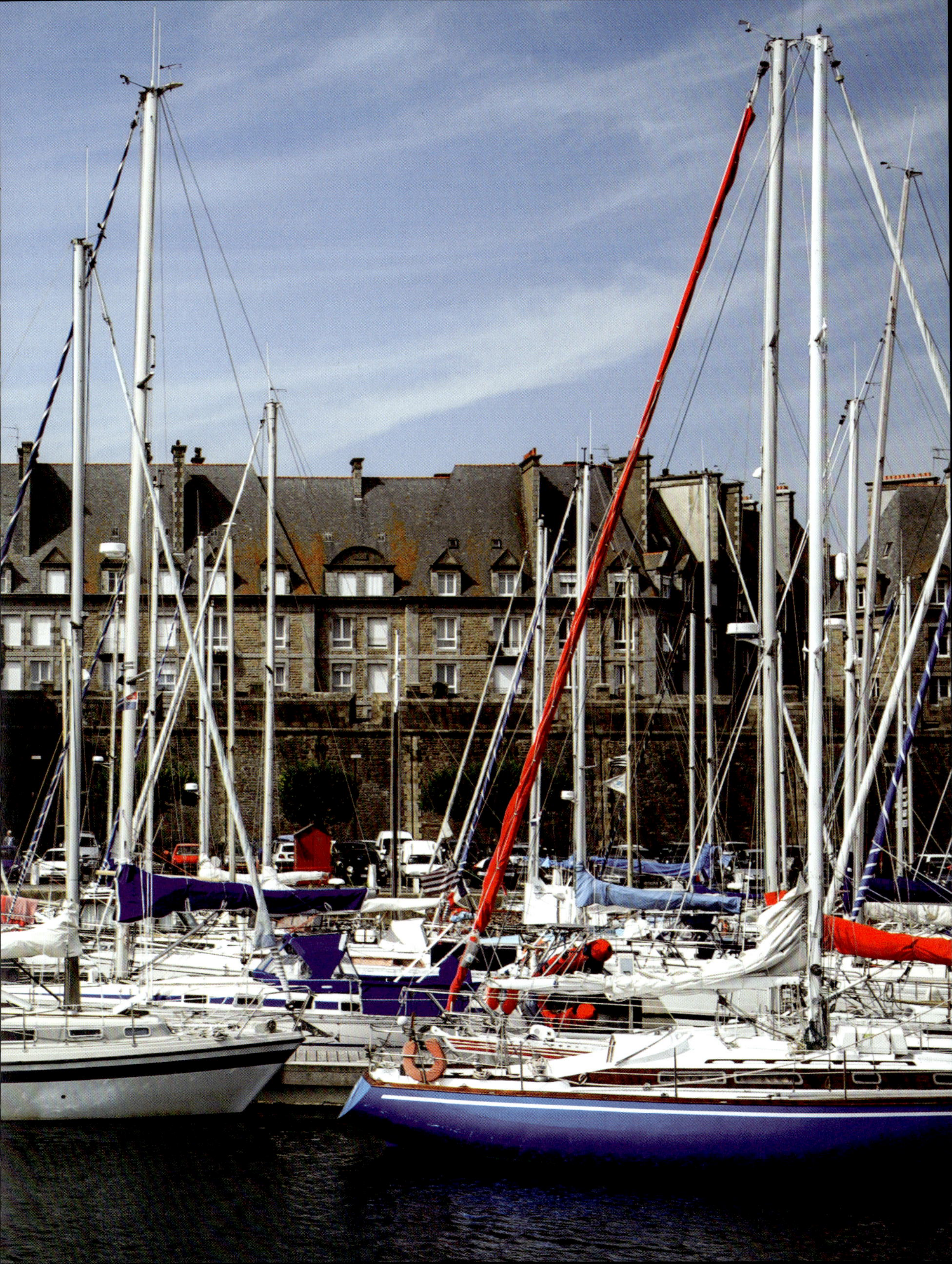

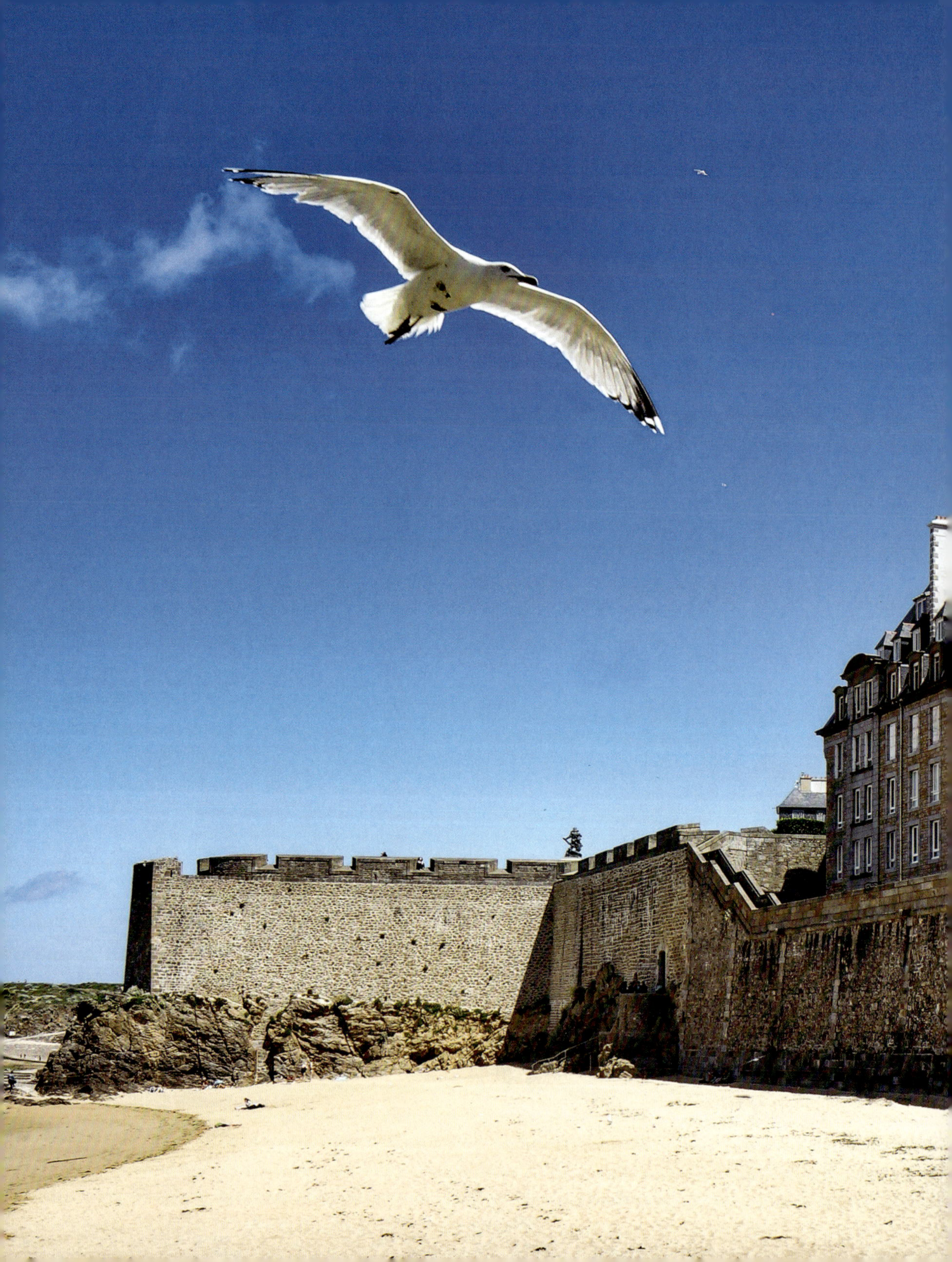

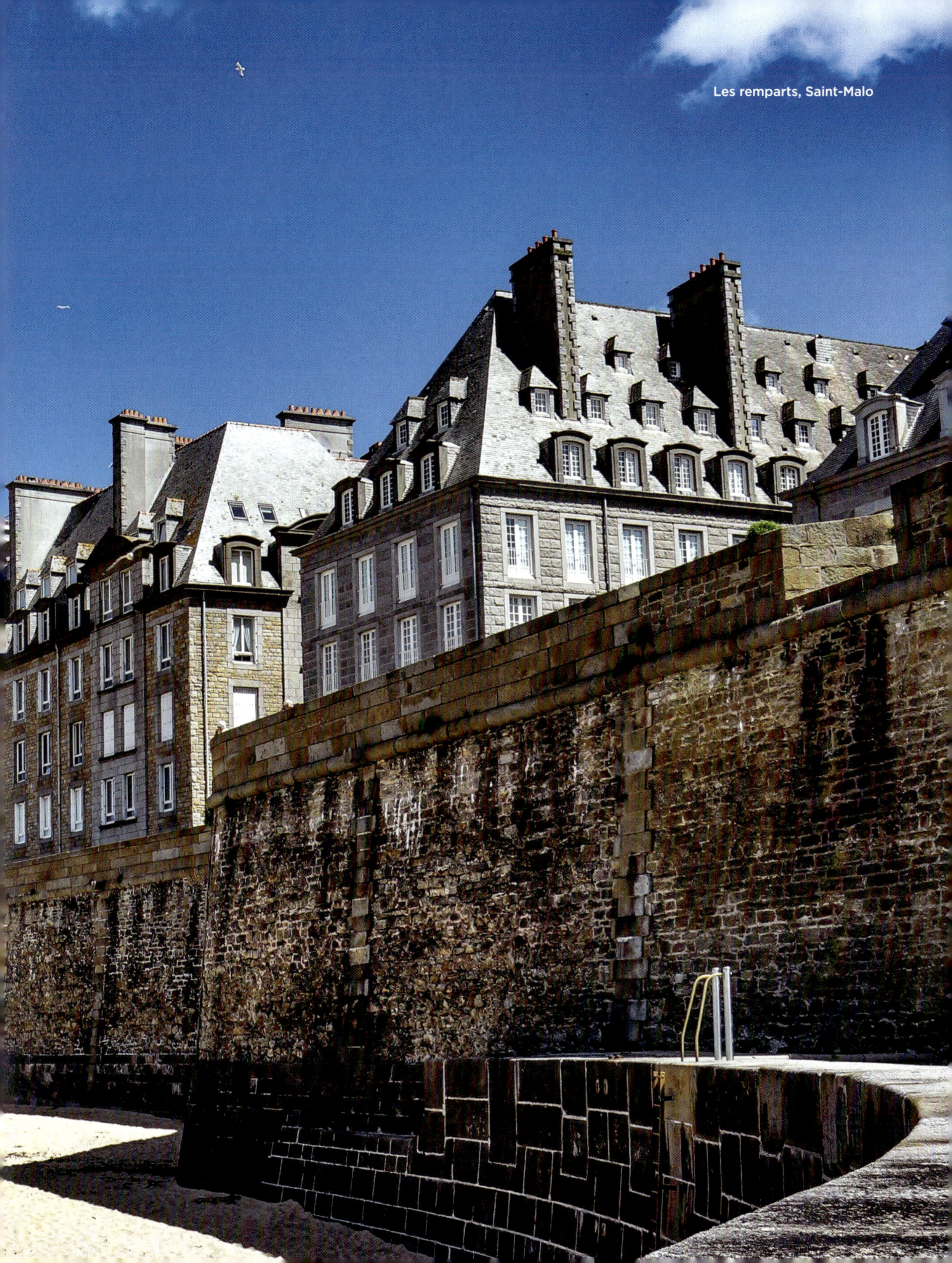
Les remparts, Saint-Malo

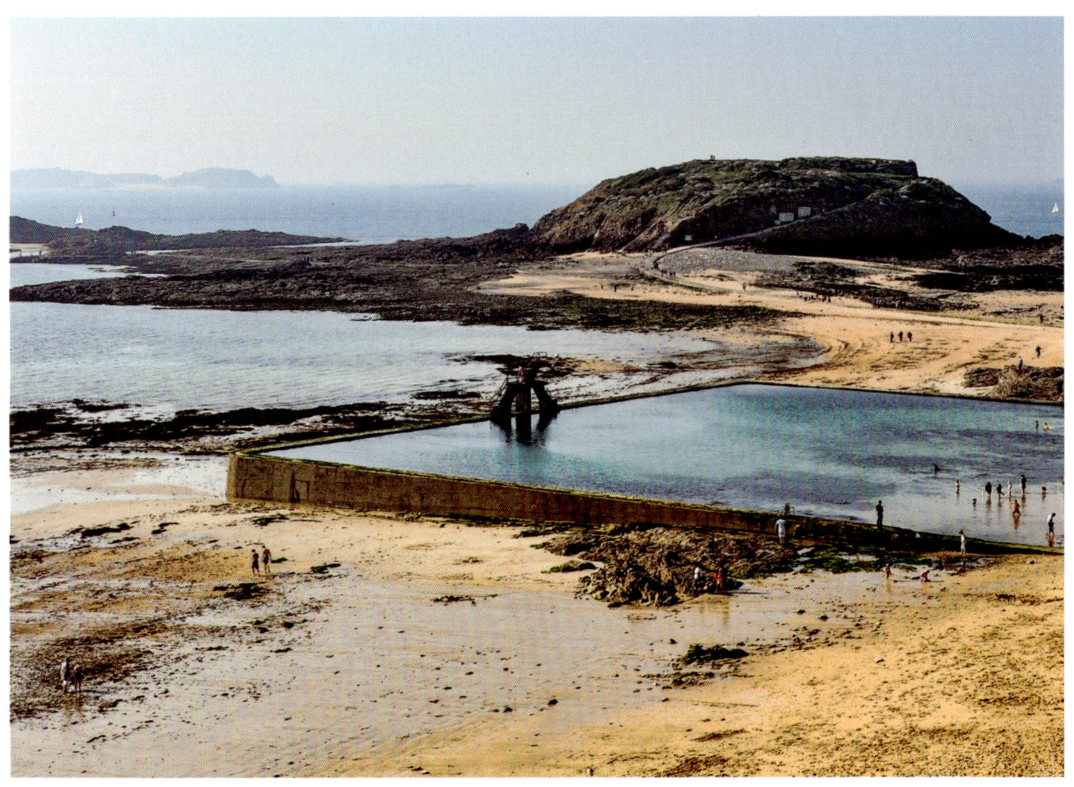

Plage de Bon Secours, l'îlot du Grand Bé, Saint-Malo

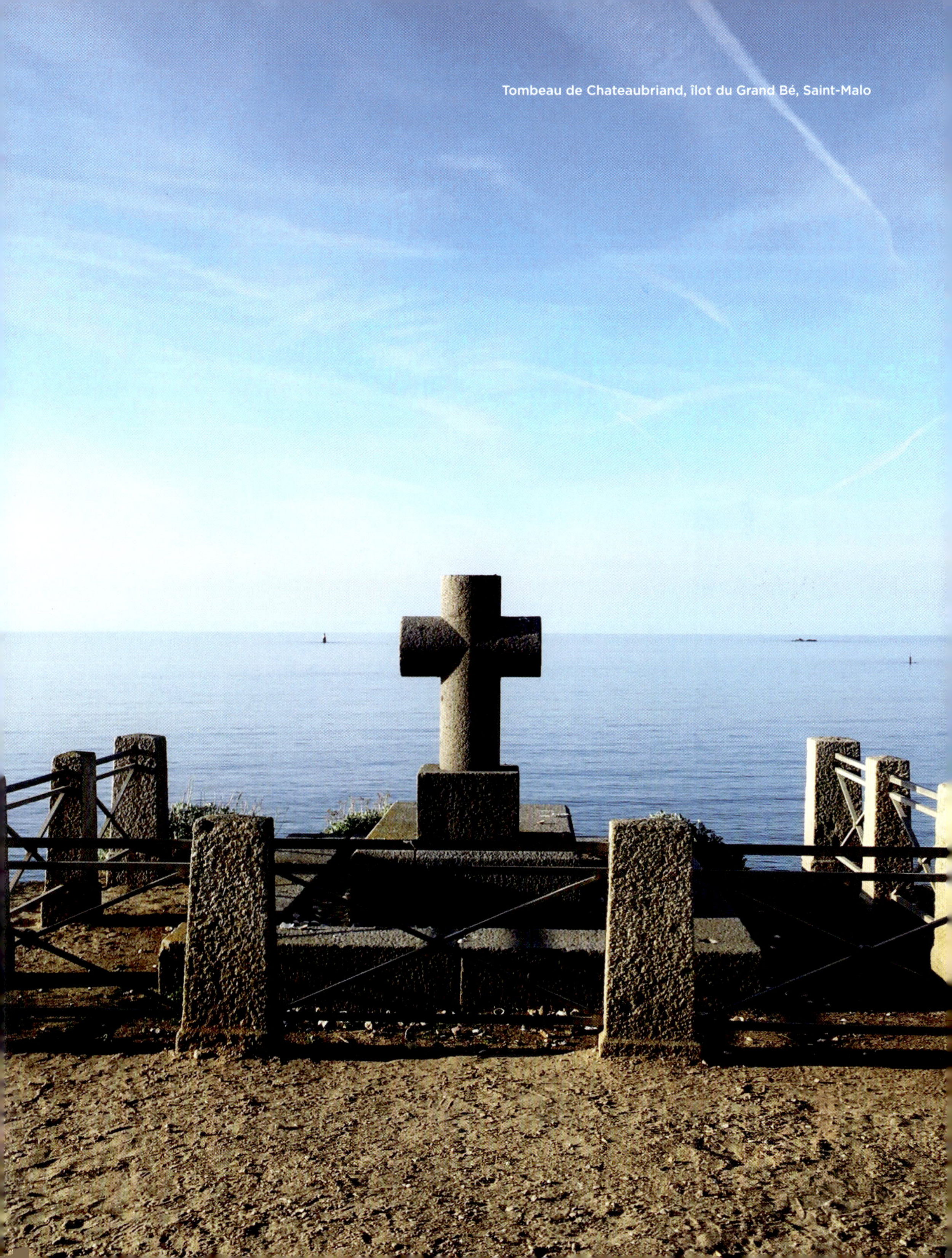
Tombeau de Chateaubriand, îlot du Grand Bé, Saint-Malo

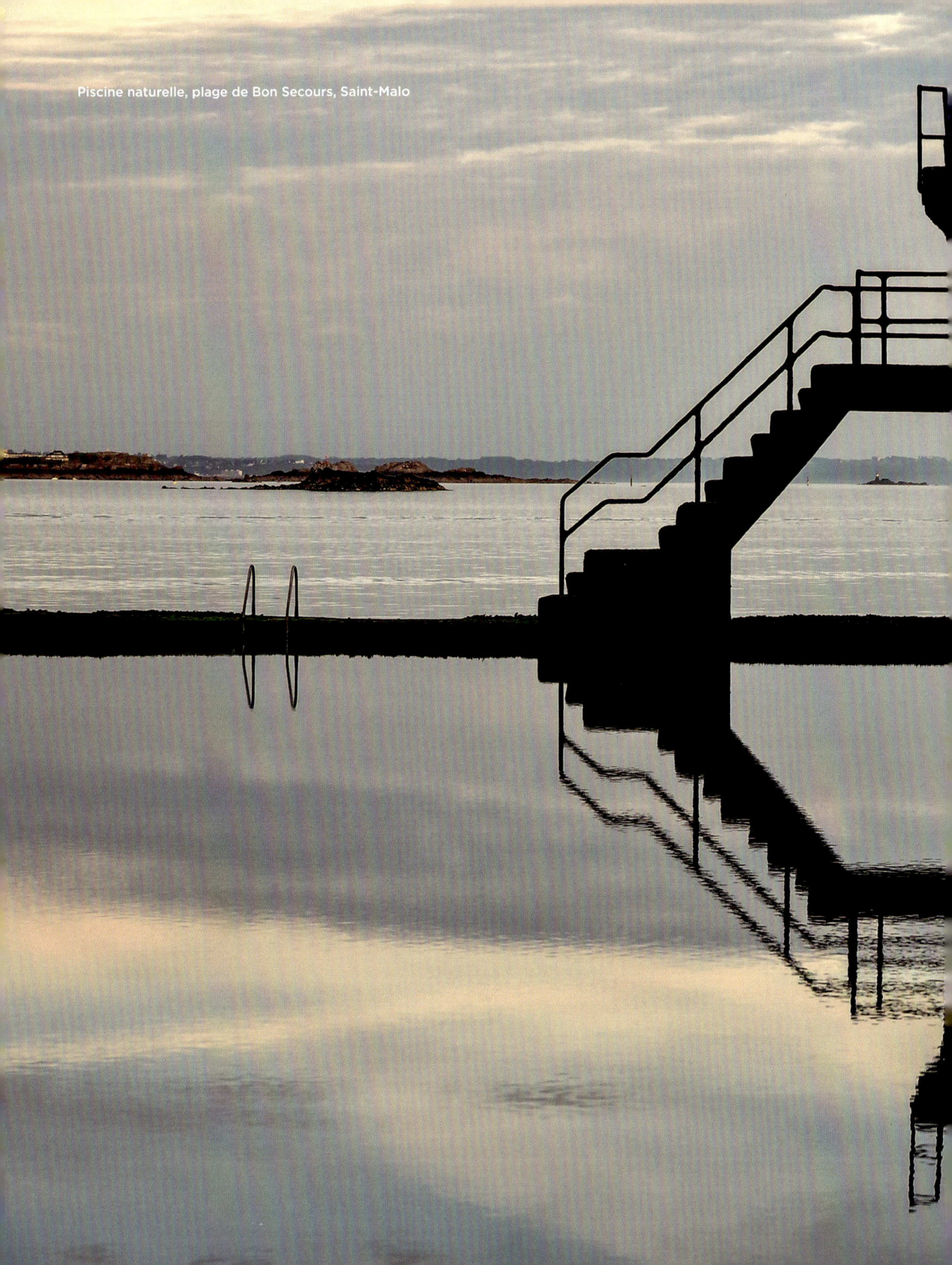

Piscine naturelle, plage de Bon Secours, Saint-Malo

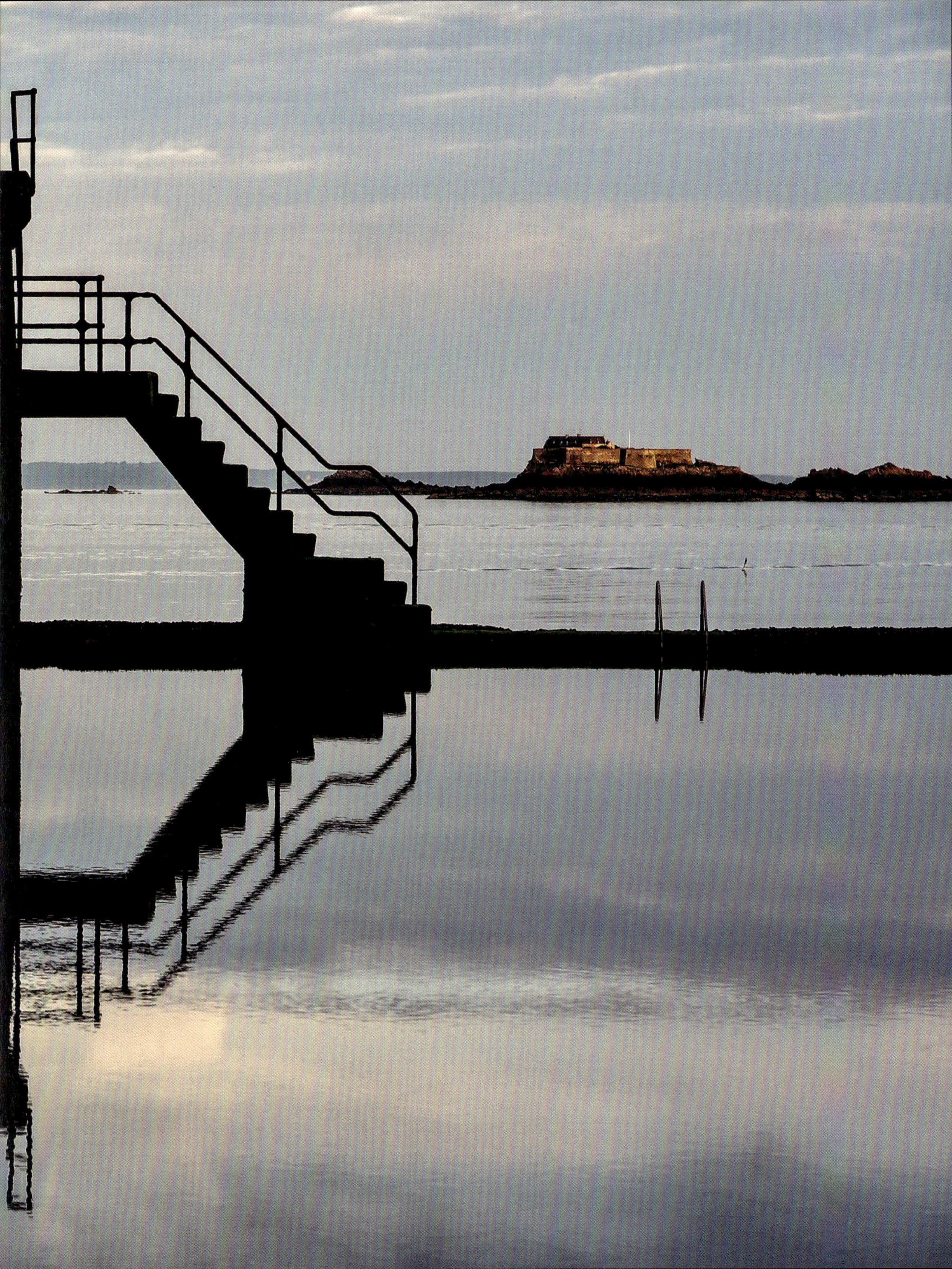

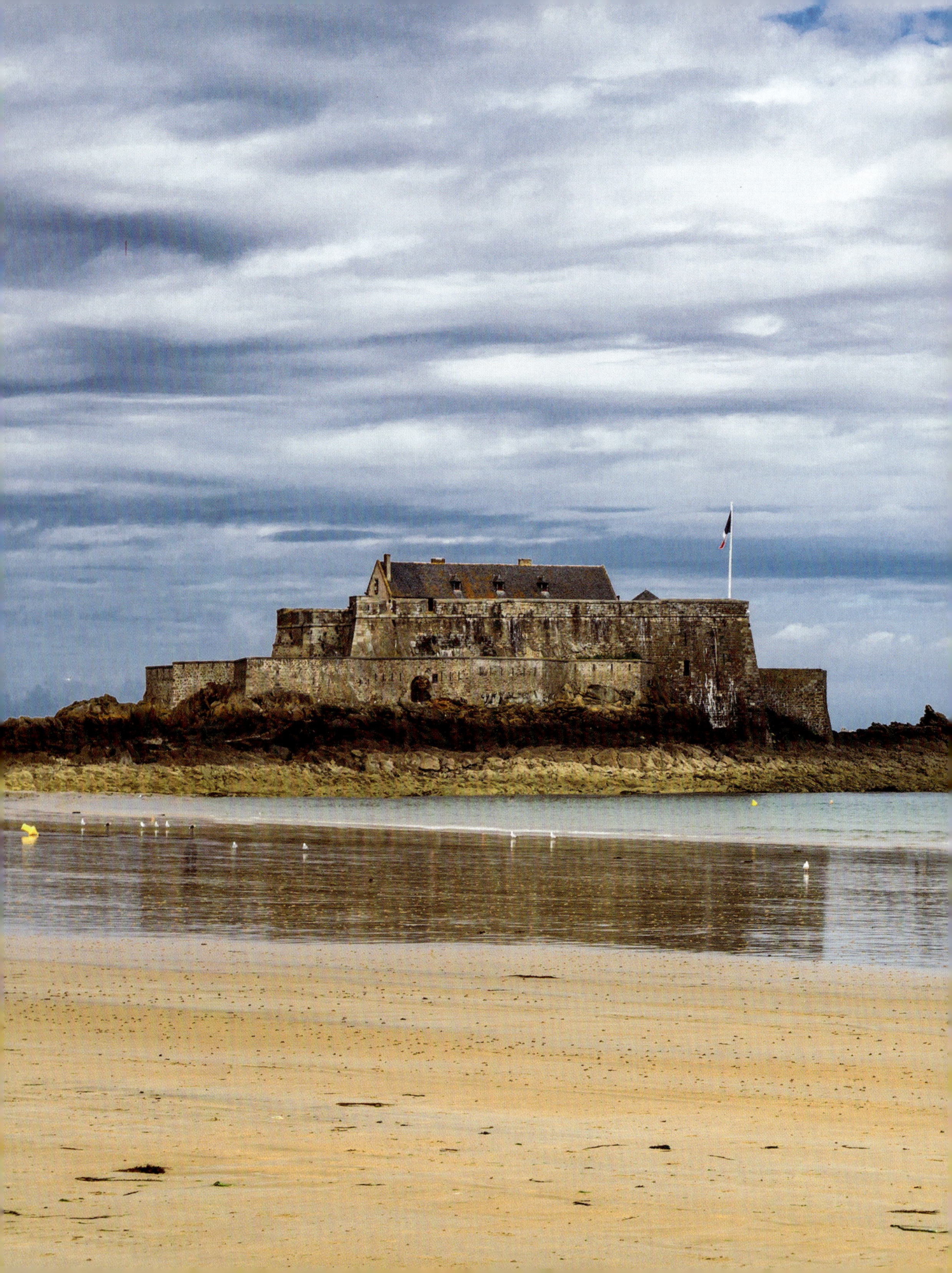

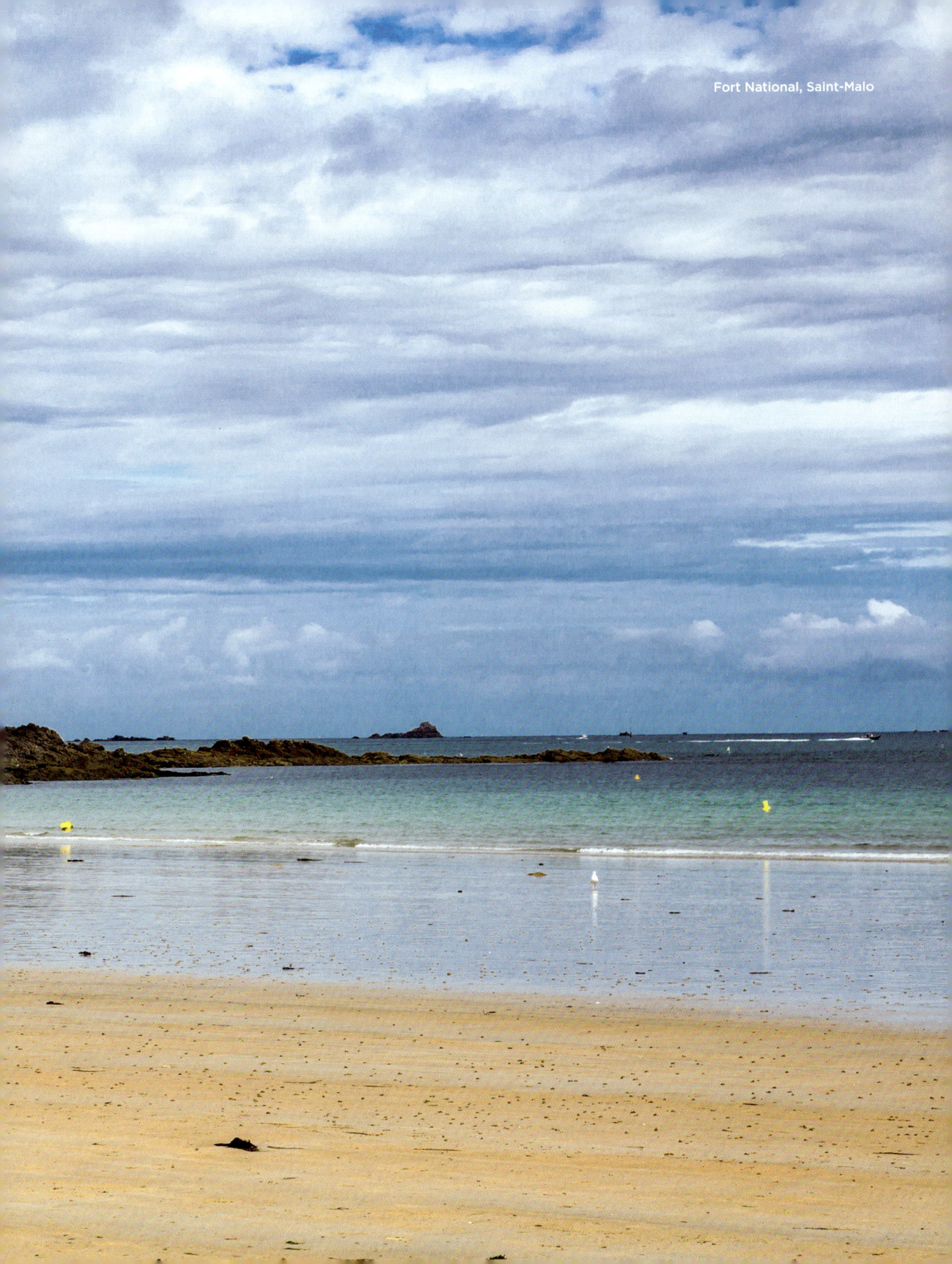
Fort National, Saint-Malo

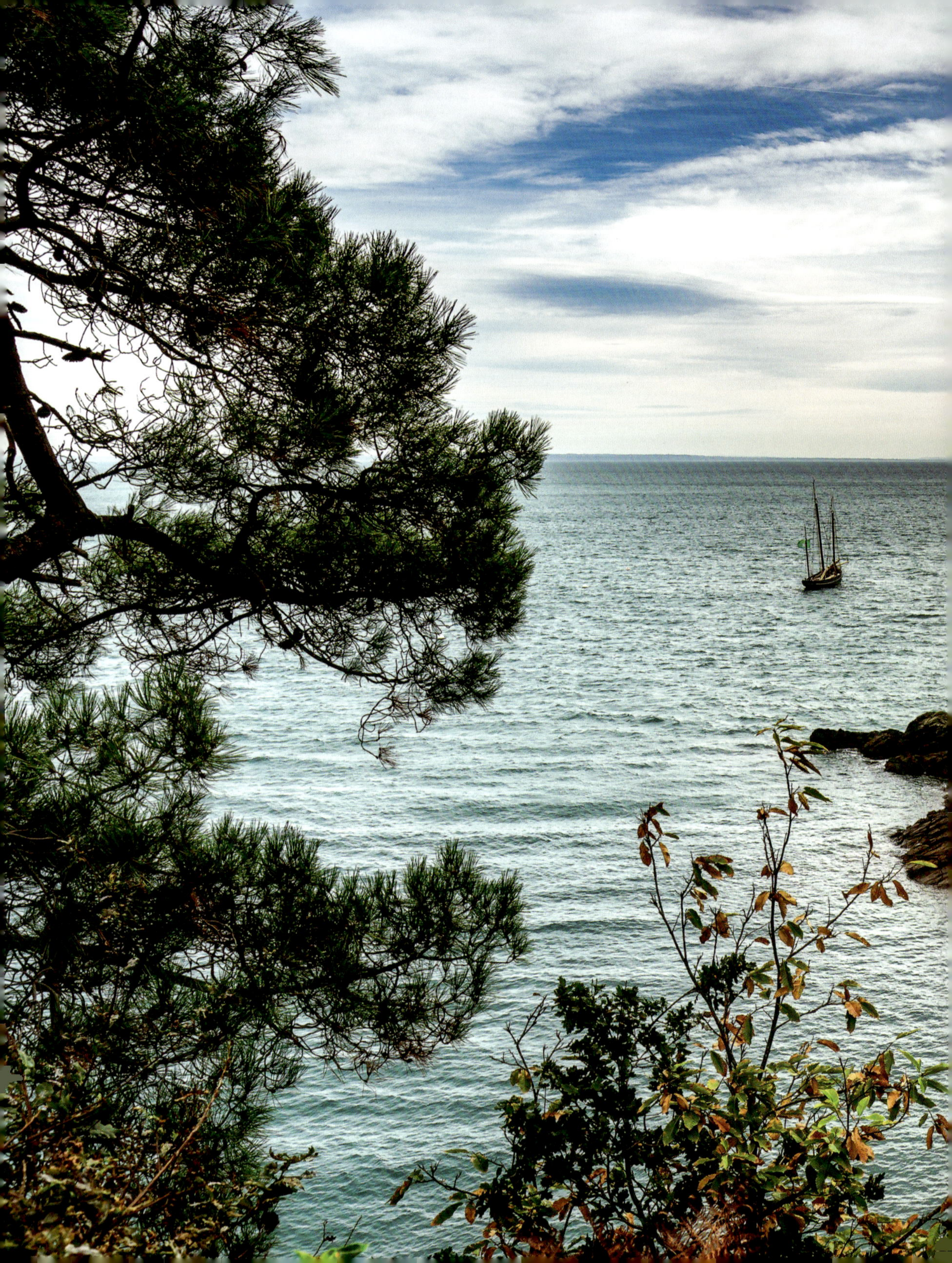

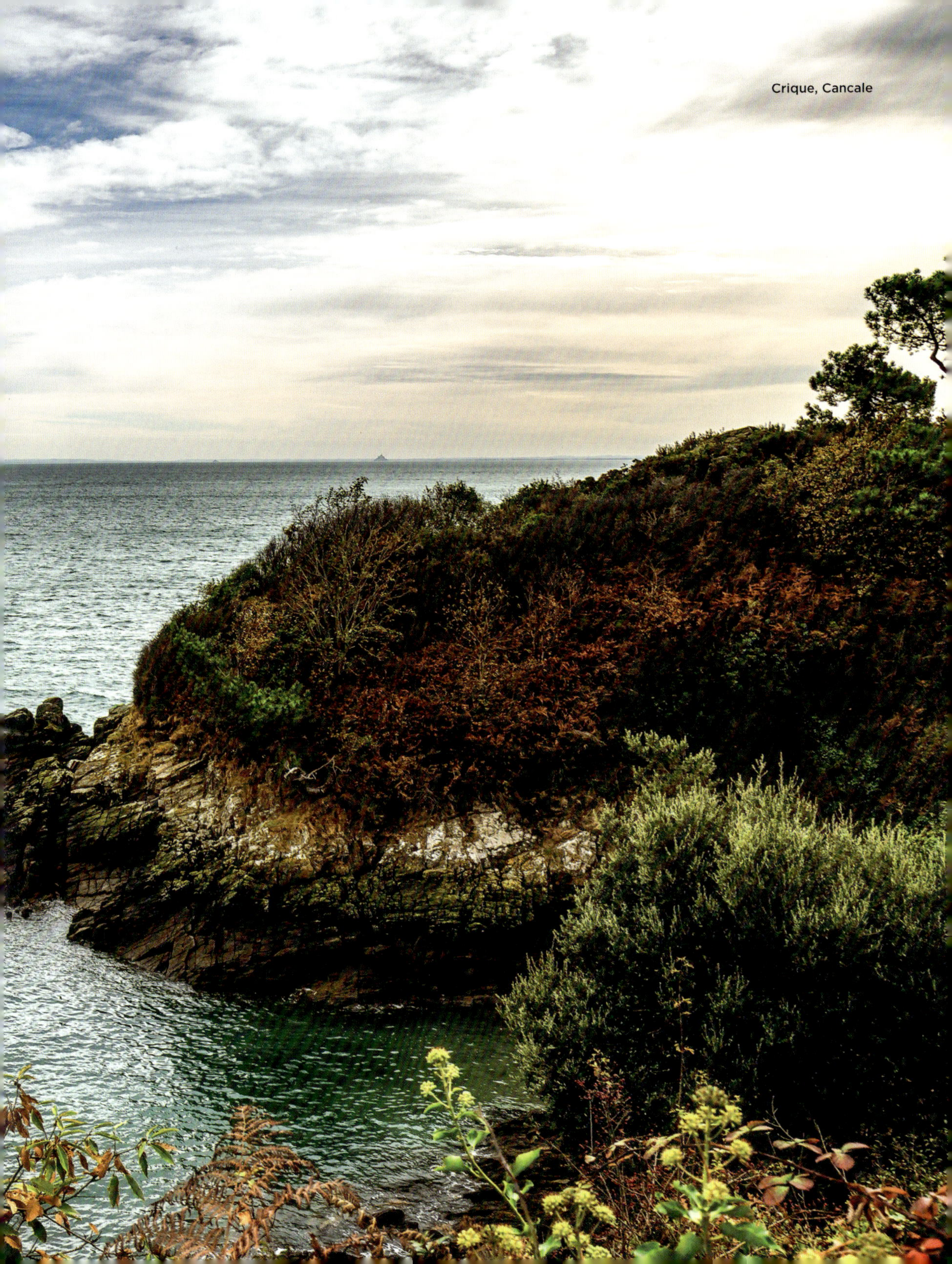

Crique, Cancale

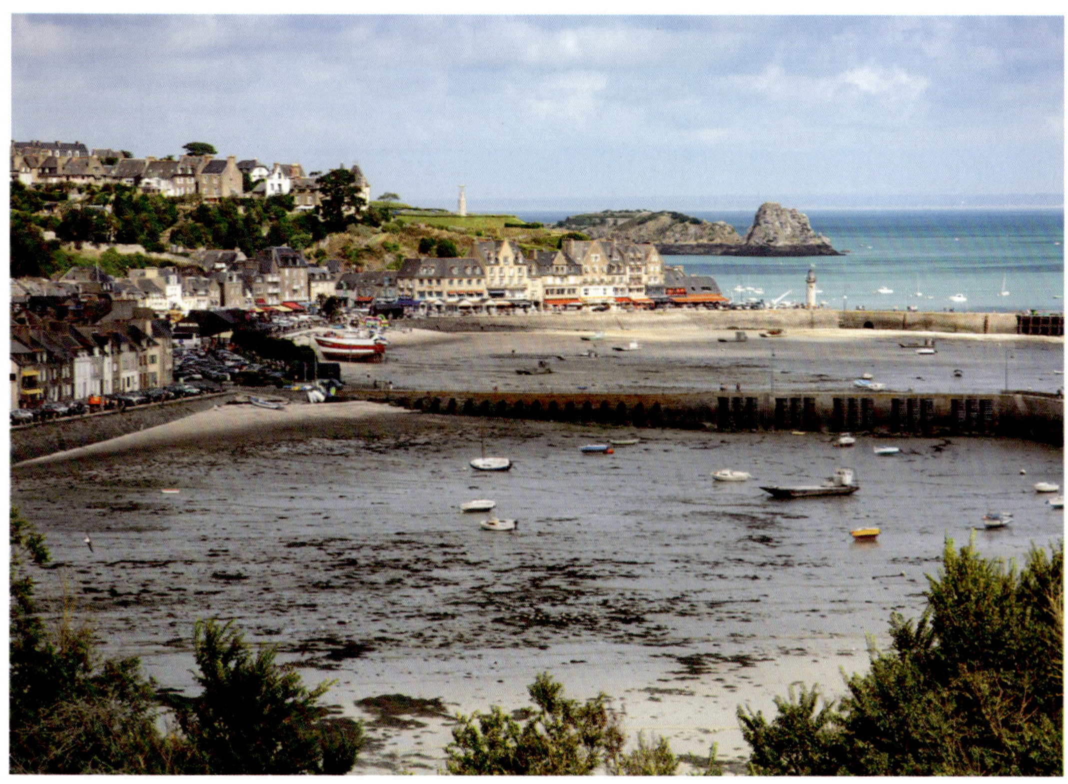

Cancale

Cancale

This small harbour is well known for its oysters and shellfish. The village offers a beautiful view of one of France's architectural wonders: the Mont-Saint-Michel, which rises in the middle of the bay.

Cancale

Cancale est un très joli petit port depuis longtemps réputé pour ses huîtres et ses coquillages. On peut les apprécier en admirant la merveille qu'est le mont Saint-Michel, qui se découvre au milieu de la baie.

Cancale

Der kleine sehenswerte Hafen ist für seine Austern und Schalentiere bekannt. Der Ort bietet einen wunderschönen Ausblick auf eines der Architekturwunder Frankreichs: den Mont-Saint-Michel, der sich in der Mitte der Bucht erhebt.

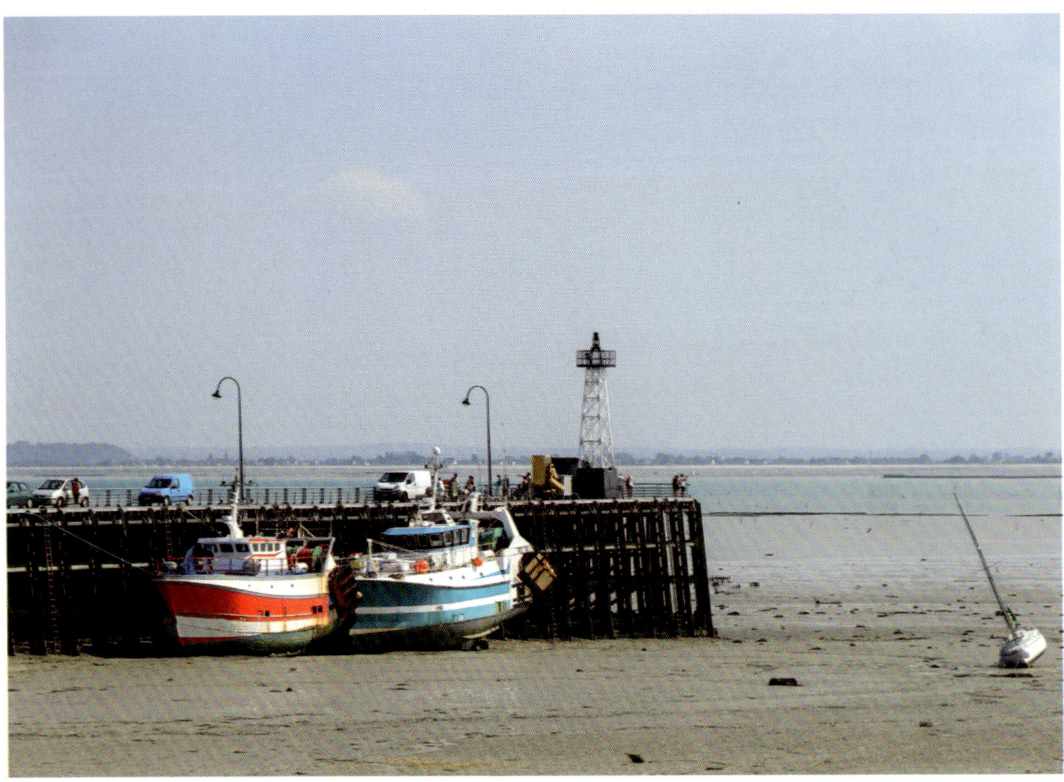

Le port à marée basse, Cancale

Cancale

El pequeño puerto, que merece la pena visitar, es bien conocido por sus ostras y mariscos. El pueblo ofrece una hermosa vista de una de las maravillas arquitectónicas de Francia: el Mont-Saint-Michel, que se levanta en medio de la bahía.

Cancale

O pequeno mas bonito porto é muito conhecido pelas suas ostras e marisco. A vila oferece uma bela vista de uma das maravilhas arquitetónicas da França: o Mont-Saint-Michel, que se ergue no meio da baía.

Cancale

Het bezienswaardige haventje staat bekend om zijn oesters en schaaldieren. De plaats biedt een prachtig uitzicht op een van de architectonische wonderen van Frankrijk: de Mont-Saint-Michel, die midden in de baai oprijst.

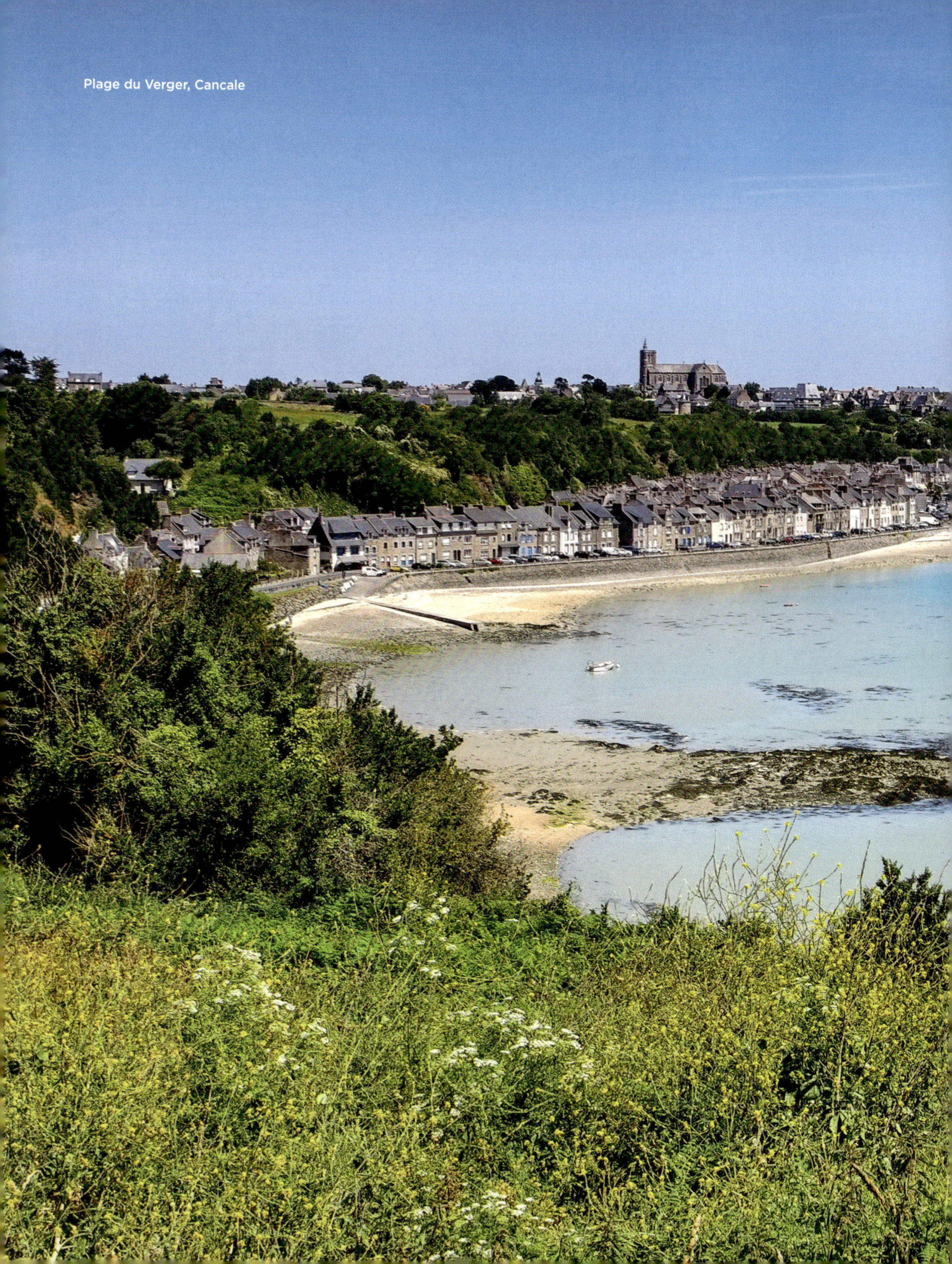
Plage du Verger, Cancale

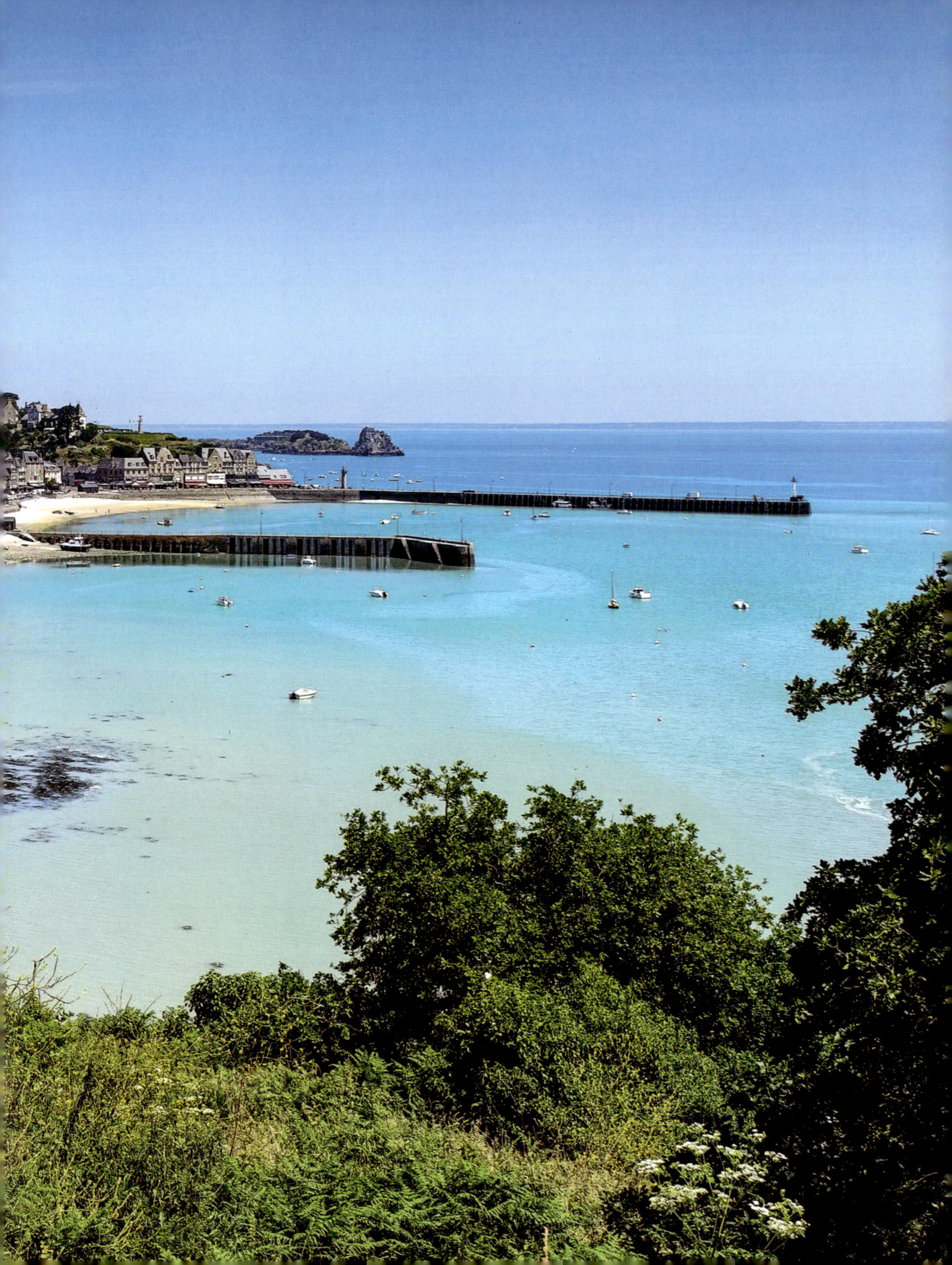

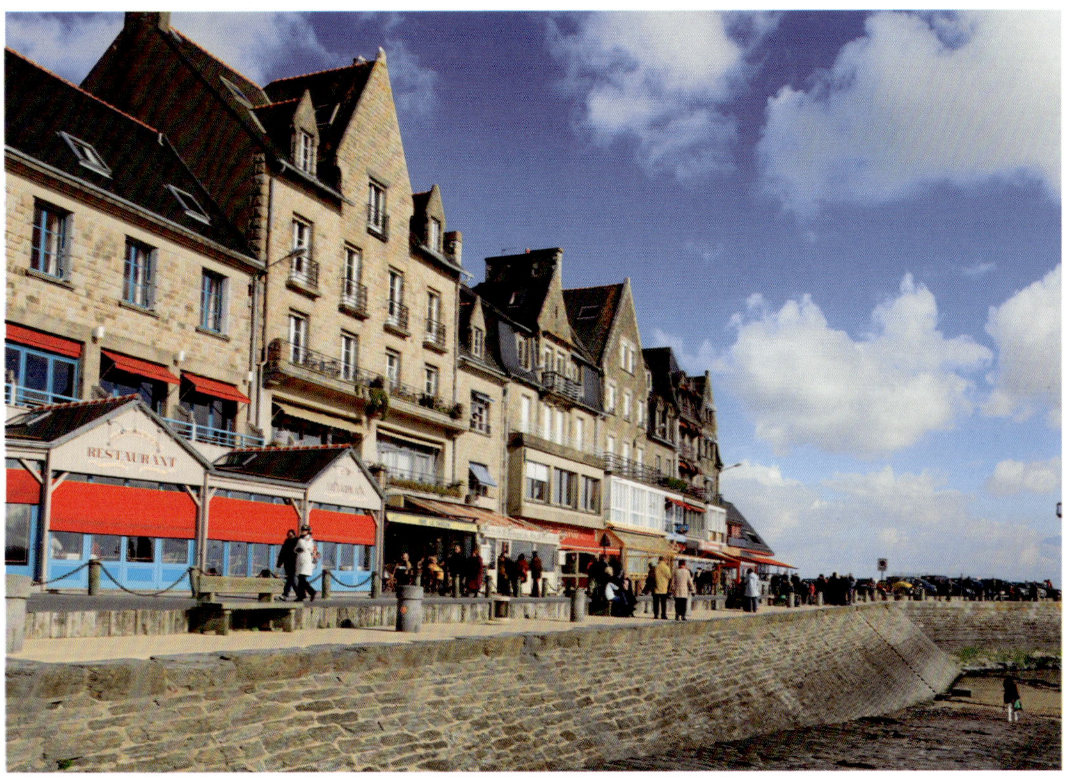

Plage de la Houle, Cancale

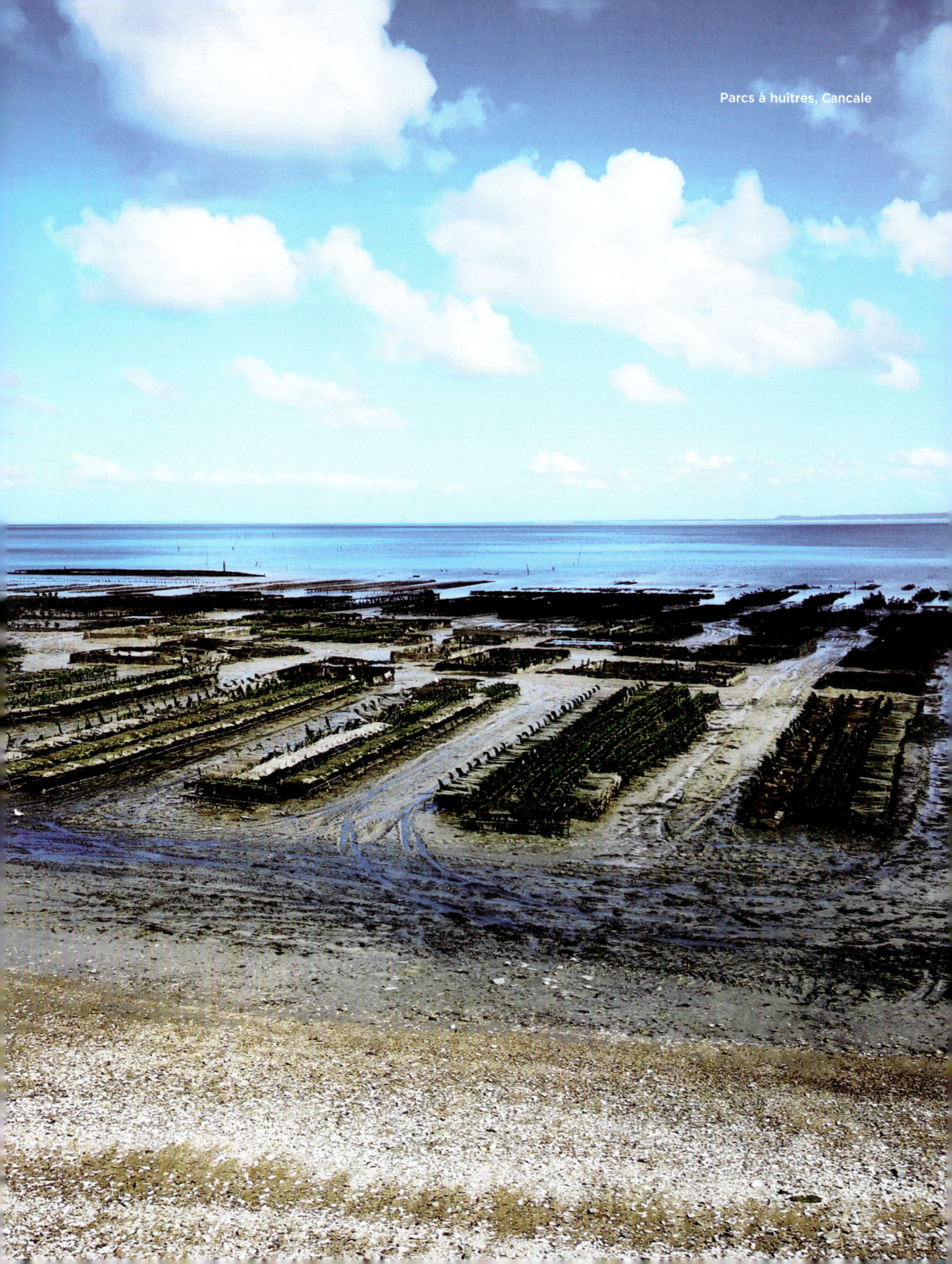
Parcs à huîtres, Cancale

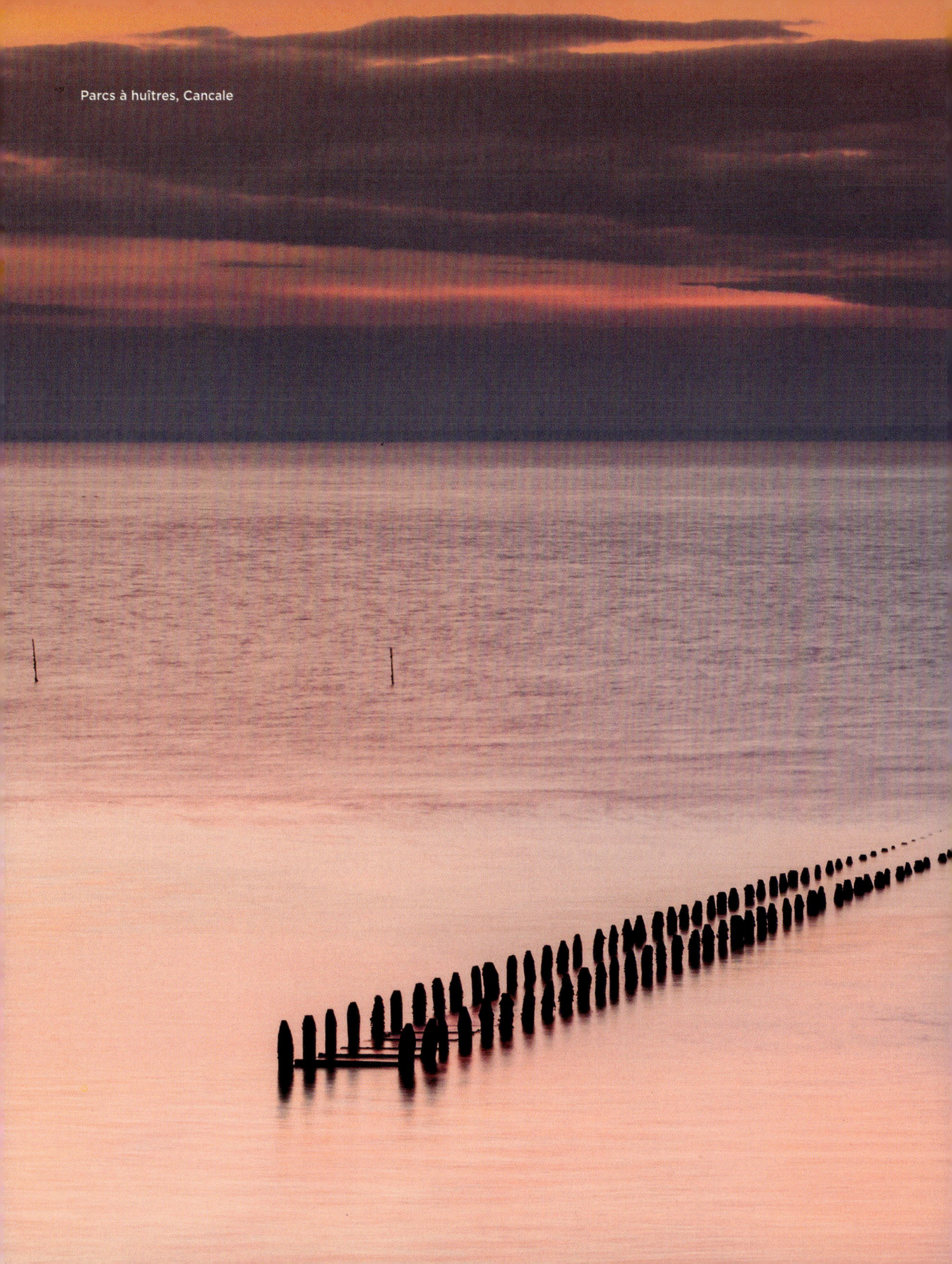
Parcs à huîtres, Cancale

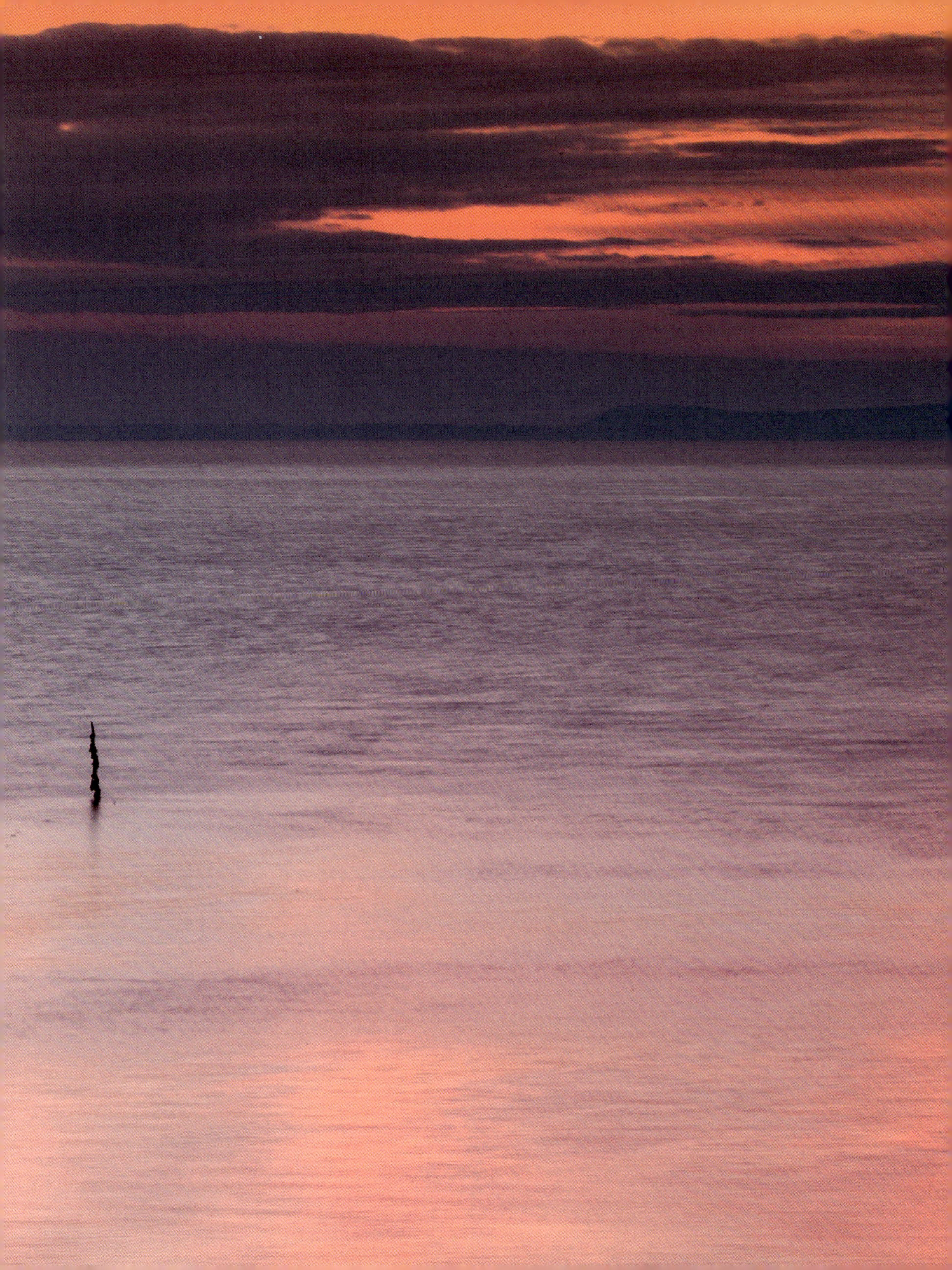

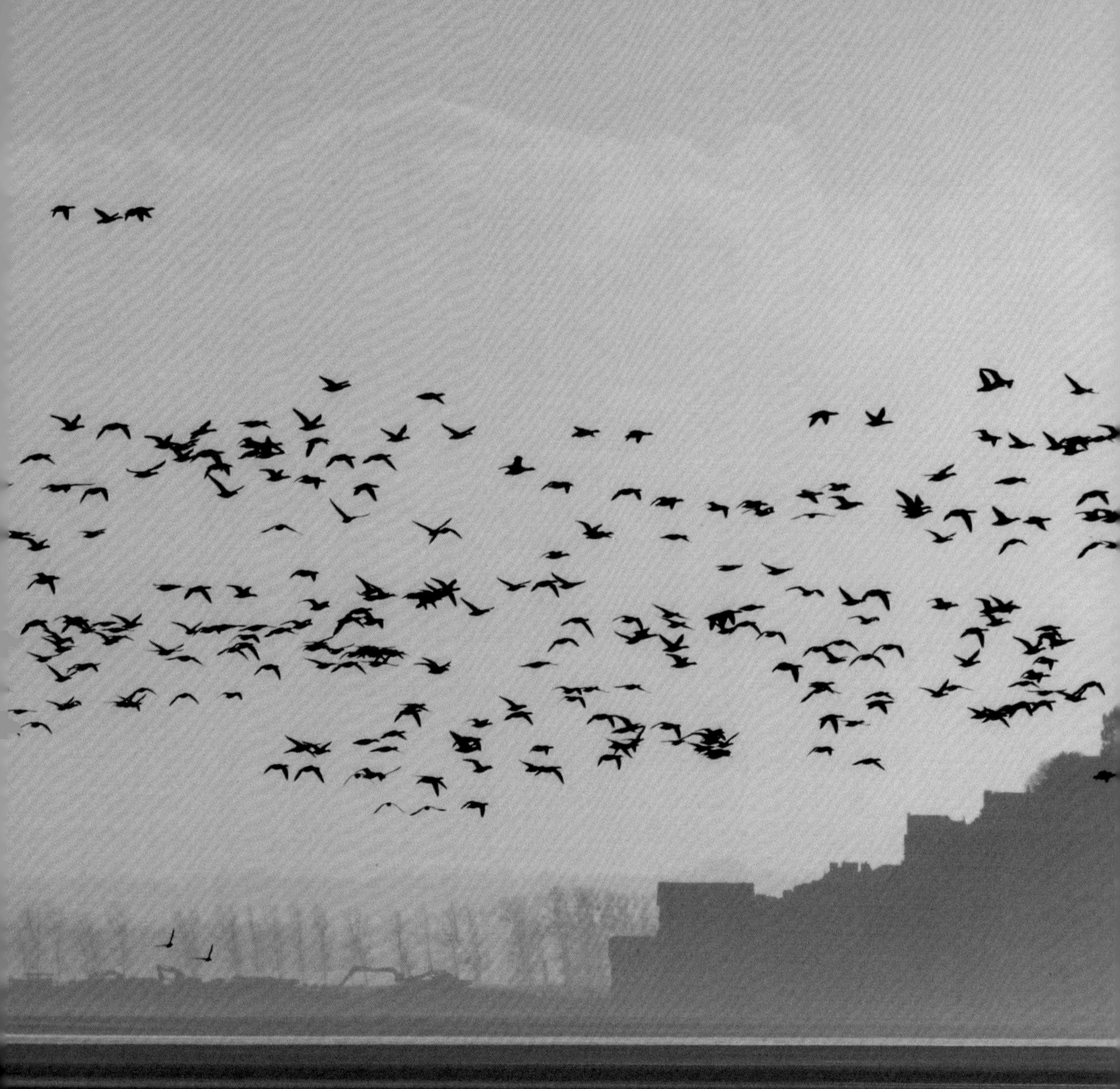

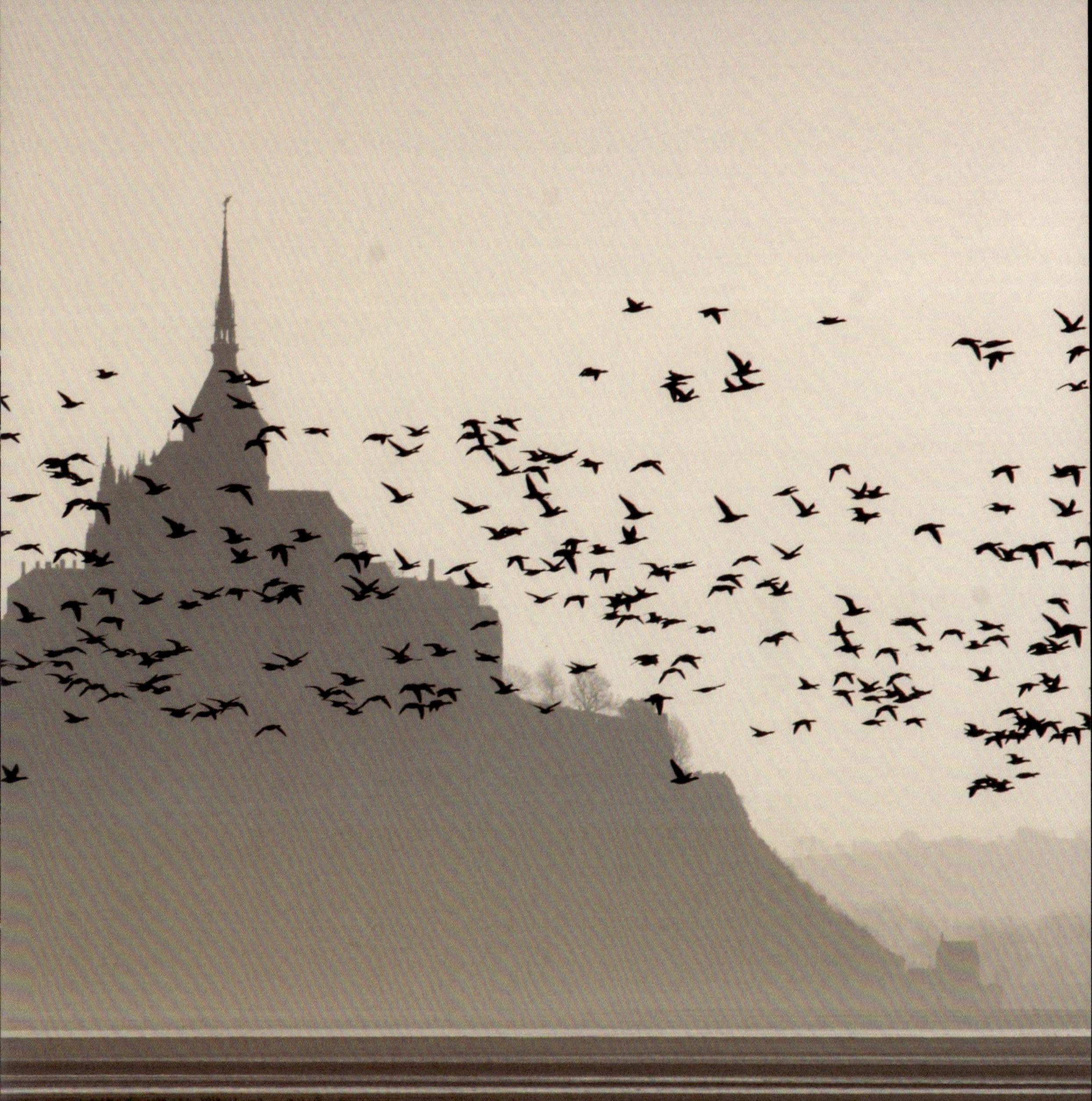

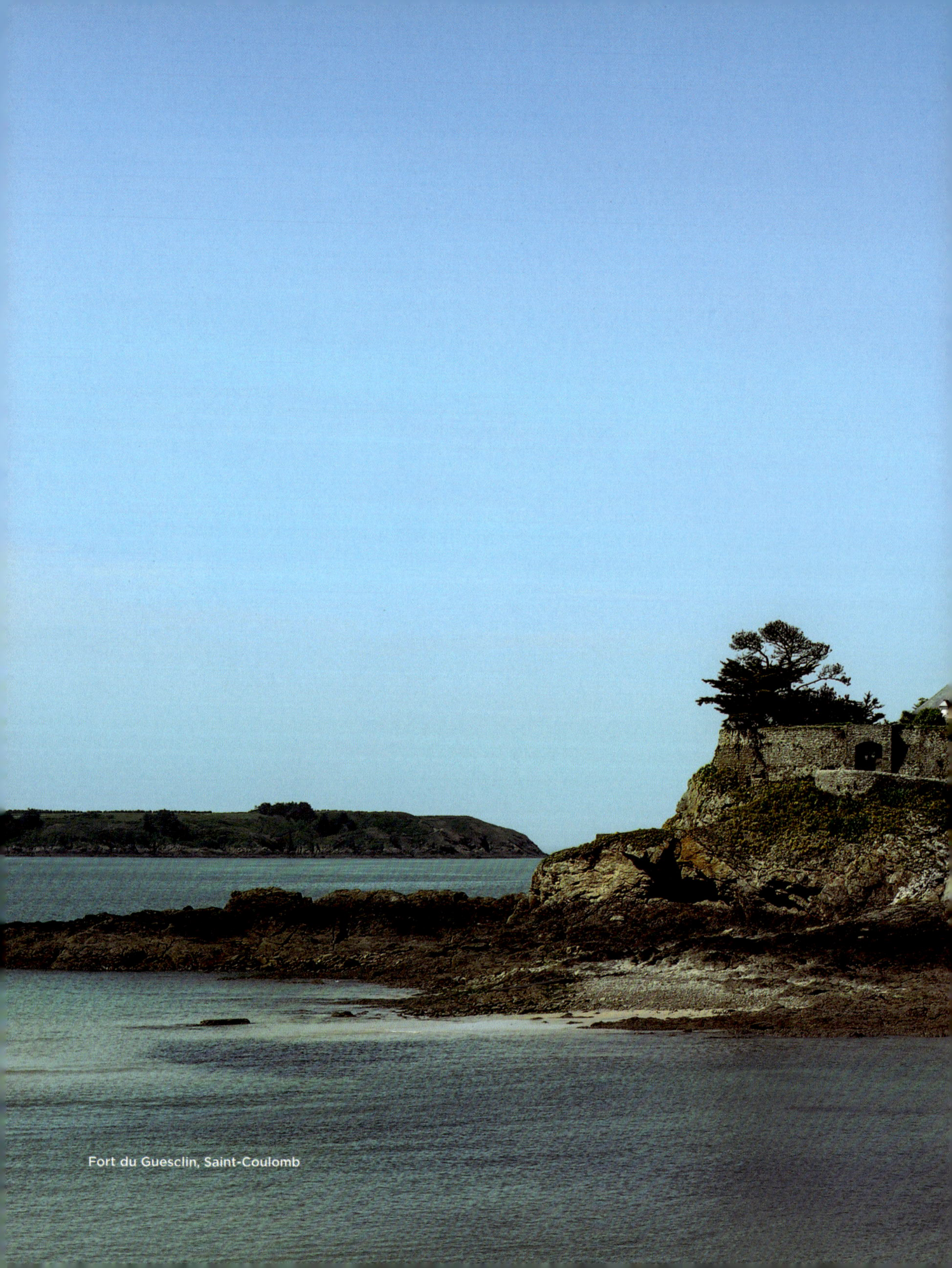

Fort du Guesclin, Saint-Coulomb

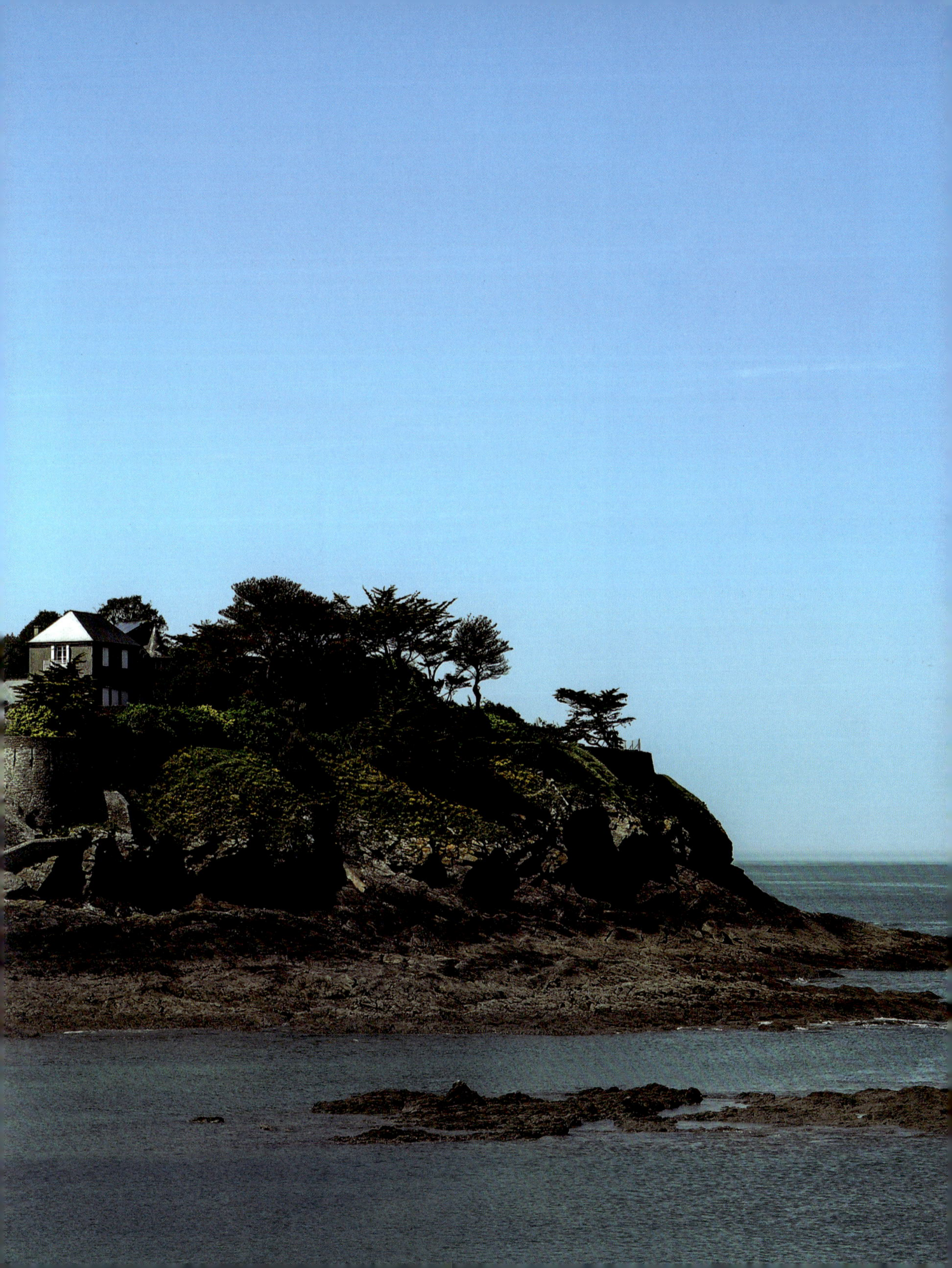

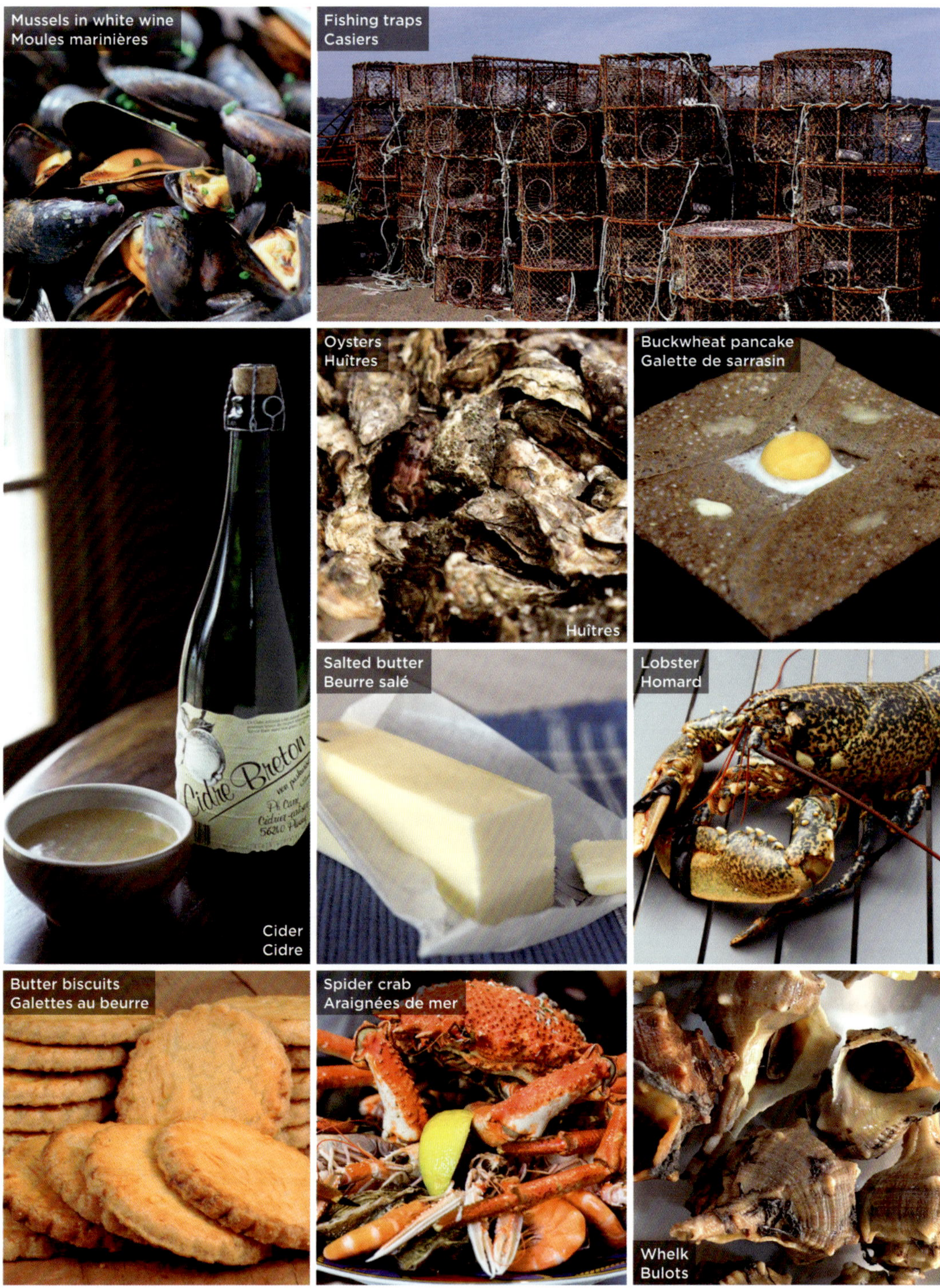

Mussels in white wine
Moules marinières
Fishing traps
Casiers
Oysters
Huîtres
Buckwheat pancake
Galette de sarrasin
Huîtres
Cidre Breton
Salted butter
Beurre salé
Lobster
Homard
Cider
Cidre
Butter biscuits
Galettes au beurre
Spider crab
Araignées de mer
Whelk
Bulots

The Cuisine

The fresh sea air makes you want to sample the culinary specialities of the region: shrimps, prawns, langoustines, oysters, crabs or sea spiders, snails, and of course Breton lobsters - there is no limit to the selection of seafood. It is served with bread and salted butter, one of Brittany's most renowned products, which is also used in large quantities in the Kouign-amann – a popular cake from Douarnenez. Another speciality are crêpes and galettes – Breton buckwheat pancakes from the Middle Ages.

La gastronomie

Le parfum iodé des côtes fait saliver nos papilles à l'idée de déguster un plateau de fruits de mer : crevettes grises et roses, langoustines, huîtres creuses ou plates, tourteaux ou araignées selon la saison, bulots, bigorneaux, et, il va sans dire, un délicieux homard breton, accompagné de tartines de pain beurrées. Le beurre salé est un produit phare sur la table. On l'utilise sans compter dans le fameux kouign-amann dont l'origine vient de Douarnenez. Quant à la crêpe bretonne et à la galette de sarrasin, leur origine remonterait au Moyen Âge.

Die Gastronomie

Die frische Meeresluft macht Lust auf die kulinarischen Spezialitäten der Region: Krabben, Garnelen, Langustinen, Austern, Taschenkrebse oder Seespinnen, Schnecken und natürlich bretonischer Hummer – der Auswahl an Meeresfrüchten ist keine Grenze gesetzt. Serviert werden dazu Brot und gesalzene Butter, eines der renommiertesten Produkte der Bretagne, die auch in großen Mengen im Kouign-amann zum Einsatz kommt – einem beliebten Kuchen aus Douarnenez. Eine weitere Spezialität sind Crêpes und Galettes – bretonische Buchweizenpfannkuchen – die aus dem Mittelalter stammen.

La gastronomía

El aire fresco del mar hace que se deseen las especialidades culinarias de la región: camarones, gambas, langostinos, langostinos, ostras, cangrejos o arañas marinas, caracoles y, por supuesto, langostas bretonas; no hay límite en la selección de mariscos. Se sirven con pan y mantequilla con sal, uno de los productos más famosos de Bretaña, que también se utiliza en grandes cantidades en el Kouign-amann (un pastel popular de Douarnenez). Otra especialidad son los crepes y las galettes (panqueques de trigo sarraceno bretón) de la Edad Media.

A gastronomia

O ar fresco do mar convida a provar as especialidades culinárias da região: camarões, lagostins, ostras, caranguejos ou aranhas do mar, caracóis e, claro, lagostas bretãs - a seleção de marisco e frutos do mar não tem limites e é acompanhada com pão e manteiga salgada, um dos produtos mais famosos da Bretanha, que também é utilizada em grandes quantidades no Kouign-amann - um bolo típico de Douarnenez, muito apreciado. Uma outra especialidade são os crepes e as galetes - panquecas de trigo mourisco bretão - da Idade Média.

De gastronomie

De frisse zeelucht maakt hongerig naar de culinaire speciliteiten van de regio: krabben, garnalen, langoustines, Japanse of gewone oesters, noordzeekrabben of spinkrabben, wulken, alikruiken en natuurlijk Bretonse kreeften – de keuze aan zeevruchten is onbegrensd. Ze worden geserveerd met brood en gezouten boter, een van de bekendste Bretonse producten, die ook in grote hoeveelheden wordt gebruikt in de kouign amann – een geliefd gebak uit Douarnenez. Een andere specialiteit zijn crêpes en galettes (Bretonse boekweitpannenkoeken), die uit de middeleeuwen stammen.

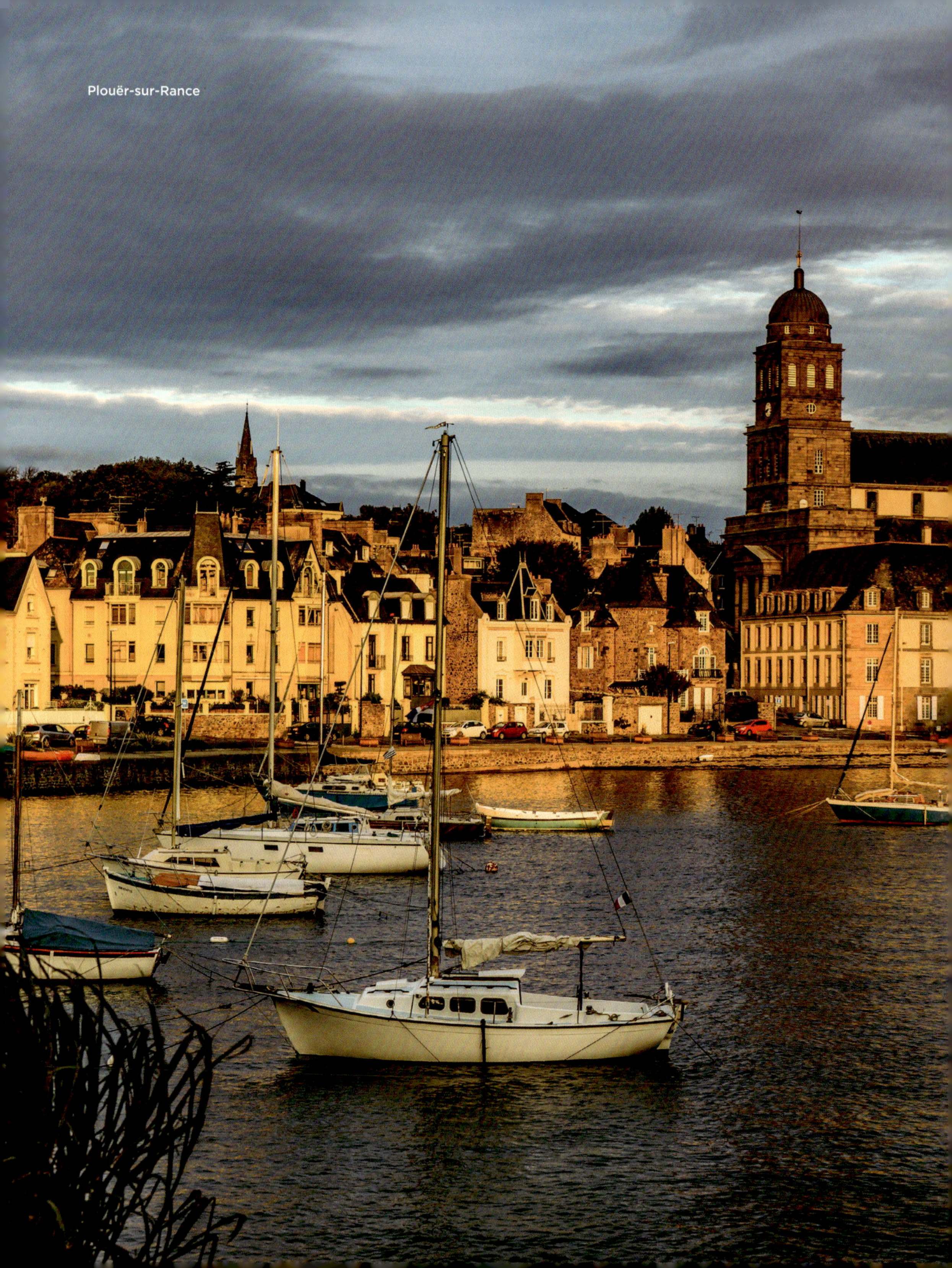
Plouër-sur-Rance

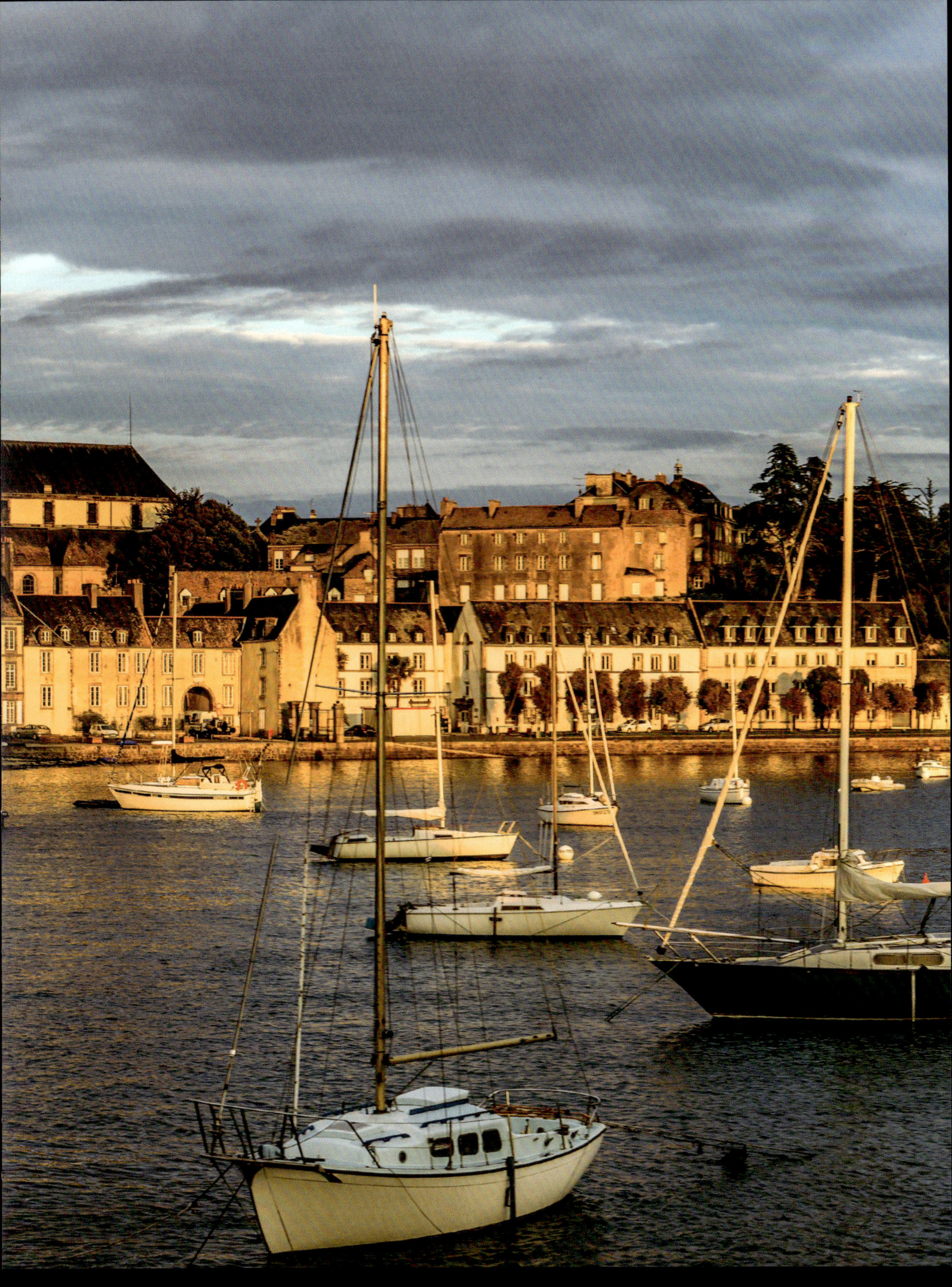

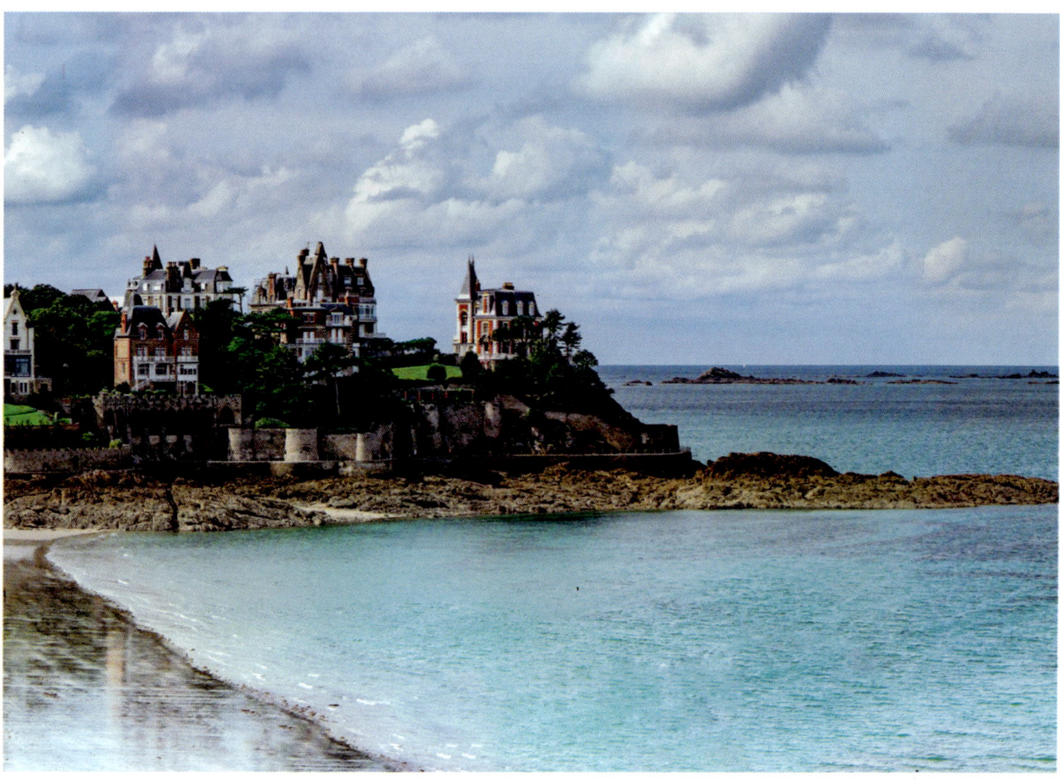

Dinard

Dinard

This popular seaside resort is known for its Belle Époque villas. On sunny days, the main beach Plage de l'Écluse with its white and blue tents attracts many visitors.

Dinard

El popular balneario es conocido por sus villas de la Belle Époque. En los días soleados, la playa principal, Plage de l'Écluse, con sus puestos blancos y azules, atrae a muchos visitantes.

Dinard

Station balnéaire de renom, avec ses villas Belle Époque, Dinard est aussi très prisée pour sa célèbre plage de l'Écluse où se dressent de jolies tentes blanche et bleue les jours de grand soleil.

Dinard

A famosa estância balnear é conhecida pelas suas casas tipo „Belle Époque". Em dias de sol, a praia principal da Plage de l'Écluse, com as suas barracas brancas e azuis, atrai muitos visitantes.

Dinard

Der beliebte Badeort ist für seine Villen der Belle Époque bekannt. An sonnigen Tagen zieht der Hauptstrand Plage de l'Écluse mit seinen weißen und blauen Zelten zahlreiche Besucher an.

Dinard

De populaire badplaats staat bekend om zijn villa's uit de belle époque. Op zonnige dagen trekt het hoofdstrand Plage de l'Écluse met zijn witte en blauwe tenten veel bezoekers.

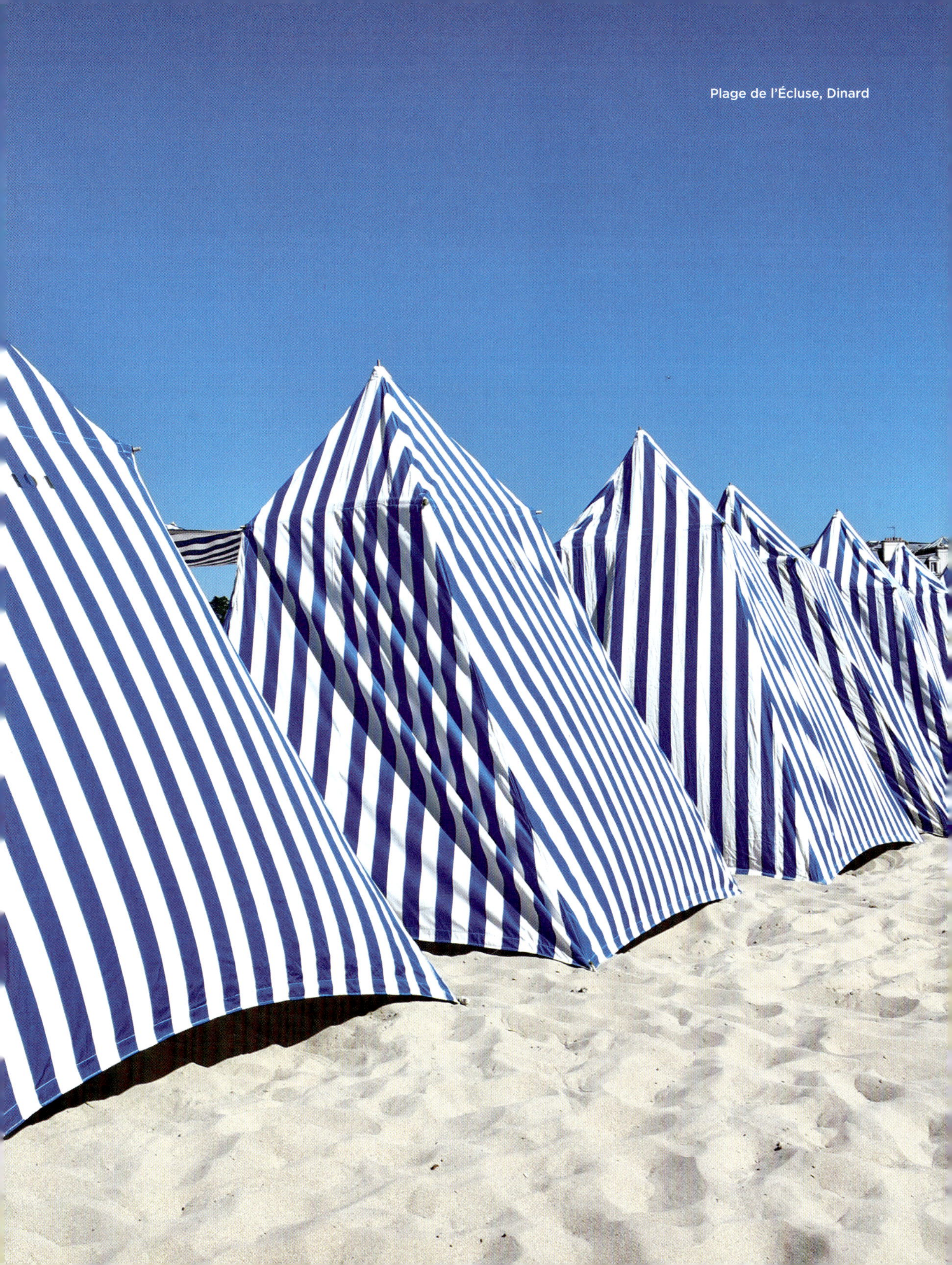

Plage de l'Écluse, Dinard

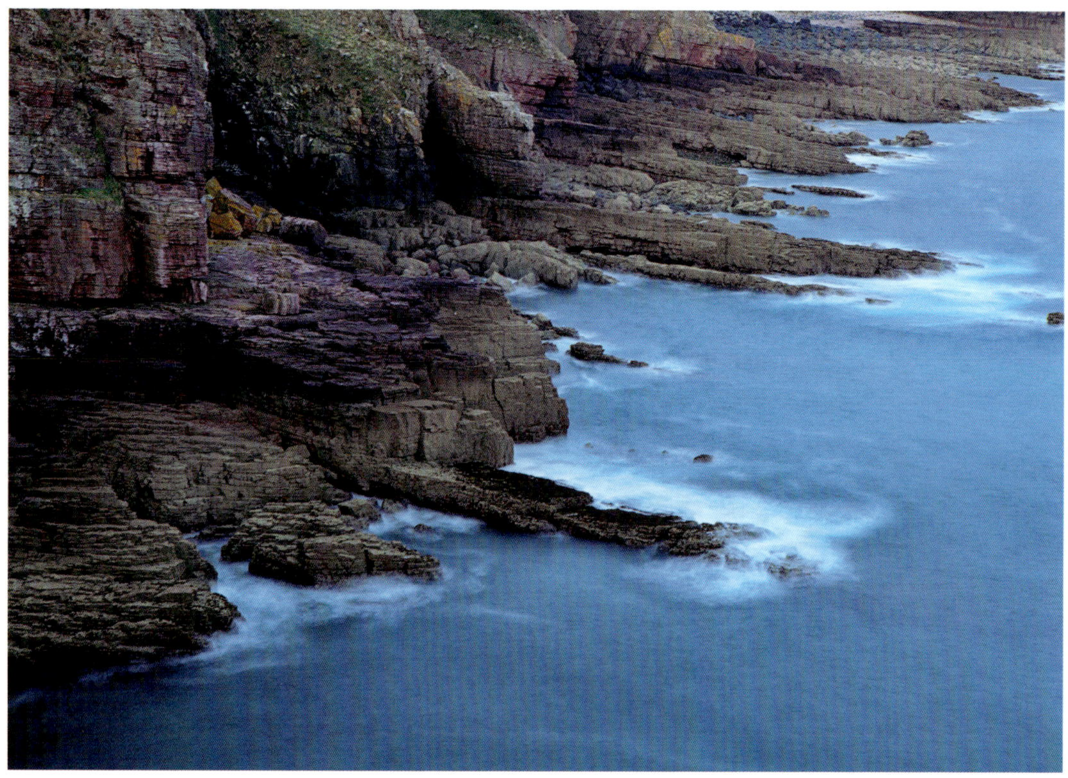

Le cap Fréhel

Cap Fréhel

The majestic cliffs of Cap Fréhel offer one of the most beautiful views of Brittany. They tower over the emerald green sea. Behind them lies a wild, colourful heath landscape, where the cries of the birds and the roar of the waves can be heard.

Le cap Fréhel

Ces majestueuses falaises offrent l'une des plus belles vues de Bretagne.
Elles surplombent une mer émeraude et se parent de landes sauvages aux couleurs changeantes où résonnent le fracas des vagues et les cris des oiseaux.

Cap Fréhel

Die majestätischen Klippen des Cap Fréhel bieten einen der schönsten Ausblicke der Bretagne. Sie überragen das smaragdgrüne Meer. Auf ihrem Rücken liegt eine wilde, farbenprächtige Heidelandschaft, über der die Schreie der Vögel und das Getöse der Wellen erklingen.

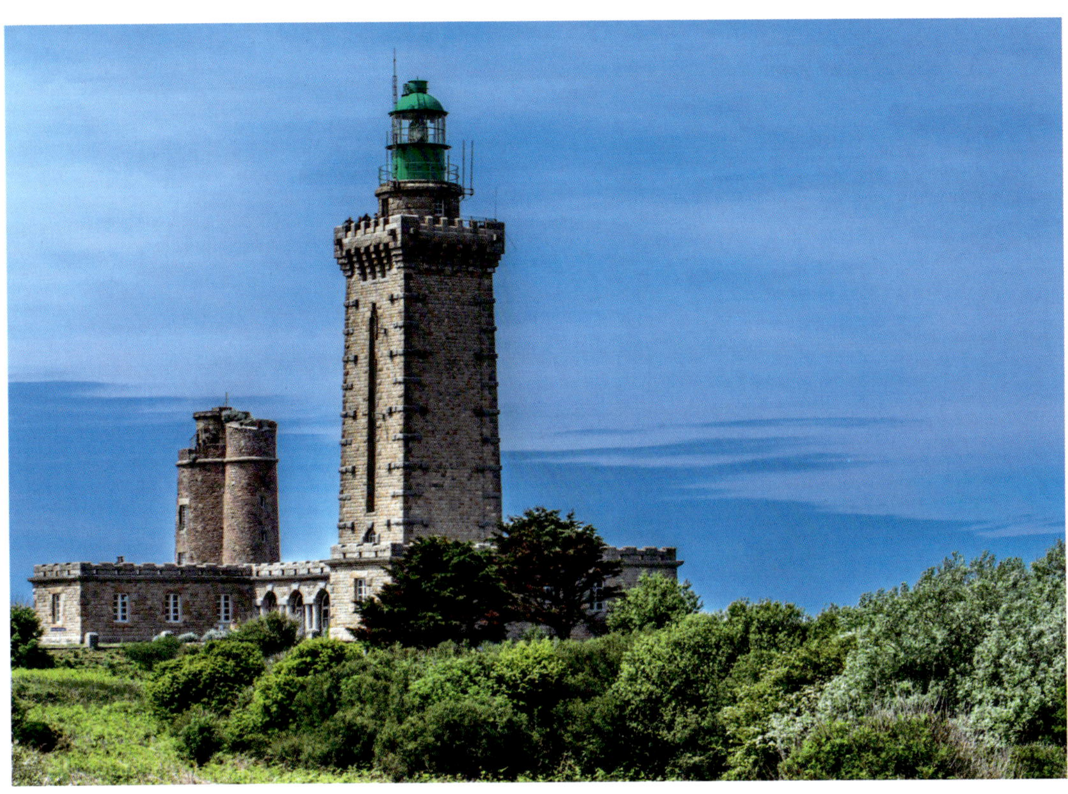

Le phare du cap Fréhel

Cap Fréhel

Los majestuosos acantilados del Cap Fréhel ofrecen una de las vistas más bellas de Bretaña. Se elevan sobre el mar verde esmeralda. A sus espaldas yace un paisaje de brezales salvaje y colorido sobre el que resuenan los gritos de los pájaros y el rugido de las olas.

Cap Fréhel

As majestosas falésias de Cap Fréhel, que proporcionam uma das mais belas vistas da Bretanha, elevam-se sobre o mar verde-esmeralda. Na sua costa desfruta-se uma paisagem selvagem, e colorida de urzes, sobre a qual soam os gritos dos pássaros e o rugido das ondas.

Cap Fréhel

De majestueuze klippen van Cap Fréhel bieden een van de mooiste uitzichten van Bretagne. Ze steken hoog uit boven de smaragdgroene zee. Op hun rug ligt een wild, kleurrijk heidelandschap waarboven het gekrijs van de vogels en het gebulder van de golven weerklinken.

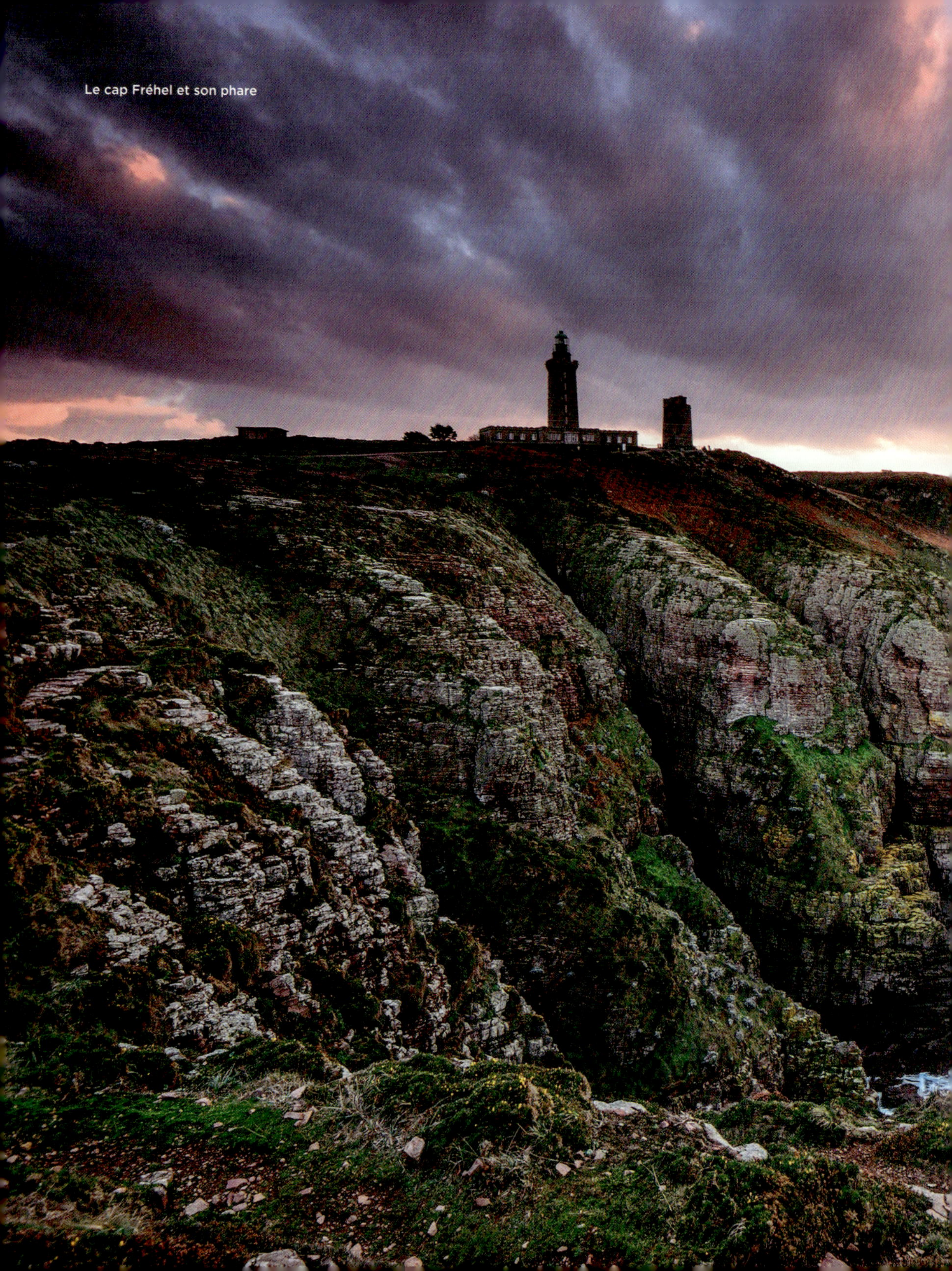

Le cap Fréhel et son phare

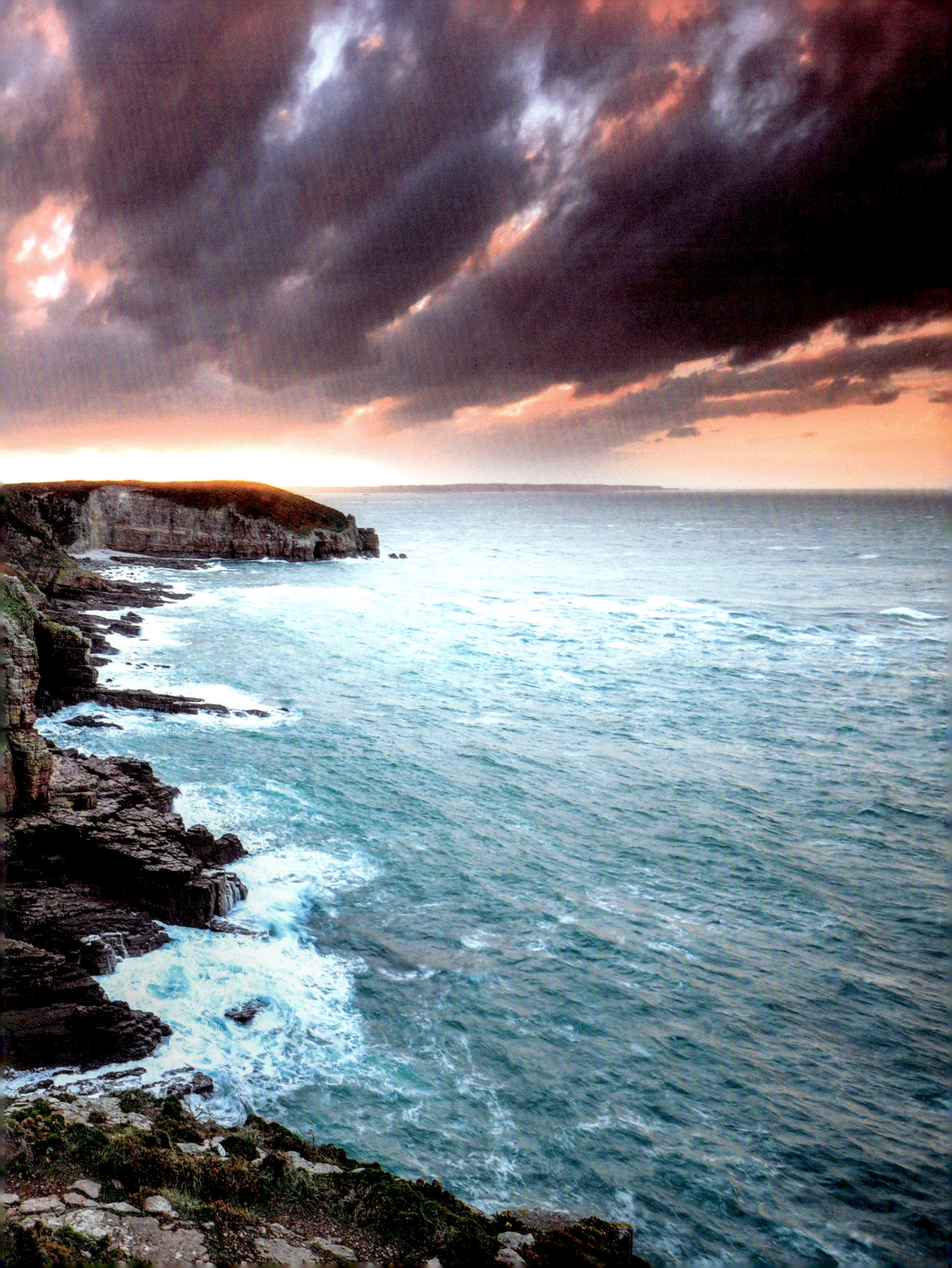

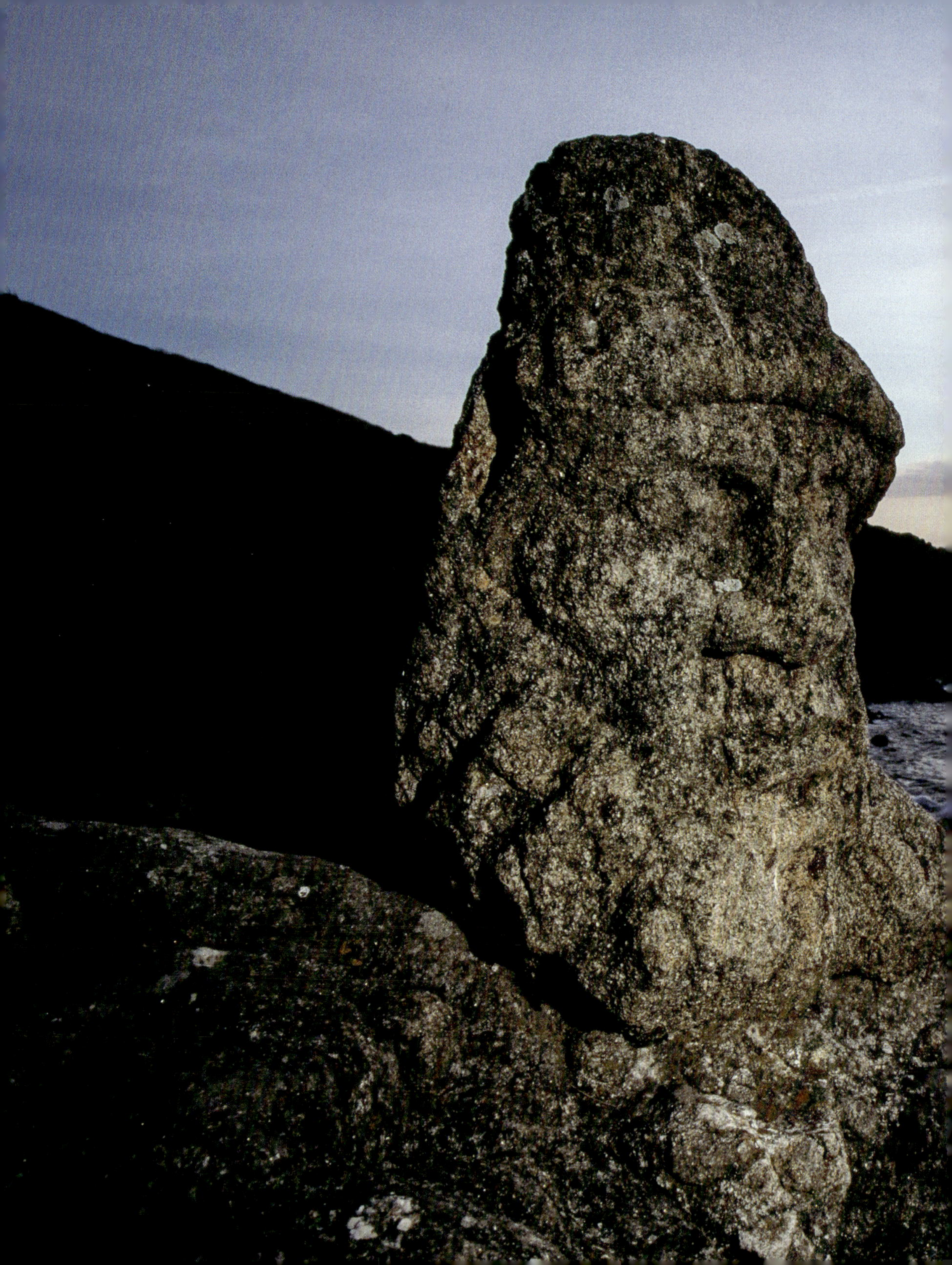

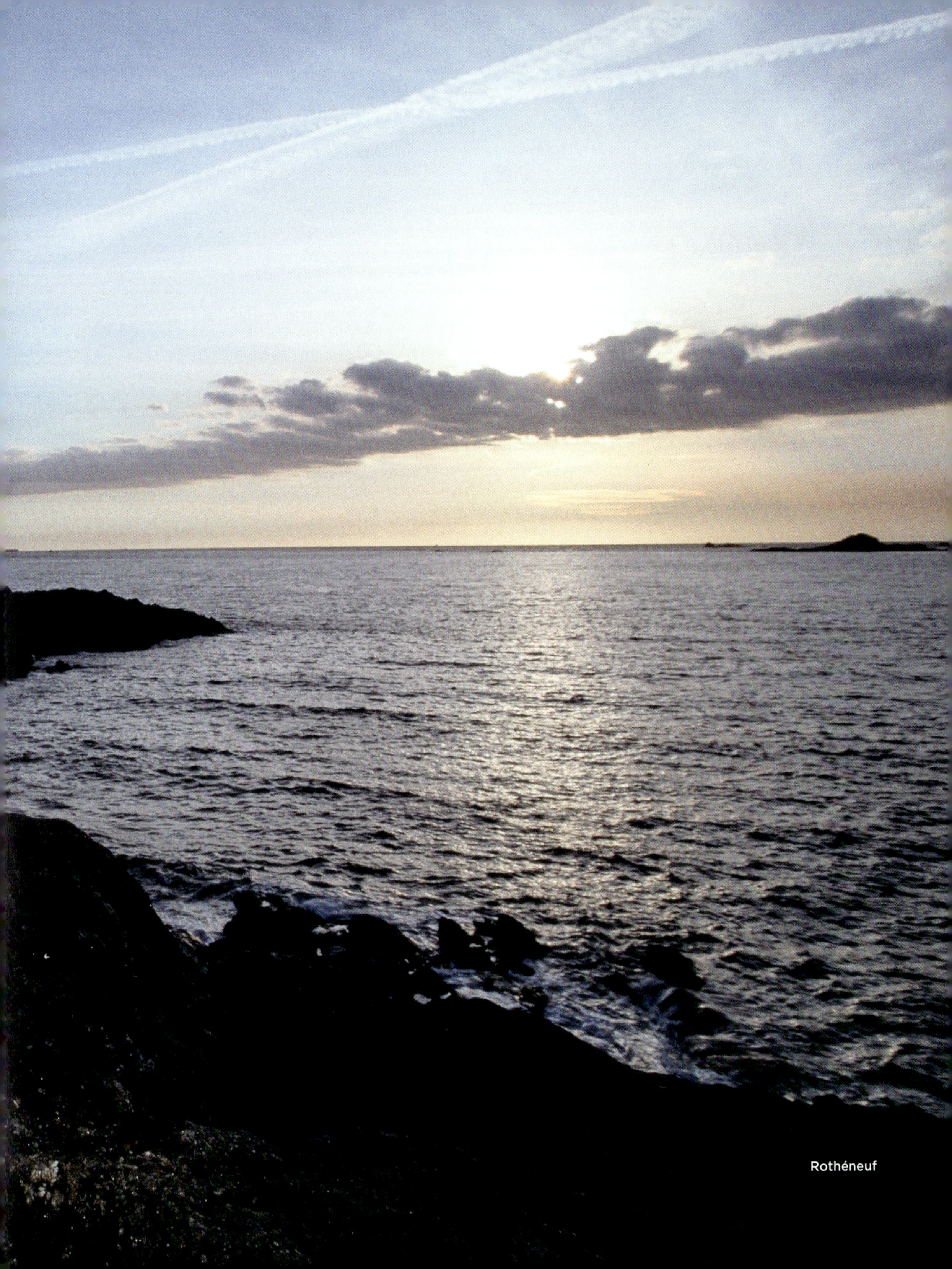
Rothéneuf

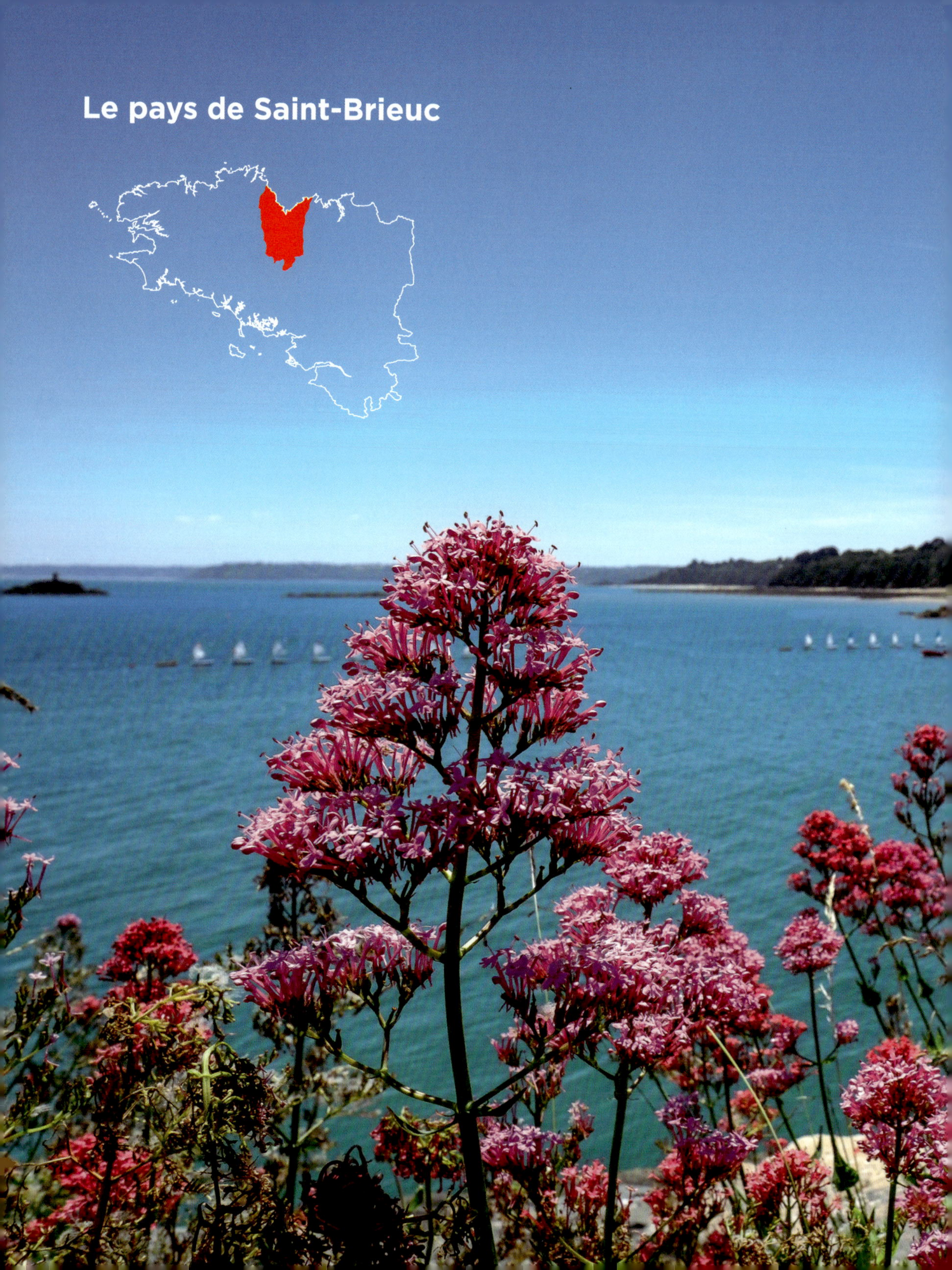

Le pays de Saint-Brieuc

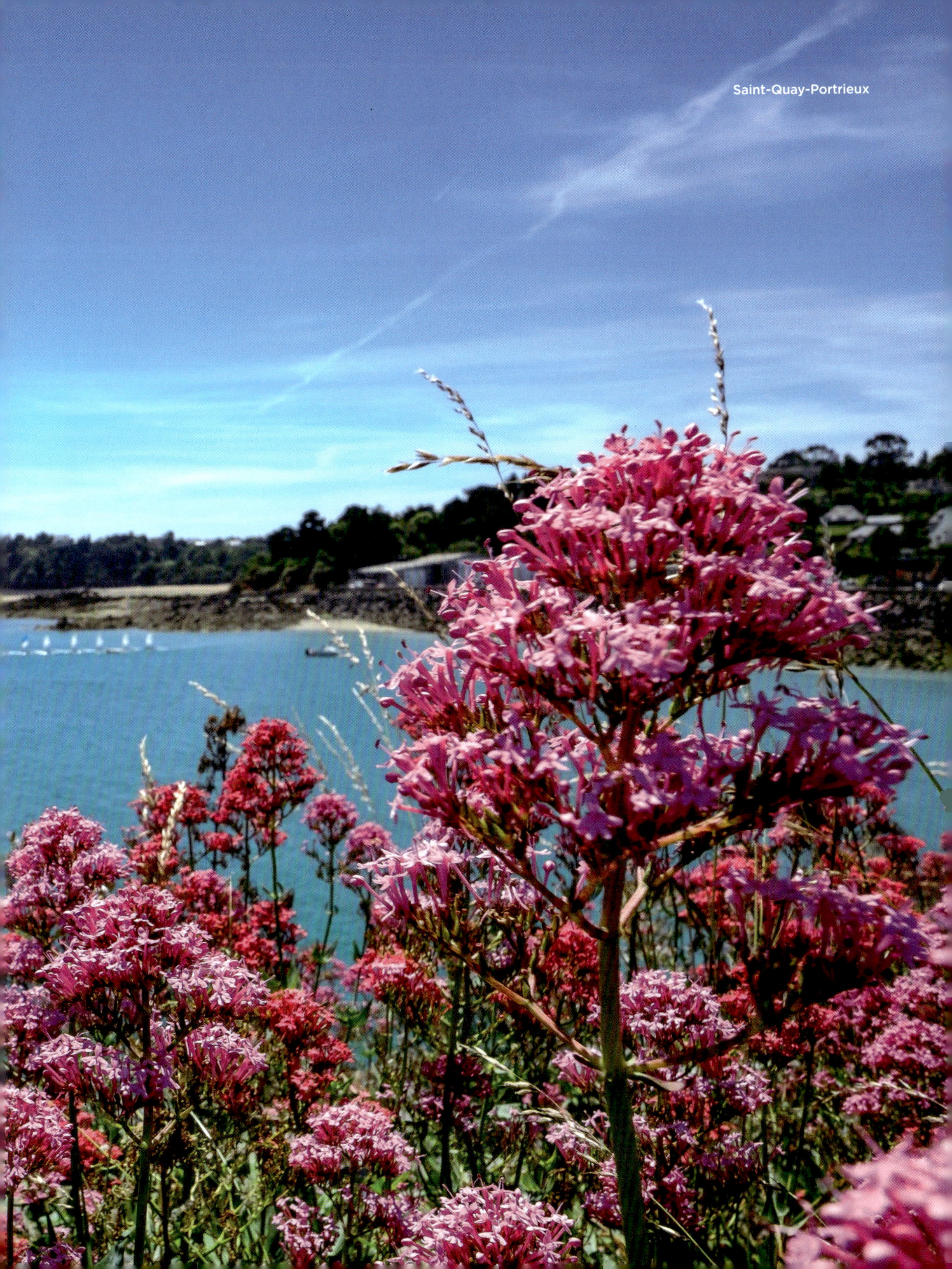
Saint-Quay-Portrieux

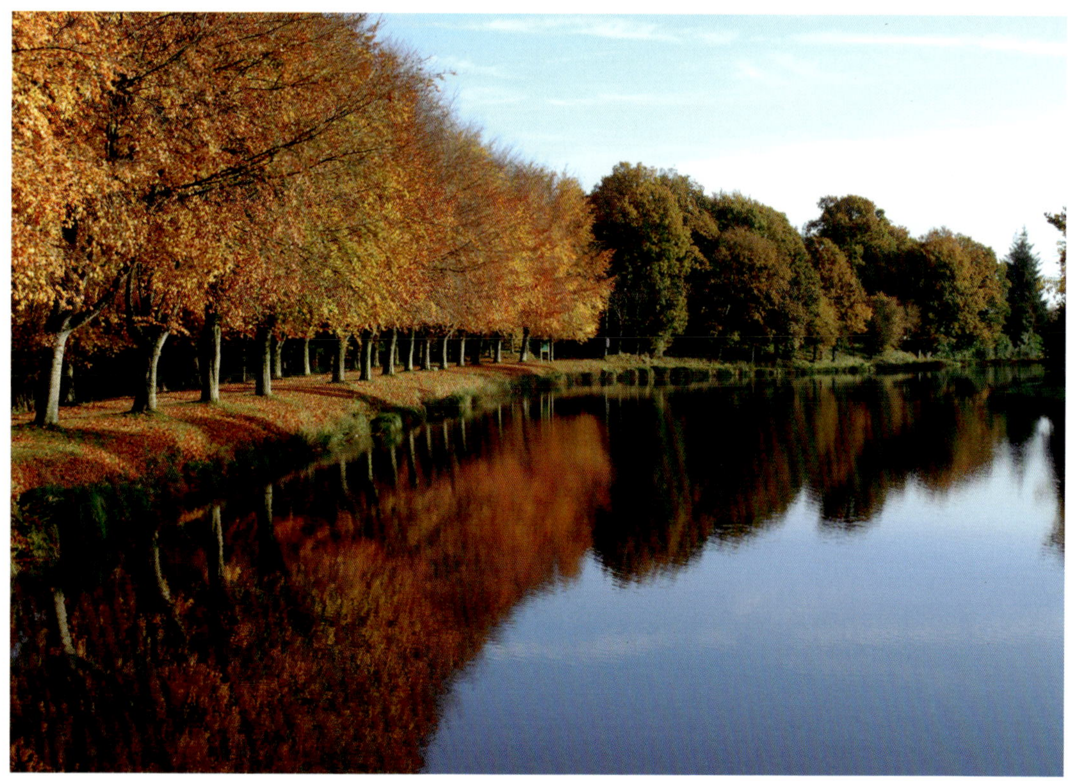

Loudéac

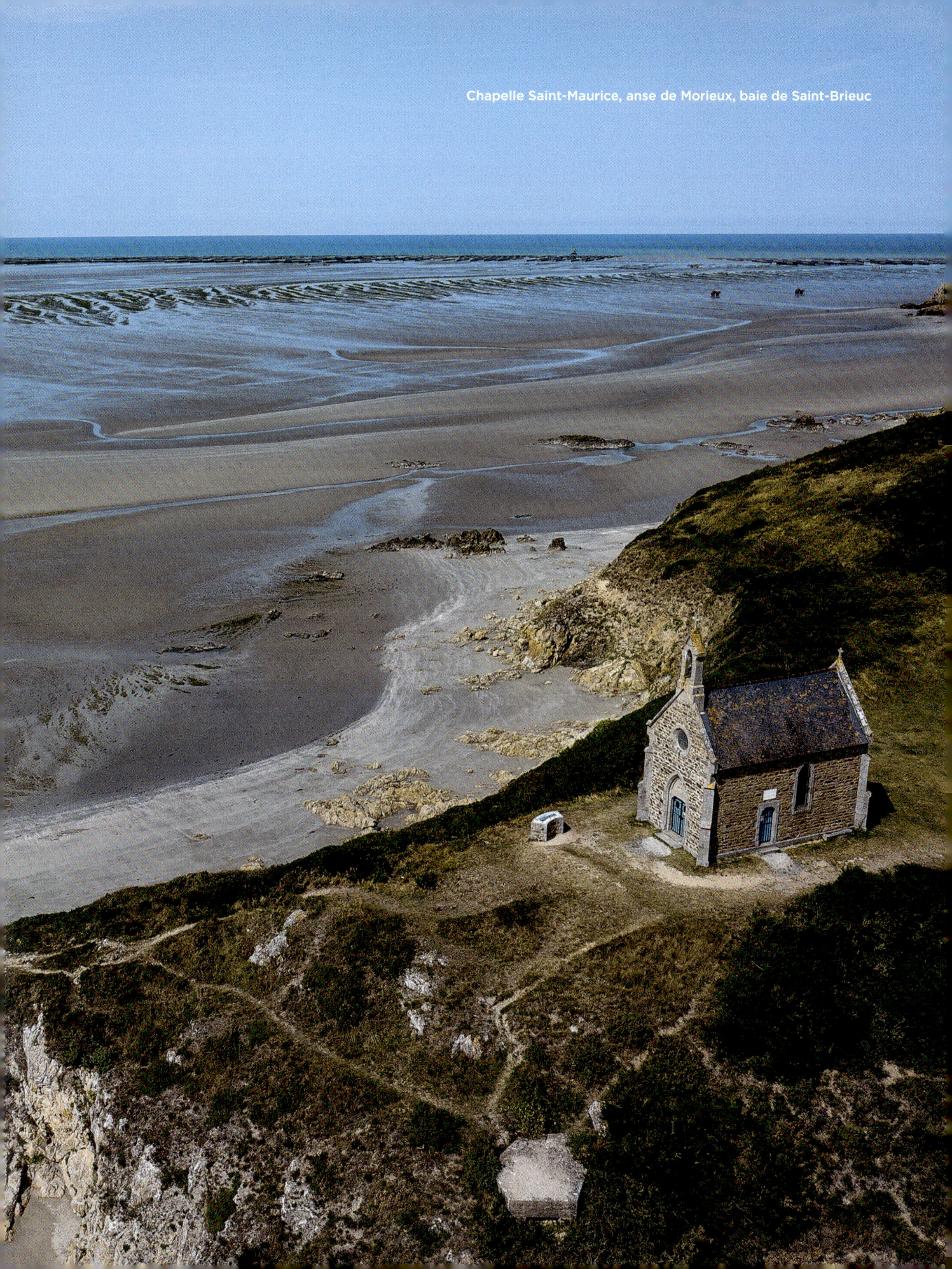

Chapelle Saint-Maurice, anse de Morieux, baie de Saint-Brieuc

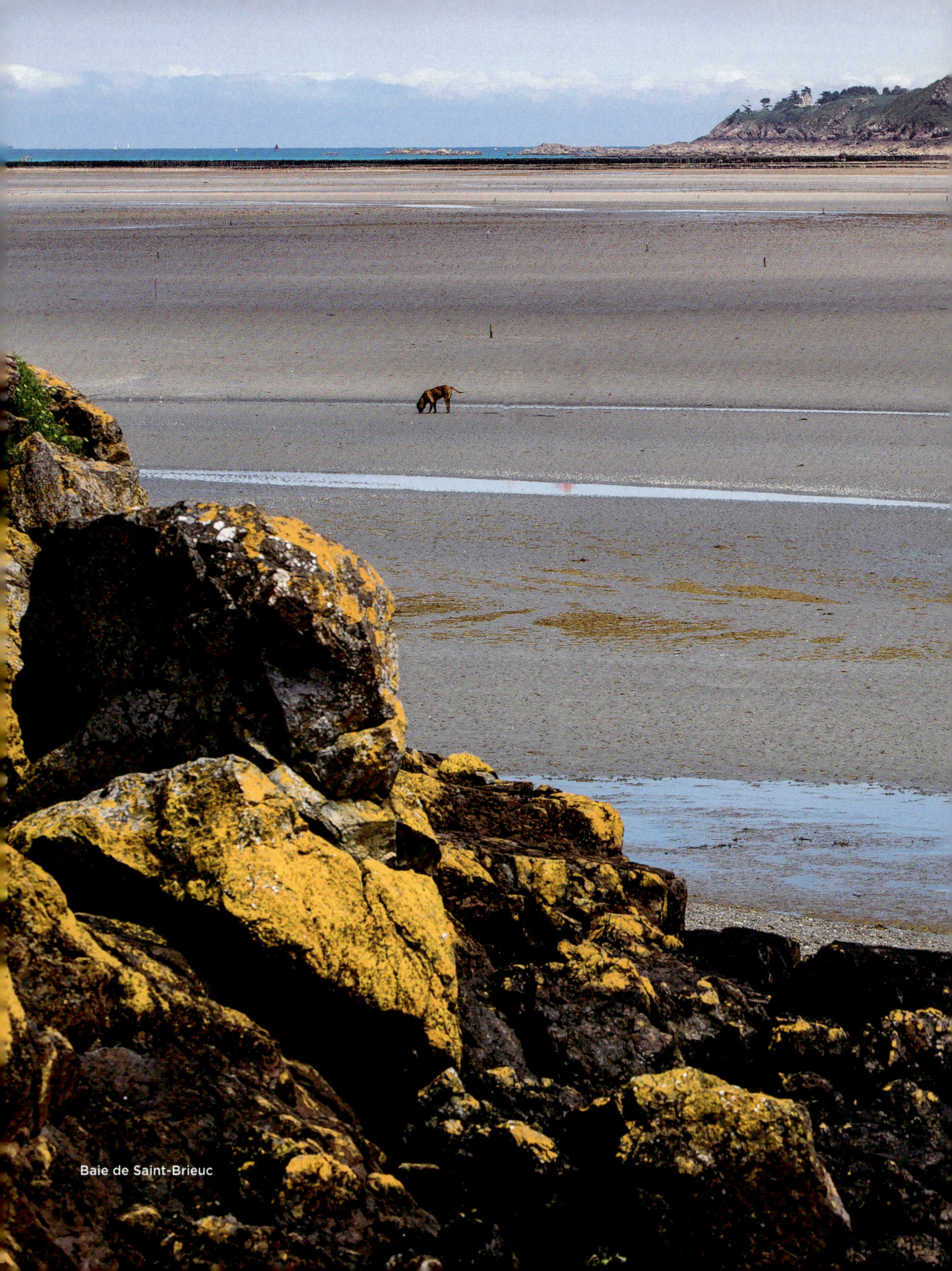
Baie de Saint-Brieuc

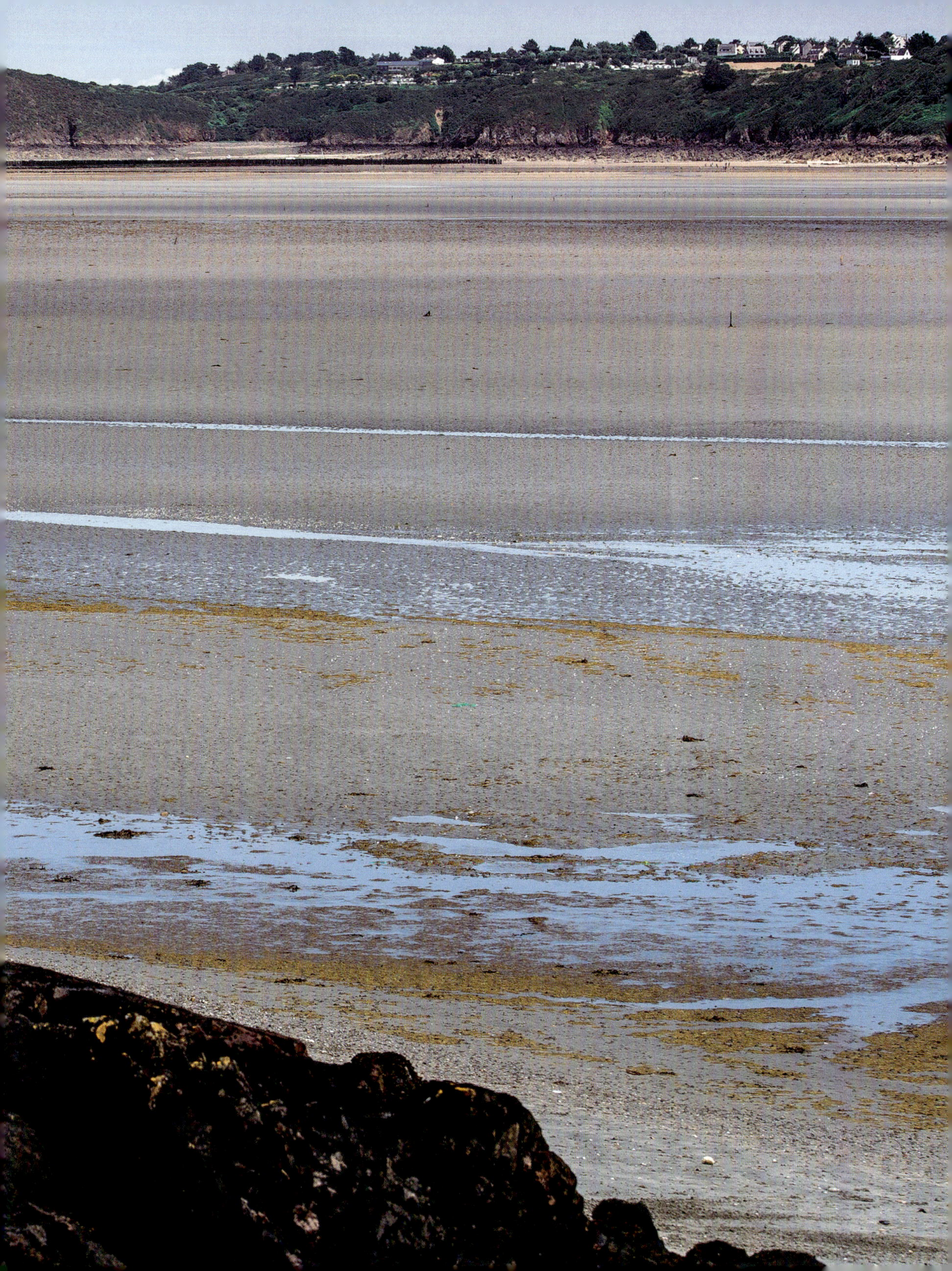

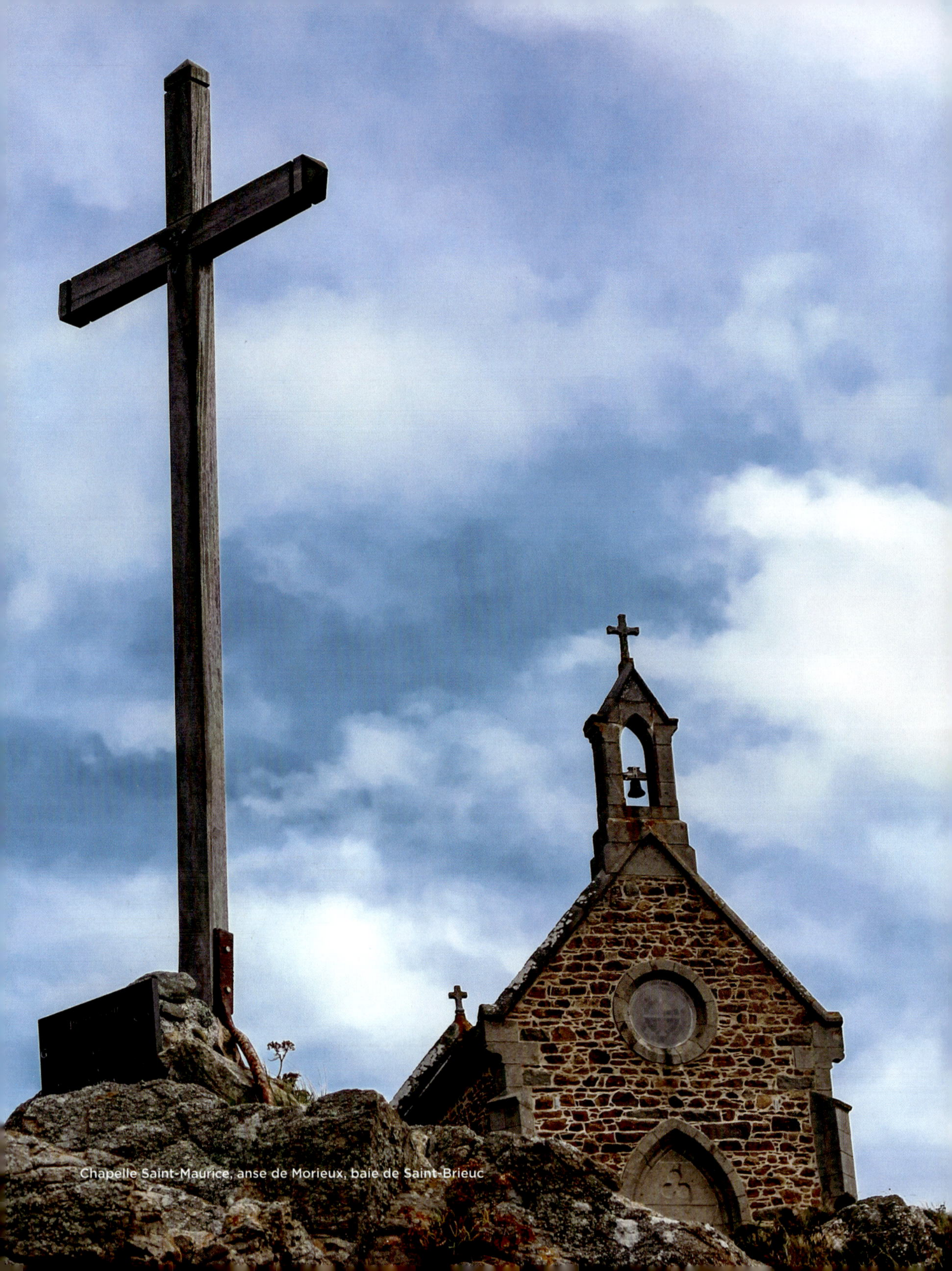

Chapelle Saint-Maurice, anse de Morieux, baie de Saint-Brieuc

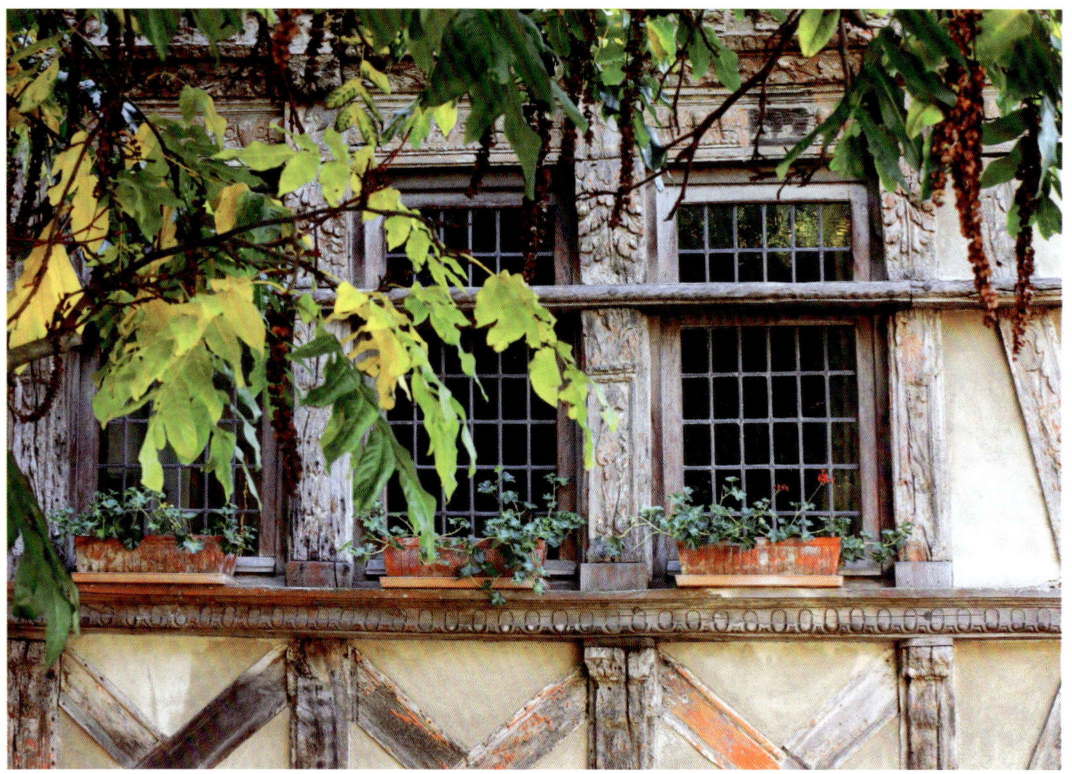

Maison traditionnelle, Saint-Brieuc

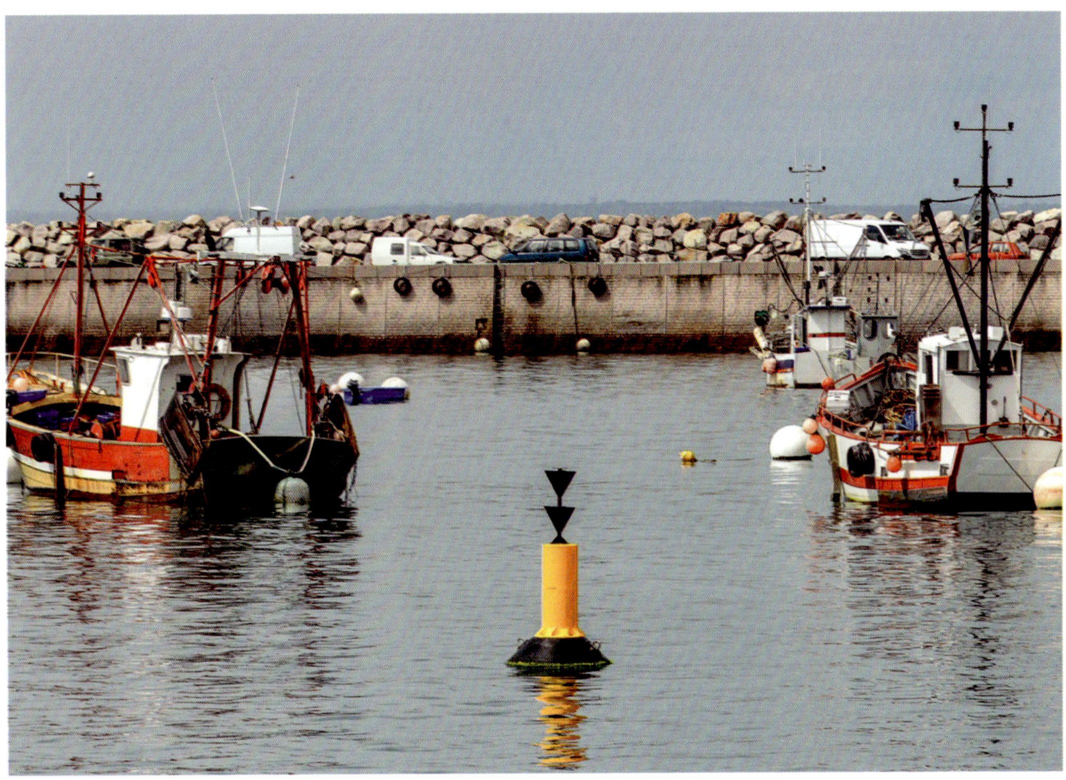

Le port de pêche, Erquy

Erquy and the Cap d'Erquy

Erquy is one of the centres of the Côte de Penthièvre, thanks to its active fishing port. The town is considered the capital of the scallop s, which are cultivated and harvested in the bay of Saint-Brieuc. Not far from the port is Cap d'Erquy, a rocky promontory covered with heathland that closes off Saint-Brieuc to the east.

Erquy et le cap d'Erquy

Erquy est une des plus importantes villes de la côte de Penthièvre et un port de pêche très actif. Il est en particulier connu pour être la capitale de la coquille Saint-Jacques, pêchée dans la baie de Saint-Brieuc. Au-dessus du port d'Erquy, le cap d'Erquy est un promontoire rocheux couvert de landes qui ferme la baie de Saint-Brieuc à l'est.

Erquy und das Cap d'Erquy

Erquy ist durch seinen aktiven Fischereihafen eines der Zentren der Côte de Penthièvre. Der Ort gilt als die Hauptstadt der Jakobs-muschel, die in der Bucht von Saint-Brieuc gezüchtet und geerntet wird. Unweit des Hafens liegt Cap d'Erquy, eine von Heide-landschaft bedeckte Felszunge, die die Bucht von Saint-Brieuc im Osten abschließt.

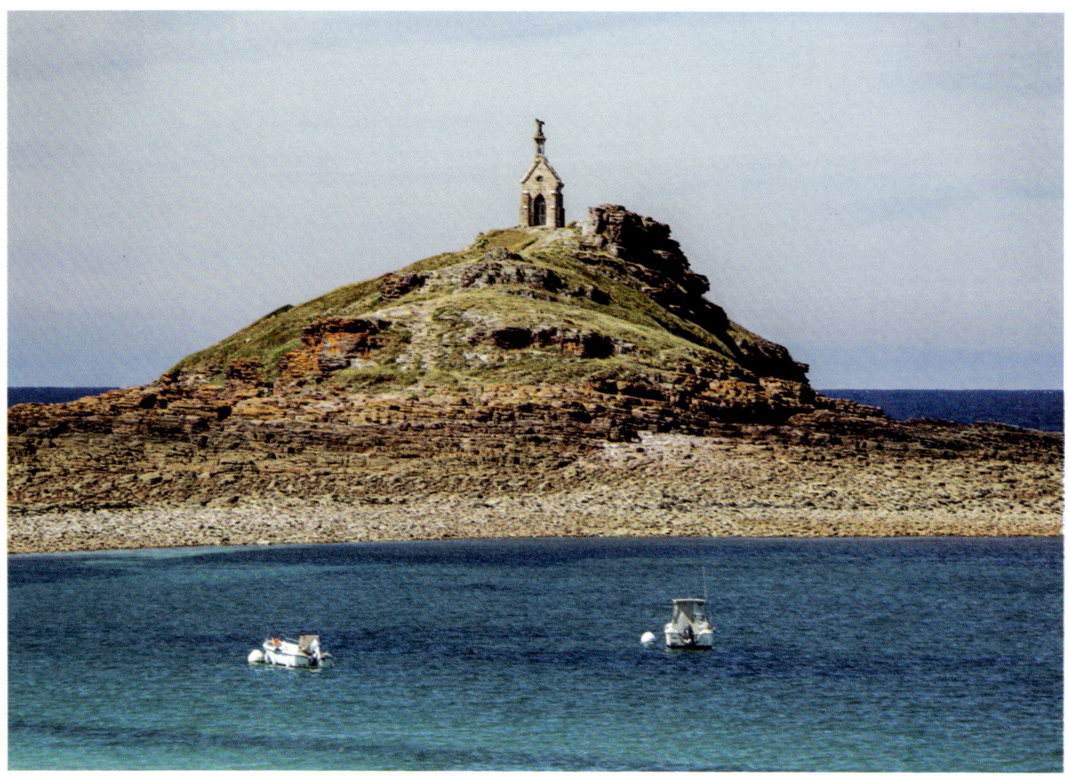

Îlot Saint-Michel, Erquy

Erquy y el Cap d'Erquy

Erquy es uno de los centros de la Côte de Penthièvre gracias a su activo puerto pesquero. La ciudad es considerada la capital de la concha de vieira, que se cultiva y cosecha en la bahía de Saint-Brieuc. No muy lejos del puerto se encuentra Cap d'Erquy, un promontorio rocoso cubierto de brezales que cierra la bahía de Saint-Brieuc al este.

Erquy e o Cap d'Erquy

Erquy é um dos principais centros da Côte de Penthièvre, graças ao seu activo porto de pesca. A cidade é considerada a capital da concha de vieira, que é cultivada e colhida na baía de Saint-Brieuc. Não muito longe do porto está o Cap d'Erquy, um promontório rochoso coberto de charneca que limita a baía de Saint-Brieuc a leste.

Erquy en de Cap d'Erquy

Erquy is dankzij zijn actieve vissershaven een van de centra van de Côte de Penthièvre. De plaats wordt beschouwd als de hoofdstad van de sint-jakobsschelp, die in de baai van Saint-Brieuc wordt gekweekt en geoogst. Niet ver van de haven ligt Cap d'Erquy, een met heide bedekte rotstong die de baai van Saint-Brieuc in het oosten afsluit.

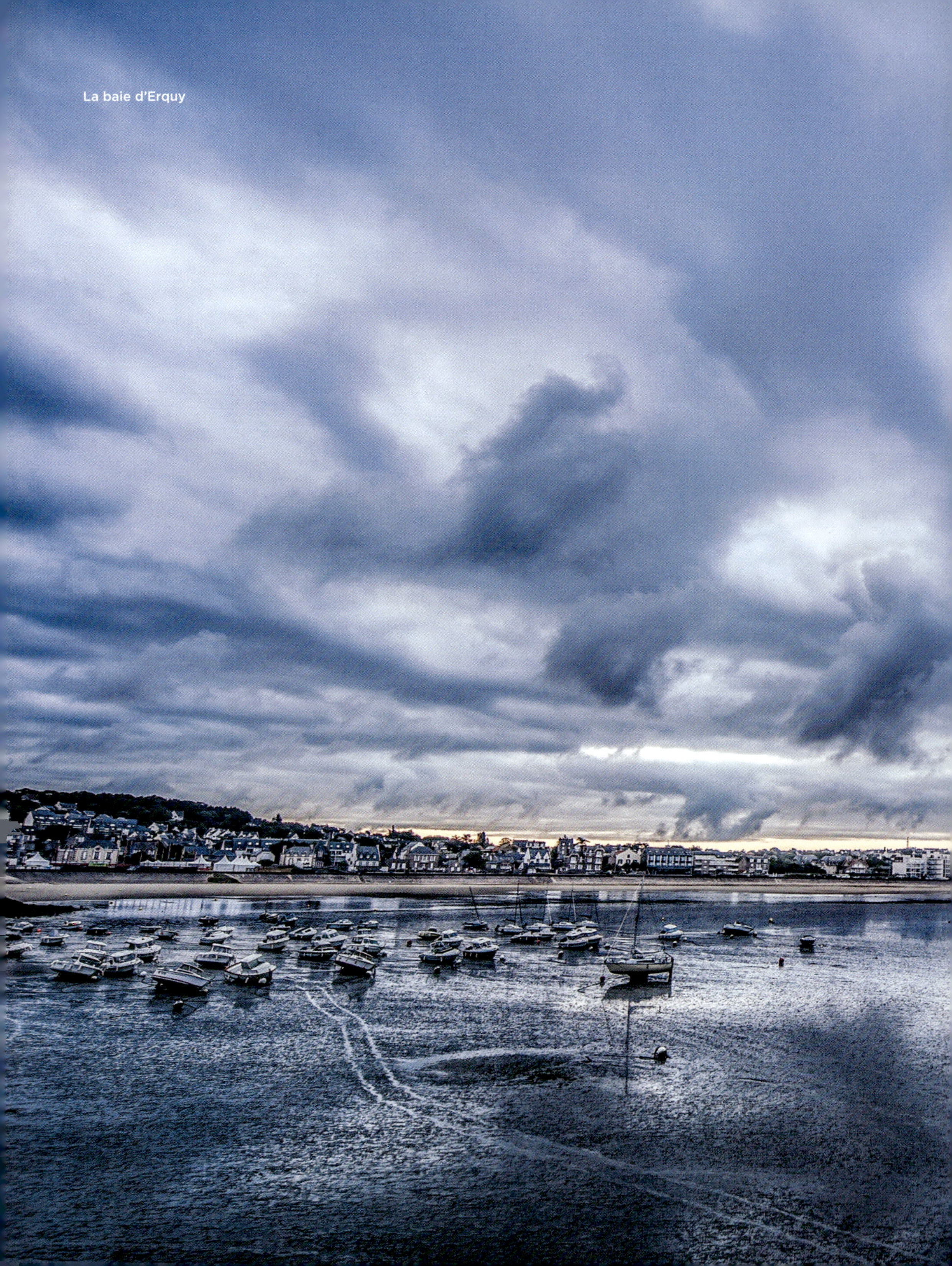
La baie d'Erquy

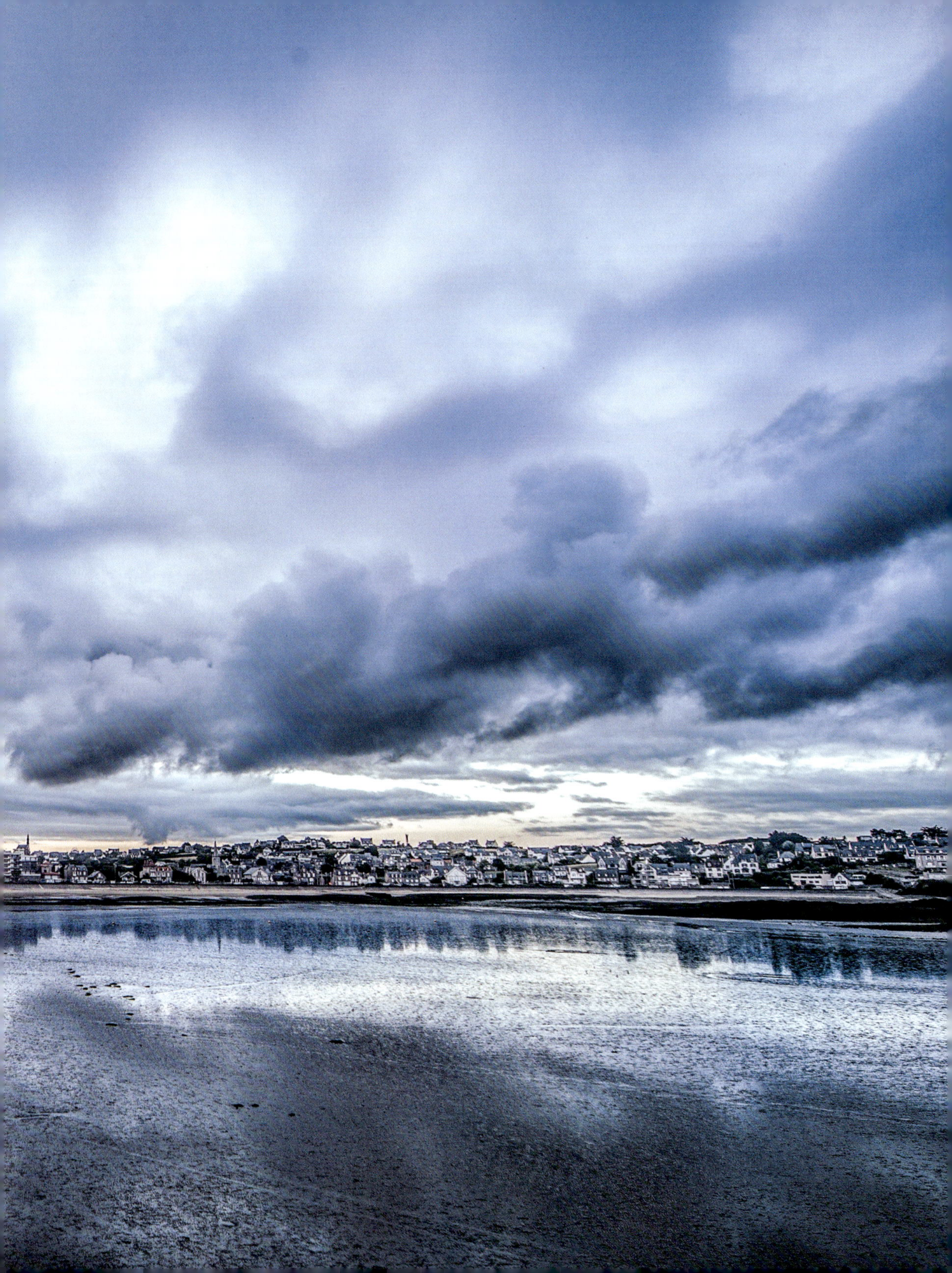

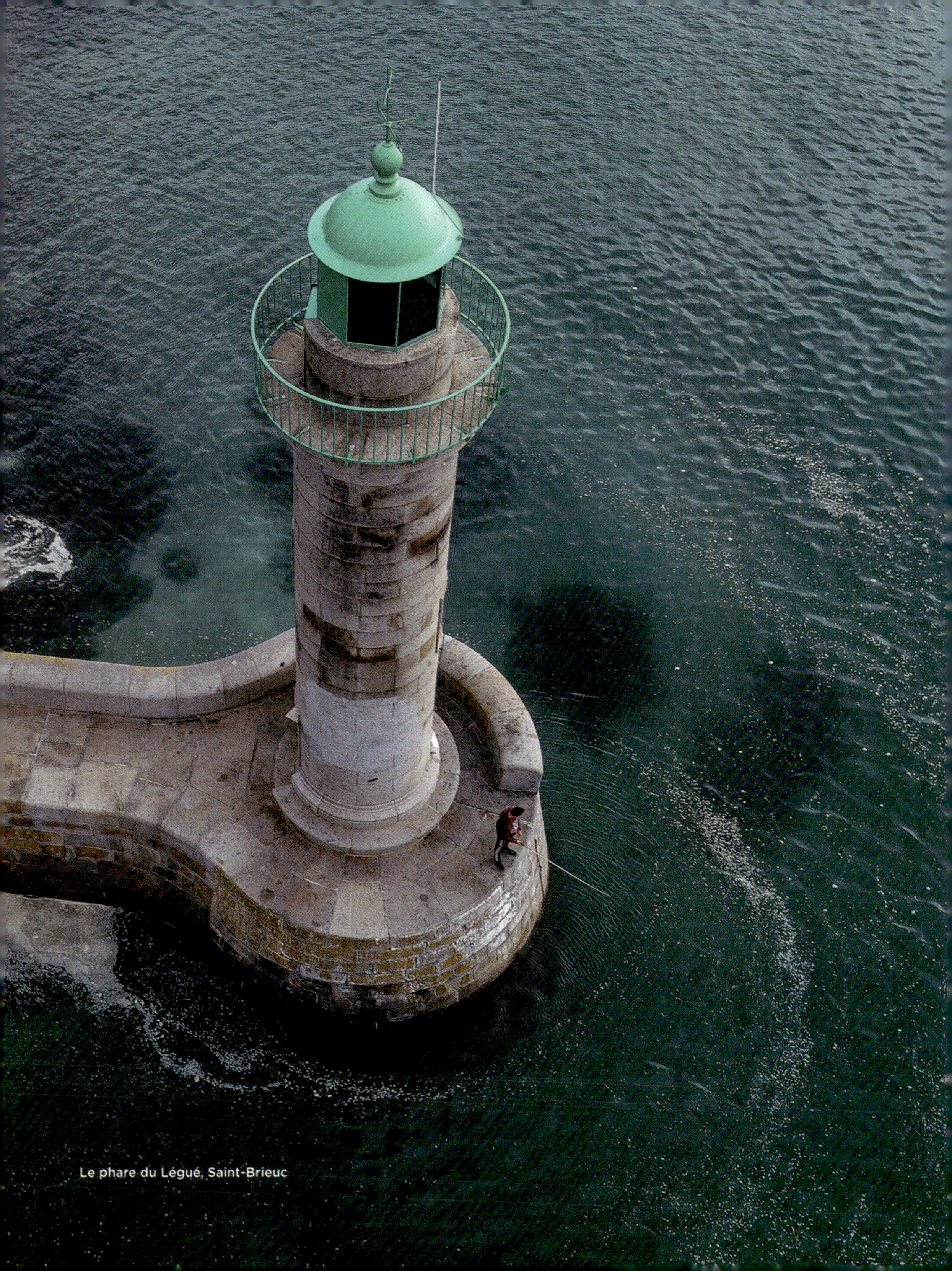

Le phare du Légué, Saint-Brieuc

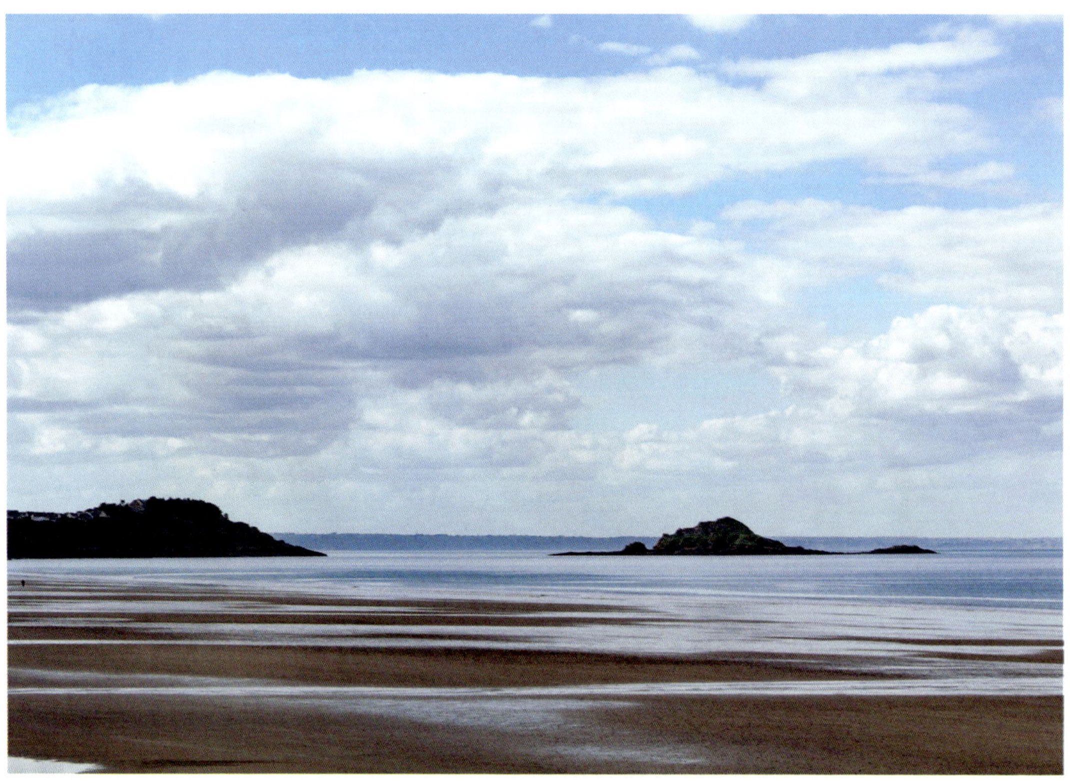

Baie de Saint-Brieuc

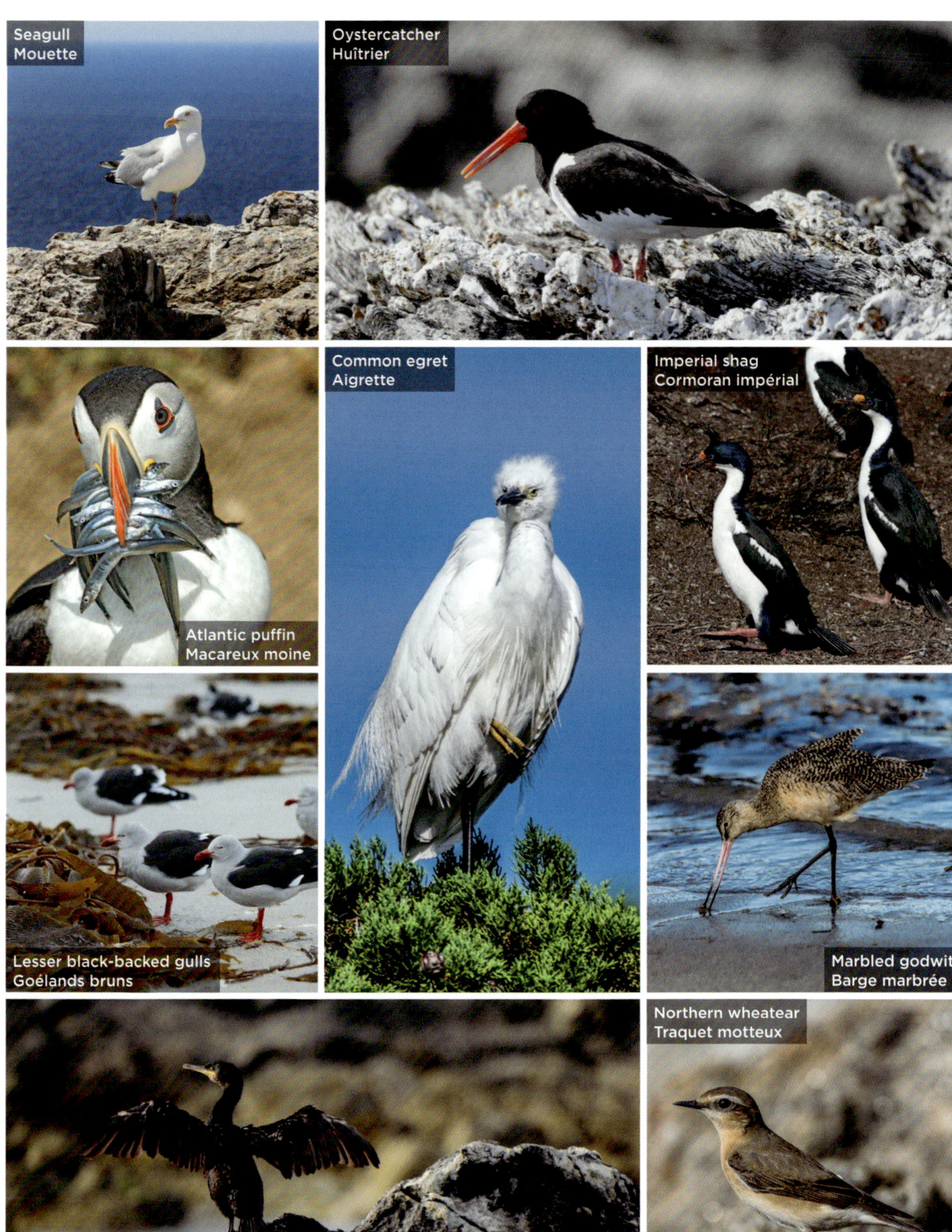

Seagull
Mouette
Oystercatcher
Huîtrier
Common egret
Aigrette
Imperial shag
Cormoran impérial
Atlantic puffin
Macareux moine
Lesser black-backed gulls
Goélands bruns
Marbled godwit
Barge marbrée
Northern wheatear
Traquet motteux
Great cormorant
Cormoran

The Bird World

Brittany is a Mecca for ornithologists. The numerous nature reserves are free of human influences, and are home to a unique flora and fauna. Numerous types of birds use the area as resting place on their flight south, while others have their nesting places there. In winter, more than 40,000 birds of 112 different species can be seen. The silver seagulls (Larus argentatus) that make up the biggest portion of the seabirds are to be found most frequently.

Les oiseaux

La Bretagne est un haut lieu de l'ornithologie. De nombreux espaces ont été classés «réserve naturelle» assurant la protection d'une faune qui prospère en toute tranquillité. Carrefour de migration, certains oiseaux aiment à faire étape dans cette région tandis que d'autres y ont élu domicile pour leur nidification. Au gré des sentiers en hiver, plus de 40 000 oiseaux de 112 espèces différentes peuvent être observés à loisir. Parmi les nombreux oiseaux marins, l'espèce la plus commune est le goéland argenté (*Larus argentatus*).

Die Vogelwelt

Die Bretagne ist ein Mekka für Ornithologen. Die zahlreichen Naturschutzgebiete sind frei von menschlichen Einflüssen und beherbergen eine einzigartige Tier- und Pflanzenwelt. Zahlreiche Vogelarten nutzen sie als Rastplatz auf ihrem Flug in den Süden, während andere dort ihre Brutstätten haben. Im Winter lassen sich dort mehr als 40.000 Tiere von 112 verschiedenen Arten beobachten. Am häufigsten anzutreffen sind die Silbermöwen (Larus argentatus), die den größten Anteil der Seevögel ausmachen.

El mundo de las aves

Bretaña es una meca para los ornitólogos. Las numerosas reservas naturales están libres de influencias humanas y albergan una flora y una fauna únicas. Numerosos tipos de aves lo utilizan como lugar de descanso en su vuelo hacia el sur, mientras que otros tienen sus lugares de cría allí. En invierno se pueden observar más de 40 000 animales de 112 especies diferentes. Las gaviotas argénteas (larus argentatus), son las aves marinas que más hay y las que con más frecuencia se encuentran.

O mundo dos pássaros

A Bretanha é uma Meca para ornitólogos. As numerosas reservas naturais estão livres de influências humanas e abrigam uma flora e fauna únicas. Muitas espécies de aves utilizam-na como local de repouso no seu voo para sul, enquanto outras a utilizam como local de nidificação. No inverno podem ser observados aí mais de 40.000 animais de 112 espécies diferentes. As gaivotas-prateadas (Larus argentatus), que constituem a maior parte das aves marinhas, são as mais frequentes.

De vogelwereld

Bretagne is een mekka voor ornithologen. De talrijke beschermde natuurgebieden zijn vrij van menselijke invloeden en herbergen een unieke flora en fauna. Talrijke vogelsoorten gebruiken ze als rustplaats op hun trek naar het zuiden, terwijl andere er juist broeden. In de winter kunnen hier meer dan 40.000 dieren van 112 verschillende soorten worden waargenomen. Zilvermeeuwen (Larus argentatus), die het leeuwendeel van de zeevogels uitmaken, komen het meest voor.

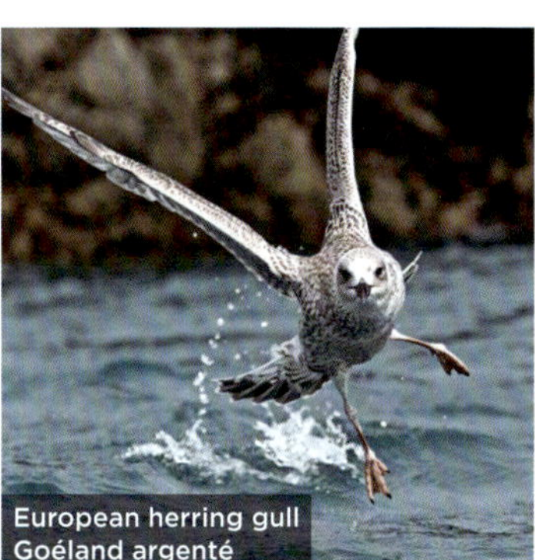

European herring gull
Goéland argenté

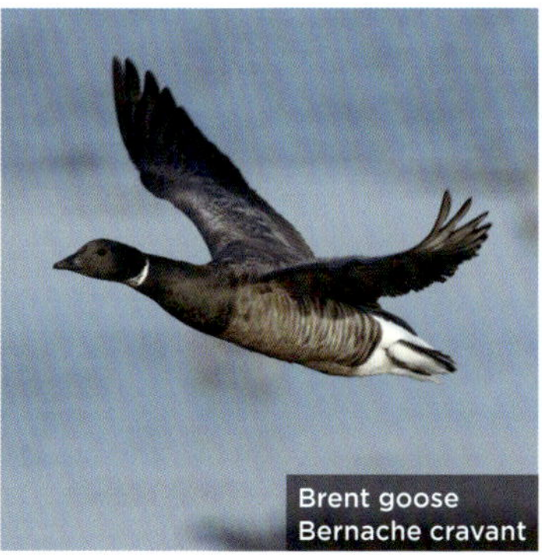

Brent goose
Bernache cravant

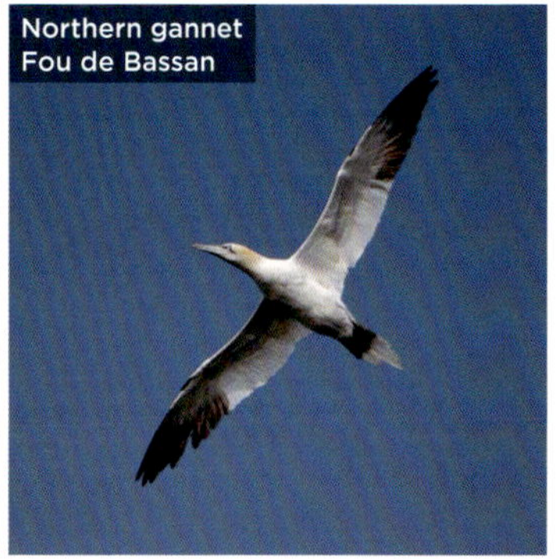

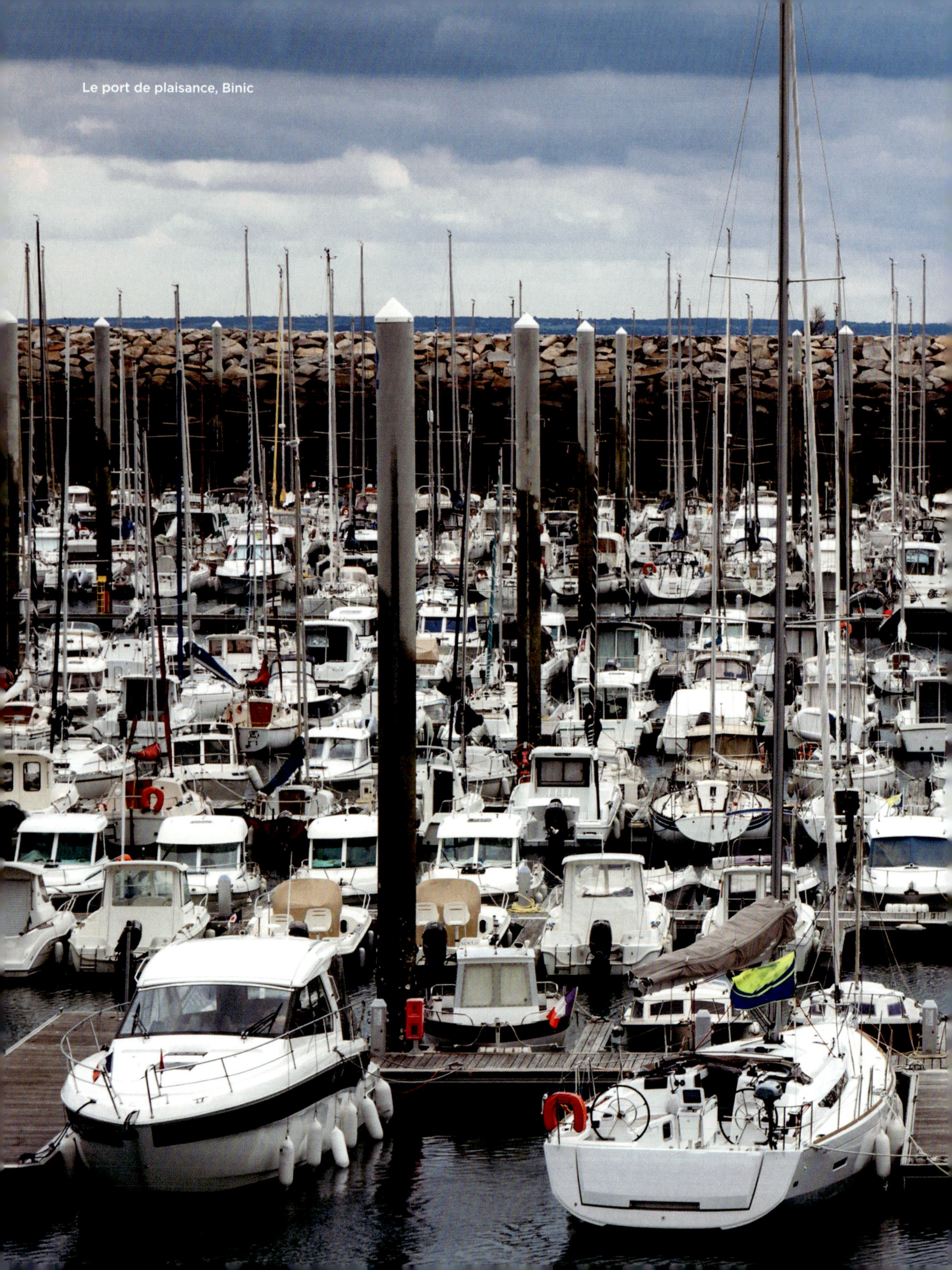
Le port de plaisance, Binic

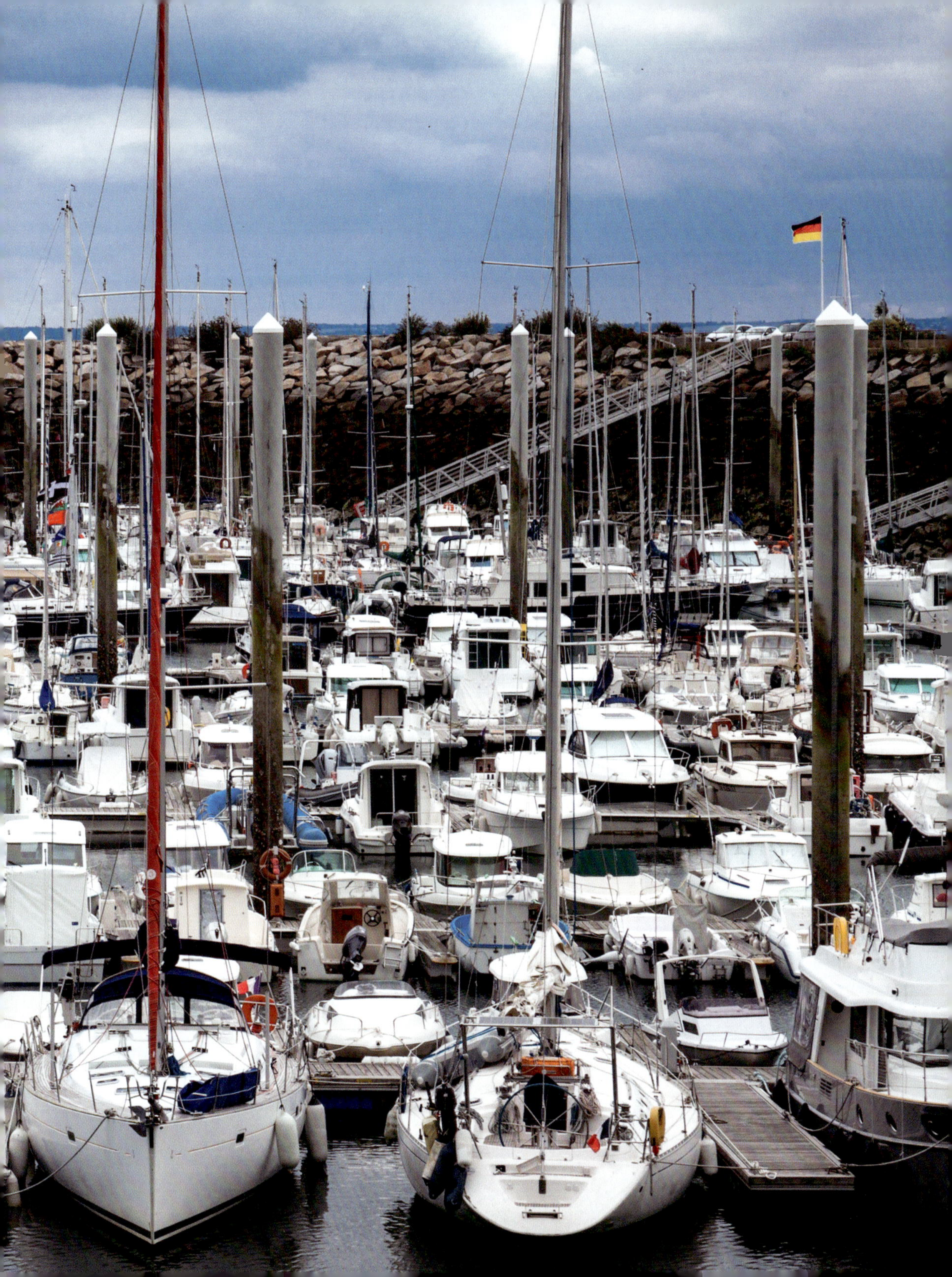

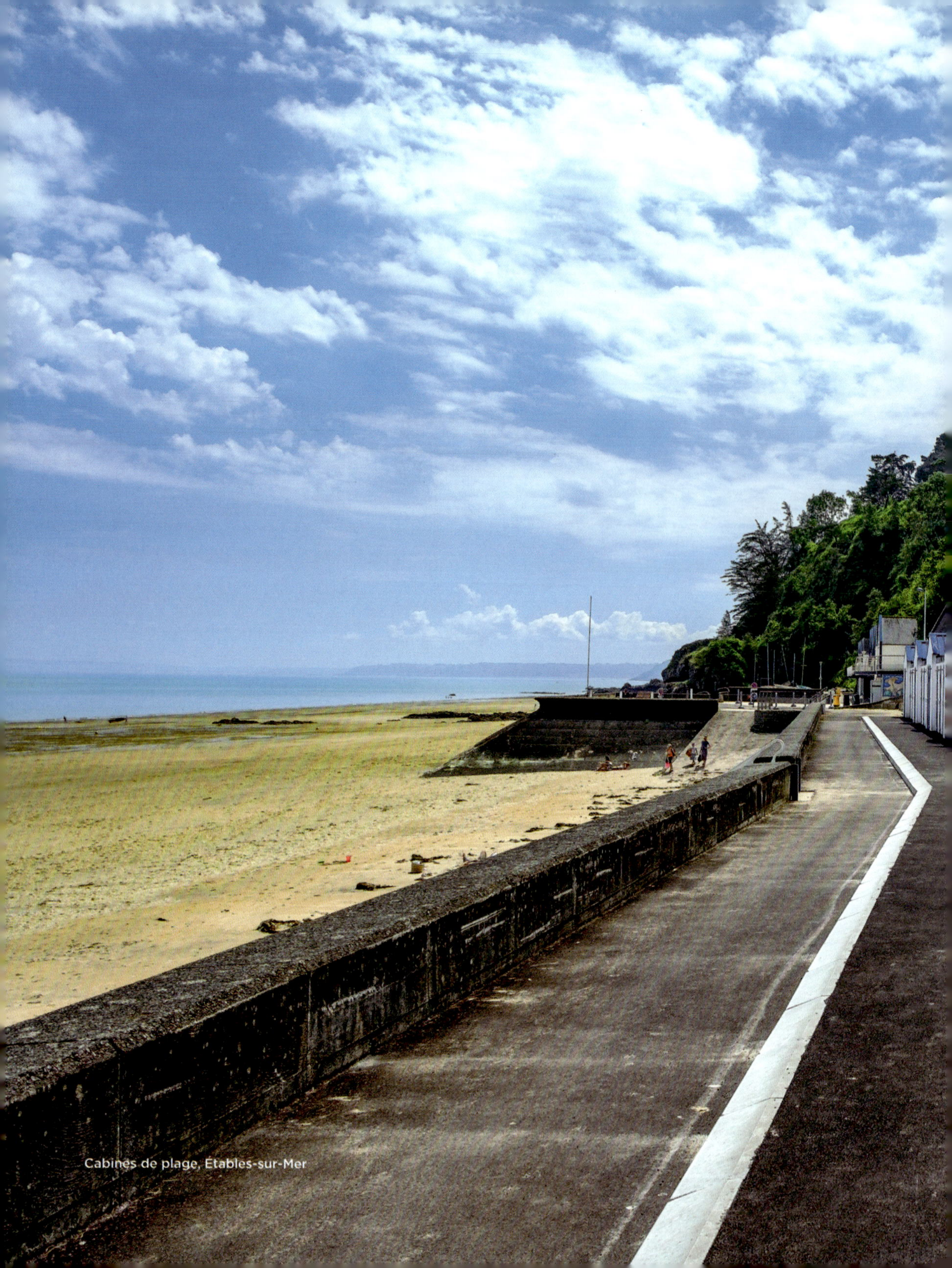

Cabines de plage, Étables-sur-Mer

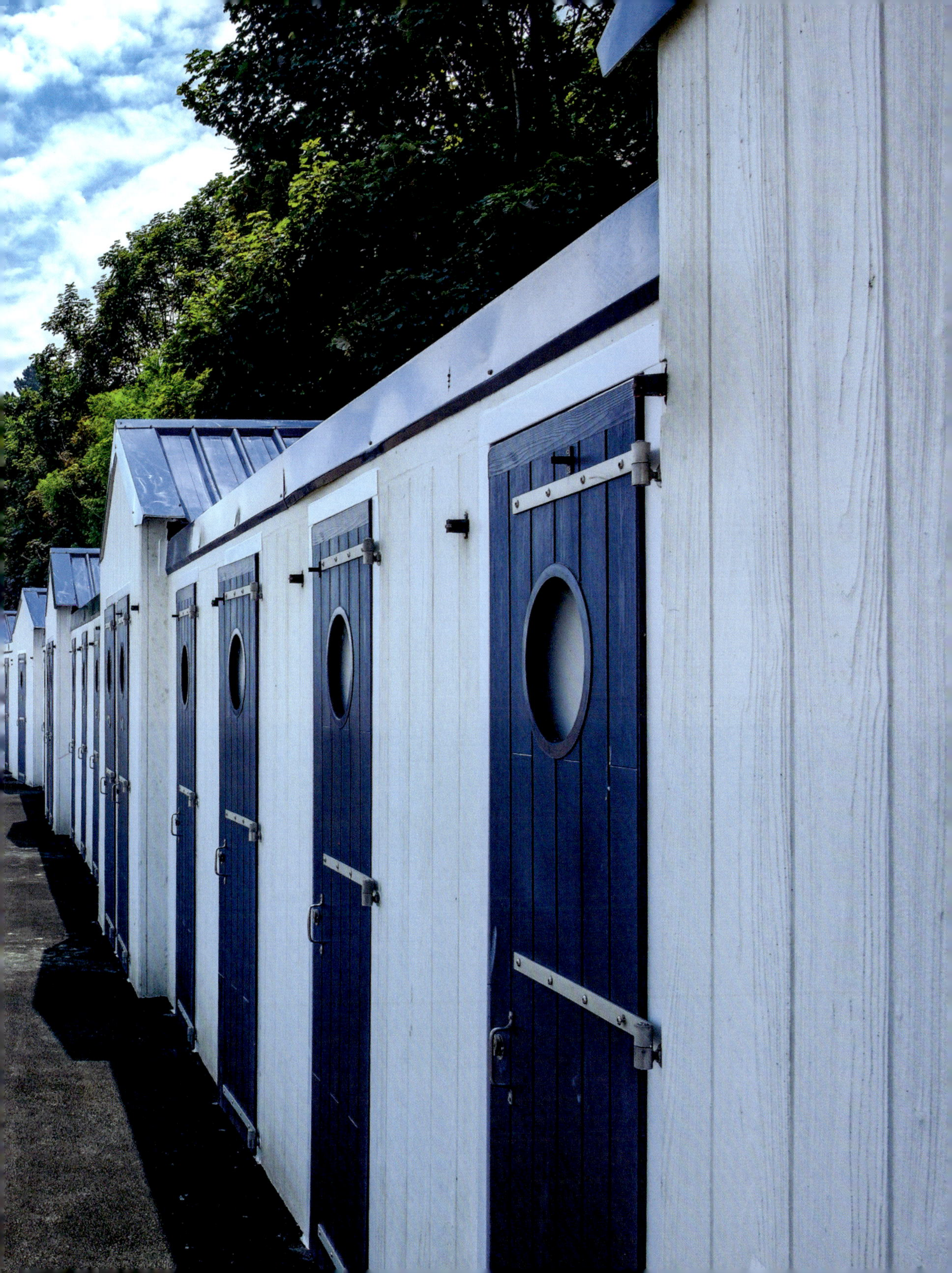

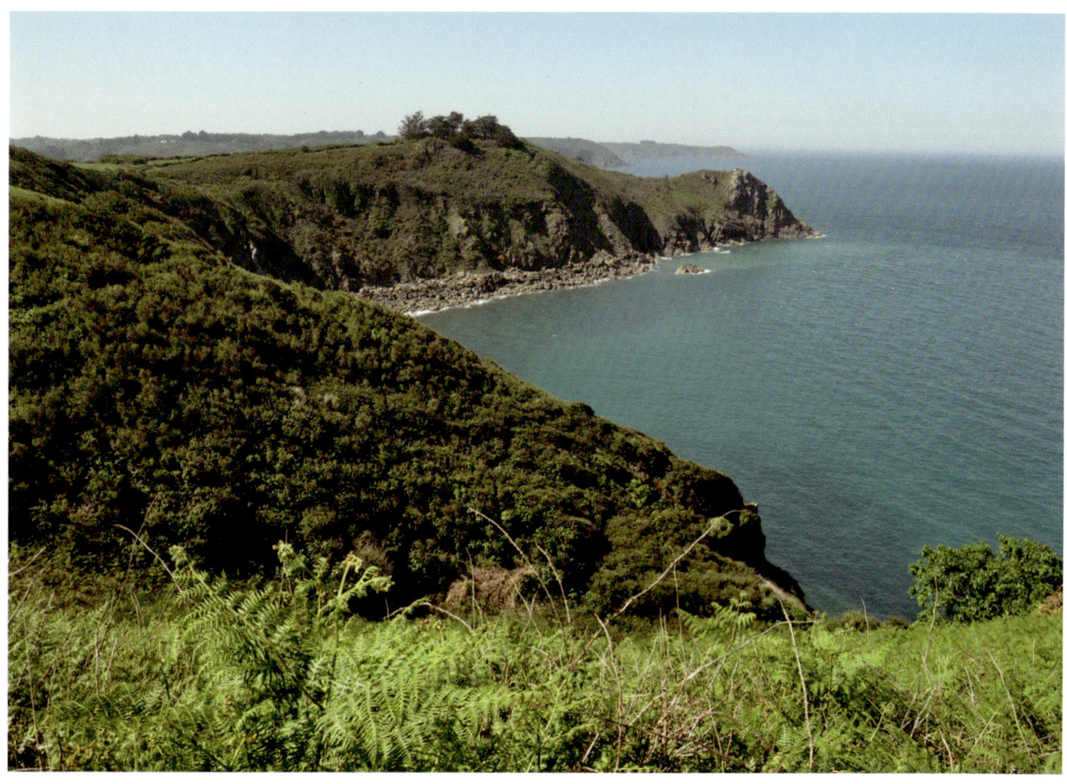

Les falaises de Plouha

The Cliffs of the Pointe de Plouha

With a height of 104 m, the Pointe de Plouha is the highest elevation on a steep 14 km long coast. Small bays, nesting places for seabirds and an old harbour hide between the cliffs. Inland there is a chapel with fearsome frescoes.

La pointe de Plouha et ses falaises

Haute de 104 mètres, la pointe de Plouha est le point culminant de la côte rocheuse longue de 14 km et abritant des criques dissimulées, des aires de nidification pour oiseaux, un ancien port ainsi qu'une chapelle renfermant des fresques terrifiantes.

Die Felsenklippen am Pointe de Plouha

Mit einer Höhe von 104 m ist die Pointe de Plouha die höchste Erhebung einer 14 km langen Steilküste. Zwischen ihren Felswänden verstecken sich kleine Buchten, Nistplätze für Seevögel und ein alter Hafen. Im Landesinneren liegt eine Kapelle mit furchterregenden Fresken.

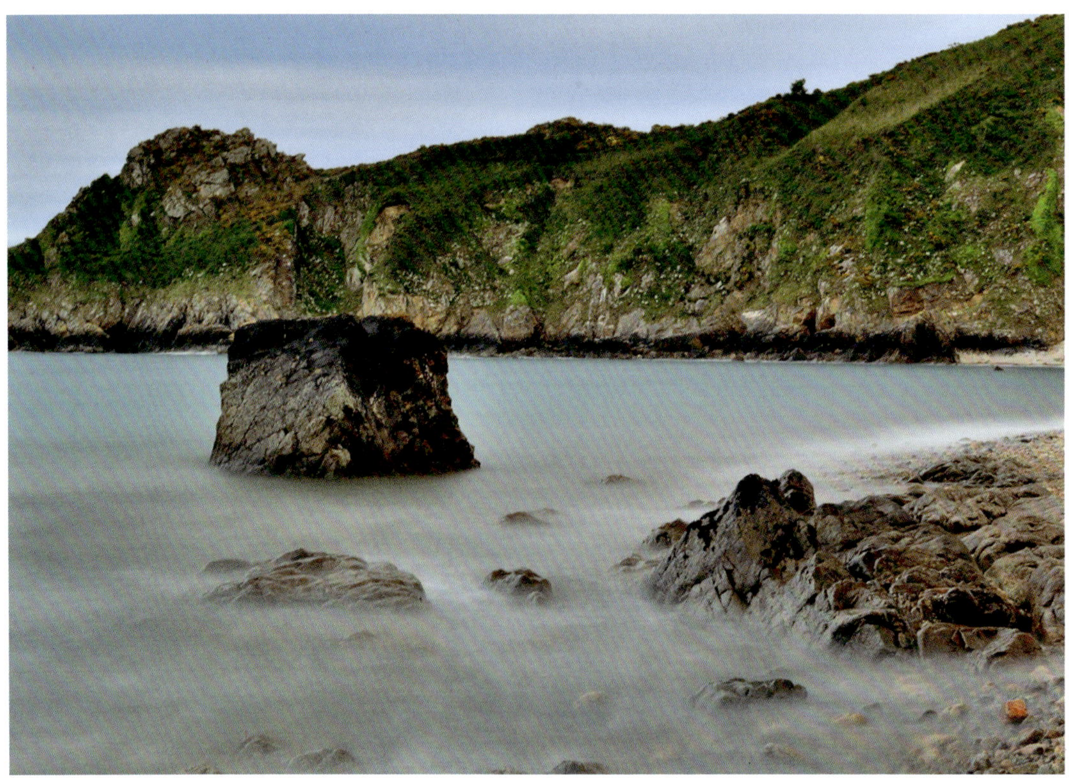

Les falaises de Plouha

Los acantilados de Pointe de Plouha

Con una altura de 104 m, Pointe de Plouha es la elevación más alta de una costa escarpada de 14 km de largo. Pequeñas bahías, nidos de aves marinas y un viejo puerto se esconden entre sus paredes rocosas. En el interior hay una capilla con frescos espantosos.

As falésias da Pointe de Plouha

Com uma altura de 104 m, a Pointe de Plouha é a maior elevação de uma costa íngreme de 14 km. Entre as suas faces rochosas, escondem-se pequenas baías e um velho porto, locais de nidificação para aves marinhas. E, no interior, existe uma capela com frescos assustadores.

De klippen van de Pointe de Plouha

Met 104 meter is de Pointe de Plouha de hoogste verheffing aan een 14 km lange steile kust. Kleine baaien, broedplaatsen voor zeevogels en een oude haven liggen verstopt tussen de rotswanden. Landinwaarts staat een kapel met angstaanjagende fresco's.

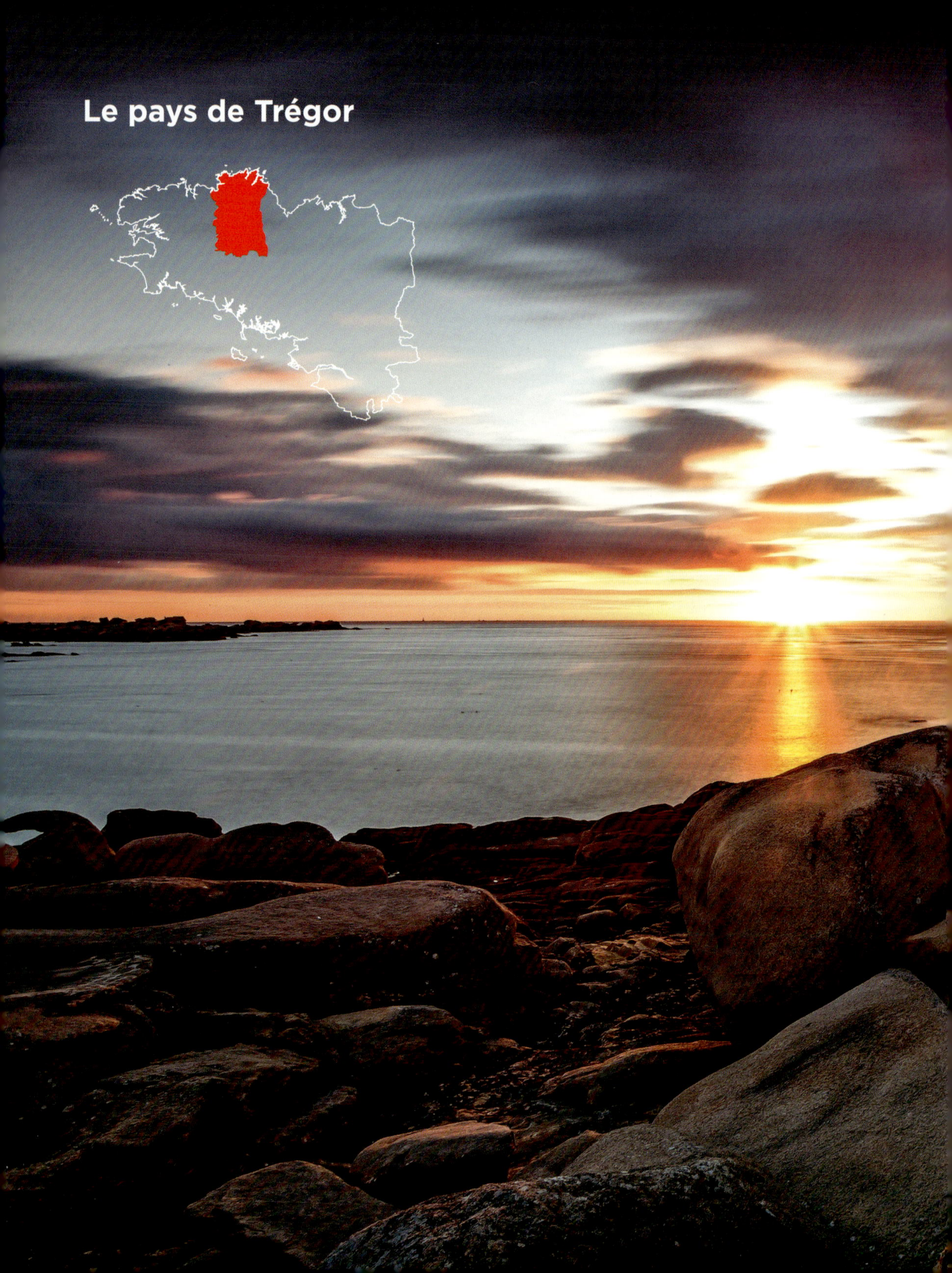

Le pays de Trégor

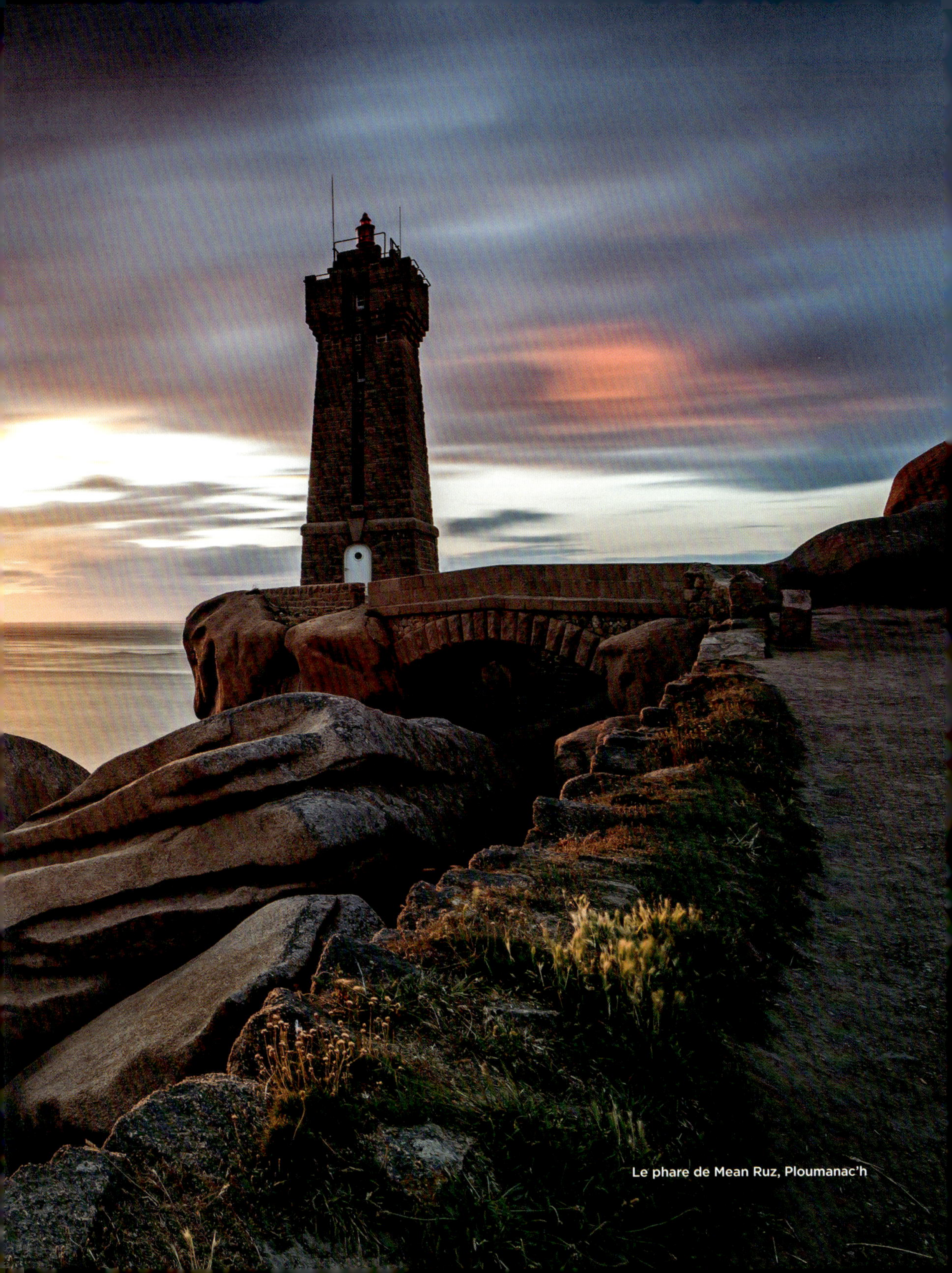

Le phare de Mean Ruz, Ploumanac'h

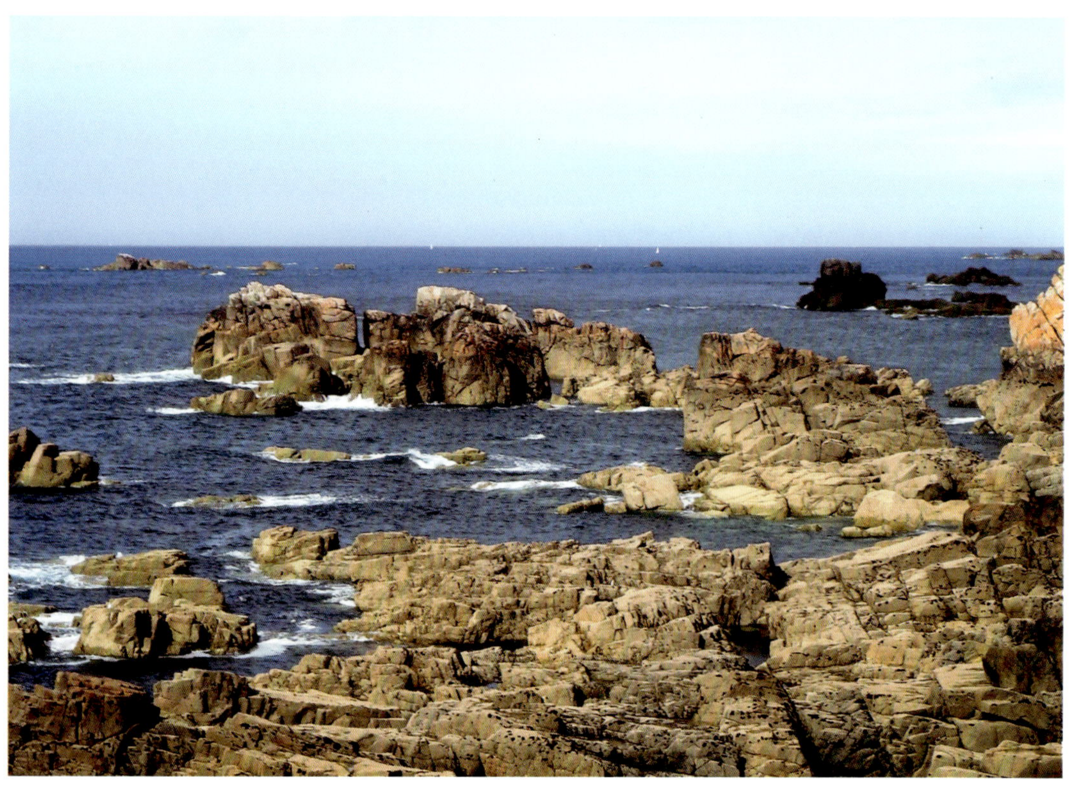

Plougrescant

Trégor-Goëlo

With its 160 km of coastline, Trégor-Goëlo is one of the most maritime regions in Brittany. It ranges from the Bréhat Islands to the Côte de Granit Rose. Between Guingamp and the bay of Paimpol there are several natural sites of national importance.

Le pays du Trégor-Goëlo

Avec 160 km de côtes, le pays du Trégor-Goëlo est l'un des plus maritimes de Bretagne. De l'archipel de Bréhat à la Côte de granit rose, il possède un riche patrimoine naturel. De la ville de Guingamp à la baie de Paimpol, on trouvera plusieurs grands sites naturels.

Trégor-Goëlo

Ihre 160 km lange Küste macht die Region Trégor-Goëlo zu einer der maritimsten der Bretagne. Sie reicht vom den Bréhat-Inseln bis zur Côte de Granit Rose. Zwischen Guingamp und der Bucht von Paimpol finden sich mehrere Naturstätten von überregionaler Bedeutung.

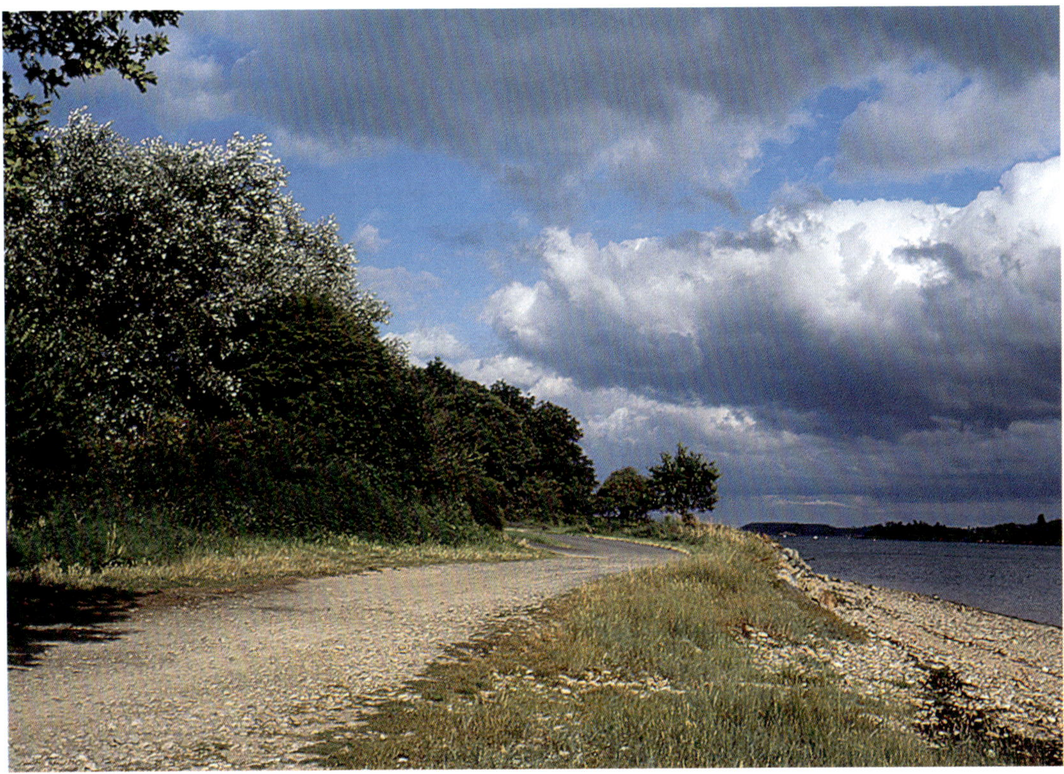

Environs de Paimpol

Trégor-Goëlo

Sus 160 km de costa hacen de la región de Trégor-Goëlo una de las más marítimas de Bretaña. Va desde las Islas Bréhat hasta la costa de granito rosa. Entre Guingamp y la bahía de Paimpol hay varios sitios naturales de importancia suprarregional.

Trégor-Goëlo

Com uma orla costeira de 160 km, a região de Trégor-Goëlo, é uma das mais marítimas da Bretanha. Estende-se das Ilhas Bréhat até à Côte de Granit Rose. Entre Guingamp e a baía de Paimpol existem vários sítios naturais de importância que excede o nível regional.

Trégor-Goëlo

De 160 km lange kust maakt van de regio Trégor-Goëlo een van de meest maritieme van Bretagne. Hij reikt van het Île-de-Bréhat tot de Côte de Granit Rose. Tussen Guingamp en de baai van Paimpol liggen verschillende natuurgebieden van supraregionaal belang.

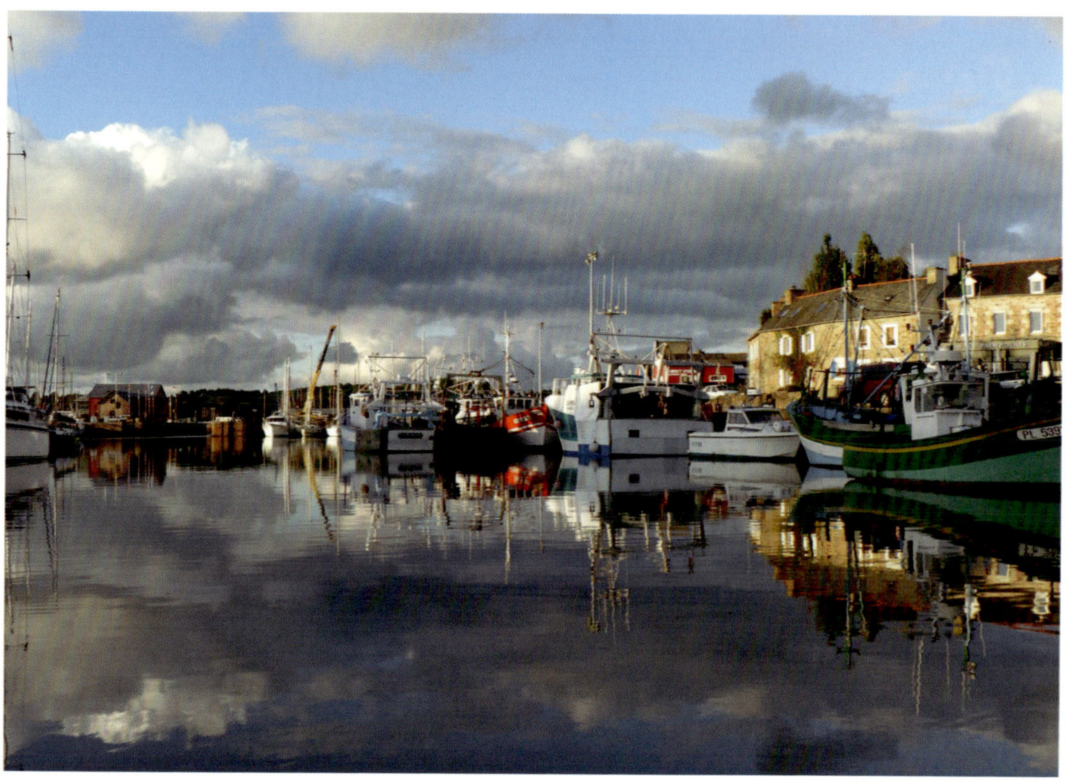

Le port de Paimpol

Paimpol

Between the Bréhat Islands, the mouth of the Trieux, and the highest cliffs of Brittany lies the village of Paimpol, which Pierre Loti referred to in his book "The Icelandic Fishermen". Today Paimpol is one of the most important fishing and marina ports on the English Channel.

Paimpol

Nichée entre l'archipel de Bréhat, l'estuaire du Trieux et les plus hautes falaises de Bretagne, Paimpol a été immortalisée par Pierre Loti dans le célèbre livre *Pêcheur d'Islande*. Paimpol est l'un des principaux ports de pêche et de plaisance donnant sur la Manche.

Paimpol

Zwischen den Bréhat-Inseln, der Mündung des Trieux und den höchsten Klippen der Bretagne liegt der Ort Paimpol, dem Pierre Loti in seinem Buch „Die Islandfischer" ein Denkmal setzte. Heute ist Paimpol einer der wichtigsten Fischerei- und Jachthäfen am Ärmelkanal.

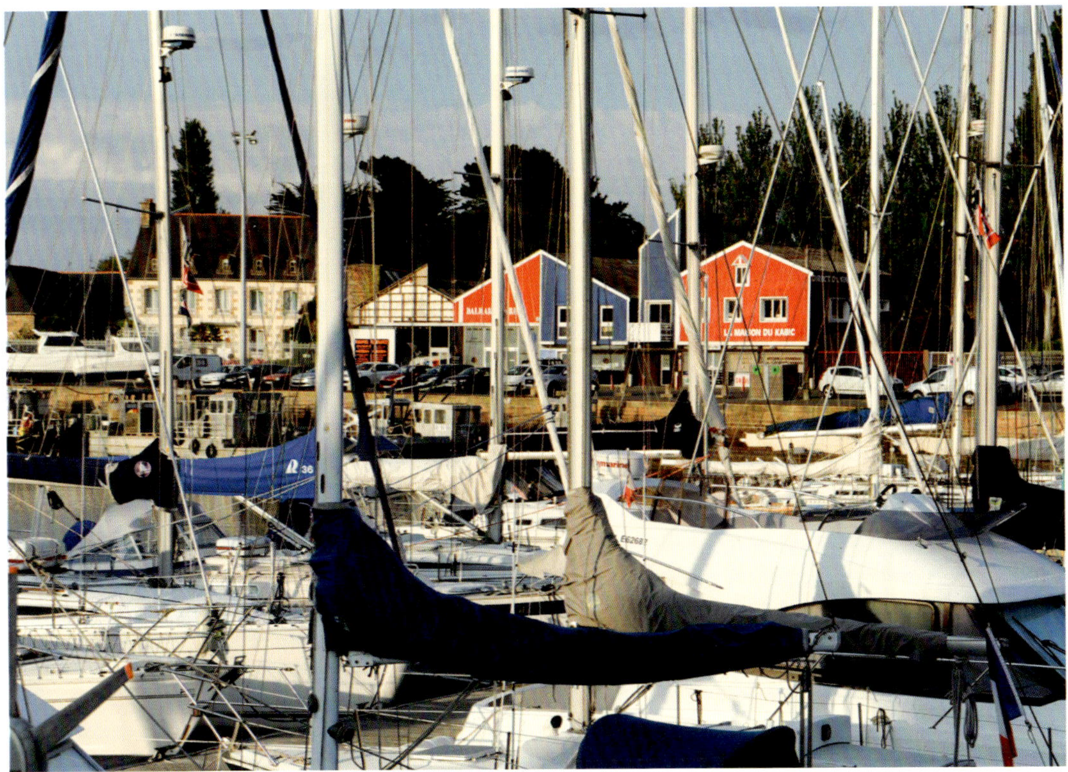

Le port et le Quai de Kernoa, Paimpol

Paimpol

Entre las islas Bréhat, la desembocadura del Trieux y los acantilados más altos de Bretaña se encuentra el pueblo de Paimpol, al que Pierre Loti hace un homenaje en su libro «El pescador de Islandia». Hoy en día, Paimpol es uno de los puertos pesqueros y deportivos más importantes del canal de la Mancha.

Paimpol

Entre as Ilhas Bréhat, a foz dos Trieux e os penhascos mais altos da Bretanha fica a aldeia de Paimpol, à qual Pierre Loti dedicou um monumento no seu livro «Os Pescadores Islandeses». Hoje em dia, Paimpol, é um dos portos de pesca e marina mais importantes do Canal da Mancha.

Paimpol

Tussen het Île-de-Bréhat, de monding van de Trieux en de hoogste klippen van Bretagne ligt het dorp Paimpol, waarvoor Pierre Loti met zijn boek Pêcheur d'Islande een monument oprichtte. Tegenwoordig is Paimpol een van de belangrijkste vissers- en jachthavenhavens aan het Kanaal.

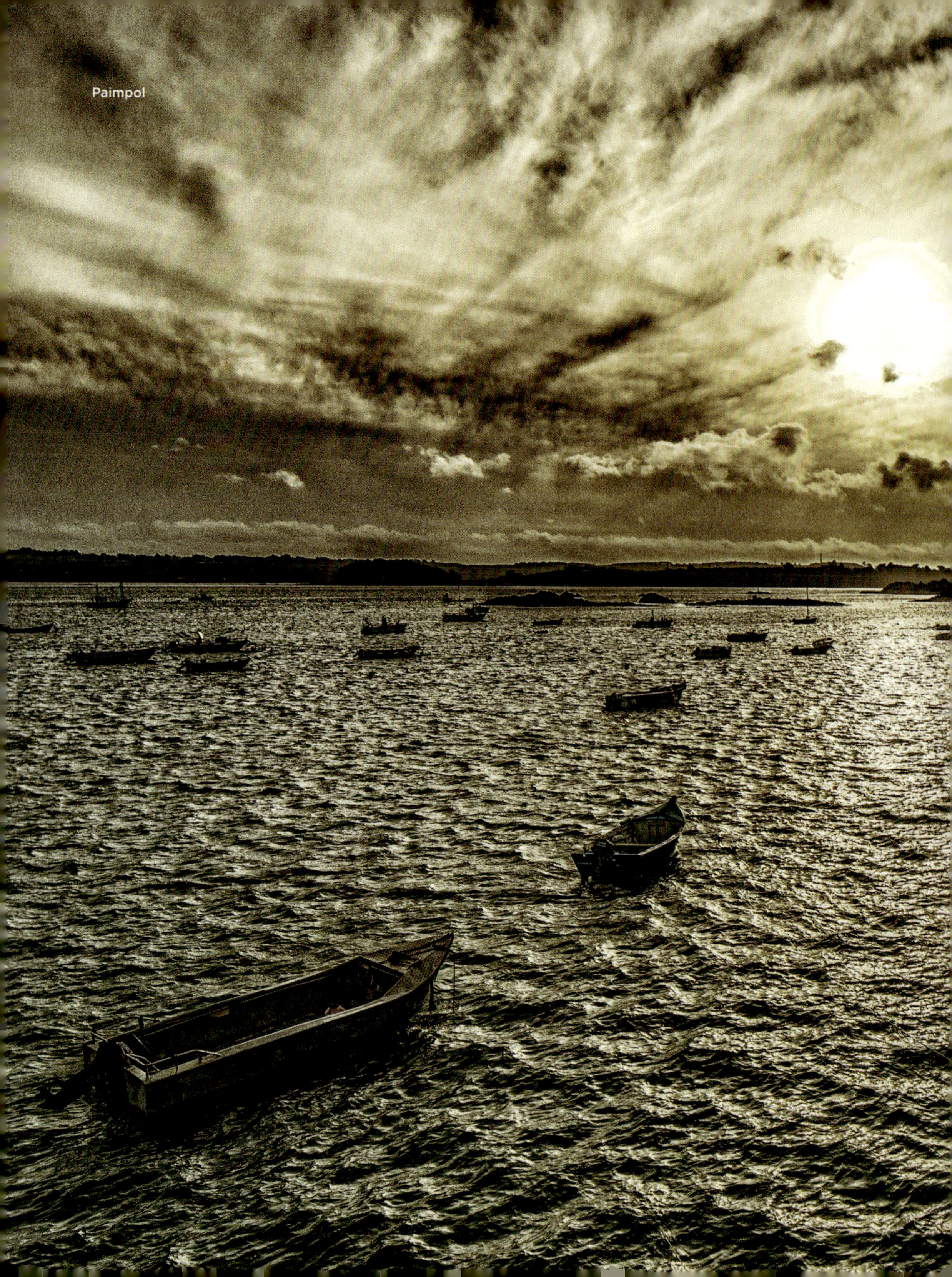

Paimpol

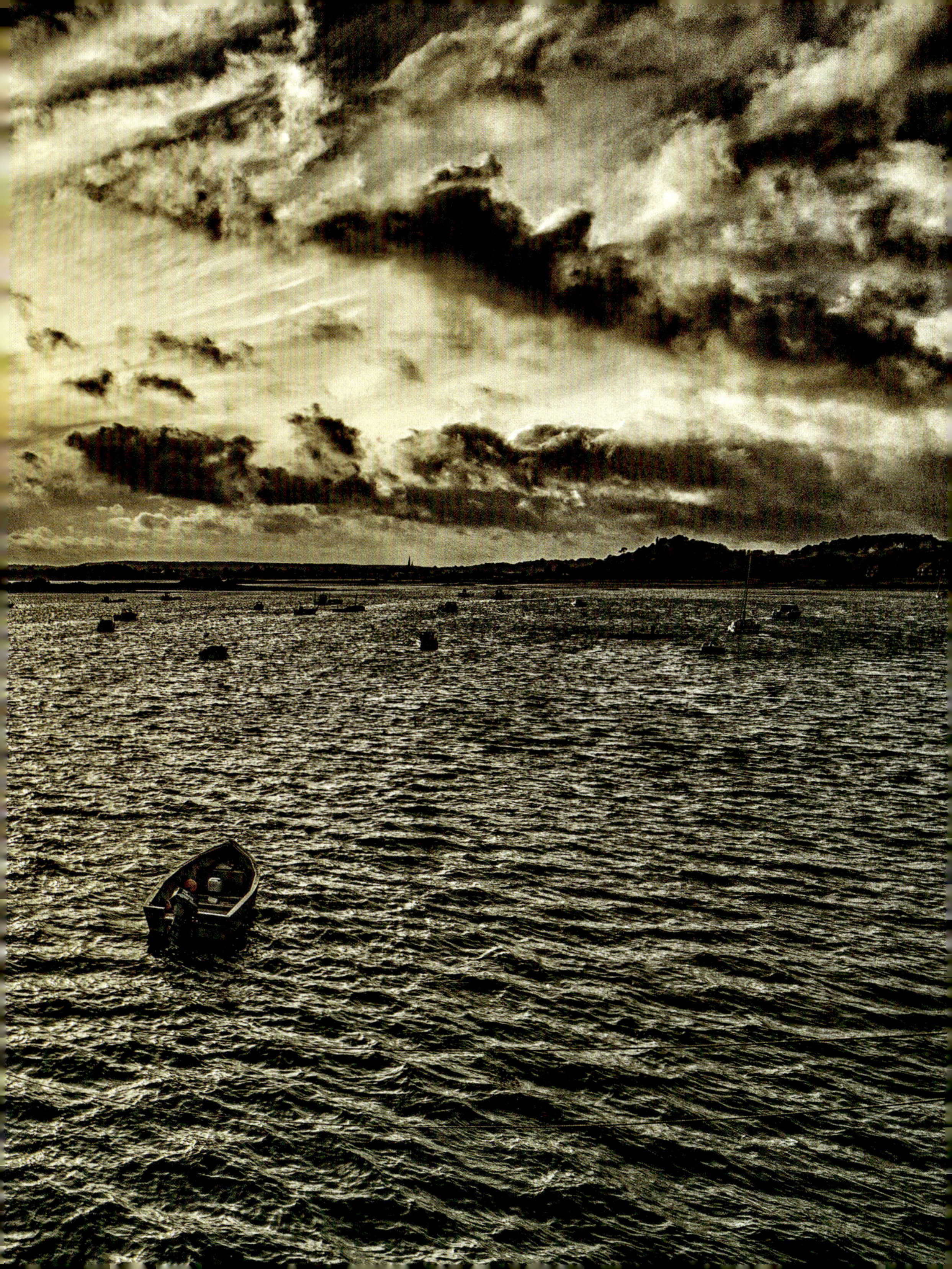

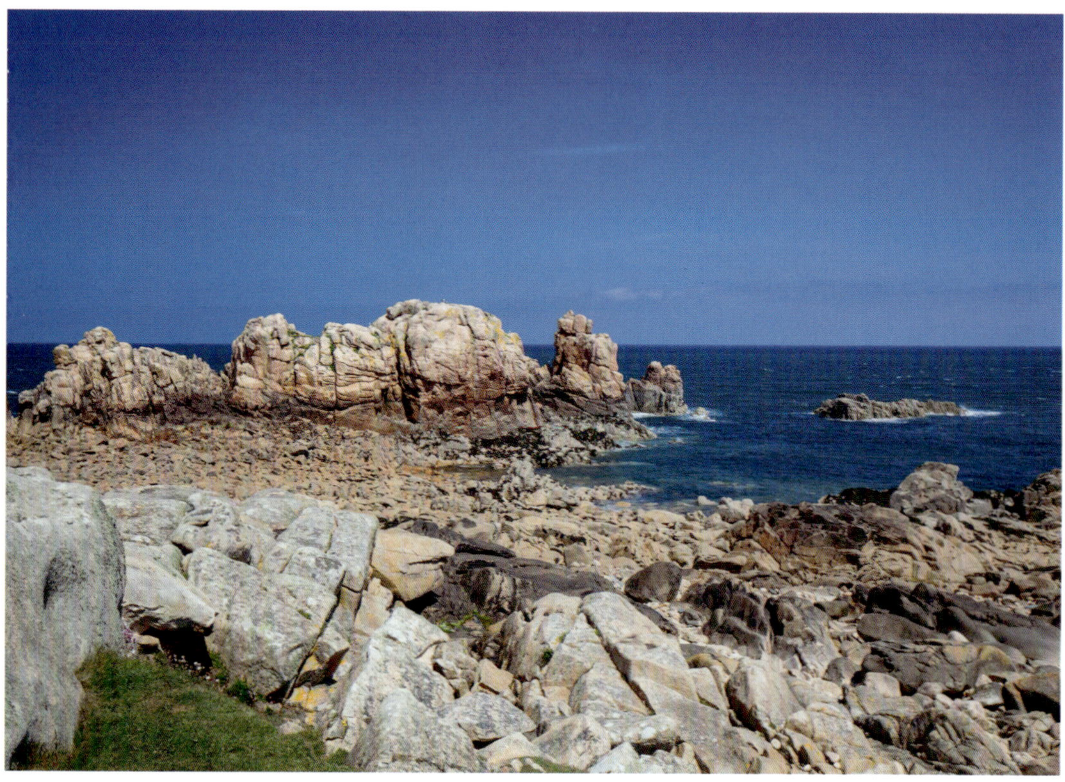

L'île de Bréhat

The Ile de Bréhat

The main island of the archipelago of the same name is also known as the "Island of Flowers". In 1907 the Île de Bréhat was declared the first nature reserve in France. The archipelago benefits from a very mild microclimate.

L'île de Bréhat

Constituée de l'archipel de Bréhat, qui doit son nom à l'île principale, surnommée « l'île aux fleurs », Bréhat fut le premier site naturel classé en France en 1907. L'archipel bénéficie d'un microclimat très doux.

Die Île de Bréhat

Die Hauptinsel des gleichnamigen Archipels wird auch „Insel der Blumen" genannt. 1907 wurde die Île de Bréhat zum ersten Naturschutzgebiet Frankreichs erklärt. Der Archipel profitiert von einem sehr milden Mikroklima.

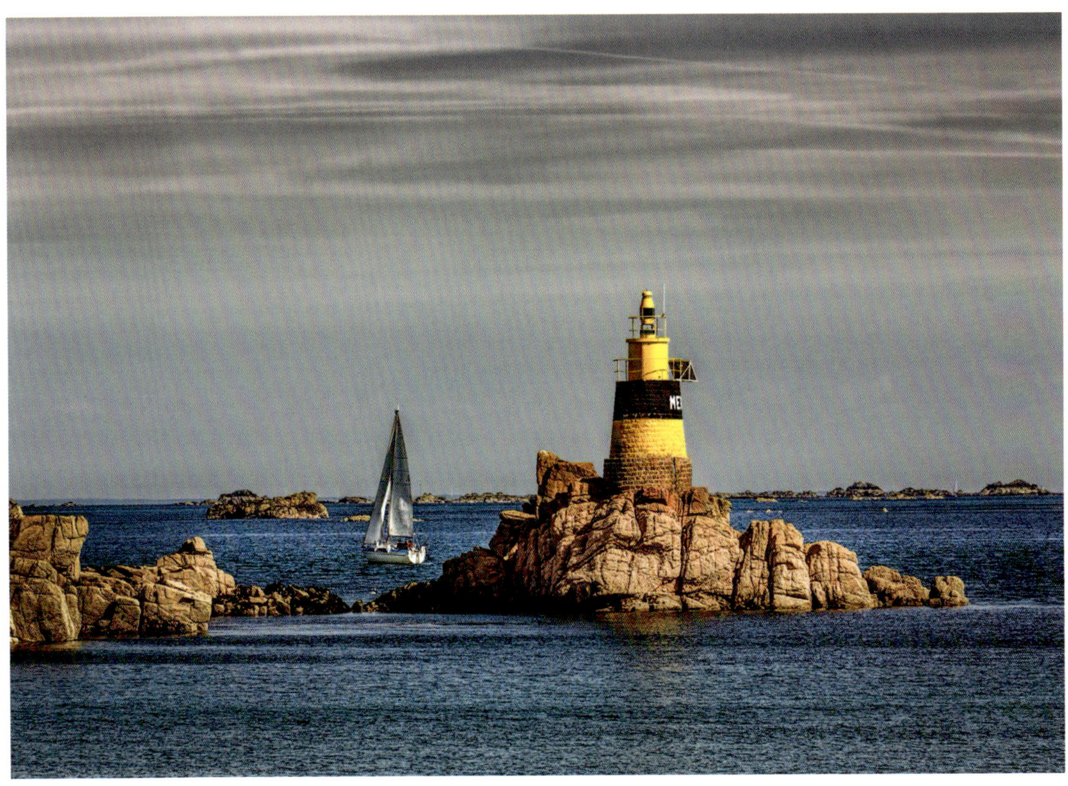

Balise maritime, Bréhat

Île de Bréhat

La isla principal del archipiélago con el mismo nombre también se llama la «isla de las flores». En 1907, la isla de Bréhat fue declarada la primera reserva natural de Francia. El archipiélago goza de un microclima muy suave.

A lle de Bréhat

A ilha principal do arquipélago com o mesmo nome é também chamada «Ilha das Flores». Em 1907, a Île de Bréhat foi declarada a primeira reserva natural de França. O arquipélago beneficia de um microclima muito suave.

Het Île-de-Bréhat

Het hoofdeiland, waar enkele kleine eilandjes omheen liggen, wordt ook wel het 'bloemeneiland' genoemd. In 1907 werd het uitgeroepen tot eerste natuurreservaat van Frankrijk. De eilandengroep profiteert van een zeer mild microklimaat.

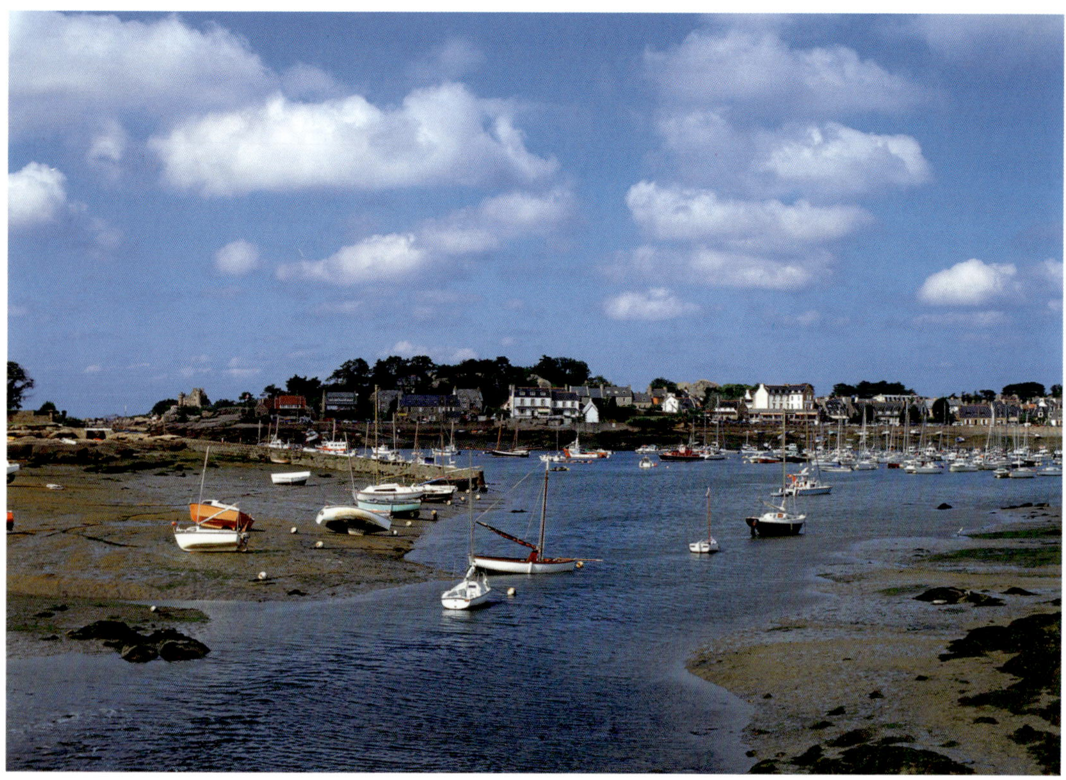

La rivière de Tréguier

Tréguier

The cathedral, narrow streets, half-timbered houses and the waterfront location create the charm of the historic capital of Tréguier. This town lies on the steep slopes of a small plateau bordered by the rivers Guindy and Jaudy, which extend as a ria - a coastal inlet penetrating deep into the interior - to the English Channel 9 km away.

Tréguier

Le charme de la capitale historique du Trégor tient à sa cathédrale, ses ruelles, ses maisons à pans de bois et à sa situation au bord de l'eau. La ville s'est développée sur les deux escarpements limitant ce lambeau de plateau jusqu'à la rive droite du Guindy et la rive gauche du Jaudy. Tréguier est une ville-port de fond de ria, située à 9 km de la Manche.

Tréguier

Die Kathedrale, die engen Gassen, die Fachwerkhäuser und die Lage am Wasser machen den Charme der historischen Hauptstadt des Trégor aus. Tréguier liegt auf den Steilhängen eines kleine Plateaus, das von den Flüssen Guindy und Jaudy begrenzt wird, die als Ria – eine tief ins Landesinnere eindringende Bucht – bis zum 9 km entfernten Ärmelkanal reichen.

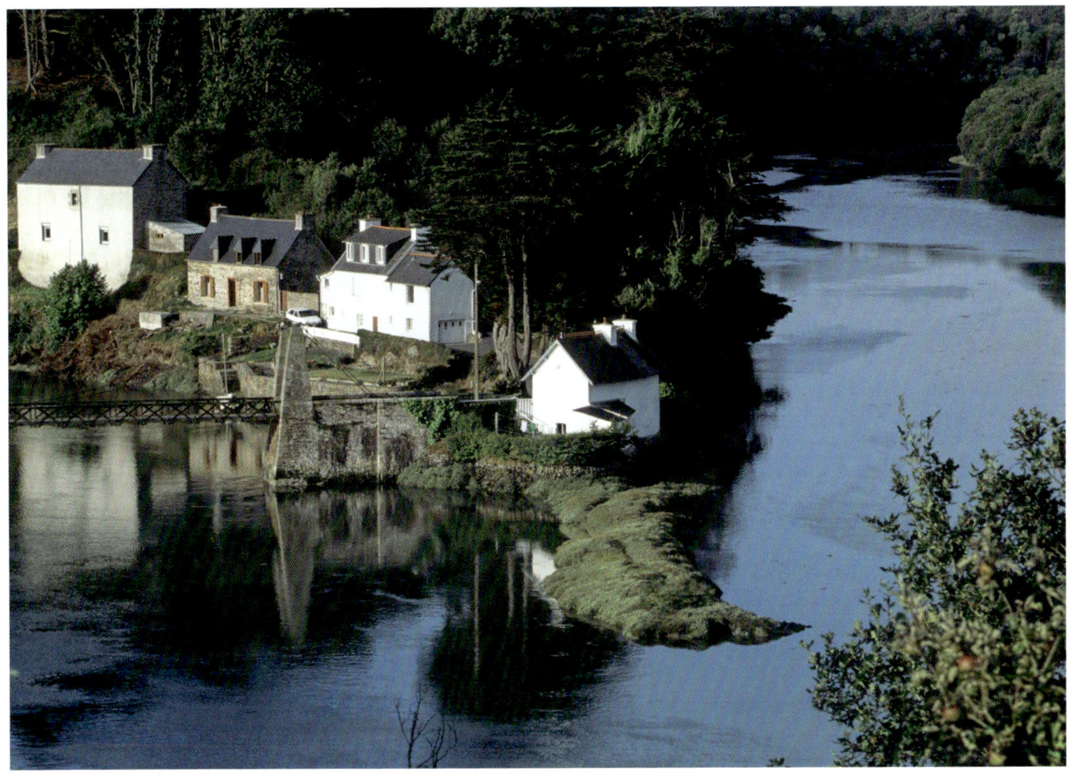

La rivière du Guindy, Tréguier

Tréguier

La catedral, las calles estrechas, las casas de entramado de madera y la ubicación junto al agua son el encanto de la histórica capital de Trégor. Tréguier se encuentra en las empinadas laderas de una pequeña meseta bordeada por los ríos Guindy y Jaudy, que se extienden como Ria (una bahía que penetra profundamente en el interior) hasta el canal de la Mancha, a 9 km de distancia.

Tréguier

A sua catedral, as ruas estreitas, as casas no estilo enxaimel e a localização junto à água traçam o encanto da capital histórica de Trégor. Tréguier situa-se nas encostas íngremes de um pequeno planalto rodeado pelos rios Guindy e Jaudy, que se estendem como uma ria - uma baía que penetra profundamente no interior - até ao Canal da Mancha a 9 km de distância.

Tréguier

De kathedraal, de smalle straatjes, de vakwerkhuizen en de ligging aan het water vormen de charme van de historische hoofdstad van Trégor. Tréguier ligt op de steile hellingen van een klein plateau dat wordt begrensd door de rivieren Guindy en Jaudy, die zich als een ria – een diep het binnenland binnendringende baai – uitstrekt tot aan het 9 km verderop gelegen Kanaal.

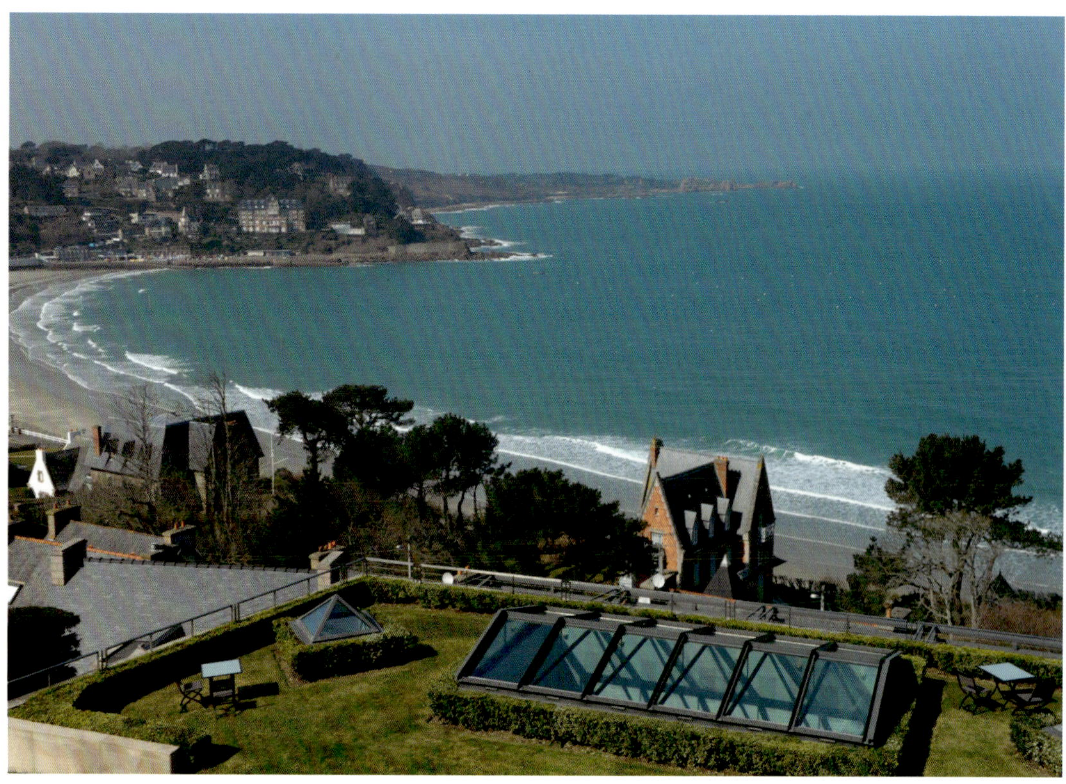

Perros-Guirec

Perros-Guirec and the Côte de Granit Rose

The charming seaside resort of Perros-Guirec is the centre of the Côte de Granit Rose. It offers a wonderful panoramic view of the Sept-Îles archipelago, one of the most important bird sanctuaries in France.

Perros-Guirec et la Côte de granit rose

Perros-Guirec est une charmante station balnéaire et la capitale de la Côte de granit rose. La ville jouit d'une vue panoramique sur l'archipel des Sept-Îles, l'une des plus importantes réserves ornithologiques de France.

Perros-Guirec und die Côte de Granit Rose

Der charmante Badeort Perros-Guirec ist das Zentrum der Côte de Granit Rose. Er bietet einen wunderschönen Panoramablick auf die Inselgruppe Sept-Îles, eines der wichtigsten Vogelschutzgebiete Frankreichs.

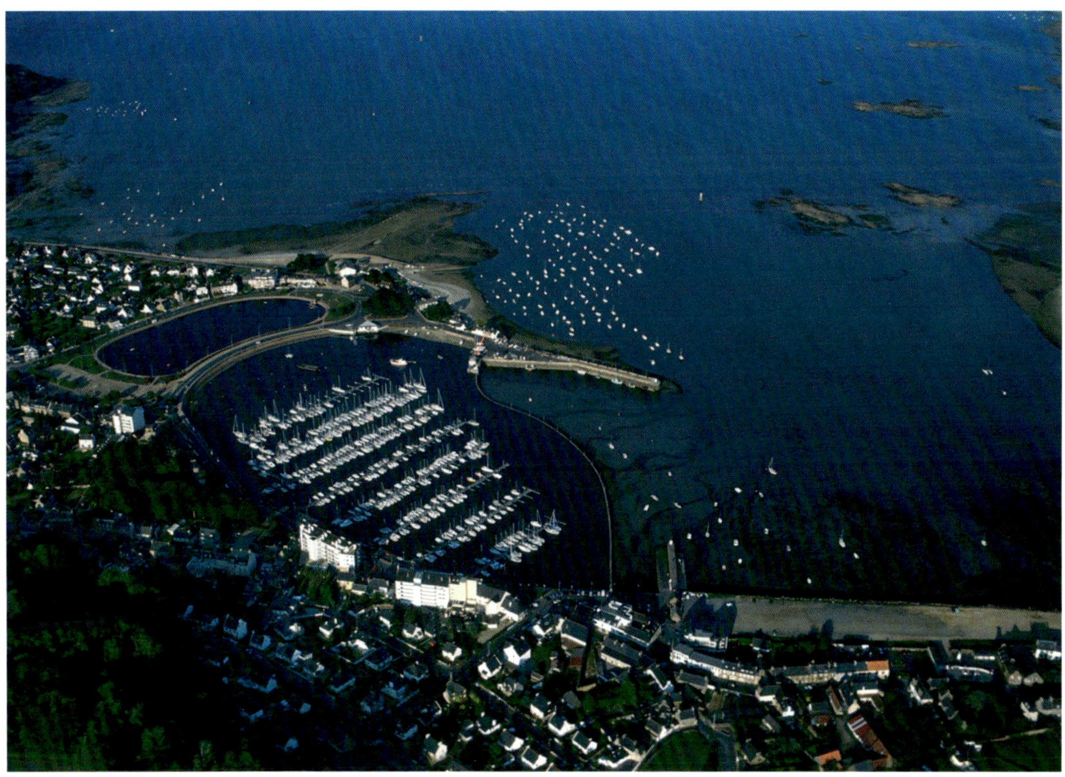

La baie de Perros-Guirec

Perros-Guirec y la costa de granito rosa

La encantadora estación balnearia de Perros-Guirec es el centro de la costa de granito rosa. Ofrece una maravillosa vista panorámica del archipiélago de Sept-Îles, una de las reservas de aves más importantes de Francia.

Perros-Guirec e a Côte de Granit Rose

A encantadora estância balnear de Perros-Guirec é o centro da Côte de Granit Rose. Oferece uma maravilhosa vista panorâmica do arquipélago de Sept-Îles, um dos mais importantes santuários de aves da França.

Perros-Guirec en de Côte de Granit Rose

De charmante badplaats Perros-Guirec is het centrum van de Côte de Granit Rose. Hij biedt een prachtig panoramisch uitzicht op de eilandengroep van Sept-Îles, een van de belangrijkste vogelreservaten van Frankrijk.

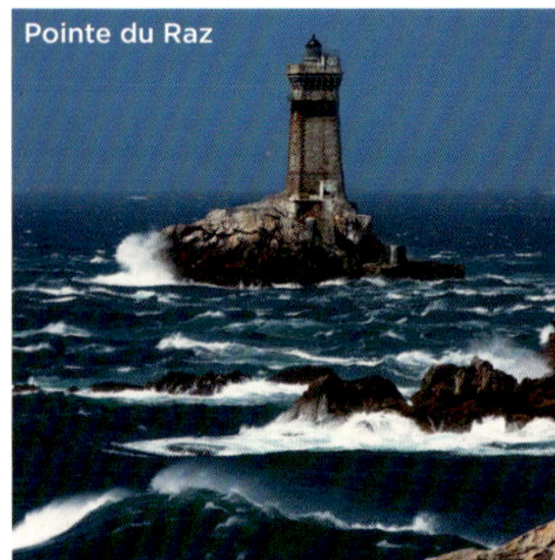

Pointe du Raz

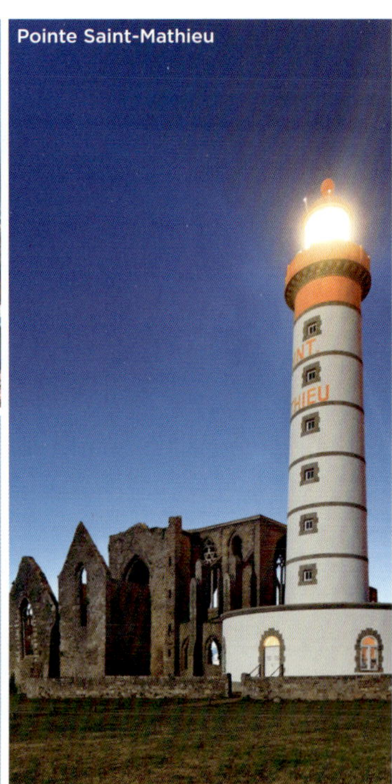

Pointe Saint-Mathieu

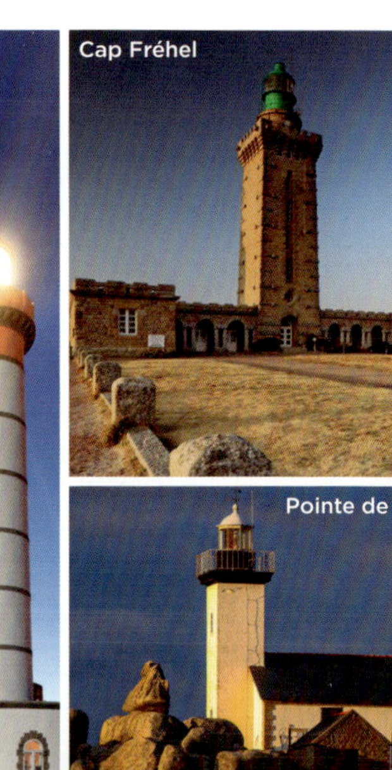

Cap Fréhel

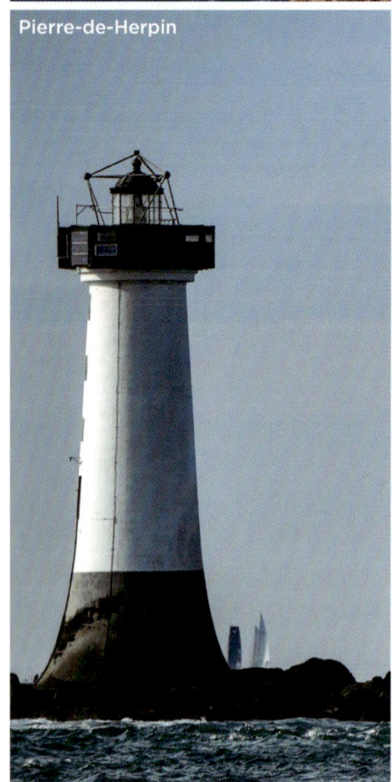

Pierre-de-Herpin

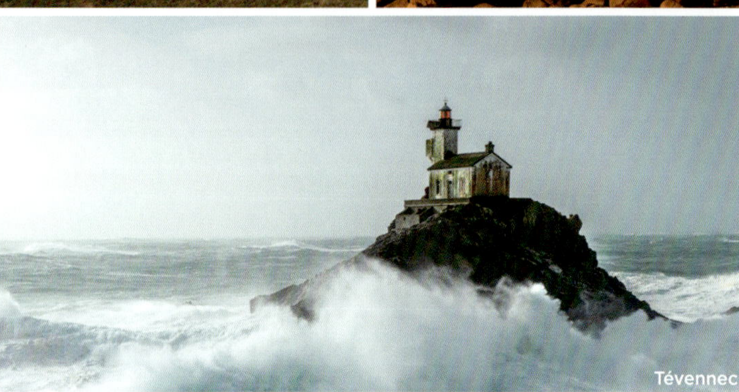

Pointe de Pontusval

Tévennec

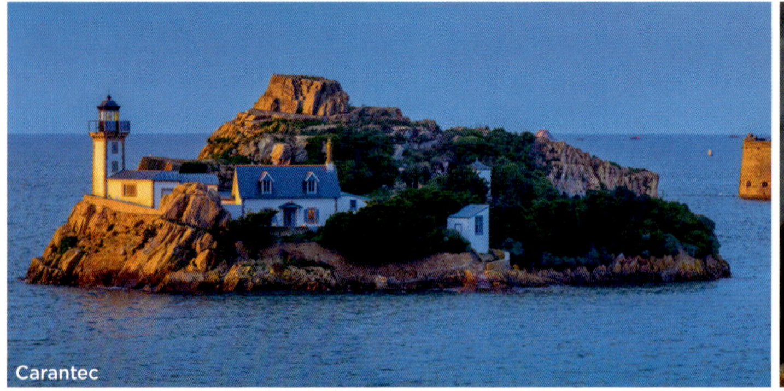

Carantec

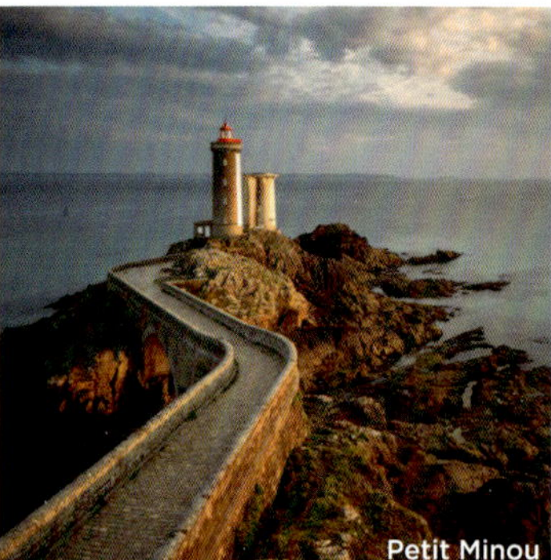

Petit Minou

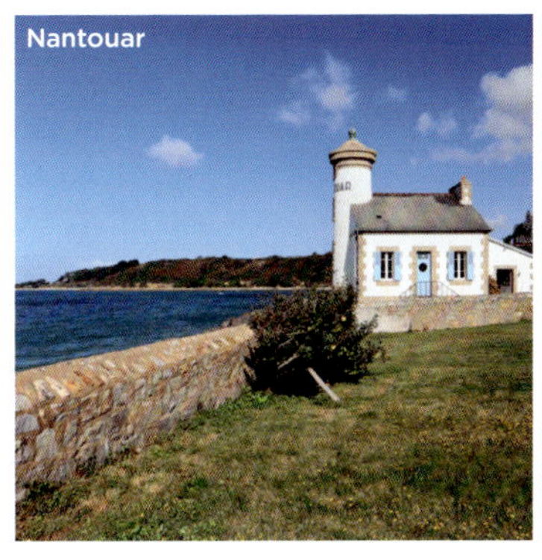

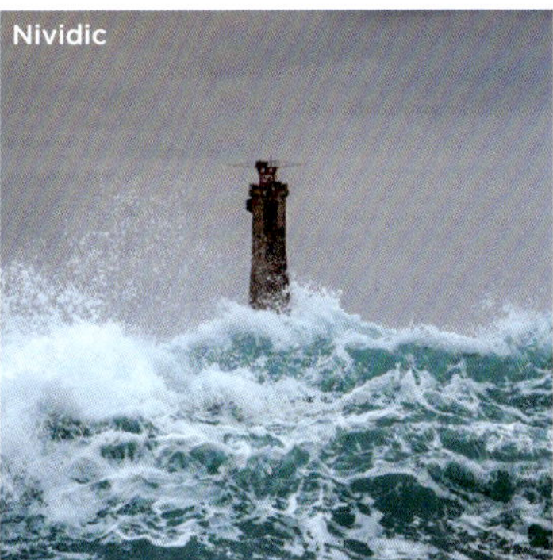

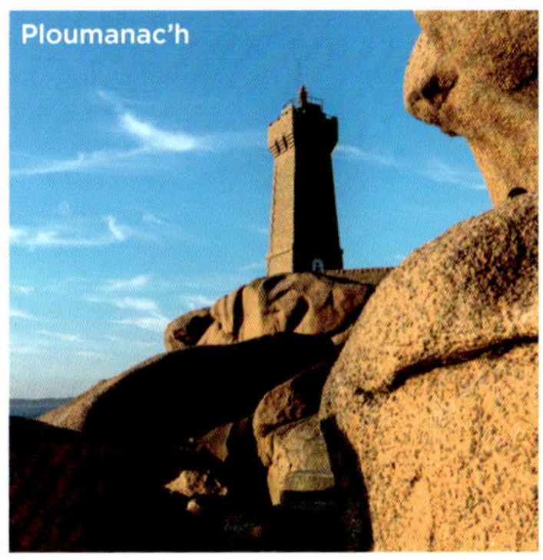

The Guardians of the Sea

Brittany is home to more than a third of all French lighthouses. These striking buildings, form landmarks for maritime navigation. Today, seven of the lighthouses are listed and invite you to visit them. Five are still permanently occupied (Sein, Créac'h, Belle-Île-en-Mer and Fréhel). The Phare de l'Île Vierge in Plouguerneau is the highest lighthouse in Europe (82.5 m, 397 steps). Built in 1700, the Phare du Stiff is the oldest lighthouse in France, and the Phare du Créac'h is the brightest in the world.

Les sentinelles de la mer

La Bretagne compte plus d'un tiers des phares français. Véritables sentinelles, grandioses, ils scandent le paysage et veillent à donner des repères aux navigateurs. Parmi ceux-ci, 7 sont classés monuments historiques et 4 sont encore gardiennés (Sein, Créac'h, Belle-Île-en-Mer et Fréhel). Certains se visitent ! Le phare de l'île Vierge à Plouguerneau est le plus haut phare d'Europe (82,5 m, 397 marches). À Ouessant, Le Stiff, construit en 1700, est le plus ancien des phares français et le phare du Créac'h le plus puissant du monde.

Die Wächter des Meeres

In der Bretagne stehen mehr als ein Drittel aller französischen Leuchttürme. Als markante Bauwerke bilden sie Orientierungspunkte für die Seefahrt. Heute stehen sieben der Leuchttürme unter Denkmalschutz und laden zu einem Besuch ein. Fünf sind noch dauerhaft besetzt (Sein, Créac'h, Belle-Île-en-Mer und Fréhel). Der Phare de l'Île Vierge in Plouguerneau ist der höchste Leuchtturm Europas (82,5 m, 397 Stufen). Der im Jahr 1700 erbaute Phare du Stiff ist der älteste Leuchtturm Frankreichs und der Phare du Créac'h der hellste der Welt.

Los guardianes del mar

Bretaña alberga más de una tercera parte de todos los faros franceses. Son edificios llamativos que constituyen puntos de referencia para la navegación marítima. Hoy en día, siete de los faros se consideran monumentos históricos e invitan a visitarlos. Cinco de ellos siguen ocupados permanentemente (Sein, Créac'h, Belle-Île-en-Mer y Fréhel). El Phare de l'Île Vierge en Plouguerneau es el faro más alto de Europa (82,5 m, 397 escalones). Construido en 1700, el Phare du Stiff es el faro más antiguo de Francia y el Phare du Créac'h el más brillante del mundo.

Os guardiões do mar

A Bretanha é a região onde se encontram mais de um terço de todos os faróis franceses. Construções impressionantes, são marcos de orientação para a navegação. Hoje, sete dos faróis são considerados como património histórico e podem ser visitados. Cinco deles estão ainda permanentemente ocupados (Sein, Créac'h, Belle-Île-en-Mer e Fréhel). O Phare de l'Île Vierge em Plouguerneau é o farol mais alto da Europa (82,5 m, 397 degraus). Construído em 1700, o Phare du Stiff é o farol mais antigo da França e o Phare du Créac'h o mais brilhante do mundo.

De bewakers van de zee

Meer dan een derde van alle Franse vuurtorens staat in Bretagne. Als markante bouwwerken vormen ze oriëntatiepunten voor de zeevaart. Tegenwoordig staan er zeven vuurtorens op de monumentenlijst en nodigen ze uit tot een bezoek. Vijf zijn nog permanent bezet (Sein, Créac'h, Belle-Île-en-Mer en Fréhel). De Phare de l'Île Vierge in Plouguerneau is de hoogste vuurtoren van Europa (82,5 meter, 397 treden). De in 1700 gebouwde Phare du Stiff is de oudste vuurtoren van Frankrijk en de Phare du Créac'h de helderste ter wereld.

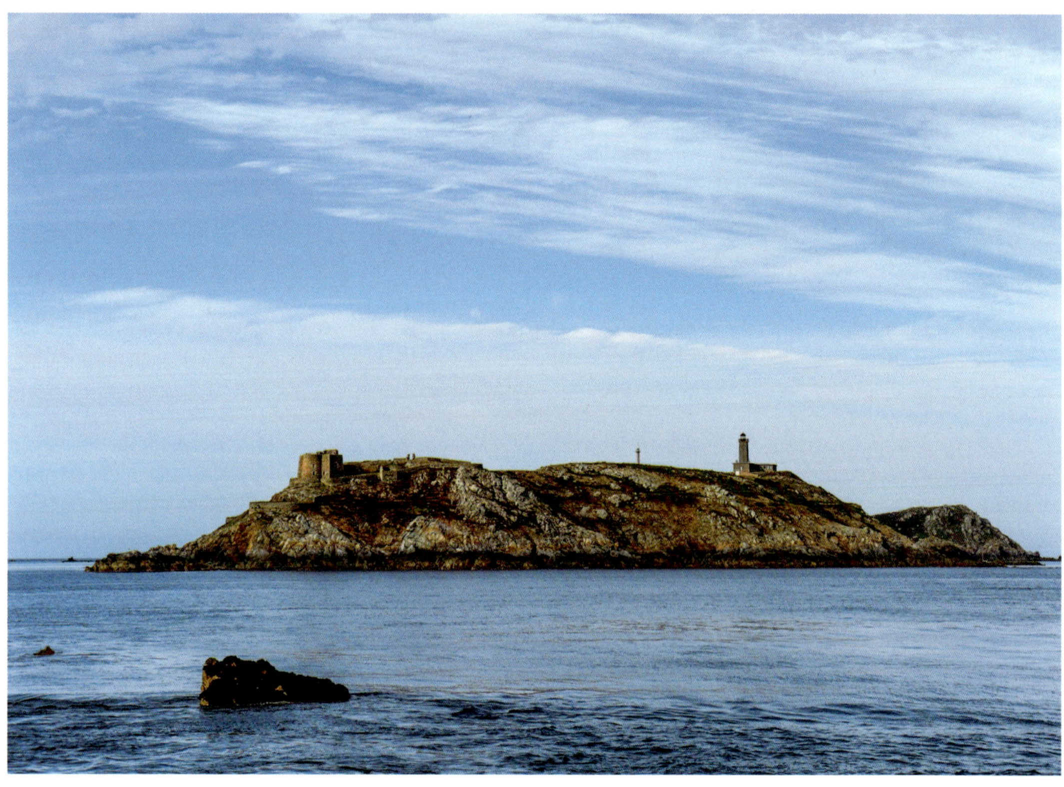

L'île-aux-Moines

The Sept-Îles

Between Perros-Guirec and Trégastel, in a nature reserve of almost 40 hectares, lies a true paradise for seabirds. The archipelago consists of seven islands: Rouzic, Malban, Bono, Plates, Le Cerf, Les Costans and the Île aux Moines. Access is subject to strict rules. The only island that can be visited is Île aux Moines - the others can only be explored by water or air.

L'archipel des Sept-Îles

Un paradis des oiseaux marins se niche entre Perros-Guirec et Trégastel, dans une réserve naturelle qui s'étend sur près de 40 hectares, composé de 5 îles : Rouzic, Malban, Plates, Bono, et l'Île-aux-Moines, et 2 îlots rocheux : le Cerf et le plateau de Costans. L'accès aux îles est réglementé et le site protégé. Elles s'admirent par la mer ou par les airs et la seule île sur laquelle il est possible d'accoster est l'Île-aux-Moines.

Die Sept-Îles

Zwischen Perros-Guirec und Trégastel, in einem Naturschutzgebiet, das fast 40 Hektar umfasst, liegt ein wahres Seevogelparadies. Die Inselgruppe setzt sich aus sieben Inseln zusammen: Rouzic, Malban, Bono, Plates, Le Cerf, Les Costans und der Île aux Moines. Der Zugang unterliegt strengen Regeln. Die einzige Insel, die besucht werden kann, ist die Île aux Moines – die übrigen lassen sich nur vom Wasser oder aus der Luft erkunden.

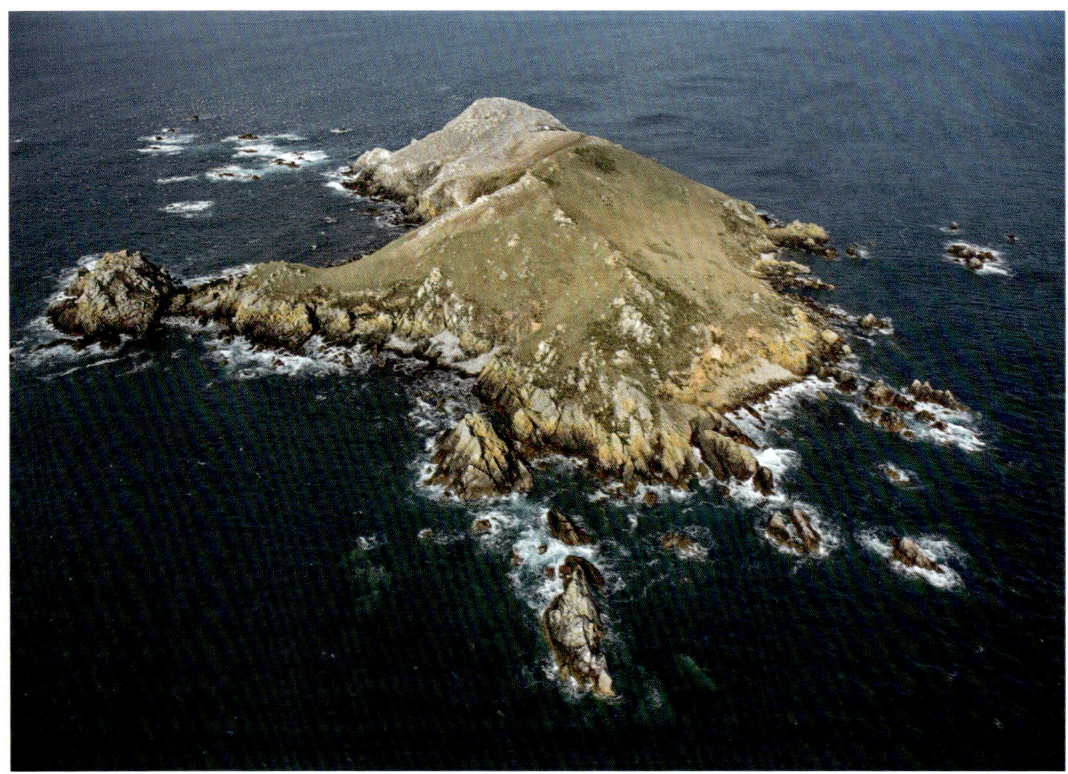

L'île Rouzic

Sept-Îles

Entre Perros-Guirec y Trégastel, en una reserva natural de casi 40 hectáreas, se encuentra un verdadero paraíso para las aves marinas. El archipiélago está formado por siete islas: Rouzic, Malban, Bono, Plates, Le Cerf, Les Costans e Île-aux-Moines. El acceso está sujeto a normas muy estrictas. La única isla que se puede visitar es Île-aux-Moines; las demás solo se pueden explorar desde el agua o el aire.

O arquipélago de Sept-Îles

Entre Perros-Guirec e Trégastel, existe uma reserva natural de quase 40 hectares, um verdadeiro paraíso para as aves marinhas. O arquipélago é constituído por sete ilhas: Rouzic, Malban, Bono, Plates, Le Cerf, Les Costans e a Île aux Moines. O acesso está sujeito a regras estritas. A única ilha que pode ser visitada é a Île aux Moines - as outras só podem ser exploradas por via marítima ou aérea.

De Sept-Îles

Tussen Perros-Guirec en Trégastel, in een beschermd natuurgebied van bijna 40 hectare, ligt een paradijs voor zeevogels. De eilandengroep omvat zeven eilanden: Rouzic, Malban, Bono, Plates, Le Cerf, Les Costans en het Île aux Moines. Voor de toegang gelden strenge regels. Het enige eiland dat kan worden bezocht, is het Île aux Moines. De andere kunnen alleen worden verkend vanaf het water of vanuit de lucht.

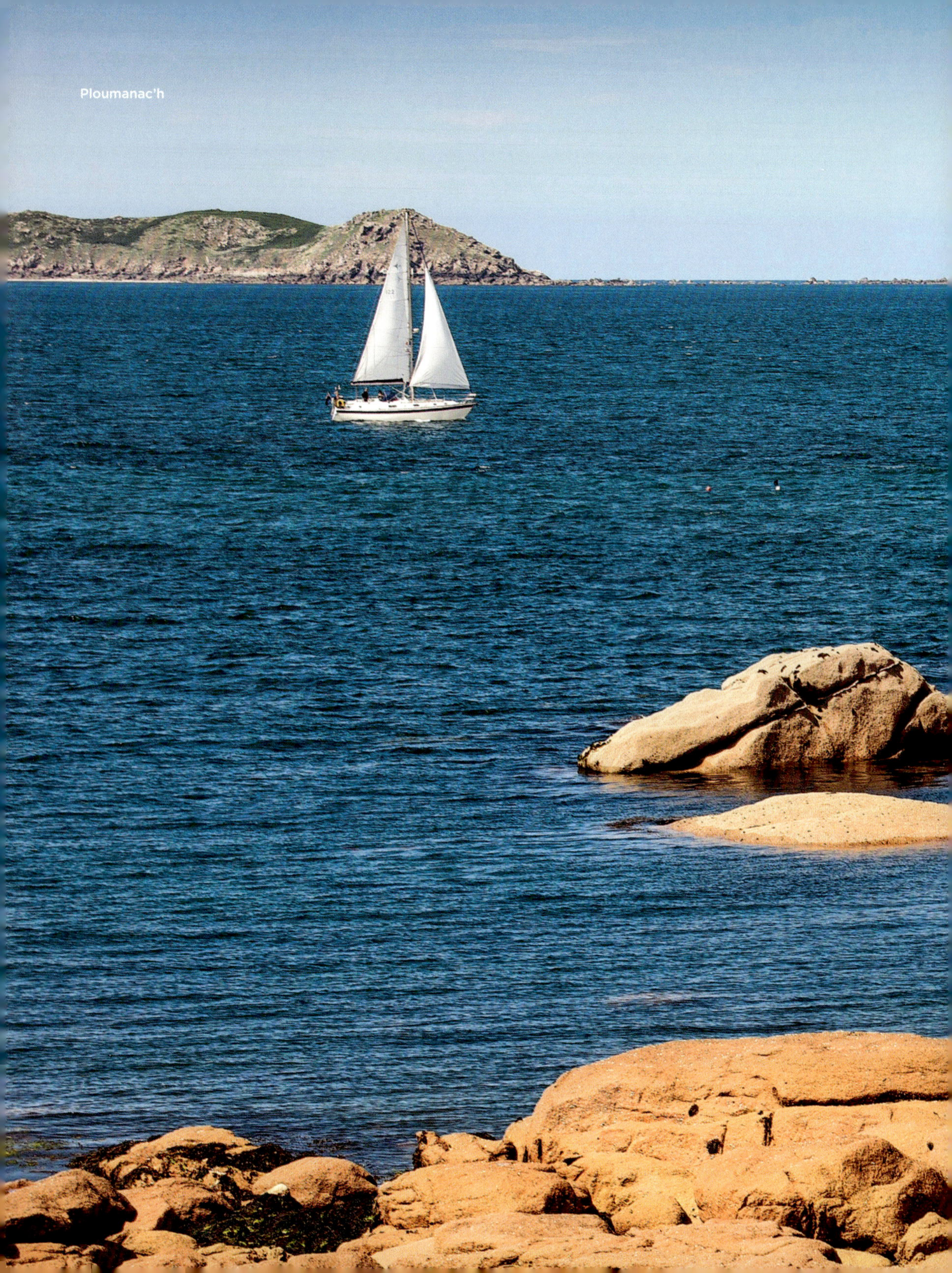
Ploumanac'h

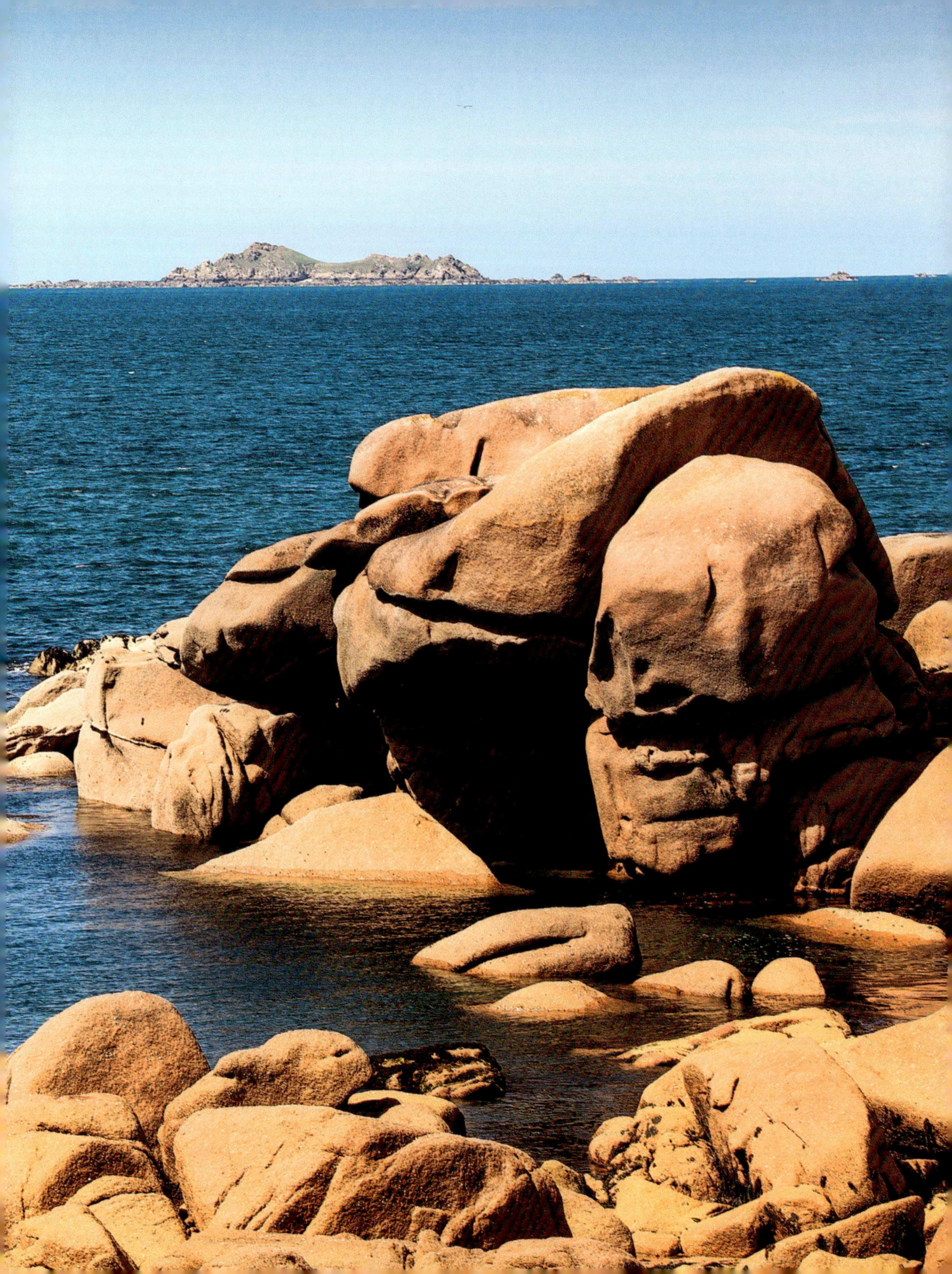

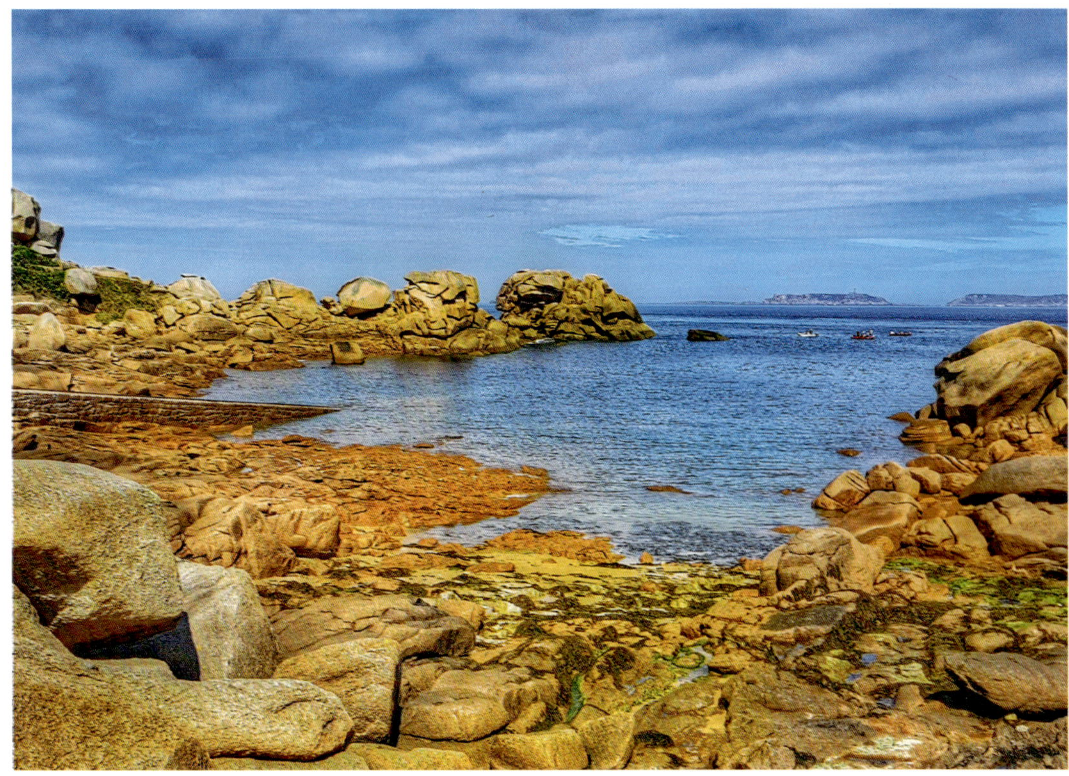

La plage de Squéouel, Ploumanac'h

Ploumanac'h

This small town in the municipality of Perros-Guirec is known for its bizarre rock formations around the harbour. The entrance is marked by a lighthouse made of pink granite. The rock of the region owes its colour to the combination of three minerals: mica, feldspar and quartz - which produce a black, a pink and a transparent grey colour.

Ploumanac'h

Ploumanac'h est un bourg de la commune de Perros-Guirec. Son célèbre phare de granit rose marque l'entrée du port entouré de ses rochers aux formes fantastiques. Le granit de cette côte tient sa couleur de la combinaison de trois minéraux dans le granit : le mica, qui lui donne sa couleur noire, le feldspath qui lui donne sa couleur rose, et le quartz avec sa teinte grise translucide.

Ploumanac'h

Die Kleinstadt in der Gemeinde Perros-Guirec ist für ihre bizarren Felsformationen um den Hafen bekannt. Die Einfahrt markiert ein Leuchtturm aus rosa Granit. Das Gestein der Region verdankt seine Farbe der Kombination aus drei Mineralien: Glimmer, Feldspat und Quarz – die eine schwarze, eine rosafarben und eine transparent graue Färbung erzeugen.

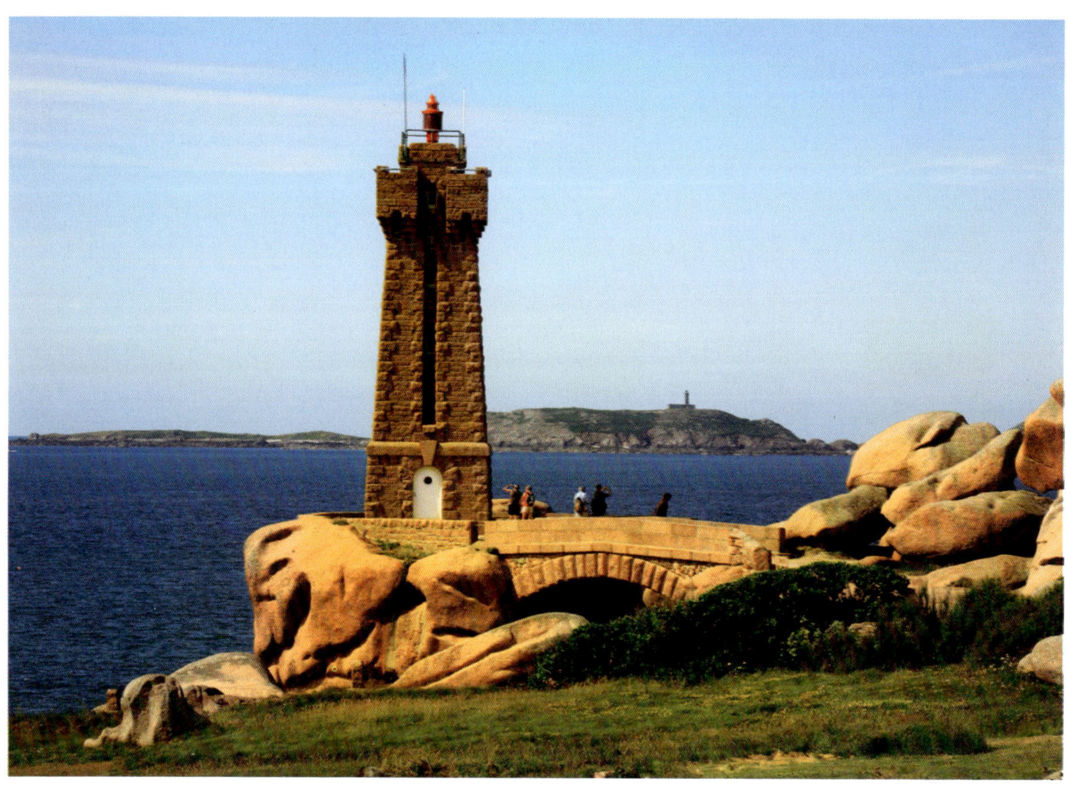

Le phare de Mean Ruz, Ploumanac'h

Ploumanac'h

El pequeño pueblo del municipio de Perros-Guirec es conocido por sus extrañas formaciones rocosas alrededor del puerto. Un faro de granito rosa señaliza la entrada. La roca de la región debe su color a la combinación de tres minerales: mica, feldespato y cuarzo, que producen un color negro, rosa y gris transparente.

Ploumanac'h

A pequena cidade no município de Perros-Guirec é conhecida pelas estranhas formações rochosas ao redor do porto. Um farol construído em granito rosa marca a entrada do porto. A rocha da região deve a sua cor à combinação de três minerais: mica, feldspato e quartzo - que produzem uma cor preta, rosa e translúcida.

Ploumanac'h

Het stadje in de gemeente Perros-Guirec staat bekend om zijn bizarre rotsformaties rond de haven. Een vuurtoren van roze graniet markeert de ingang. Het regionale gesteente dankt zijn kleur aan de combinatie van drie mineralen: mica, veldspaat en kwarts. Ze leveren een zwarte, roze en transparant grijze kleur op.

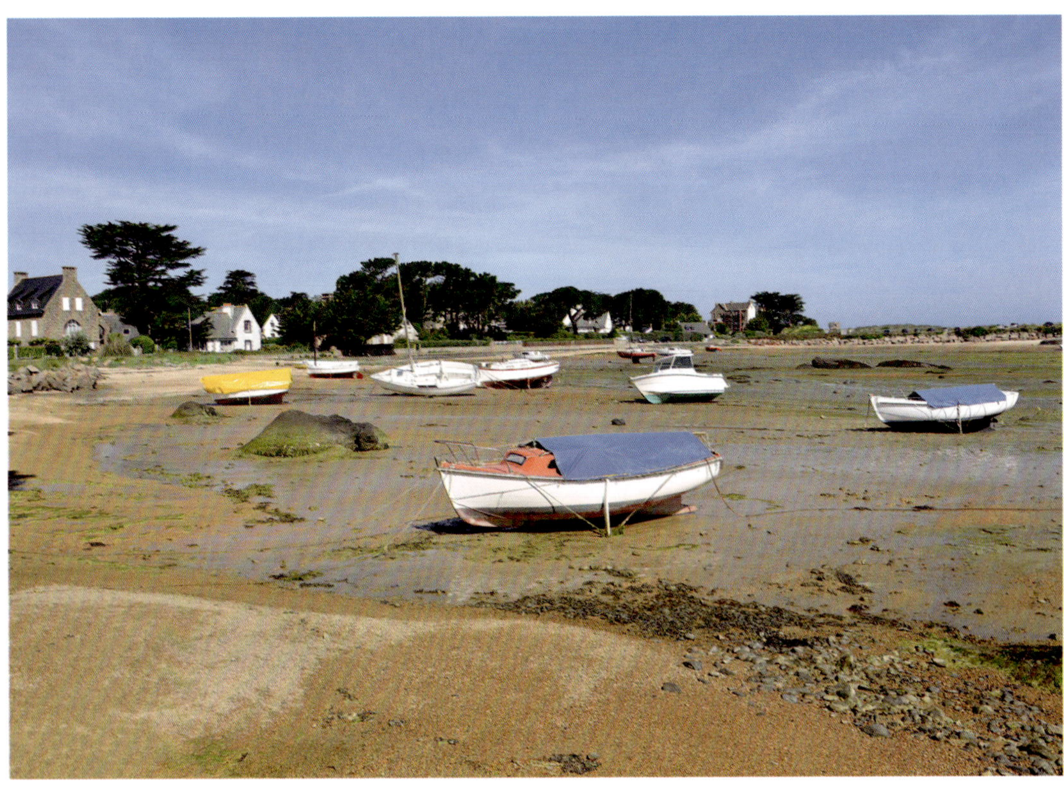

L'île Renote, Trégastel

Trégastel and the Île Renote

The emerald green sea contrasts with the pink rocks of Trégastel. The Île Renote, which can be reached from there, can be explored on a hiking trail in less than an hour. From here you can discover sandy beaches and coves, turquoise waters and pink granite rocks, as well as views of the Ploumanac'h lighthouse and Costaérès Castle.

Trégastel et l'île Renote

Les rochers de Trégastel sont roses en bordure d'une mer émeraude tout comme ceux de Ploumanac'h. Sur l'île Renote, à laquelle on peut accéder par Trégastel, un sentier des douaniers permet d'en faire le tour en une heure environ. Plages et criques sablonneuses, eaux turquoise, rochers de granit rose, vues sur le phare de Ploumanac'h et le château de Costaérès.

Trégastel und die Île Renote

Das smaragdgrüne Meer kontrastiert mit den rosafarbenen Felsen von Trégastel. Die Île Renote, die von dort aus erreichbar ist, kann auf einem Wanderweg innerhalb einer Stunde erkundet werden. Von ihm aus lassen sich Sandstrände und Buchten, türkisfarbenes Wasser, rosa Granitfelsen, Ausblicke auf den Leuchtturm von Ploumanac'h und das Schloss Costaérès entdecken.

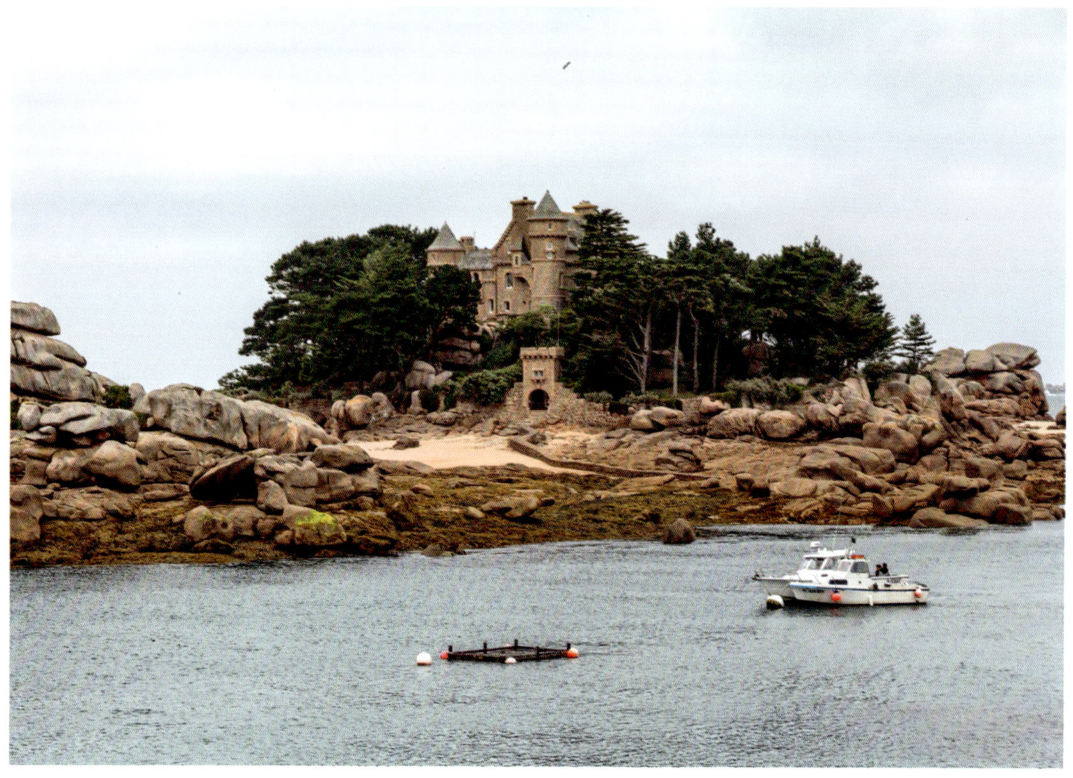

Le château de Costaérès, Trégastel

Trégastel e Île Renote

El mar verde esmeralda contrasta con las rocas rosadas de Trégastel. Île Renote, a la que se puede llegar desde allí, se puede explorar en una ruta de senderismo en menos de una hora. Desde aquí podrá descubrir playas de arena y bahías, aguas turquesas, rocas graníticas de color rosa, y vistas al faro de Ploumanac'h y al castillo de Costaérès.

Trégastel e a Île Renote

O mar verde-esmeralda contrasta com a cor rosa das falésias de Trégastel. A Île Renote, que facilmente se pode alcançar daqui, pode ser visitada numa hora de caminhada, ao longo da qual se vão descobrindo praias de areia e enseadas, águas azul-turquesa, rochedos de granito rosa e uma vista panorâmica do Farol de Ploumanac'h e do Castelo Costaérès.

Trégastel en het Île Renote

De smaragdgroene zee contrasteert met de roze rotsen van Trégastel. Het Île Renote, dat van daaruit te bereiken is, kan via een wandelpad binnen een uur worden verkend. Van hieruit kunt u zandstranden en baaien, turquoise wateren, roze granietrotsen, uitzichten op de vuurtoren van Ploumanac'h en het Château de Costaérès bewonderen.

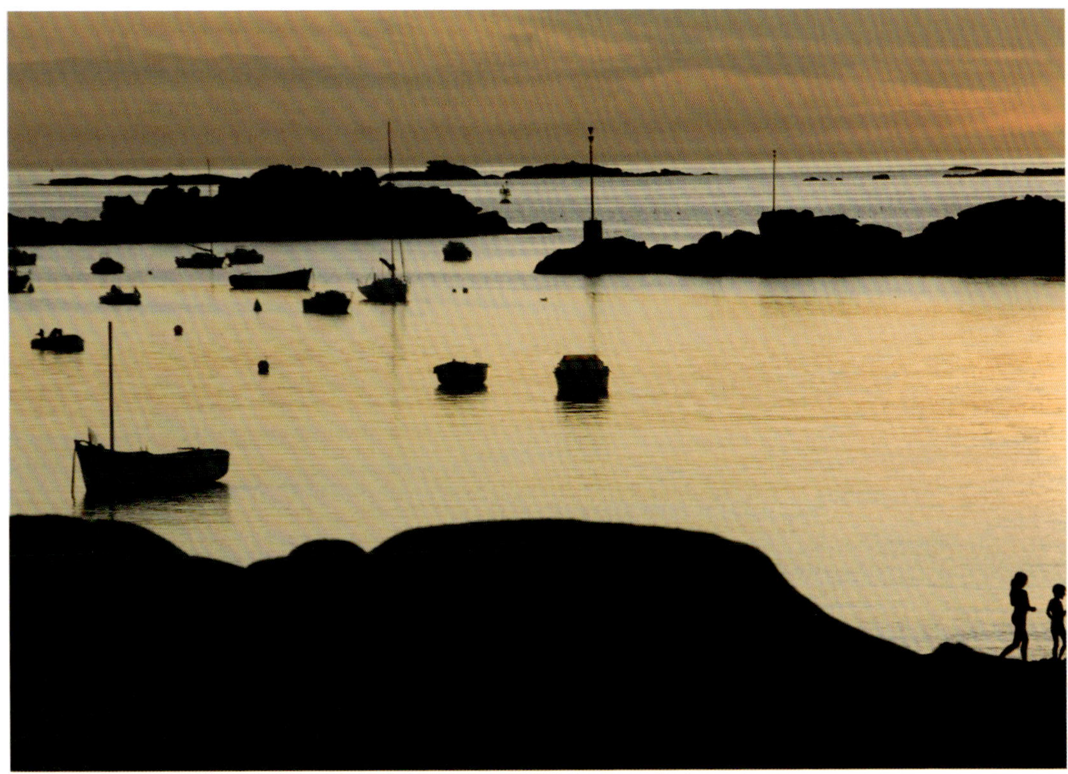

Trébeurden

Trébeurden

This small fishing and bathing resort with its beautiful landscape is framed by the headlands of Pointe de Bihit and Pointe du Castel. In front of the Pointe du Castel is the Île Milliau, which is accessible on foot on some days at low tide. In addition to its heath landscape, it offers farms and a Neolithic gallery grave.

Trébeurden

Petit port et petit village balnéaire, encadré des pointes de Bihit sur la gauche et du Castel sur la droite, il bénéficie d'un environnement de toute beauté. En face de la pointe du Castel, l'île Milliau offre aux regards ses landes, ses fermes, son allée couverte. Certains jours, il est possible de s'y rendre à pied quand la marée est assez basse.

Trébeurden

Der kleine Fischer- und Badeort mit seiner wunderschönen Landschaft wird von den Landzungen Pointe de Bihit und Pointe du Castel eingerahmt. Vor der Pointe du Castel liegt die Île Milliau, die an manchen Tagen bei Ebbe zu Fuß zugänglich ist. Neben ihrer Heidelandschaft bietet sie Bauernhöfe und ein jungsteinzeitliches Galeriegrab.

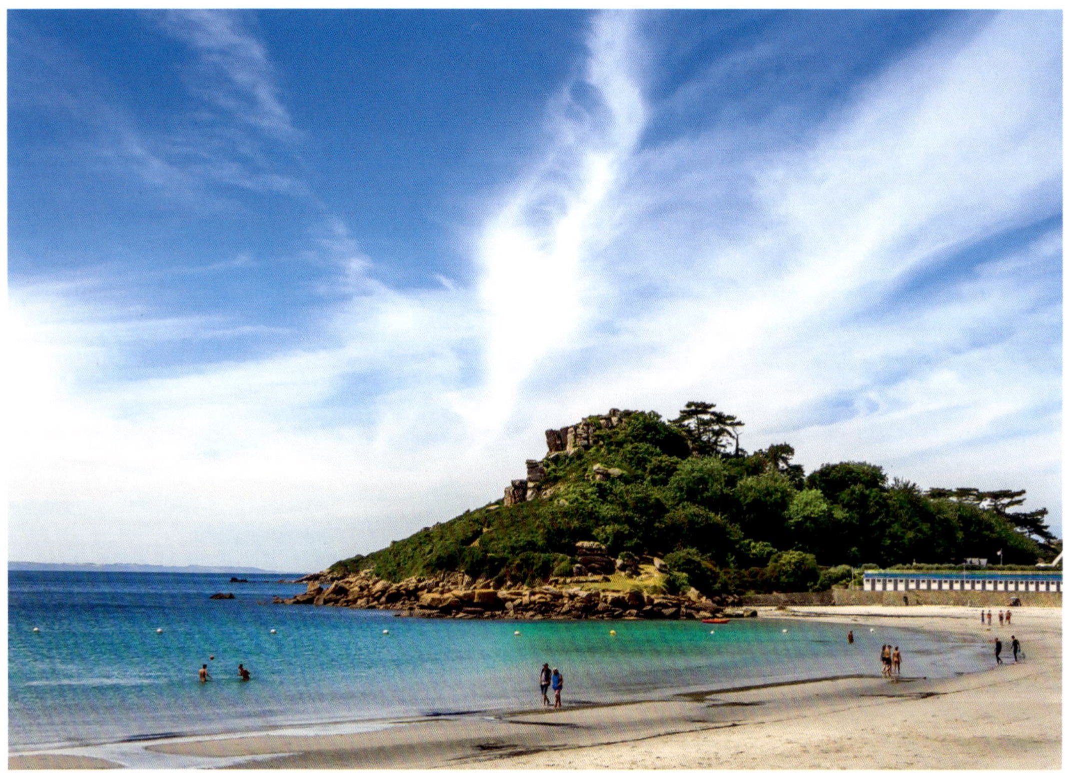

La plage de Tresmeur, Trébeurden

Trébeurden

El pequeño centro de pesca y baño, con su hermoso paisaje, está enmarcado por los cabos Pointe de Bihit y Pointe du Castel. Frente a Pointe du Castel se encuentra Île Milliau, a la que se puede acceder a pie algunos días de marea baja. Además de su paisaje de brezales, ofrece granjas y una galería neolítica de tumbas.

Trébeurden

A pequena vila piscatória e estância balnear, com a sua paisagem maravilhosa, é emoldurada pelas penínsulas Pointe de Bihit e Pointe du Castel. Em frente à Pointe du Castel está a Île Milliau, acessível a pé durante alguns dias na maré baixa. Além da sua paisagem de urzes, podem-se encontrar algumas quintas e uma sepultura de galeria neolítica.

Trébeurden

De kleine vissers- en badplaats met zijn prachtige landschap wordt omlijst door de landtongen Pointe de Bihit en Pointe du Castel. Voor de Pointe du Castel ligt het Île Milliau, dat op sommige dagen bij eb te voet bereikbaar is. Hier zijn behalve heidevelden boerderijen en een neolithisch galerijgraf.

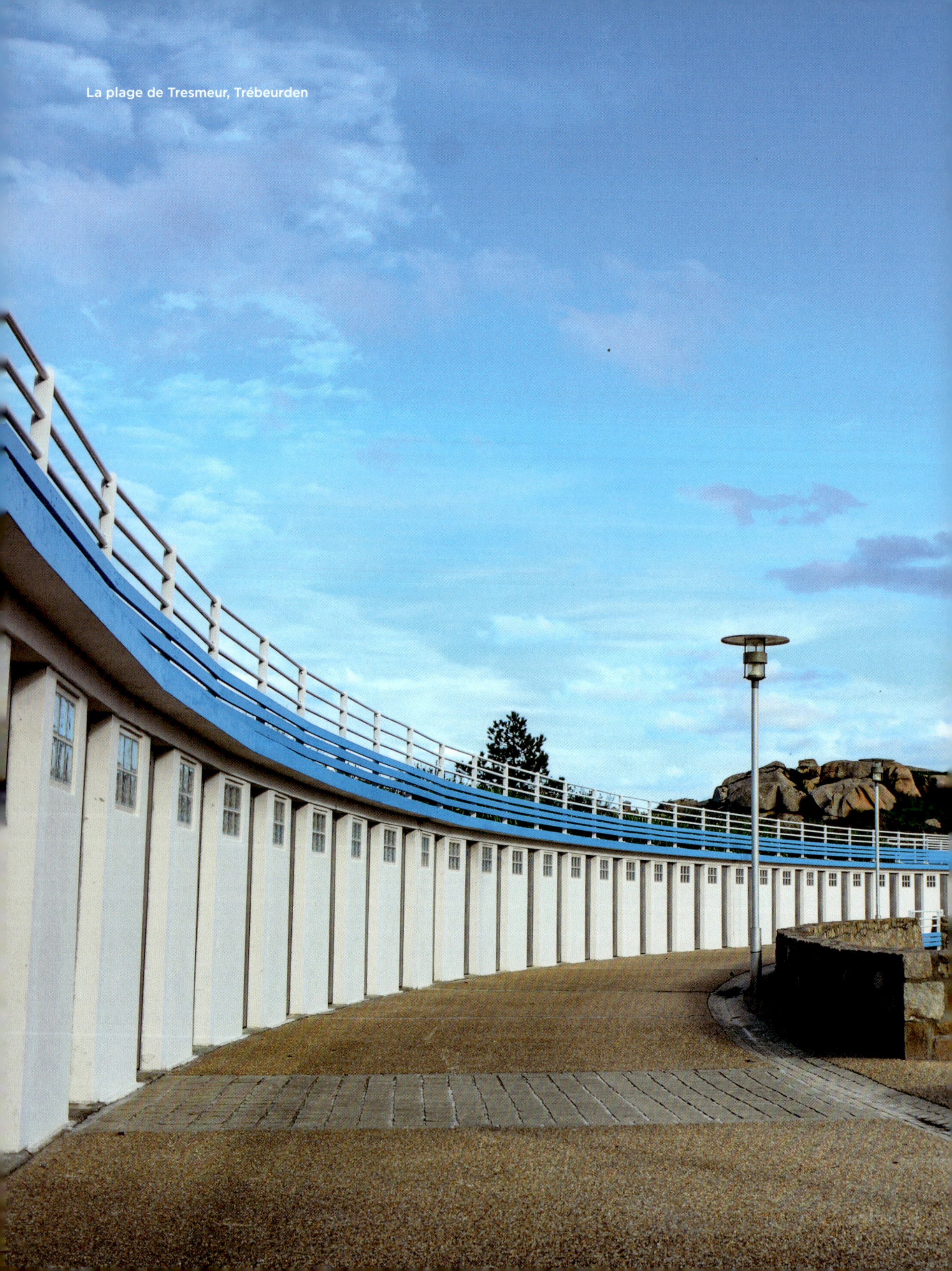
La plage de Tresmeur, Trébeurden

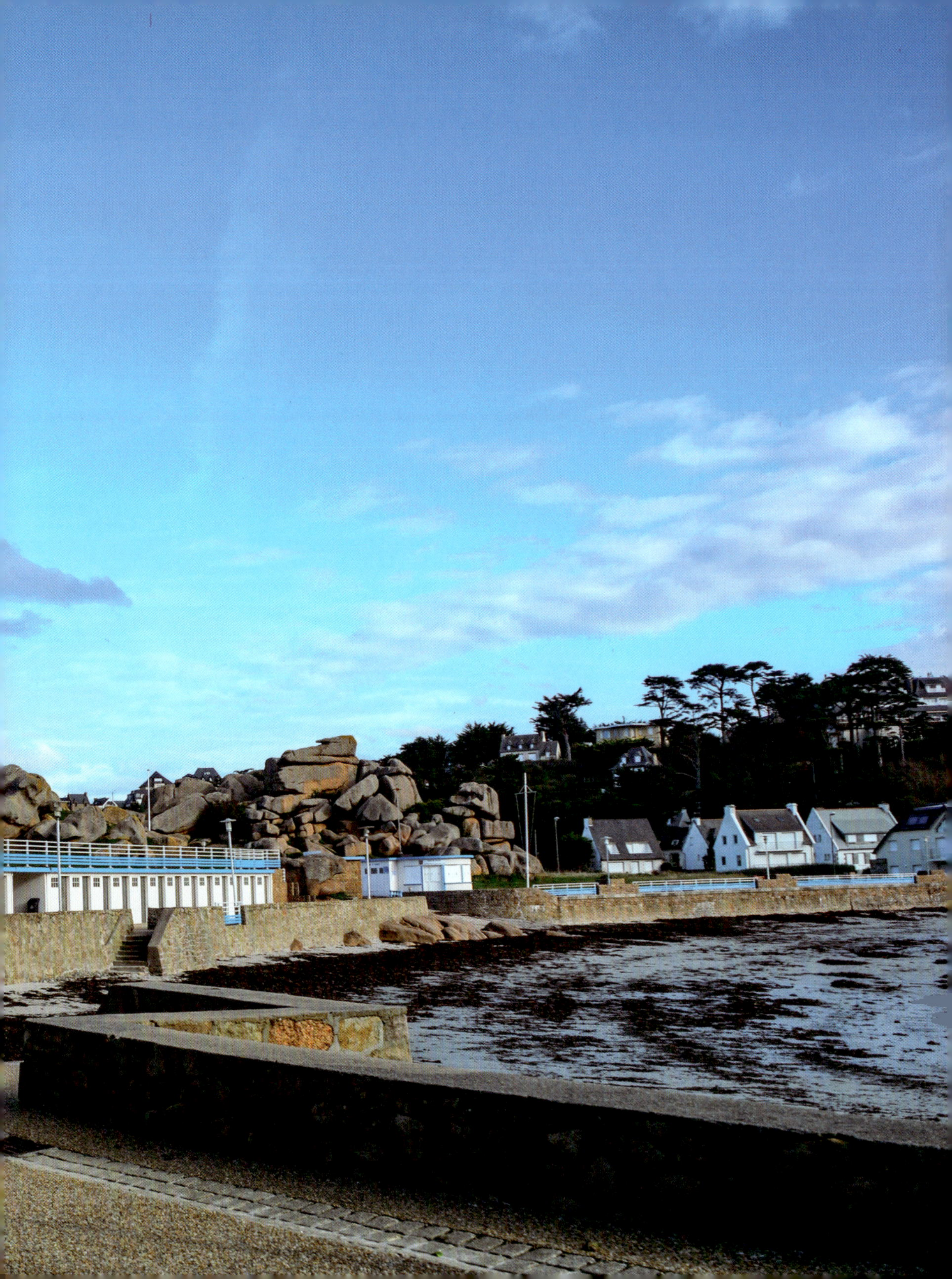

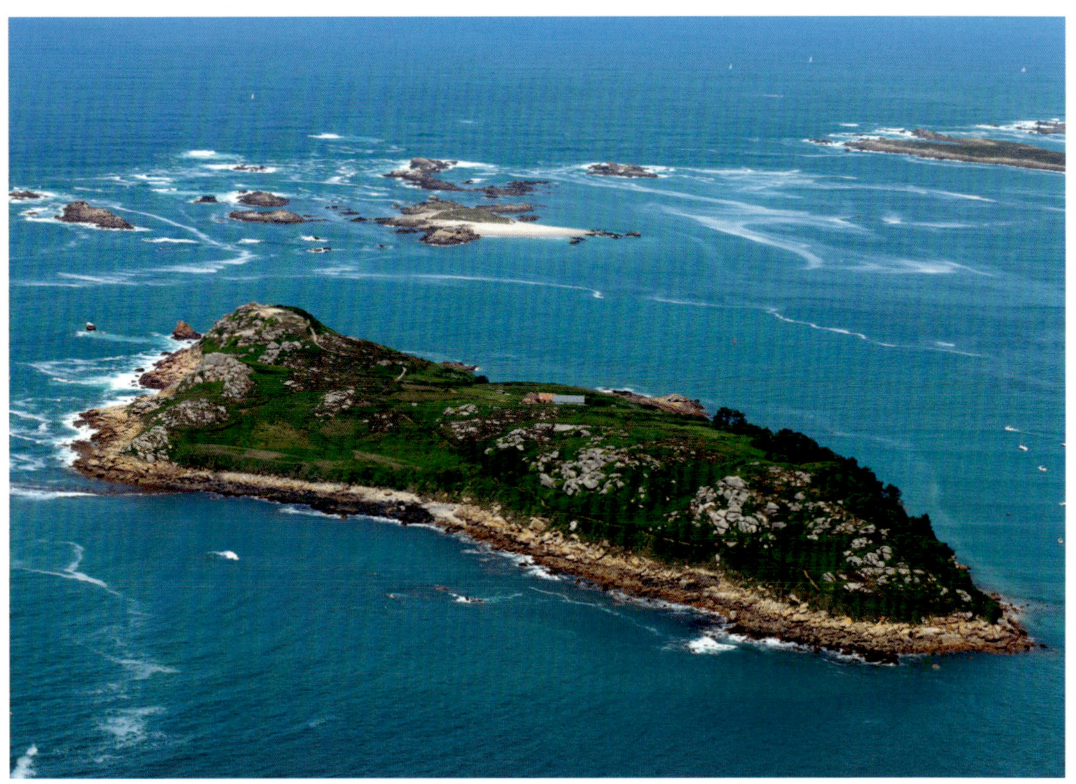

L'île Milliau, Trébeurden

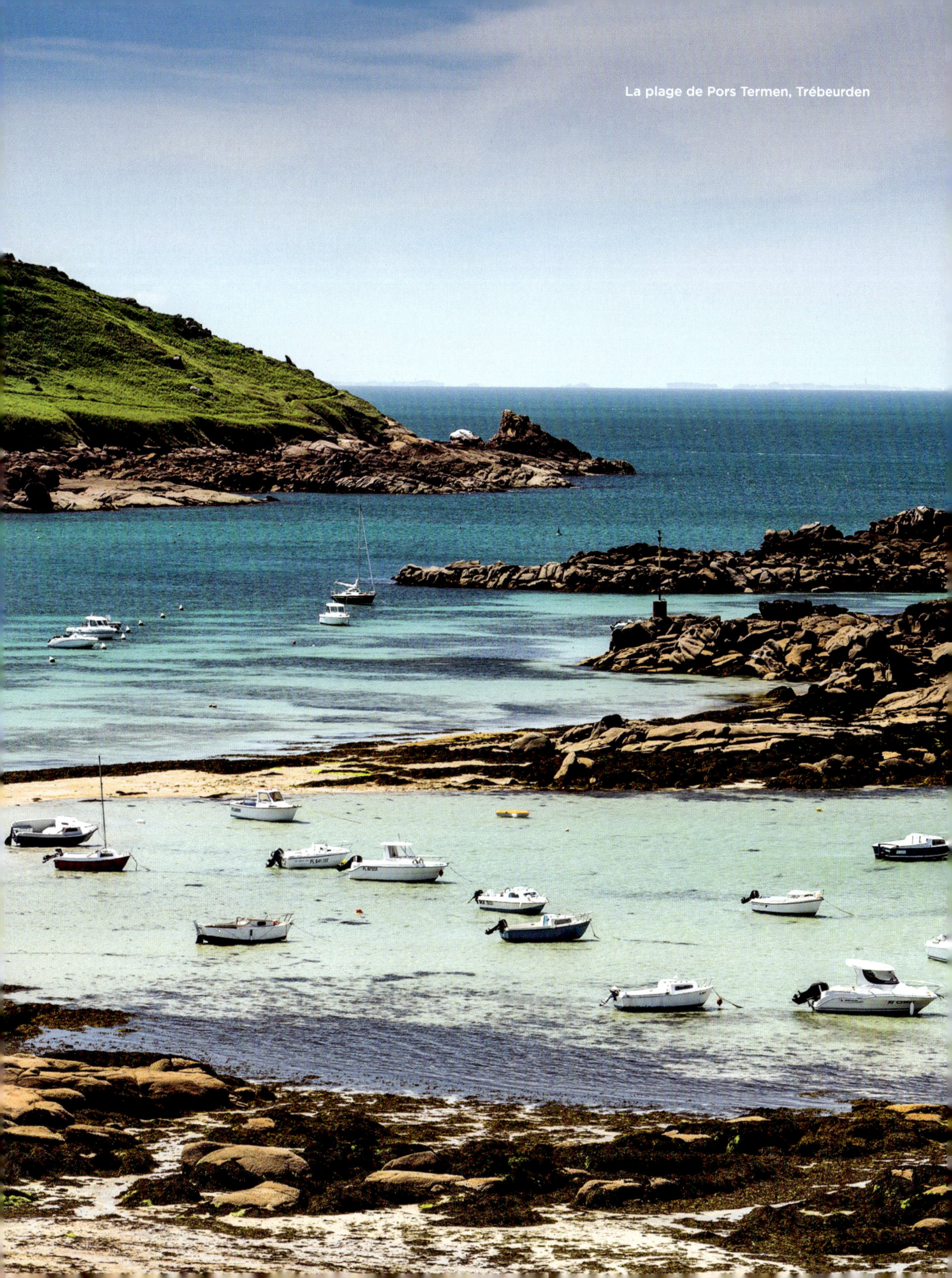
La plage de Pors Termen, Trébeurden

Le Finistère Nord et le pays de Léon

Baie de la Vierge, Le Yaudet

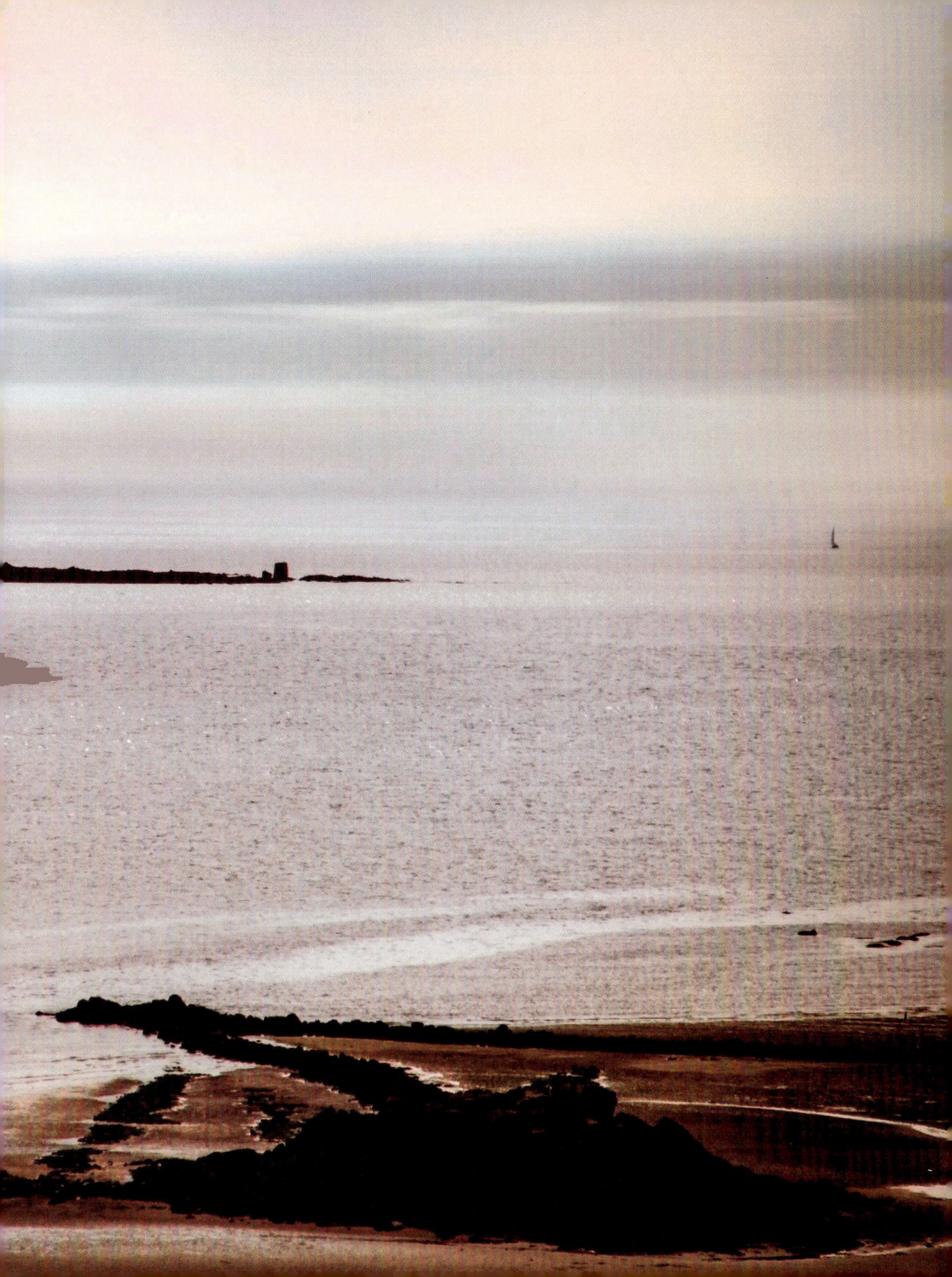

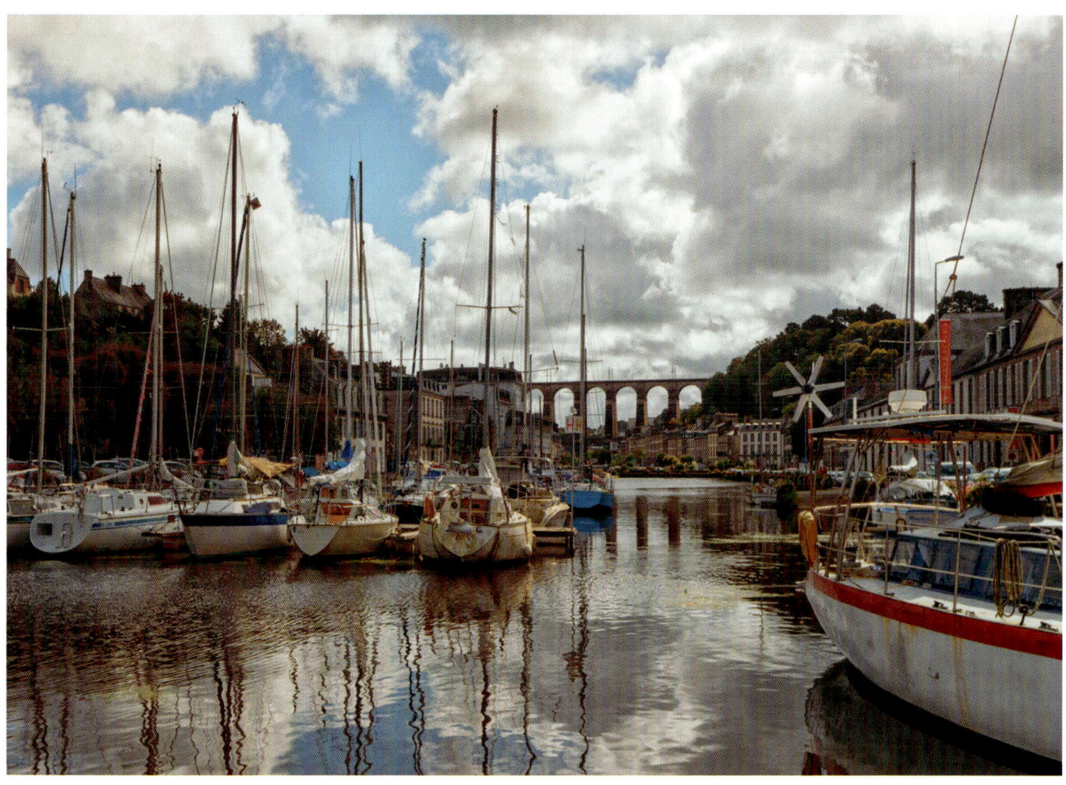

Le port de Morlaix

Morlaix, "The City of the Viaduct"

Morlaix lies inland at the end of a long bay - the bay of Morlaix - into which two rivers flow. The city is spanned by an imposing viaduct which gives it its nickname. It is part of the Trégor and Léon regions.

Morlaix, « La cité du viaduc »

Morlaix que l'on nomme « la cité du viaduc » car elle est située en retrait de la côte, en fond de ria, au creux d'un estuaire. Cette ville-pont est au confluent de deux rivières qui se jettent dans la Manche, en baie de Morlaix. Elle fait partie à la fois du pays du Trégor et du pays du Léon.

Morlaix, „Die Stadt des Viadukts"

Morlaix liegt im Landesinneren am Ende einer langen Meeresbucht – der Bucht von Morlaix – in die zwei Flüsse münden. Die Stadt wird von einem imposanten Viadukt überspannt, das ihr ihren Spitznamen verleiht. Sie ist Teil der Region Trégor und der Region Léon.

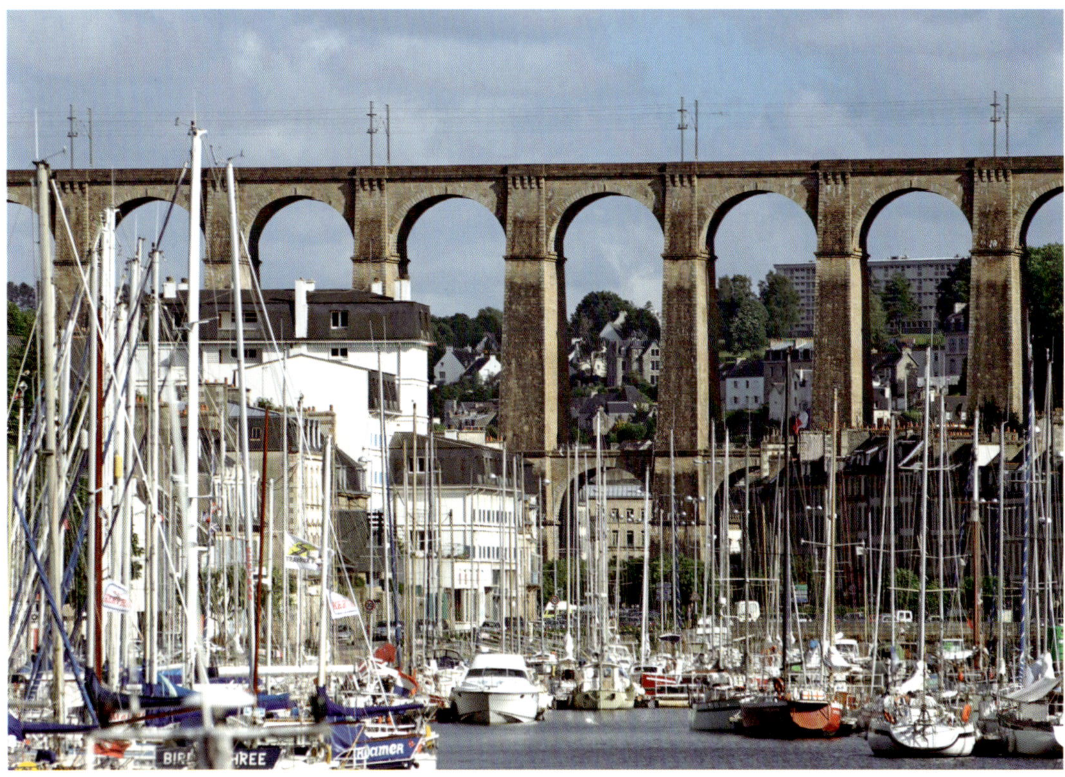

Le viaduc et le port, Morlaix

Morlaix, «La ciudad del viaducto»

Morlaix se encuentra en el interior, al final de una larga bahía (la bahía de Morlaix) en la que desembocan dos ríos. La ciudad está atravesada por un imponente viaducto (de ahí el apodo que recibe la ciudad). Forma parte de la región de Trégor y de la región de Léon.

Morlaix, «A Cidade do Viaduto»

Morlaix fica no interior, no fim de uma longa baía - a baía de Morlaix – onde desaguam dois rios. A cidade é atravessada por um imponente viaduto, que lhe dá o seu nome. Faz parte da região de Trégor e da região de Leão.

Morlaix, 'De stad van het viaduct'

Morlaix ligt landinwaarts aan het einde van een lange baai (de baai van Morlaix) waarin twee rivieren uitmonden. De stad wordt overspannen door een imposant viaduct, waaraan hij zijn bijnaam dankt. Morlaix maakt deel uit van de regio's Trégor en Léon.

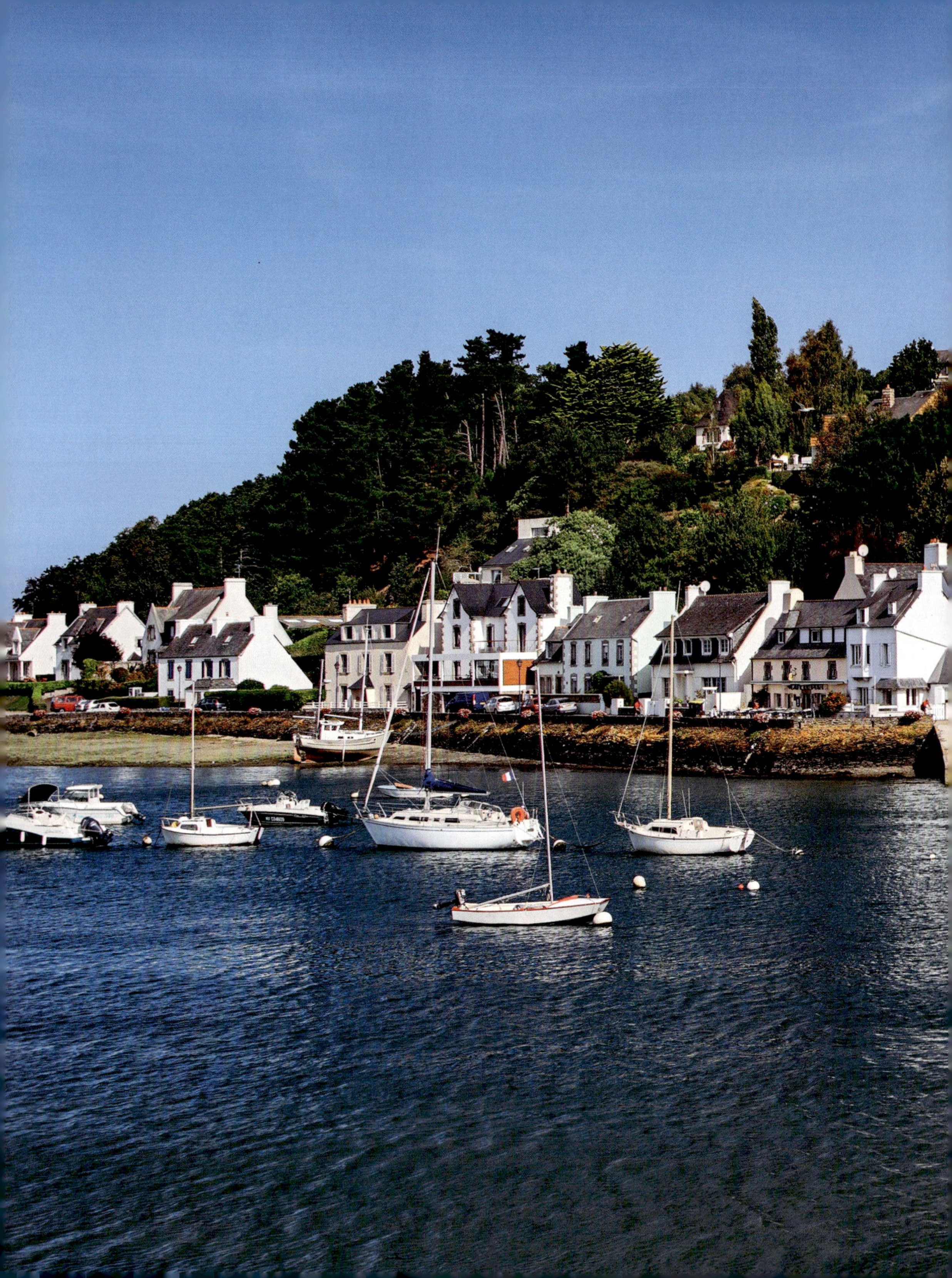

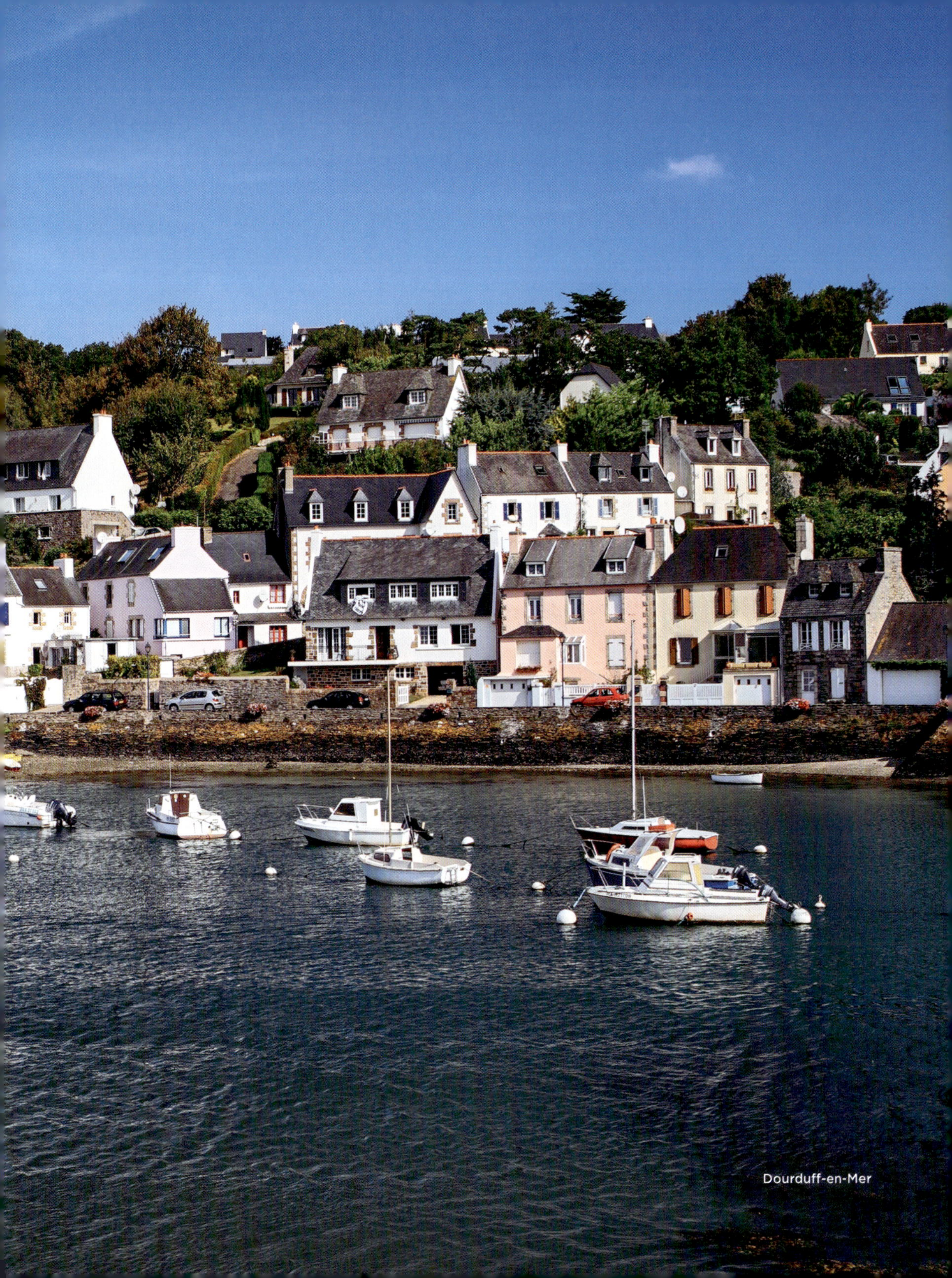

Dourduff-en-Mer

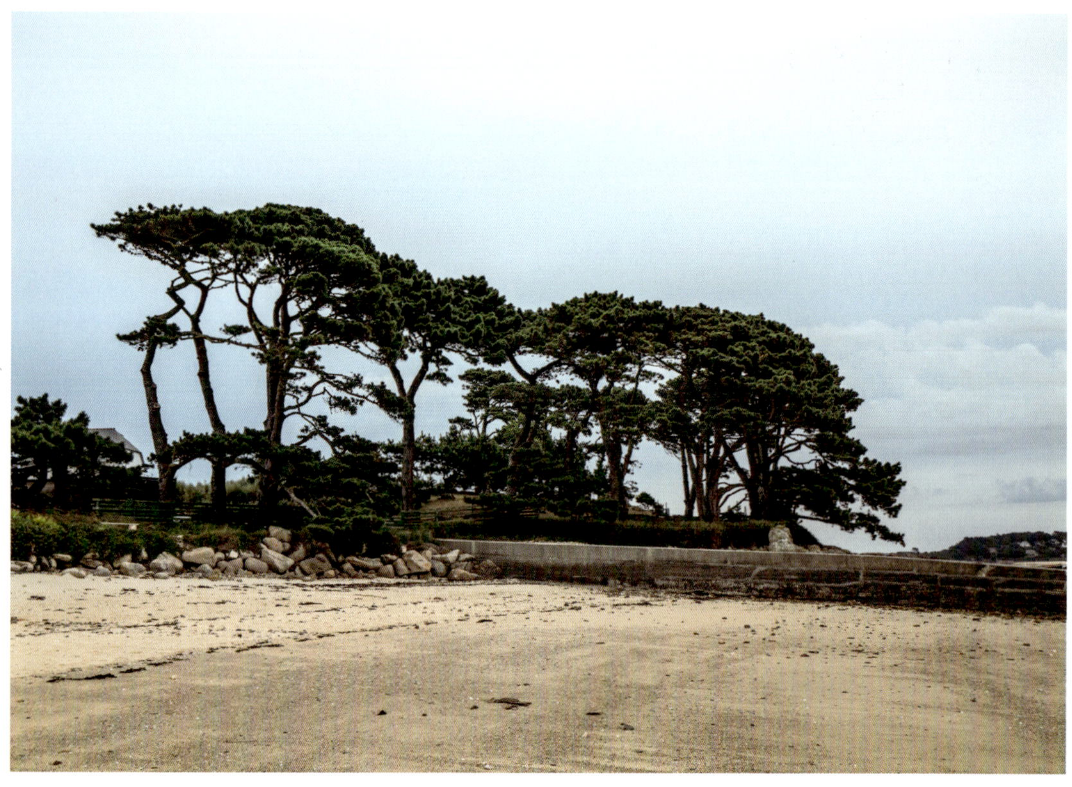

L'île Callot, Carantec

Carantec

Carantec, in the bay of Morlaix, has been a popular tourist destination for over 100 years. This village at the end of a 2 km long peninsula is situated on a beach that extends up to 2 km into the sea at low tide. Special sights are the islands Louët and Callot, the beaches La Grêve Blanche, Kelenn and Le Clouet, the steep rocky coast at the Chaise du Curé or Pointe de Pen-al-Lann and the viewpoint of the Château du Taureau.

Carantec

Carantec, en baie de Morlaix, est une destination touristique depuis les années 1900. Le village est installé à l'extrémité d'une presqu'île de 2 km de large et le long d'une grève qui se découvre jusqu'à 2 km au large lors des grandes marées. Prisée, avec les îles Louët et Callot, pour ses plages (la grève Blanche, la plage du Kelenn et la plage du Clouet), ses falaises qui offrent des paysages remarquables (la « Chaise du Curé » et la pointe de Pen-al-Lann) et son point de vue magnifique sur le château du Taureau.

Carantec

Carantec, in der Bucht von Morlaix, ist seit über 100 Jahren ein bei Touristen beliebtes Ziel. Das Dorf am Ende einer 2 km langen Halbinsel liegt an einem Strand, der sich bei Ebbe bis zu 2 km in das Meer ausdehnt. Besondere Sehenswürdigkeiten sind die Inseln Louët und Callot, die Strände La Grêve Blanche, Kelenn und Le Clouet, die steile Felsenküste am Chaise du Curé oder Pointe de Pen-al-Lann und der Aussichtspunkt auf das Château du Taureau.

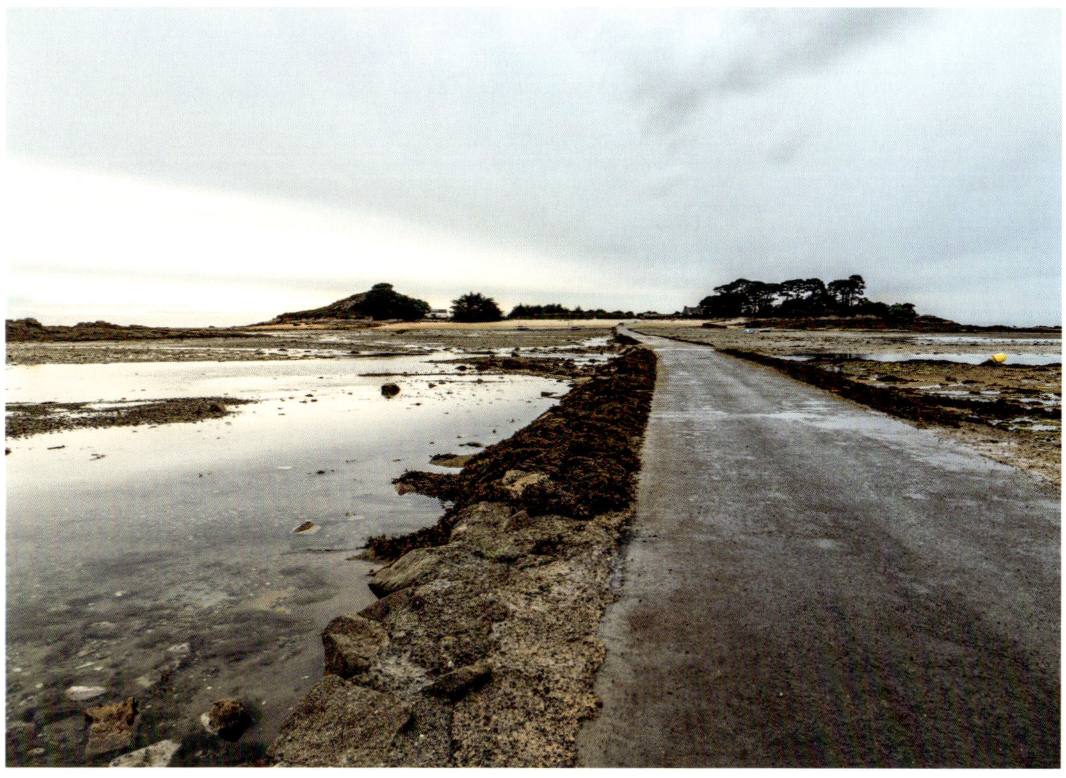

L'île Callot, Carantec

Carantec

Carantec, en la bahía de Morlaix, ha sido un destino turístico popular durante más de 100 años. El pueblo, que se encuentra en el extremo de una península de 2 km de largo, está situado en una playa que se extiende hasta 2 km en el mar en marea baja. Las mayores atracciones turísticas son las islas Louët y Callot, las playas La Grêve Blanche, Kelenn y Le Clouet, la escarpada costa rocosa de la Chaise du Curé o Pointe de Pen-al-Lann y el mirador del Château du Taureau.

Carantec

Carantec, na baía de Morlaix, é um destino turístico popular há mais de 100 anos. A aldeia, na extremidade de uma península de 2 km de comprimento, está situada numa praia que chega a atingir 2 km na maré baixa. Destacam-se as ilhas Louët e Callot, as praias La Grêve Blanche, Kelenn e Le Clouet, a costa rochosa e íngreme do Chaise du Curé ou Pointe de Pen-al-Lann e o miradouro do Château du Taureau.

Carantec

Carantec in de baai van Morlaix is al ruim honderd jaar een populaire toeristenplaats. Het dorp aan het einde van een 2 km lang schiereiland ligt aan een strand dat bij laag water 2 km de zee in loopt. Bijzondere bezienswaardigheden zijn de eilanden Louët en Callot, de stranden La Grêve Blanche, Kelenn en Le Clouet, de steile rotskust bij de Chaise du Curé of Pointe de Pen-al-Lann en het uitzicht op het Château du Taureau.

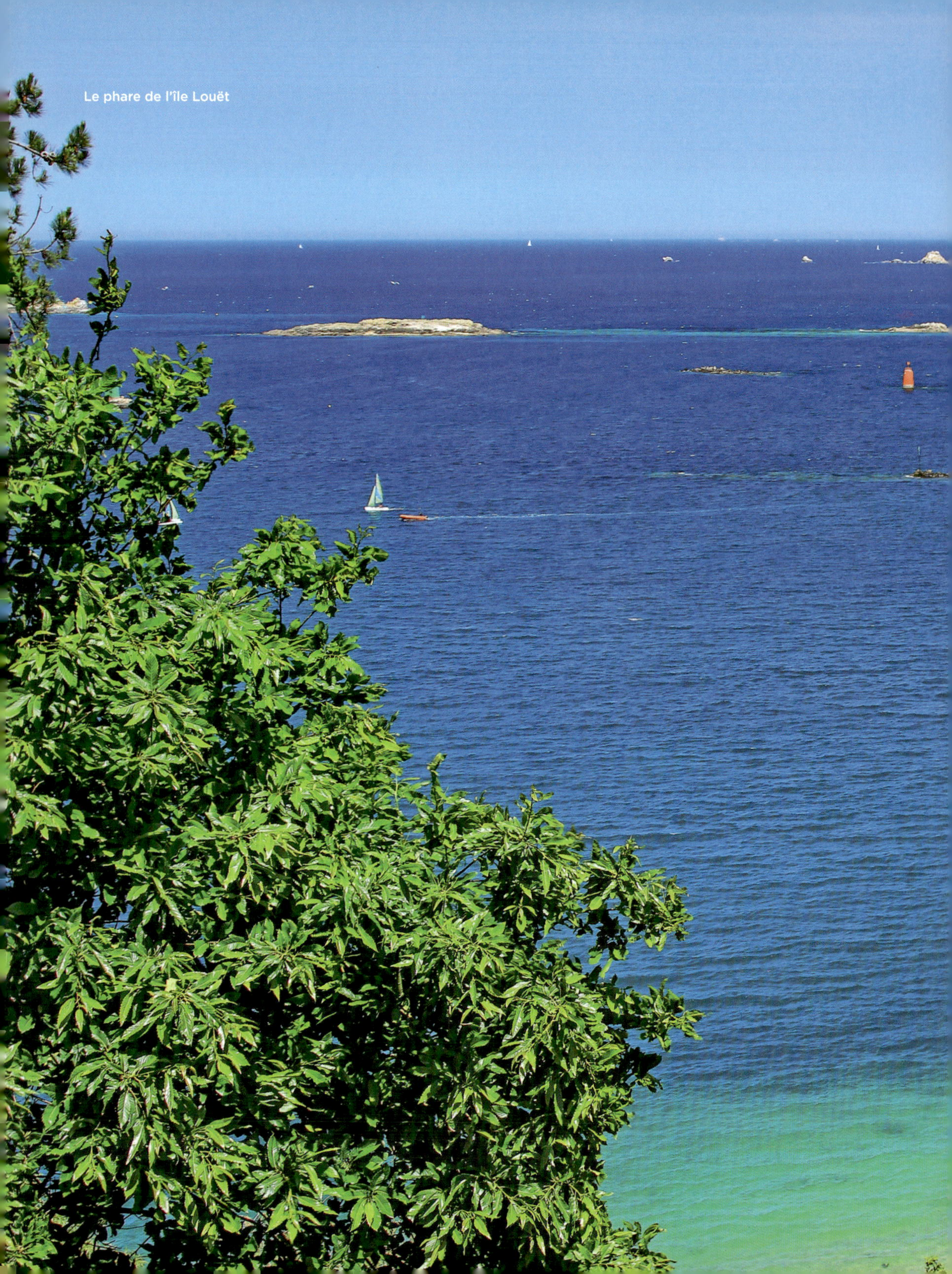
Le phare de l'île Louët

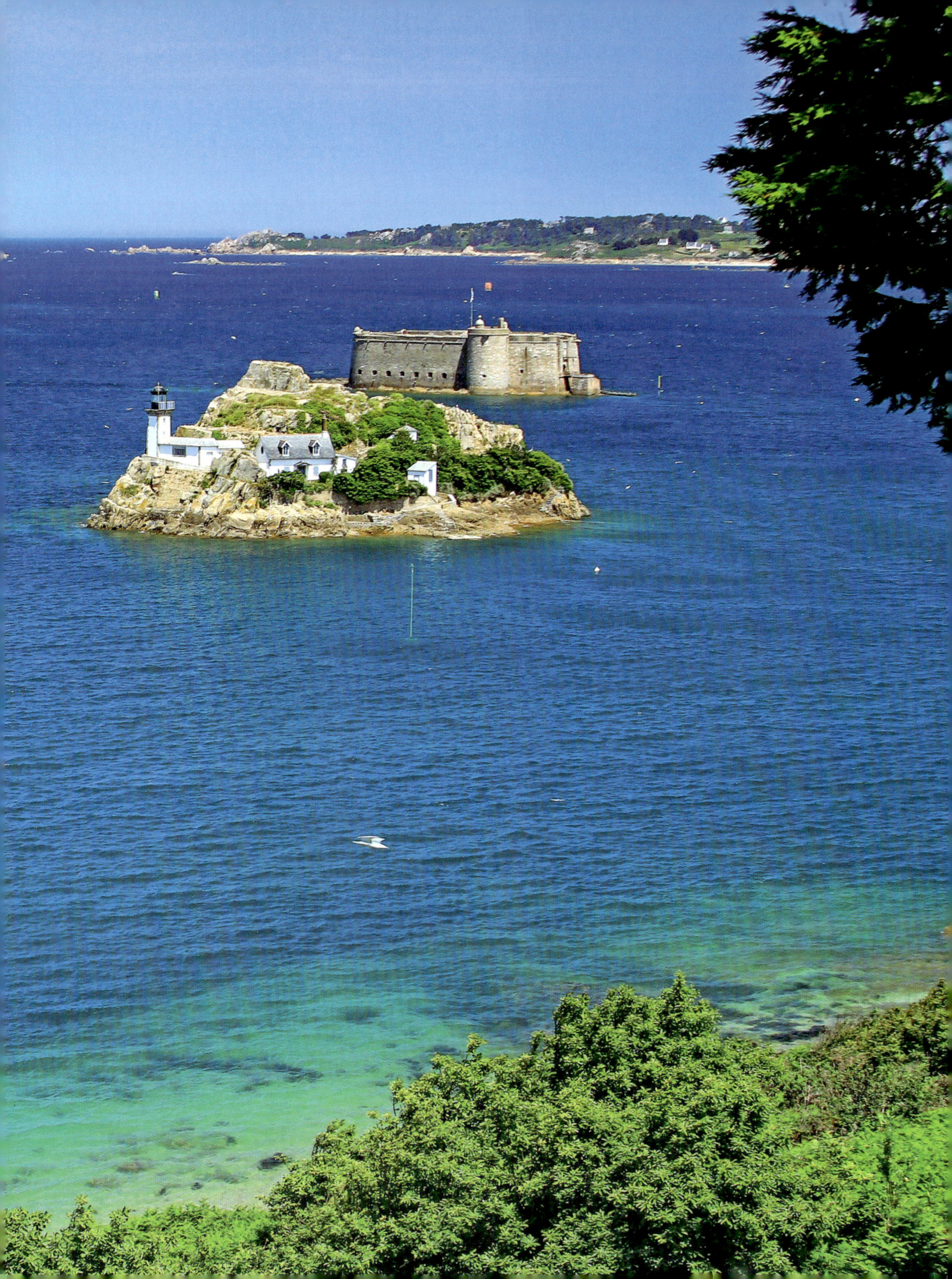

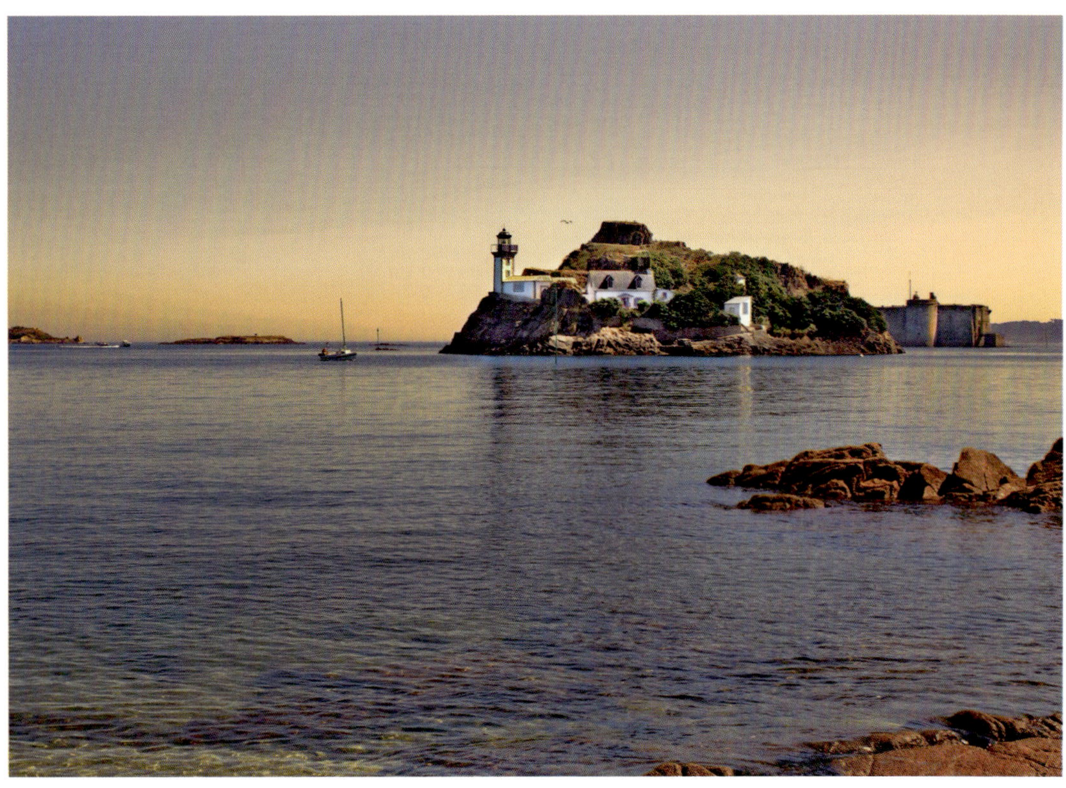

L'île Louët et le château du Taureau

Saint-Pol-de-Léon

This small town in the department of Finistère captivates with its historical and religious heritage. The 13 km long coastline not only gives Saint-Pol-de-Léon the charm of a harbour town, but the bay also houses a seabird reserve with a high biodiversity.

Saint-Pol-de-Léon

Cette petite ville est une commune dotée d'un patrimoine civil et religieux exceptionnel. Posée sur le littoral finistérien et riche de 13 km de côtes, elle a le charme d'une cité portuaire dont la baie abrite une réserve d'oiseaux marins d'une grande variété.

Saint-Pol-de-Léon

Die kleine Stadt im Département Finistère besticht durch ihr geschichtliches und religiöses Erbe. Die 13 km lange Küste verleiht Saint-Pol-de-Léon nicht nur den Charme einer Hafenstadt, die Bucht beherbergt auch ein Seevogelreservat mit einer hohen Artenvielfalt.

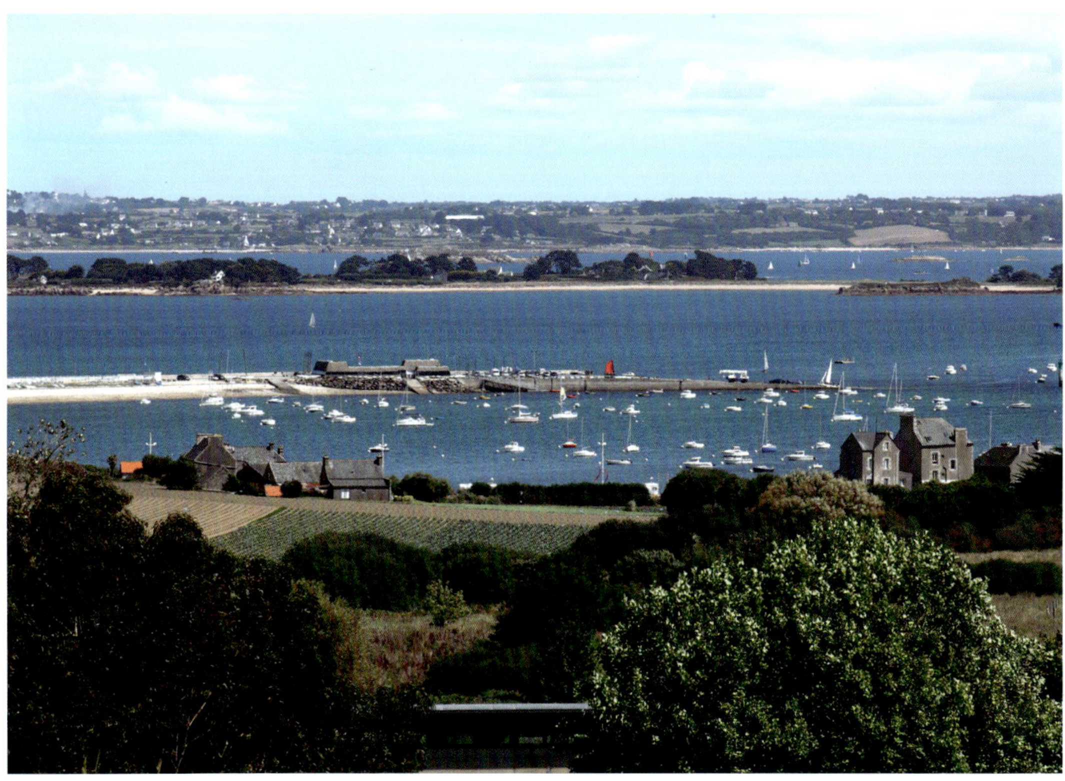

Saint-Pol-de-Léon

Saint-Pol-de-Léon

La pequeña ciudad del departamento de Finisterre cautiva por su patrimonio histórico y religioso. Los 13 km de costa no solo confieren a Saint-Pol-de-Léon el encanto de una ciudad portuaria, sino que la bahía también alberga una reserva de aves marinas con una gran biodiversidad.

Saint-Pol-de-Léon

Esta pequena cidade, do departamento de Finistère, cativa pelo seu património histórico e religioso. Os 13 km de orla costeira dão a Saint-Pol-de-Léon o encanto de uma cidade portuária. Além disso, a baía abriga uma reserva de aves marinhas de elevada biodiversidade.

Saint-Pol-de-Léon

Dit stadje in het departement Finistère boeit met zijn historische en religieuze erfgoed. De 13 km lange kust verleent Saint-Pol-de-Léon niet alleen de charme van een havenstad, maar de baai herbergt ook een zeevogelreservaat met een grote soortenrijkdom.

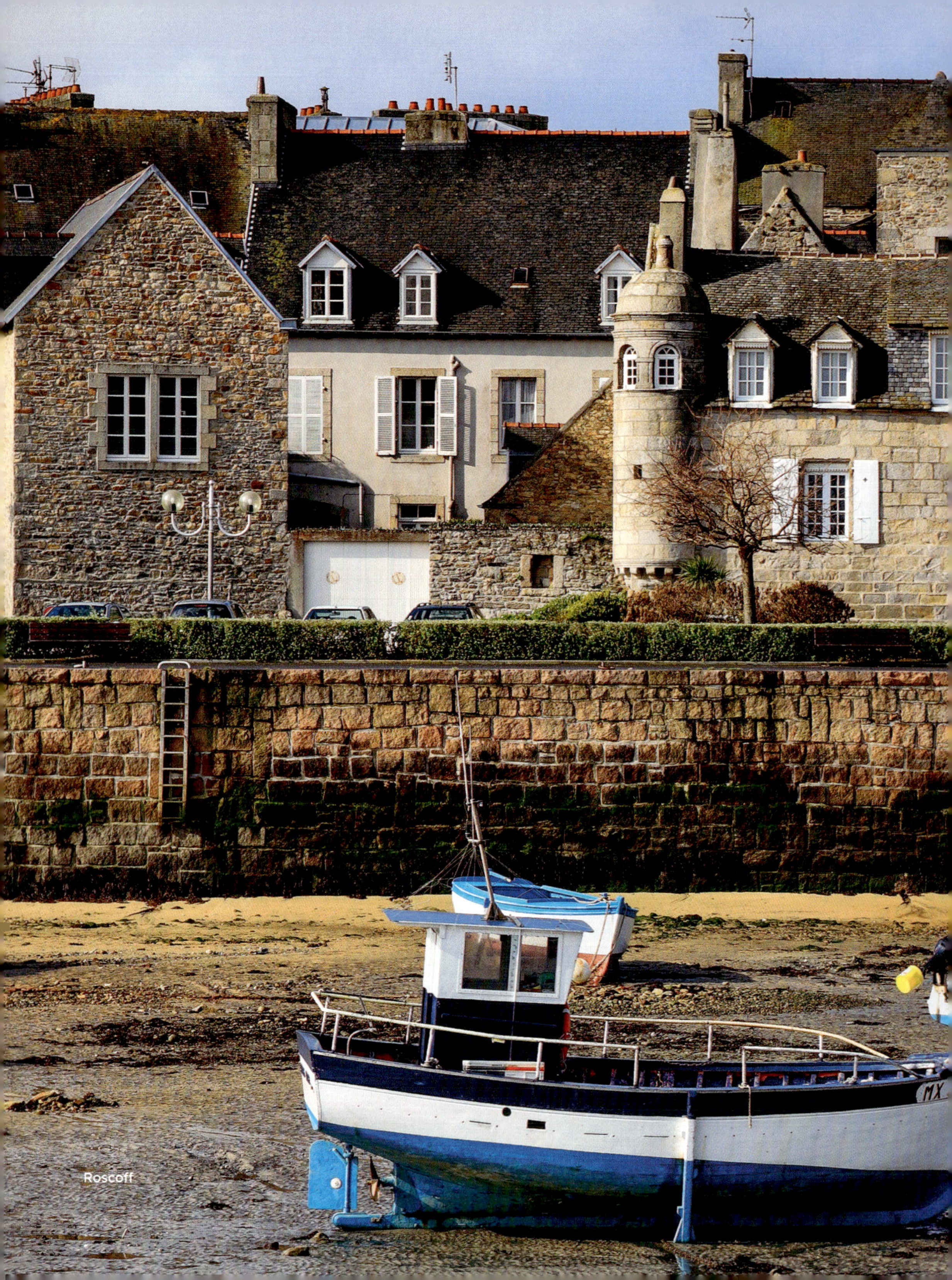

Roscoff

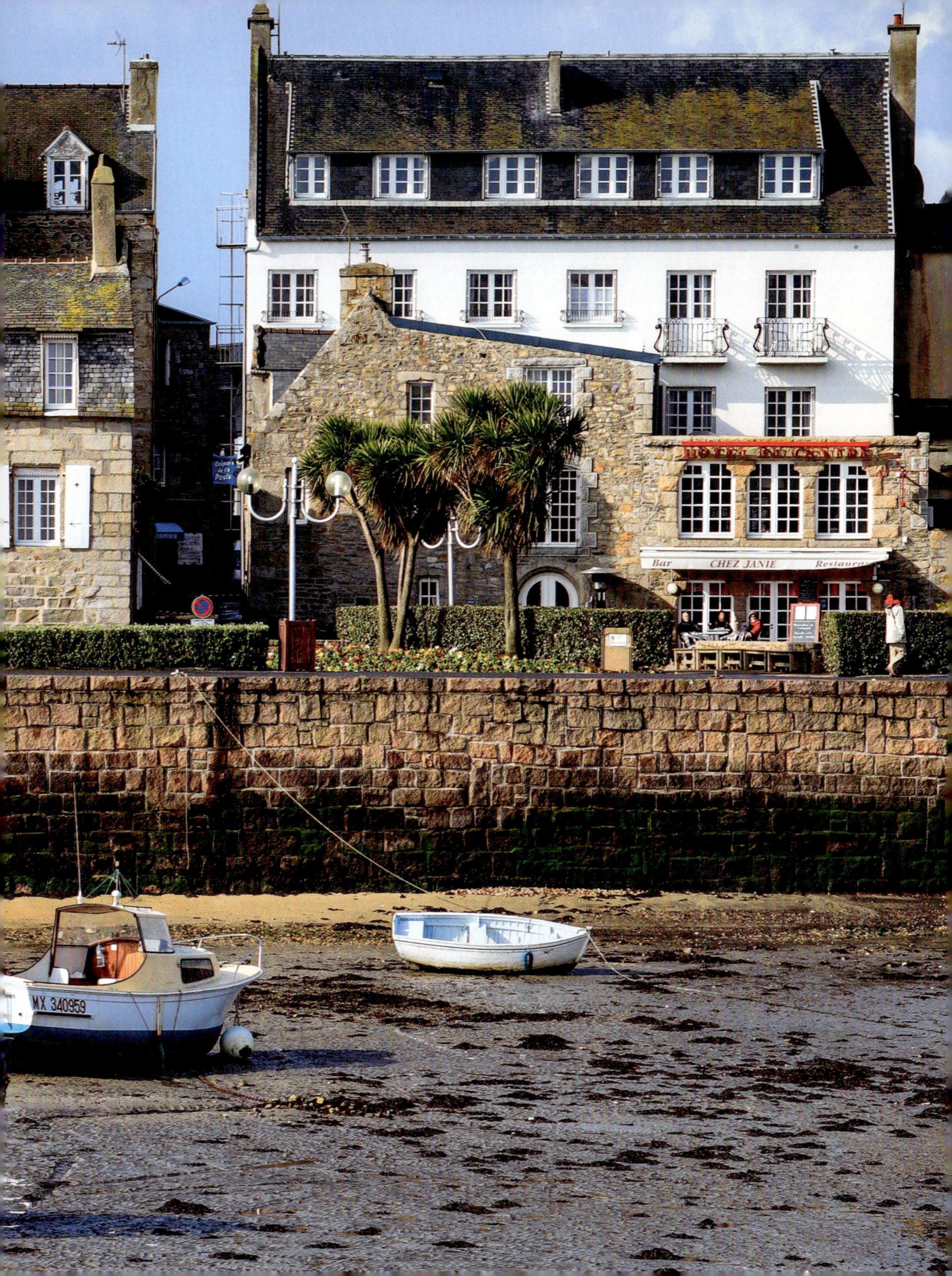

CHEZ JANIE
Bar
Restaurant
MX 340959

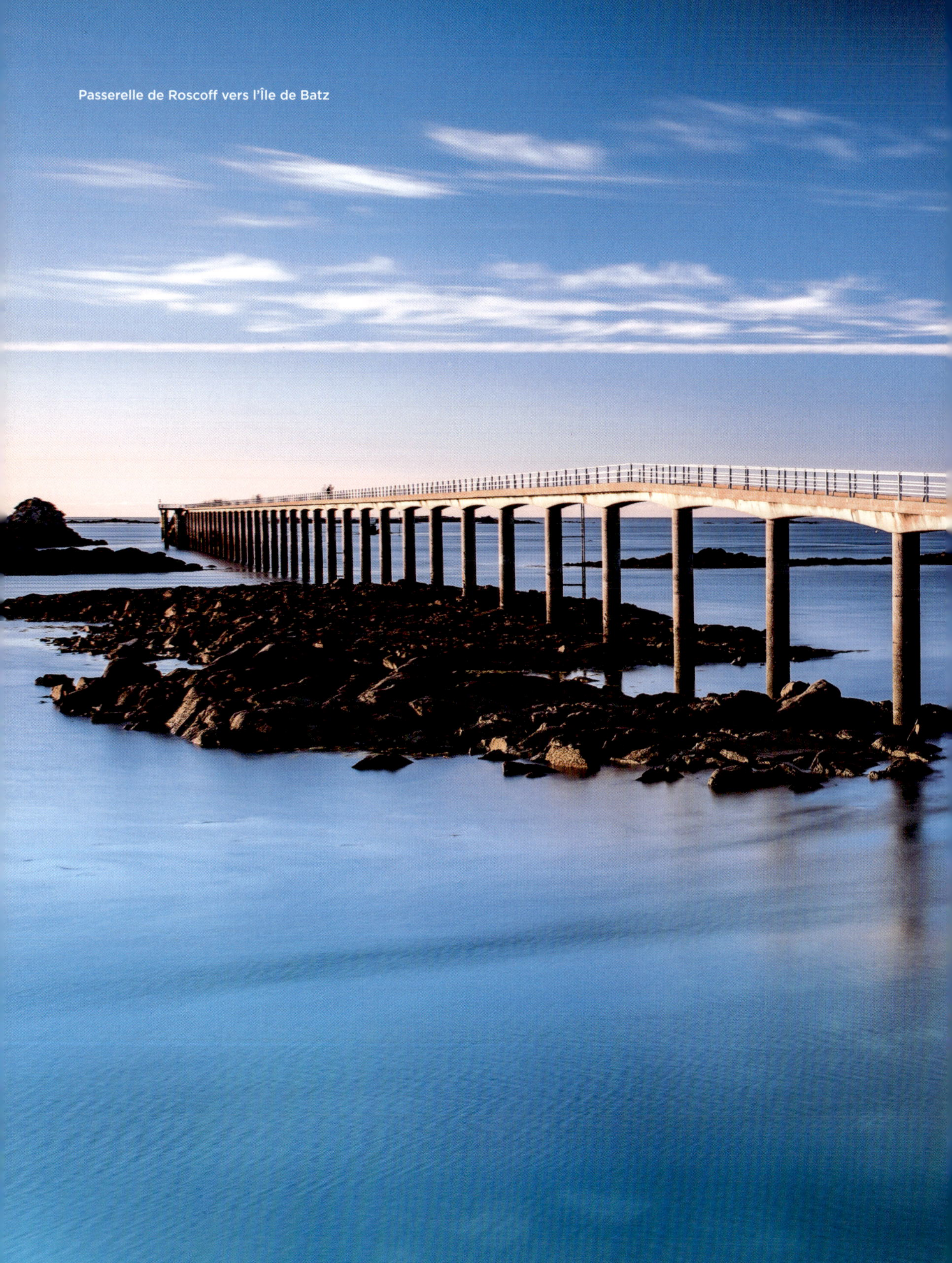
Passerelle de Roscoff vers l'Île de Batz

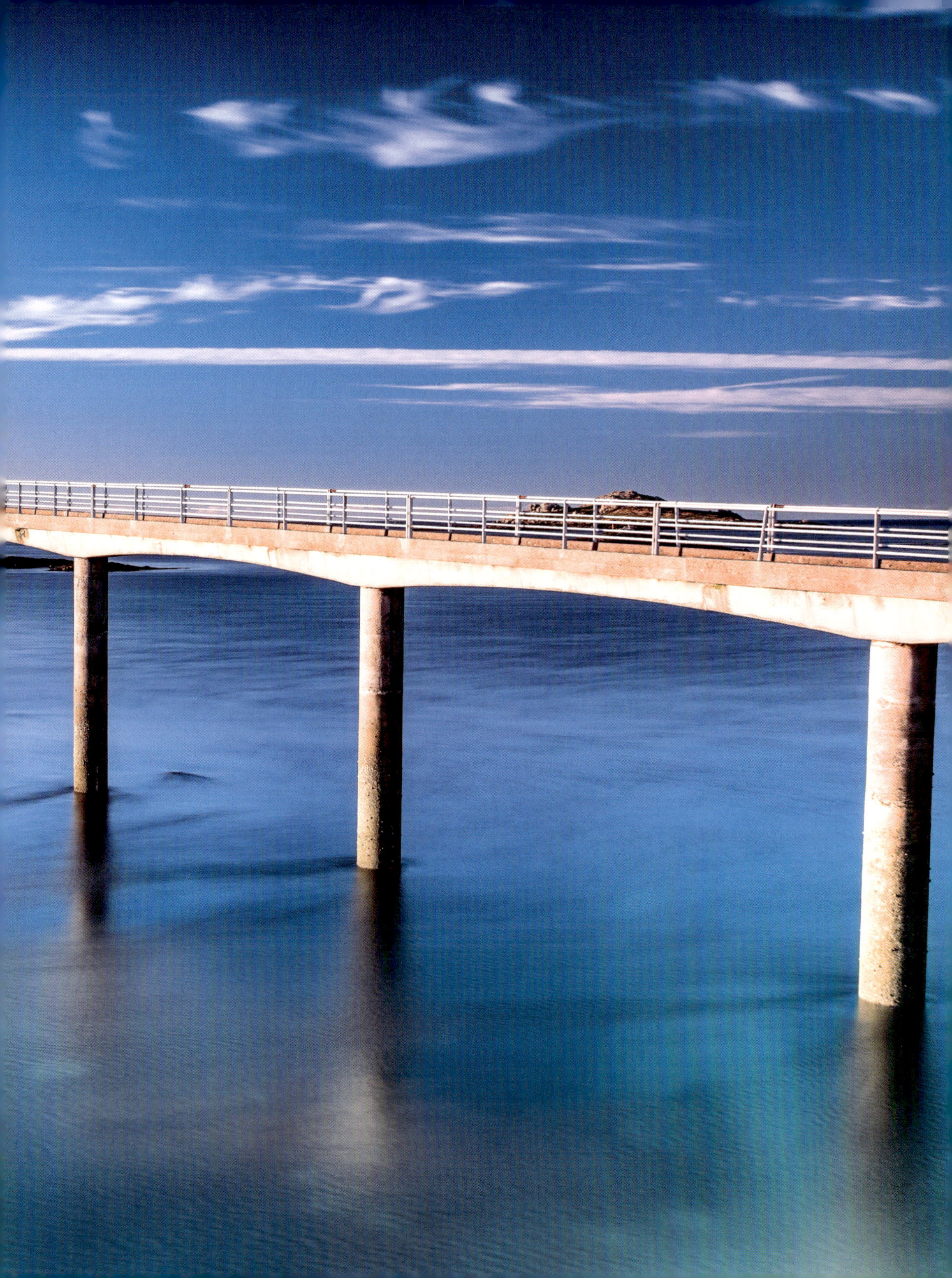

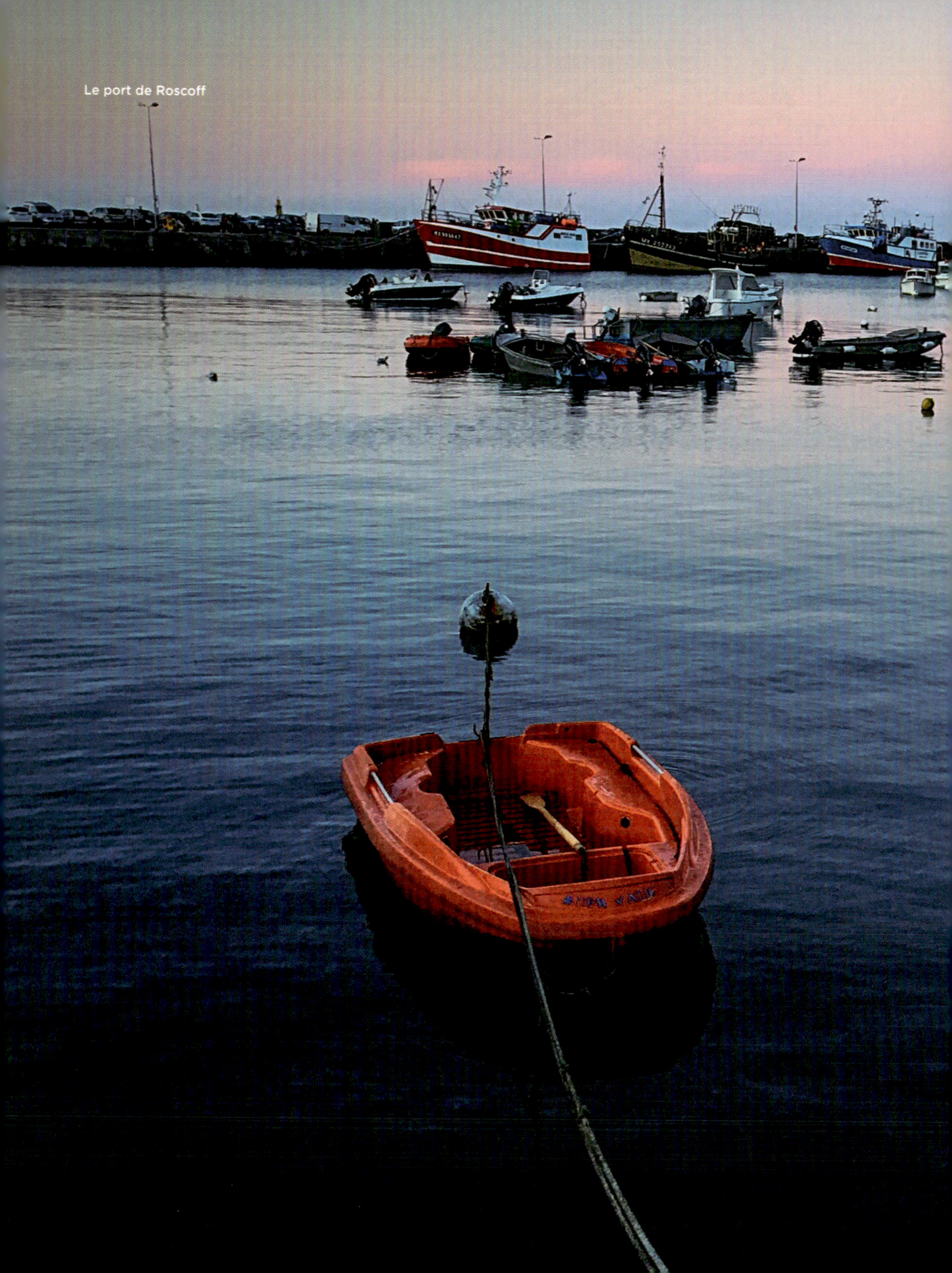

Le port de Roscoff

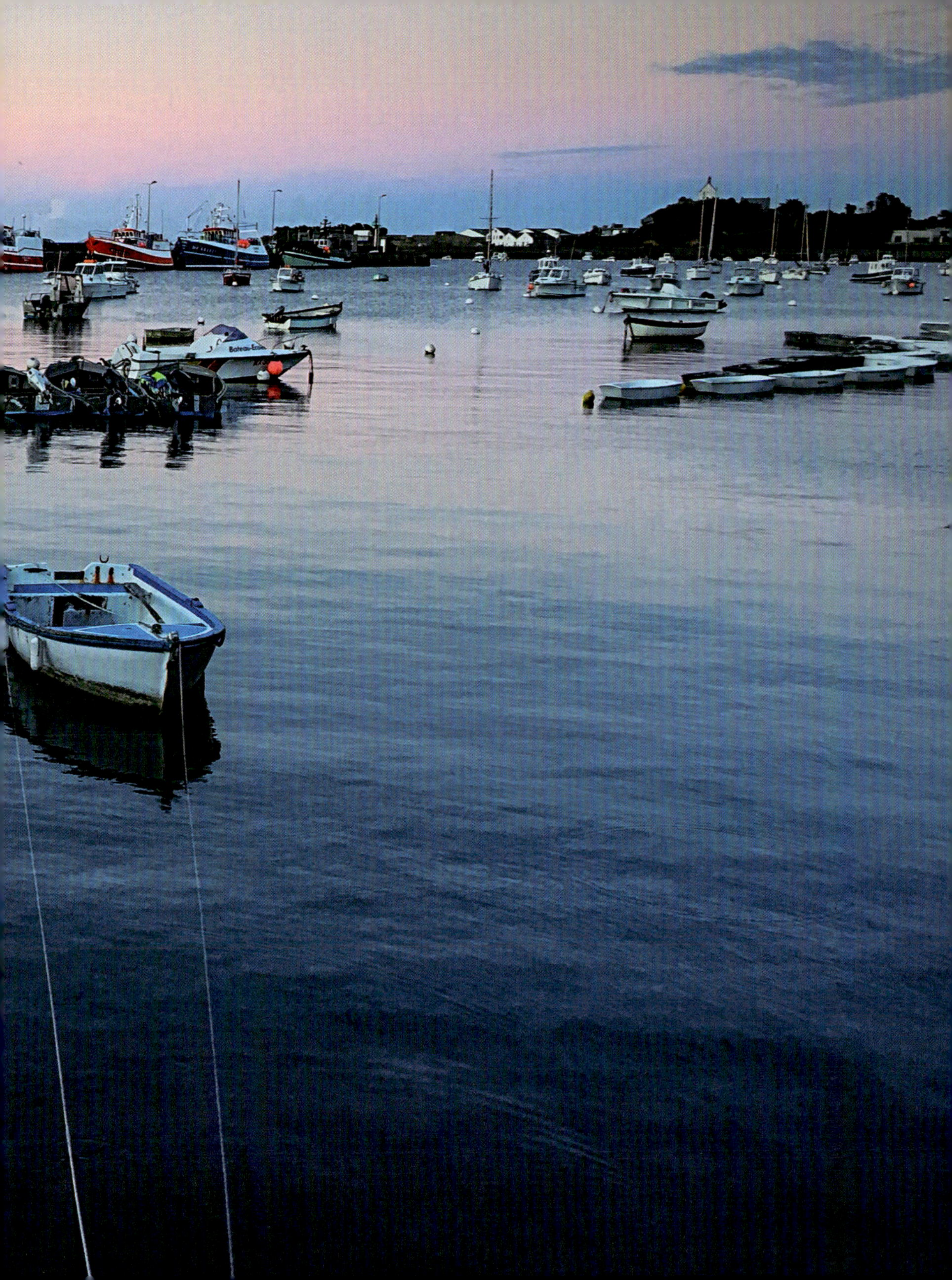

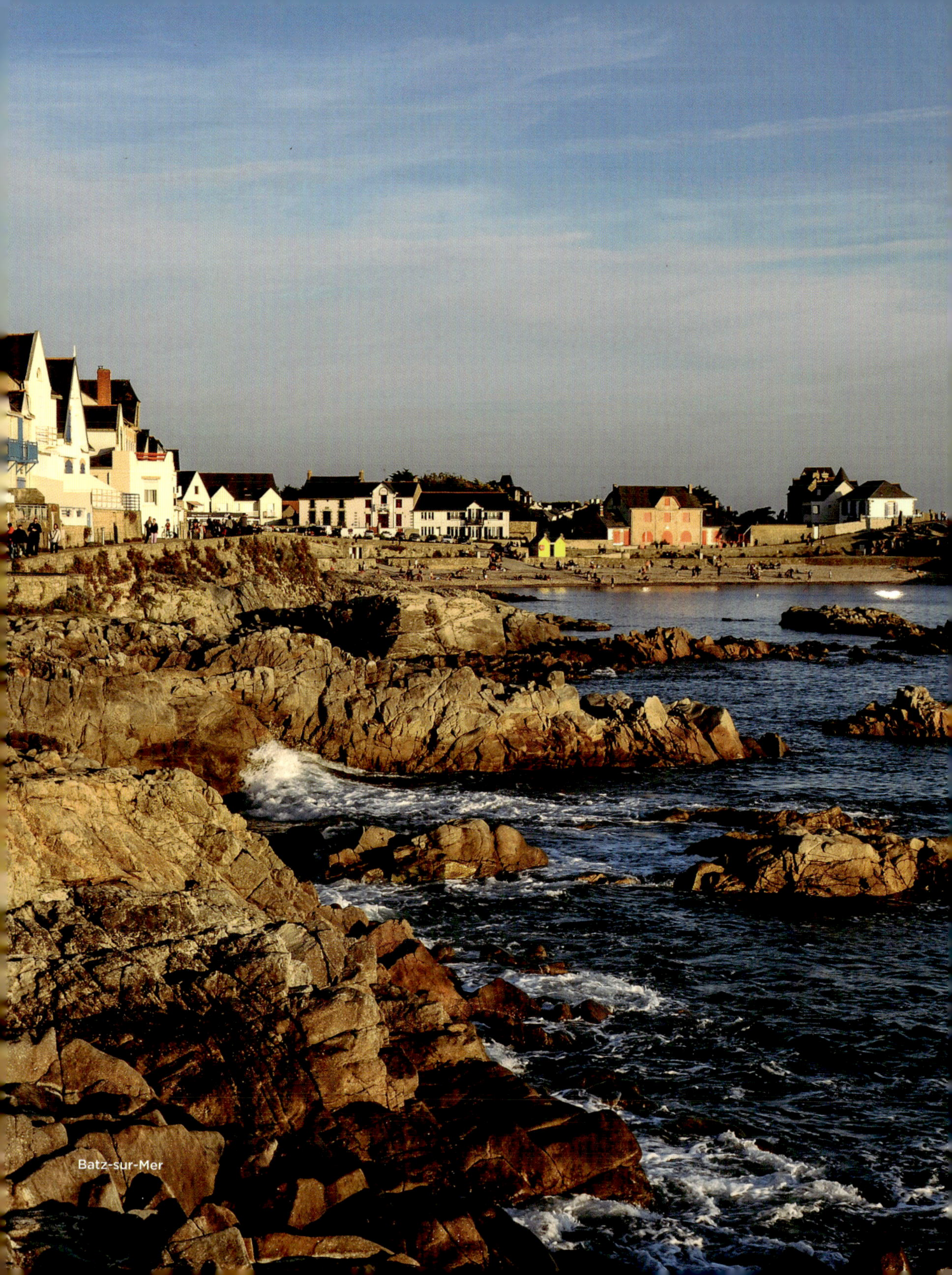

Batz-sur-Mer

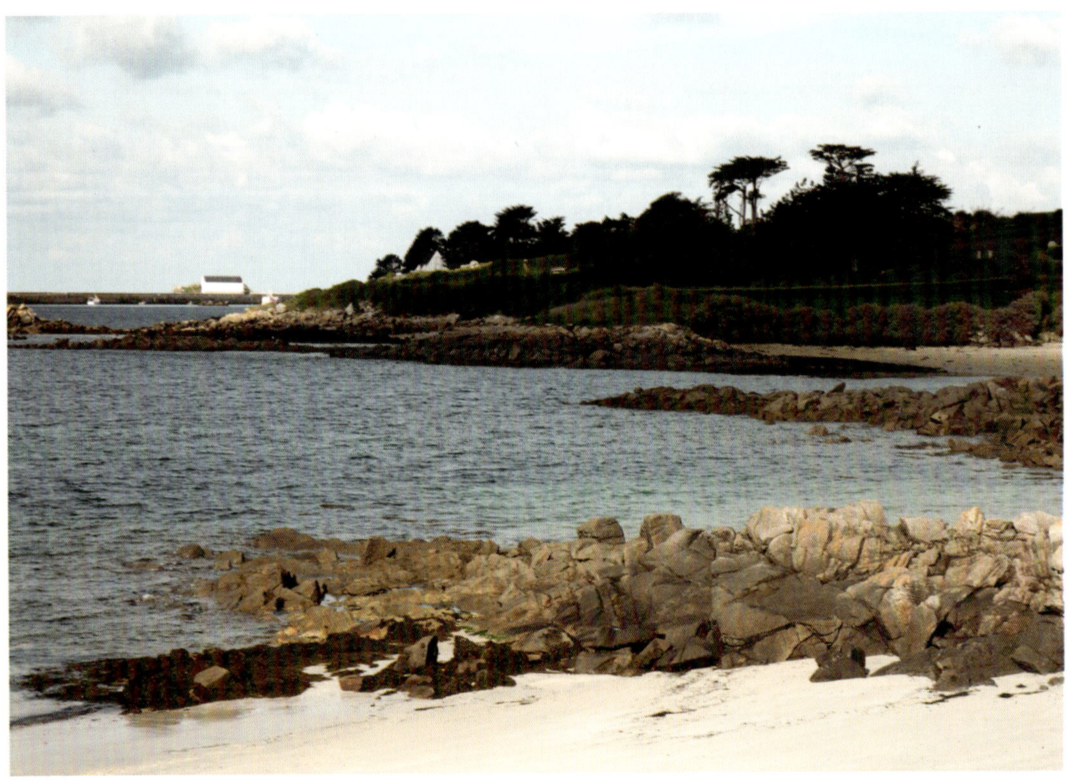

La pointe de Perharidy, Île de Batz

The Île de Batz

In the sea before Roscoff lies the small island Île de Batz. At first sight inconspicuous, it surprises visitors with its rich flora and fauna, and is considered a national natural heritage.

Île de Batz

En el mar frente a Roscoff se encuentra la pequeña isla Île de Batz. A primera vista parece insignificante, pero sorprende a los visitantes con sus ricas flora y fauna, y está considerada patrimonio natural nacional.

L'île de Batz

L'île de Batz est une petite île située au large de Roscoff. Souvent décrite comme « discrète », elle séduit par la richesse de sa faune, de sa flore et de son patrimoine naturel.

A Île de Batz

No mar em frente a Roscoff fica a pequena ilha Île de Batz. À primeira vista discreta, surpreende os visitantes com uma rica flora e fauna e é considerada património natural nacional.

Die Île de Batz

Im Meer vor Roscoff liegt die kleine Insel Île de Batz. Auf den ersten Blick unscheinbar, überrascht sie Besucher durch eine reiche Flora und Fauna und gilt als nationales Naturerbe.

Het Ile de Batz

In de zee voor Roscoff ligt het eilandje Île de Batz. Dit op het eerste gezicht onopvallende eilandje verrast bezoekers met een rijke flora en fauna, en is nationaal natuurerfgoed.

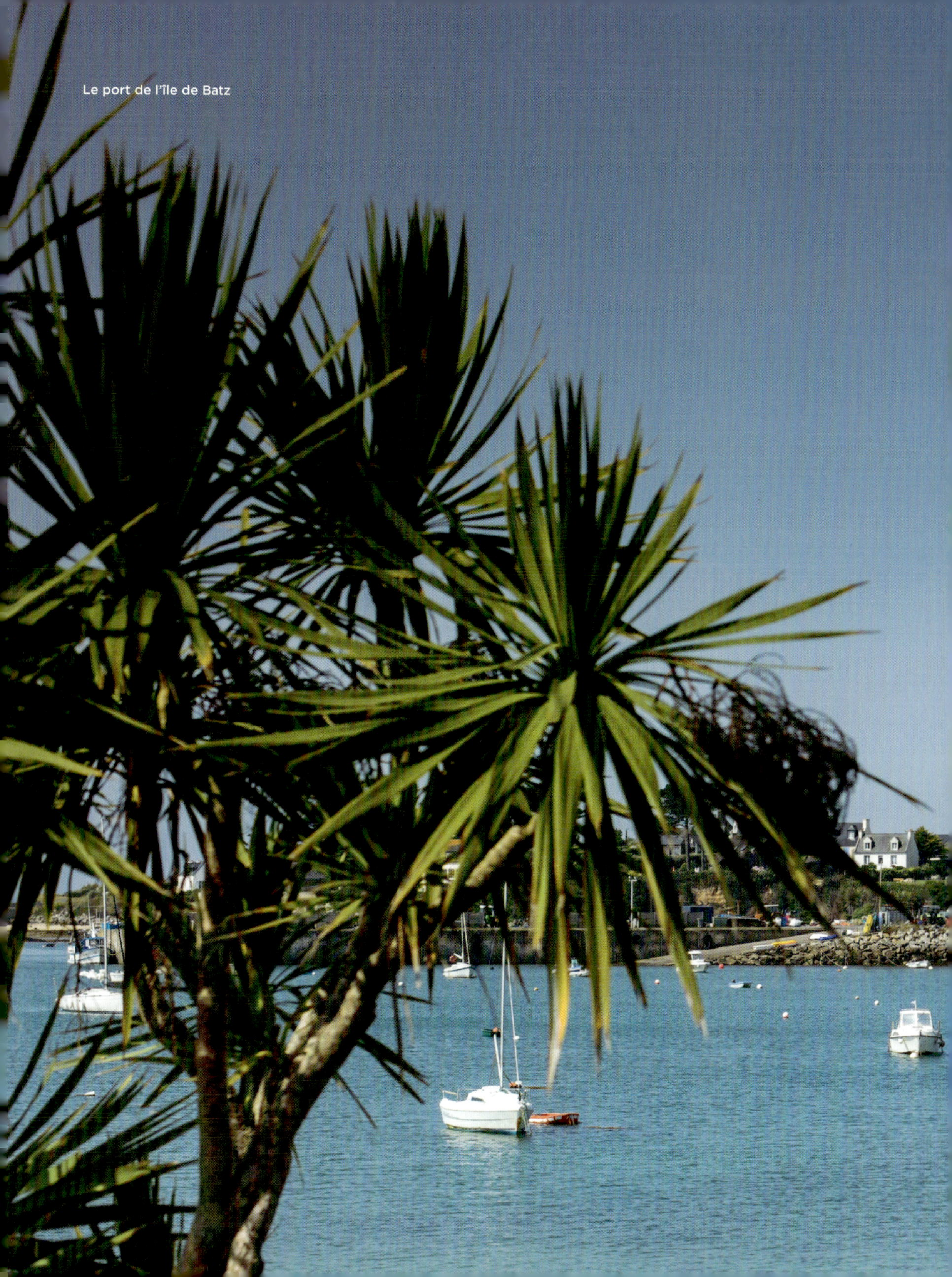

Le port de l'île de Batz

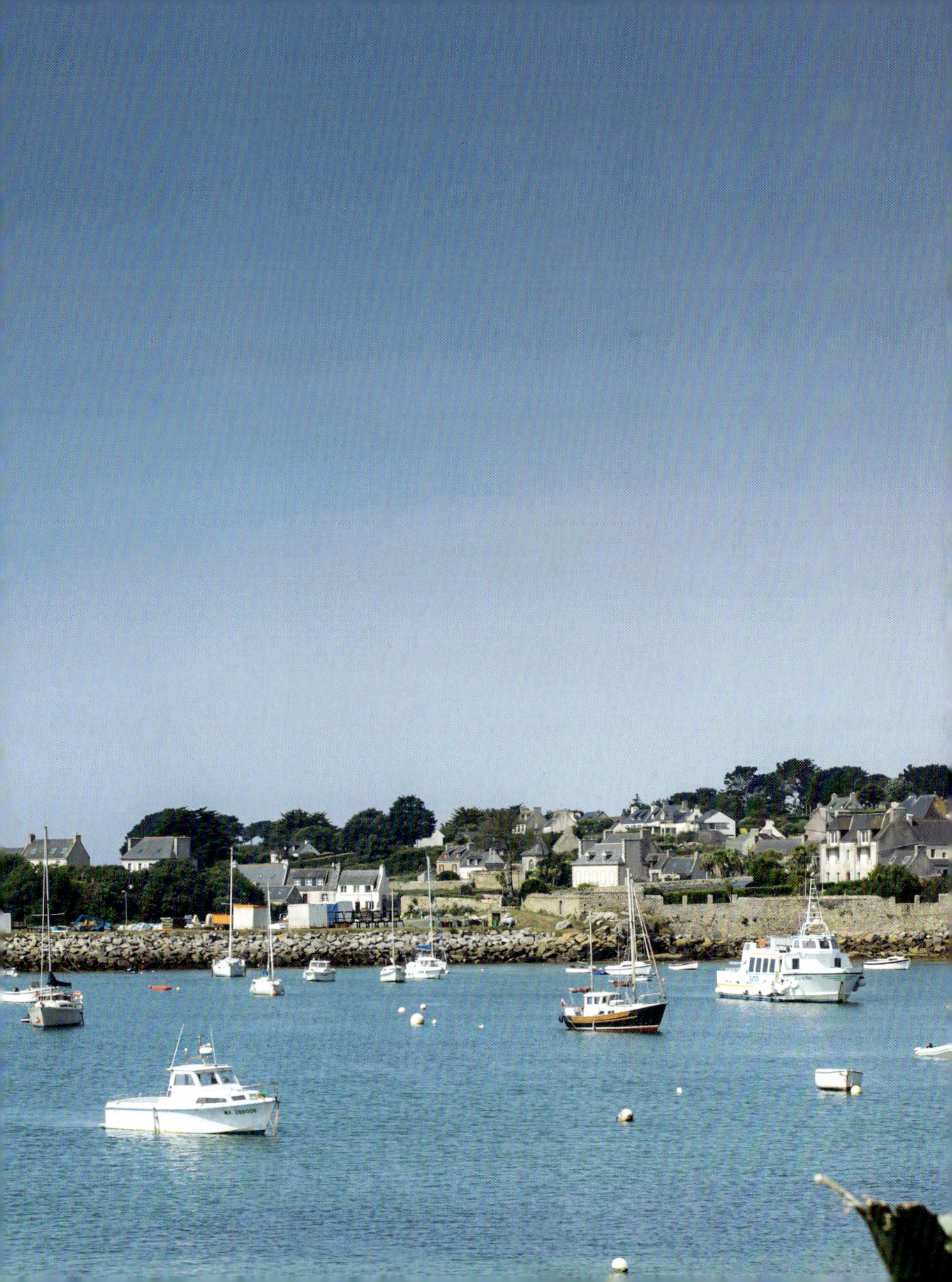

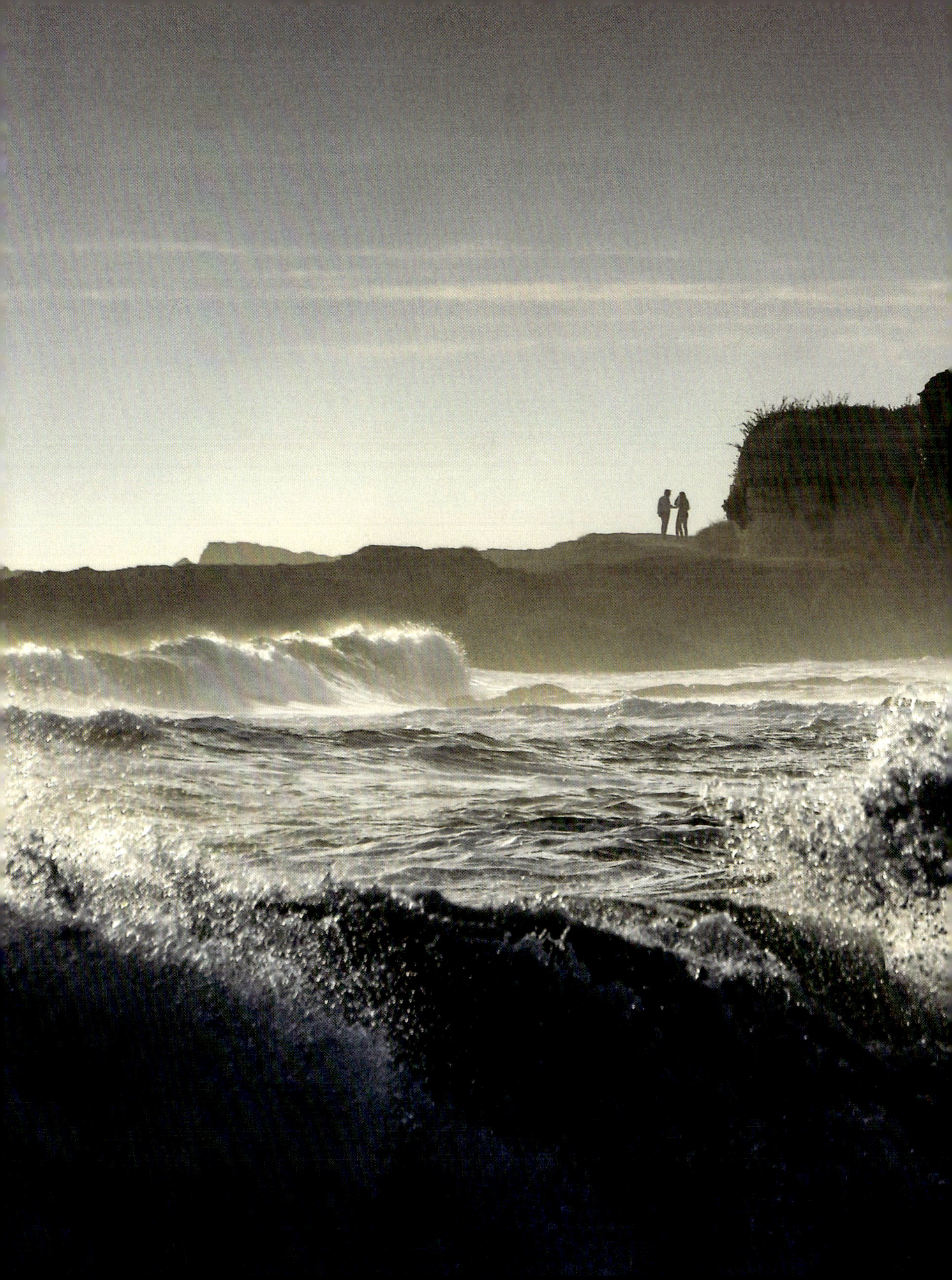

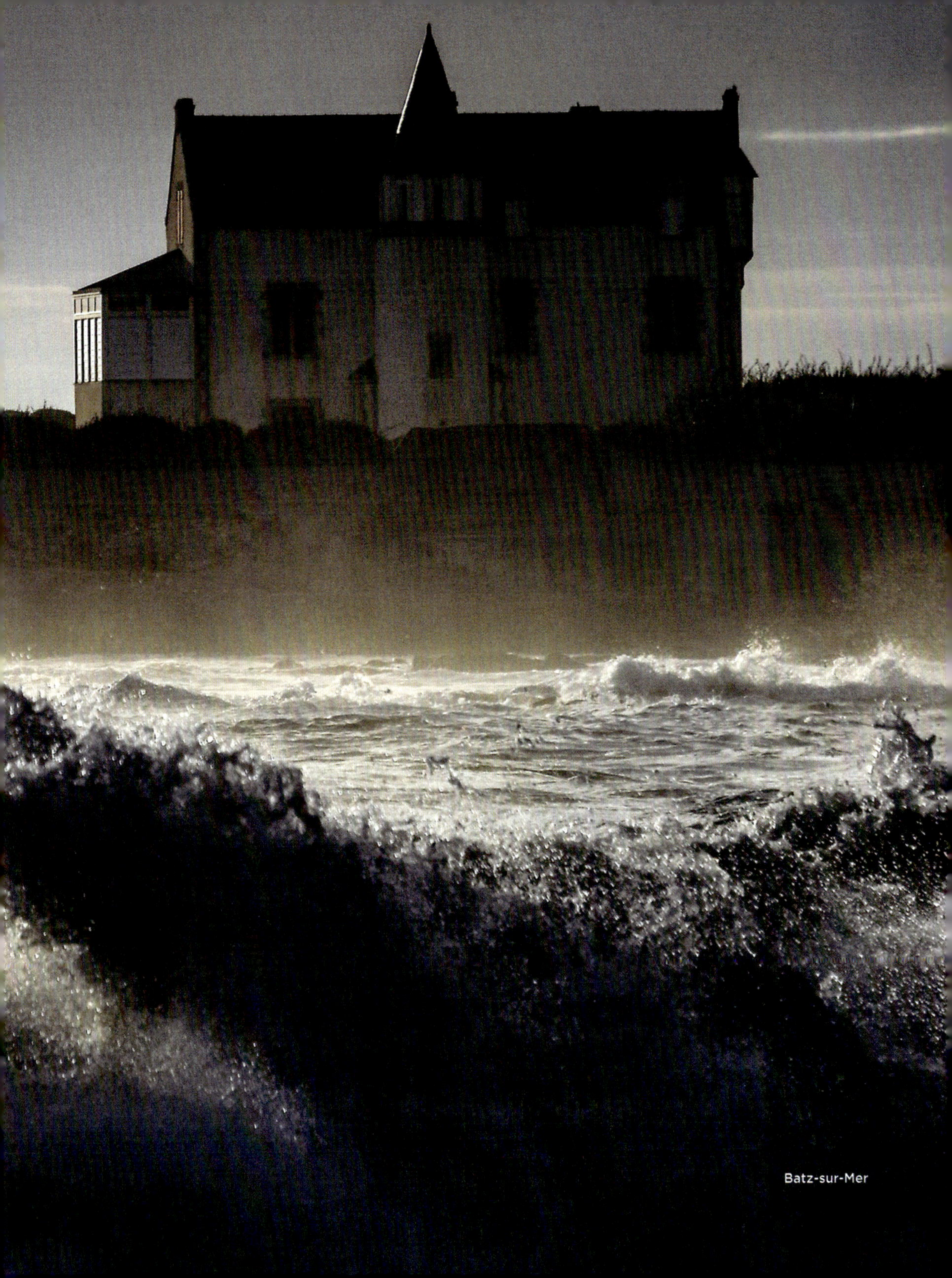
Batz-sur-Mer

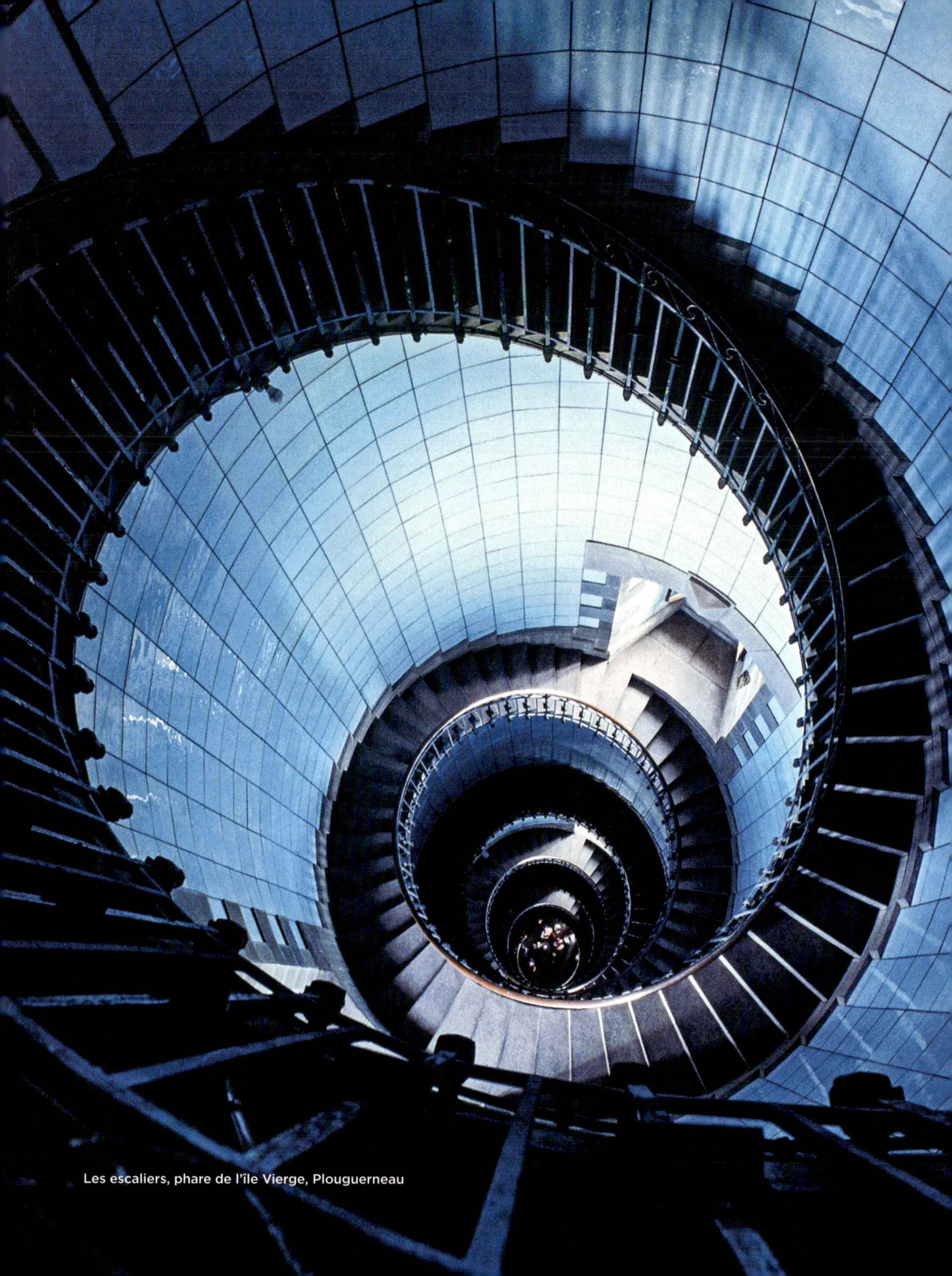

Les escaliers, phare de l'île Vierge, Plouguerneau

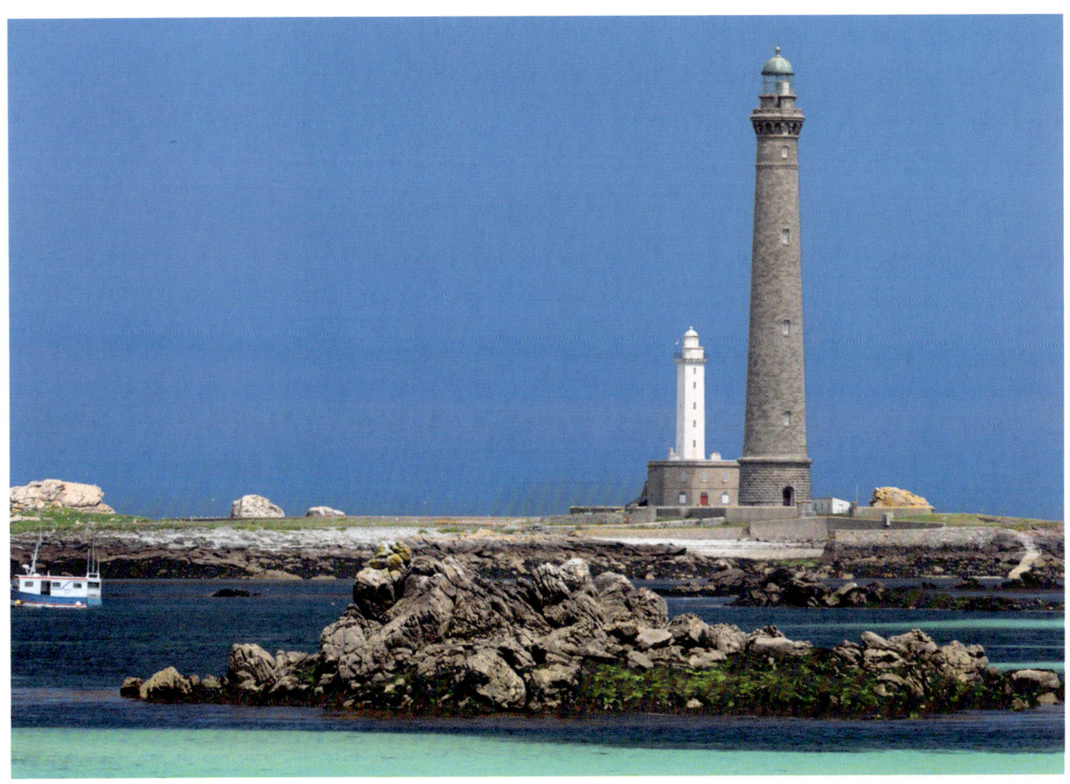

Le phare de l'île Vierge, Plouguerneau

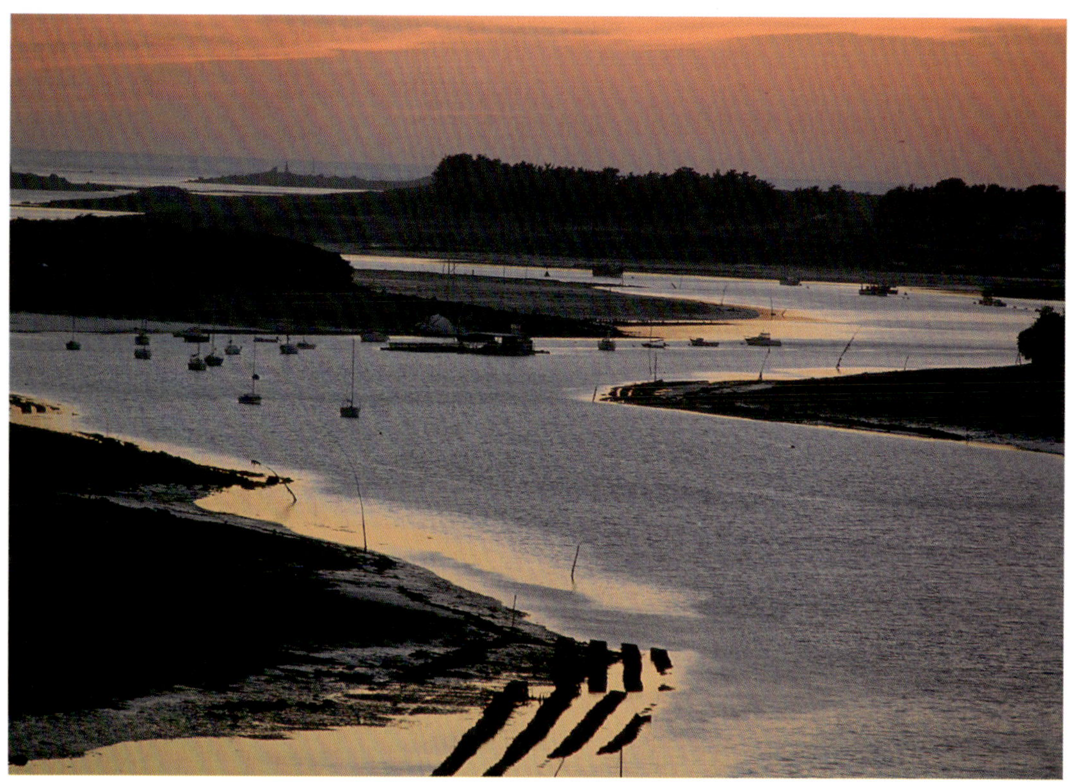

L'Aber-Wrac'h

The Pays des Abers

The Pays des Abers is characterised by river mouths that penetrate deep into the interior of the country - the Abers. They form an untouched landscape between the land and the sea.

El Pays des Abers

El Pays des Abers se caracteriza por sus desembocaduras que penetran profundamente en el interior del país: el Abers. Forman un paisaje intacto entre la tierra y el mar.

Le pays des Abers

Les abers sont des estuaires (ria) qui pénètrent à l'intérieur des terres et offrent des paysages sauvages entre terre et mer.

O Pays des Abers

O Pays des Abers é caracterizado por desembocaduras de rios que penetram no interior da região - os Abers ou estuários. Eles formam uma paisagem intocada entre a terra e o mar.

Das Pays des Abers

Das Pays des Abers ist geprägt von tief in das Landesinnere vordringenden Flussmündungen – die Abers. Sie bilden eine unberührte Landschaft zwischen dem Land und dem Meer.

Het Pays des Abers

Het Pays des Abers wordt getekend door riviermondingen die diep het binnenland (de Abers) in dringen. Ze vormen een ongerept landschap tussen land en zee.

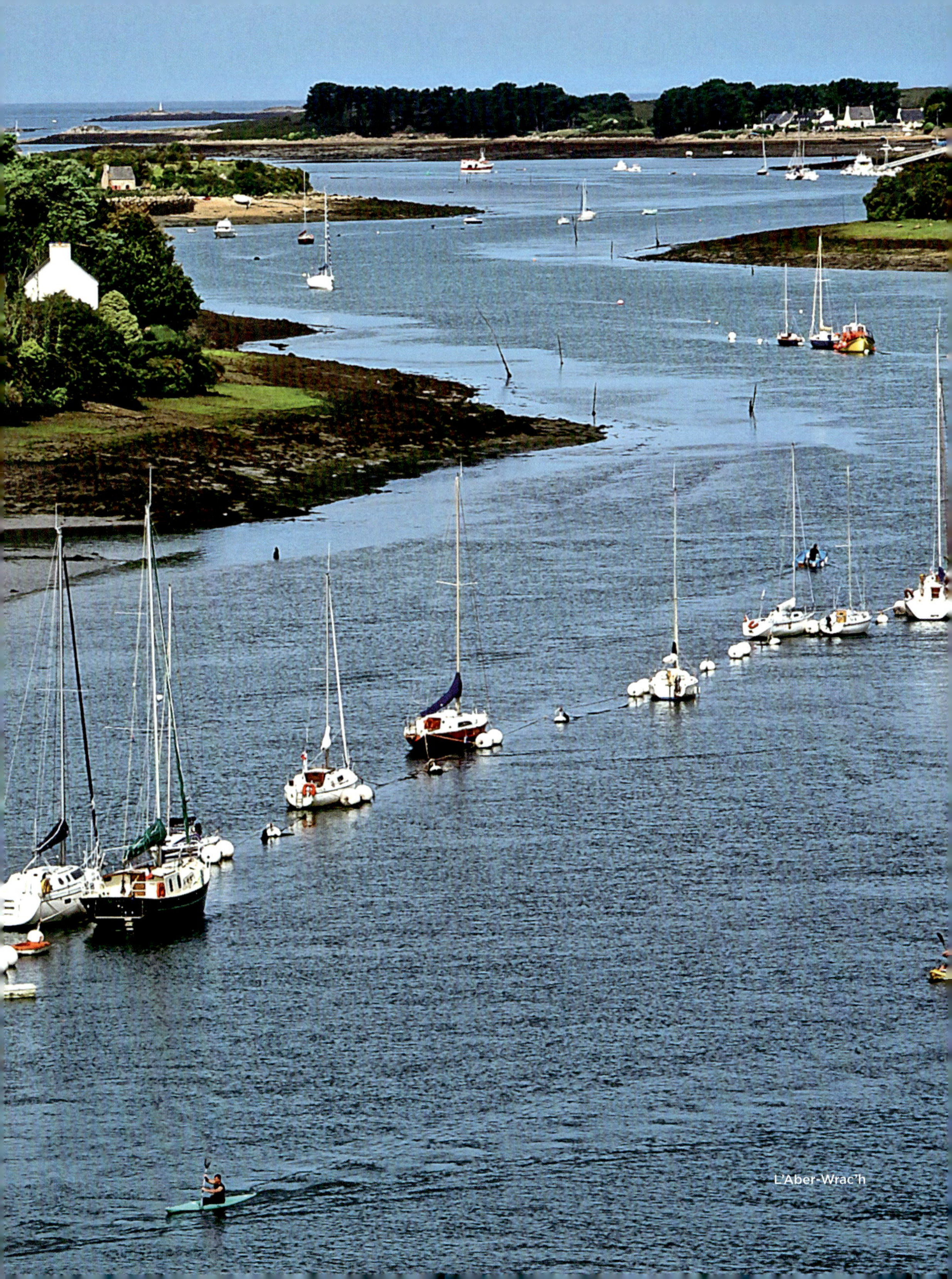

L'Aber-Wrac'h

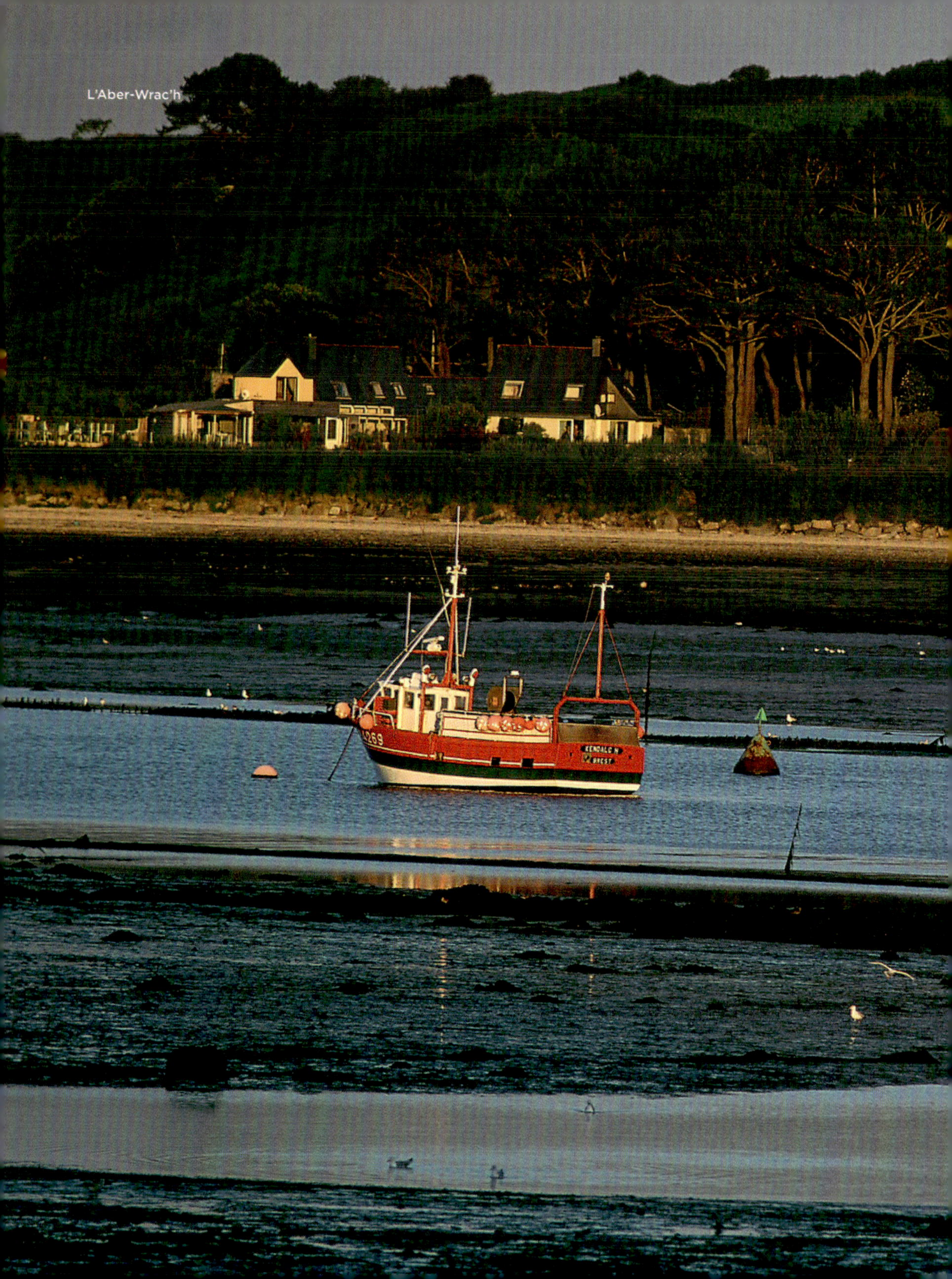

L'Aber-Wrac'h

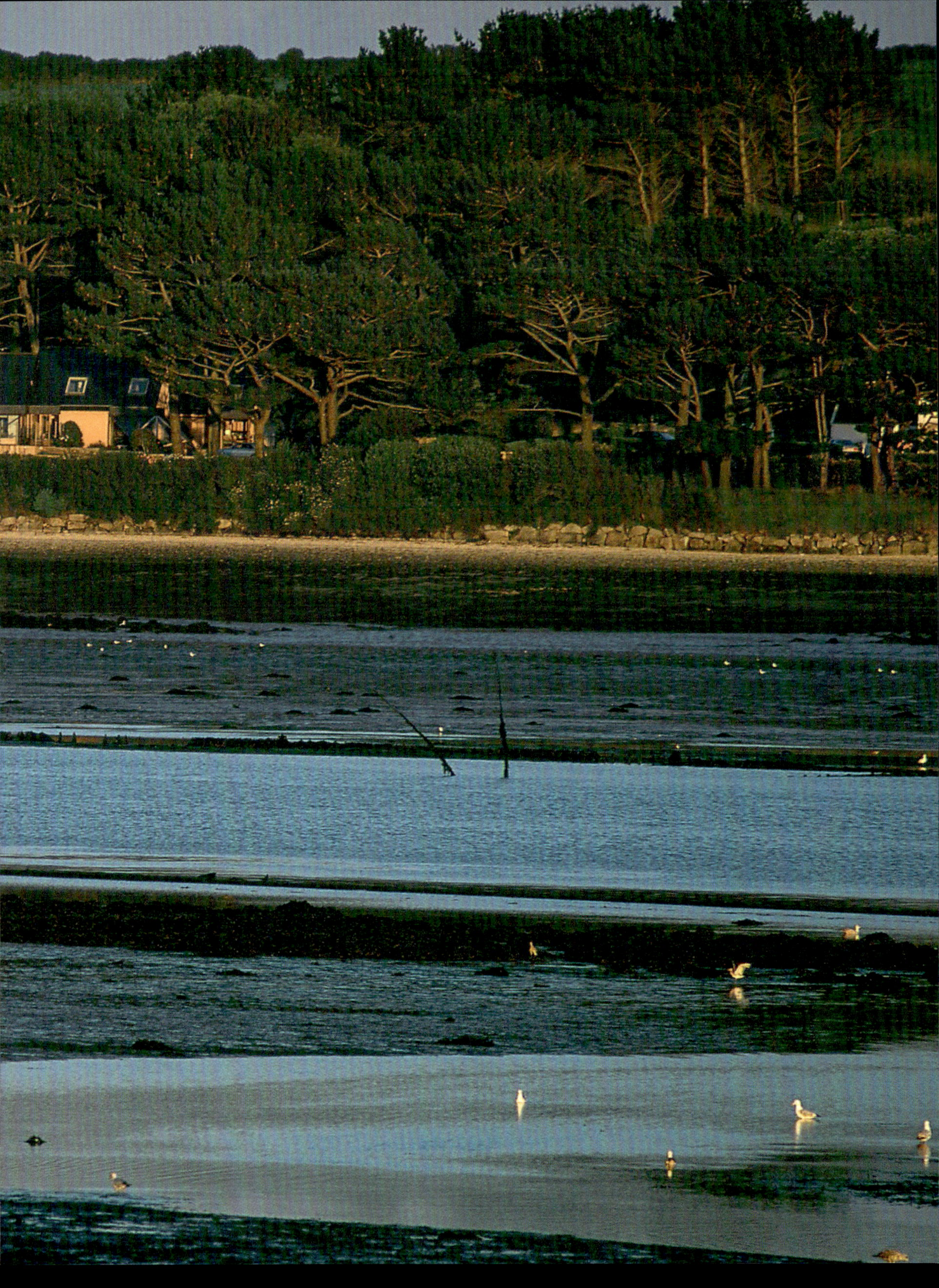

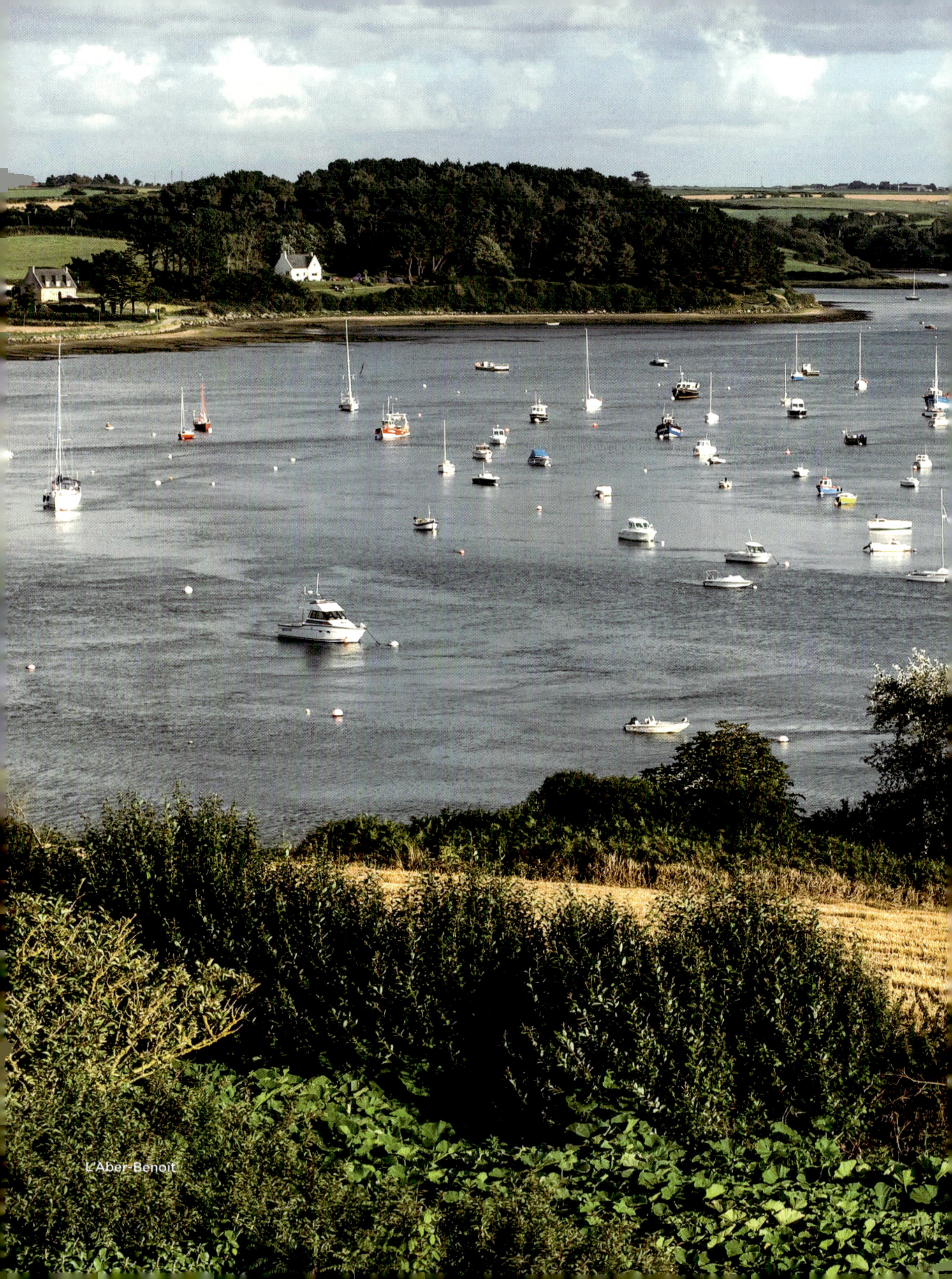

L'Aber-Benoît

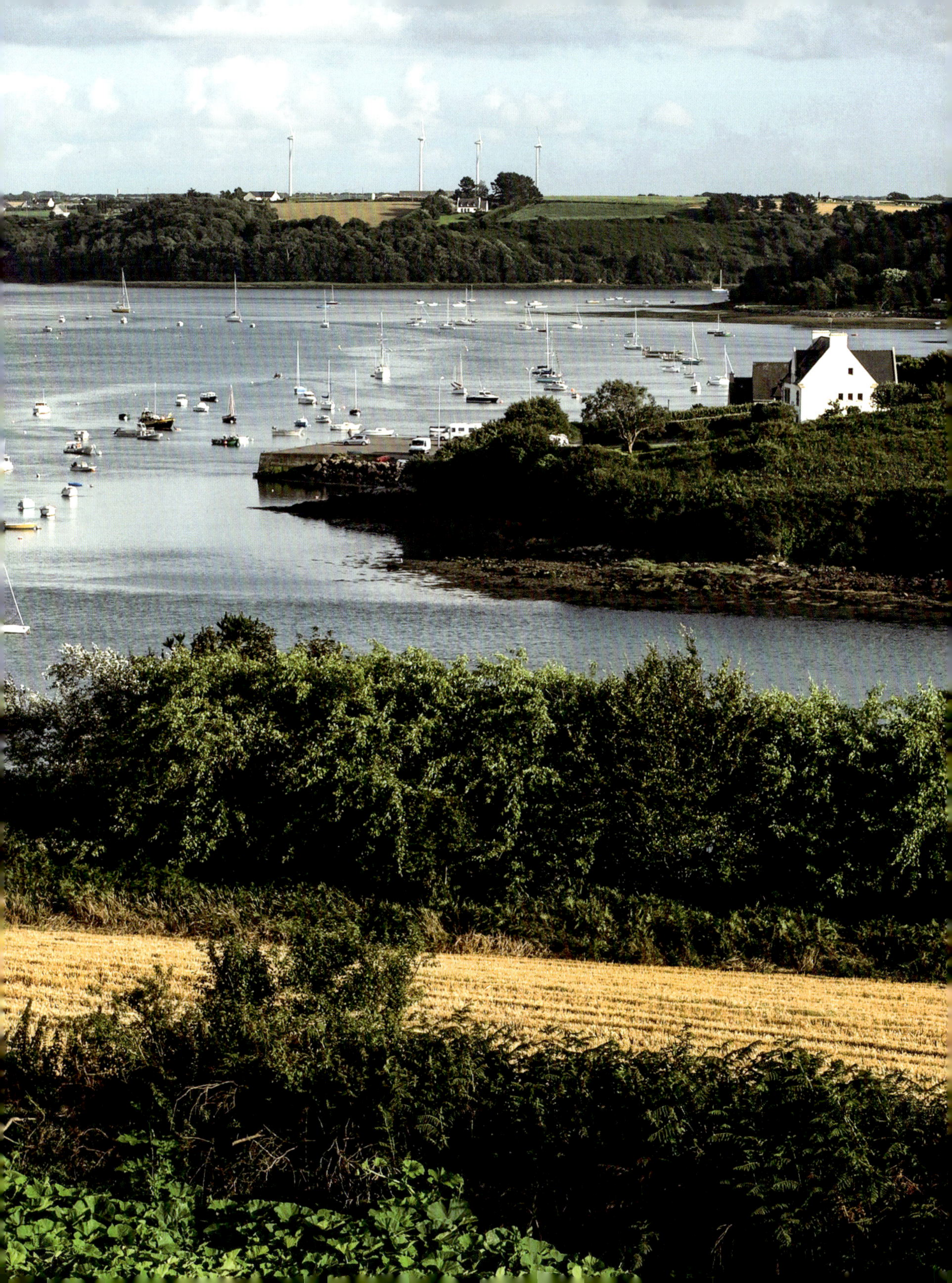

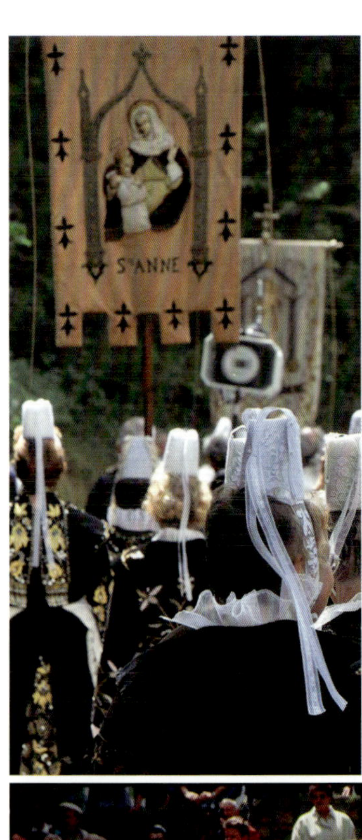
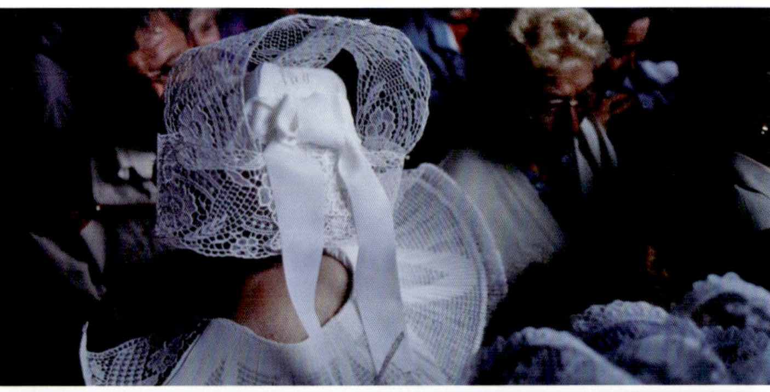
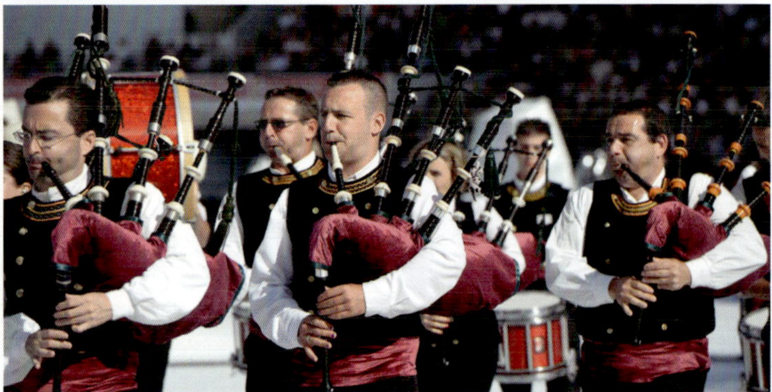
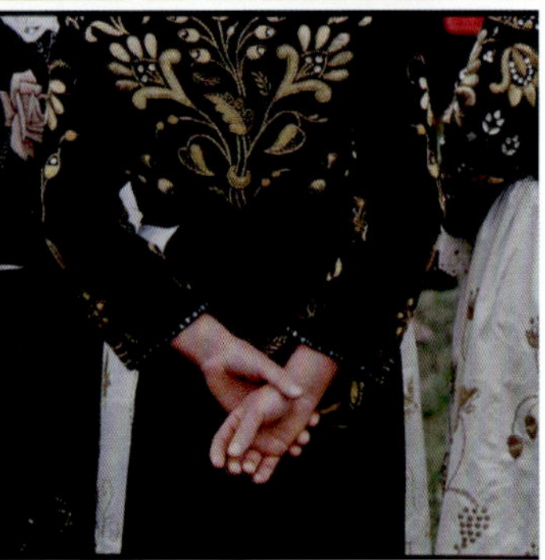
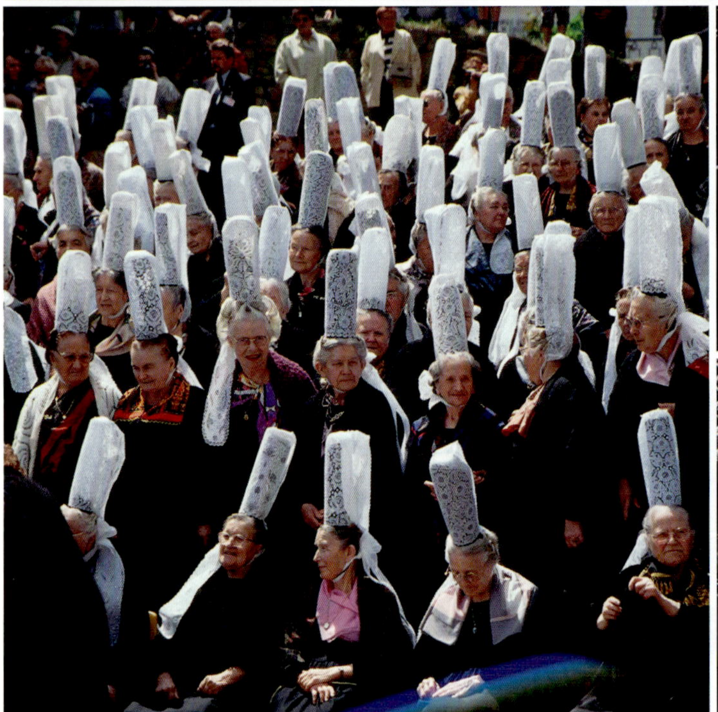
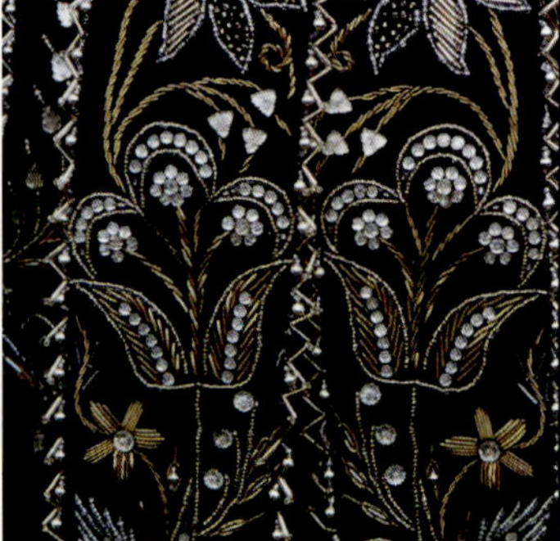

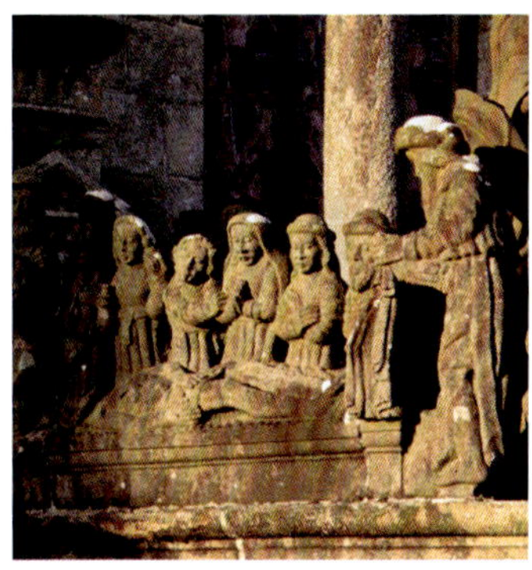 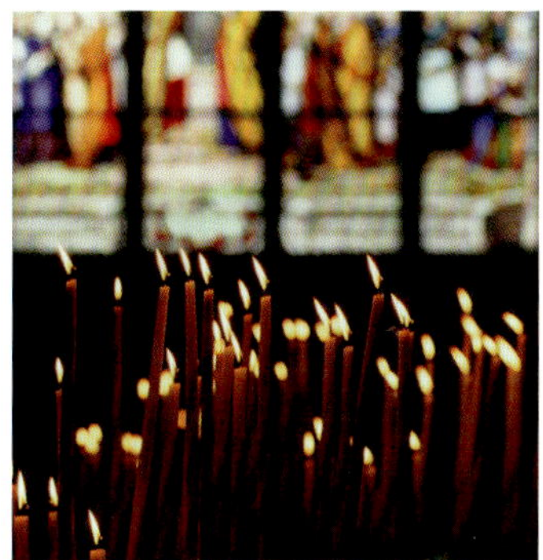 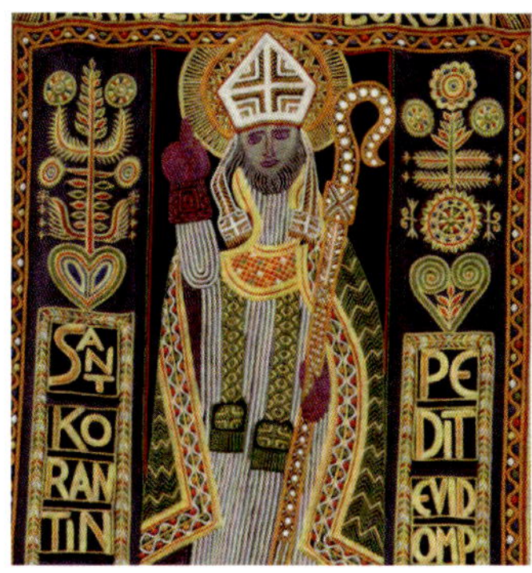

Traditions

The traditional hairstyles and costumes of the individual regions form a distinctive regional feature. In total there are 66 different types. Whereas in the past they were worn only for special festivities, today they are also seen on occasions such as processions or the holidays of local saints. Religion still plays an important role in Brittany, as can be seen in the many sacred buildings: churches with unique bell towers, suffering paths and processional sites line the landscape.

Traditions

Coiffes et costumes d'autrefois constituaient un signe de reconnaissance sociologique de la Bretagne. On dénombre 66 modes bretonnes différentes ! Alors qu'ils étaient portés pour de grandes occasions, aujourd'hui on les sort les jours de pardons, jours de fête du saint local, entre religion et croyances populaires. La présence de la religion est forte et la Bretagne possède une architecture religieuse unique : des églises dont les clochers étaient de vrais morceaux de bravoure, calvaires et croix disposés en pleine nature...

Traditionen

Die traditionellen Frisuren und Trachten der einzelnen Regionen bilden ein typisches regionales Erkennungszeichen. Insgesamt gibt es 66 verschieden Arten. Während sie früher nur zu besonderen Festen getragen wurden, sieht man sie heute auch bei Anlässen wie Prozessionen oder den Feiertagen der lokalen Heiligen. Die Religion spielt immer noch eine große Rolle in der Bretagne, was sich in den vielfältigen Sakralbauten zeigt: Kirchen mit einzigartigen Glockentürmen, Leidenswege und Prozessionsstätten säumen die Landschaft.

Costumbres

Los peinados y los trajes tradicionales tradicionales de las distintas regiones forman una marca distintiva típica de la región. En total hay 66 tipos diferentes. Mientras que en el pasado se usaban solo para fiestas especiales, hoy en día también se ven en ocasiones como las procesiones o las fiestas de los santos locales. La religión sigue desempeñando un papel importante en Bretaña, como se puede ver en los numerosos edificios sagrados: el paisaje está bordeado por iglesias con campanarios únicos, vidas de calvario y sitios de procesiones.

Tradições

Os penteados e os trajes tradicionais de cada região formam uma marca distintiva regional típica. Ao todo, existem 66 espécies diferentes. Enquanto que no passado eram usados apenas para festividades especiais, hoje também são vistos em ocasiões como procissões ou feriados de santos locais. A religião ainda desempenha um papel importante na Bretanha, como se pode ver em muitos edifícios de funções sagradas: igrejas com torres de sinos singulares, calvários e locais de peregrinação que orlam a paisagem.

Tradities

De traditionele kapsels en klederdrachten van de afzonderlijke regio's vormen een typisch regionaal herkenningsteken. Er zijn in totaal 66 verschillende. Waar klederdracht vroeger alleen bij speciale feesten werd gedragen, is die nu ook te zien bij processies en feestdagen van plaatselijke heiligen. Godsdienst speelt nog steeds een belangrijke rol in Bretagne, zoals te zien is aan de vele sacrale gebouwen: kerken met unieke klokkentorens, lijdenswegen en processiestations omzomen het landschap.

Plein ouest

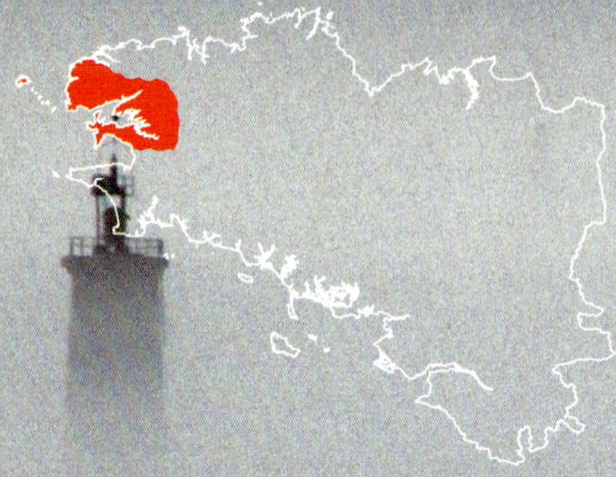

Le phare de la Vieille, Brest

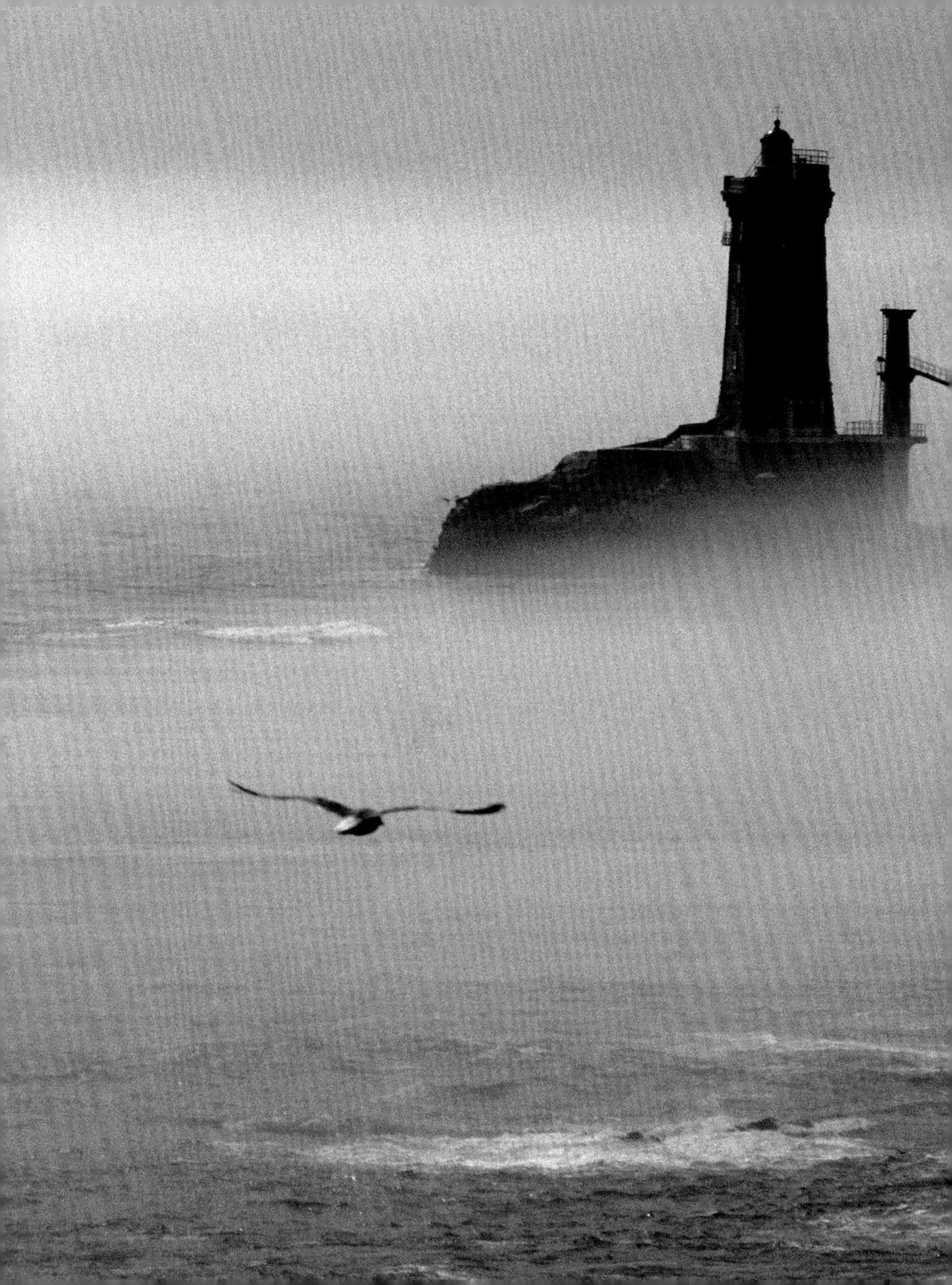

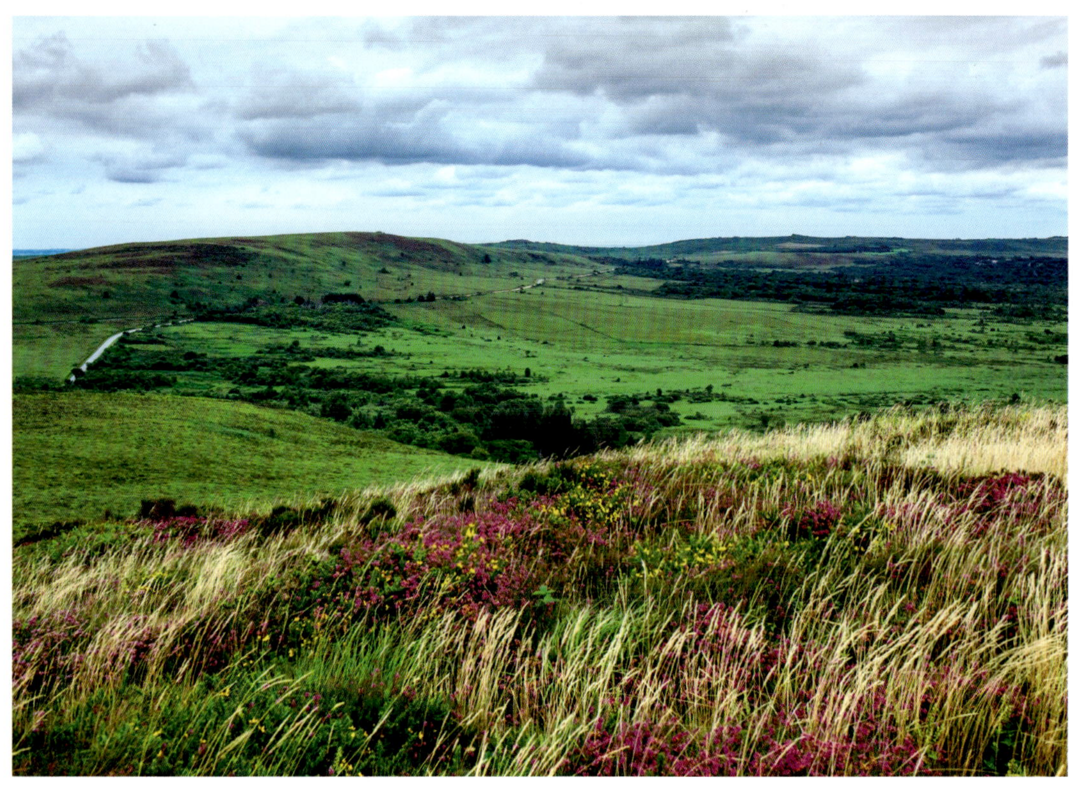

Mont Saint-Michel de Brasparts, monts d'Arrée

The Monts d'Arrée

This mountain range divides the department of Finistère into two parts. Deep in the heart of the Armorique Nature Park, it offers heath landscapes, peat bogs and impressive rock formations. At 385 m, the Roc'h Ruz is the highest elevation.

Les monts d'Arrée

Ce massif montagneux sépare le Finistère en deux. Situé au sein du parc régional d'Armorique en plein cœur de la Bretagne, il est constitué de landes, tourbières et rocs. Son plus haut sommet, le Roc'h Ruz, culmine à 385 mètres.

Die Monts d'Arrée

Der Gebirgszug trennt das Département Finistère in zwei Teile. Tief im Herzen des Naturparks Armorique bietet er Heide-landschaften, Torfmoore und beeindruckende Felsformationen. Mit 385 m ist der Roc'h Ruz die höchste Erhebung.

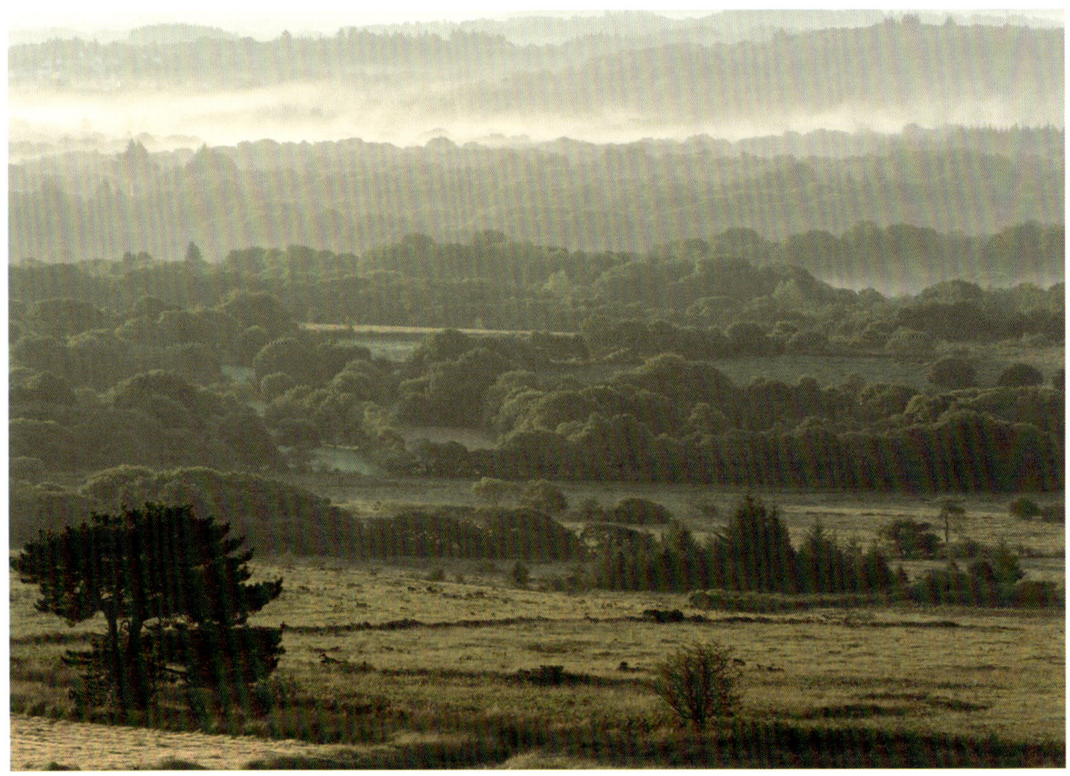

Saint-Rivoal, monts d'Arrée

Los Monts d'Arrée

La cordillera divide el departamento de Finisterre en dos partes. En el corazón del Parque Natural de Armorique, ofrece paisajes de brezales, turberas e impresionantes formaciones rocosas. Con 385 m, el Roc'h Ruz es el punto más alto.

Os Monts d'Arrée

A cadeia montanhosa divide o departamento de Finistère em duas partes. O Parque Natural Armorique, oferece paisagens de urze, turfeiras e impressionantes formações rochosas. A maior elevação com 385m de altura é a Roc'h Ruz.

De Monts d'Arrée

De bergketen deelt het departement Finistère in tweeën. Diep in het hart van het natuurpark Armorique biedt hij heidelandschappen, veengebieden en indrukwekkende rotsformaties. Met zijn 385 meter is de Roc'h Ruz de hoogste top.

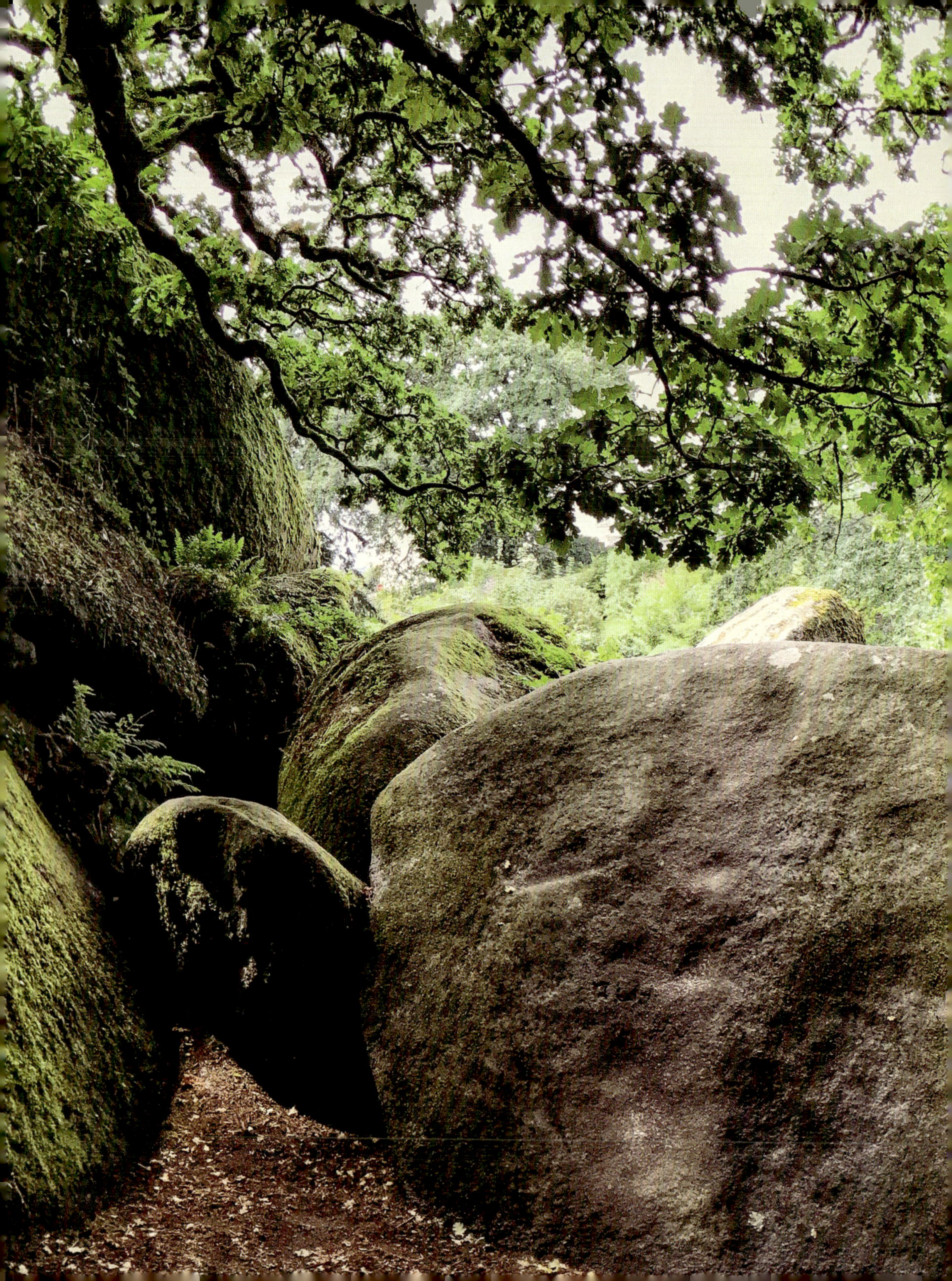

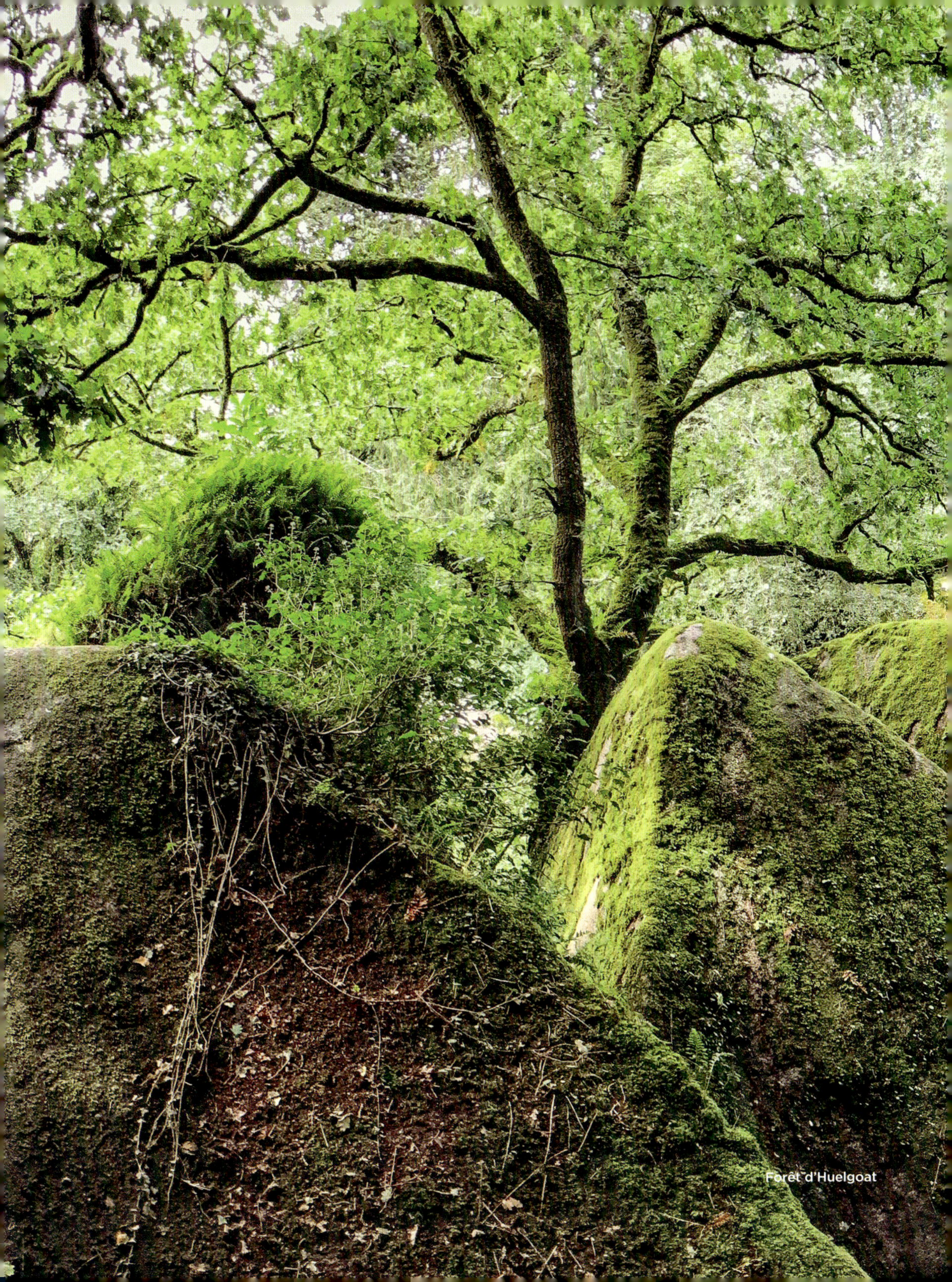
Forêt d'Huelgoat

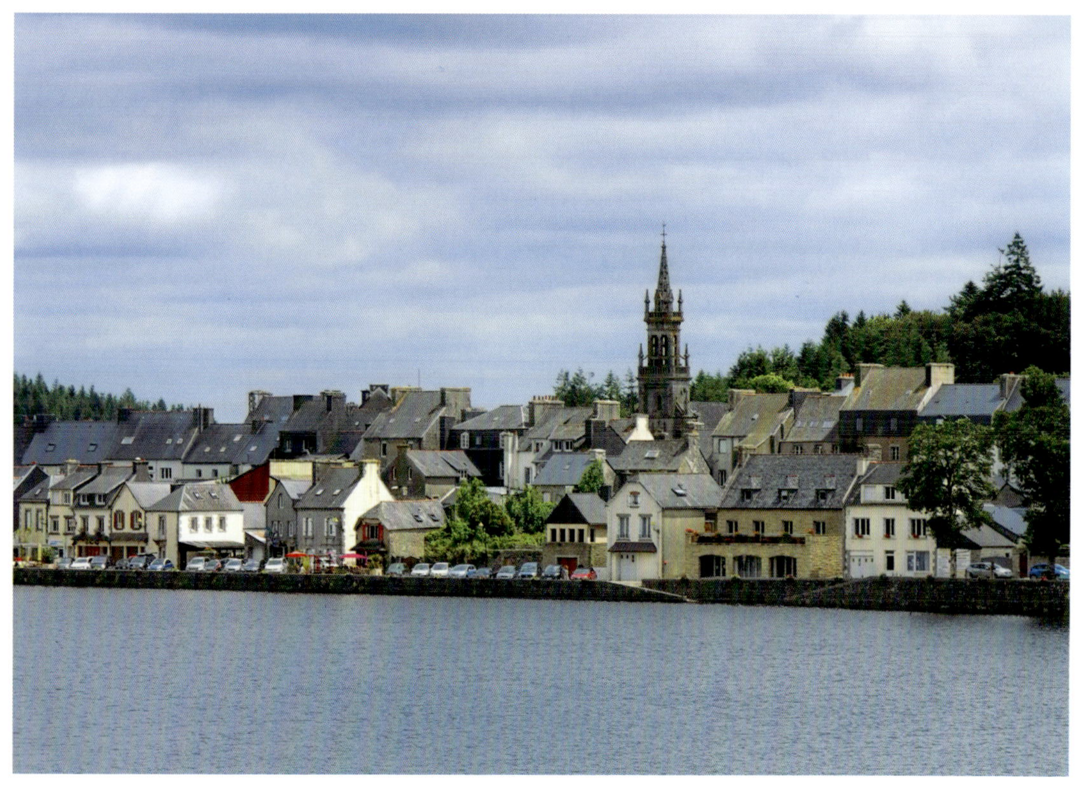

Huelgoat

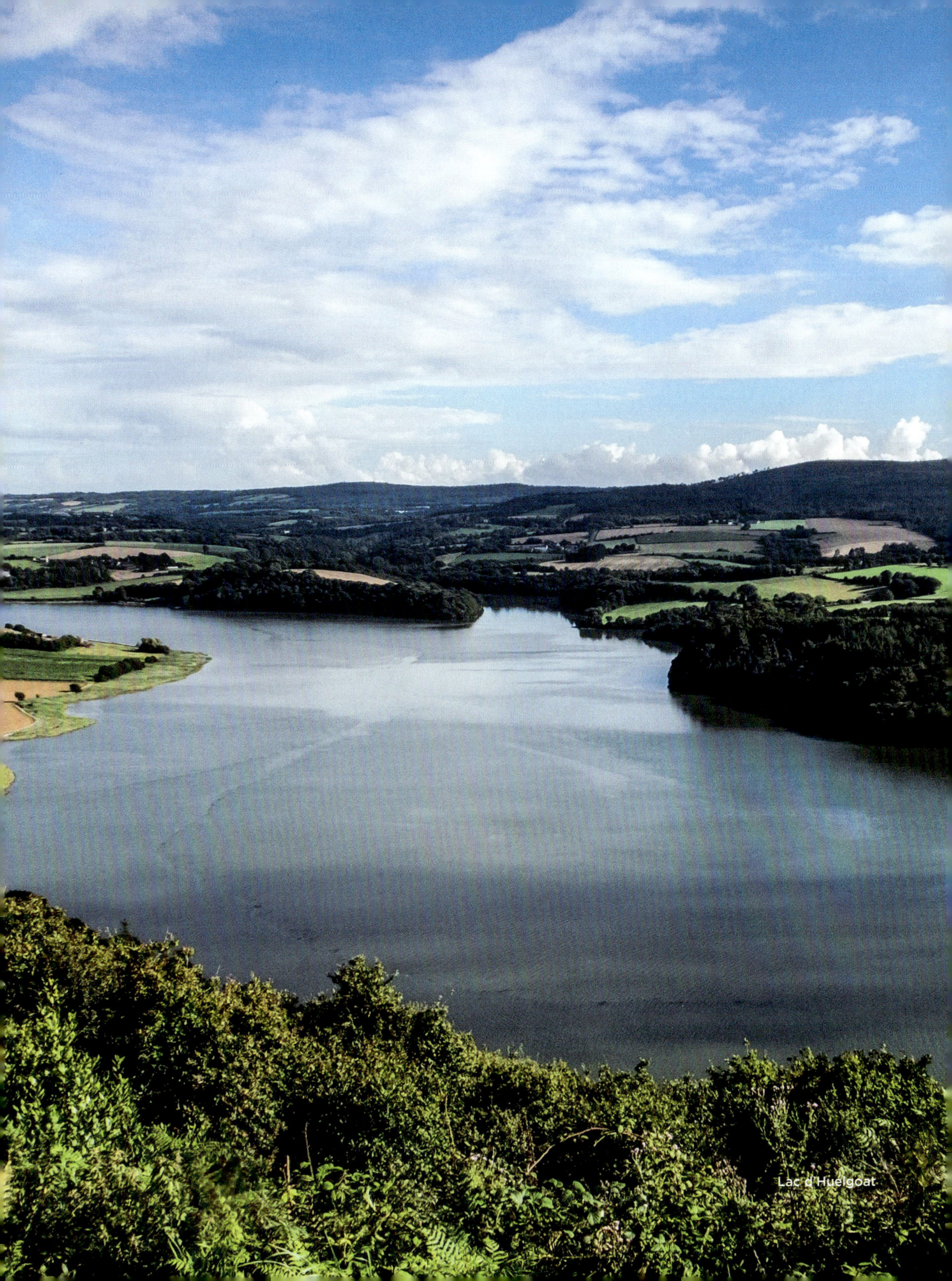
Lac d'Huelgoat

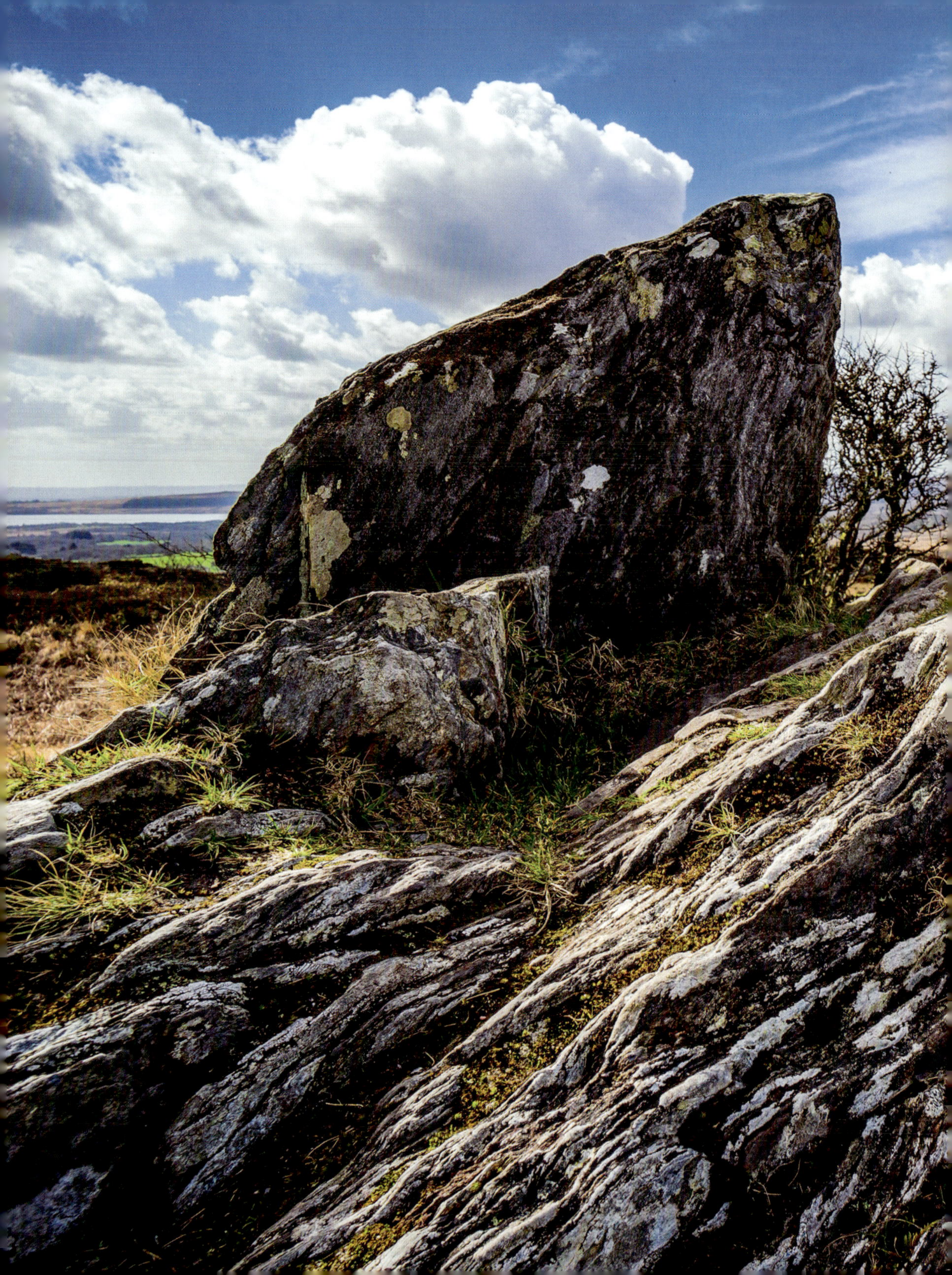

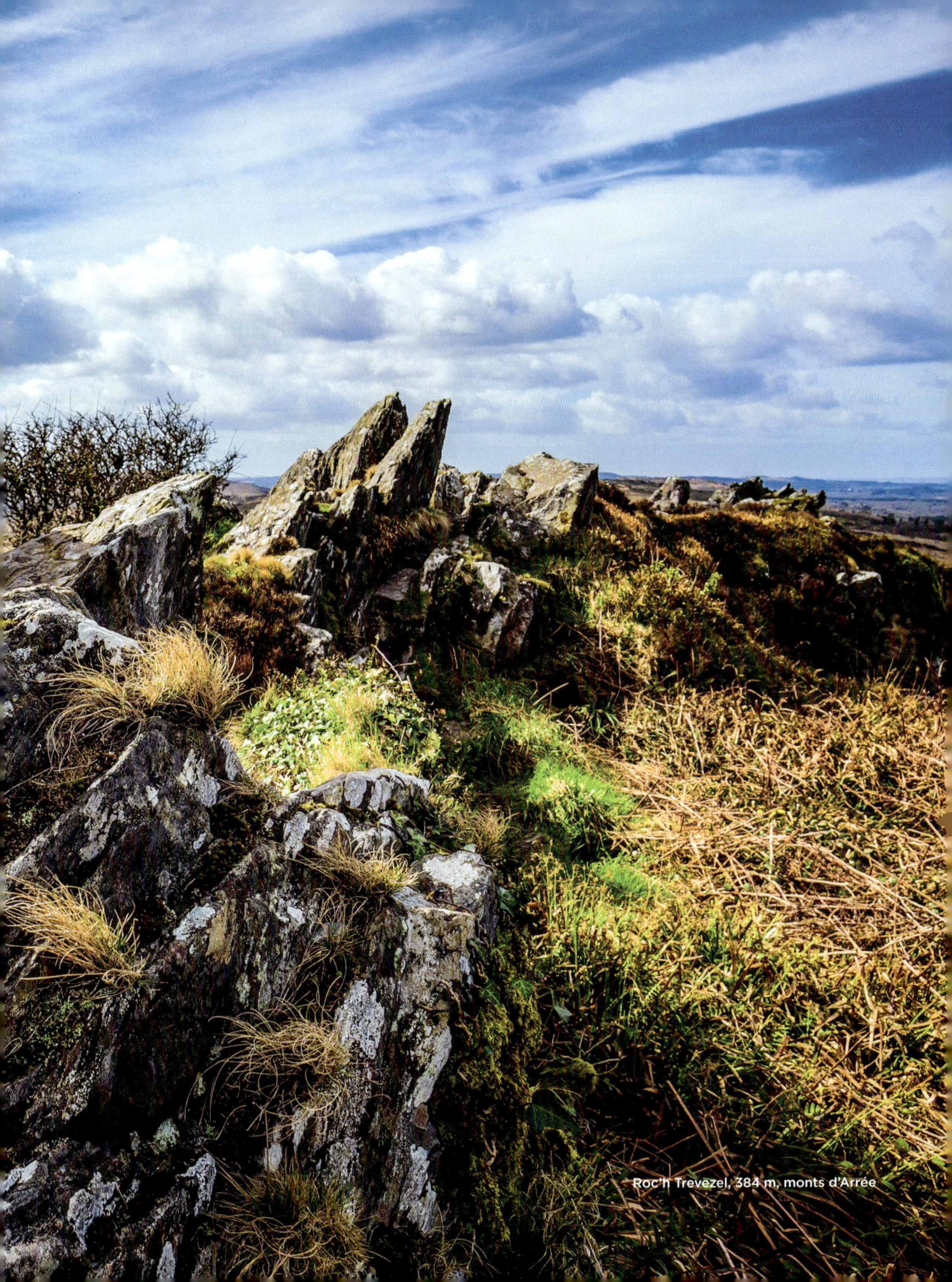

Roc'h Trevezel, 384 m, monts d'Arrée

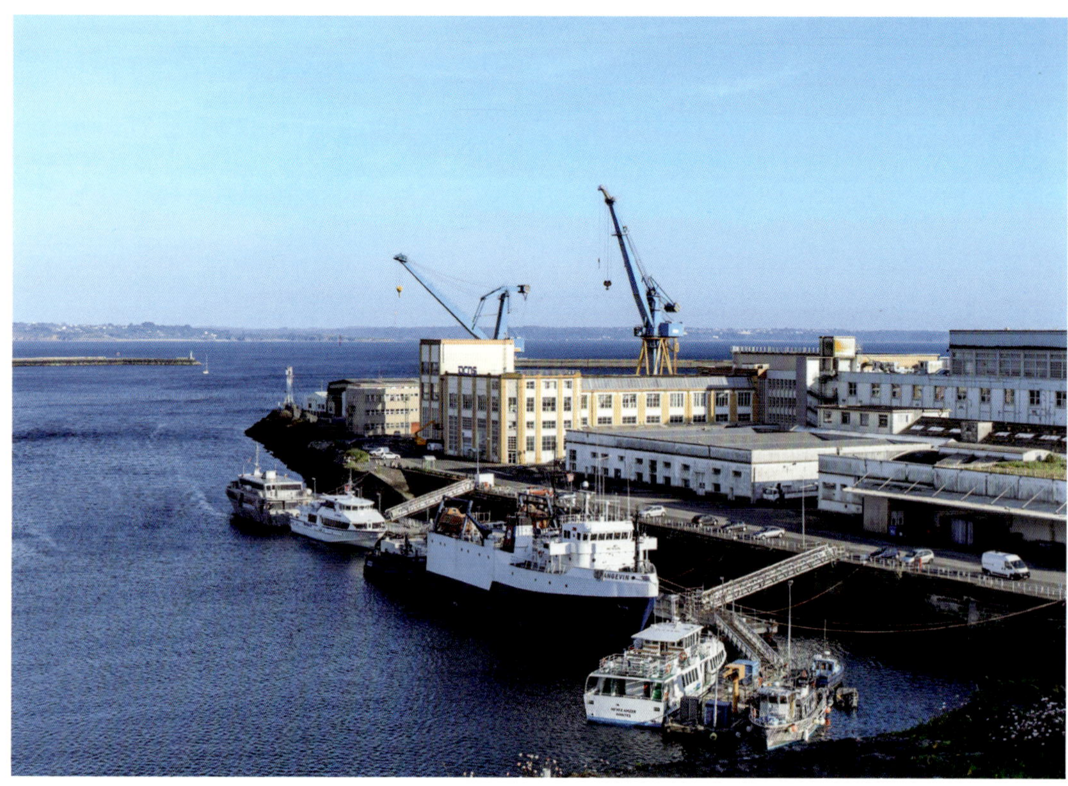

Le port de Brest

Brest

This city at the western end of Brittany is the second largest military port in France after Toulon. Due to its proximity to the Atlantic Ocean, it benefits from a maritime climate with moderate temperatures. Every four years the "Fêtes Maritimes" takes place in Brest - a meeting of traditional boats from all over the world.

Brest

Deuxième port militaire en France après Toulon, Brest est située à l'extrémité ouest de la Bretagne. Grâce à la proximité de l'océan Atlantique, Brest subit rarement des extrêmes au niveau des températures et son climat est tempéré océanique.
Tous les quatre ans, les fêtes maritimes de Brest offrent un rassemblement de bateaux traditionnels venant des quatre coins du globe.

Brest

Die Stadt am westlichen Ende der Bretagne ist nach Toulon der zweitgrößte Militärhafen Frankreichs. Durch die Nähe zum Atlantik profitiert sie von einem maritimen Klima mit gemäßigten Temperaturen. Alle vier Jahre finden in Brest die „Fêtes Maritimes" statt – ein Treffen traditioneller Boote aus aller Welt.

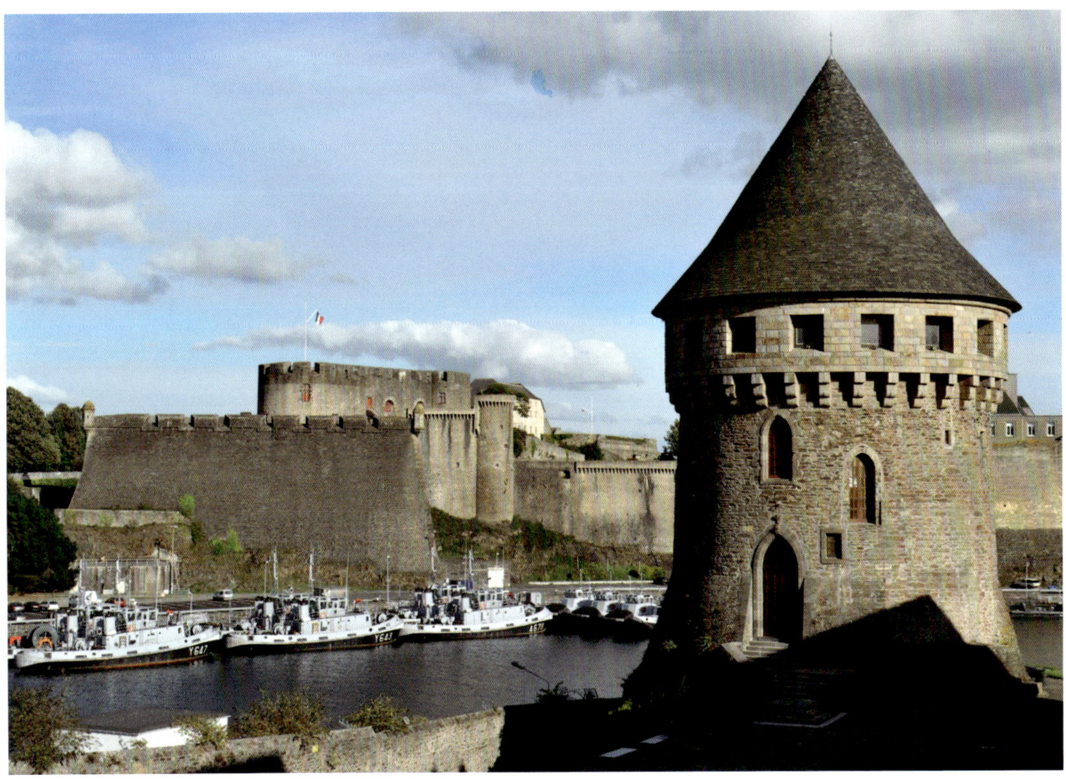

La tour Tanguy et le château, Brest

Brest

Esta ciudad, situada en el extremo occidental de Bretaña, es el segundo puerto militar más grande de Francia después de Toulon. Debido a su proximidad al océano Atlántico, se beneficia de un clima marítimo con temperaturas moderadas. Cada cuatro años se celebran en Brest las «Fêtes Maritimes», un encuentro de barcos tradicionales de todo el mundo.

Brest

A cidade no extremo oeste da Bretanha é o segundo maior porto militar da França, a seguir a de Toulon. Devido à sua proximidade com o Oceano Atlântico, beneficia de um clima marítimo com temperaturas moderadas. De quatro em quatro anos, realizam-se em Brest as Festas Marítimas „Les Fêtes Maritimes"- um encontro de barcos tradicionais de todo o mundo.

Brest

De stad aan het westelijke uiteinde van Bretagne is na Toulon de grootste militaire haven van Frankrijk. Door de nabijheid van de Atlantische Oceaan profiteert hij van een zeeklimaat met gematigde temperaturen. Om de vier jaar vinden in Brest de 'Fêtes Maritimes' plaats, waar traditionele boten uit de hele wereld op afkomen.

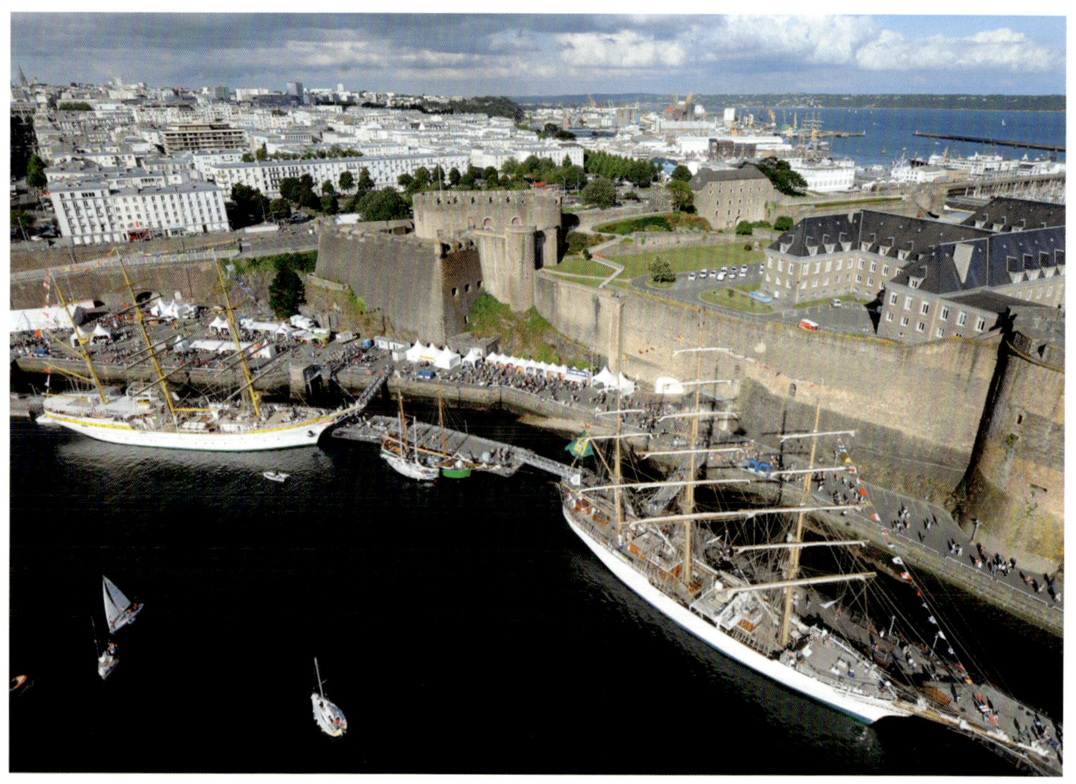

Le port de Brest

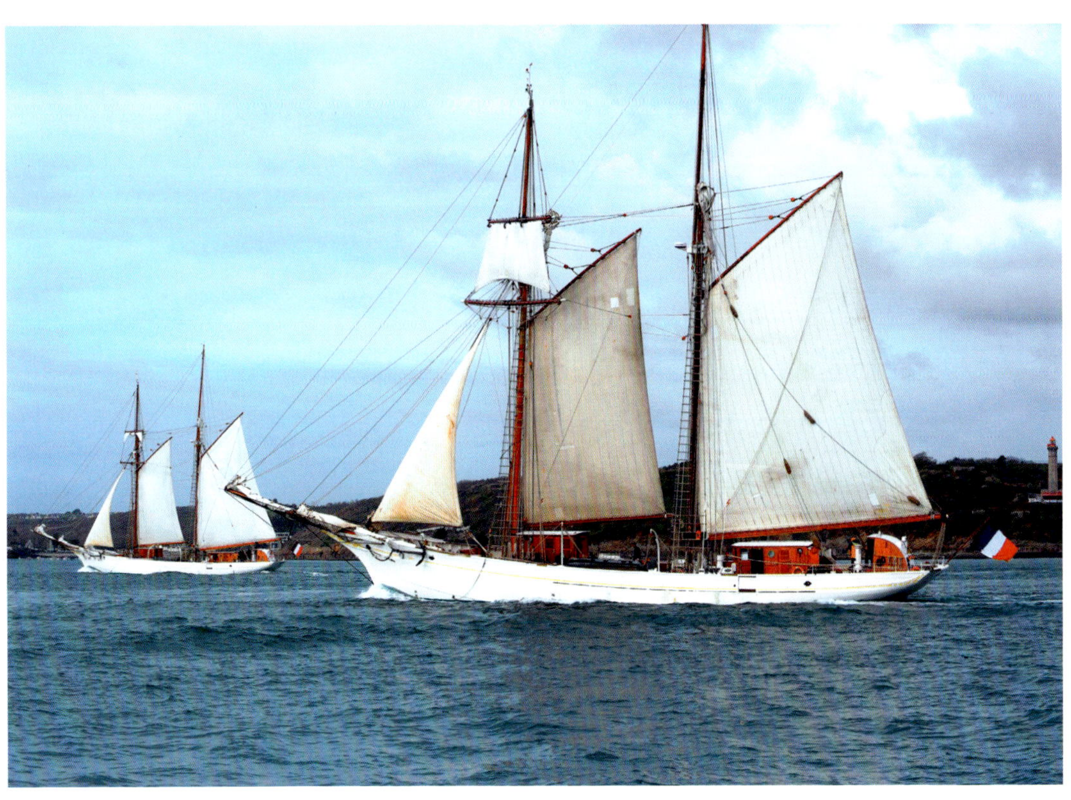

La *Belle Poule* et *L'Étoile*, goélettes dans le port de Brest

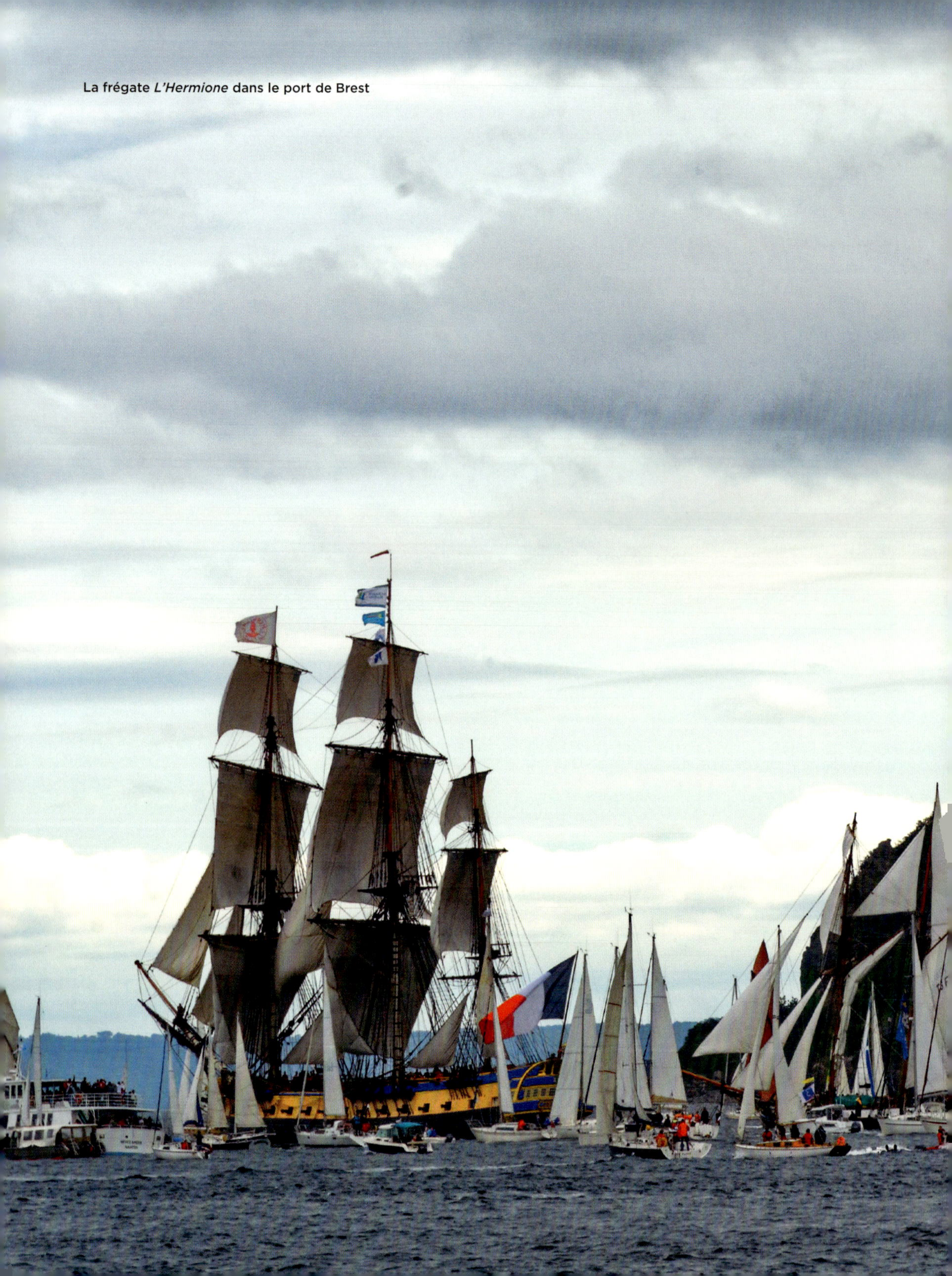

La frégate *L'Hermione* dans le port de Brest

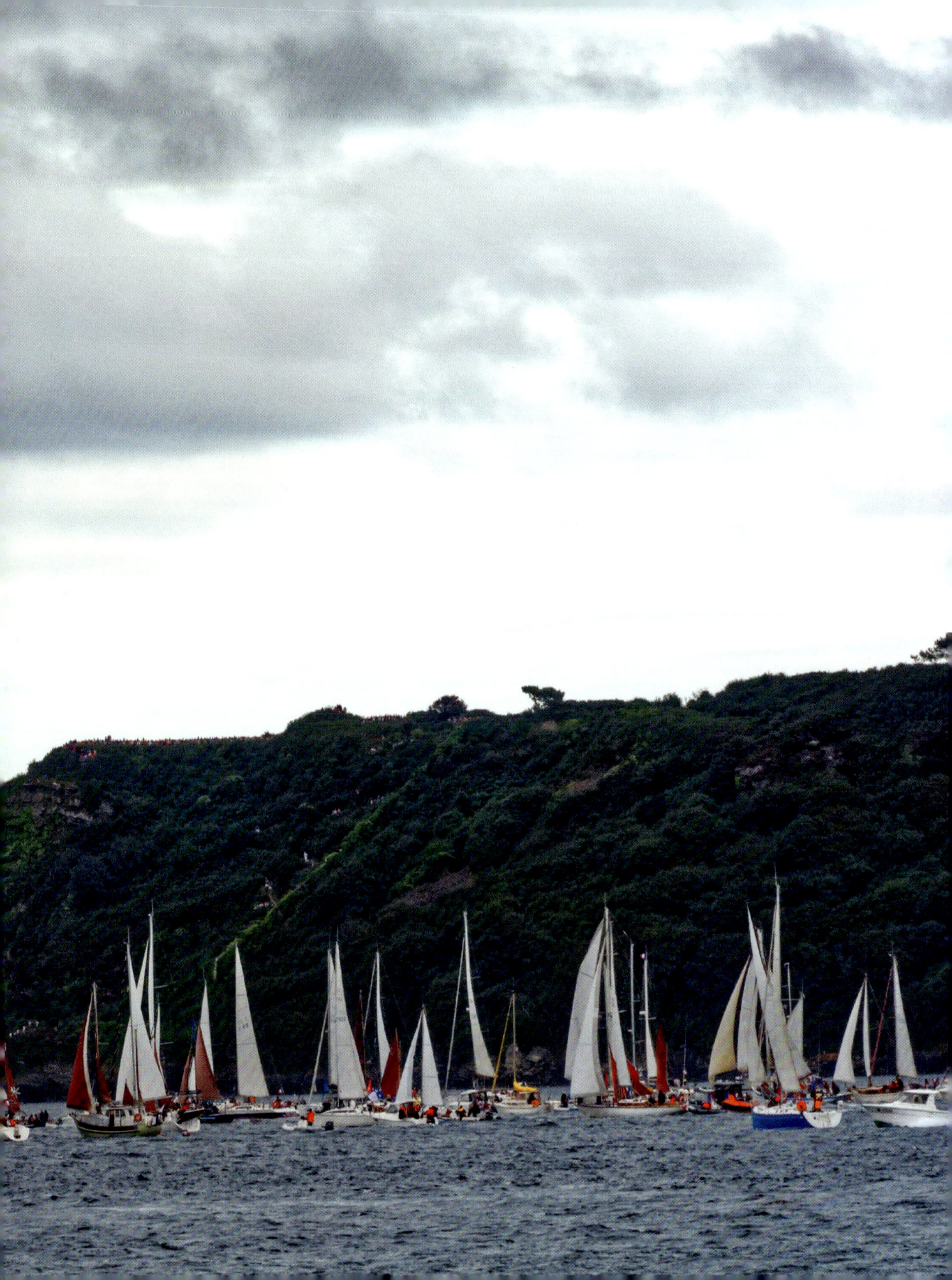

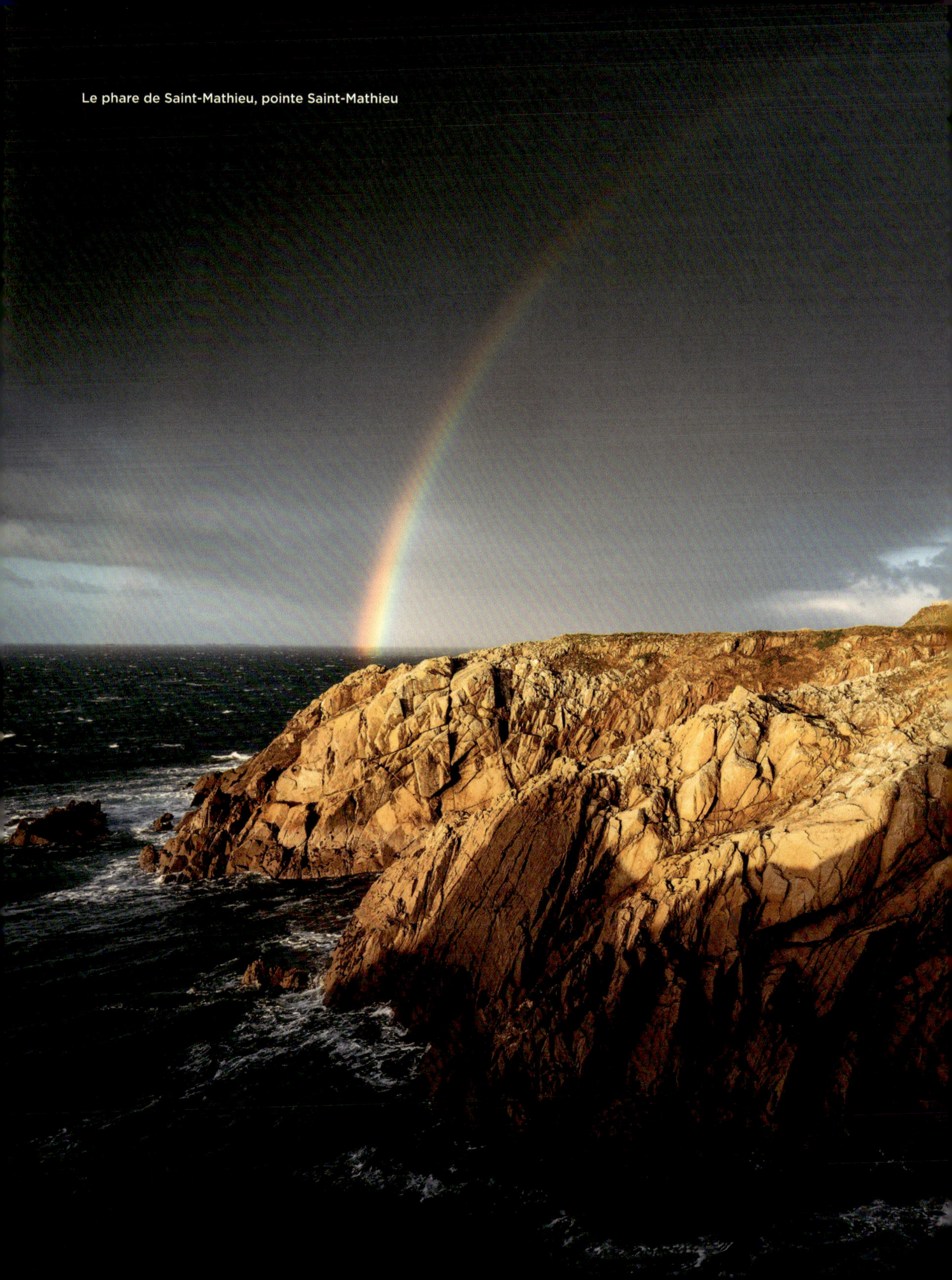

Le phare de Saint-Mathieu, pointe Saint-Mathieu

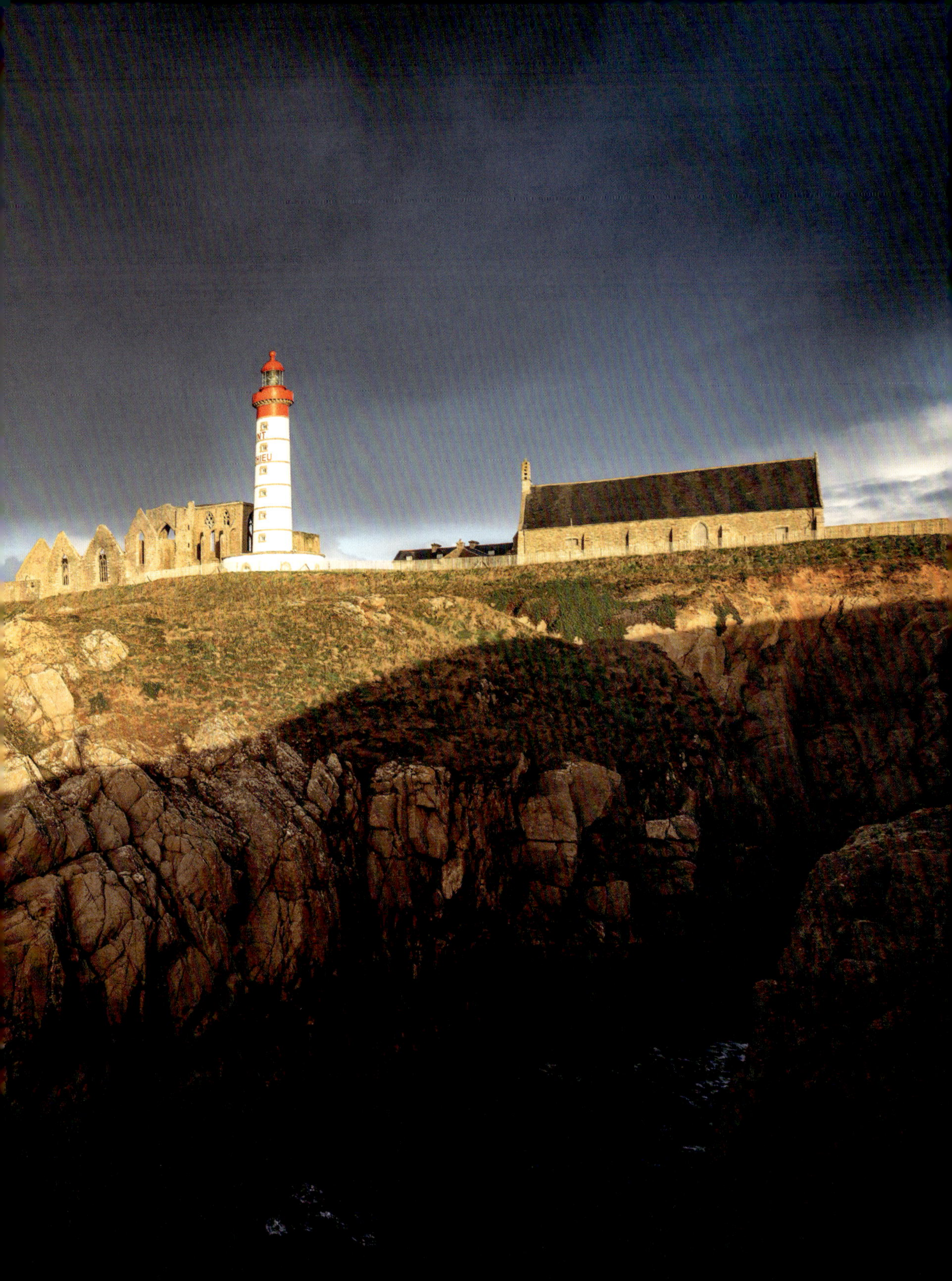

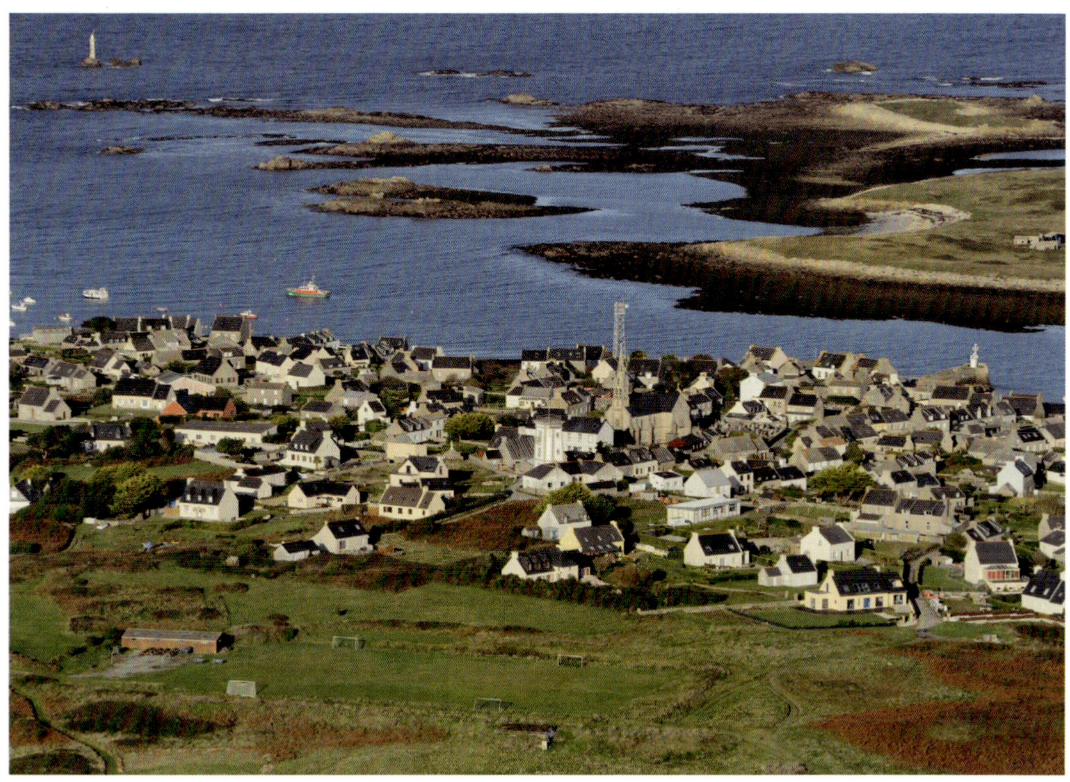

L'île de Molène

The Île de Molène

The Île de Molène stands out from the other Breton islands because of its rich biodiversity and varied landscapes. Depending on the seasons, the viewpoints offer ever different views of the coastline, which changes with the tides.

L'île de Molène

L'île de Molène ne ressemble à aucune autre de par sa biodiversité et ses paysages changeants. Selon les heures de la journée, les saisons et les points de vue, au rythme des marées montantes et descendantes, des îlots disparaissent quand d'autres poussent à vue d'œil.

Die Île de Molène

Die Île de Molène hebt sich durch ihren Artenreichtum und ihre vielfältigen Landschaften von den anderen bretonischen Inseln ab. Abhängig von den Jahreszeiten bieten die Aussichtspunkte immer wieder neue Ansichten der Küste, die sich im Wechsel der Gezeiten wandelt.

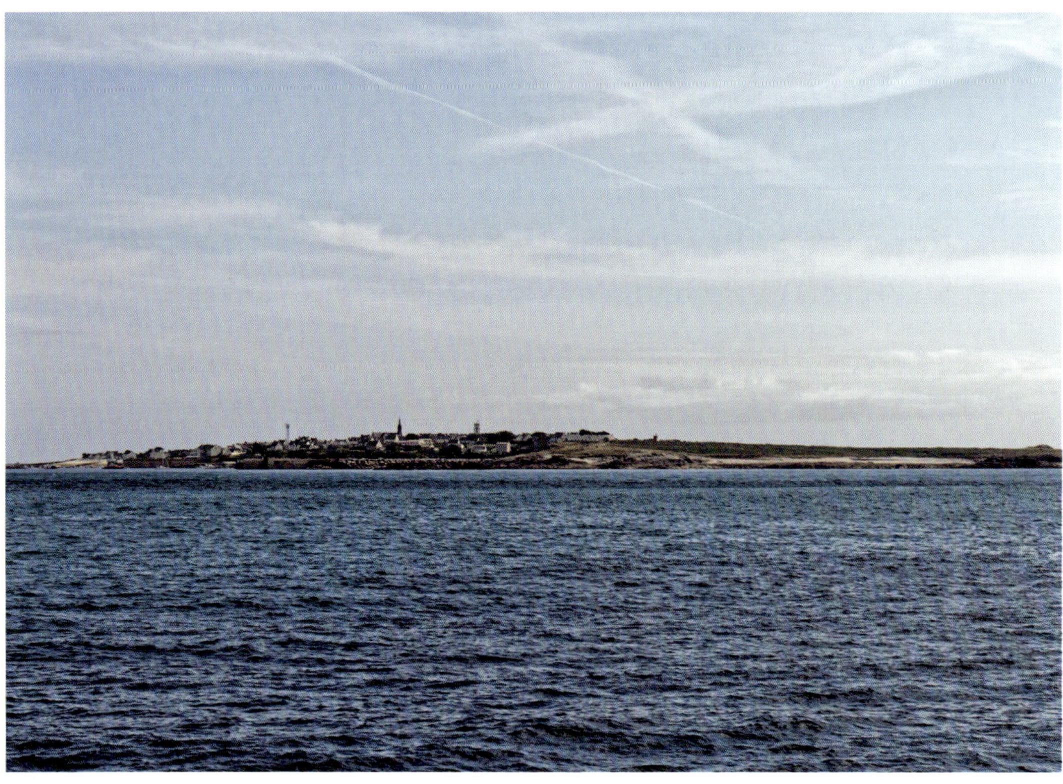

L'île de Molène

La Île de Molène

La Île de Molène se distingue del resto de las islas bretonas por su rica biodiversidad y sus variados paisajes. Dependiendo de las estaciones, los miradores ofrecen nuevas vistas de la costa, que cambian a medida que lo hacen las mareas.

A Île de Molène

A Île de Molène destaca-se das outras ilhas bretãs pela sua rica biodiversidade e paisagens variadas. Dependendo das estações do ano, os miradouros oferecem vistas panorâmicas da costa renovadas, que mudam também consoante as marés.

Het Île de Molène

Het Île de Molène onderscheidt zich van de andere Bretonse eilanden door zijn soortenrijkdom en gevarieerde landschappen. Afhankelijk van de seizoenen bieden de uitkijkpunten steeds nieuwe uitzichten over de kust, die veranderen met de wisselende getijden.

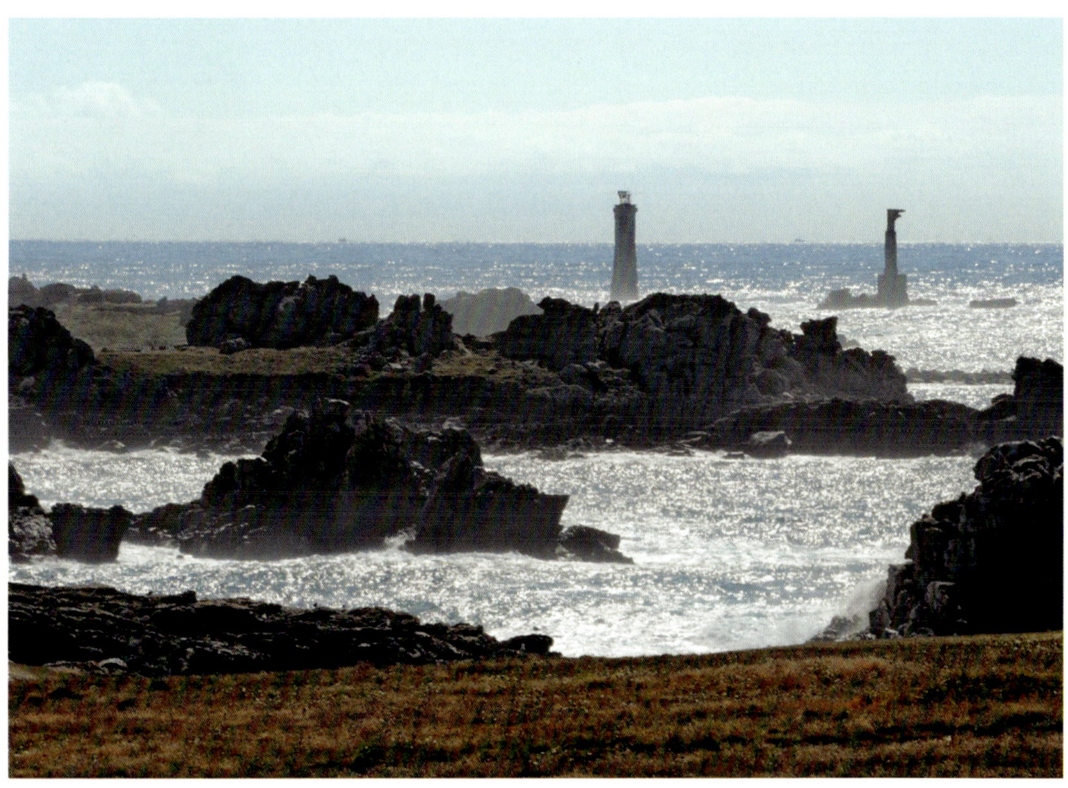

L'île d'Ouessant

Ouessant

The isolated island of Ouessant is just 8 km long and 4 km wide. In winter, violent storms rage over the harsh landscape, as evidenced by the rugged cliffs formed by the power of the sea.

L'île d'Ouessant

Symbole de l'isolement, Ouessant ne fait que 8 km de long et 4 km de large. Théâtre de tempêtes hivernales spectaculaires, l'île offre des paysages majestueux. Ses hautes falaises ciselées par l'océan disent la puissance des éléments.

Ouessant

Die isolierte Insel Ouessant ist gerade mal 8 km lang und 4 km breit. Im Winter toben über ihrer rauen Landschaft heftige Stürme, von denen die schroffen Klippen zeugen, die durch die Kraft des Meeres geformt wurden.

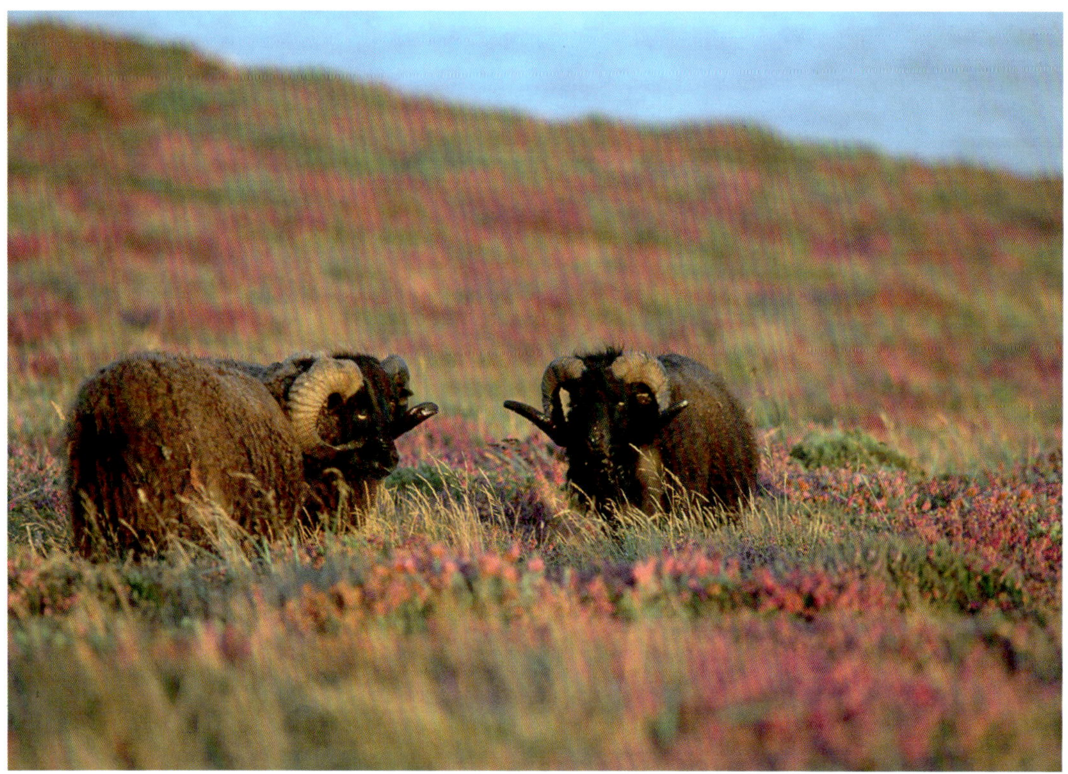

L'île d'Ouessant

Ouessant

La apartada isla de Ouessant tiene solo 8 km de largo y 4 km de ancho. En invierno, violentas tormentas se ciernen sobre su escarpado paisaje, que se caracteriza por los escarpados acantilados formados por el poder del mar.

Ouessant

A ilha isolada de Ouessant tem apenas 8 km de comprimento e 4 km de largura. No inverno, ocorrem tempestades violentas que varrem a sua paisagem acidentada, bem e testemunhado pelas falésias escarpadas formadas pela força do mar.

Ouessant

Het geïsoleerde eiland Ouessant is slechts 8 km lang en 4 km breed. In de winter woeden hevige stormen over het ruige landschap. Hiervan getuigen de ruige klippen die door de kracht van de zee gevormd worden.

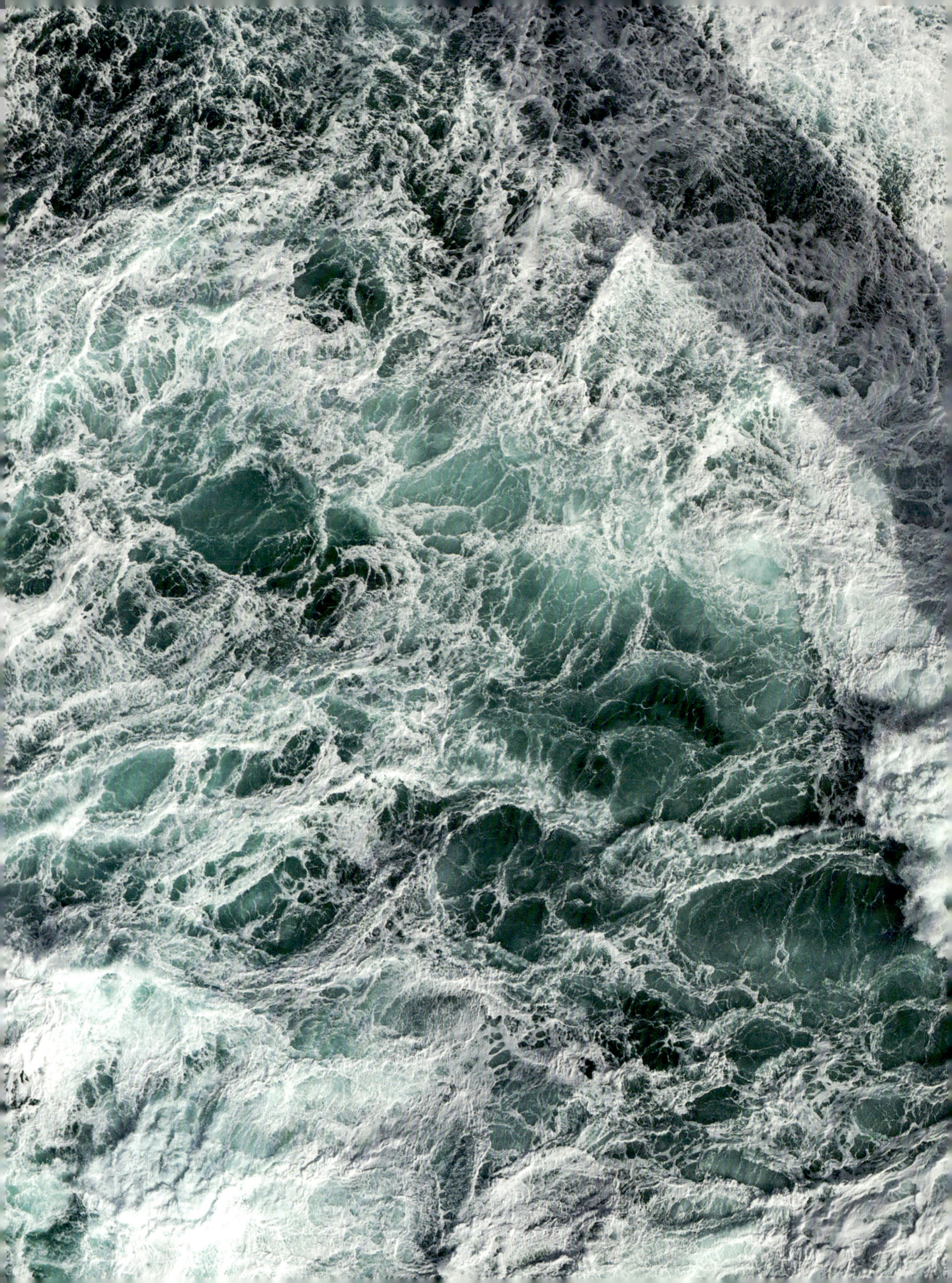

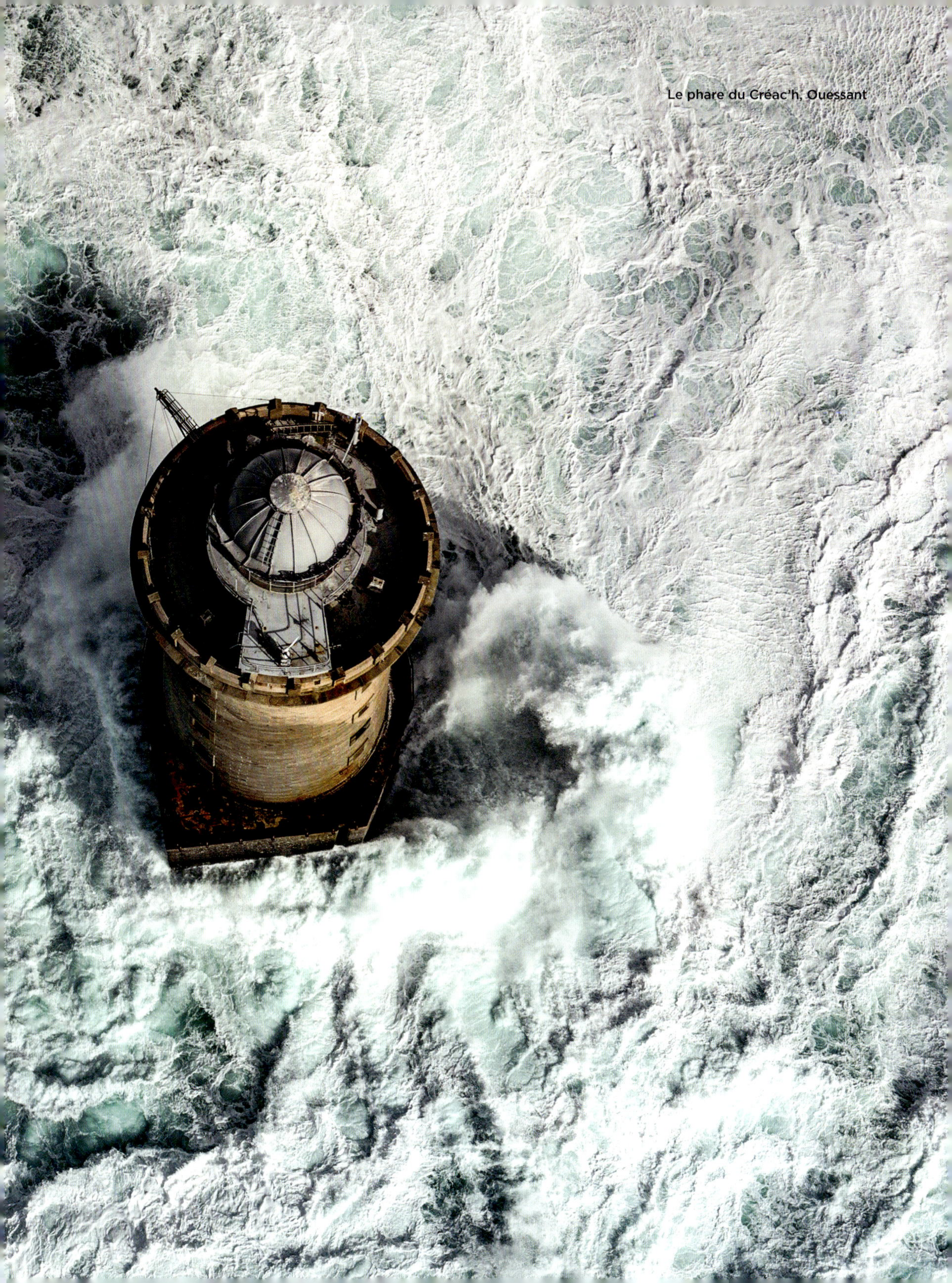

Le phare du Créac'h, Ouessant

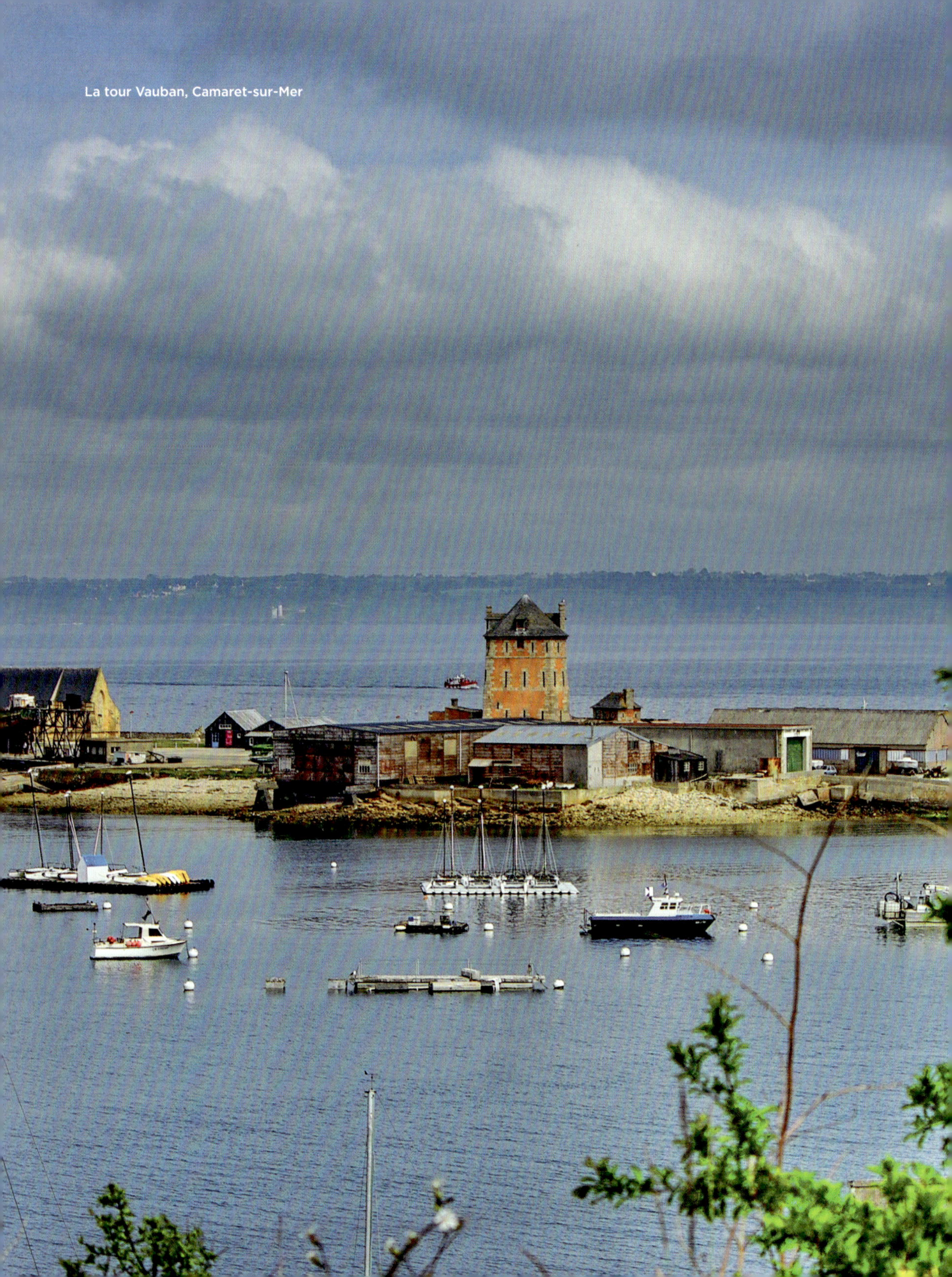

La tour Vauban, Camaret-sur-Mer

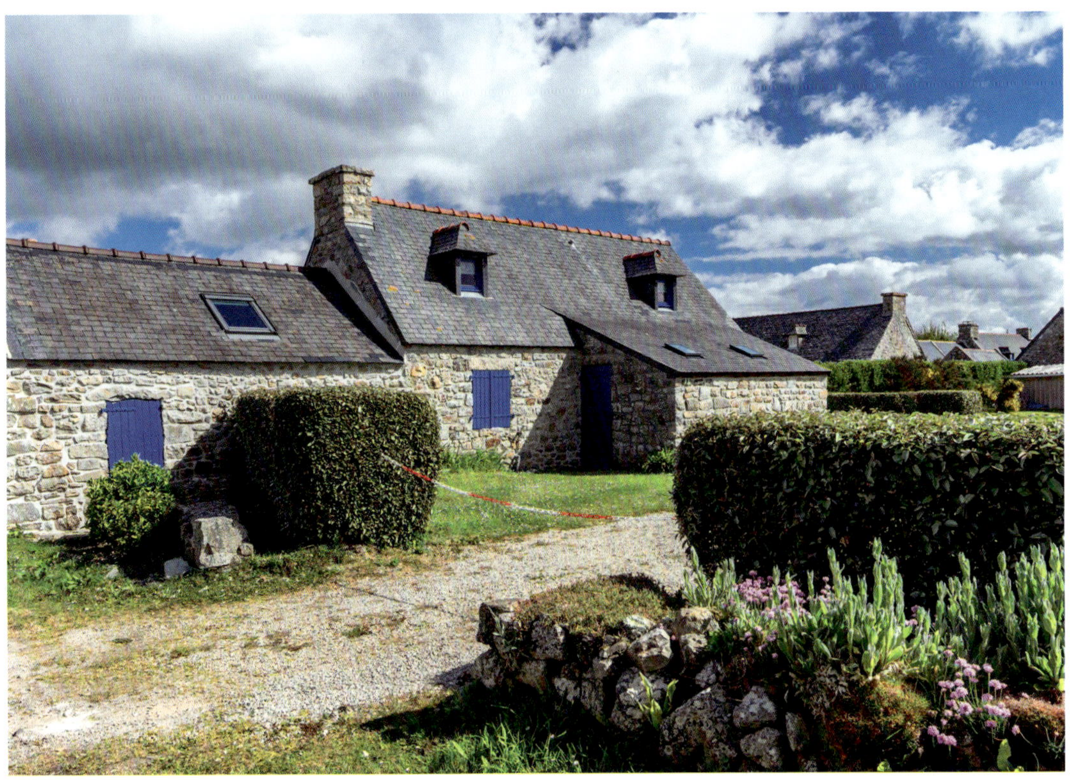

Rostudel, presqu'île de Crozon

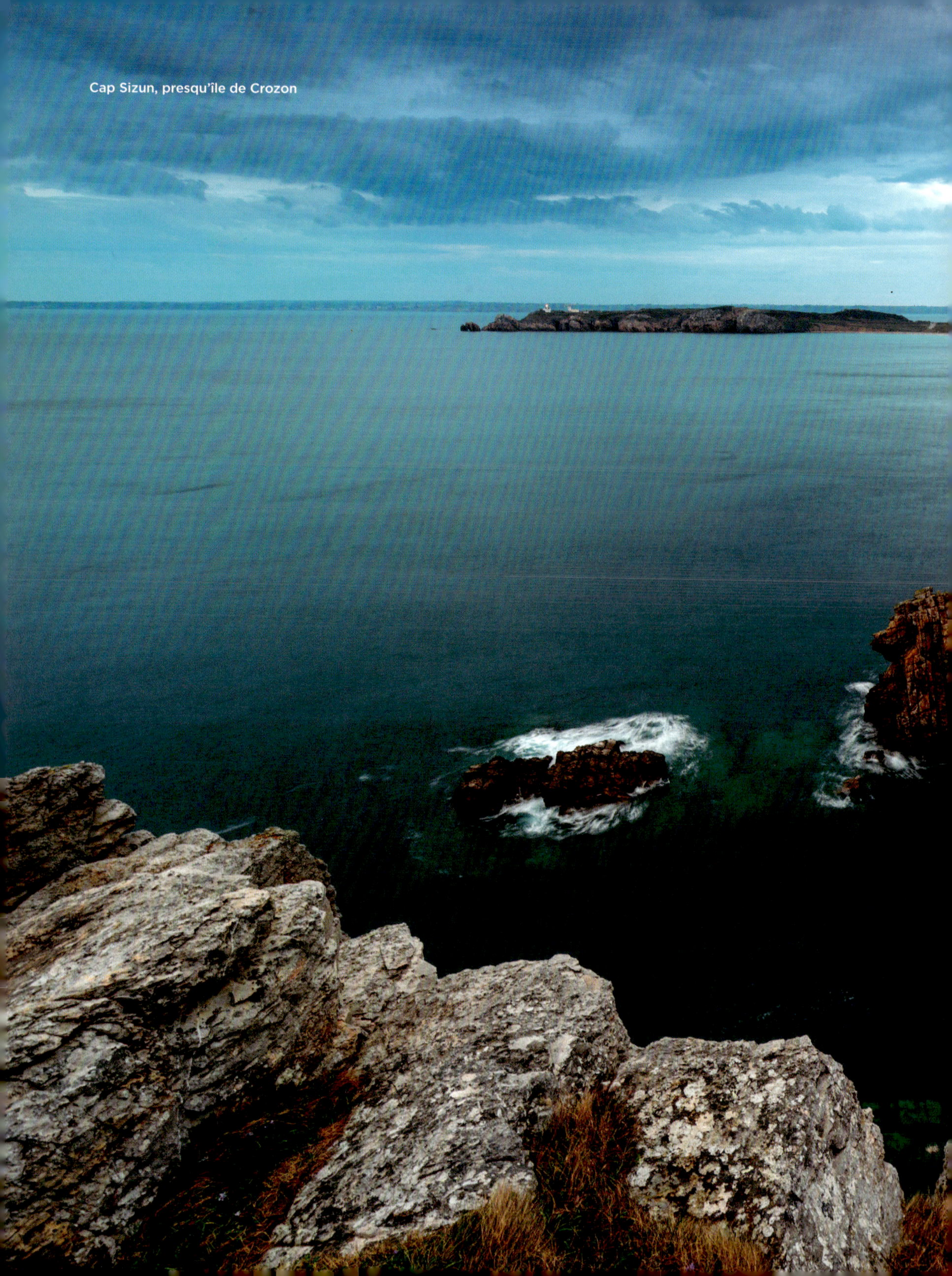
Cap Sizun, presqu'île de Crozon

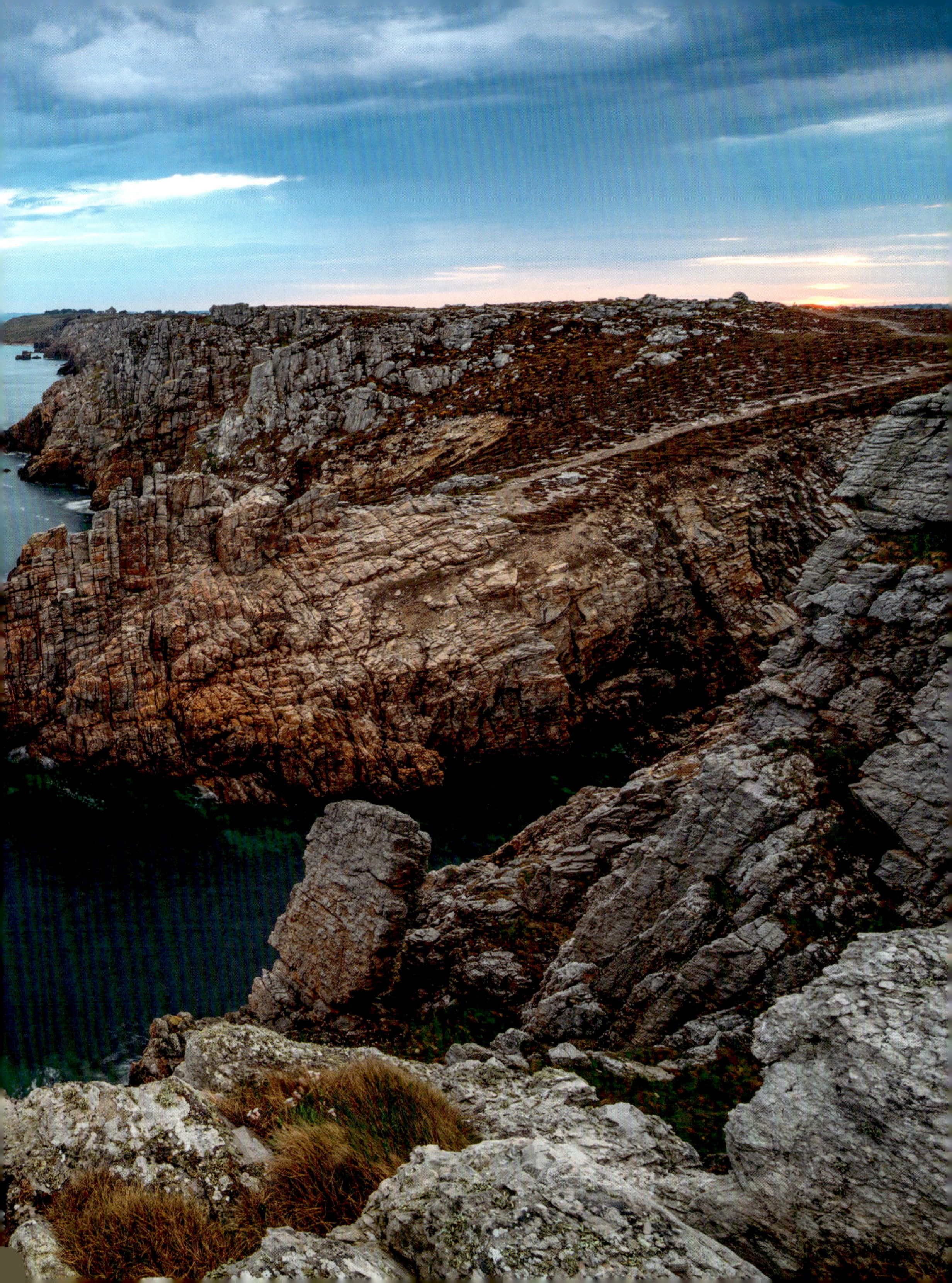

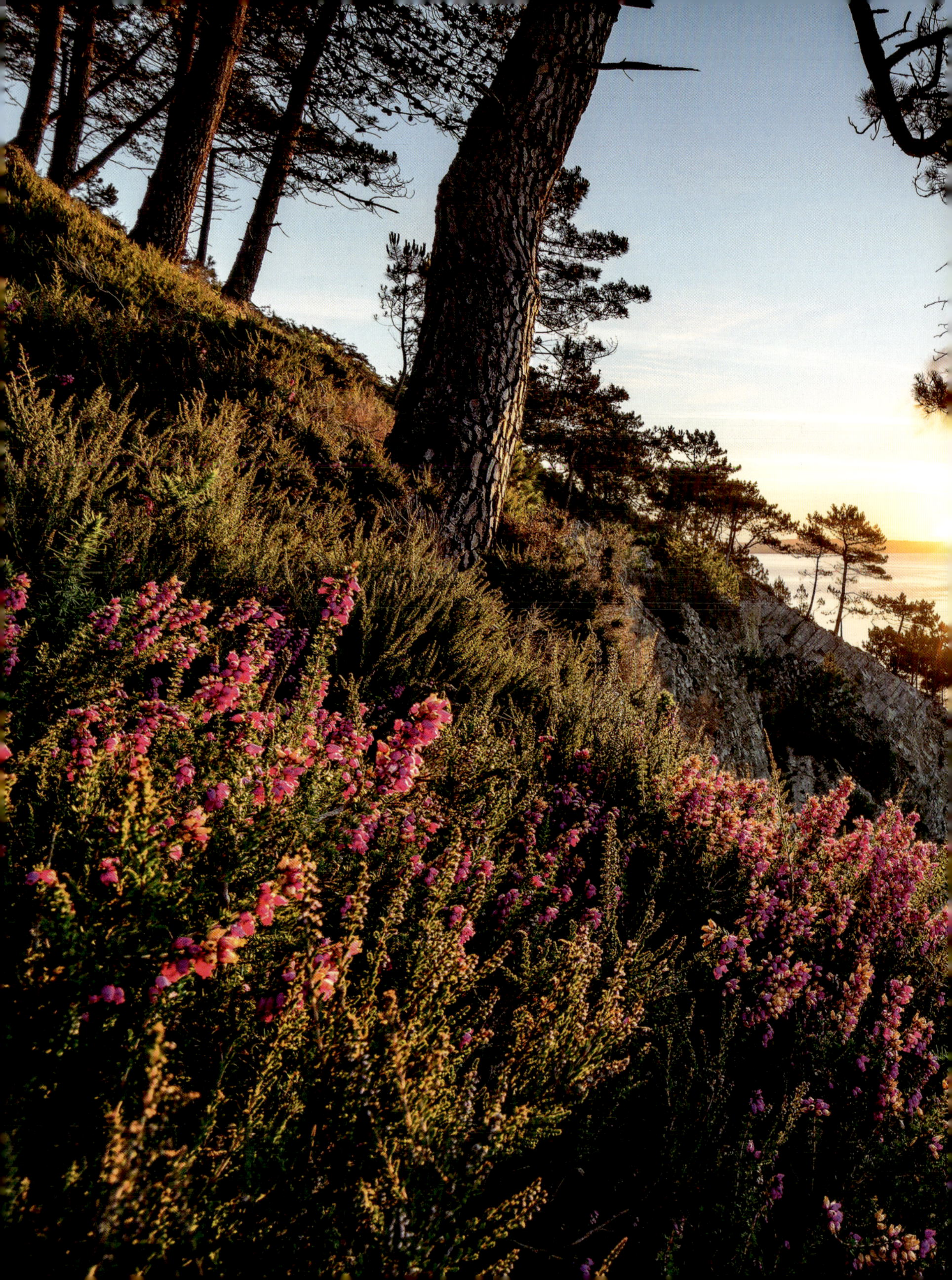

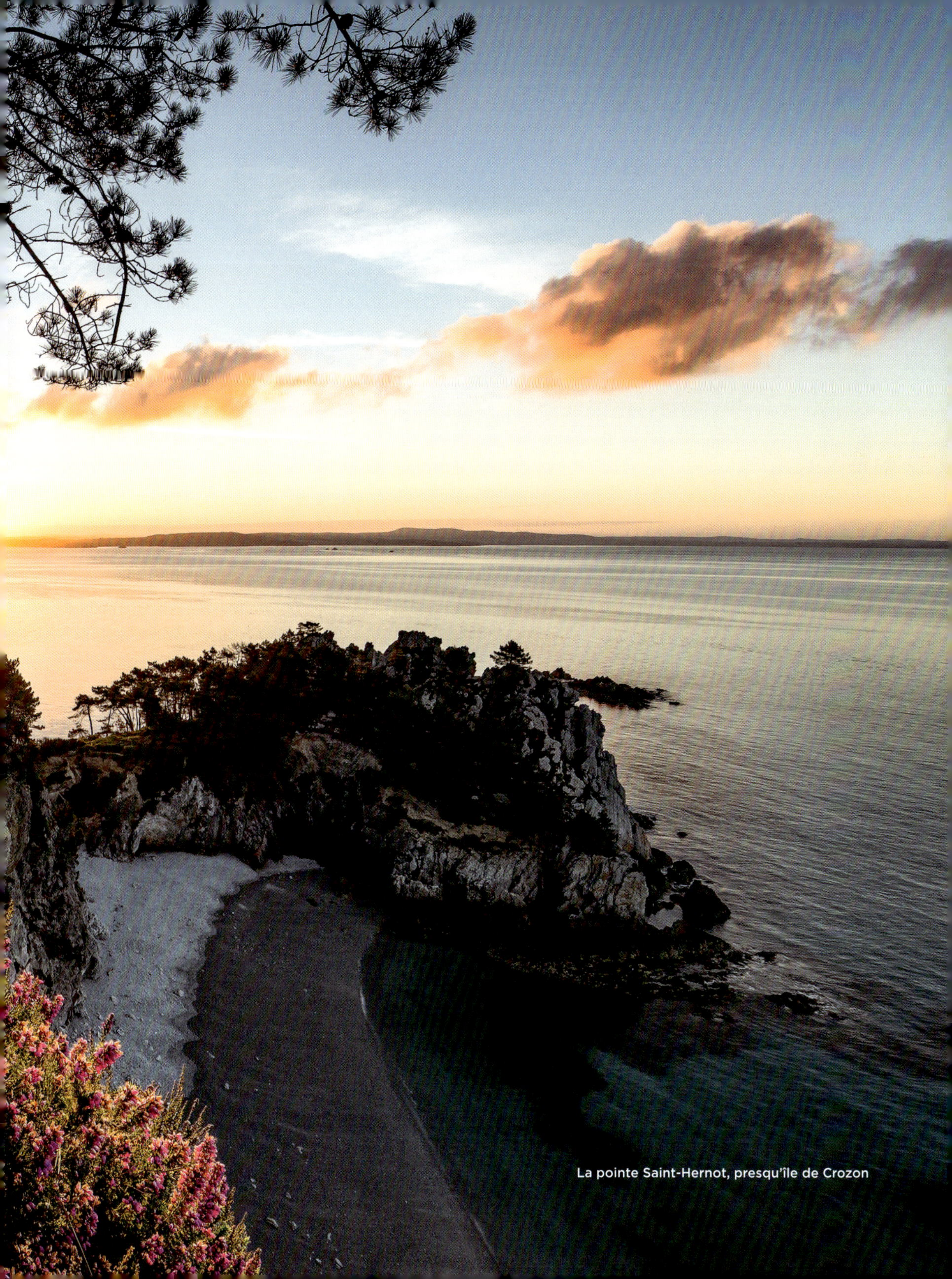

La pointe Saint-Hernot, presqu'île de Crozon

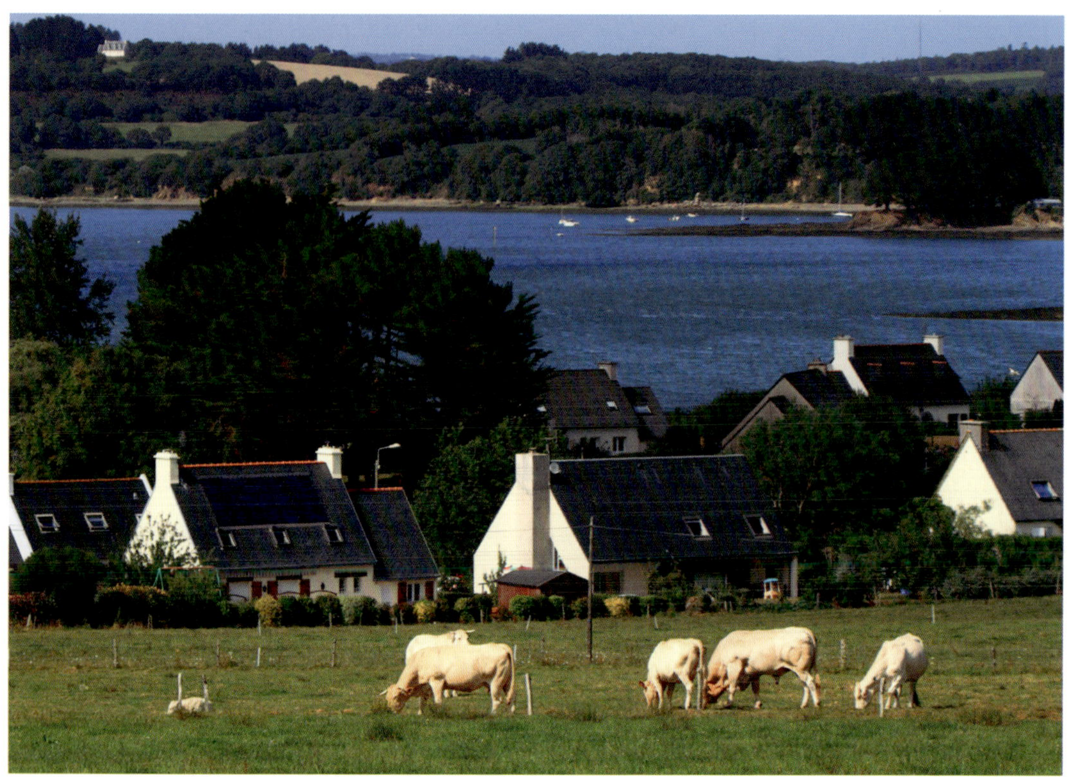

Lanvéoc, presqu'île de Crozon

The Crozon Peninsula

Opposite Brest is the peninsula
Crozon, which belongs to the
Armorique nature park. The
surrounding marine areas are also
partly protected. They belong to
the Iroise Marine Nature Park.

La presqu'île de Crozon

La presqu'île de Crozon, entourée
par la mer, est située en face de
Brest et elle appartient au parc
naturel régional d'Armorique. Les
espaces maritimes qui l'entourent
sont en partie englobés dans le
parc naturel marin d'Iroise.

Die Halbinsel Crozon

Gegenüber von Brest befindet sich
die Halbinsel Crozon, die zum
Naturpark Armorique gehört. Auch
die sie umgebenden Meeresgebiete
stehen zum Teil unter Schutz. Sie
gehören dem Meeresnaturpark
Iroise an.

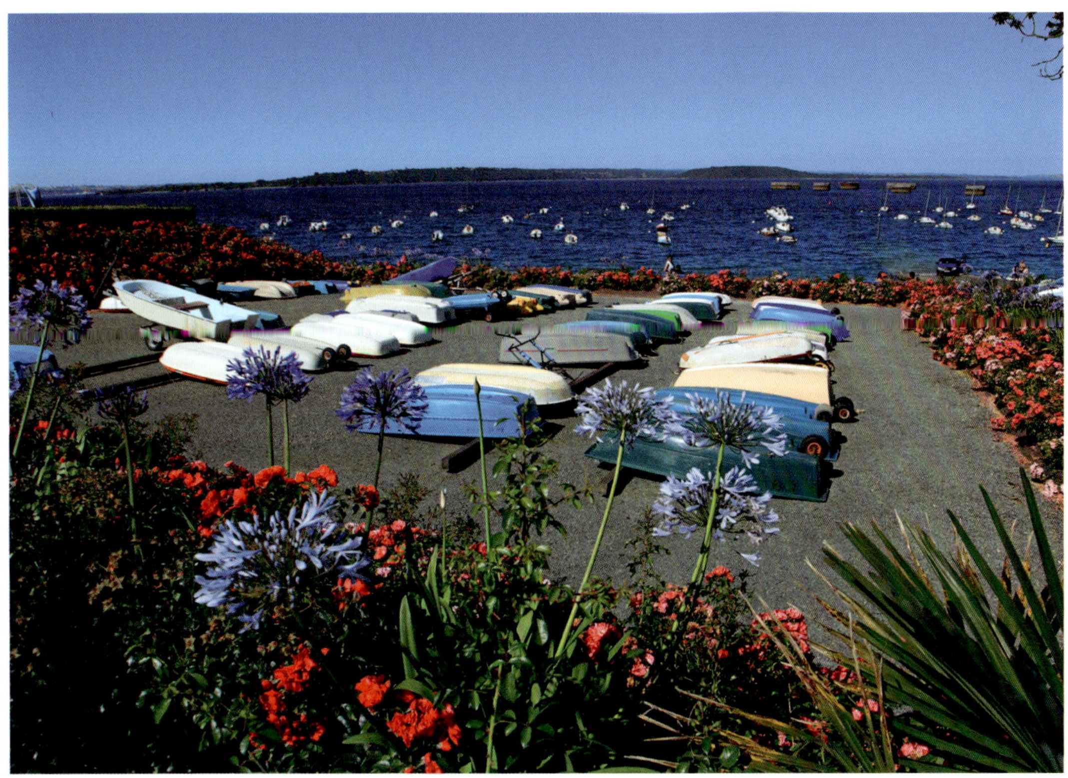

Lanvéoc, presqu'île de Crozon

La Península de Crozon

Frente a Brest se encuentra la península de Crozon, que pertenece al Parque Natural de Armórica. Las áreas marinas circundantes también están parcialmente protegidas. Pertenecen al Parque Natural Marino de Iroise.

A Península de Crozon

Em frente a Brest, encontra-se a península de Crozon, que pertence ao parque natural Armorique. As áreas marinhas circundantes também estão parcialmente protegidas. Pertencem ao Parque Natural Marinho Iroise.

Het schiereiland Crozon

Tegenover Brest ligt het schiereiland Crozon, dat bij het natuurpark Armorique hoort. Ook de omliggende zeegebieden zijn gedeeltelijk beschermd. Ze horen bij het Parc naturel marin Iroise.

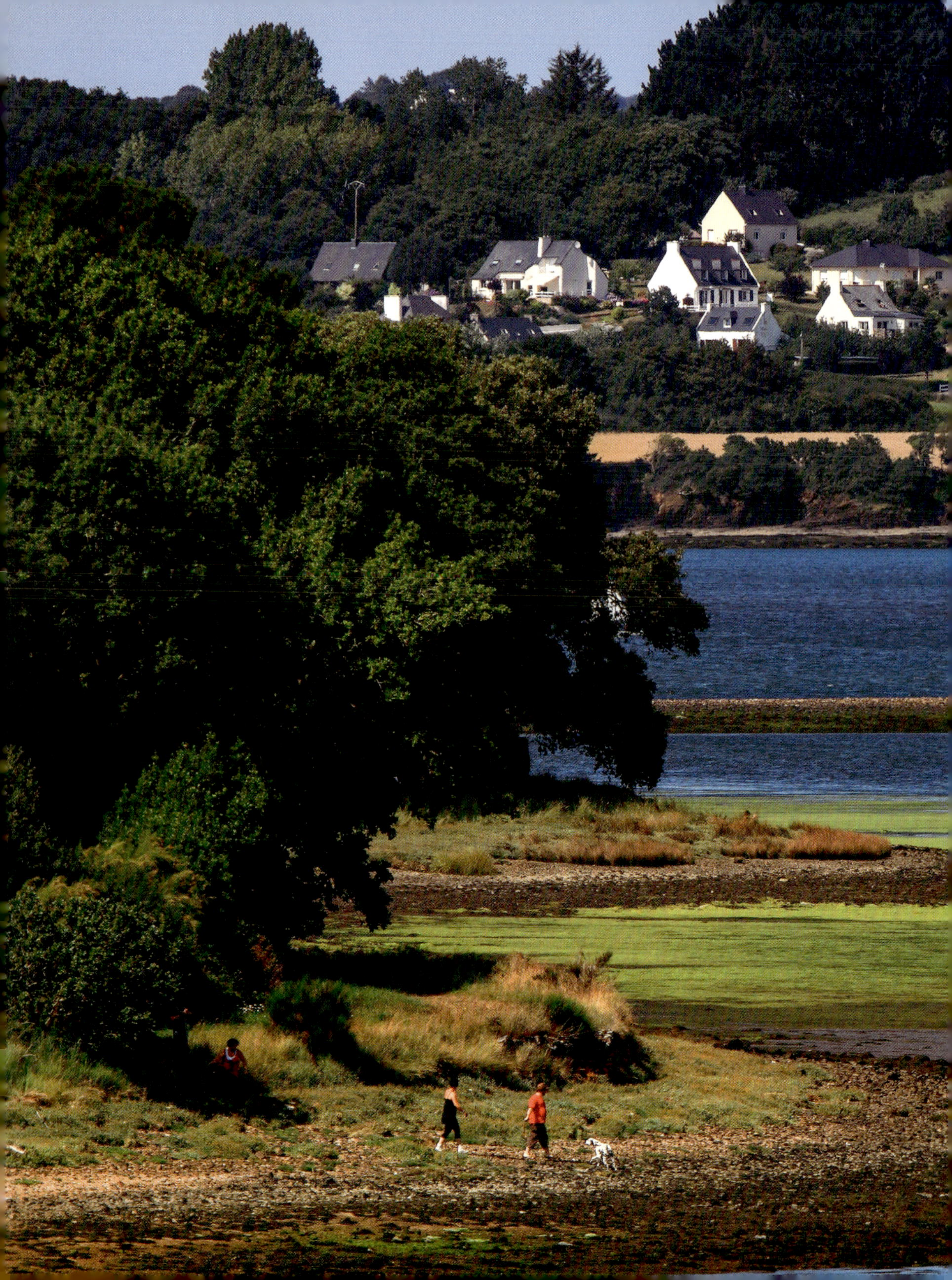

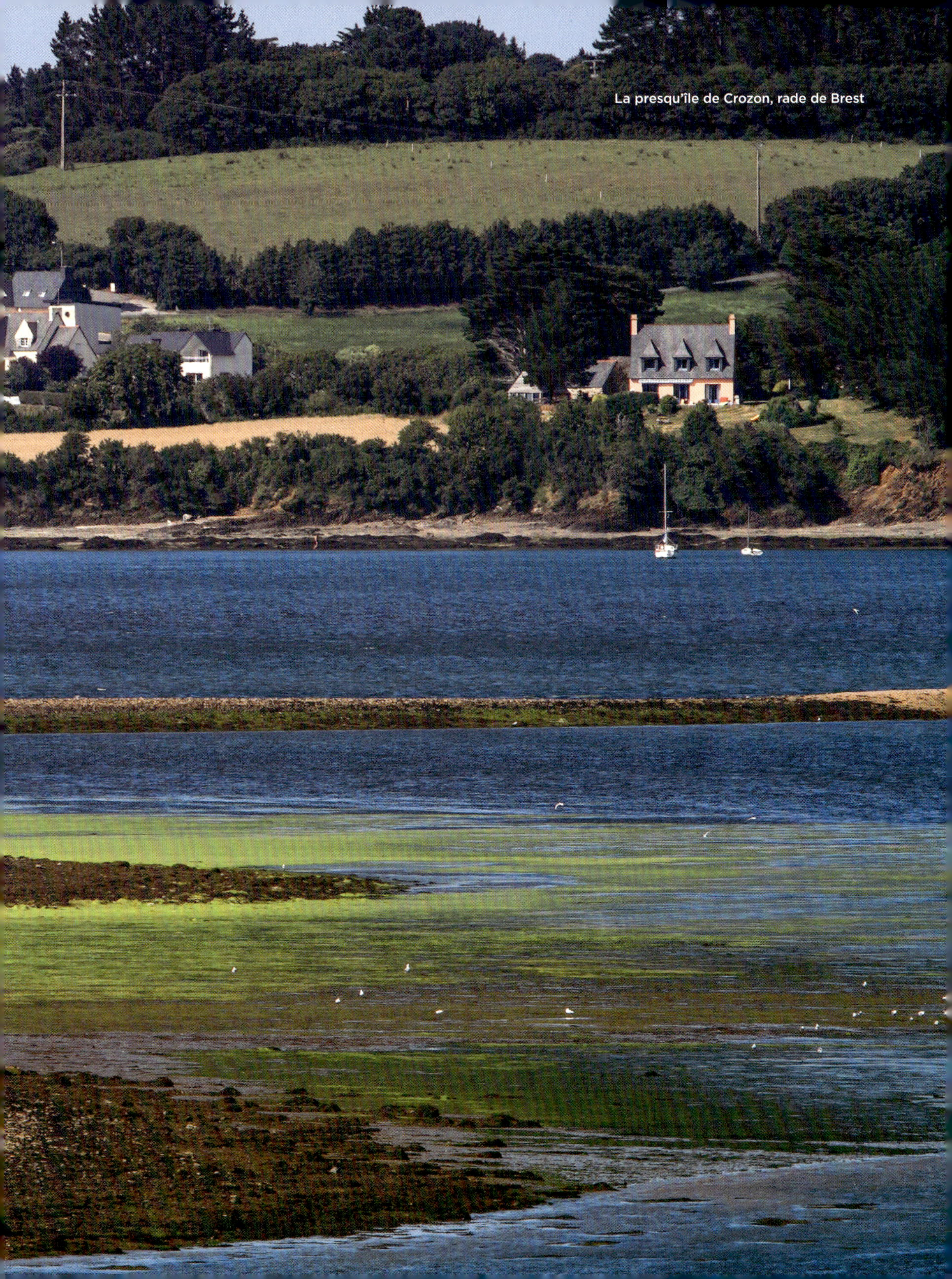

La presqu'île de Crozon, rade de Brest

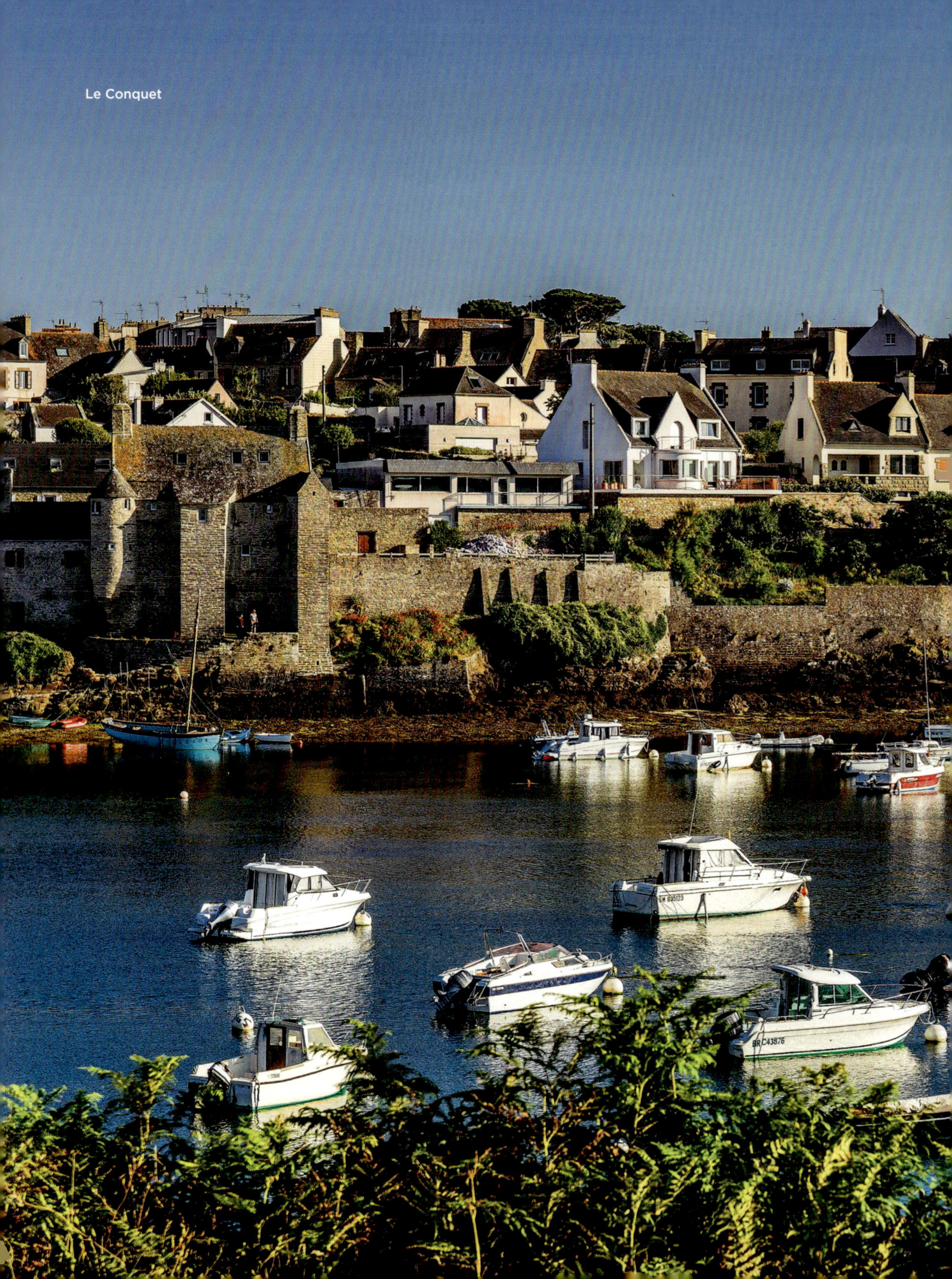
Le Conquet

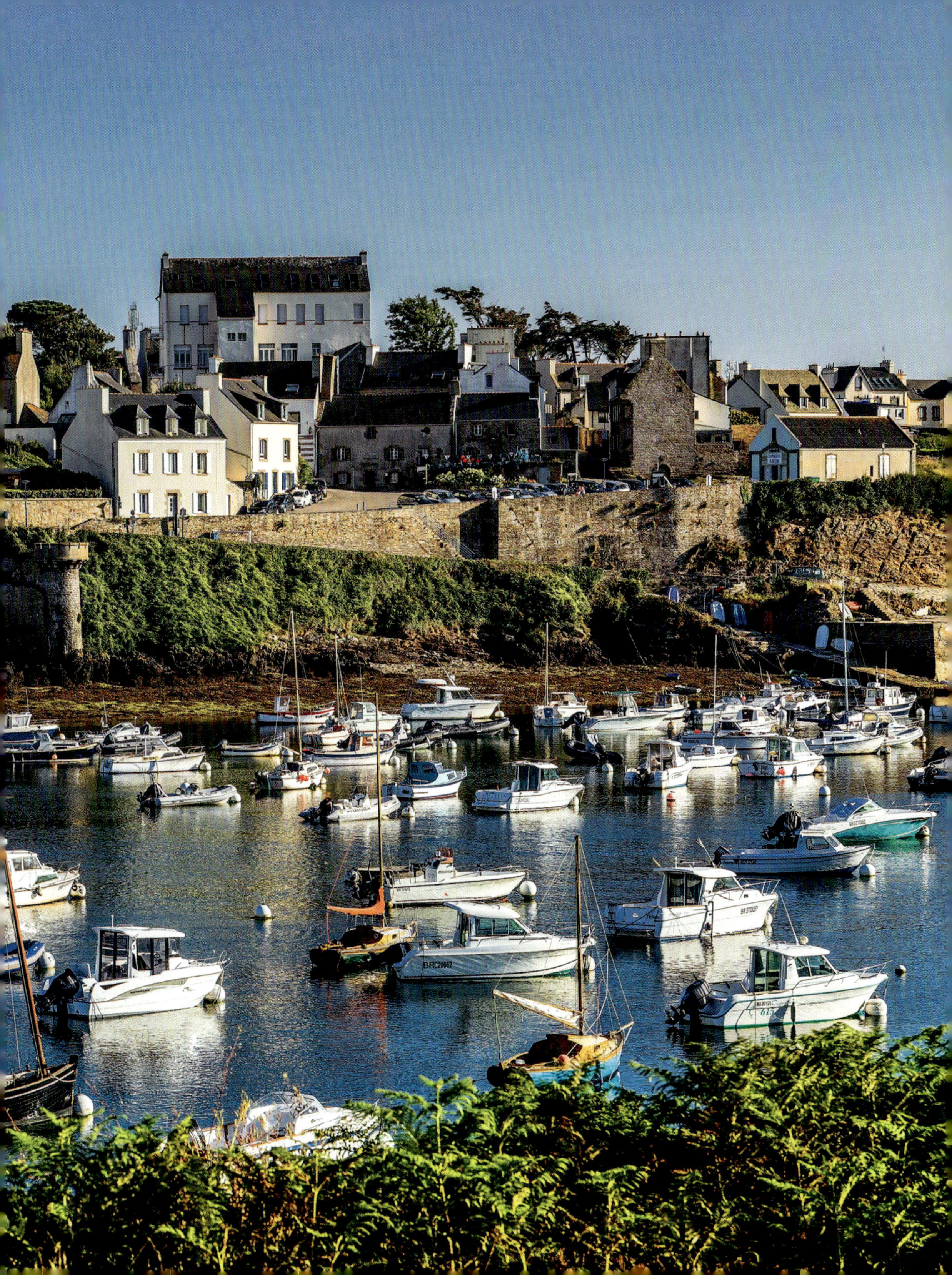

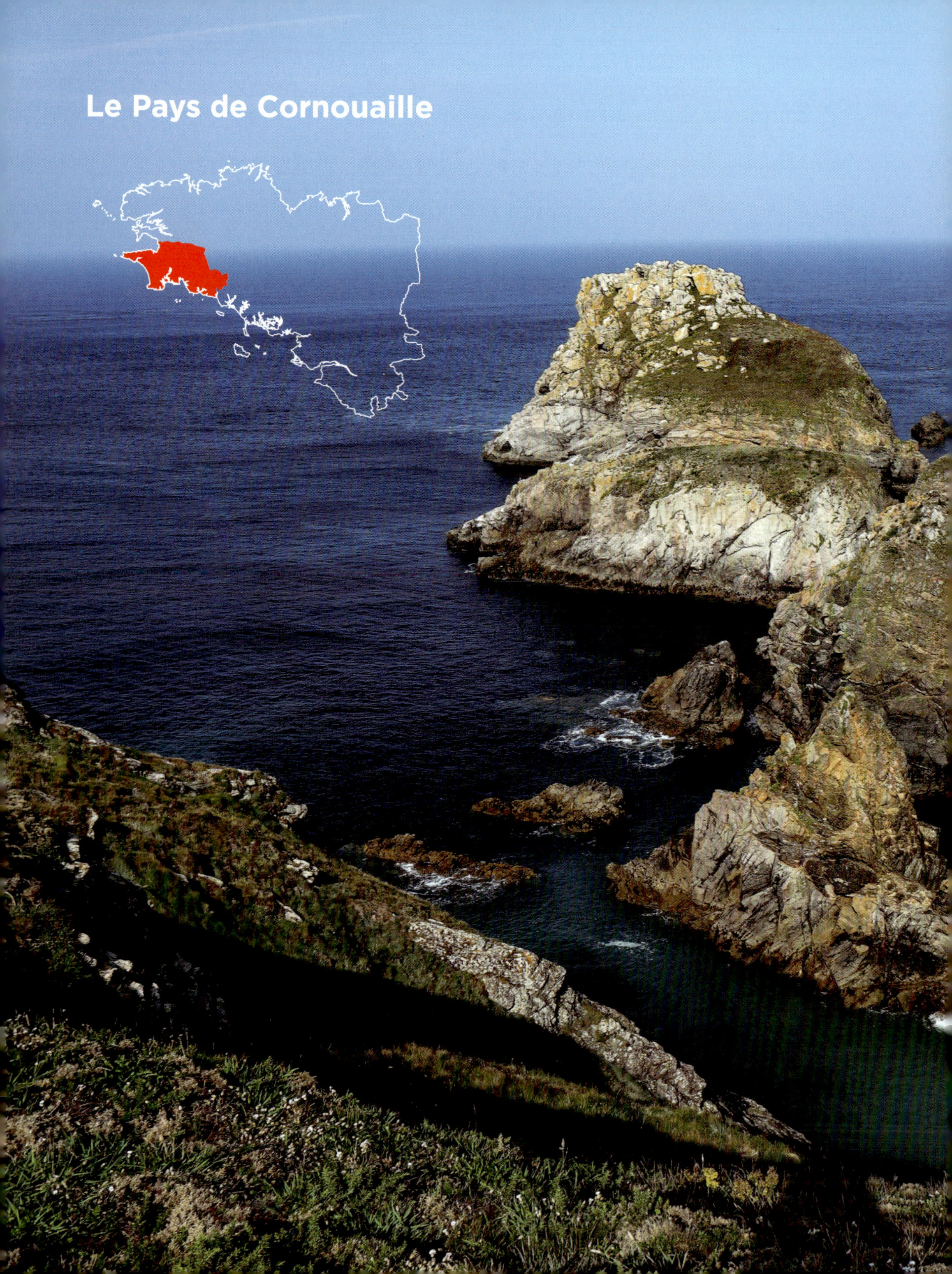
Le Pays de Cornouaille

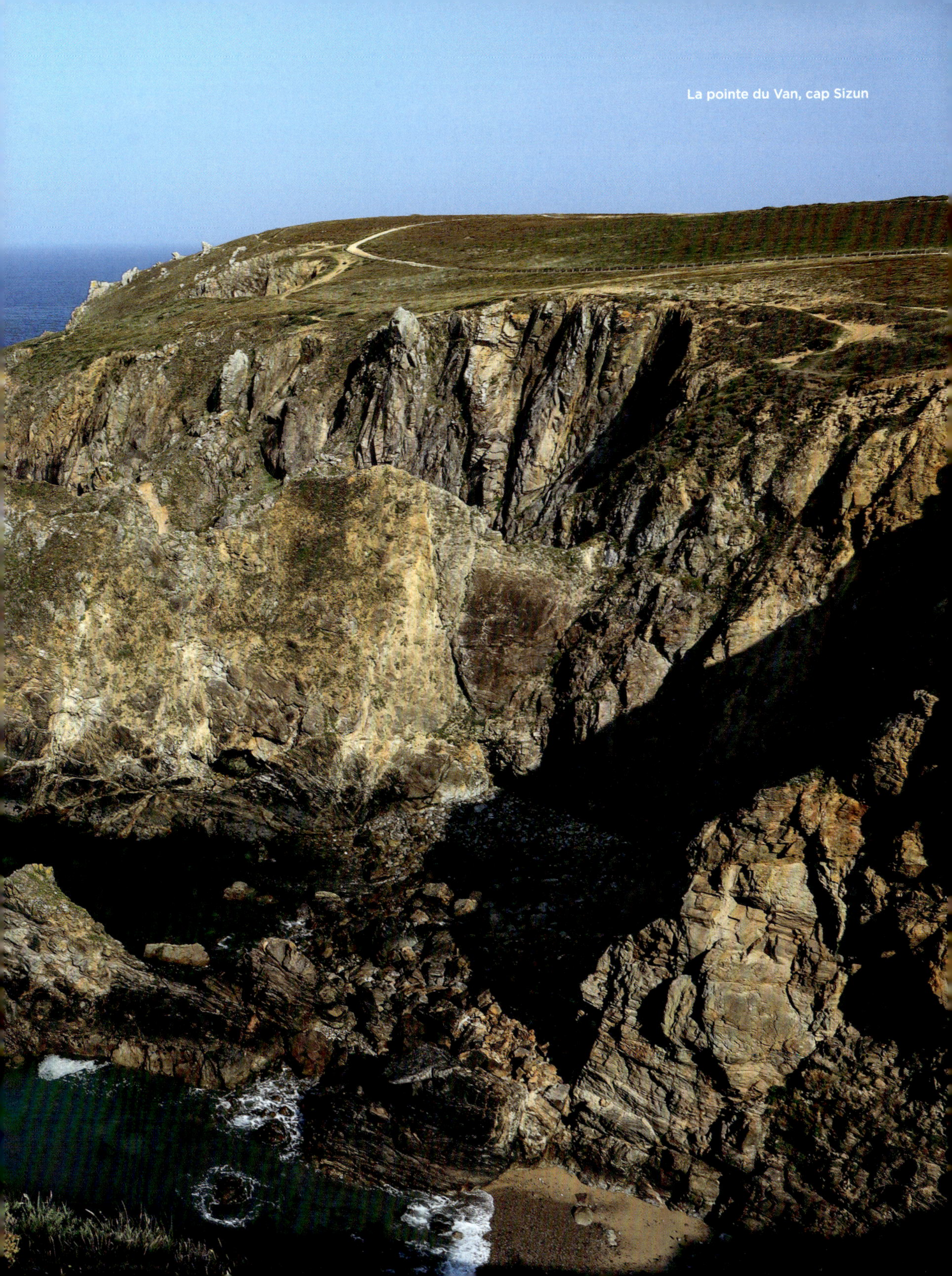

La pointe du Van, cap Sizun

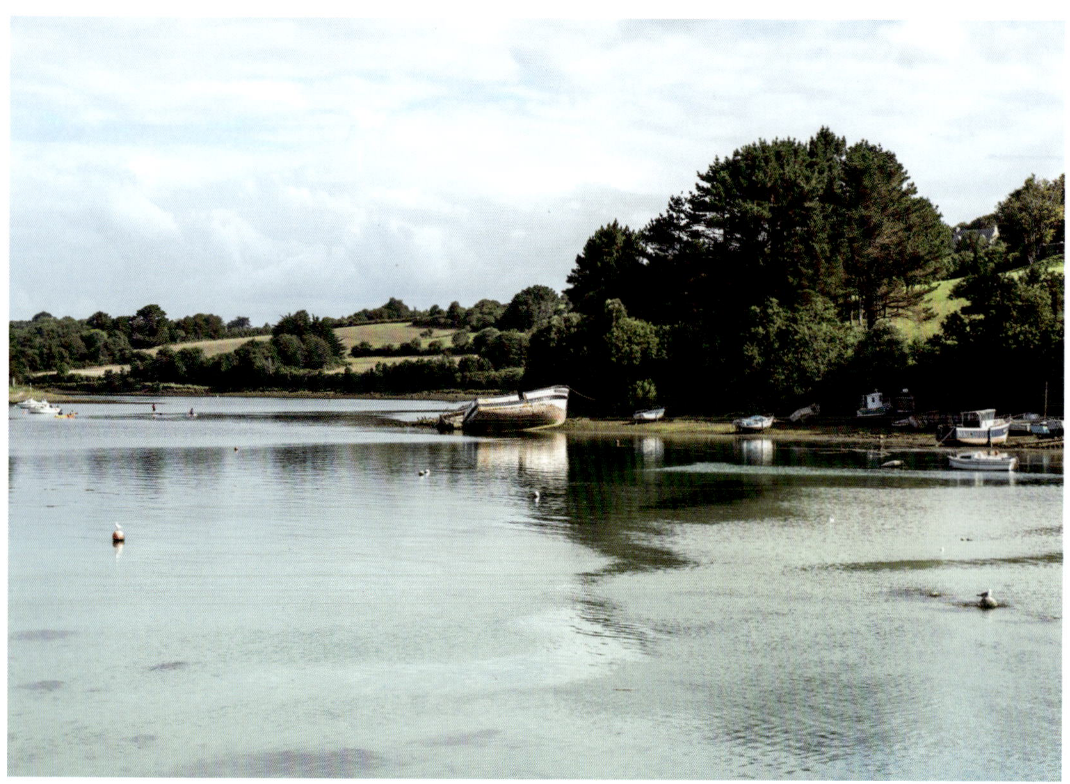

Le port d'Audierne

Audierne

Audierne, at the mouth of the Goyen, is nicknamed "La Belle du Cap". A few kilometres from the Pointe du Raz, this charming fishing village has a lively harbour where you can find the largest covered fishponds in Europe. The narrow alleys, wide beach and listed shipping graveyards make the place a worthwhile stopover.

Audierne

Audierne que l'on appelle « la belle du Cap », située dans l'estuaire du Goyen, à quelques kilomètres de la pointe du Raz, est un petit port charmant et actif. Ses quais sont animés et abritent les plus grands viviers couverts d'Europe. Ses ruelles à flanc de coteaux, sa grande plage, son cimetière de bateaux classé monument historique, en font une étape incontournable.

Audierne

Audierne an der Mündung des Goyen trägt den Spitznamen „La belle du Cap". Der wenige Kilometer von der Pointe du Raz entfernte Fischerort besticht durch seine Charme und seinen belebten Hafen, in dem die größten überdachten Fischteiche Europas zu finden sind. Die engen Gassen, der weite Strand und der denkmalgeschützte Schiffsfriedhof machen den Ort zu einem lohnenswerten Zwischenstopp.

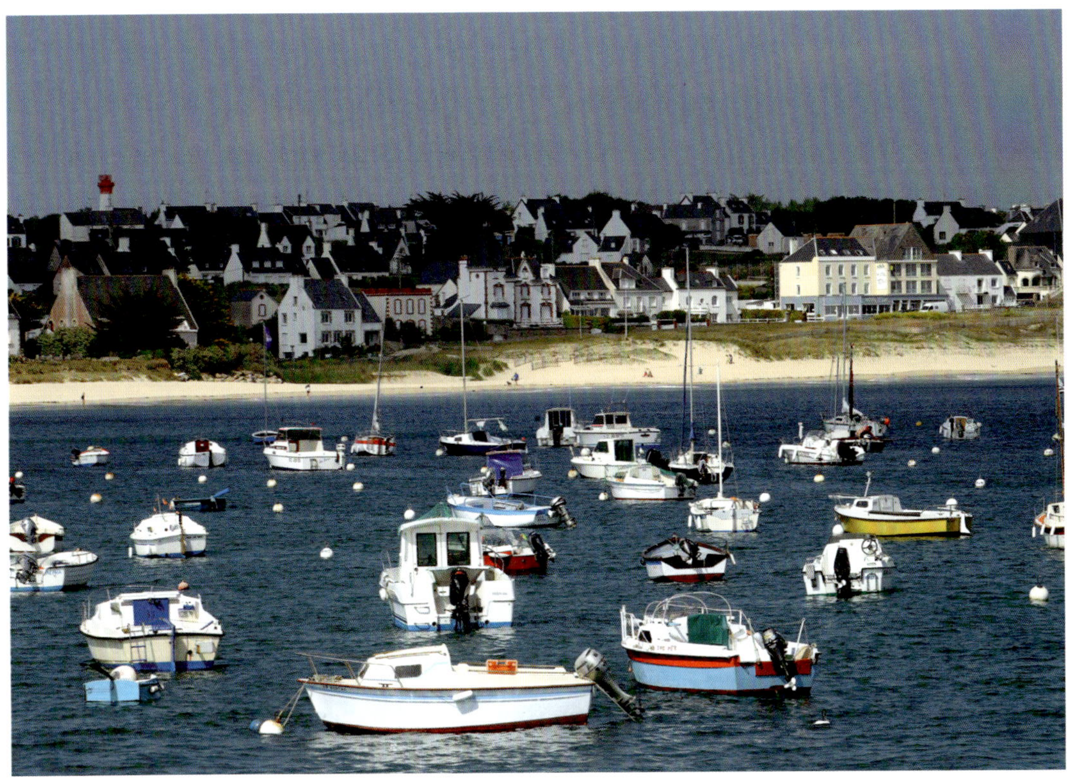

Le port d'Audierne

Audierne

Audierne, en la desembocadura del Goyen, recibe el apodo de «La belle du Cap». A pocos kilómetros de la Pointe du Raz, este pueblo de pescadores tiene un encanto y un puerto animado, donde se encuentran los mayores criaderos de peces cubiertos de Europa. Los callejones estrechos, la amplia playa y el cementerio de barcos que figura en la lista hacen de este lugar una parada que vale realmente la pena.

Audierne

Audierne na boca do Goyen é apelidada de «La belle du Cap». A poucos quilómetros da Pointe du Raz, esta vila piscatória tem um encanto e um porto animado, onde pode encontrar os maiores viveiros cobertos da Europa. Os becos estreitos, a praia larga e o cemitério de navios, considerado patrimonio histórico fazem do local uma escala importante.

Audierne

Audierne aan de monding van de Goyen heeft de bijnaam 'La belle du Cap'. Dit vissersdorpje op enkele kilometers van de Pointe du Raz bekoort met zijn charme en levendige haven. Hier zijn de grootste overdekte visvijvers van Europa. De smalle steegjes, het brede strand en het door monumentenzorg beschermde scheepskerkhof maken de plaats tot een lonende tussenstop.

Audierne

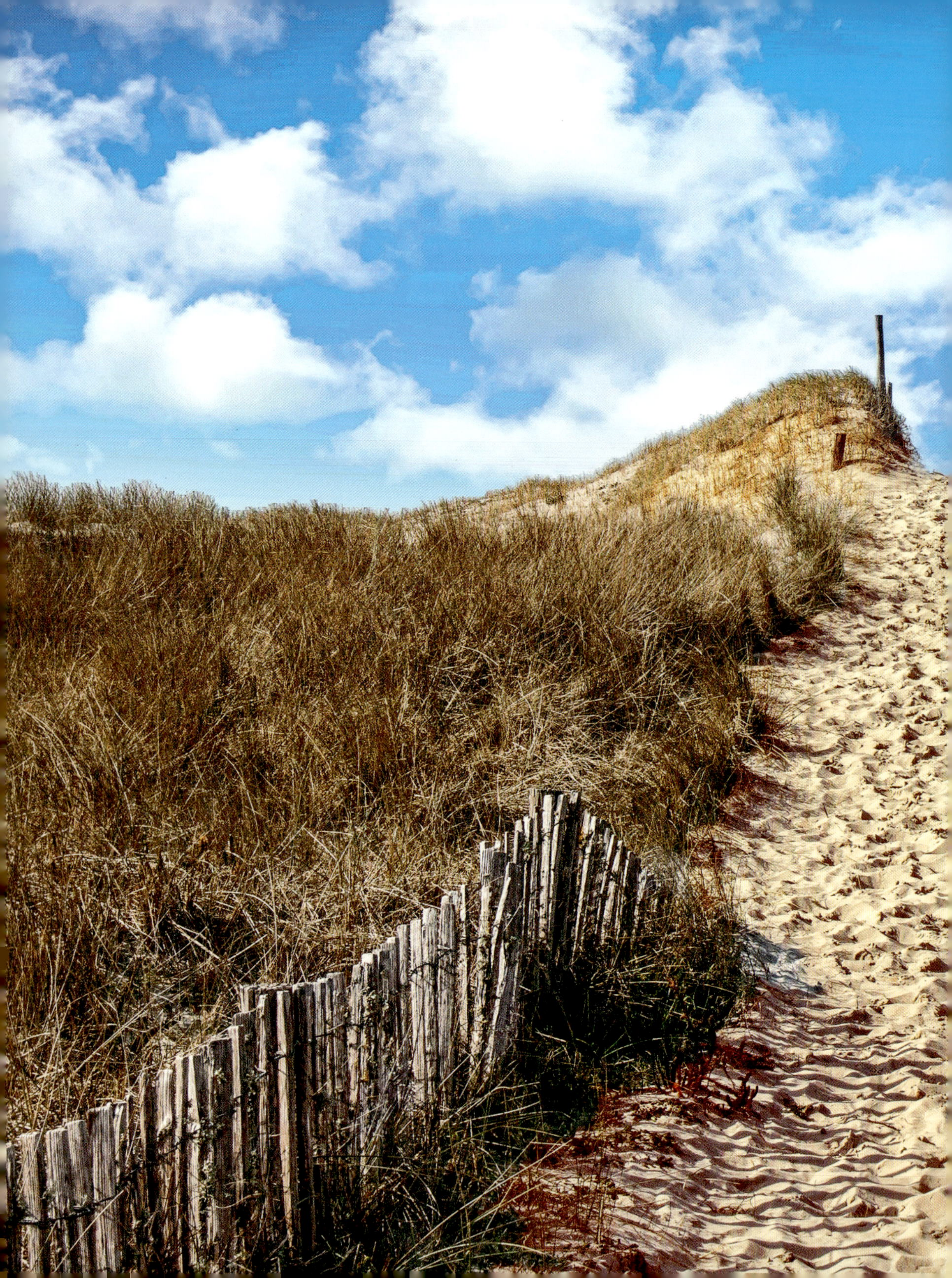

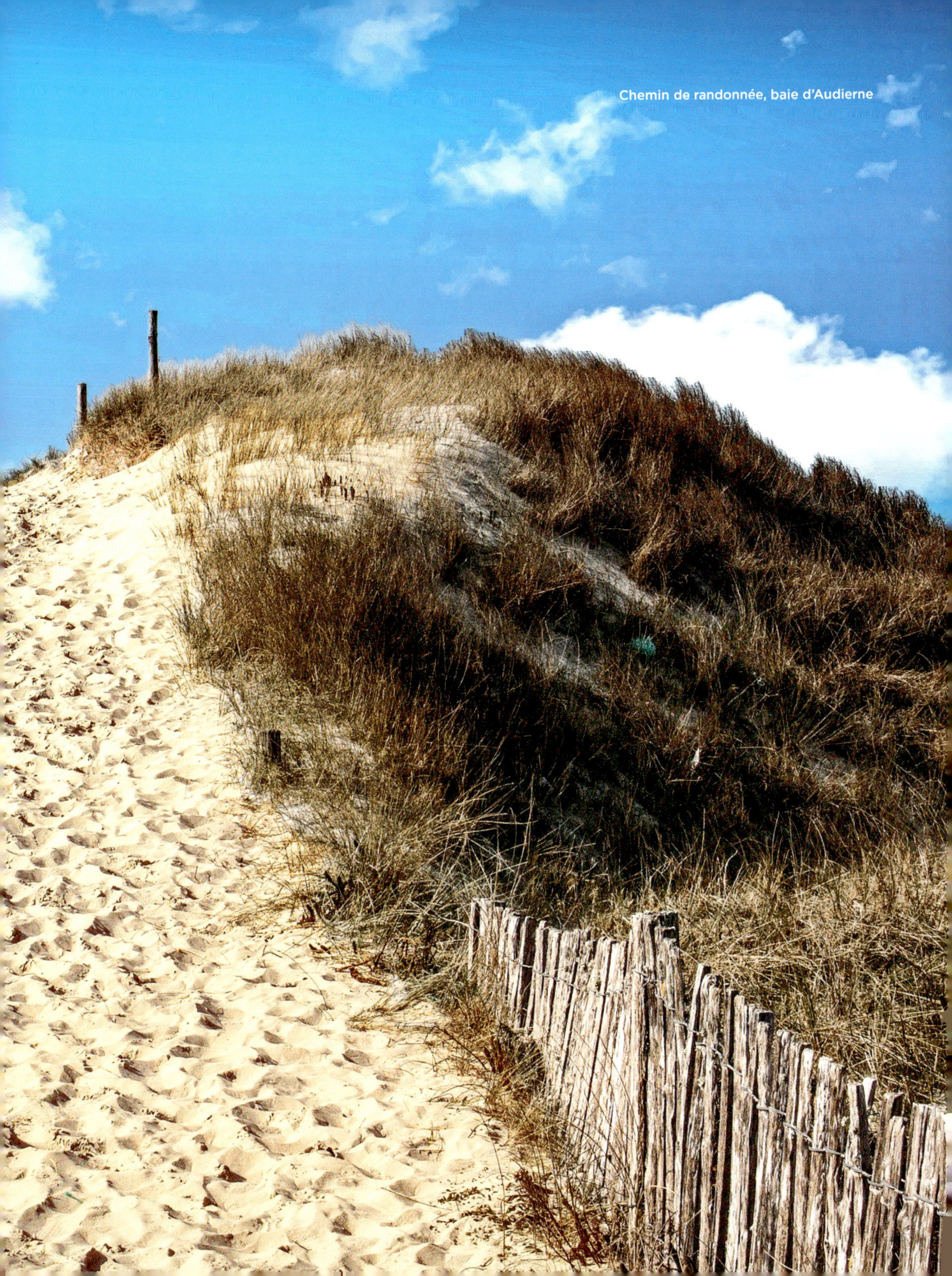
Chemin de randonnée, baie d'Audierne

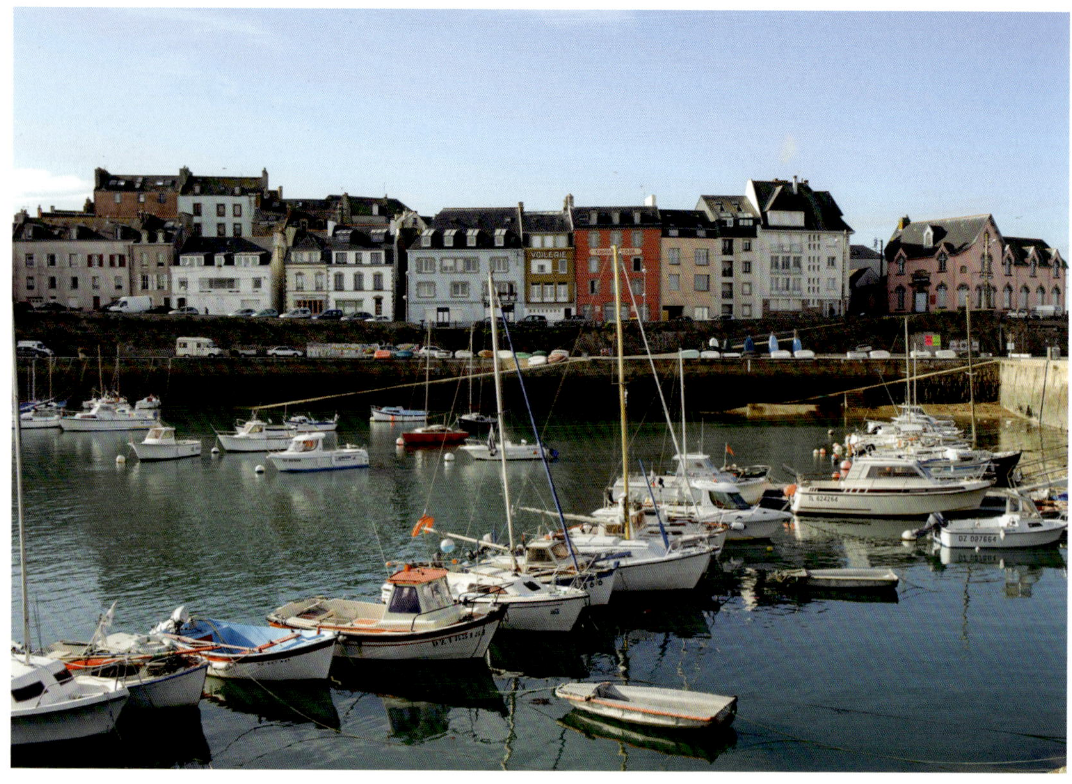

Le port du Rosmeur, Douarnenez

Douarnenez

Located 20 km from Quimper, Douarnenez is a city with three ports and a sardine industry. The maritime past is very present in the cityscape. In front of it stretches an extensive bay, in which the Île Tristan invites a visit.

Douarnenez

Douarnenez, ville aux 3 ports, ville de l'histoire sardinière, située à 20 km de Quimper, affiche sa personnalité bien trempée par son passé. La ville domine une large baie où il ne faut pas manquer l'île Tristan.

Douarnenez

20 km von Quimper entfernt liegt Douarnenez – die Stadt der drei Häfen und der Sardinenindustrie. Die maritime Vergangenheit ist im Stadtbild sehr präsent. Vor ihr erstreckt sich eine ausgedehnte Bucht, in der die Île Tristan zu einem Besuch einlädt.

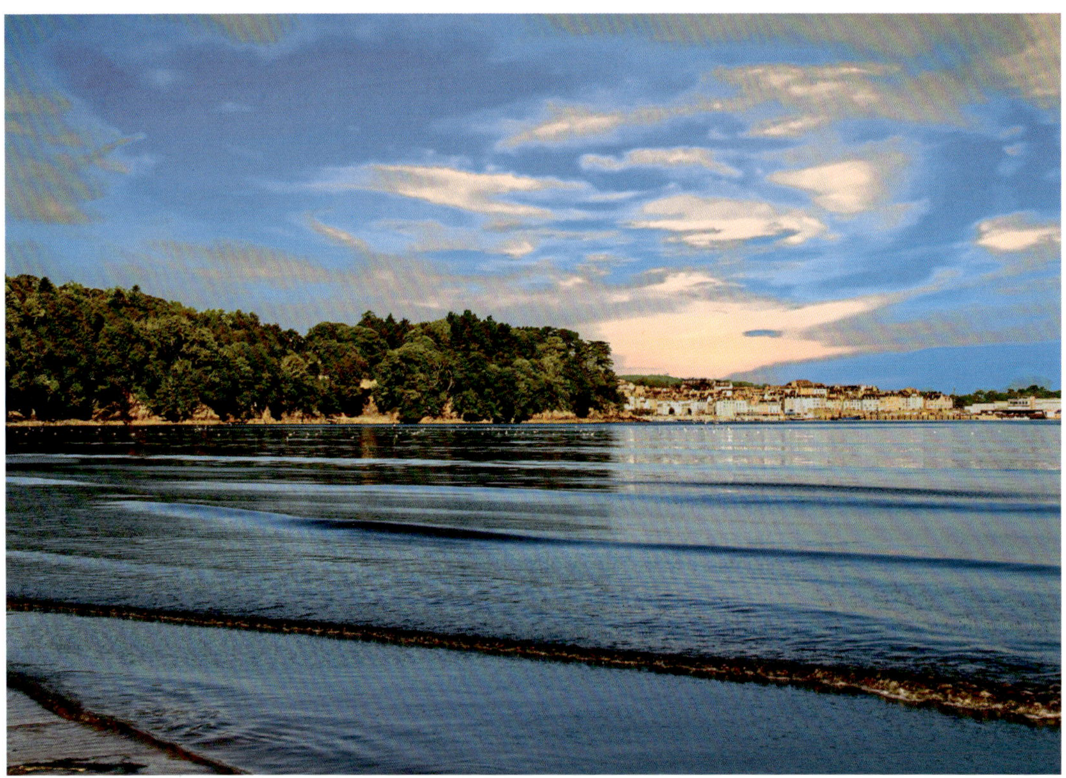

La plage du Ris, Douarnenez

Douarnenez

A 20 km de Quimper se encuentra Douarnenez, la ciudad de los tres puertos y de la industria sardinera. El pasado marítimo está muy presente en el paisaje urbano. Frente a ella se extiende una extensa bahía, en la que la Île Tristan invita a una visita.

Douarnenez

A 20 km de Quimper está Douarnenez - a cidade dos três portos e da indústria da sardinha. O passado marítimo está muito presente na paisagem urbana. Em frente estende-se uma extensa baía, na qual a Île Tristan convida a uma visita.

Douarnenez

Op 20 km van Quimper ligt Douarnenez – de stad van de drie havens en de sardine-industrie. Het maritieme verleden is sterk aanwezig in het stadsbeeld. Ervoor ligt een uitgestrekte baai, waar het Île Tristan uitnodigt tot een bezoek.

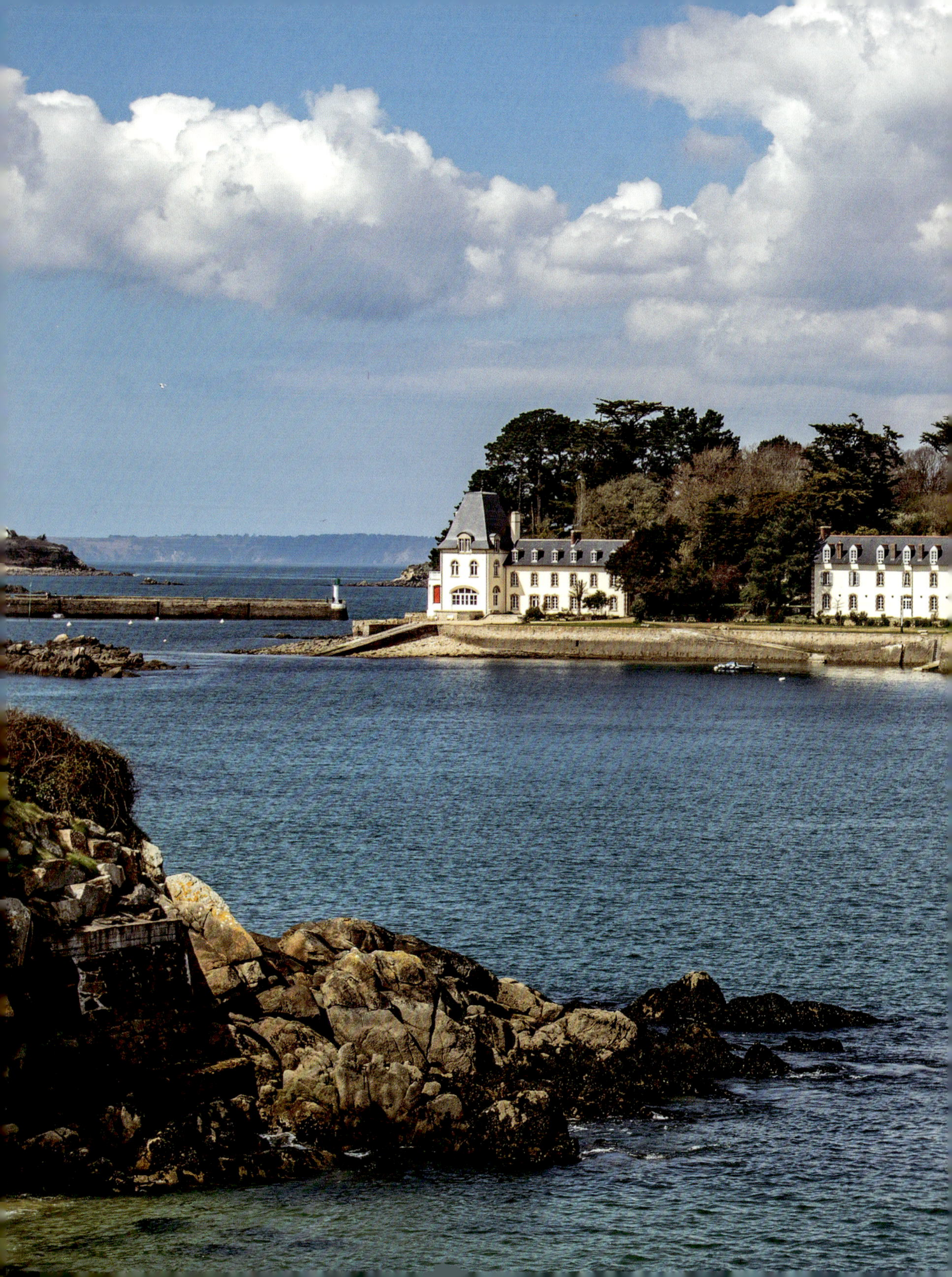

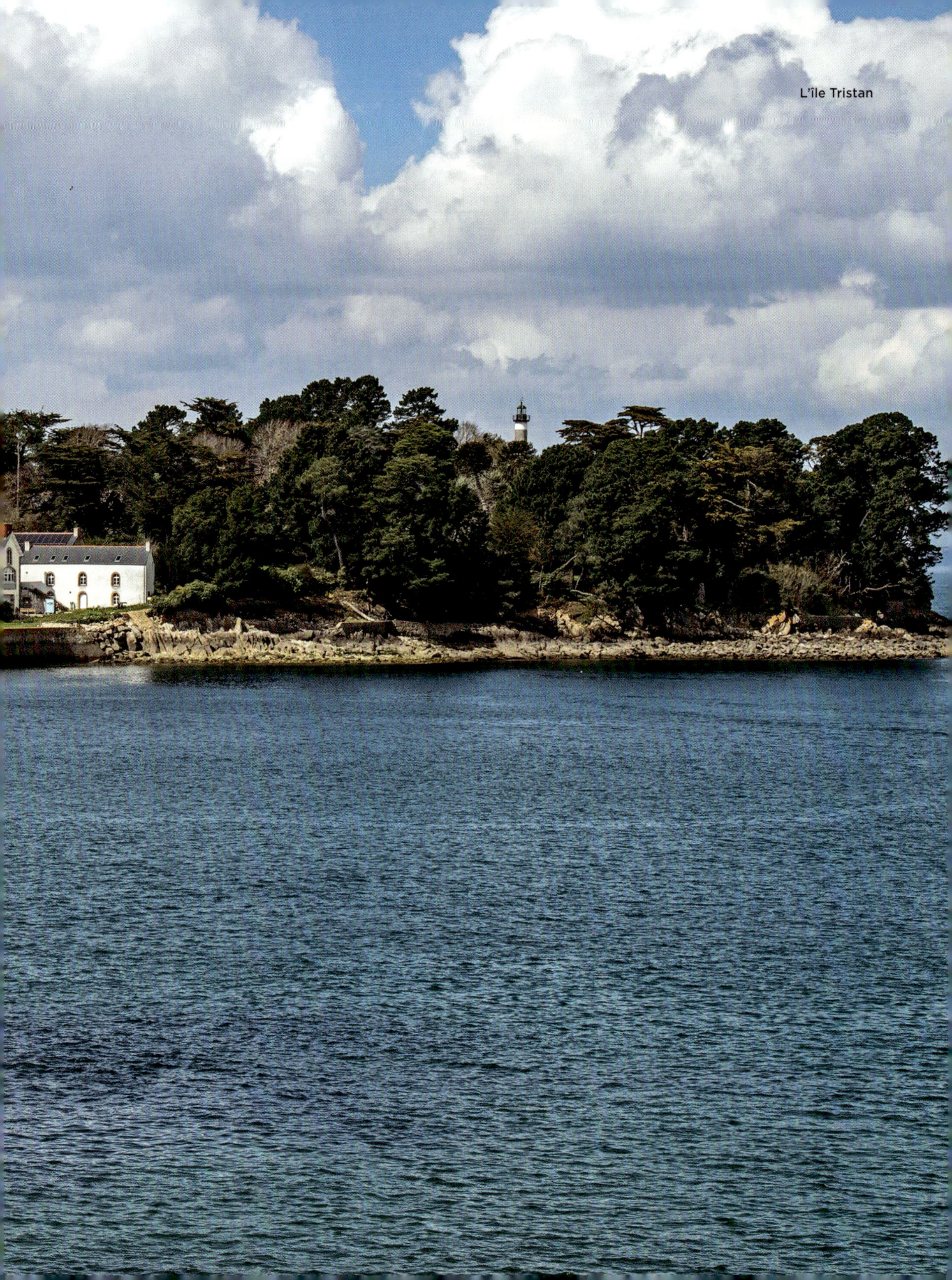

L'île Tristan

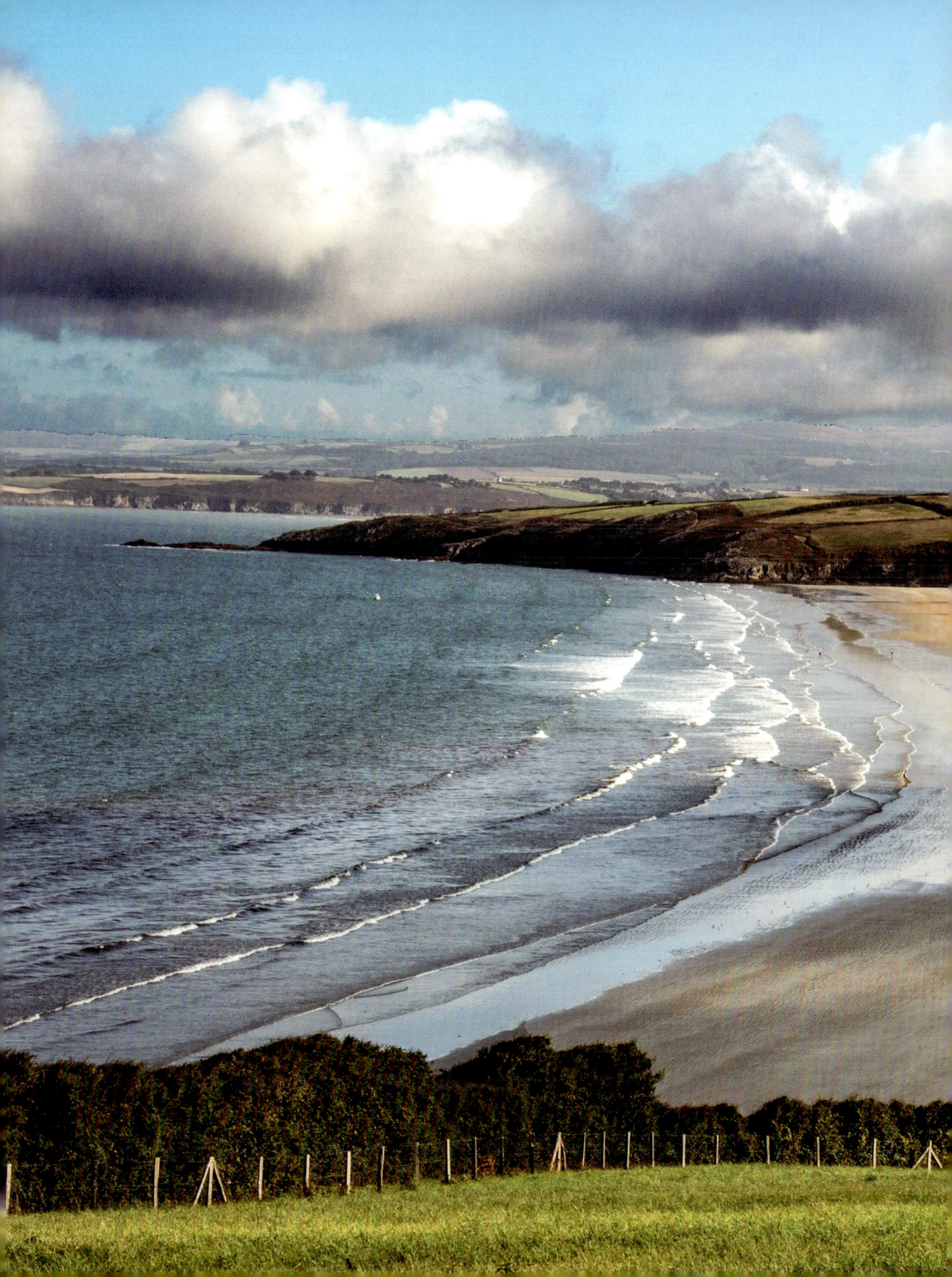

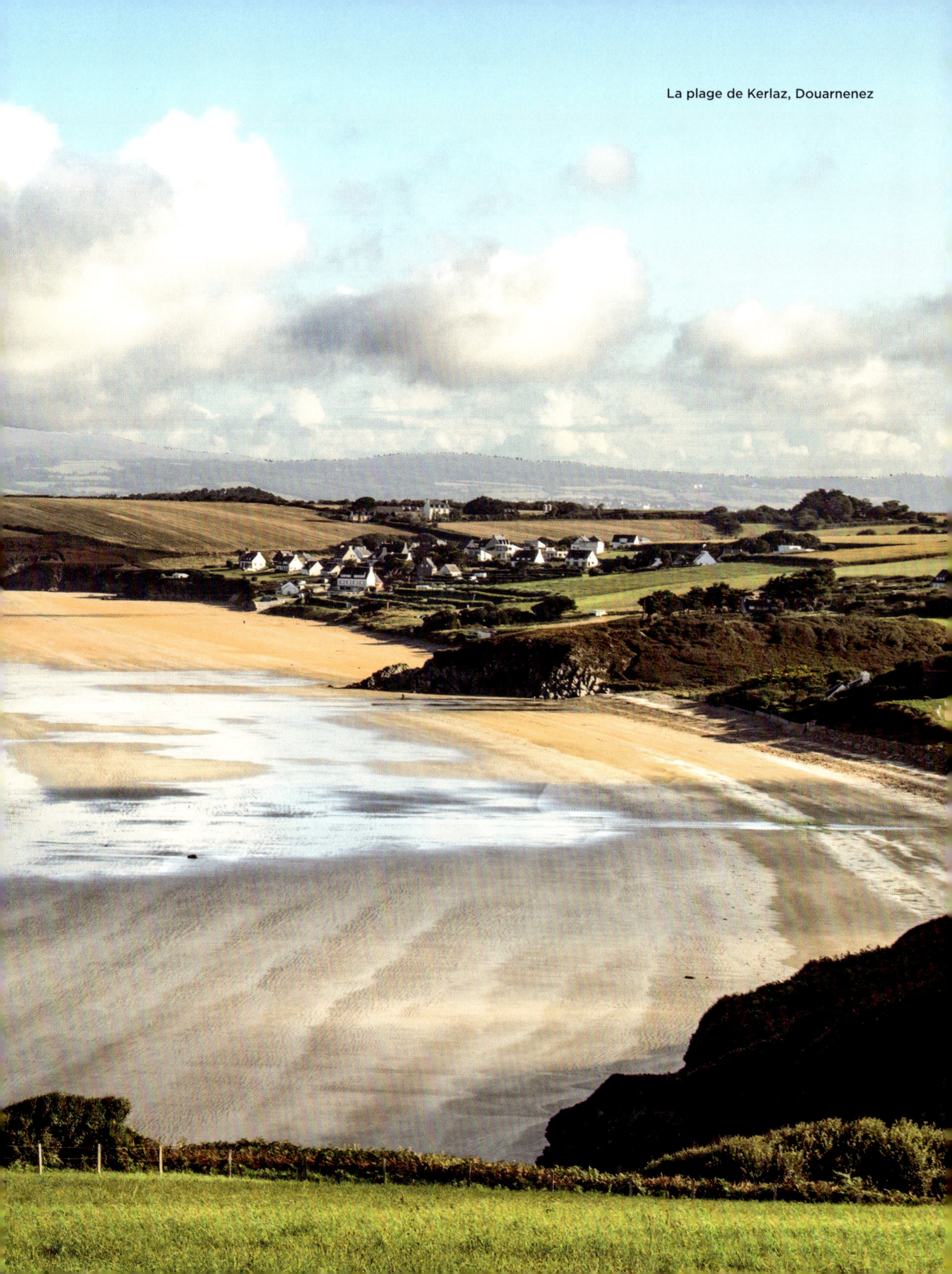

La plage de Kerlaz, Douarnenez

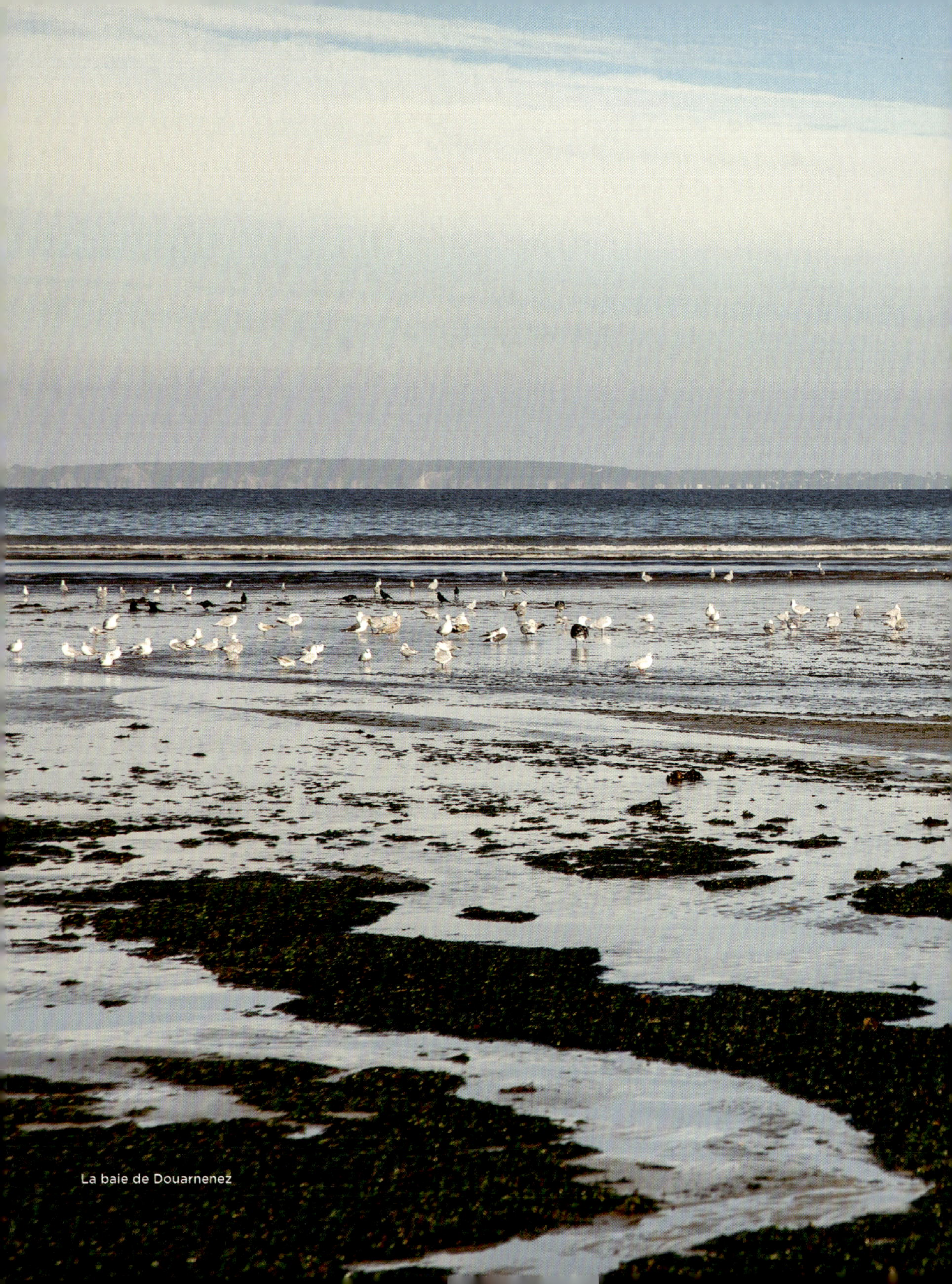

La baie de Douarnenez

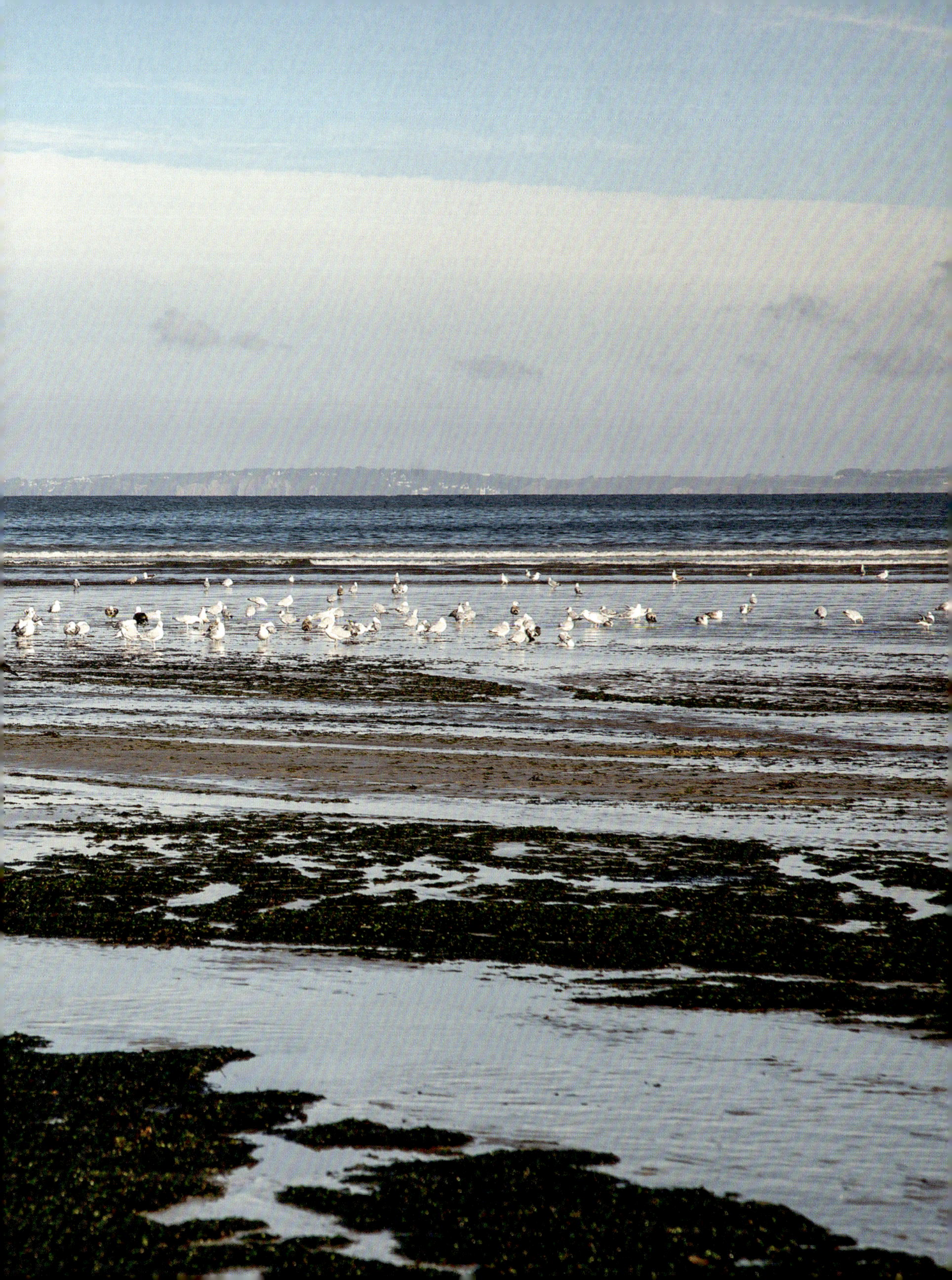

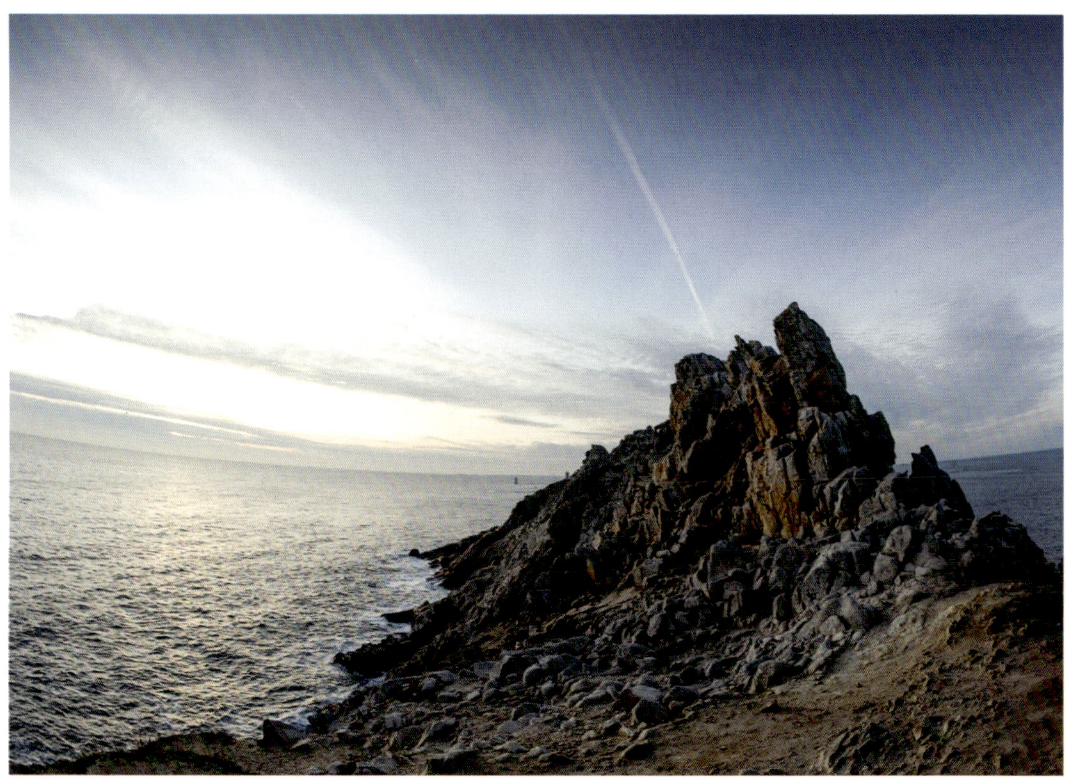

La pointe du Raz

The Pointe du Raz

The Finistère - in German "Ende der Erde" - is characterised by rugged cliffs and rocky capes. One of these is the Pointe du Raz, which reaches a height of 70 metres and is classified as a "Grand Site de France". The Phare de la Vieille lighthouse, which has been in operation since 1887, rises in front of the headland. The cape offers a view of the Île de Sein, and in clear weather even up to the lighthouse Ar Men.

La pointe du Raz

Le Finistère, qui signifie « la fin des terres », se caractérise par un défilé de caps et de promontoires. Classée « Grand Site de France », la pointe du Raz s'élève à quelque 70 mètres de hauteur. Face à elle, le phare carré de l'îlot de la Vieille, allumé en 1887.
Le panorama sur le large permet d'admirer l'île de Sein et, par temps clair, le phare d'Ar-Men.

Die Pointe du Raz

Das Finistère – auf Deutsch „Ende der Erde" – ist geprägt durch schroffe Klippen und felsige Kaps. Eines davon ist die Pointe du Raz, die eine Höhe von 70 Metern erreicht und als „Grand Site de France" eingestuft ist. Vor der Landzunge erhebt sich der Leuchtturm Phare de la Vieille, der sich seit 1887 in Betrieb befindet. Das Kap bietet einen Blick auf die Île de Sein, bei klarem Wetter sogar bis zu dem Leuchtturm Ar Men.

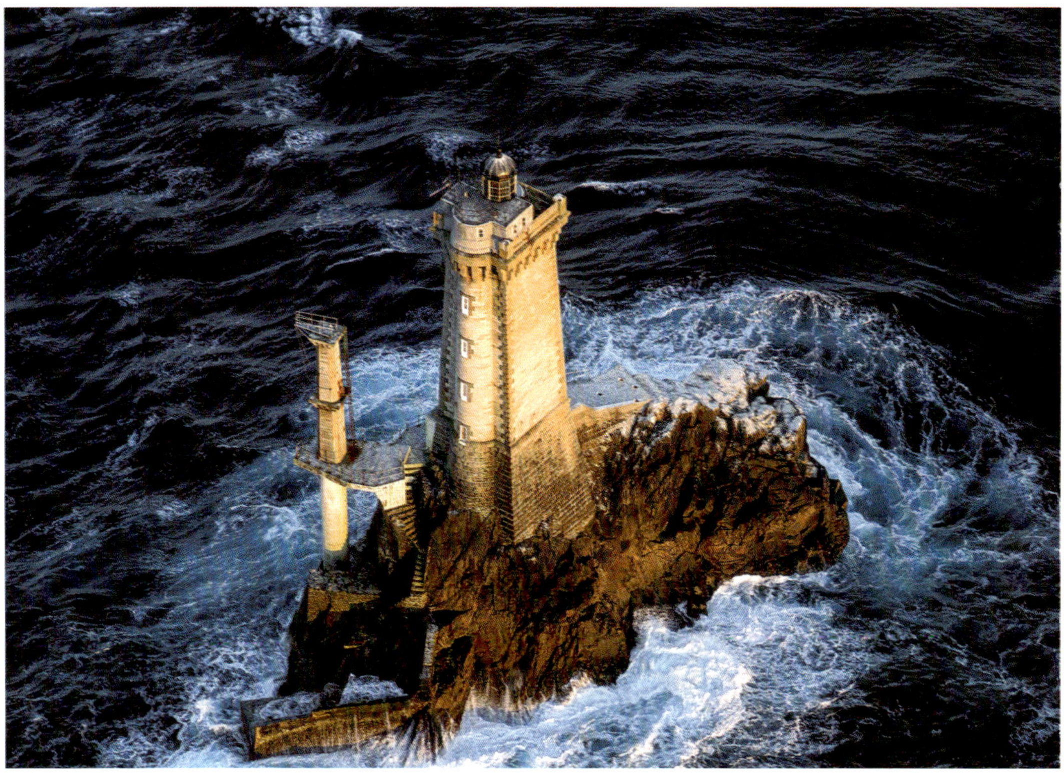

Le phare de la Vieille, en face de la pointe du Raz

La Pointe du Raz

Finisterre (en español, «fin del mundo») se caracteriza por acantilados escarpados y cabos rocosos. Uno de ellos es la Pointe du Raz, que alcanza una altura de 70 metros y está clasificada como «Grand Site de France». El faro Phare de la Vieille, en funcionamiento desde 1887, se levanta frente al promontorio. El cabo ofrece una vista de la Île de Sein y, cuando el tiempo está despejado, incluso hasta del faro Ar Men.

A Pointe du Raz

O Finistère - em alemão «Ende der Erde»(fim do mundo) - é caracterizado por falésias escarpadas e cabos rochosos. Um deles é a Pointe du Raz, que atinge uma altura de 70 metros e é classificado como «Grand Site de France». O farol Phare de la Vieille, em funcionamento desde 1887, ergue-se em frente ao promontório. O cabo oferece uma vista da Île de Sein, em tempo limpo até ao farol Ar Men.

De Pointe du Raz

Finistère (Ned. 'eind van de aarde') wordt getekend door ruige klippen en rotsachtige kapen. Een daarvan is de 70 meter hoge Pointe du Raz, die geclassificeerd is als 'Grand Site de France'. De Phare de la Vieille, die vanaf 1887 in bedrijf is, rijst op voor de landtong. De kaap biedt een blik op het Île de Sein, bij helder weer zelfs tot aan de vuurtoren Ar Men.

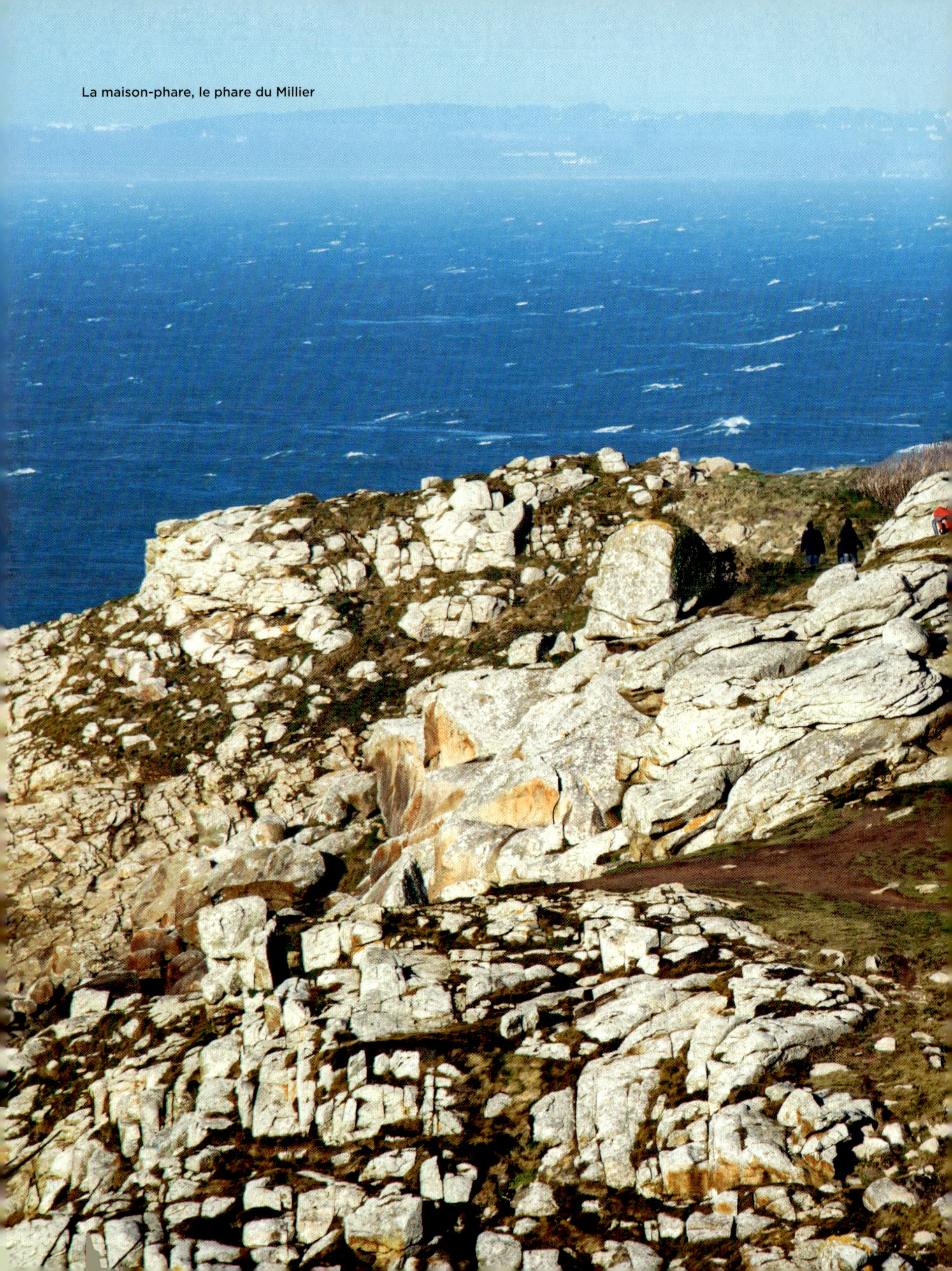

La maison-phare, le phare du Millier

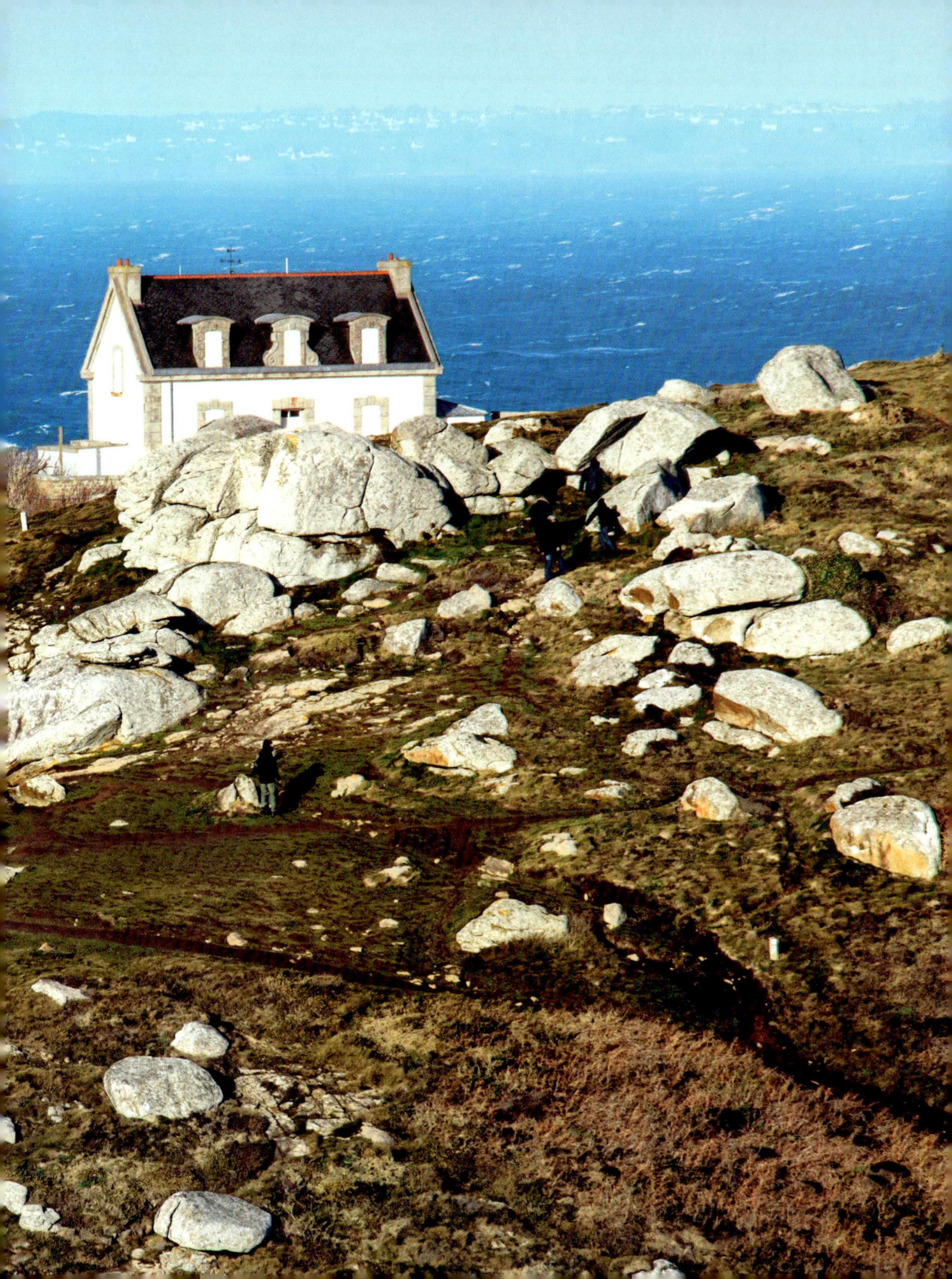

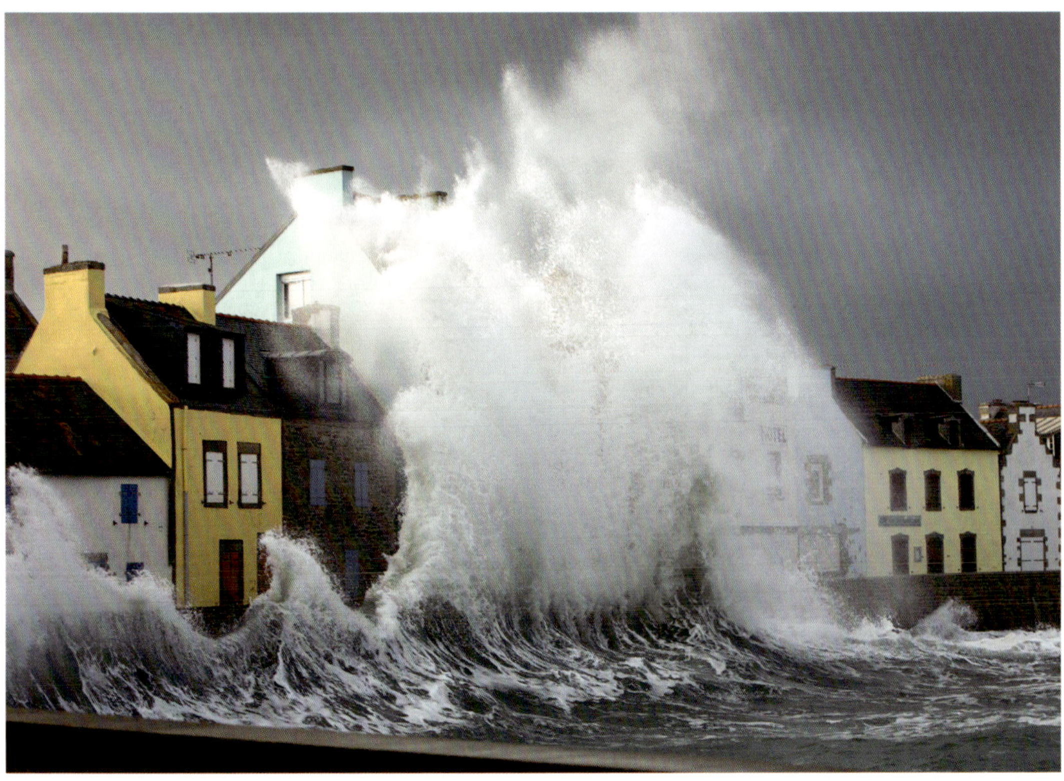

L'île de Sein

Île de Sein

The Île de Sein appears to be an accumulation of sand and rocks in the vastness of the ocean. In no other place can the force of the sea be experienced better than on this small 2 km long island. The island is situated 7 km from Cape Pointe du Raz and can be reached by a one-hour crossing from Audierne or Douarnenez.

L'île de Sein

L'île de Sein semble née de l'union de la roche et de l'océan.
Sereine ou déchaînée, noyée d'embruns et de vagues projetées contre ses digues, elle s'étend sur seulement 2 km. Elle est située à 7 km de la pointe du Raz dont elle est séparée par le raz de Sein. On y accède par Audierne ou Douarnenez et la traversée dure environ une heure.

Die Île de Sein

Die Île de Sein wirkt wie eine Ansammlung aus Sand und Felsen in der Weite des Ozeans.
An keinen anderen Ort lässt sich die Wucht des Meeres besser erleben, als auf diesem kleinen Eiland, das sich über eine Länge von 2 km erstreckt. Die Insel liegt 7 km vor dem Kap Pointe du Raz und kann mit einer einstündigen Überfahrt von Audierne oder Douarnenez aus erreicht werden.

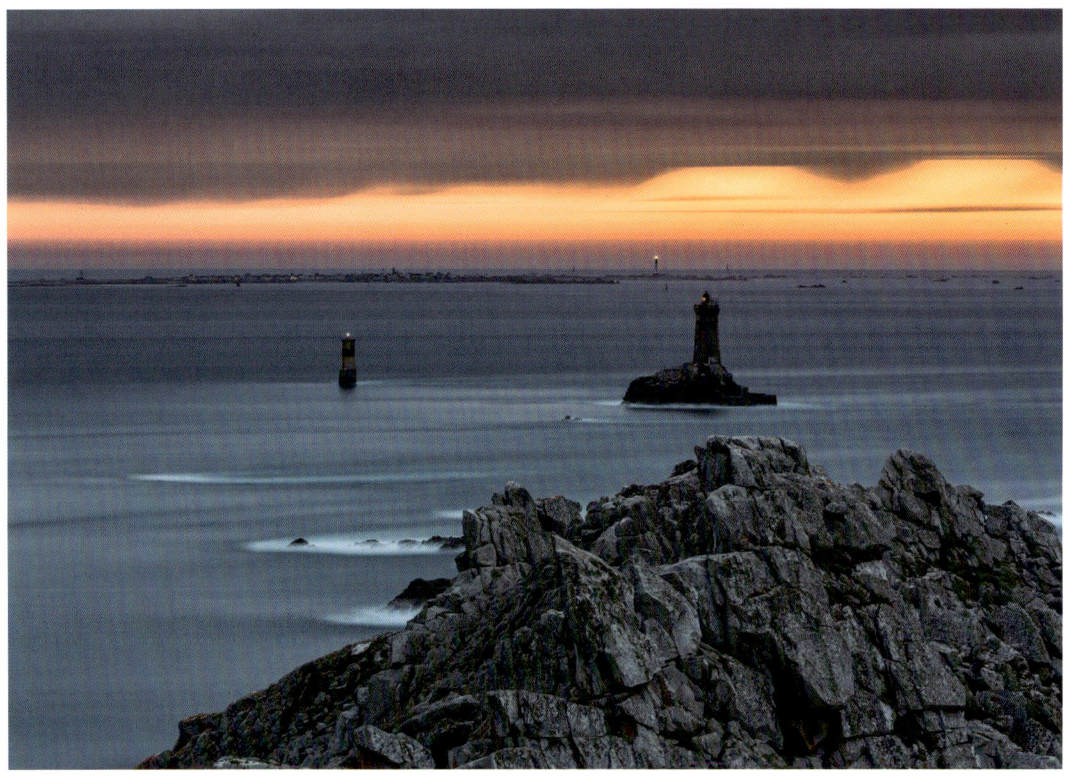

Les phares de l'île de Sein

L'île de Sein

La Île de Sein parece una acumulación de arena y rocas en la inmensidad del océano.

En ningún otro lugar se puede experimentar mejor la fuerza del mar que en esta pequeña isla, que se extiende sobre una longitud de 2 km. La isla está situada a 7 km del cabo Pointe du Raz y se puede llegar a ella a través de una travesía de una hora desde Audierne o Douarnenez.

A Île de Sein

A Île de Sein parece uma acumulação de areia e rochas na vastidão do oceano.

Em nenhum outro lugar a força do mar pode ser melhor experienciada do que nesta pequena ilha, que se estende ao longo de uma extensão de 2 km. A ilha está situada a 7 km do Cabo Pointe du Raz e pode ser alcançada após uma travessia de uma hora a partir de Audierne ou de Douarnenez.

Île de Sein

Het Île de Sein oogt als een opeenhoping van zand en rotsen in de uitgestreke oceaan. Op geen enkele andere plaats kun je de kracht van de zee beter ervaren dan op dit kleine eiland, dat zich over een lengte van 2 km uitstrekt. Het eiland ligt op 7 km afstand van Cape Pointe du Raz en is via een overtocht van een uur vanuit Audierne of Douarnenez te bereiken.

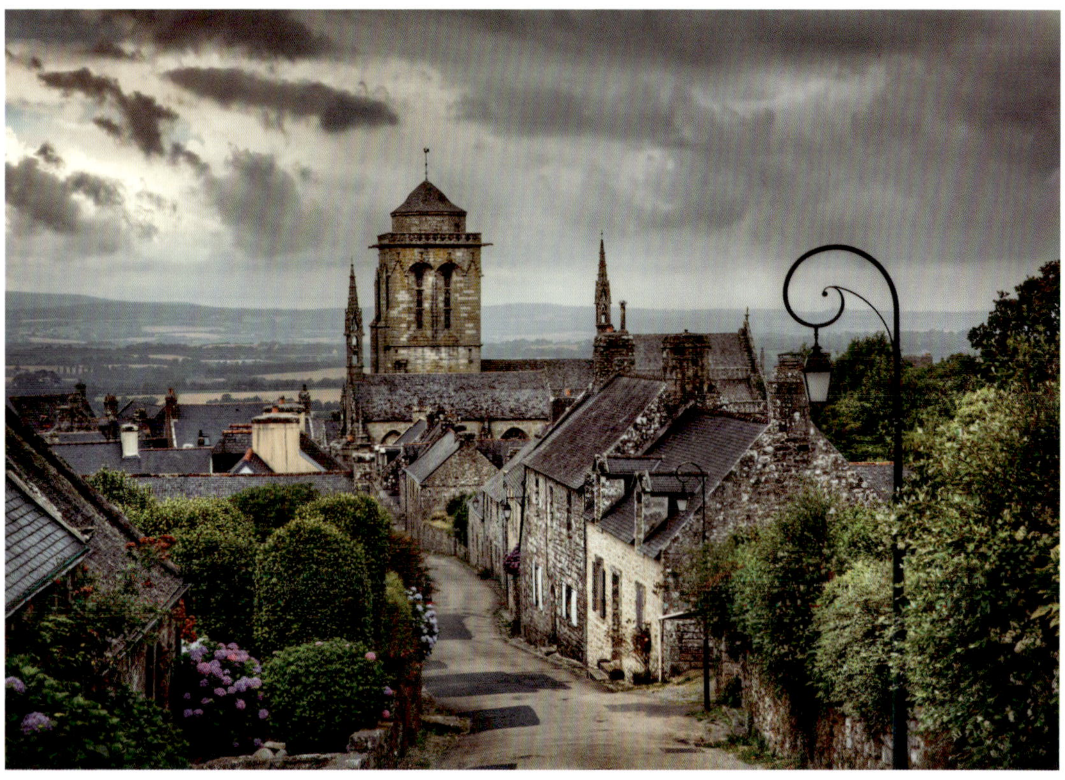

Locronan

Locronan

Locronan is one of the most beautiful villages in France and one of the most interesting places in Brittany. It has been a protected monument since 1924 and is situated 5 km from the sea on a mountain in the middle of a unique landscape. To this day it has preserved its religious and popular traditions, which are still lived there.

Locronan

Locronan est l'un des sites les plus prestigieux de Bretagne, classé au titre des monuments historiques depuis 1924. Situé sur une montagne, dans un cadre naturel exceptionnel à 5 km de la mer, le village fidèle aux traditions religieuses et folkloriques est aussi aujourd'hui gratifié du label des plus beaux villages de France.

Locronan

Locronan zählt zu den schönsten Dörfern Frankreichs und zu den sehenswertesten Orten der Bretagne. Es steht seit 1924 unter Denkmalschutz und liegt 5 km vom Meer entfernt auf einem Berg inmitten einer einmaligen Landschaft. Bis heute hat es sich seine religiösen und volkstümlichen Traditionen bewahrt, die dort immer noch gelebt werden.

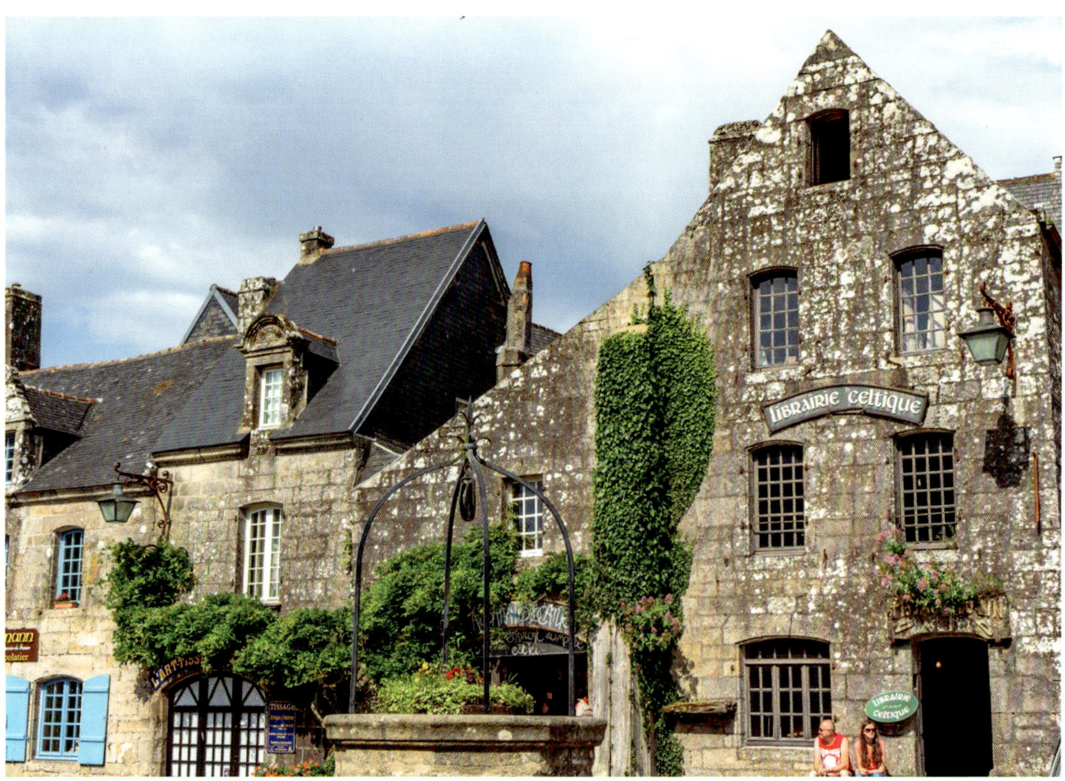

Locronan

Locronan

Locronan es uno de los pueblos más bellos de Francia y uno de los lugares más interesantes de Bretaña. Es un edificio protegido desde 1924 y está situado a 5 km del mar en una montaña en medio de un paisaje único. Hasta el día de hoy ha conservado sus tradiciones religiosas y populares, que todavía se viven allí.

Locronan

Locronan é uma das aldeias mais bonitas da França e um dos lugares mais interessantes de visitar da Bretanha. Está classificada como património cultural nacional desde 1924 e está situada a 5 km do mar numa montanha no meio de uma paisagem única. Até hoje tem preservado as suas tradições religiosas e populares, que ainda lá são vividas.

Locronan

Locronan is een van de mooiste dorpen van Frankrijk en een van de bezienswaardigste plekken van Bretagne. Het valt sinds 1924 onder monumentenzorg en staat 5 km van zee op een berg midden in een uniek landschap. Het heeft zijn religieuze en folkloristische tradities tot op heden bewaard en leeft er nog altijd naar.

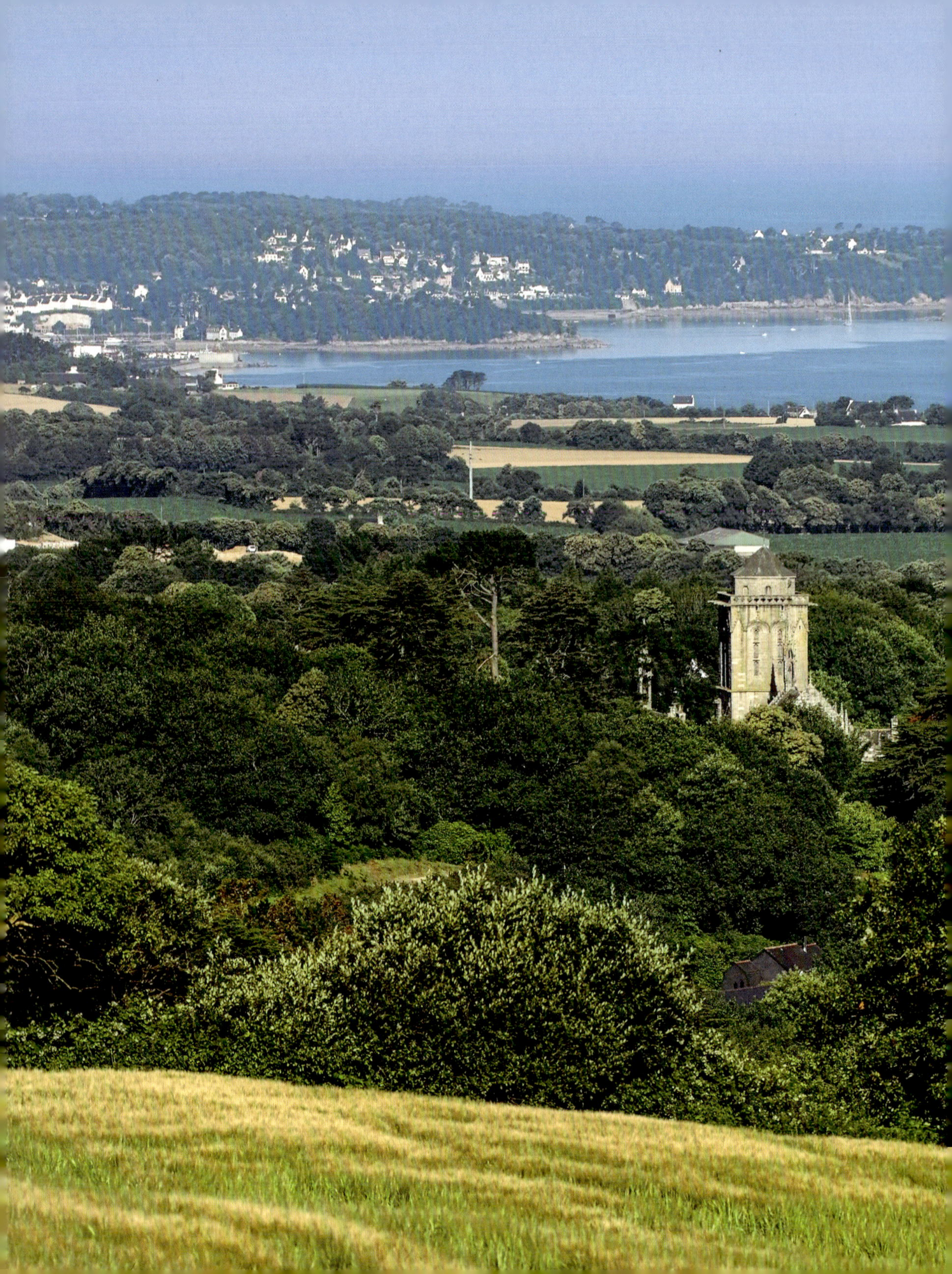

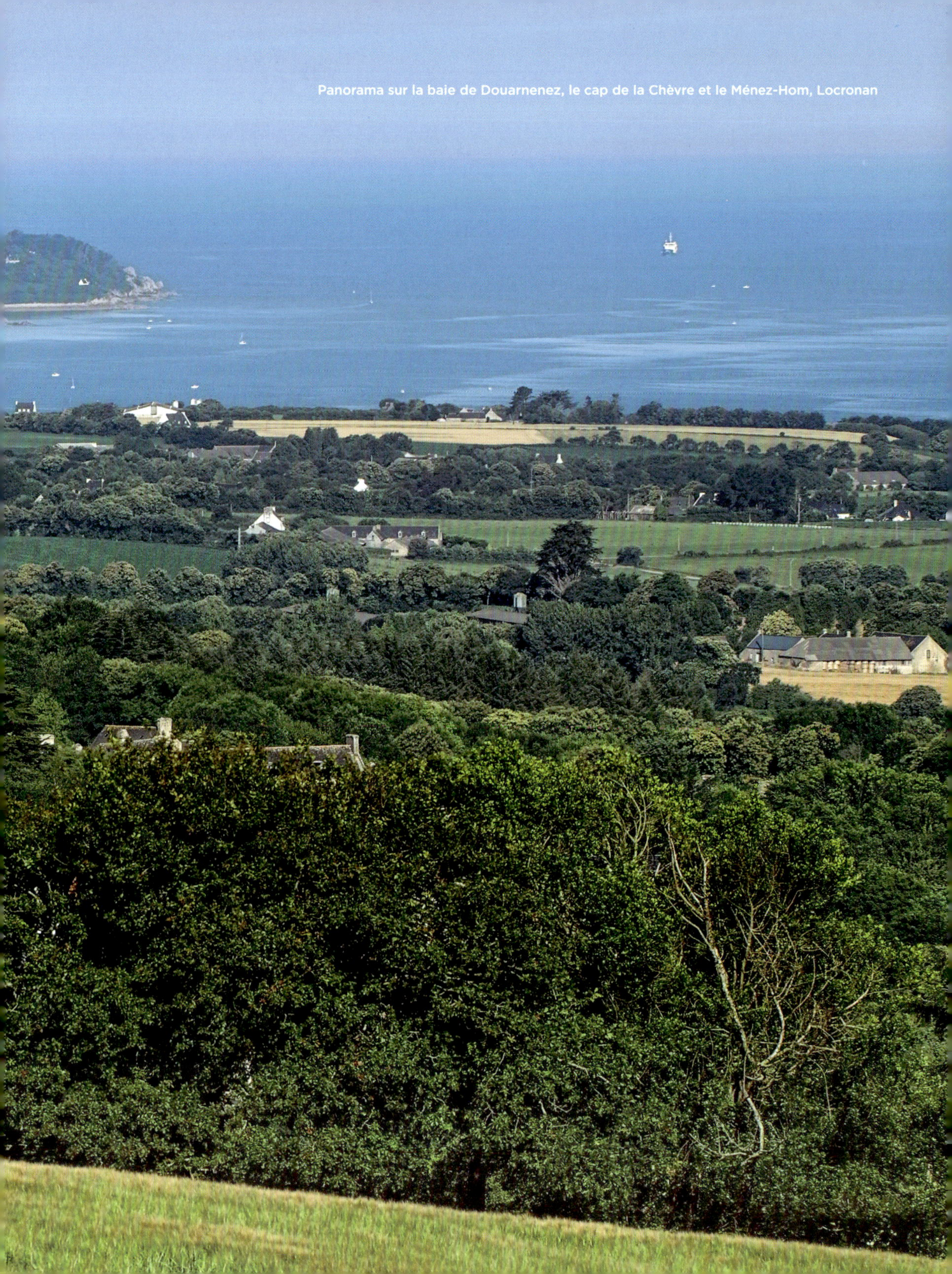
Panorama sur la baie de Douarnenez, le cap de la Chèvre et le Ménez-Hom, Locronan

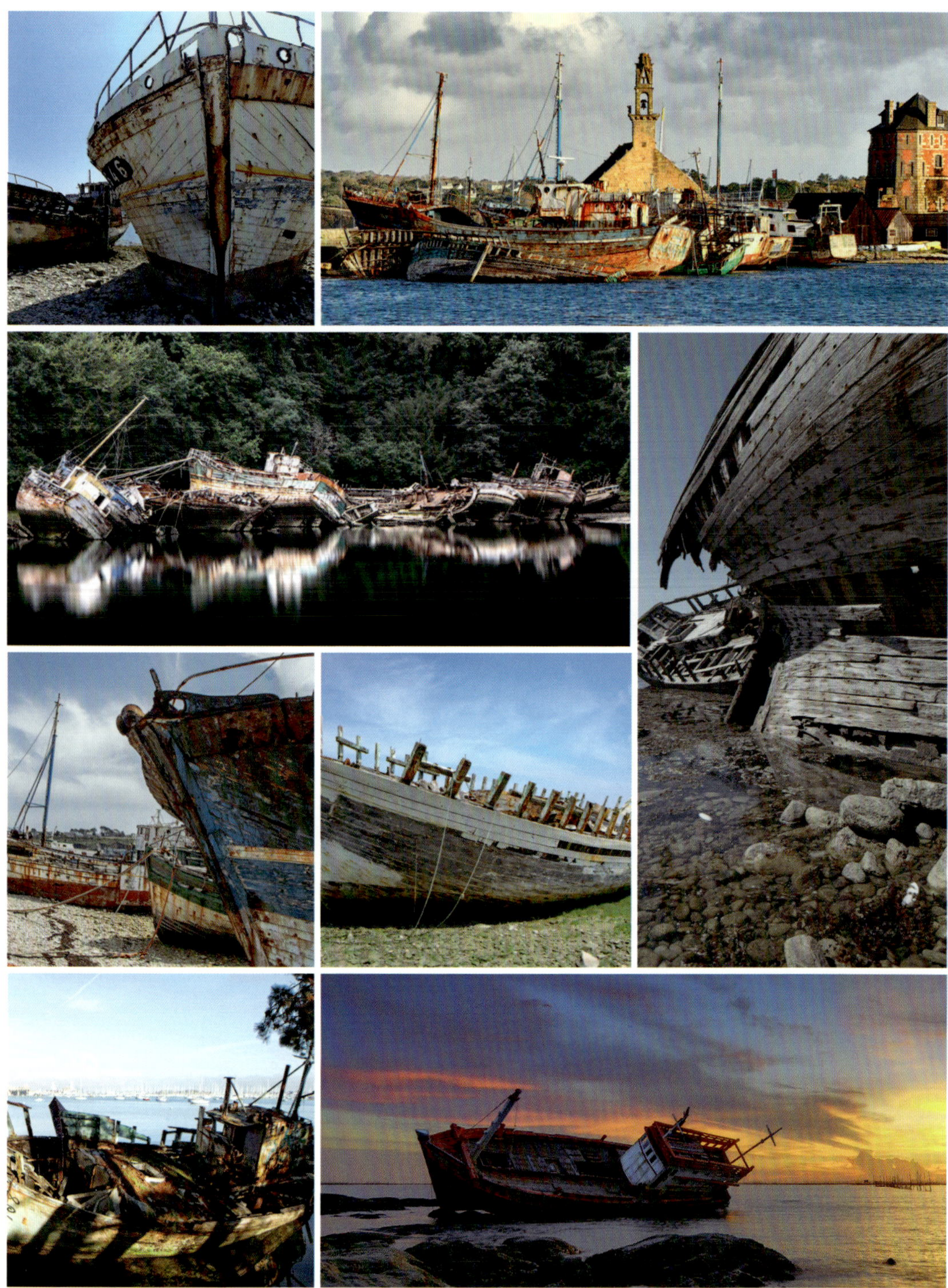

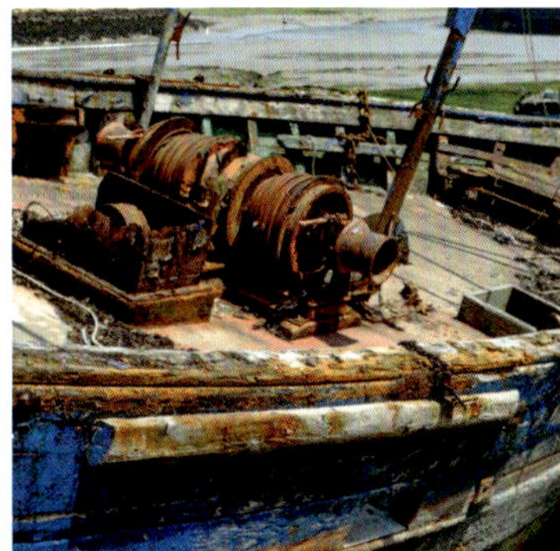
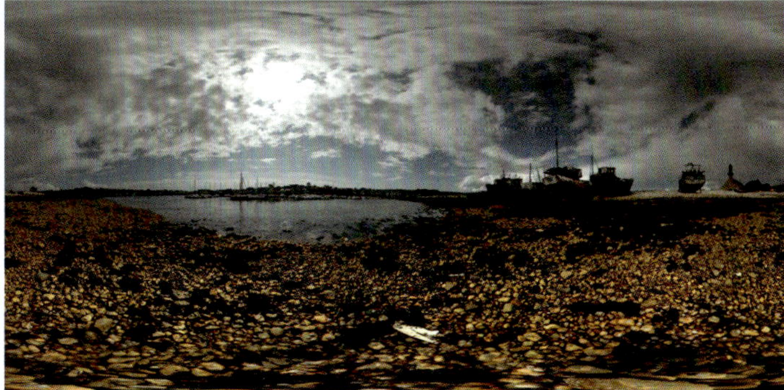
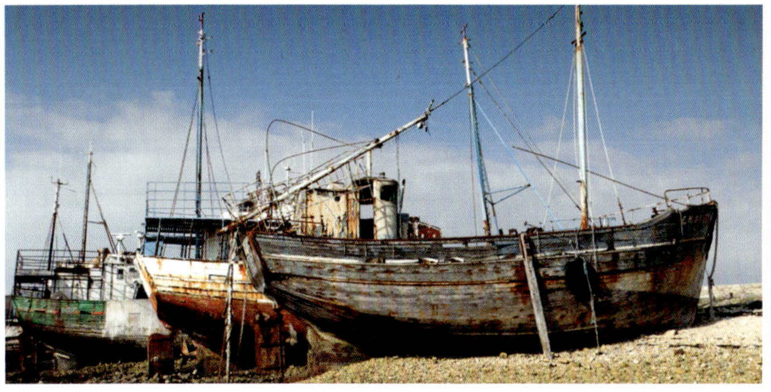
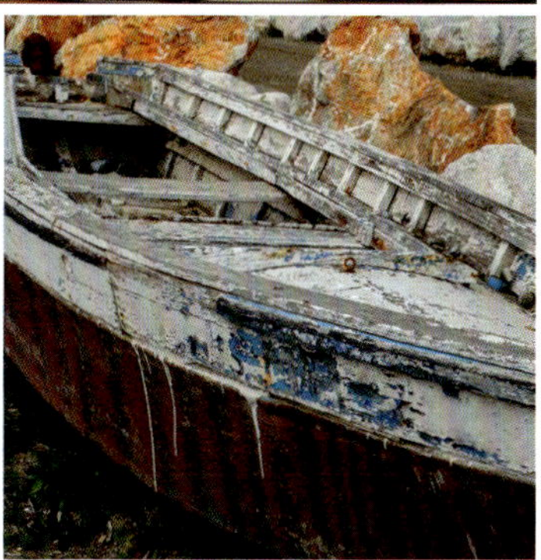

The Shipping Graveyards

Brittany's shipping graveyards are a reminder of the wooden boats of the past . Their silhouettes still populate the Breton coast, even though they have long since been replaced by ships made of modern materials. Deprived of their purpose and stuck in the mud, they are the witnesses of a bygone era.

Los cementerios de barcos

Los cementerios de barcos de Bretaña recuerdan el pasado de los barcos de madera. Sus siluetas siguen poblando la costa bretona, a pesar de que hace tiempo que han sido sustituidas por barcos de materiales modernos. Privados de su propósito y atrapados en el barro, son testigos de una época pasada.

Épaves et cimetières de bateaux

En Bretagne, les cimetières de bateaux déchaînent les passions. Les bateaux en bois ont été délaissés, remplacés par des embarcations aux matériaux plus « modernes », mais leurs silhouettes surannées peuplent toujours les côtes bretonnes. Englués dans la vase, à l'abandon, ils sont les témoins d'une époque révolue.

Os cemitérios de navios

Os cemitérios de navios da Bretanha lembram o passado dos barcos de madeira. Embora estes tenham sido substituídos, há muito tempo, por navios feitos de materiais modernos, as suas silhuetas ainda estão presentes na costa bretã. Impossibilitados de se realizarem e presos na lama, eles são testemunhas de uma era passada.

Die Schiffsfriedhöfe

Die Schiffsfriedhöfe der Bretagne erinnern an die vergangene Zeit der Holzboote. Ihre Silhouetten bevölkern immer noch die bretonische Küste, auch wenn sie heute längst durch Schiffe aus modernen Materialien ersetzt wurden. Ihrem Zweck beraubt und im Schlamm stecken geblieben sind sie die Zeugen einer vergangenen Ära.

De scheepskerkhoven

De scheepskerkhoven in Bretagne herinneren aan het verleden met houten boten. Hun silhouetten steken nog altijd af tegen de Bretonse kust, ook al zijn ze al lang geleden vervangen door schepen van moderne materialen. Beroofd van hun doel en vastgelopen in de modder zijn zij de getuigen van een vervlogen tijdperk.

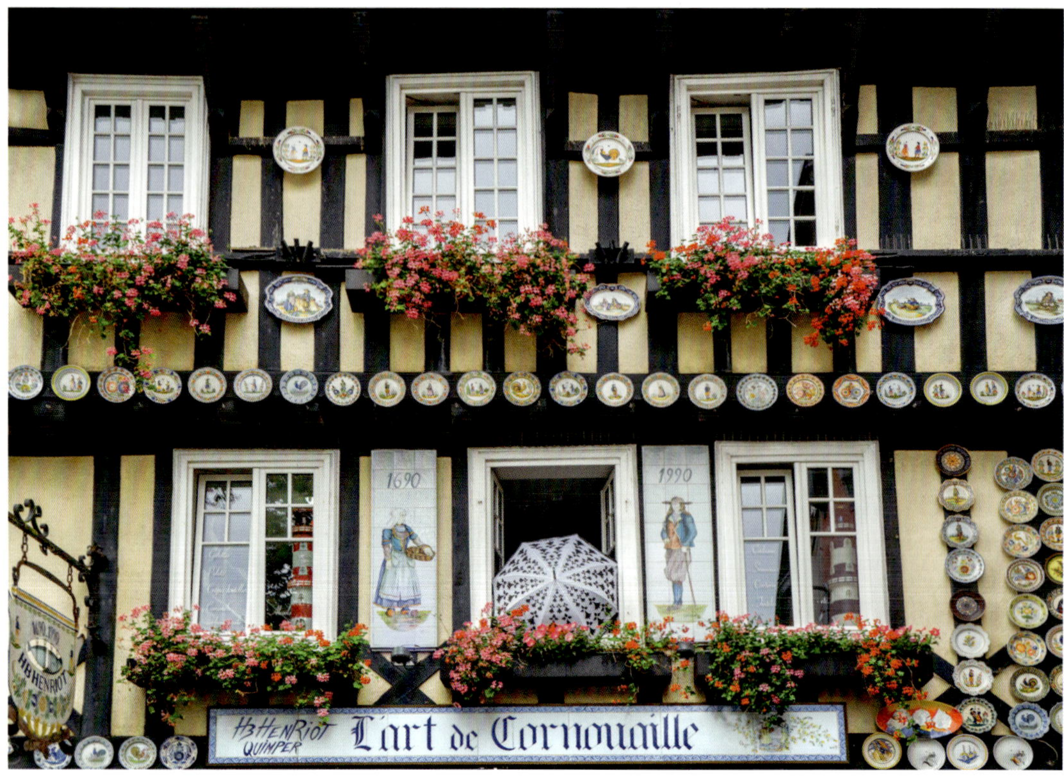

Quimper

Quimper

The capital of the department of Finistère is known far beyond its borders. With its half-timbered houses, flower-lined waterfront promenades, picturesque bridges and its ceramic workshops, the Locmaria district worth seeing. Quimper is at the centre of southern Finistère.

Quimper

Chef-lieu du département du Finistère, le rayonnement de Quimper va bien au-delà de son statut de ville. Avec ses maisons à colombages, ses quais fleuris, ses passerelles de l'Odet jusqu'au quartier de Locmaria, berceau des faïenceries, Quimper est la capitale du Finistère Sud.

Quimper

Die Hauptstadt des Departements Finistère ist weit über dessen Grenzen hinaus bekannt. Mit den Fachwerkhäusern, den von Blumen gesäumten Uferpromenaden, den pittoresken Brücken, den sehenswerten Stadtteil Locmaria und den Keramikwerkstätten ist Quimper das Zentrum des Süd-Finistère.

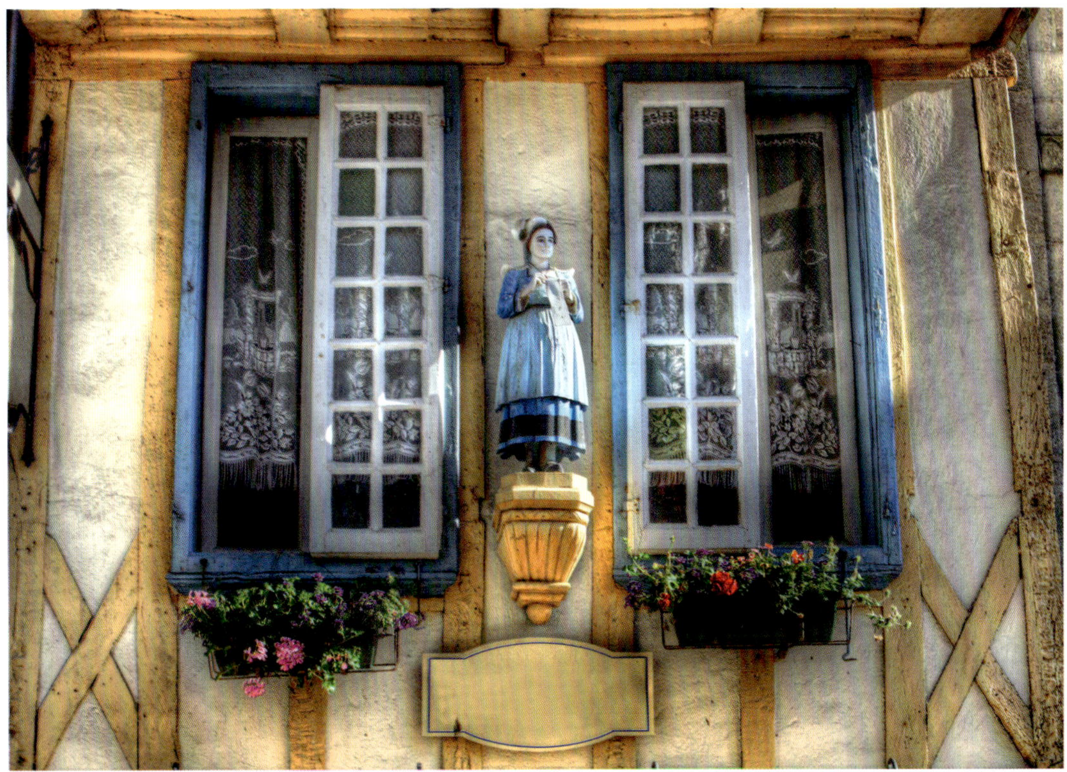

Quimper

Quimper

La capital del departamento de Finisterre es conocida mucho más allá de sus fronteras. Con sus casas de entramado de madera, sus paseos marítimos floridos, sus pintorescos puentes, su bonito barrio Locmaria y sus talleres de cerámica, Quimper es el centro del sur del Finisterre.

Quimper

A capital do departamento de Finistère é conhecida muito além das suas fronteiras. Com as suas casas em estilo enxaimel, os passeios à beira-mar floridos, as pontes pitorescas, o notável bairro de Locmaria e as oficinas de cerâmica, Quimper torna-se o centro do sul de Finistère.

Quimper

De hoofdstad van het departement Finistère is tot ver buiten de provinciegrenzen bekend. Met zijn vakwerkhuizen, de met bloemen omzoomde promenades, pittoreske bruggen, de bezienswaardige wijk Locmaria en keramiekwerkplaatsen is Quimper het centrum van Zuid-Finistère.

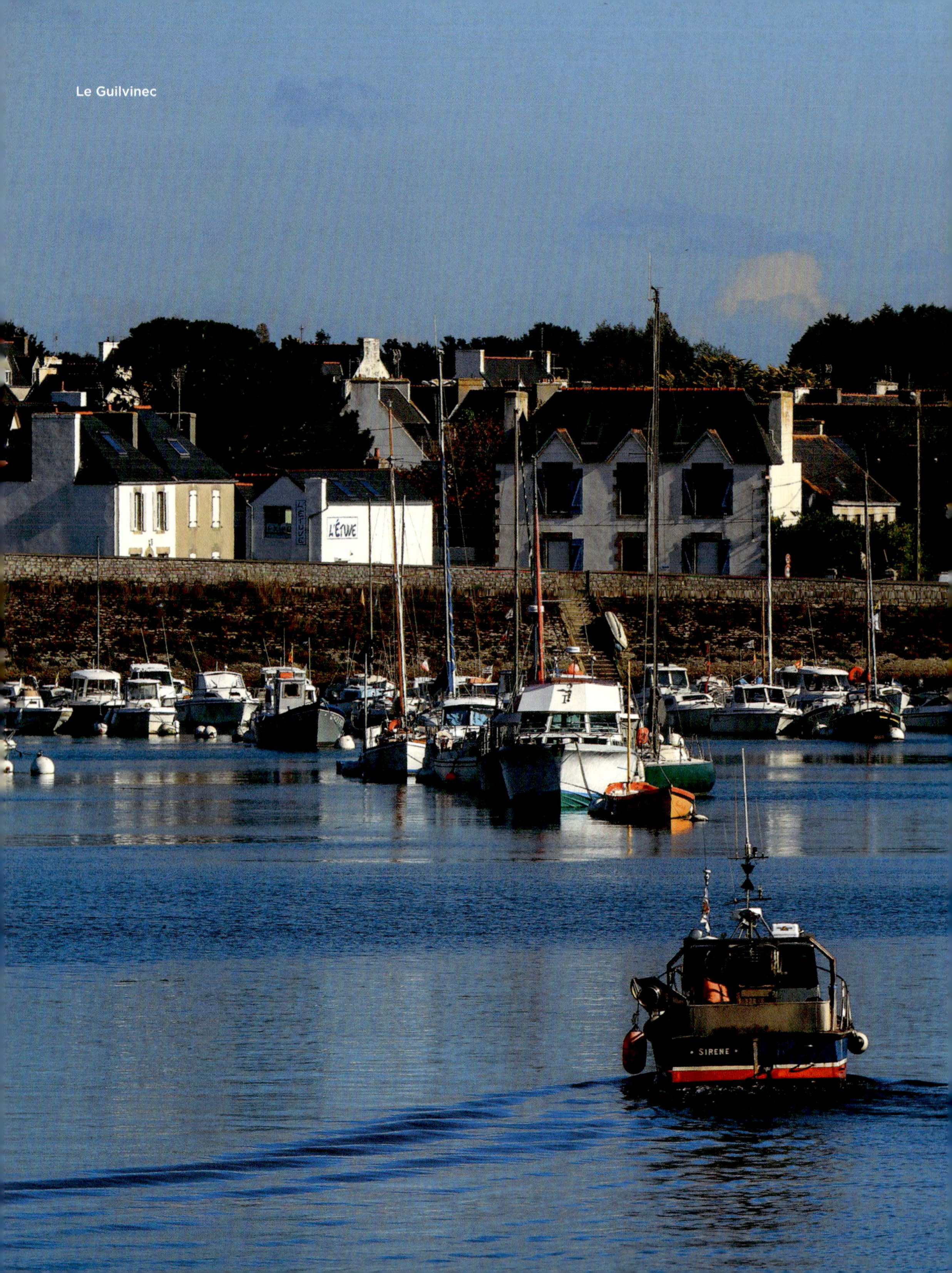

Le Guilvinec

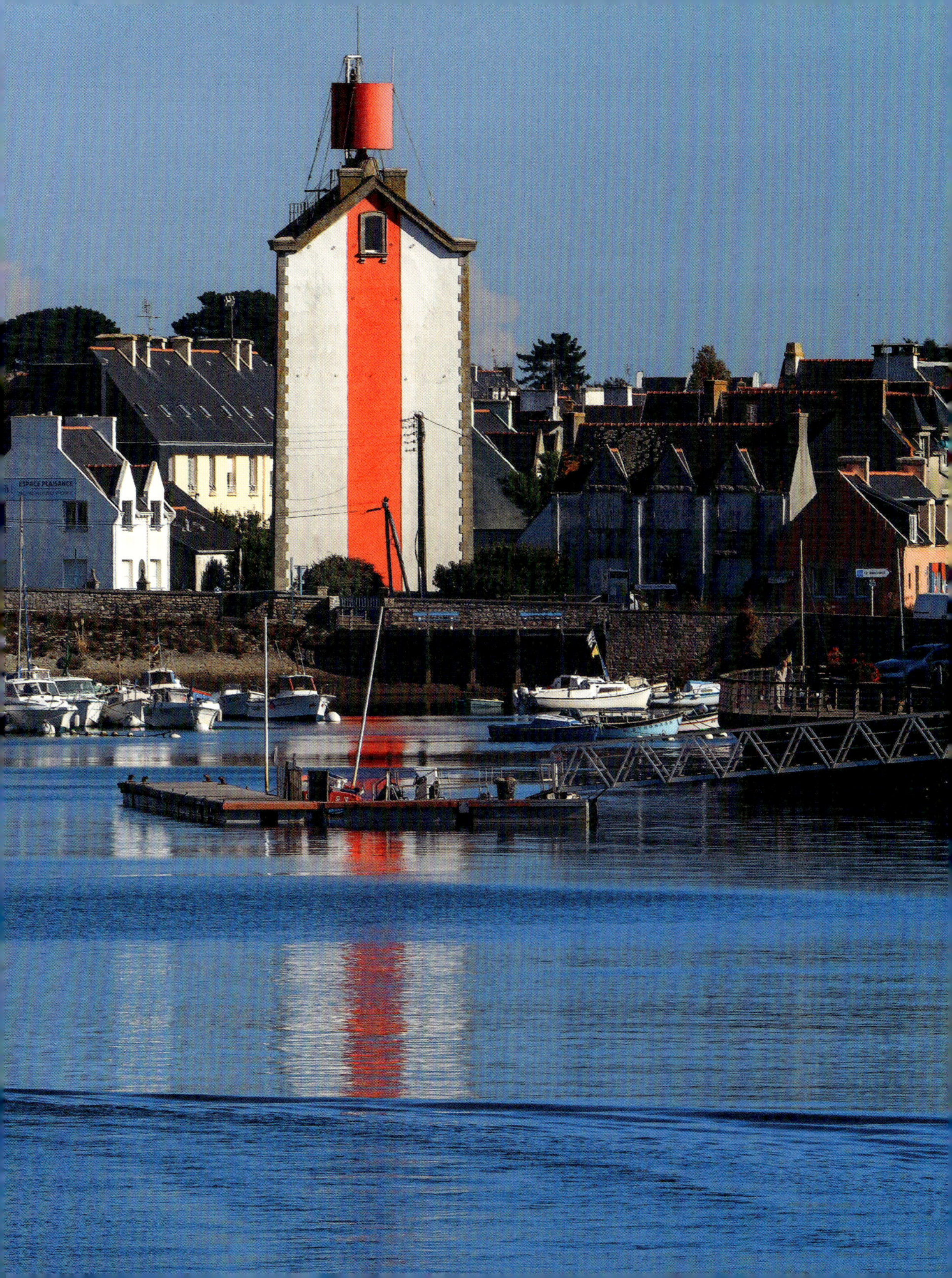
ESPACE PLAISANCE

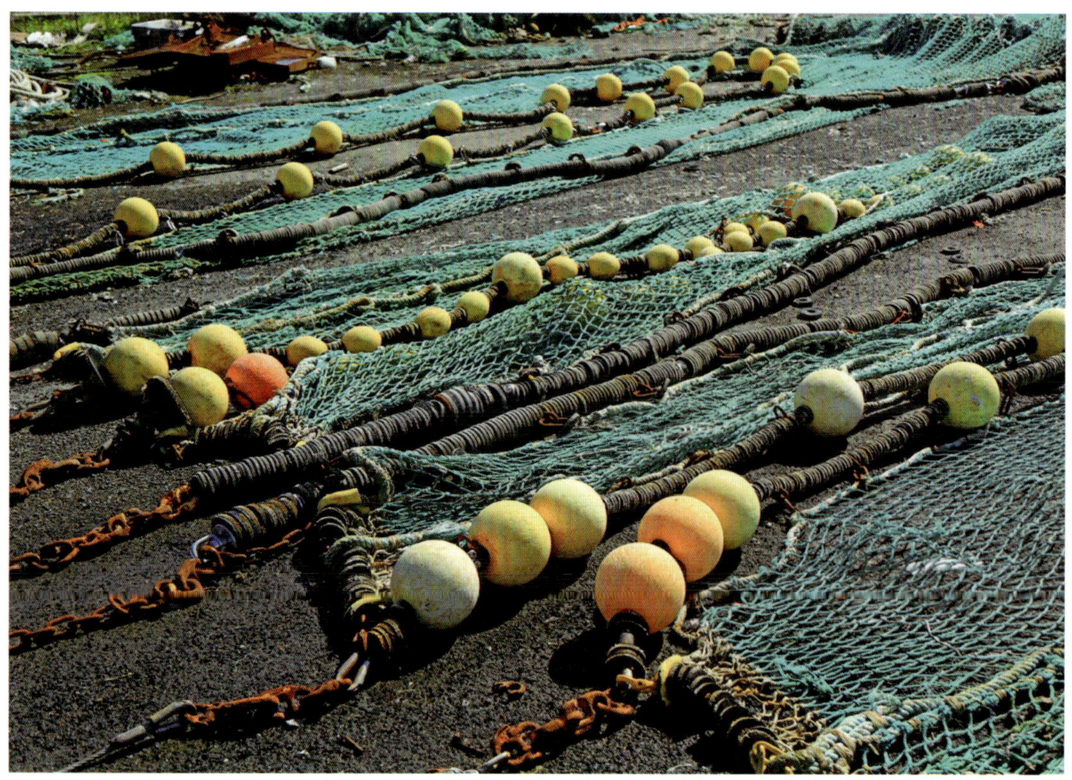

Filets de pêche, Loctudy

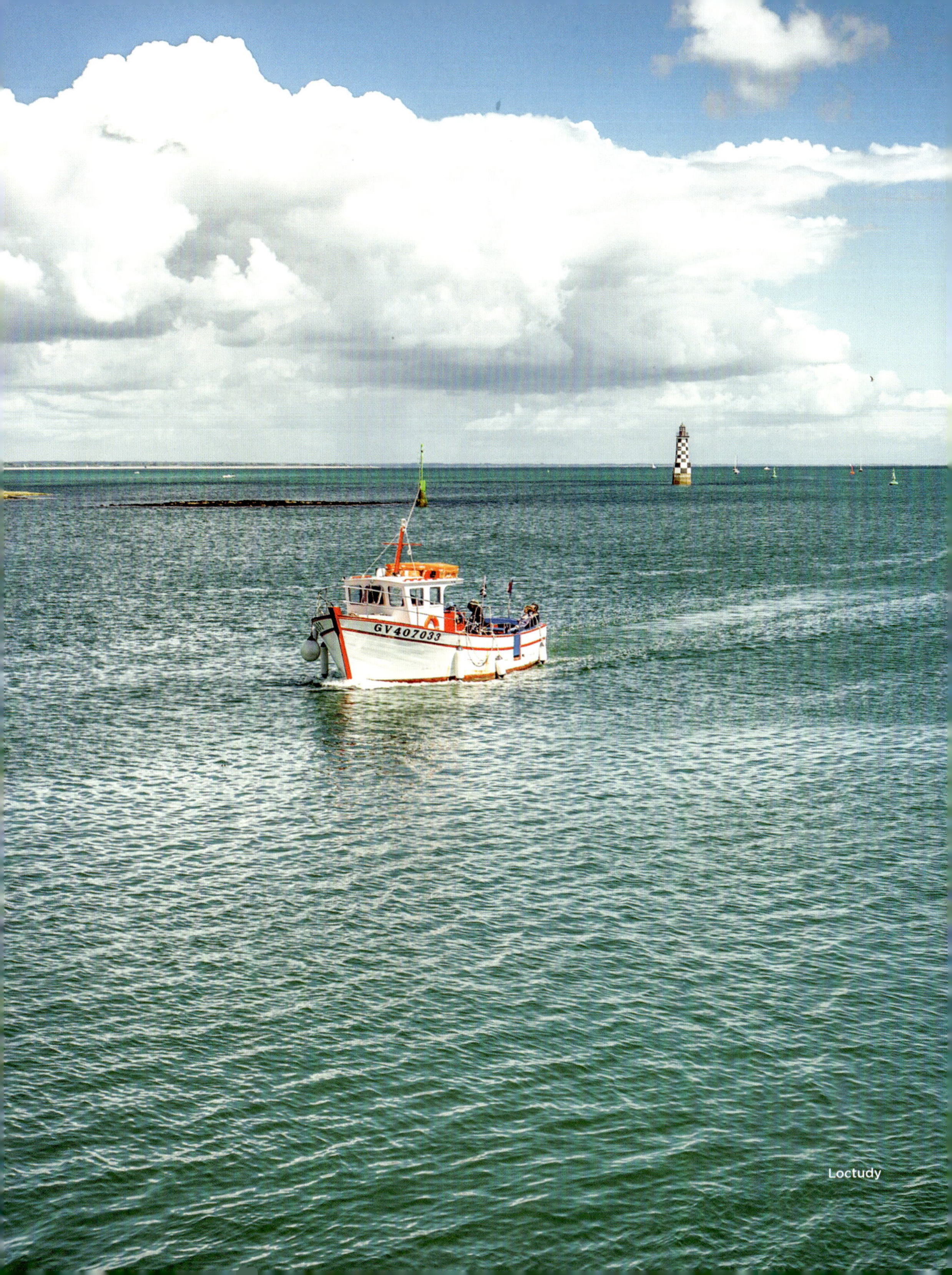

Loctudy

Bénodet, au bord de la rivière de l'Odet

Bénodet

Bénodet lies in the heart of the Breton Riviera in Bigoudenland. Opposite the picturesque village is the small port of Sainte-Marine, which invites you to take a stroll overlooking the open sea and the Glénan Islands.

Bénodet

Au cœur de la Riviera bretonne, en pays bigouden, Bénodet est une destination de rêve. En face, le minuscule port de Sainte-Marine invite à la flânerie en contemplant le grand large, face à l'archipel des Glénan.

Bénodet

Bénodet liegt im Herzen der bretonischen Riviera im Bigoudenland. Gegenüber dem malerischen Ort befindet sich der kleine Hafen von Sainte-Marine, der zu Spaziergängen mit Blick auf das offene Meer und die Glénan-Inseln einlädt.

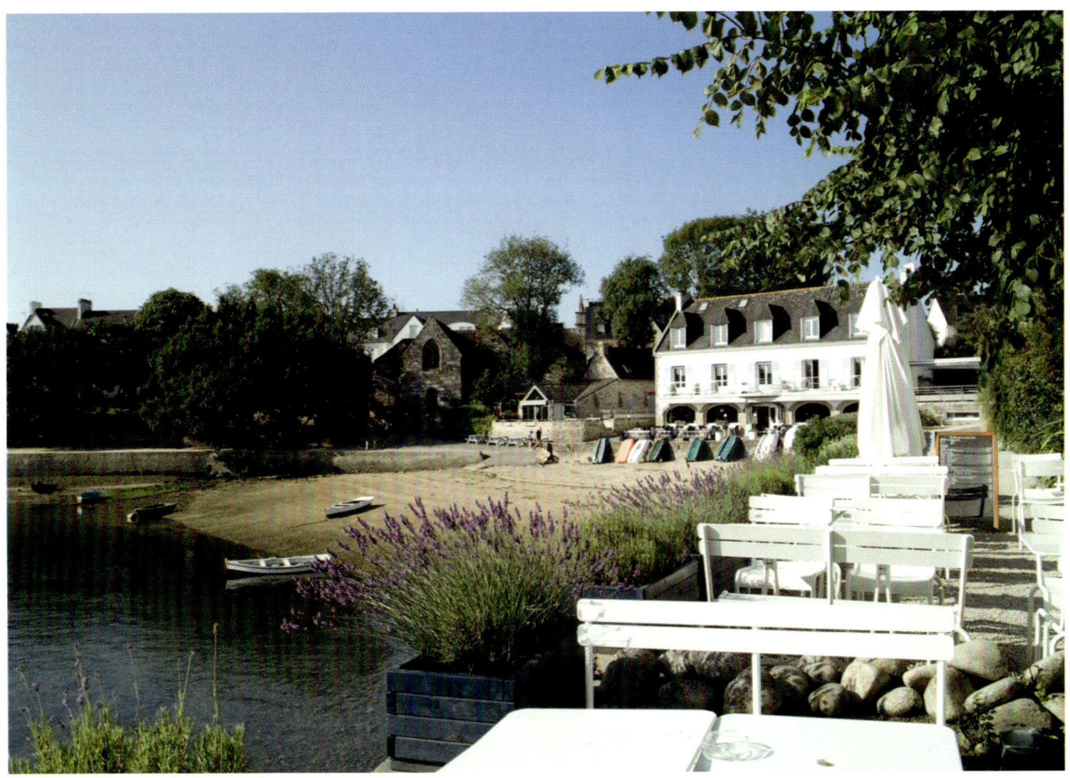

Le port de Sainte-Marine

Bénodet

Bénodet se encuentra en el corazón de la riviera bretona en Bigoudenland. Frente al pintoresco pueblo se encuentra el pequeño puerto de Sainte-Marine, que invita a dar un paseo con vistas al mar abierto y a las islas Glénan.

Bénodet

Bénodet fica no centro da Riviera Bretã em Bigoudenland. Em frente à vila pitoresca encontra-se o pequeno porto de Sainte-Marine, que convida a dar um passeio com vistas para o mar aberto e para as Ilhas Glénan.

Bénodet

Bénodet ligt in het hart van de Bretonse Rivièra in het Pays Bigouden. Tegenover het pittoreske dorpje ligt de kleine haven van Sainte-Marine, die u uitnodigt voor een wandeling met uitzicht op de open zee en de Glénan-archipel.

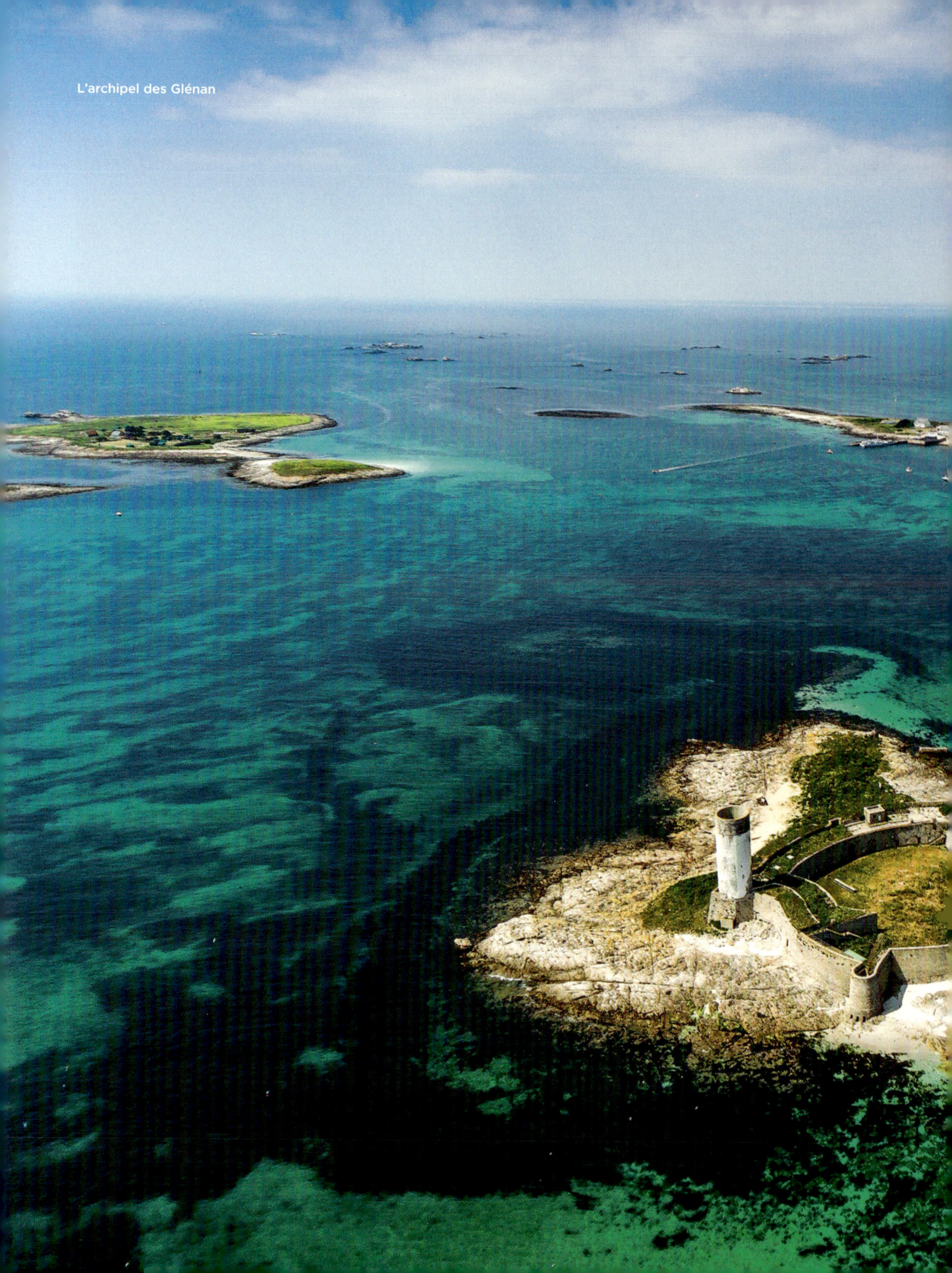
L'archipel des Glénan

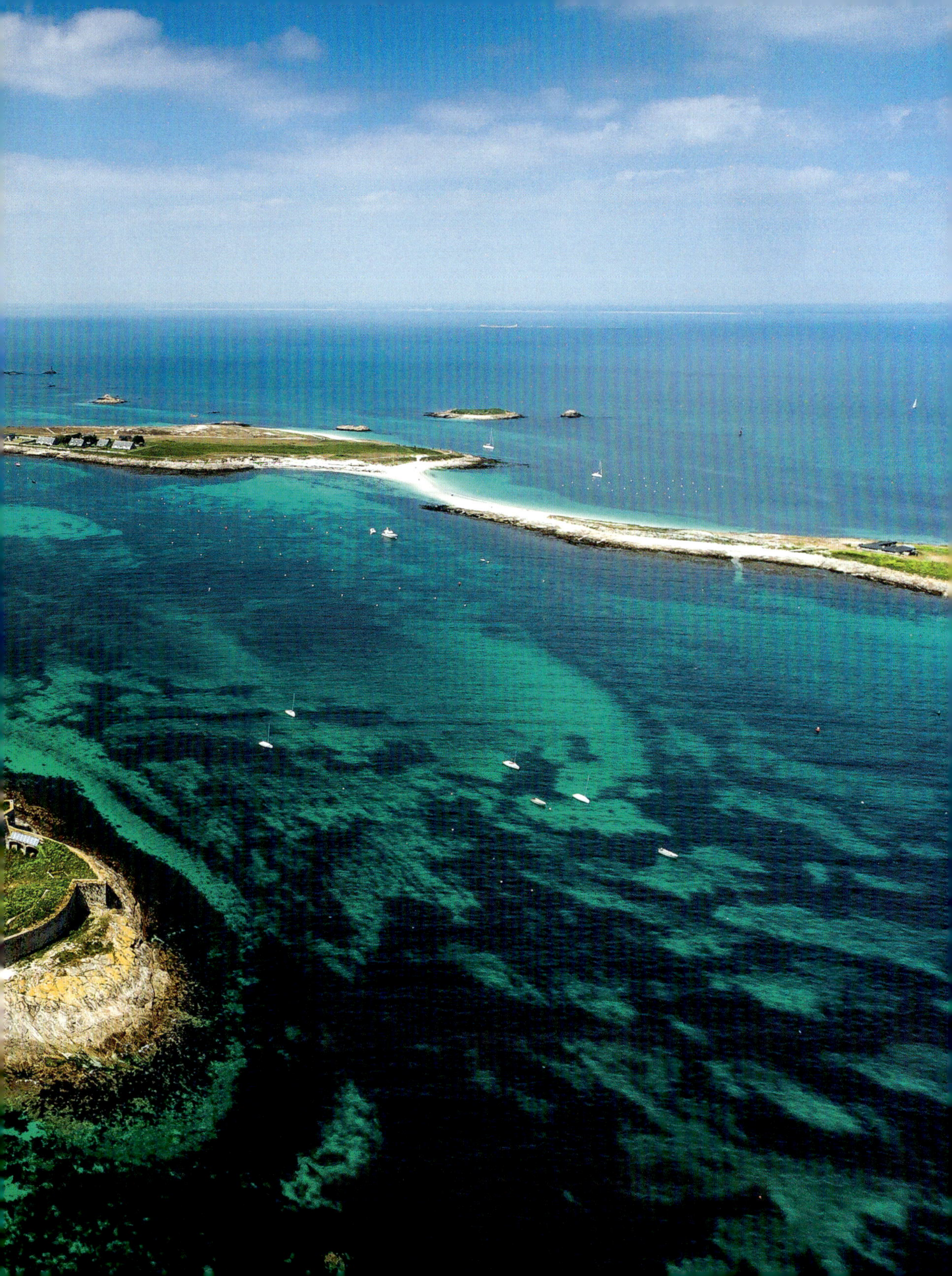

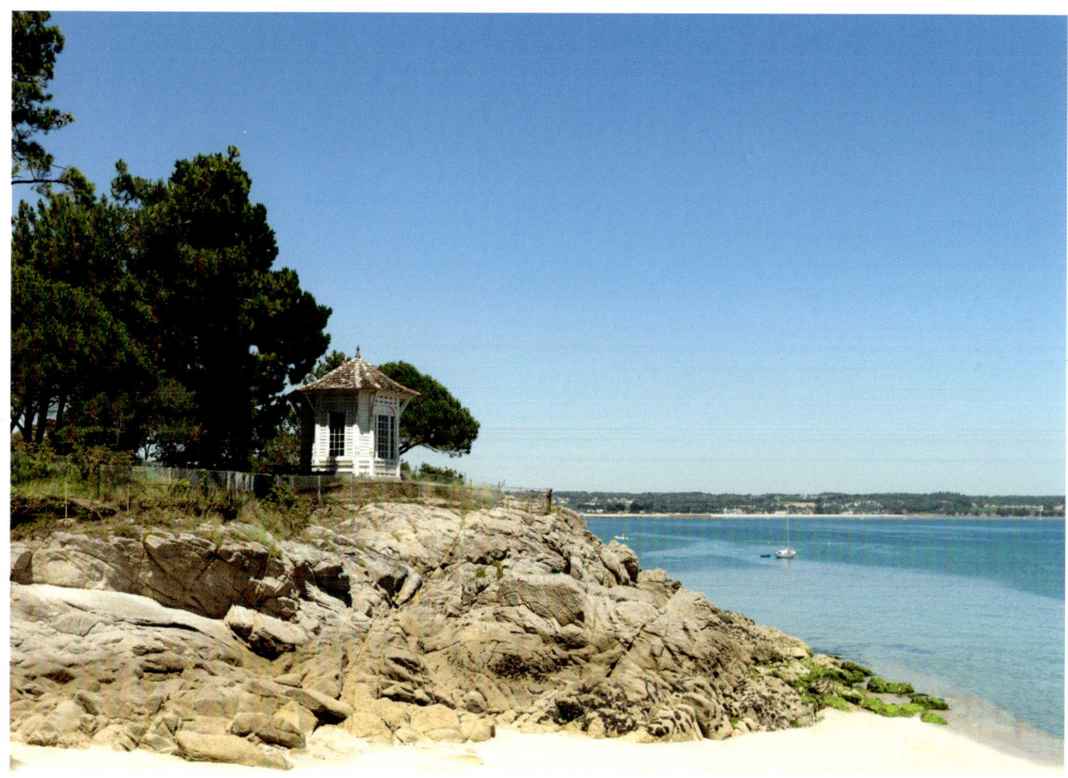

La plage de Beg Meil, Fouesnant

La Forêt-Fouesnant

Between Bénodet and Concarneau lies the village of La Forêt-Fouesnant. Numerous hiking and walking trails lead through the wooded surroundings. The old port, the wide sandy beach or the marina Port-La-Forêt, which is a centre for ocean racing, invite you to linger.

La Forêt–Fouesnant

La Forêt–Fouesnant est un village situé entre Bénodet et Concarneau. Très boisé, entre ses sentiers de balades et de randonnées, on fait une pause sur le vieux port, devant sa longue plage de sable fin, ou encore au port de plaisance Port-La-Forêt, où l'on peut croiser les plus grands skippers de la course au large.

La Forêt–Fouesnant

Zwischen Bénodet und Concarneau liegt das Dorf La Forêt-Fouesnant. Zahlreiche Wander- und Spazierwege führen durch die bewaldete Umgebung. Der alte Hafen, der weite Sandstrand oder der Jachthafen Port-La-Forêt, der ein Zentrum der Hochseeregatten ist, laden zum Verweilen ein.

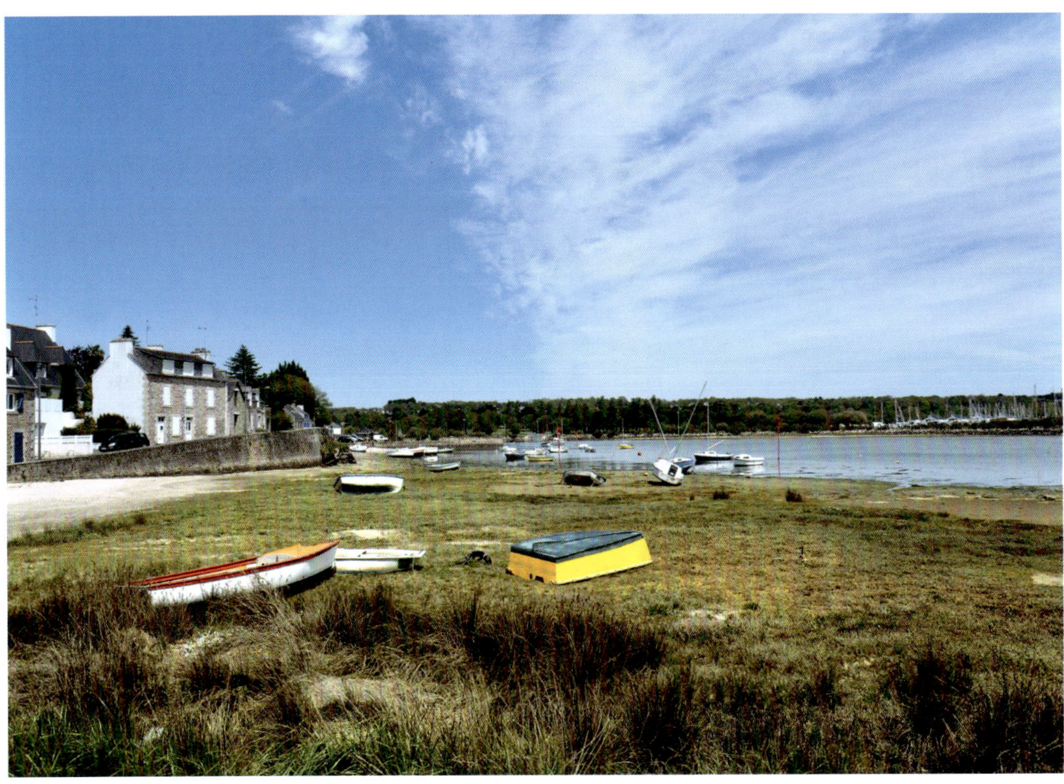

La Forêt-Fouesnant

La Forêt-Fouesnant

Entre Bénodet y Concarneau se encuentra el pueblo La Forêt-Fouesnant. Numerosas rutas de senderismo y caminos para pasear conducen a través de los alrededores boscosos. El puerto viejo, la amplia playa de arena o el puerto deportivo Port-La-Forêt, que es un centro de regatas en alta mar, invitan a quedarse.

La Forêt-Fouesnant

Entre Bénodet e Concarneau situa-se a aldeia de La Forêt-Fouesnant ao redor da qual se encontram numerosas trilhas e caminhos pelos arredores arborizados. O antigo porto, a praia de areia larga e a marina Port-La-Forêt, que é um centro de regatas de alto mar, convidam a permanecer algum tempo.

La Forêt-Fouesnant

Tussen Bénodet en Concarneau ligt het dorp La Forêt-Fouesnant. Er lopen talrijke wandelpaden door de bosrijke omgeving. De oude haven, het brede zandstrand en de jachthaven Port-La-Forêt, een centrum voor zeilwedstrijden op zee, nodigen uit tot een verblijf.

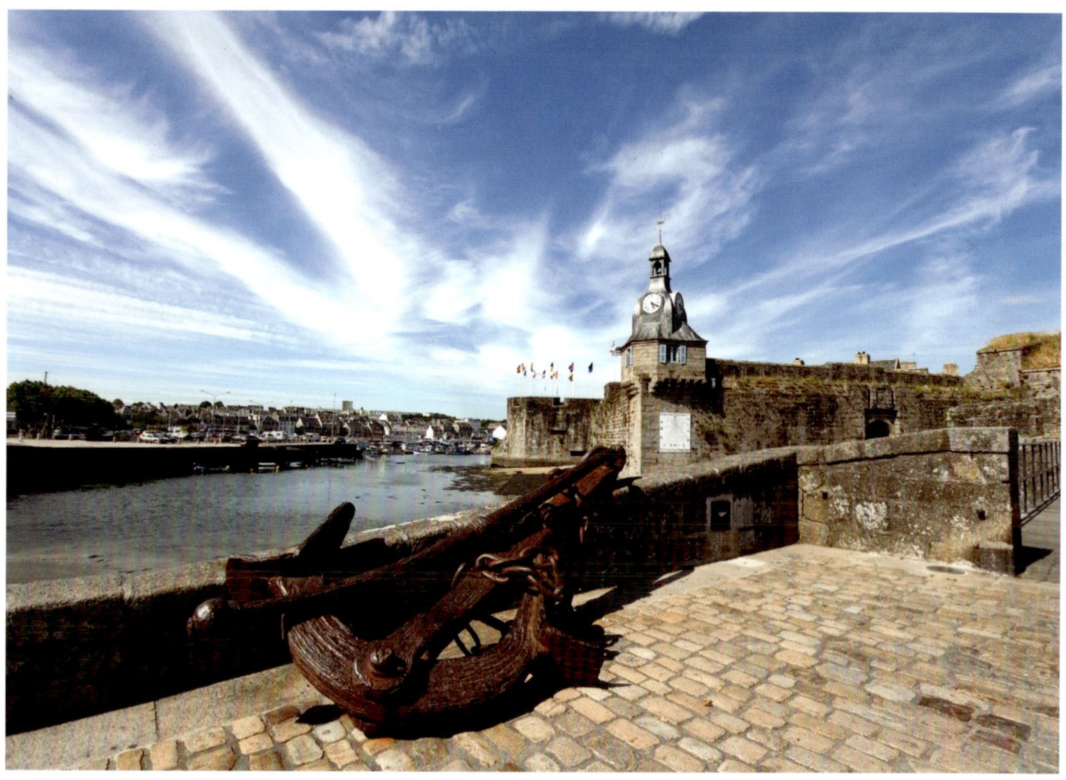

L'entrée de la Ville close, Concarneau

Concarneau

Concarneau - a city of art and history - impresses with its walled city centre. The fortifications date back to 1300, and a bridge connects the town, which developed into a fishing centre, to the mainland.

Concarneau

Ville d'art et d'histoire, Concarneau, particulièrement connue et appréciée pour sa pittoresque Ville close et ses fortifications datant des années 1300, est rattachée au continent par un pont. La ville s'est développée autour de son port, grâce à l'industrie de la pêche.

Concarneau

Concarneau – die Stadt der Kunst und Geschichte – beeindruckt durch ihren von Mauern umgebenen Stadtkern. Die Befestigungsanlagen stammen aus dem Jahr 1300. Über eine Brücke ist die Stadt, die sich als ein Zentrum der Fischerei entwickelte, mit dem Festland verbunden.

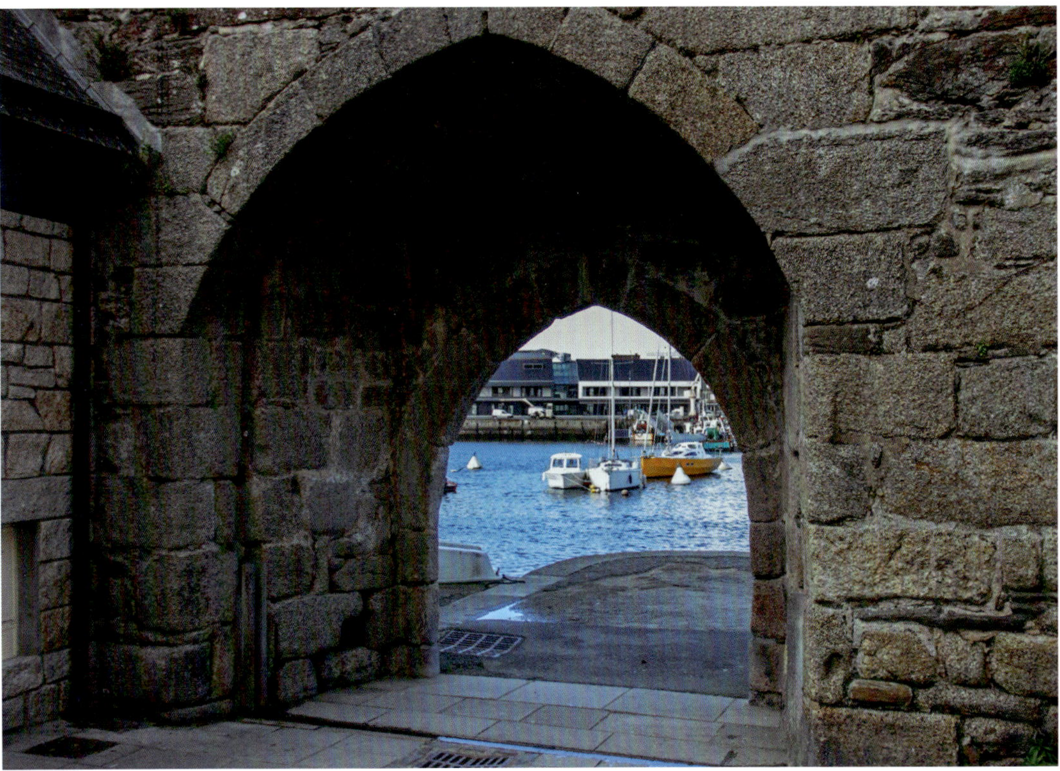

La porte du vin, Concarneau

Concarneau

Concarneau, la ciudad de arte e historia, impresiona por su centro amurallado. Las fortificaciones datan de 1300 y un puente conecta la ciudad, que se convirtió en un centro de pesca, con el continente.

Concarneau

Concarneau - a cidade da arte e da história - impressiona pelo seu centro muralhado. As fortificações remontam a 1300 e uma ponte liga a cidade, que se transformou num centro de pesca, ao continente.

Concarneau

Concarneau, de stad van kunst en geschiedenis, maakt indruk met zijn ommuurde binnenstad. De vestingwerken dateren van 1300. Een brug verbindt de stad, die is uitgegroeid tot een centrum van visserij, met het vasteland.

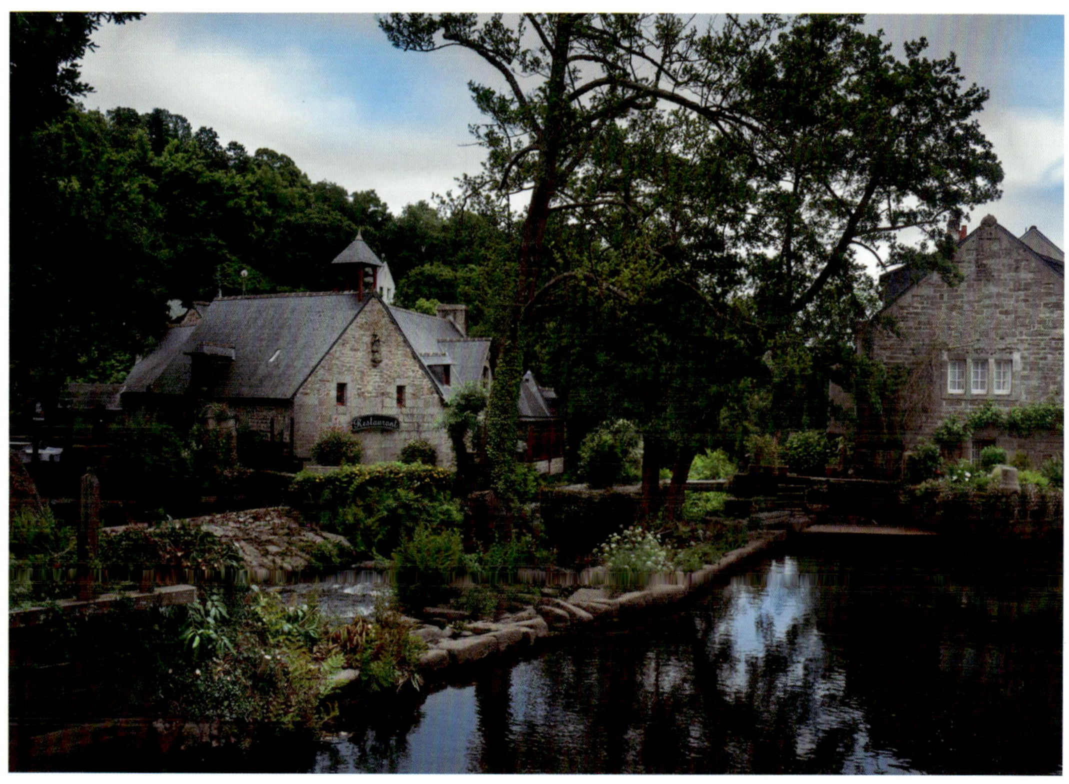

La rivière de l'Aven, Pont-Aven

Pont Aven

Located at the mouth of a river, Pont-Aven is nicknamed the "city of painters". The Aven, which changes from a wild river into a quiet estuary, divides the village into two halves. The beauty of the landscape, the picturesque little harbour with its yachts and the play of the tides make Pont-Aven a destination worth seeing.

Pont-Aven

Pont-Aven, au cœur d'un estuaire, est surnommée « la cité des peintres ». La poésie de ses paysages et la luminosité de son petit port sur l'Aven qui traverse la ville, se transformant d'une rivière capricieuse en paisible estuaire remonté par les marées et quelques bateaux de plaisance, en font une étape inspirante.

Pont-Aven

Das an einer Flussmündung gelegene Pont-Aven trägt den Spitznamen „Stadt der Maler". Der Aven, der sich von einem wilden Strom in eine ruhige Mündung verwandelt, teilt das Dorf in zwei Hälften. Die Schönheit der Landschaft, der malerische kleine Hafen mit seinen Jachten und das Spiel der Gezeiten machen Pont-Aven zu einem sehenswerten Ziel.

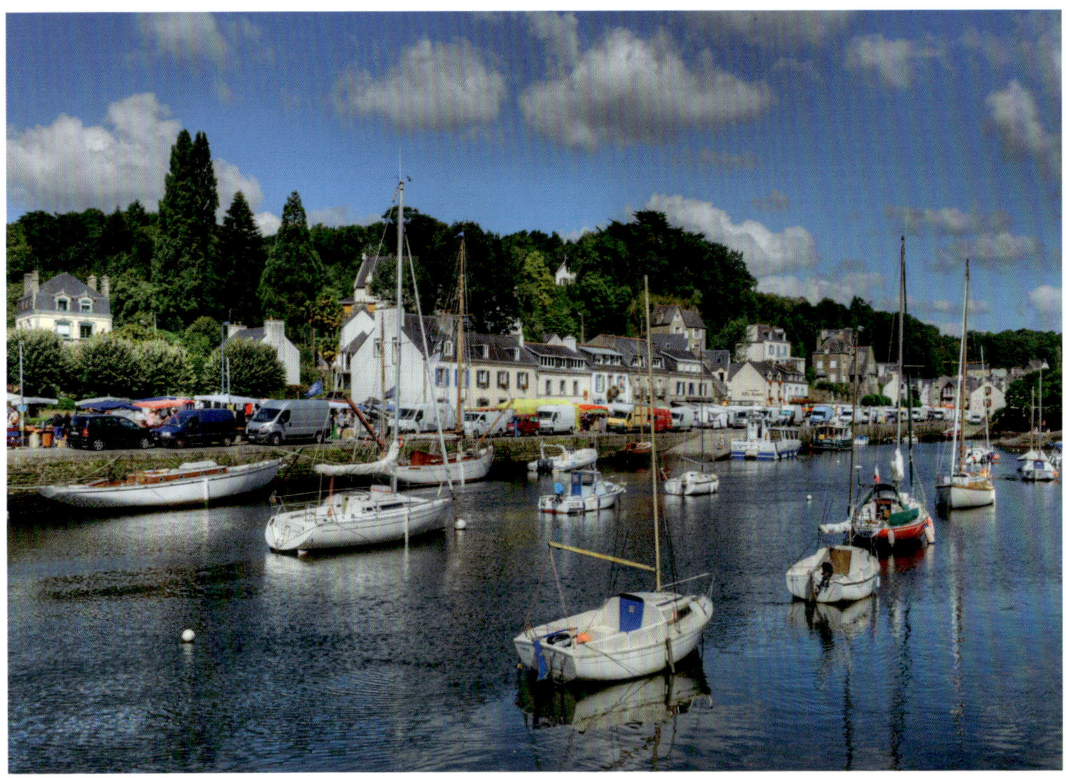

Le port de Pont-Aven

Pont-Aven

Situada en la desembocadura de un río, Pont-Aven es conocida como la «ciudad de los pintores». El Aven, que pasa de ser un río salvaje a ser una ría tranquila, divide el pueblo en dos mitades. La belleza del paisaje, el pintoresco puerto pequeño con sus yates y el juego de las mareas hacen de Pont-Aven un destino digno de ver.

Pont-Aven

Localizada na foz de um rio, Pont-Aven é também chamada a «cidade dos pintores». O rio Aven, que se tornou de um rio de forte caudal num estuário tranquilo, divide a aldeia ao meio. Devido à grandiosa beleza da sua paisagem, ao pitoresco pequeno porto com os seus iates e barcos de recreio e ao jogo das marés, Pont-Aven é um destino que vale a pena conhecer.

Pont-Aven

Het aan een riviermonding gelegen Pont-Aven heet ook wel 'stad van de schilders'. De Aven, die van een wilde rivier verandert in een rustige monding, verdeelt het dorp in tweeën. Het landschapsschoon, het pittoreske haventje met zijn jachten en het spel van de getijden maken van Pont-Aven een bezienswaardige bestemming.

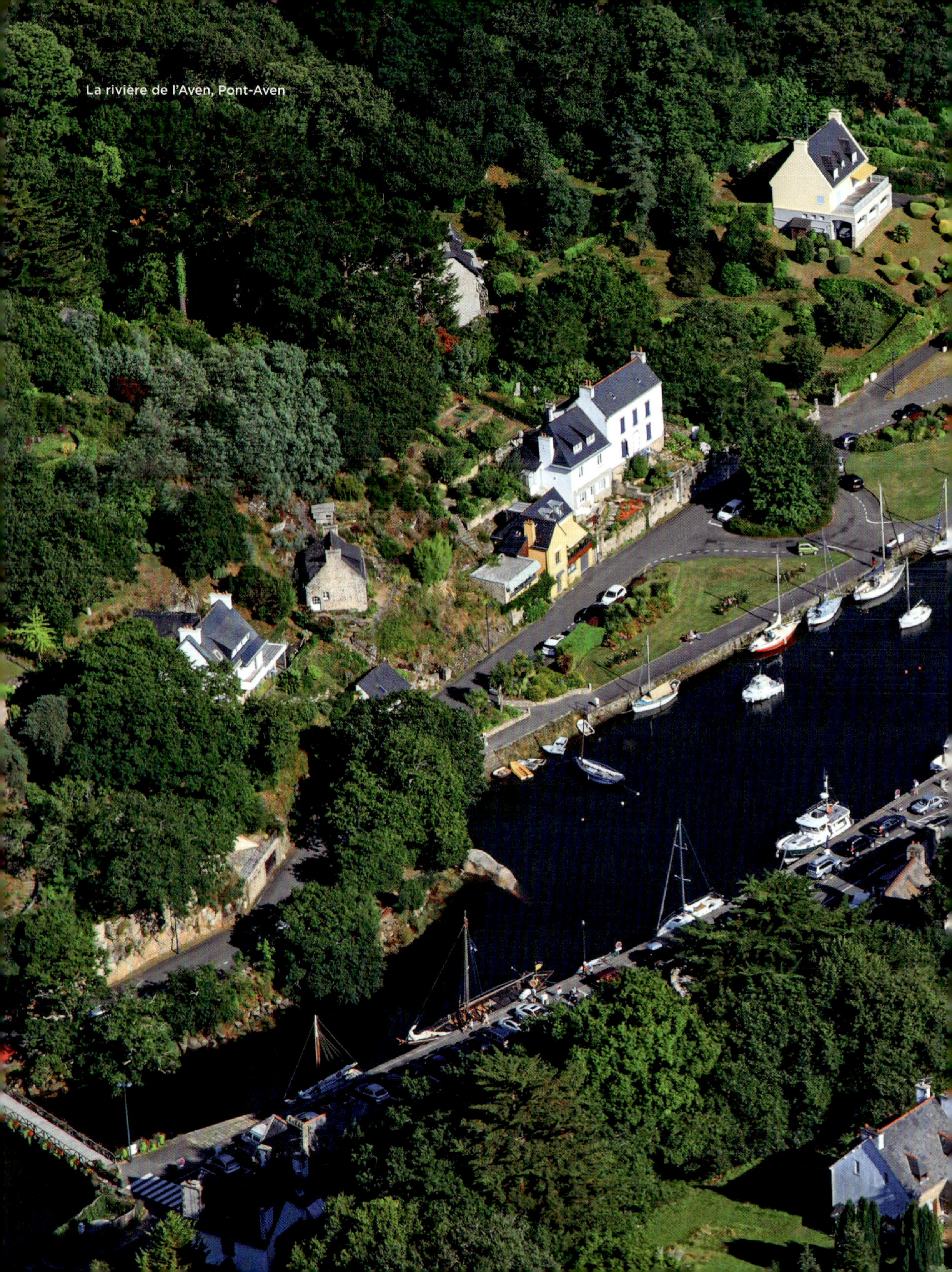

La rivière de l'Aven, Pont-Aven

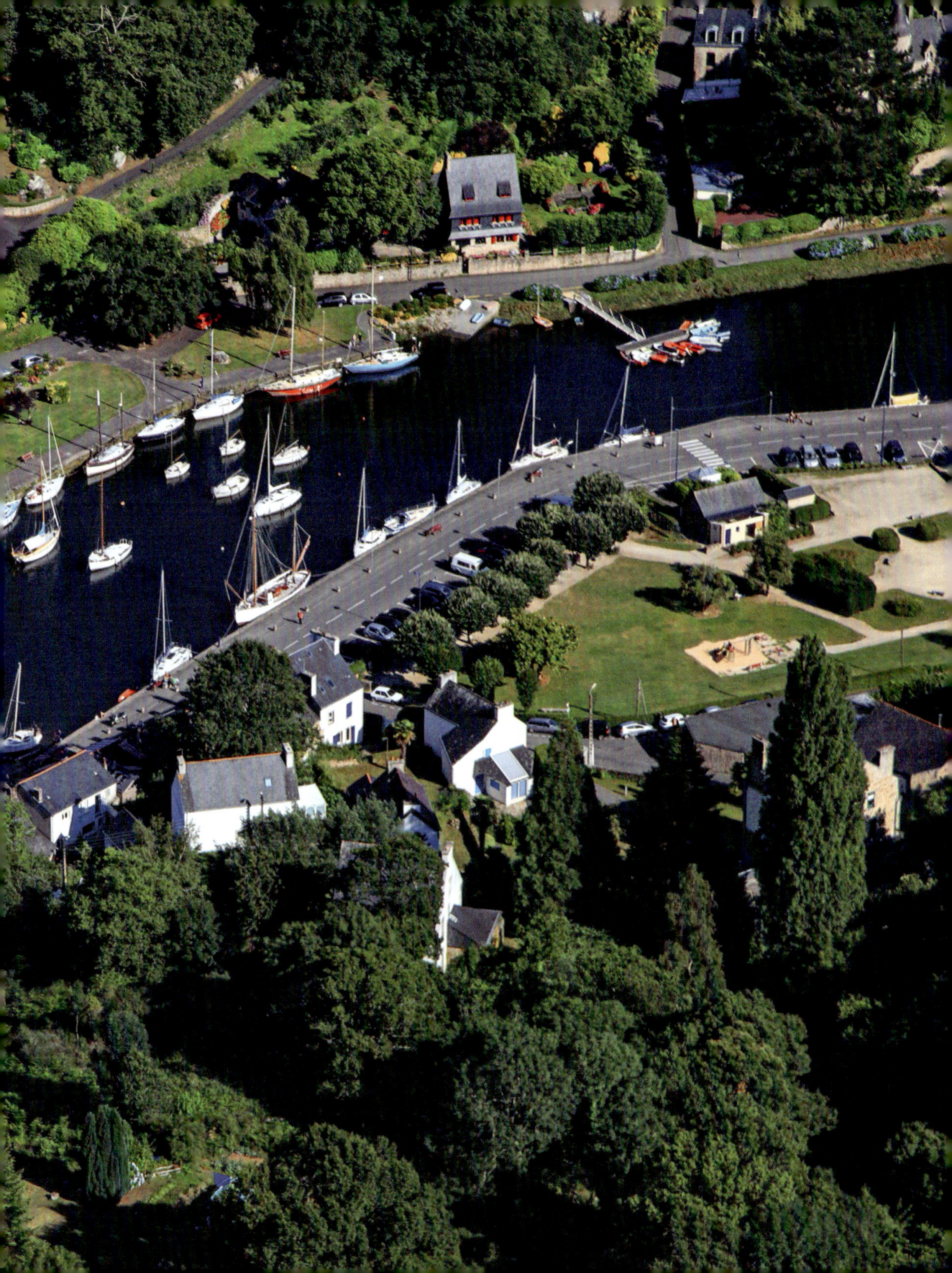

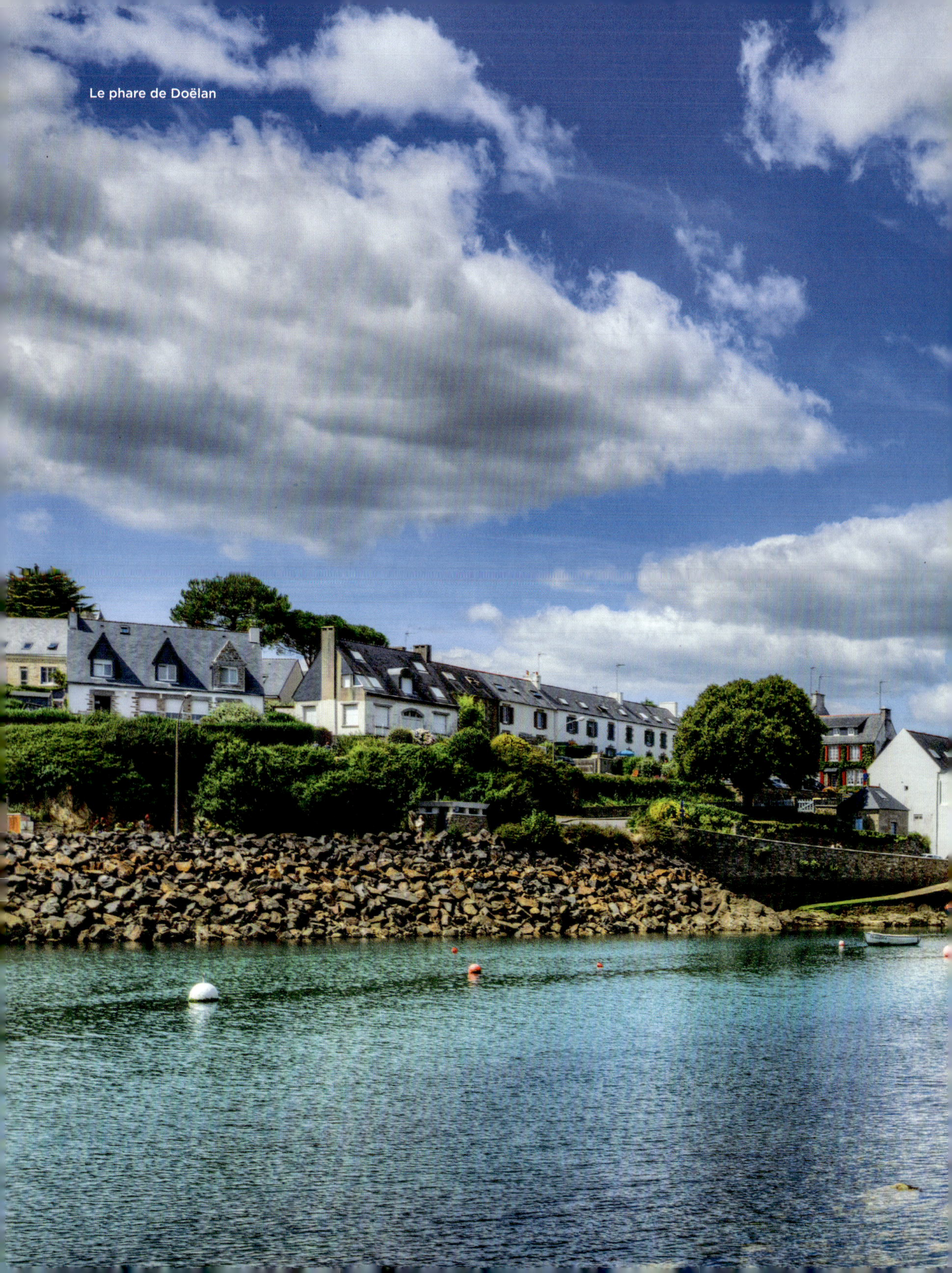
Le phare de Doëlan

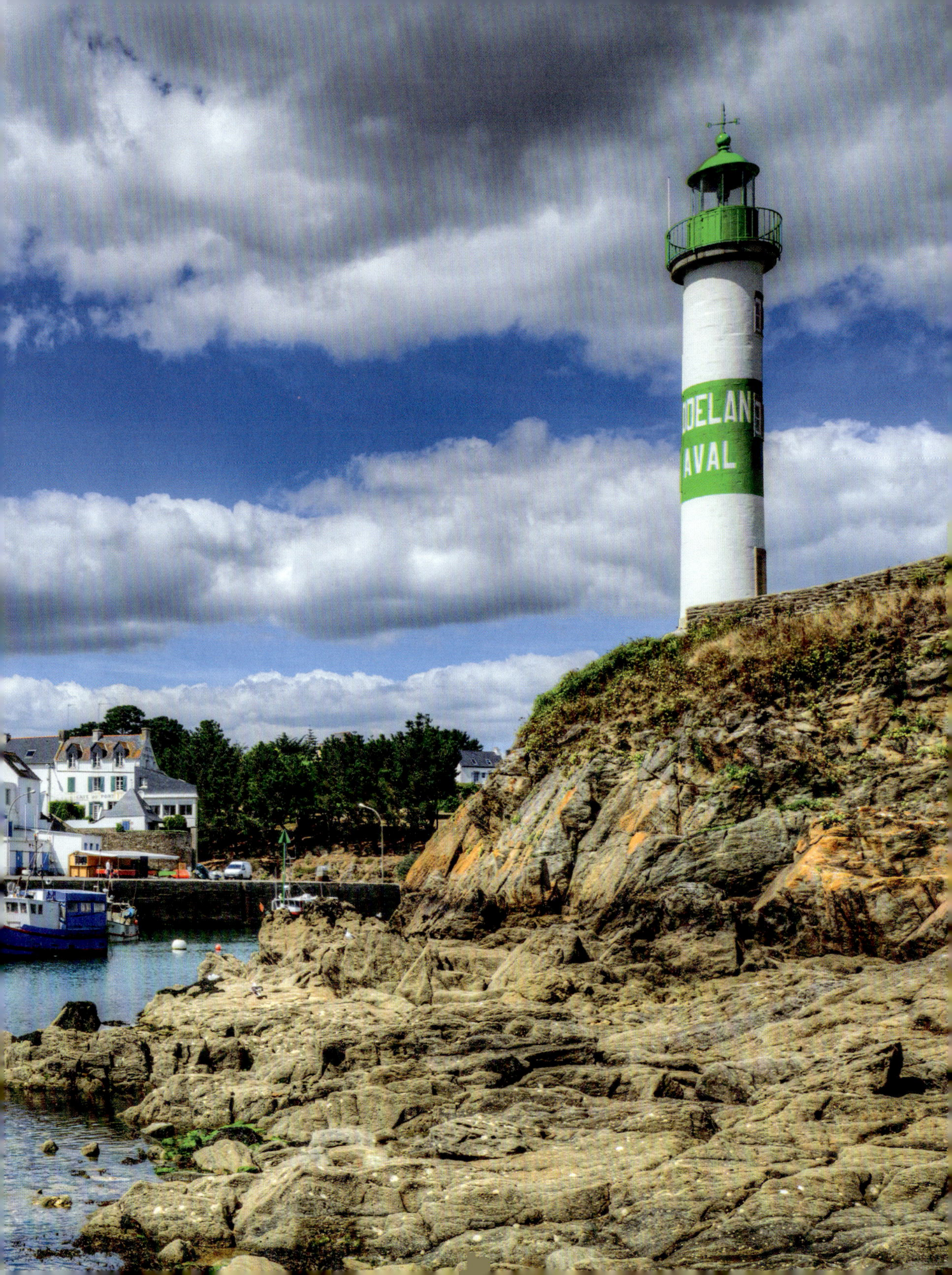
DOELAN
AVAL

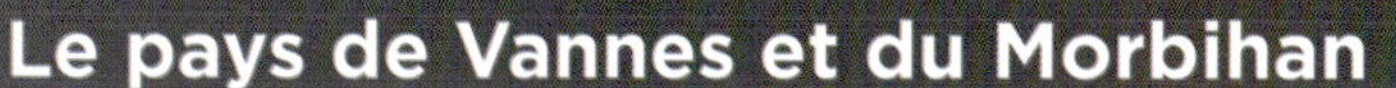

Le pays de Vannes et du Morbihan

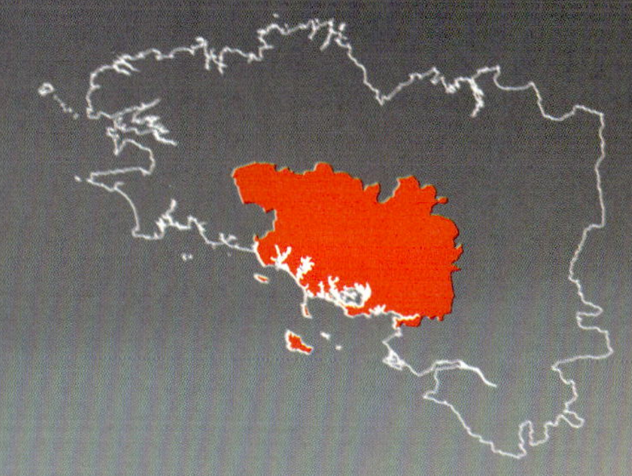

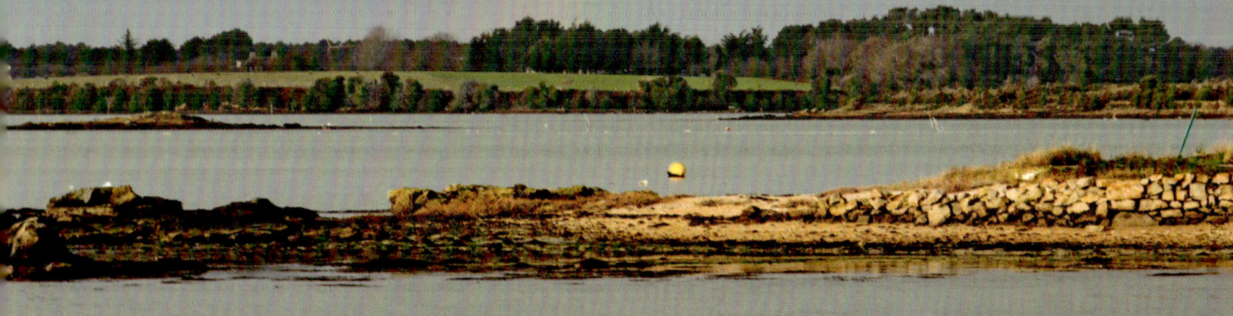

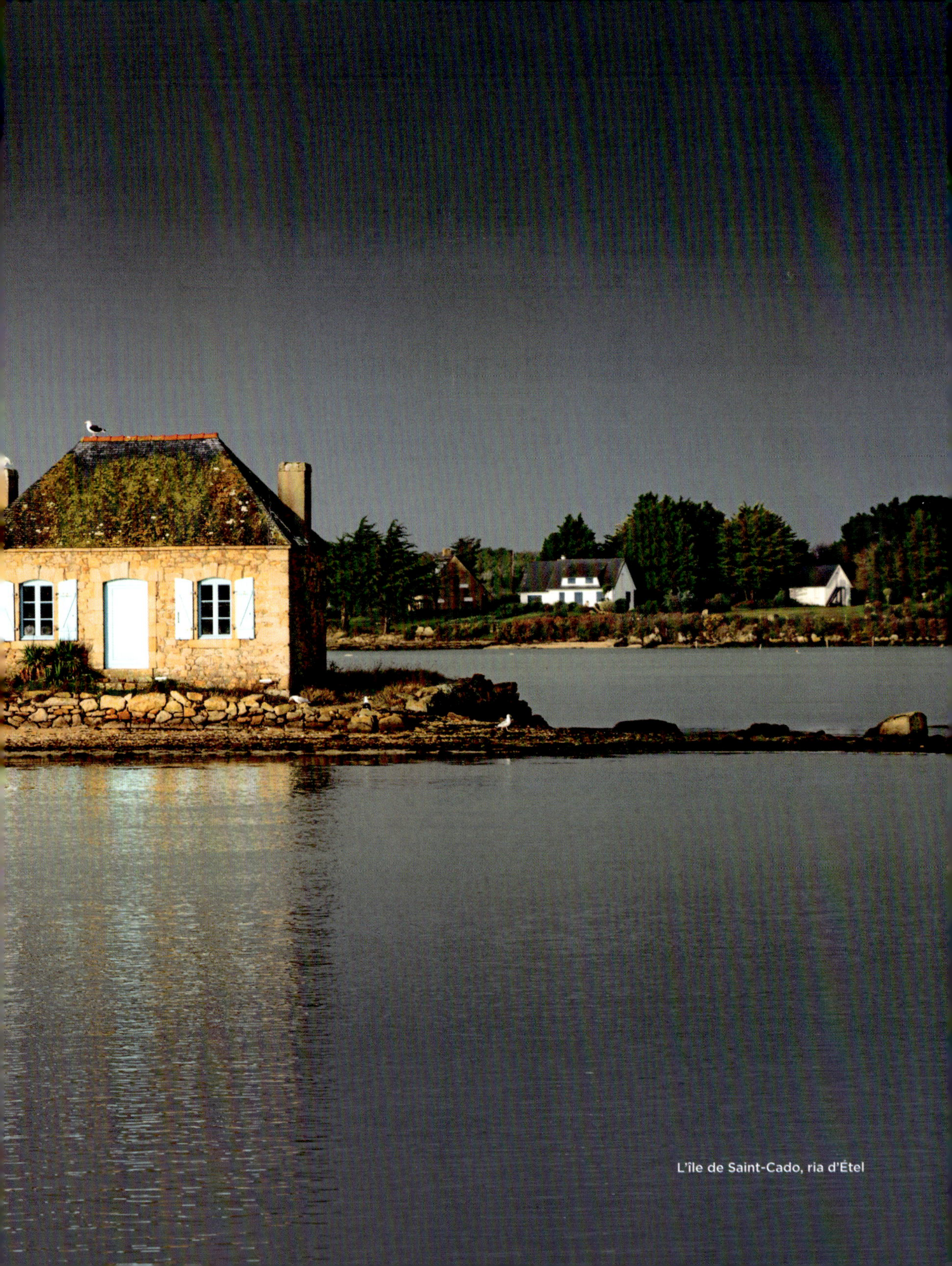

L'île de Saint-Cado, ria d'Étel

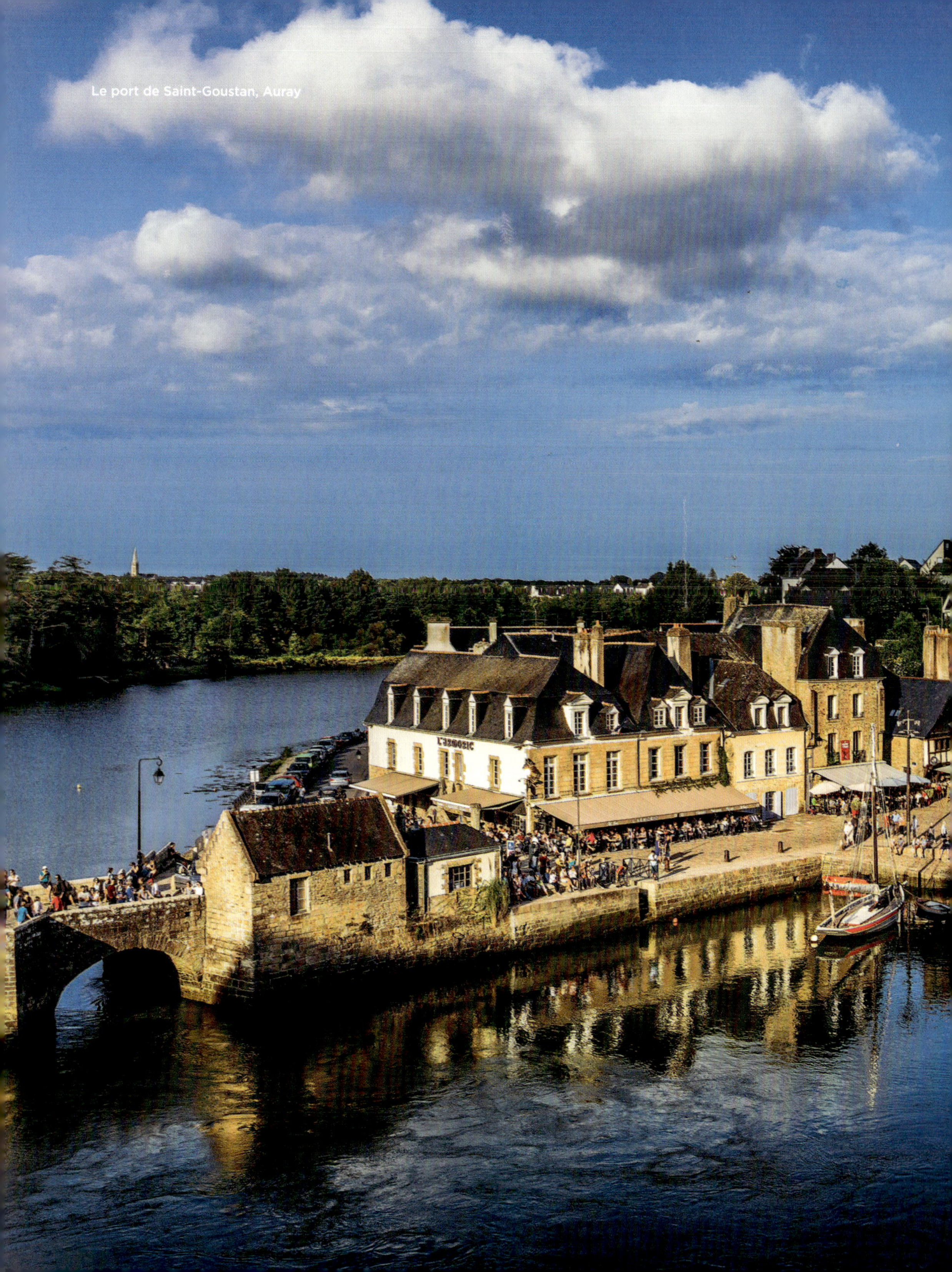

Le port de Saint-Goustan, Auray

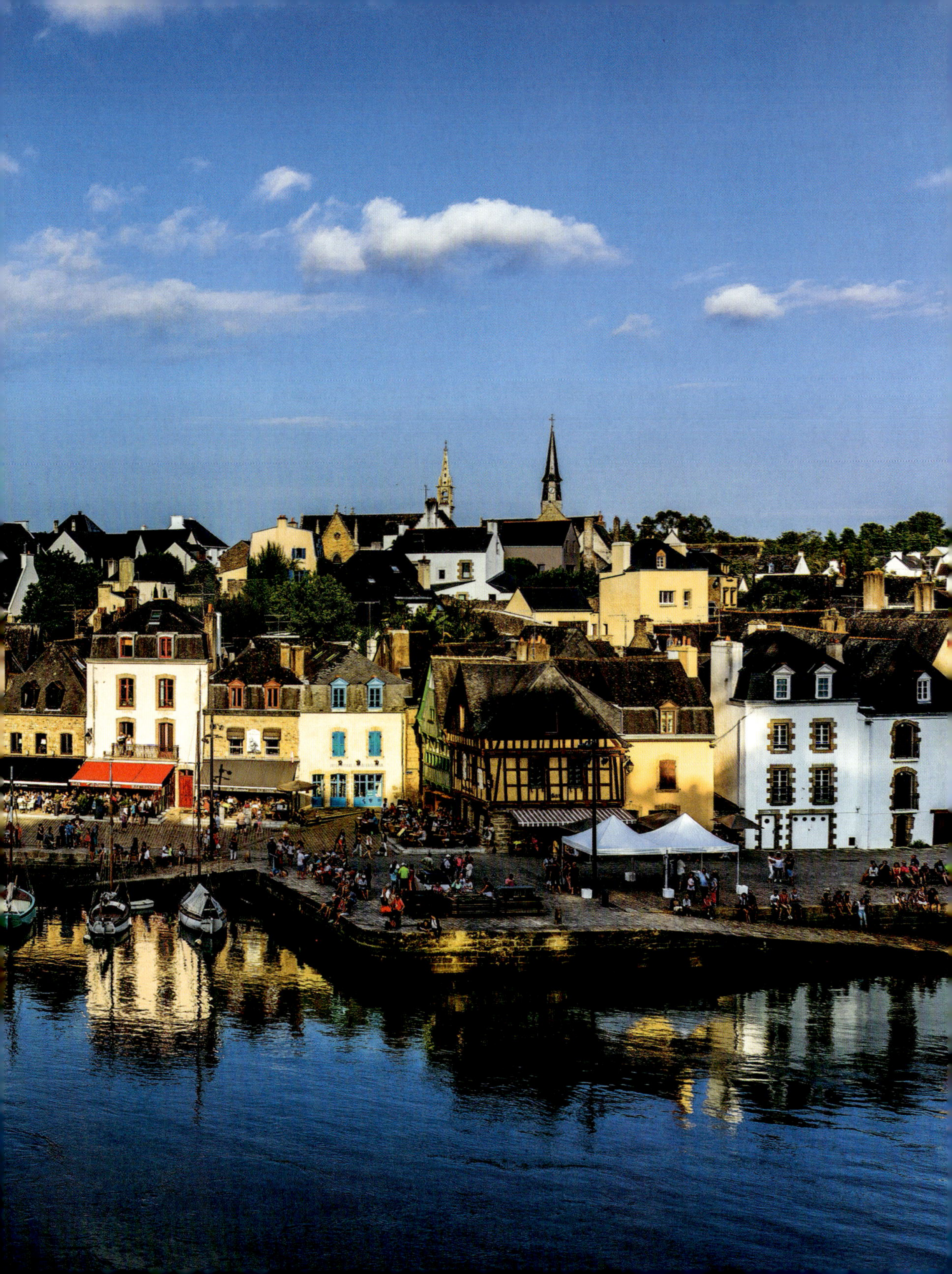

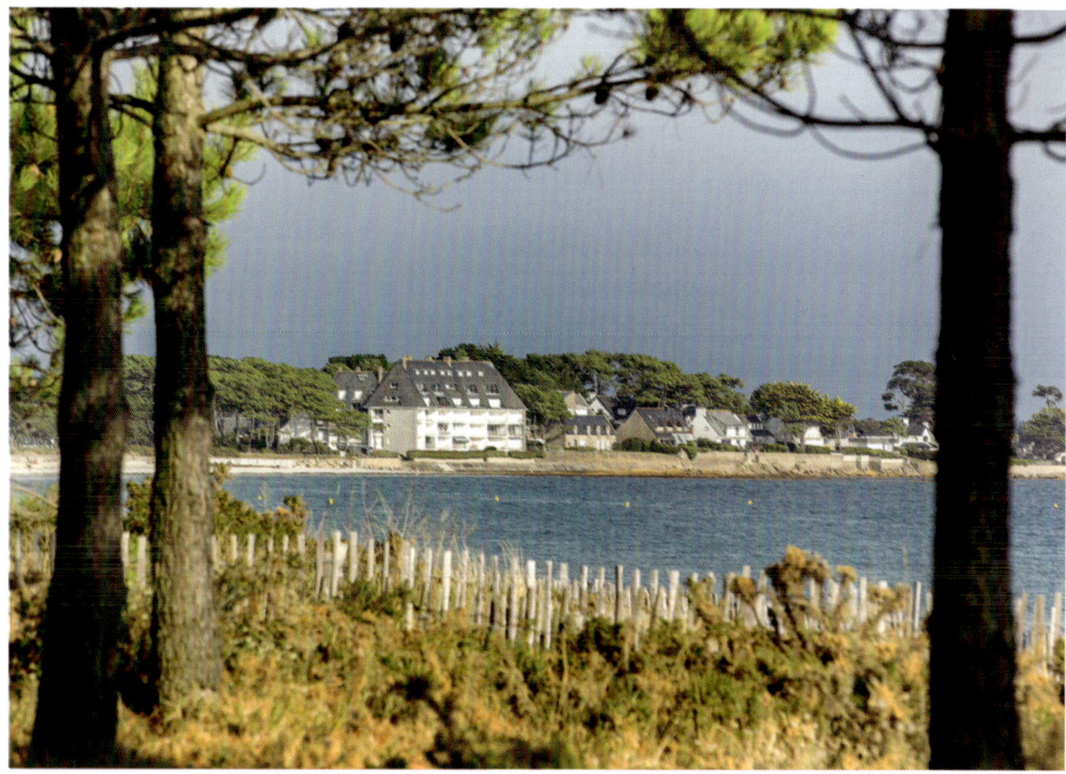

Le boulevard de plage, Carnac

Carnac

Morbihan has more than 550 megalithic sites, including the 7,000-year-old stone rows of Carnac. They consist of 2,934 menhirs, which are arranged in rows over a length of 4 km. In 1889 they were already classified as a monument. Another attraction is the sheltered beaches between the Gulf of Morbihan and the Bay of Quiberon.

Carnac

Plus de 550 sites mégalithiques sont recensés dans le Morbihan. Vieux de 7 000 ans, le site mégalithique de Carnac est le plus célèbre, classé au titre des monuments historiques depuis 1889, et compte 2 934 menhirs. Leurs alignements s'étendent sur près de 4 km. Un autre atout de Carnac : ses plages abritées entre le golfe du Morbihan et la baie de Quiberon.

Carnac

Morbihan zählt mehr als 550 megalithische Stätten, darunter die 7.000 Jahre alten Steinreihen von Carnac. Sie bestehen aus 2.934 Menhiren, die auf einer Länge von 4 km in Reihen angeordnet sind. Bereits 1889 wurden sie als Denkmal klassifiziert. Eine weitere Sehenswürdigkeit sind die geschützten Strände zwischen dem Golf von Morbihan und der Bucht von Quiberon.

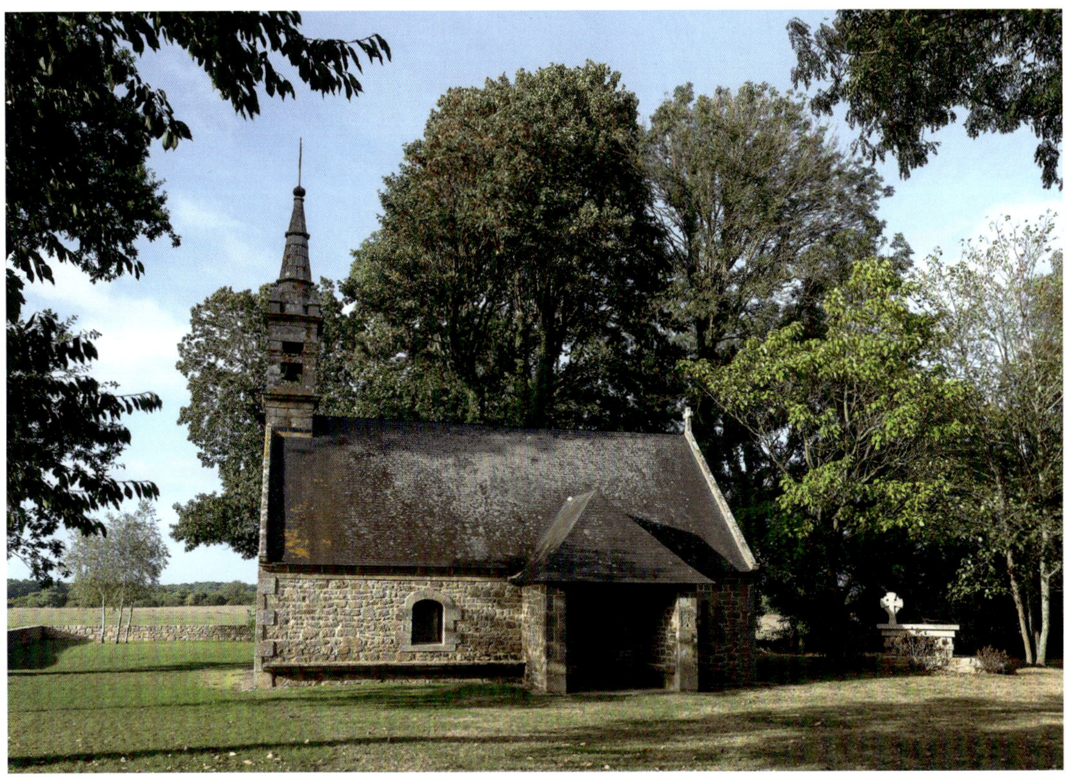

La chapelle de la Madeleine, Kerguéarec, Carnac

Carnac

Morbihan tiene más de
550 yacimientos megalíticos,
incluyendo los alineamientos de
piedra de Carnac, de 7000 años de
antigüedad. Consisten en
2934 menhires, que están
dispuestos en filas a lo largo de
4 km. Ya en 1889 fueron clasificados
como monumentos. Otro atractivo
son las playas protegidas entre el
golfo de Morbihan y la bahía de
Quiberon.

Carnac

Morbihan tem mais de 550
monumentos megalíticos, entre
eles os alinhamentos de pedra de
Carnac, mais conhecidos pelas
Rochas de Carnac, com 7.000 anos.
São 2.934 menires, dispostos em
linhas ao longo de um
comprimento de 4 km. Estão
classificados como monumento
desde 1889. Outra atração são as
praias abrigadas entre o Golfo de
Morbihan e a Baía de Quiberon.

Carnac

Morbihan heeft meer dan 550
megalithische sites, waaronder de
7.000 jaar oude rijen stenen van
Carnac. Ze bestaan uit 2.934
menhirs, die over een lengte van 4
km in rijen zijn opgesteld. In 1889
werden ze al geclassificeerd als
monument. Een andere
bezienswaardigheid zijn de
beschutte stranden tussen de Golf
van Morbihan en de baai van
Quiberon.

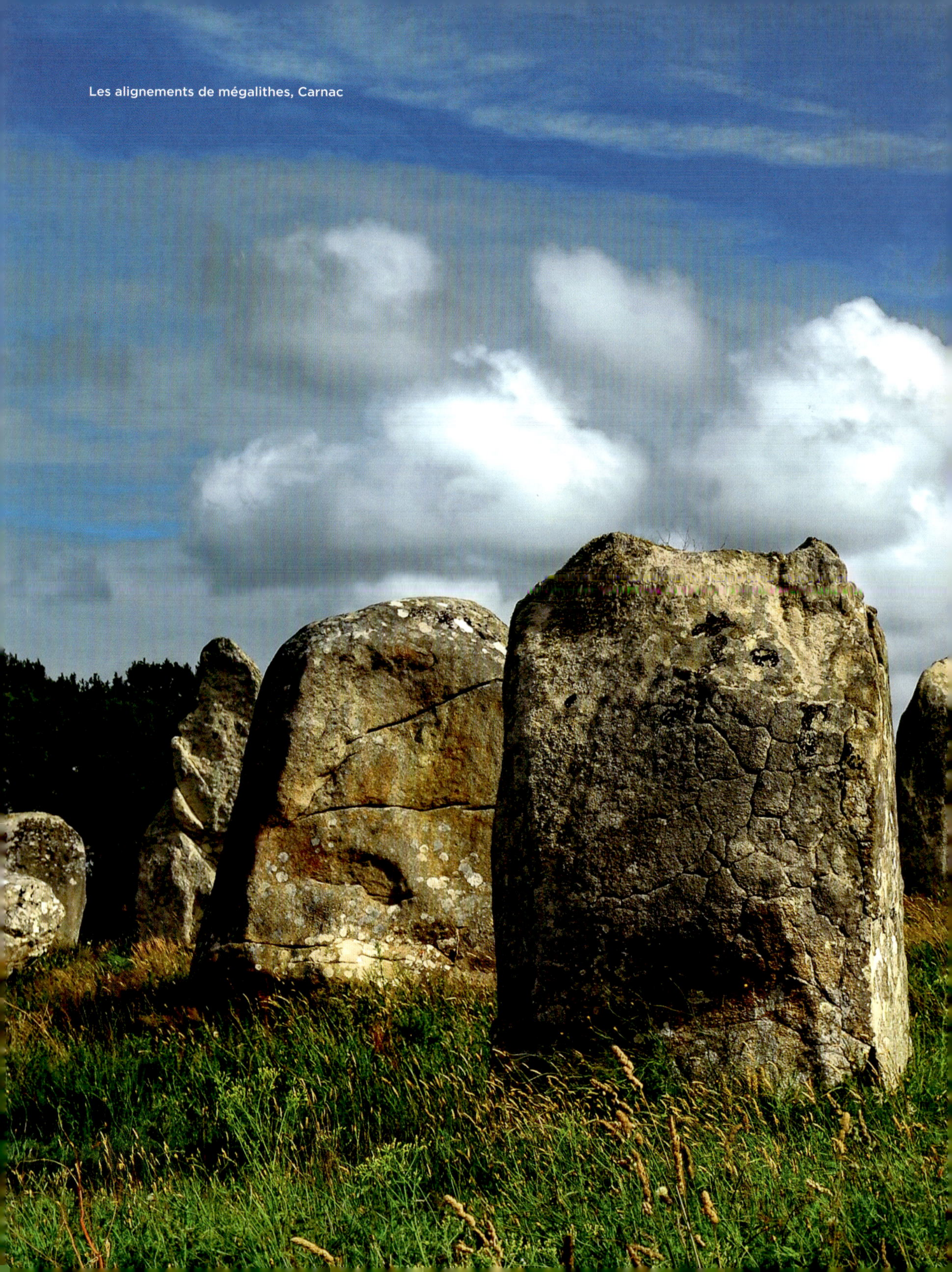
Les alignements de mégalithes, Carnac

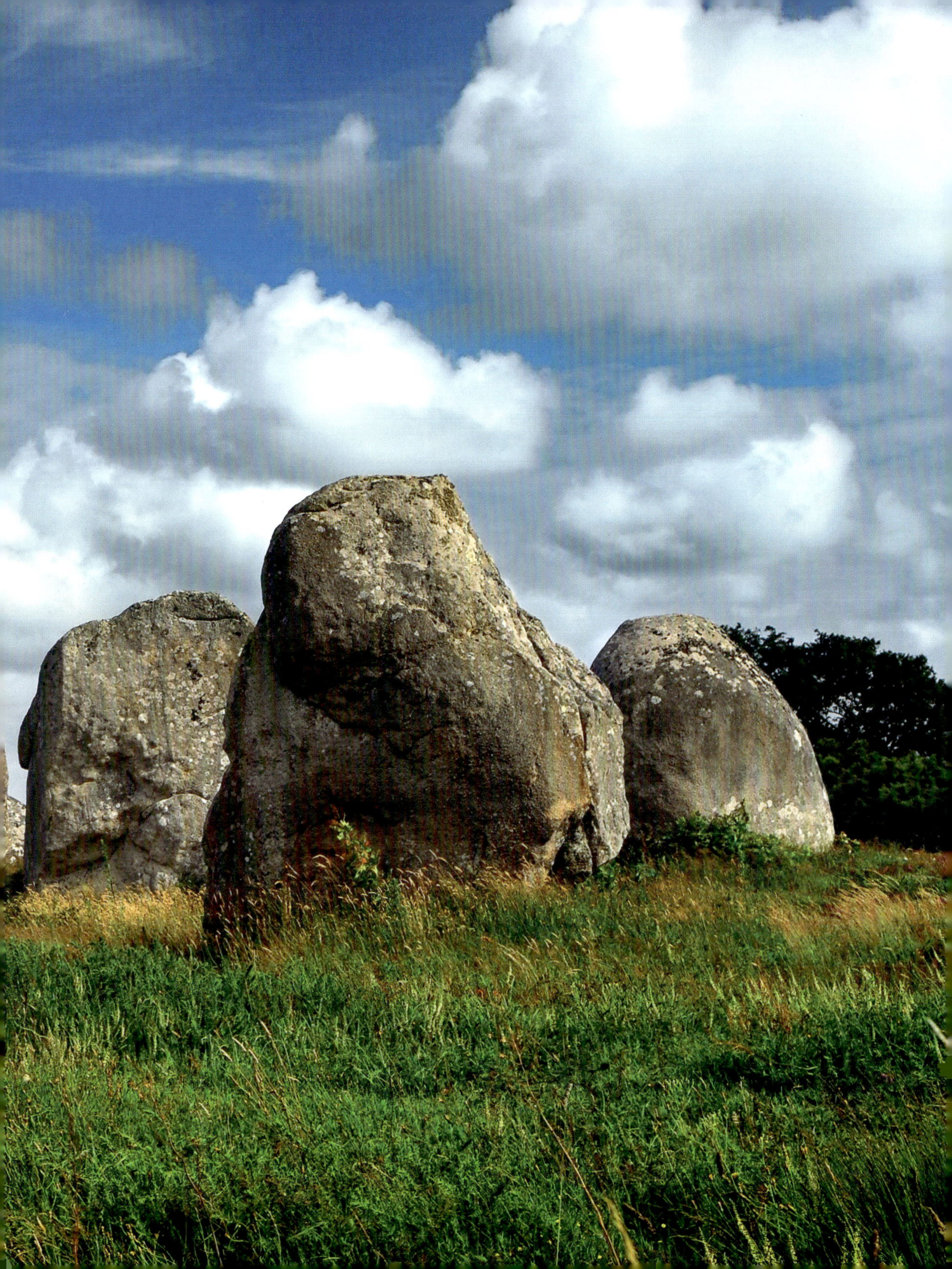

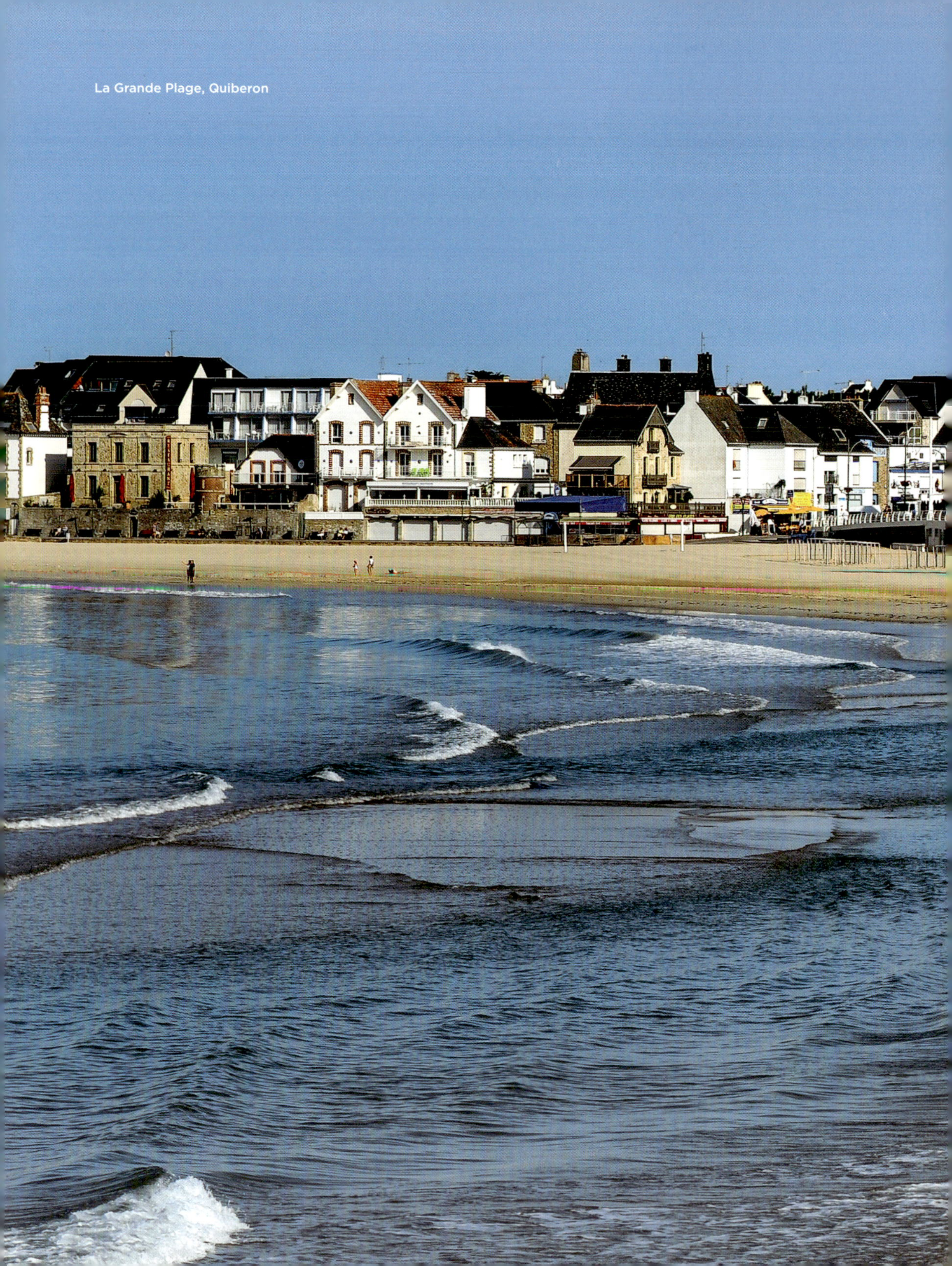
La Grande Plage, Quiberon

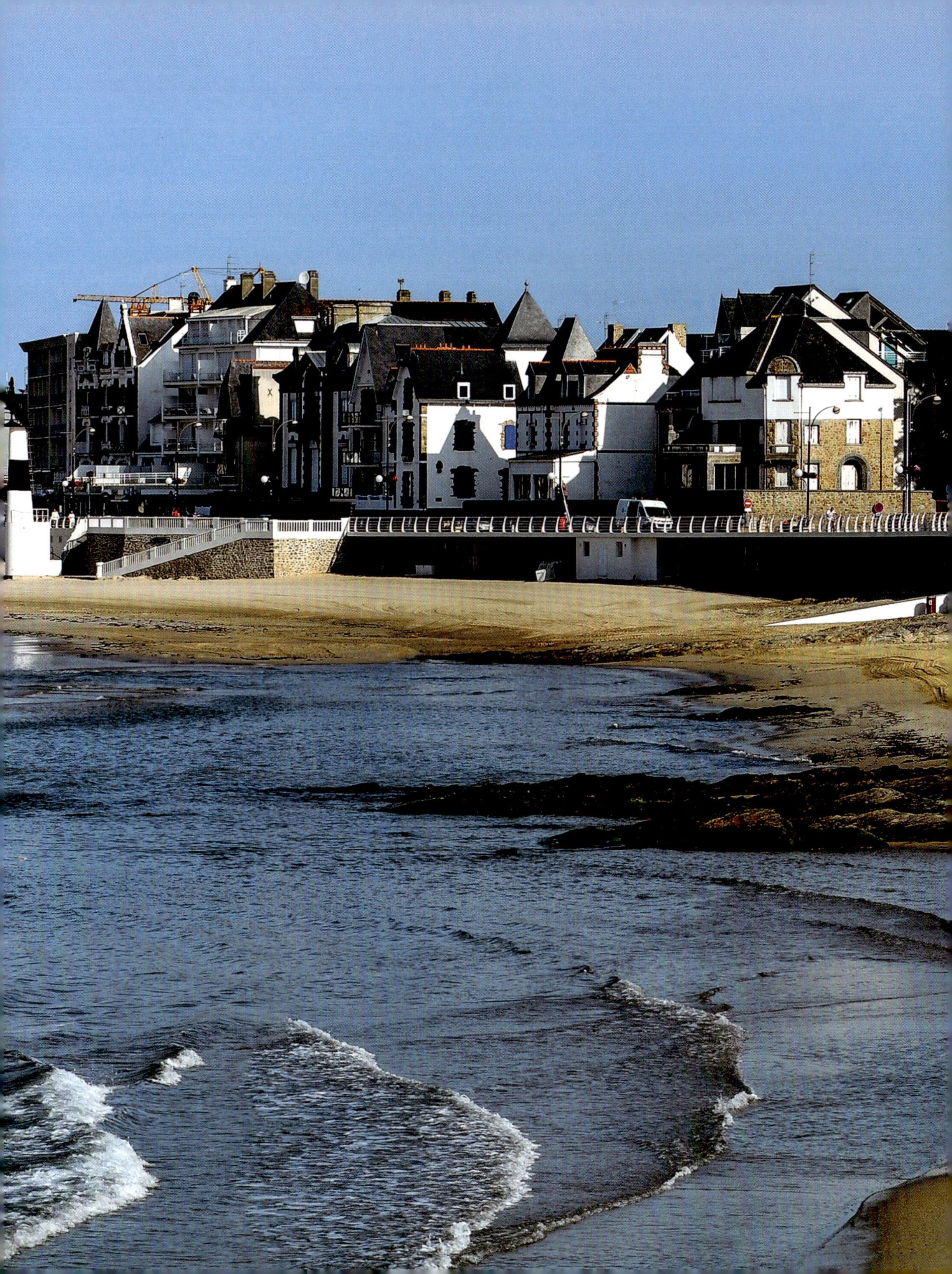

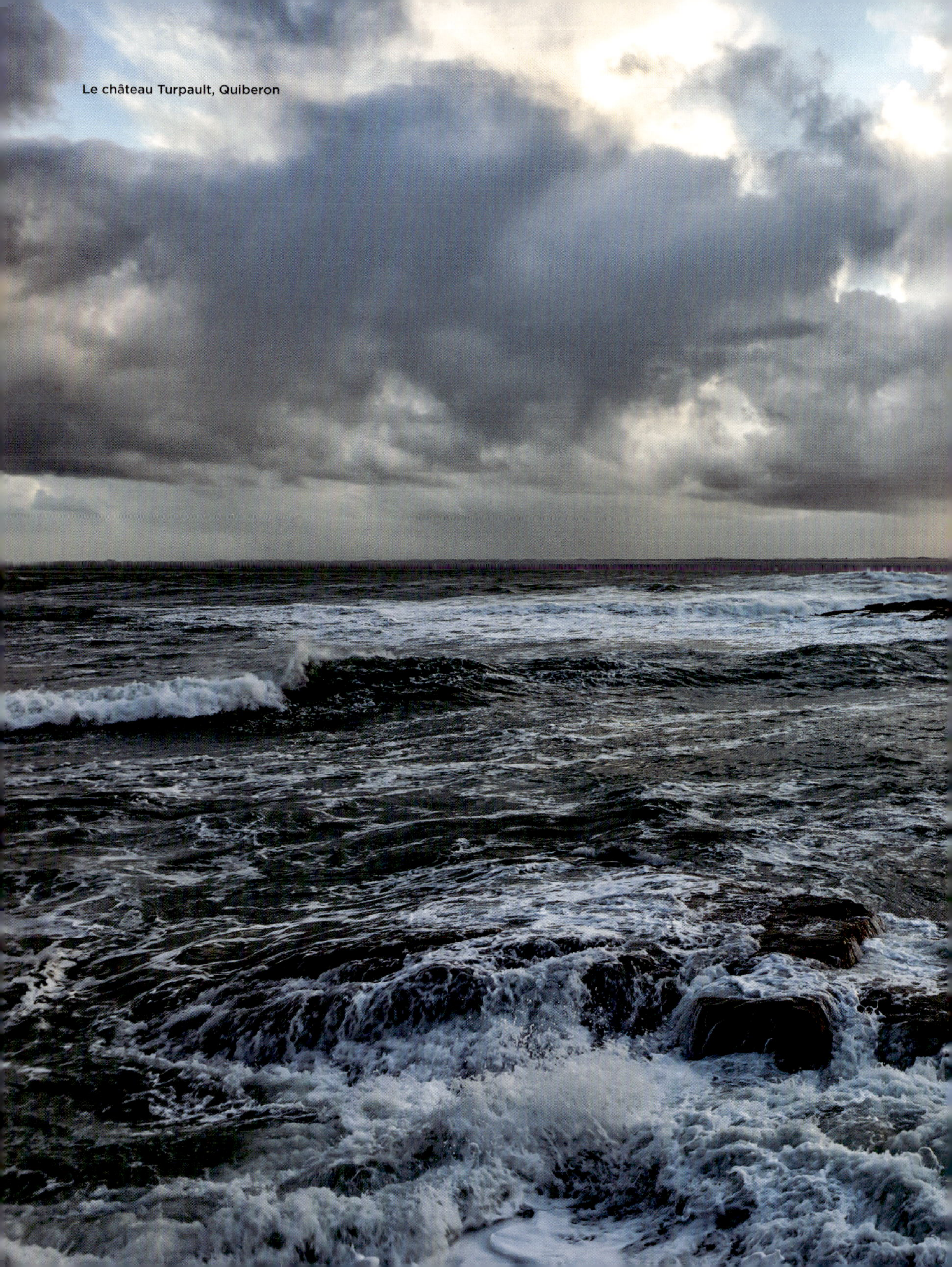

Le château Turpault, Quiberon

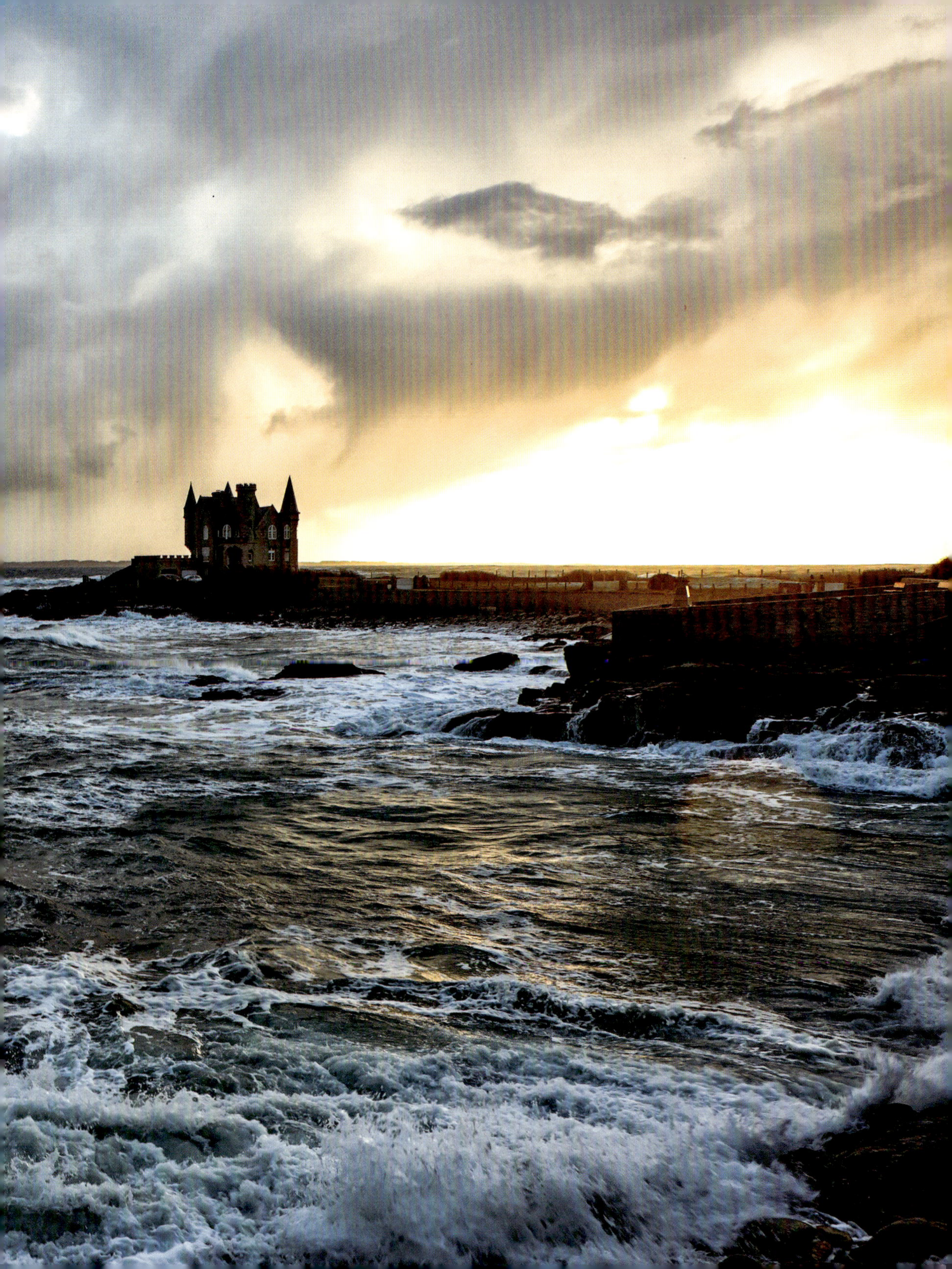

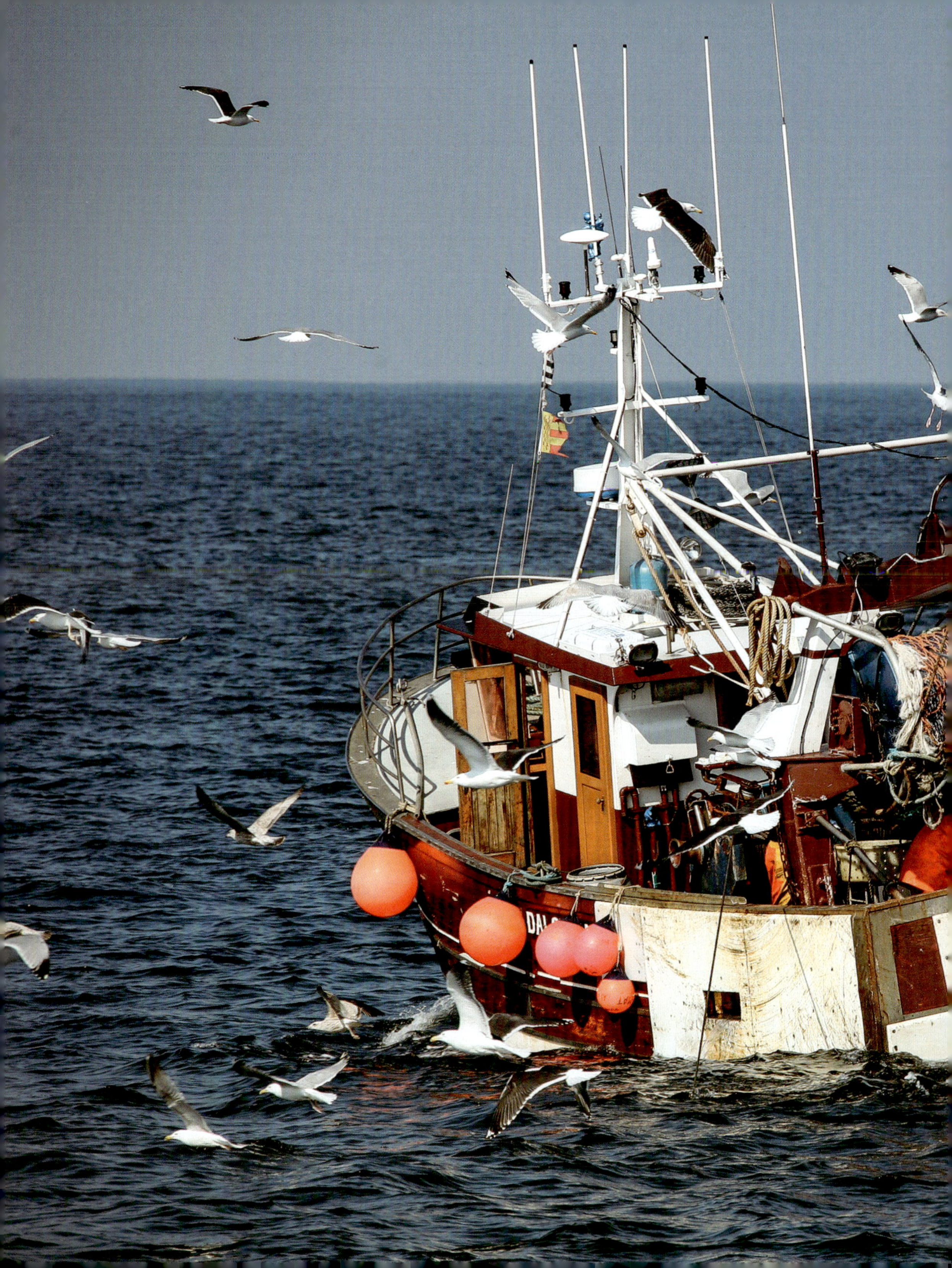

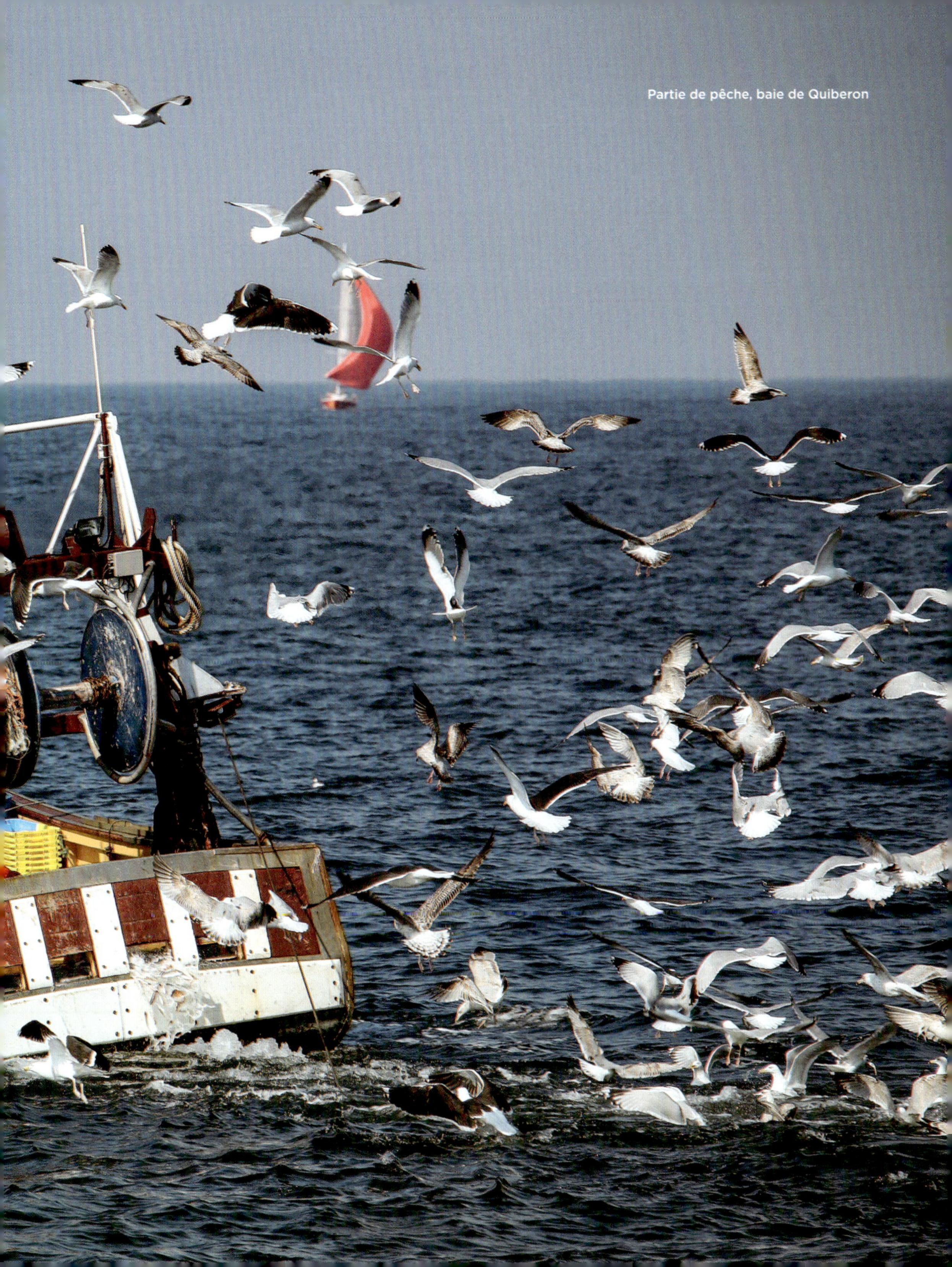

Partie de pêche, baie de Quiberon

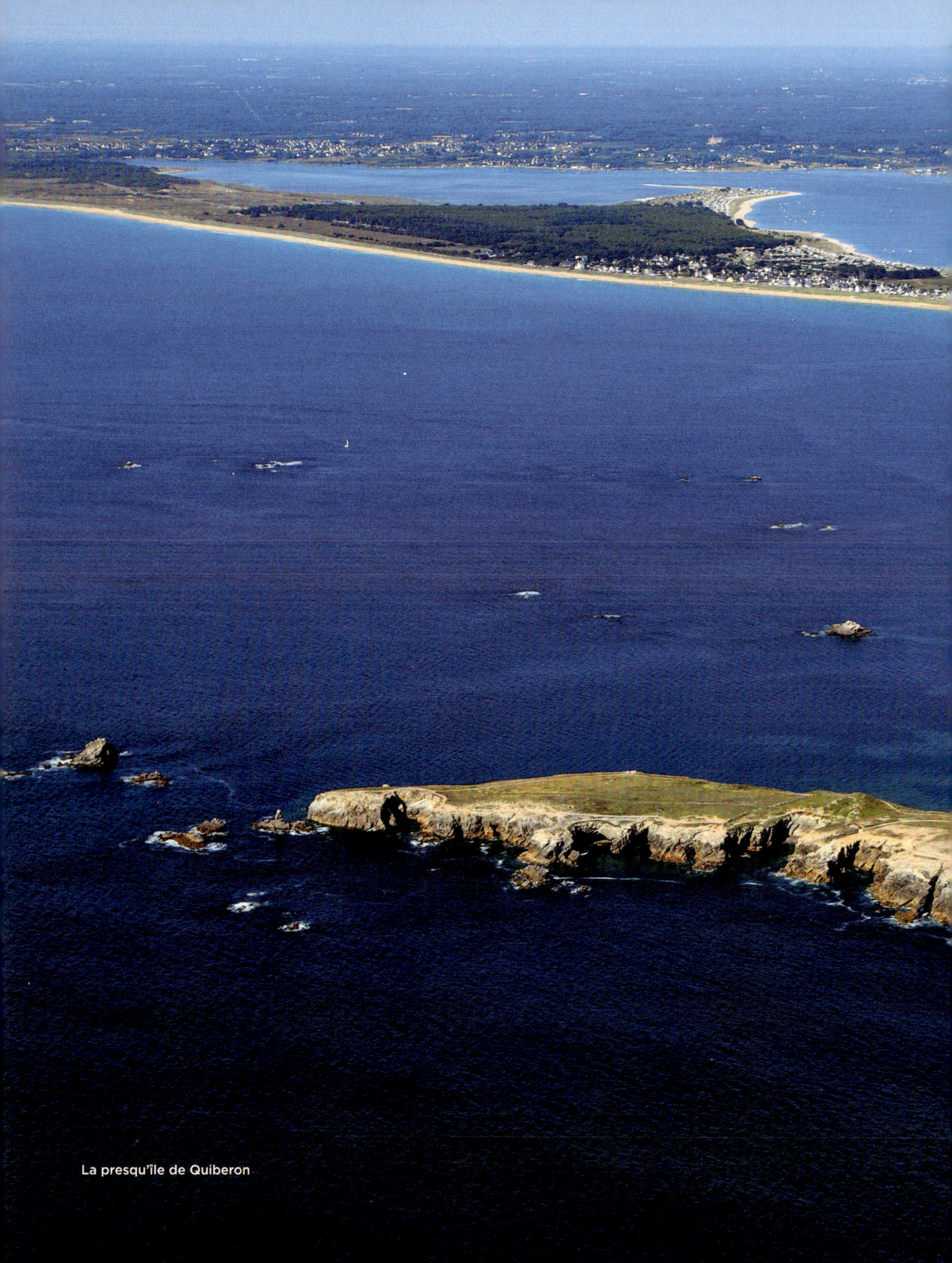

La presqu'île de Quiberon

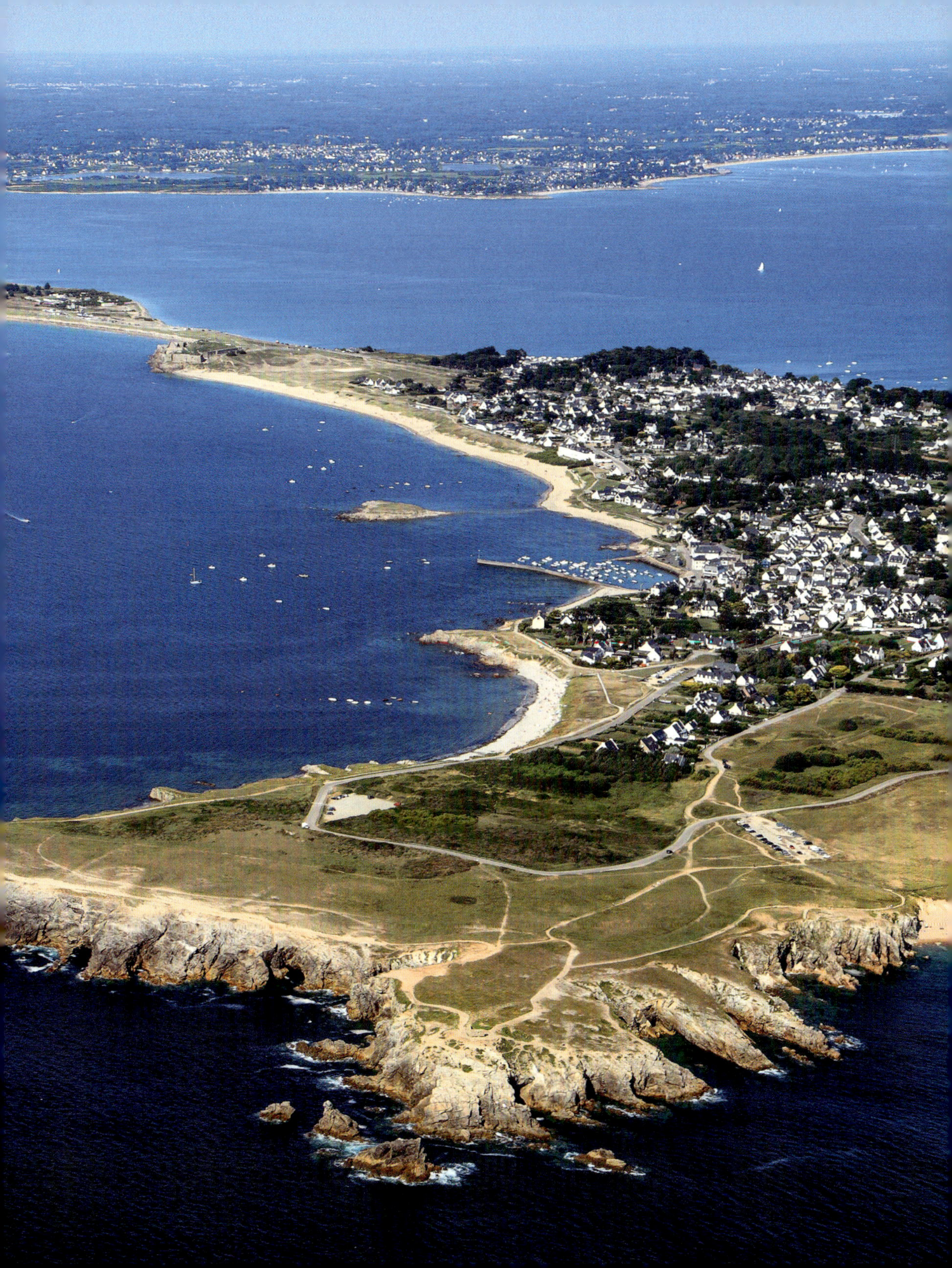

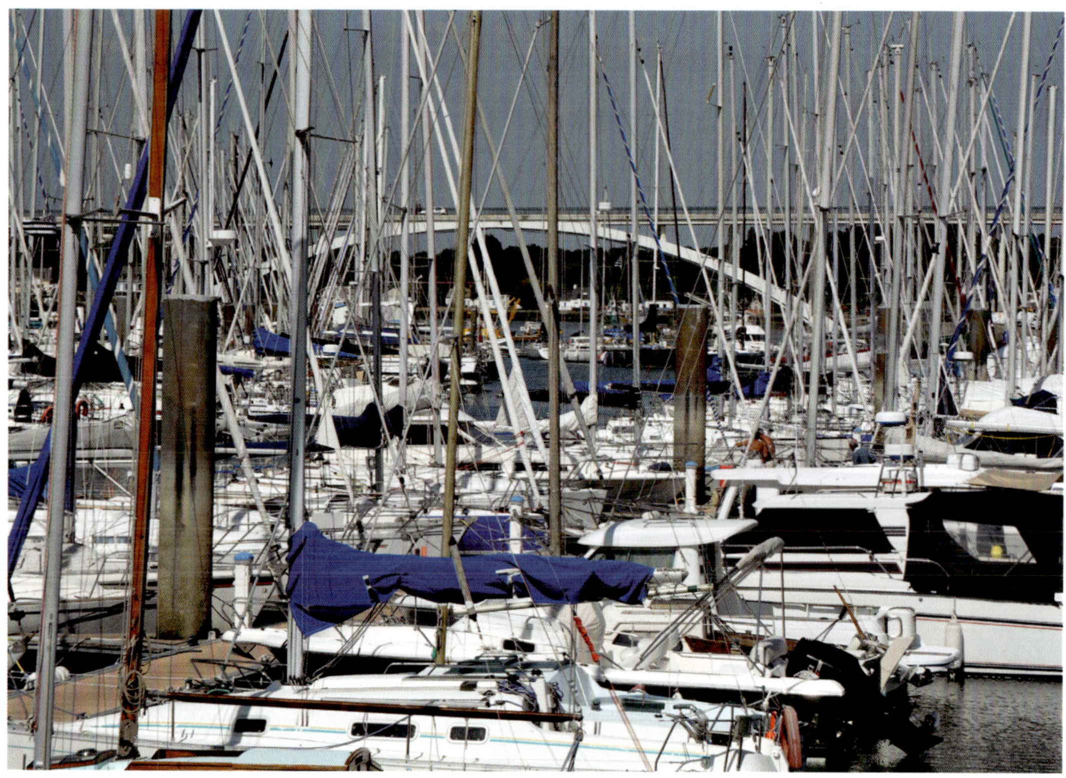

Le port de plaisance, La Trinité-sur-Mer

La Trinité-sur-Mer

From traditional sailing boats to
state-of-the-art racing yachts,
La Trinité-sur-mer and the Gulf
of Morbihan are the heart of sailing
in Brittany.

La Trinité-sur-Mer

Desde veleros tradicionales hasta
yates de competición de última
generación, La Trinité-sur-mer y el
golfo de Morbihan son el corazón
de la navegación en Bretaña.

La Trinité-sur-Mer

Des voiles traditionnelles aux
bateaux de course dont les
technologies ne cessent de se
moderniser, à la Trinité-sur-Mer et
dans le golfe du Morbihan, nous
sommes au cœur de la Bretagne
qui navigue.

La Trinité-sur-Mer

La Trinité-sur-mer e o Golfo de
Morbihan são o centro da vela na
Bretanha e podem-se encontrar
tanto barcos à vela tradicionais
como veleiros e iates de corrida
ultra-modernos.

La Trinité-sur-Mer

Von traditionellen Segelbooten,
bis hin zu Rennjachten auf dem
neuesten Stand der Technik – in
La Trinité-sur-mer und dem Golf
von Morbihan schlägt das Herz des
Segelsports in der Bretagne.

La Trinité-sur-Mer

Van traditionele zeilboten tot
racejachten met de modernste
technieken – La Trinité-sur-mer en
de Golf van Morbihan zijn het
kloppende hart van de zeilsport in
Bretagne.

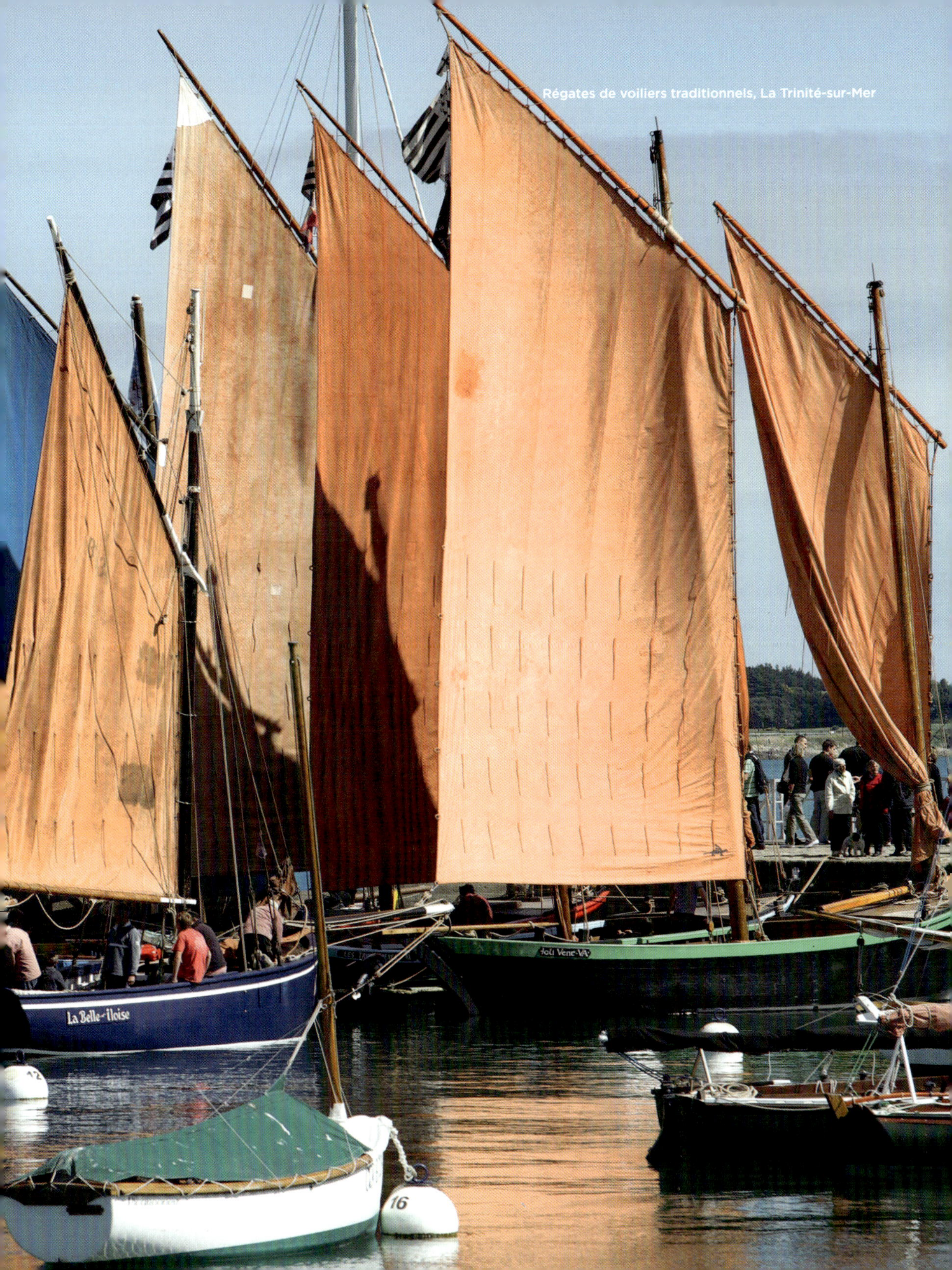
Régates de voiliers traditionnels, La Trinité-sur-Mer

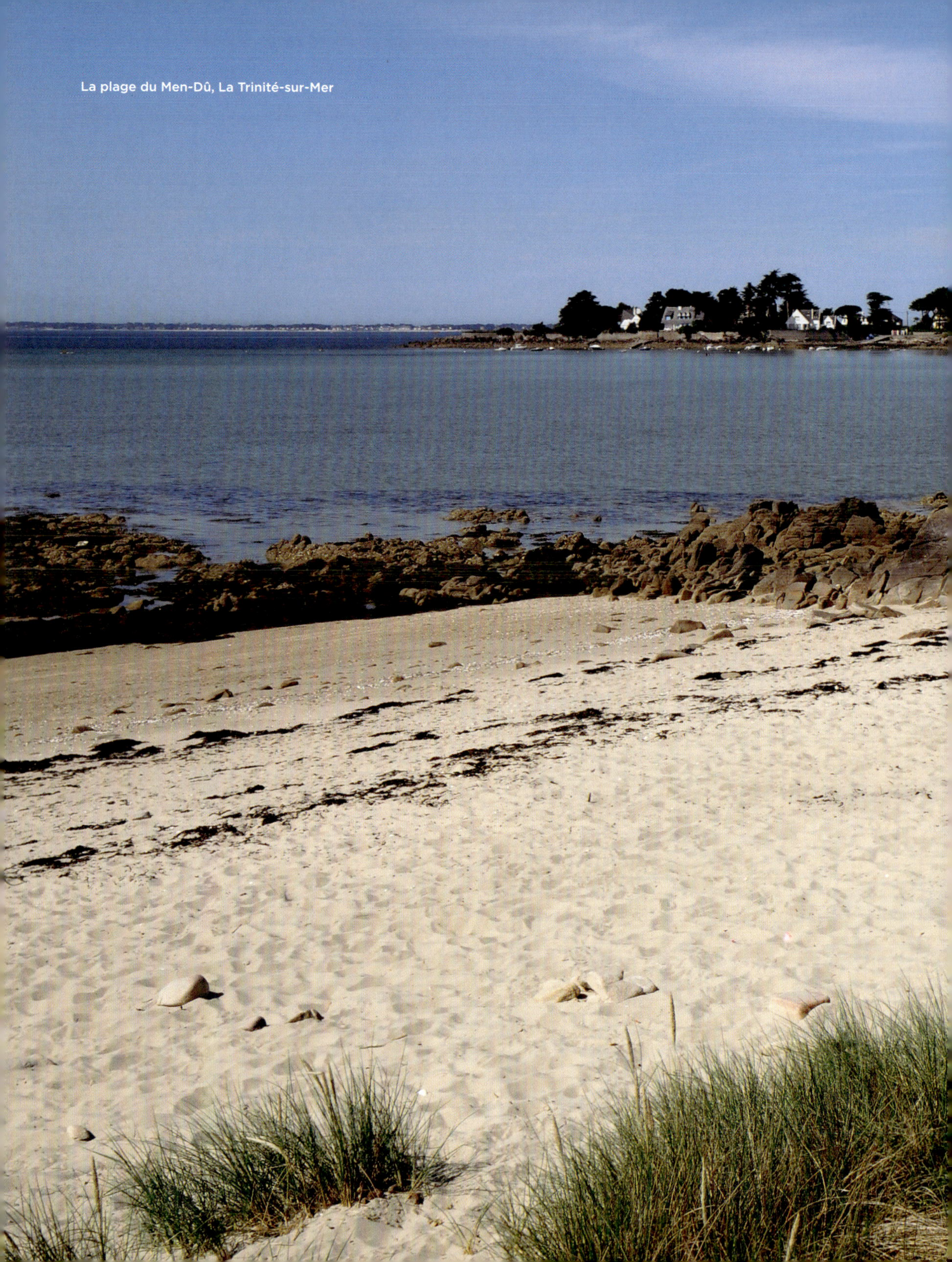

La plage du Men-Dû, La Trinité-sur-Mer

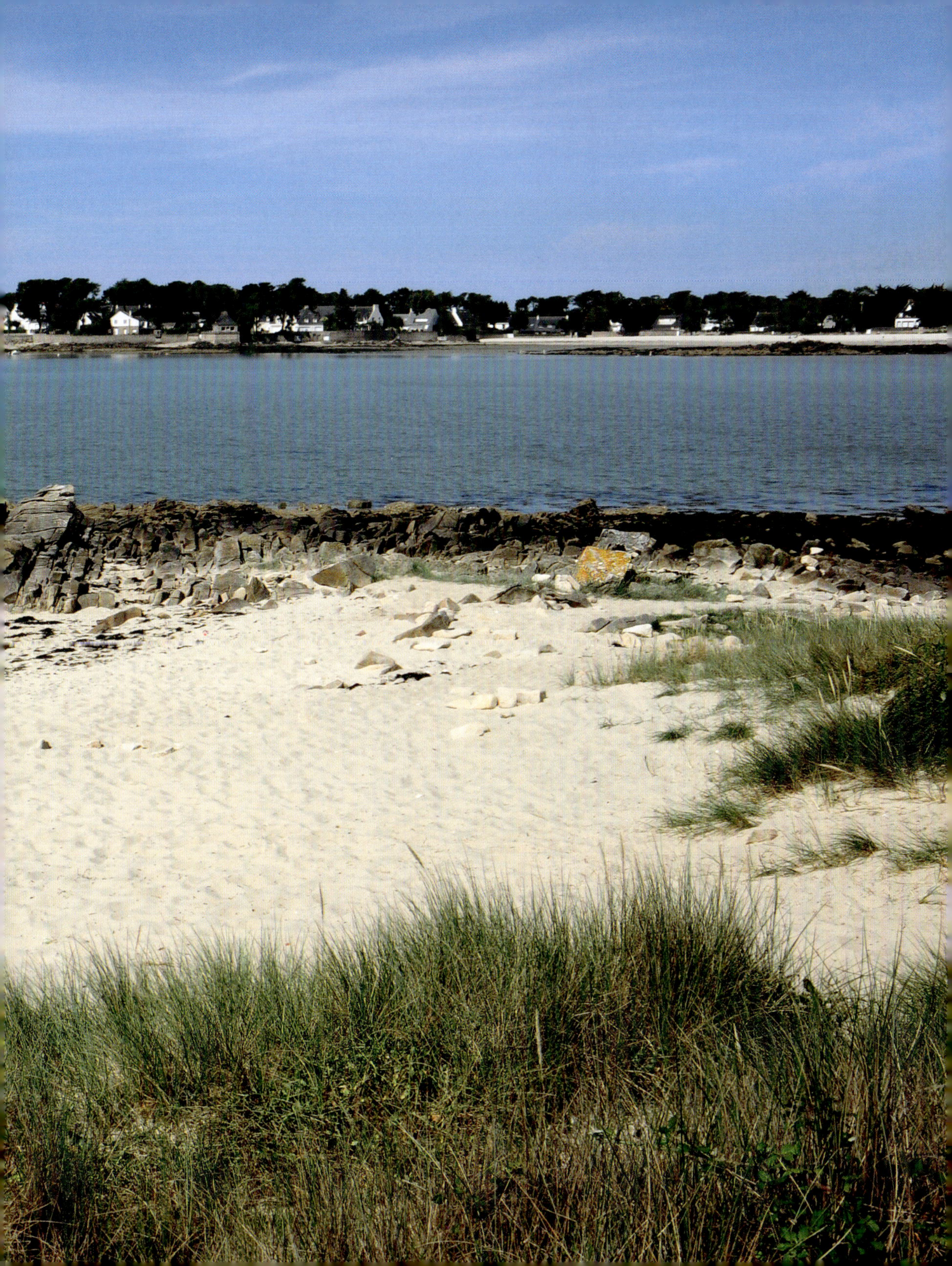

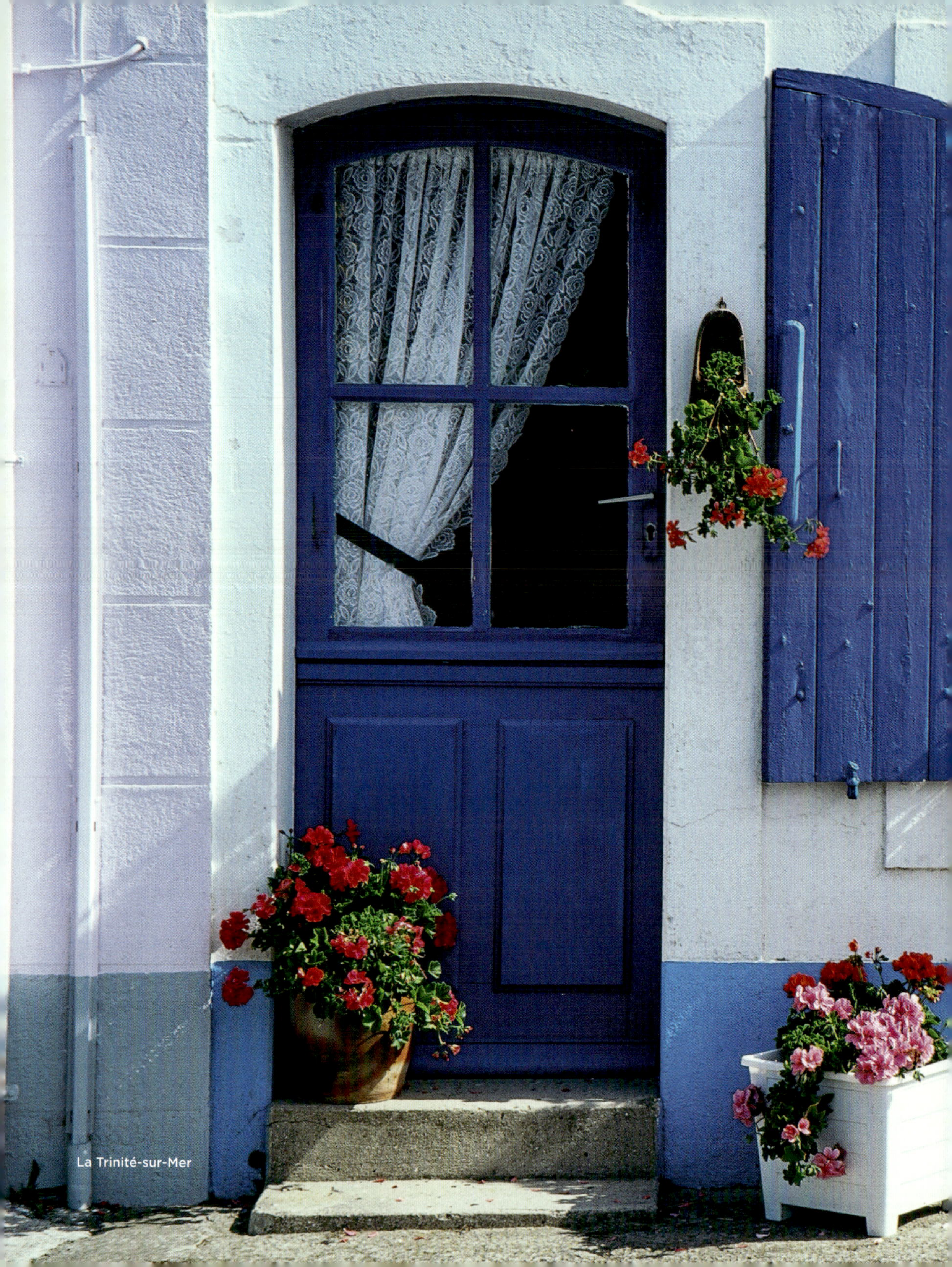
La Trinité-sur-Mer

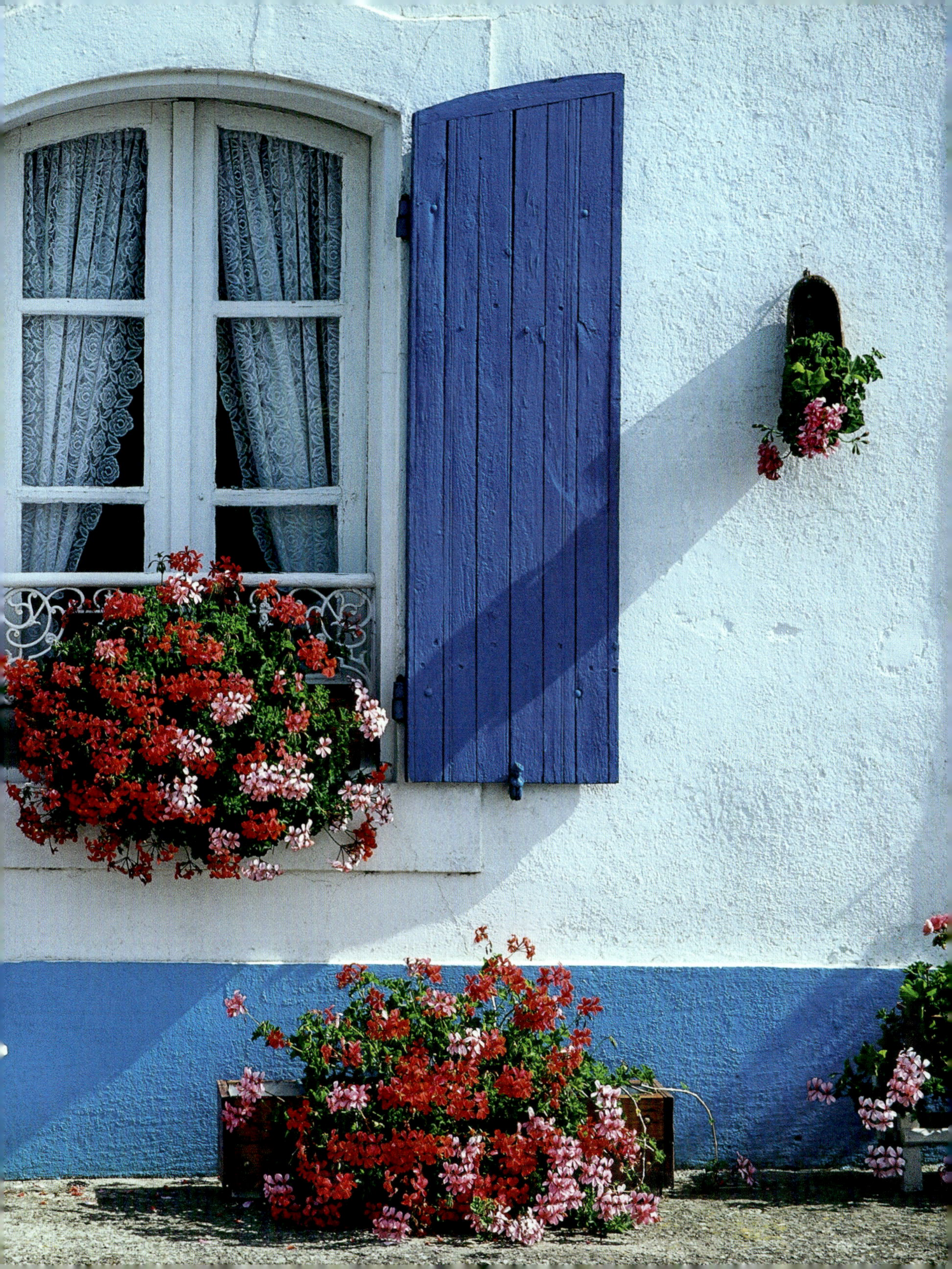

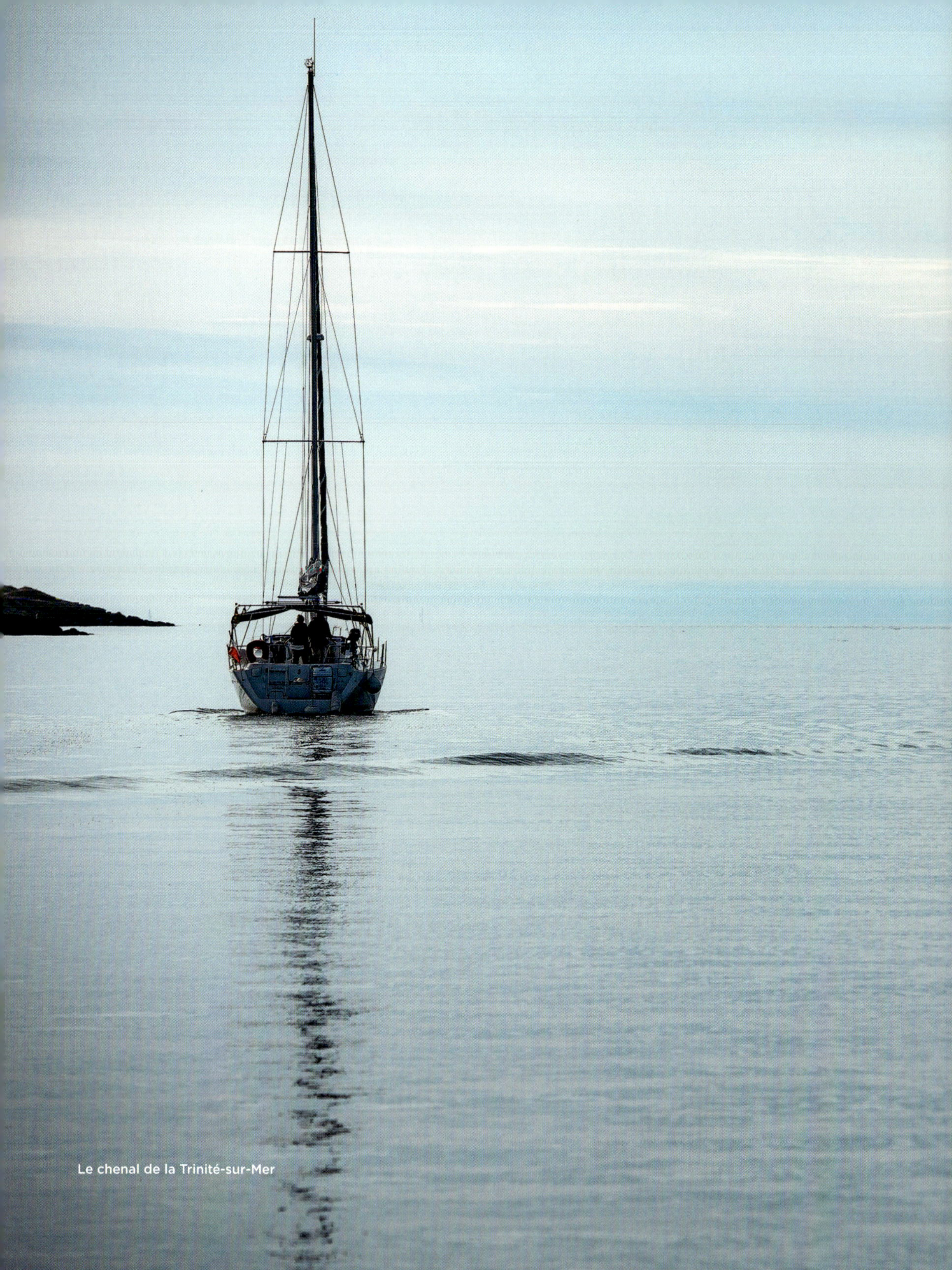

Le chenal de la Trinité-sur-Mer

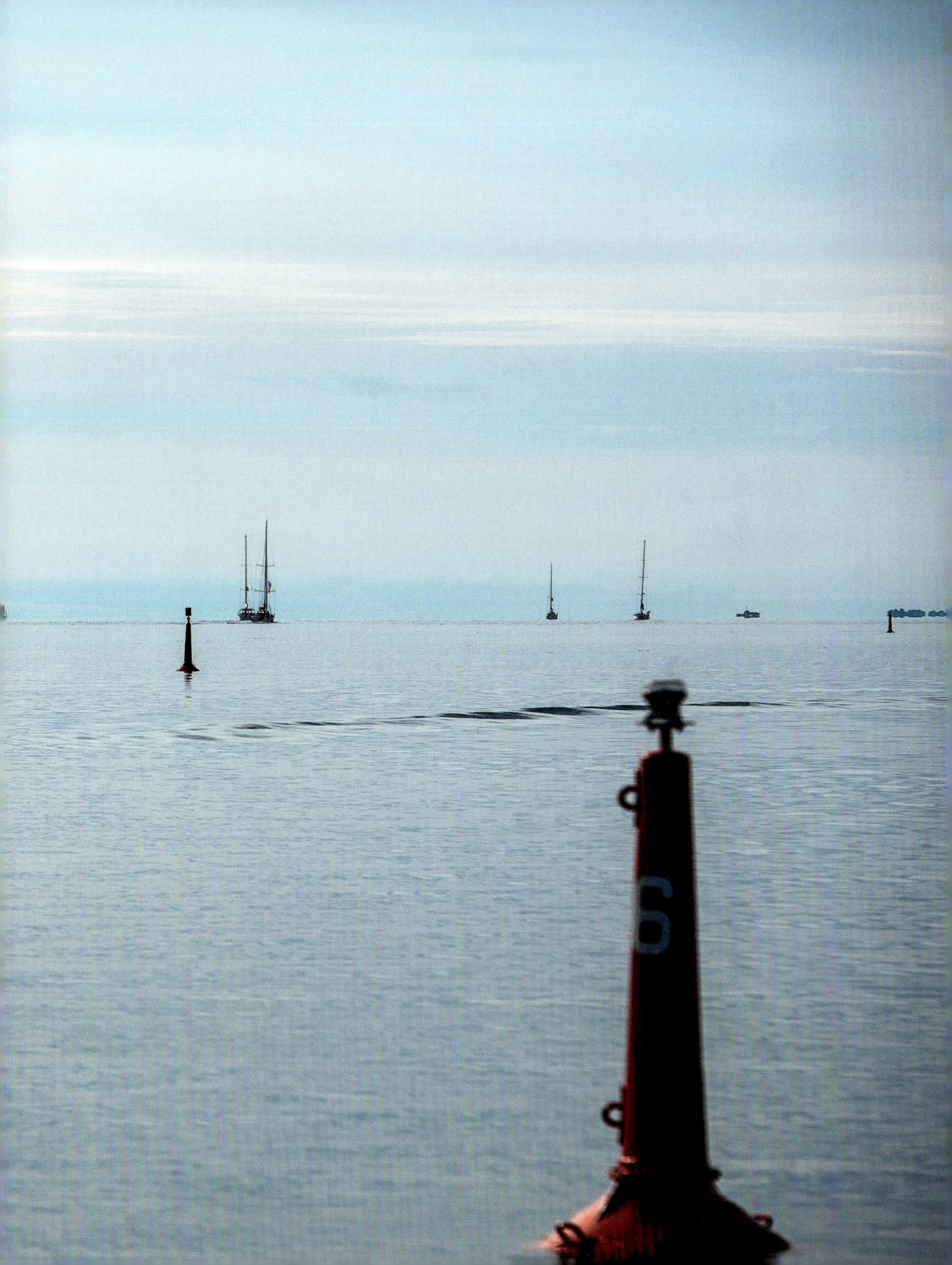

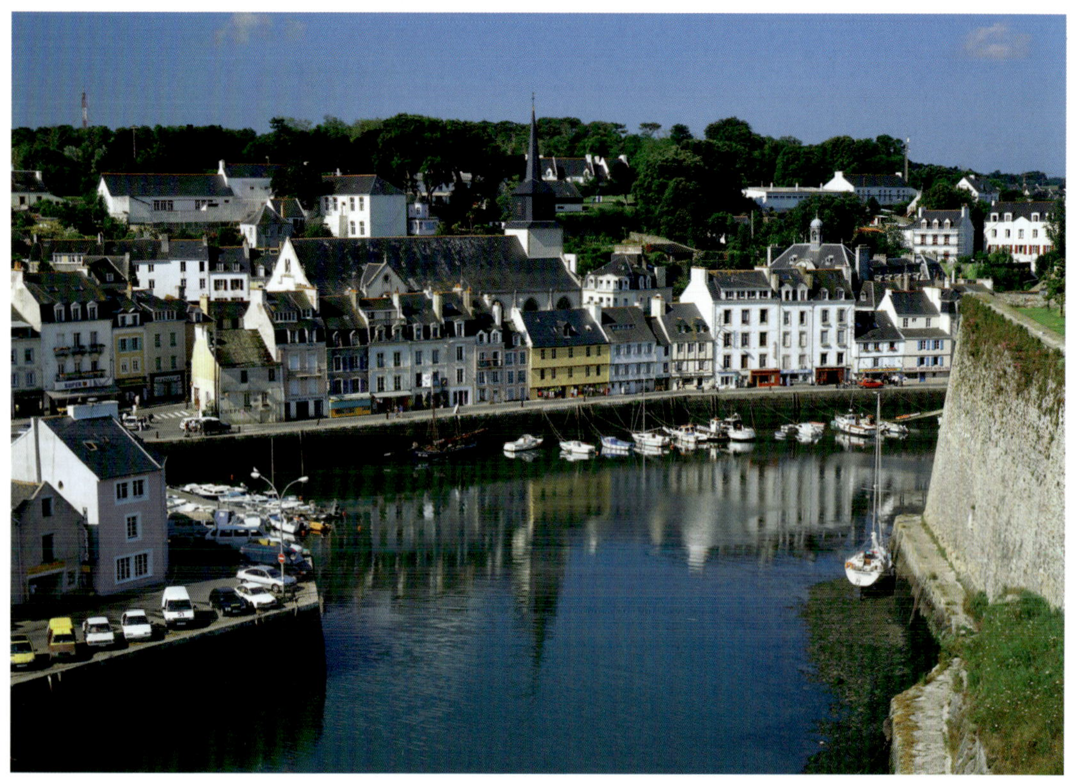

Le port du Palais, Belle-Île-en-Mer

Belle-Île-en-Mer

Upon arrival at Le Palais, the main town on the island, the red and green lighthouses immediately catch the eye. Behind them lies the imposing citadel of Vauban.

Belle-Île-en-Mer

Al llegar a Le Palais, la ciudad principal de la isla, los faros rojos y verdes llaman inmediatamente la atención. Detrás se encuentra la imponente ciudadela de Vauban.

Belle-Île-en-Mer

Arrivé au Palais, on laisse à tribord le phare vert et à bâbord le phare rouge, avant de découvrir que le port est surplombé par l'imposante citadelle Vauban.

Belle-Île-en-Mer

Ao chegar a Le Palais, a cidade principal da ilha, o farol vermelho e o verde chamam imediatamente a atenção. Atrás dela está a imponente cidadela de Vauban.

Belle-Île-en-Mer

Bei der Ankunft in Le Palais, dem Hauptort der Insel, fallen sofort der rote und der grüne Leuchtturm ins Auge. Dahinter liegt die imposante Zitadelle Vauban.

Belle-Île-en-Mer

Bij aankomst in Le Palais, de belangrijkste plaats op het eiland, vallen de rode en groene vuurtorens meteen op. Daarachter ligt de imposante citadel van Vauban.

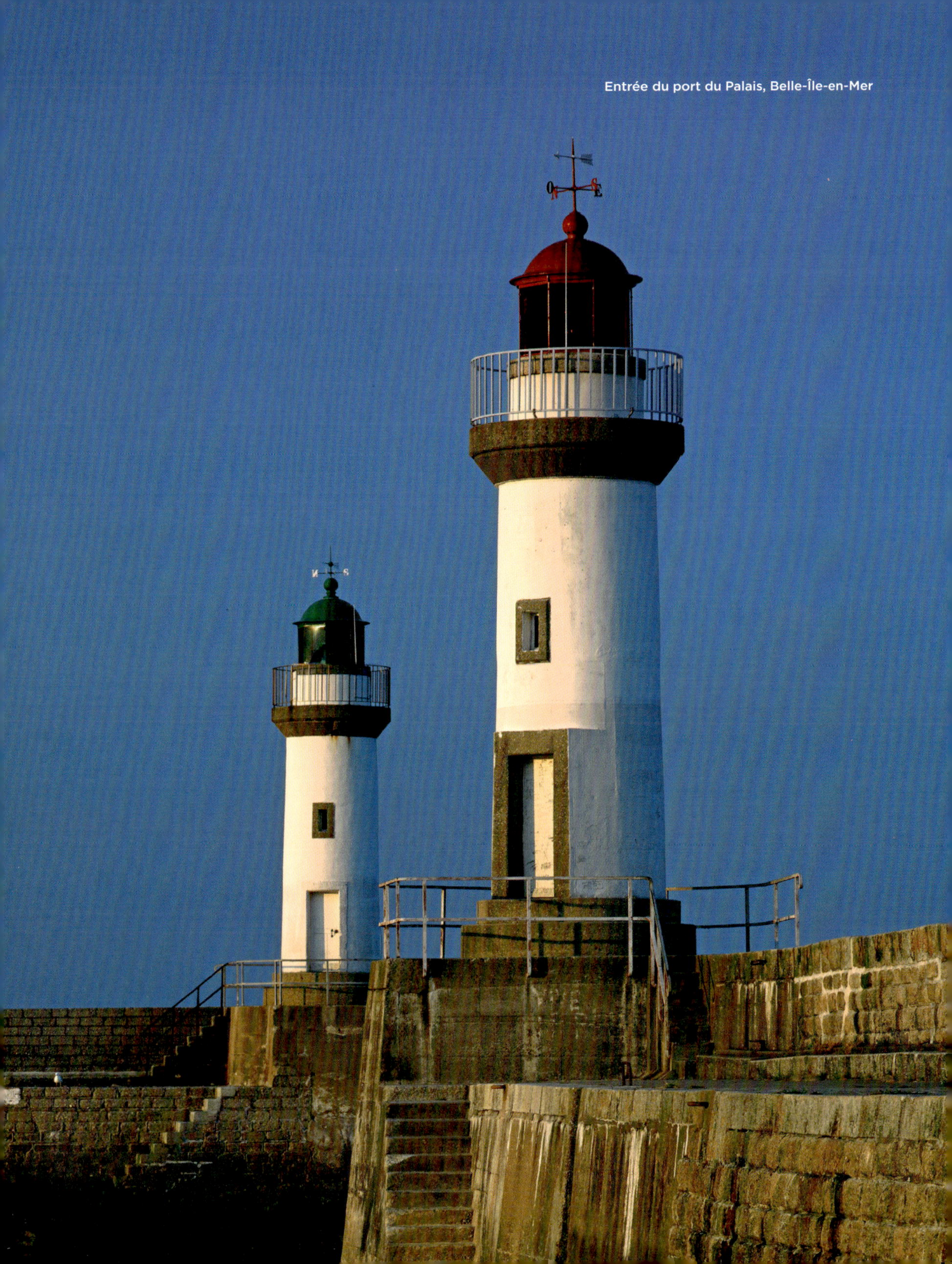

Entrée du port du Palais, Belle-Île-en-Mer

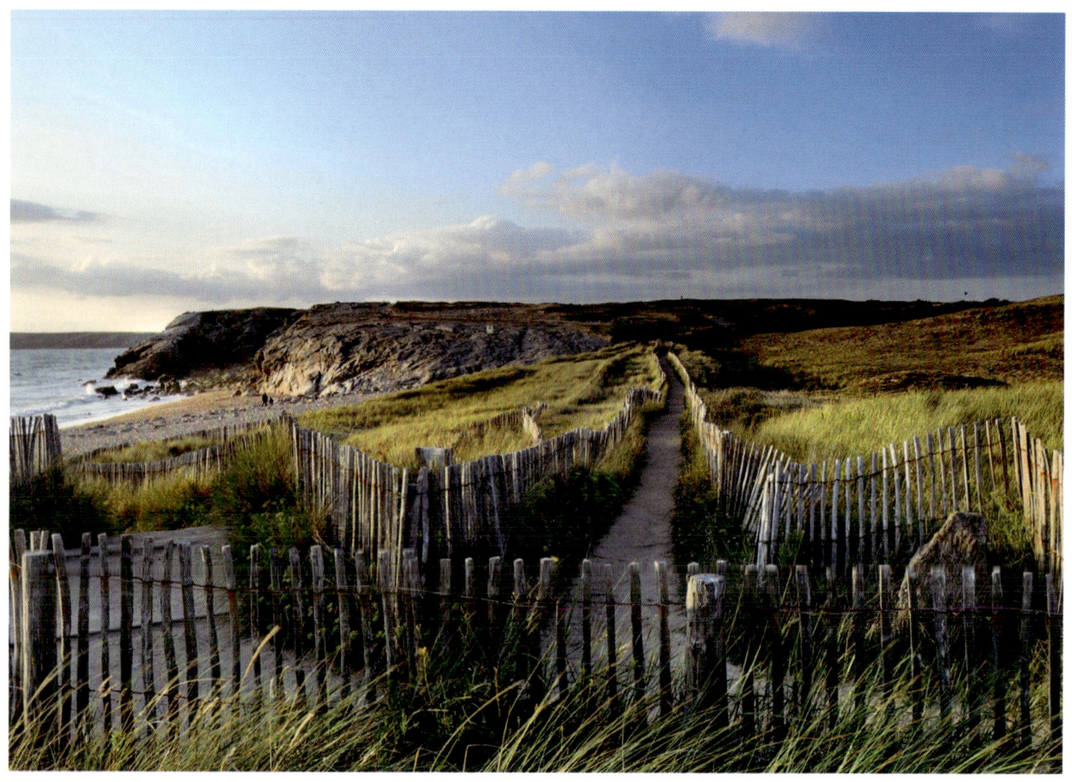

Chemin de randonnée, Belle-Île-en-Mer

Belle-Île-en-Mer

Hiking trails lead directly along the Atlantic coast over a length of 82 km. On them you can discover authentic landscapes and maritime perspectives, marked by the colours, the light, the scents and the wild beauty of the island.

Belle-Île-en-Mer

Pour les amoureux de la randonnée, 82 km de sentiers longent le littoral atlantique, permettant de contempler des paysages et des perspectives marines authentiques ainsi que les couleurs, la lumière, les parfums et la beauté sauvage de l'île.

Belle-Île-en-Mer

Auf 82 km Länge führen Wanderpfade direkt an der Atlantikküste entlang. Auf ihnen lassen sich authentische Land-schaften und maritime Perspektiven entdecken, die durch die Farben, das Licht, die Düfte und die wilde Schönheit der Insel geprägt sind.

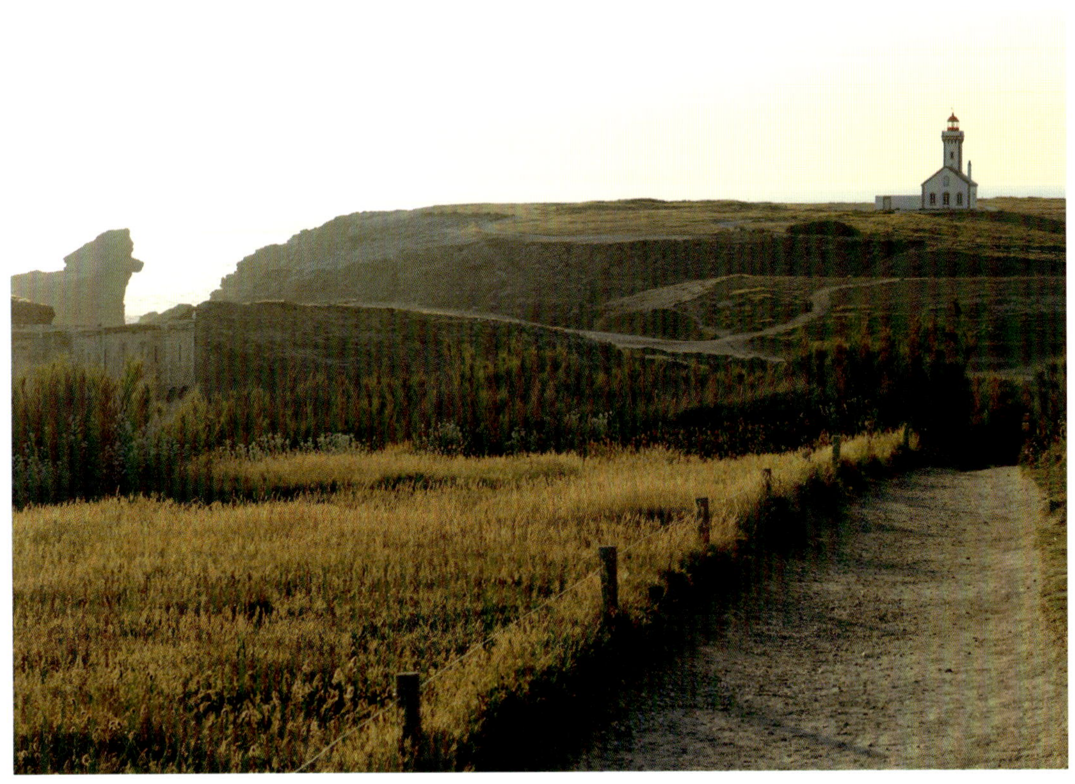

La pointe des Poulains, Belle-Île-en-Mer

Belle-Île-en-Mer

Las rutas de senderismo conducen directamente a lo largo de la costa atlántica a lo largo de 82 km. En ellas se pueden descubrir paisajes auténticos y perspectivas marítimas, marcadas por los colores, la luz, los aromas y la belleza salvaje de la isla.

Belle-Île-en-Mer

Ao longo da costa atlântica existem trilhas para caminhadas com uma extensão de 82 km onde se podem descobrir paisagens bem autênticas e belas perspectivas do mar, marcadas pelas cores, pela luz, pelos aromas e pela beleza selvagem da ilha.

Belle-Île-en-Mer

Wandelpaden lopen over een lengte van 82 km direct langs de Atlantische kust. Vanaf deze paden kunt u authentieke landschappen en maritieme perspectieven bewonderen, die getekend worden door de kleuren, het licht, de geuren en wilde schoonheid van het eiland.

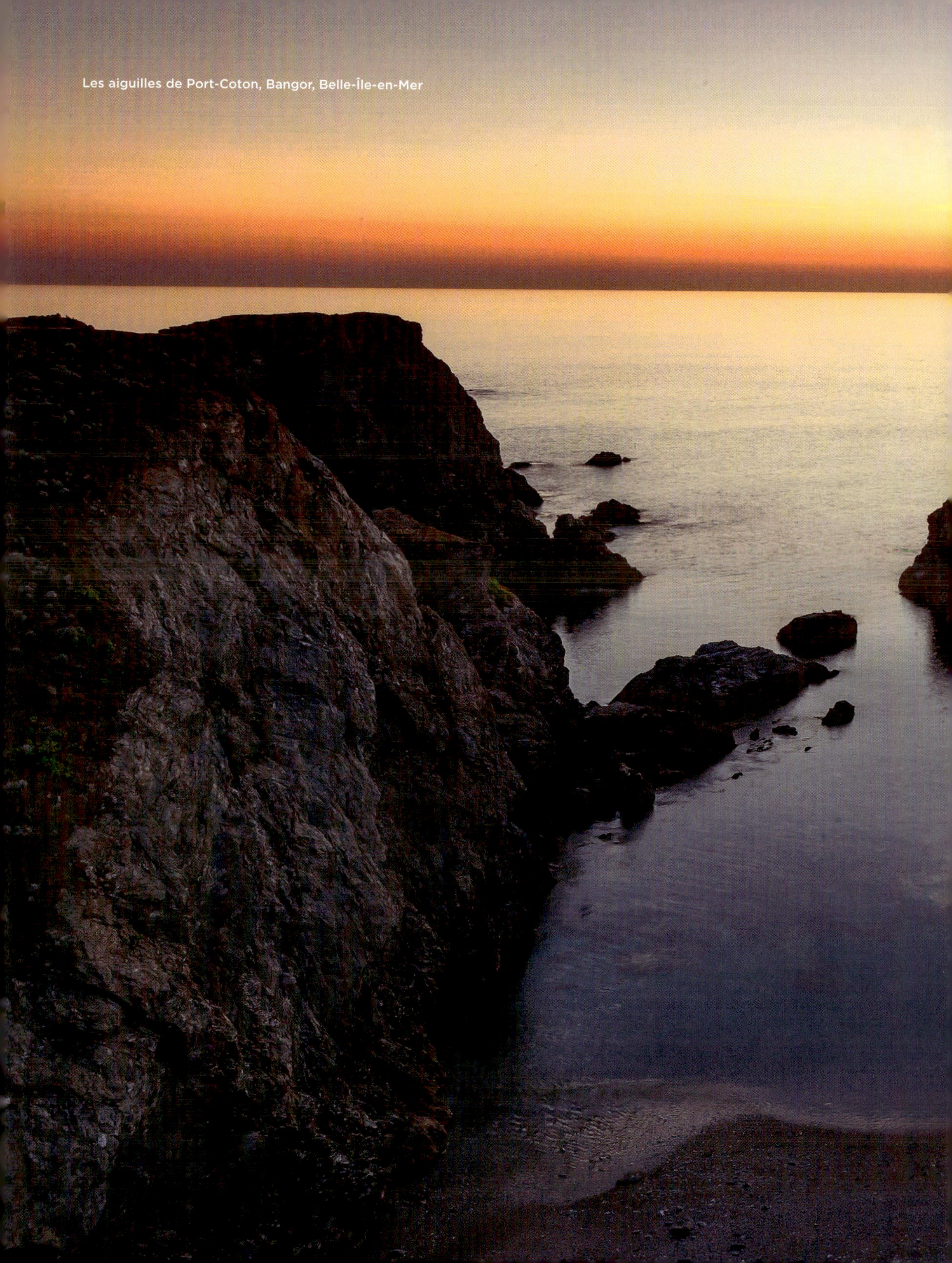
Les aiguilles de Port-Coton, Bangor, Belle-Île-en-Mer

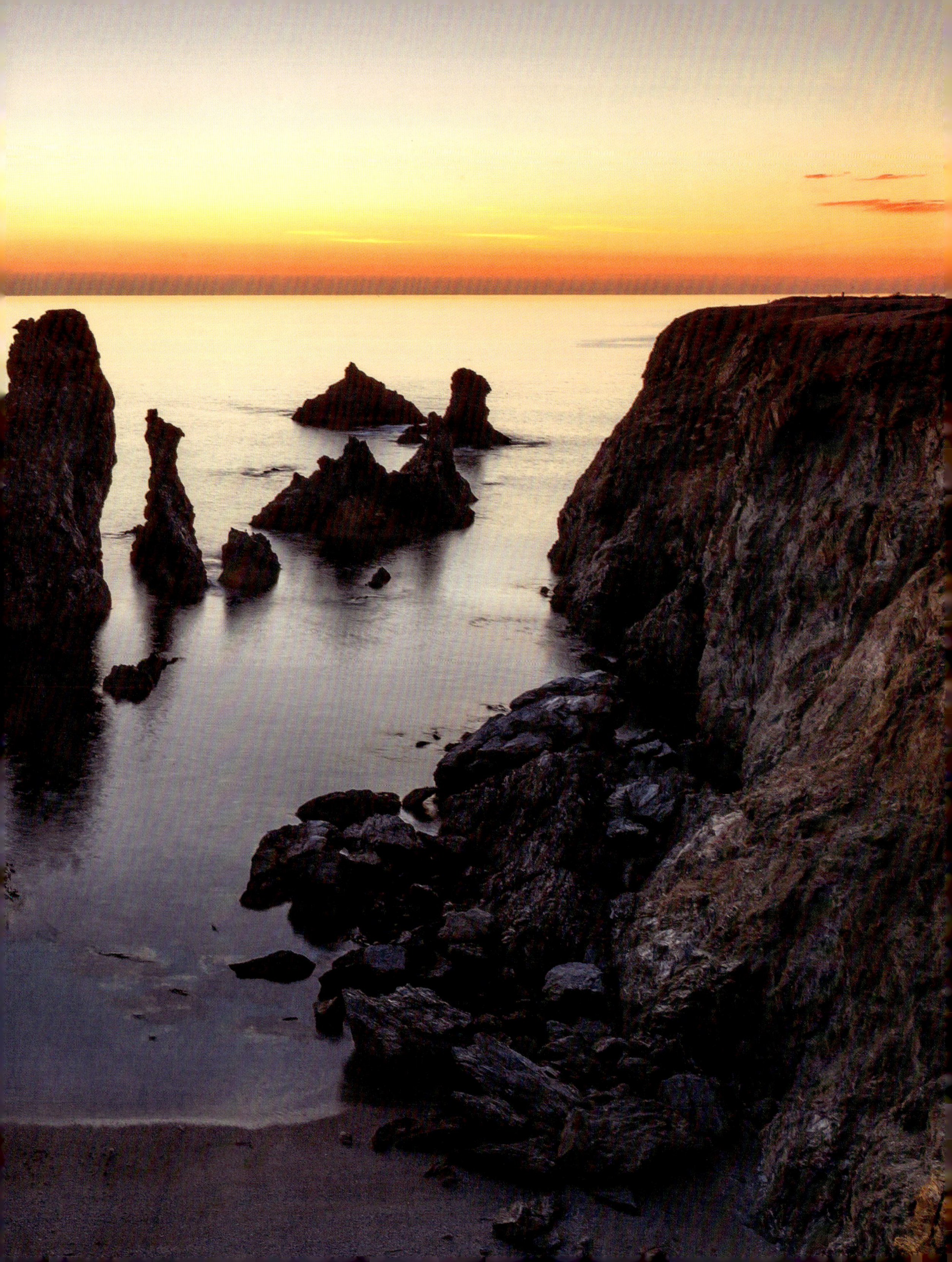

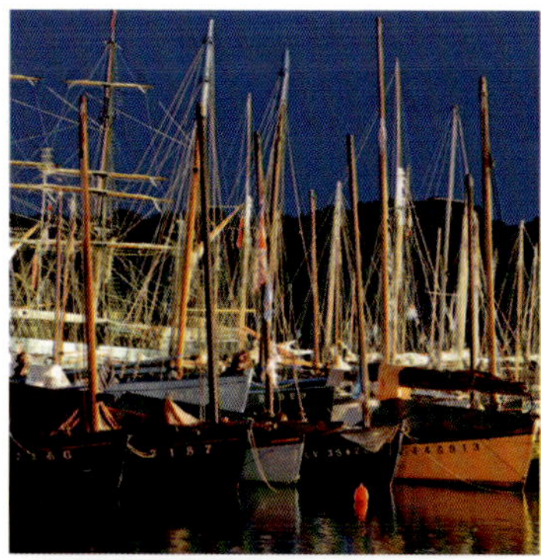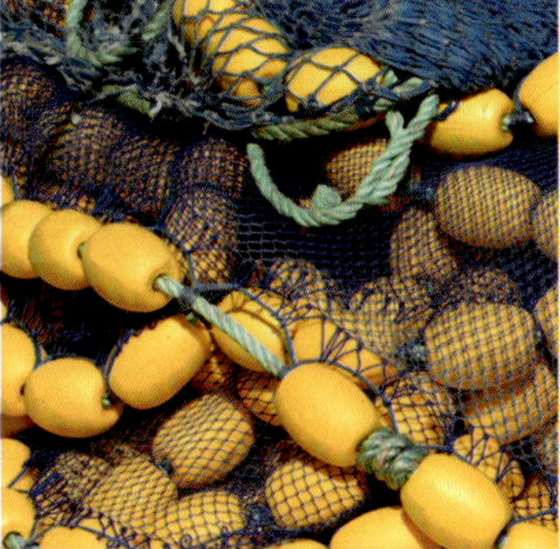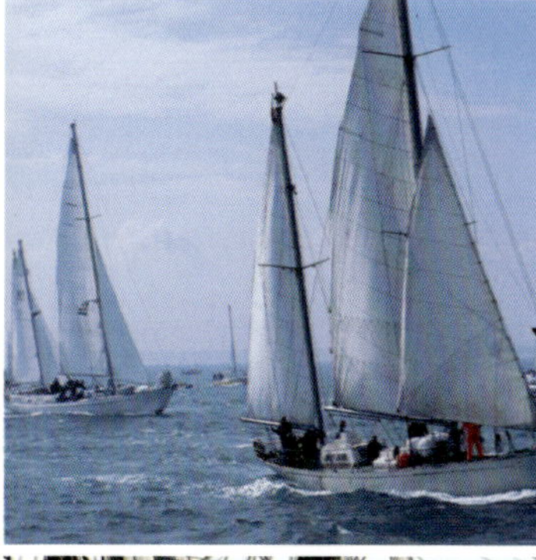

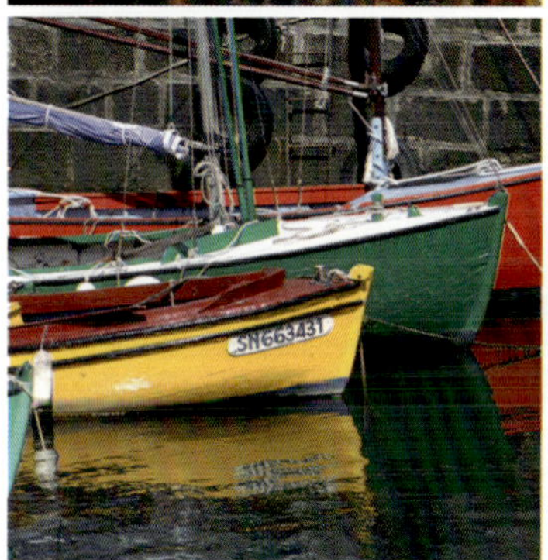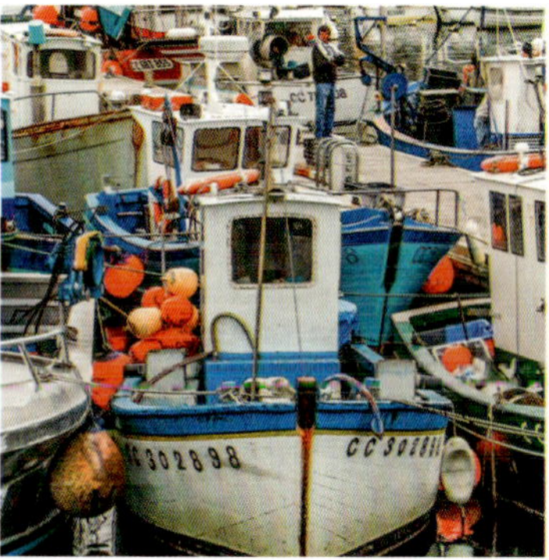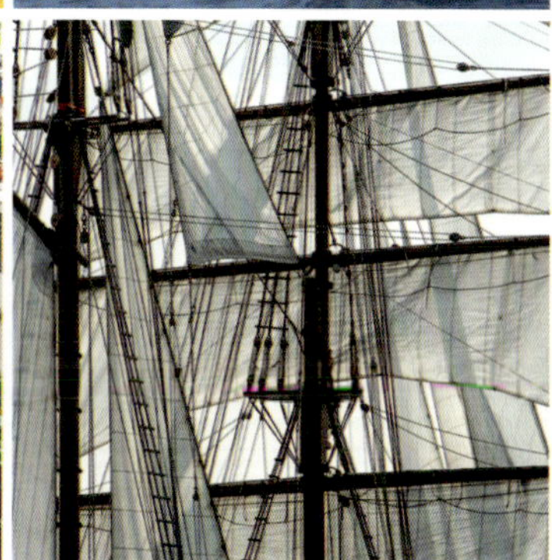

Sailing and Fishing Boats

Brittany is the land of the sea - the possibilities for water sports are numerous, as are the means of transport on the water. Modern regatta yachts cross the paths of traditional sailing boats such as the Sinagot in the Gulf of Morbihan. Old types of ships such as tuna boats or lobster fishing boats are being restored and are finding a new life on the water. Off the coast, the ferries to the islands share the sea with the numerous fishing boats.

Voiles et pêche

En Bretagne, il faut avoir le pied marin. D'ailleurs, les activités nautiques ne manquent pas et les embarcations sont des plus variées. Les bateaux de pêche croisent les bateaux à voiles traditionnels de la plaisance (le Sinagot dans le golfe du Morbihan par exemple) ou les bateaux de la course au large. De vieux gréements (dundee, langoustier, thonier…) ont été restaurés pour notre plus grand plaisir. Et les barques de pêche des côtes sont chahutées par le tangage généré par les navettes naviguant entre les îles.

Segel- und Fischerboote

Die Bretagne ist das Land des Meeres – die Wassersportmöglichkeiten sind zahlreich, genauso wie die Fortbewegungsmittel auf dem Wasser. Modernen Regattajachten kreuzen die Wege von traditionellen Segelbooten, wie dem Sinagot im Golf von Morbihan. Alte Schiffstypen wie Thunfischfänger oder Langustenfischer werden restauriert und finden ein neues Leben auf dem Wasser. Vor der Küste teilen sich die Fähren zu den Inseln das Meer mit den zahlreichen Fischerbooten.

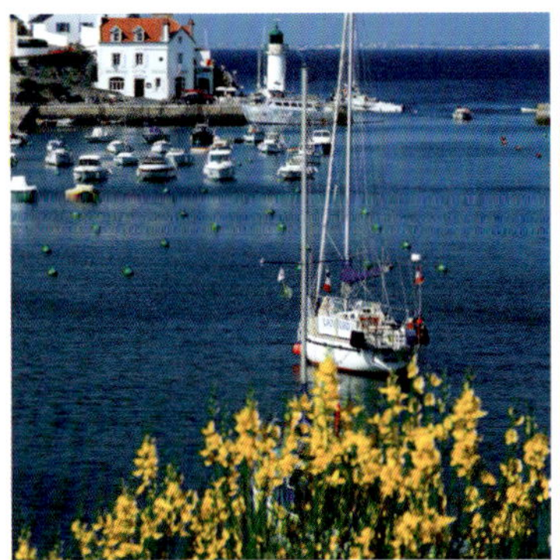
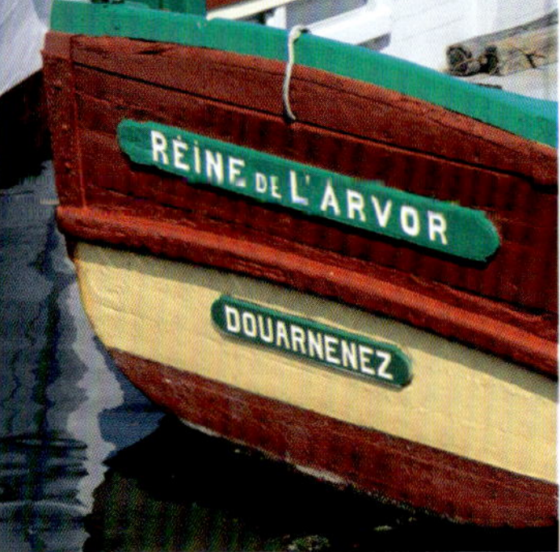

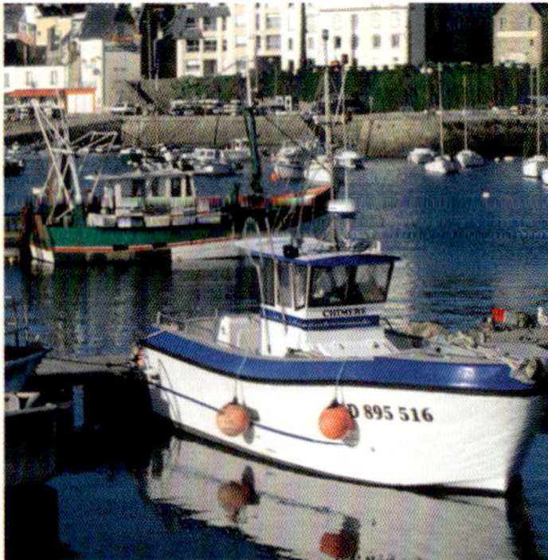
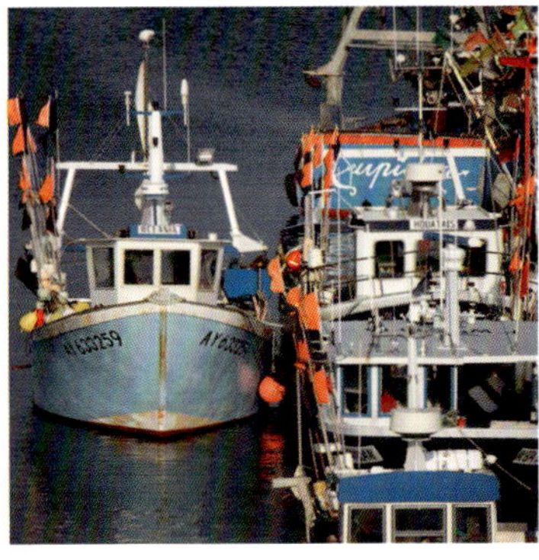
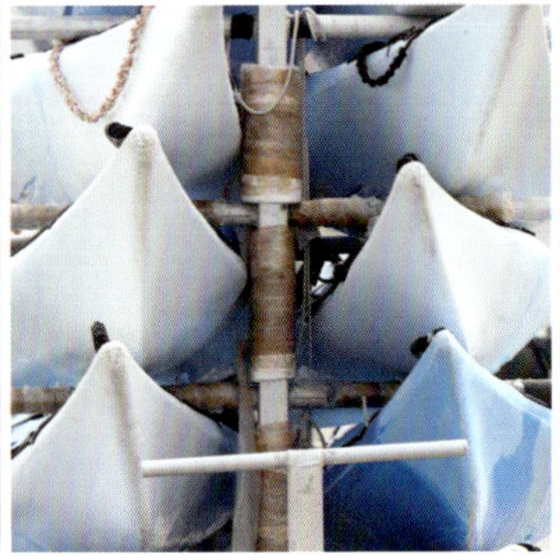
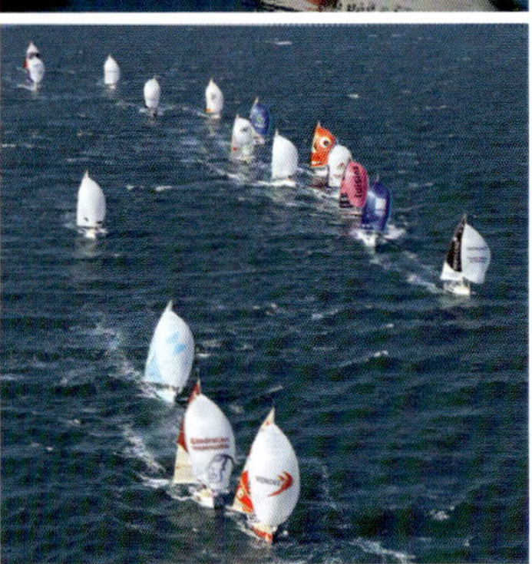

Veleros y barcos de pesca

Bretaña es la tierra del mar; los deportes acuáticos son numerosos, así como los medios de transporte sobre el agua. Los modernos yates de regata cruzan los caminos de los veleros tradicionales, como el Sinagot en el golfo de Morbihan. Antiguos tipos de barcos como los atuneros o los pescadores de langosta están siendo restaurados y están encontrando una nueva vida en el agua. Frente a la costa, los transbordadores a las islas comparten el mar con los numerosos barcos de pesca.

Veleiros e barcos de pesca

A Bretanha é a terra do mar - os desportos náuticos são numerosos, bem como os meios de transporte na água. Os modernos iates de regata cruzam os caminhos dos barcos à vela tradicionais, como o Sinagot, no Golfo de Morbihan. Vários tipos de barcos antigos, como os atuneiros ou os pescadores de lagosta, estão a ser restaurados e, em breve, voltam a cruzar as águas. Ao largo da costa, os ferries para as ilhas partilham o mar com os numerosos barcos de pesca.

Zeil- en vissersboten

Bretagne is het land van de zee, en de watersporten zijn talrijk, evenals de vervoermiddelen op het water. Moderne zeiljachten kruisen de vaarroutes van traditionele zeilboten zoals de sinagots in de Golf van Morbihan. Oude scheepstypen, zoals die voor de tonijn- en langoestenvangst, worden gerestaureerd en krijgen een nieuw bestaan op het water. Voor de kust delen de veerboten naar de eilanden de zee met talloze vissersboten.

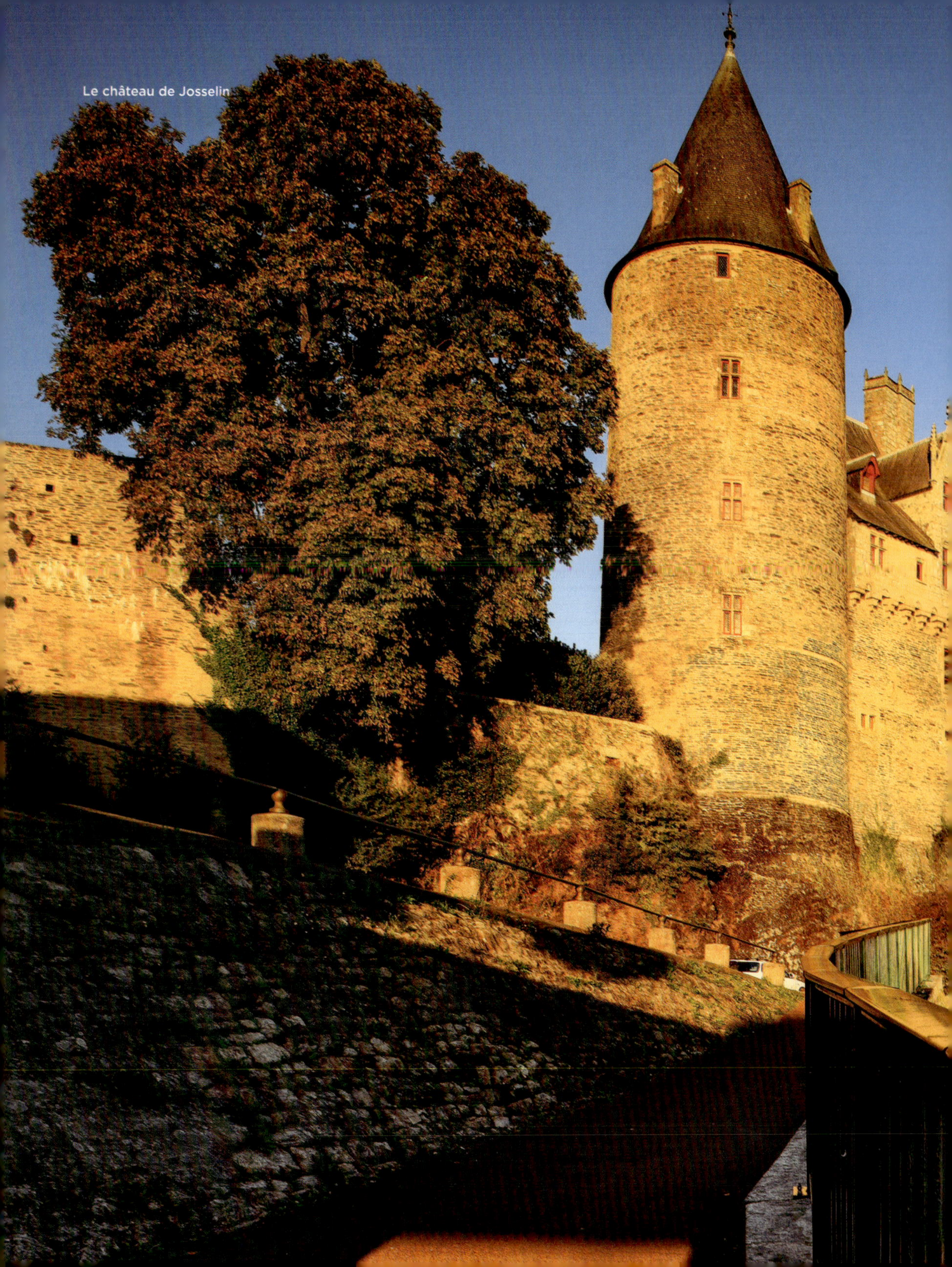

Le château de Josselin

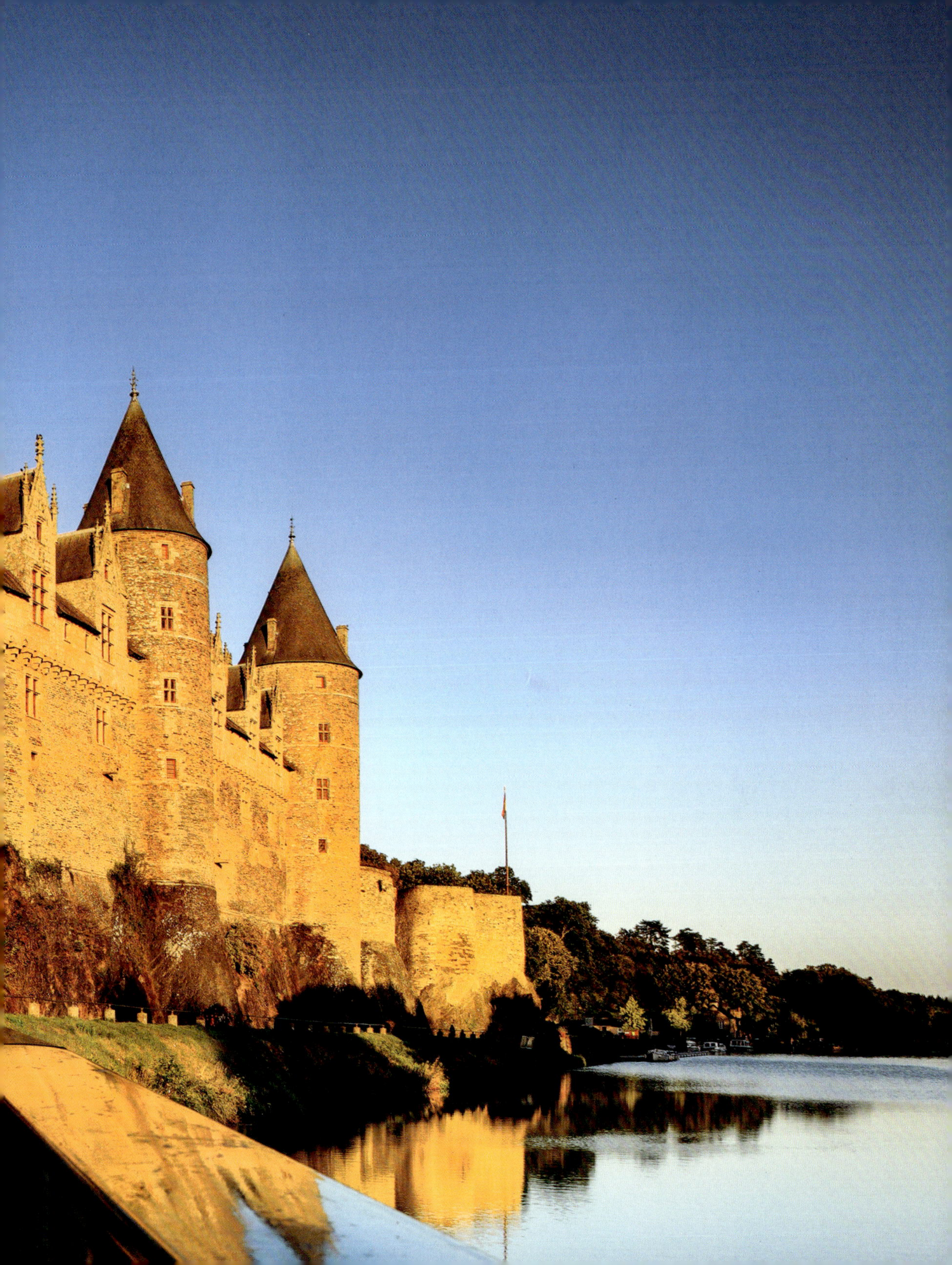

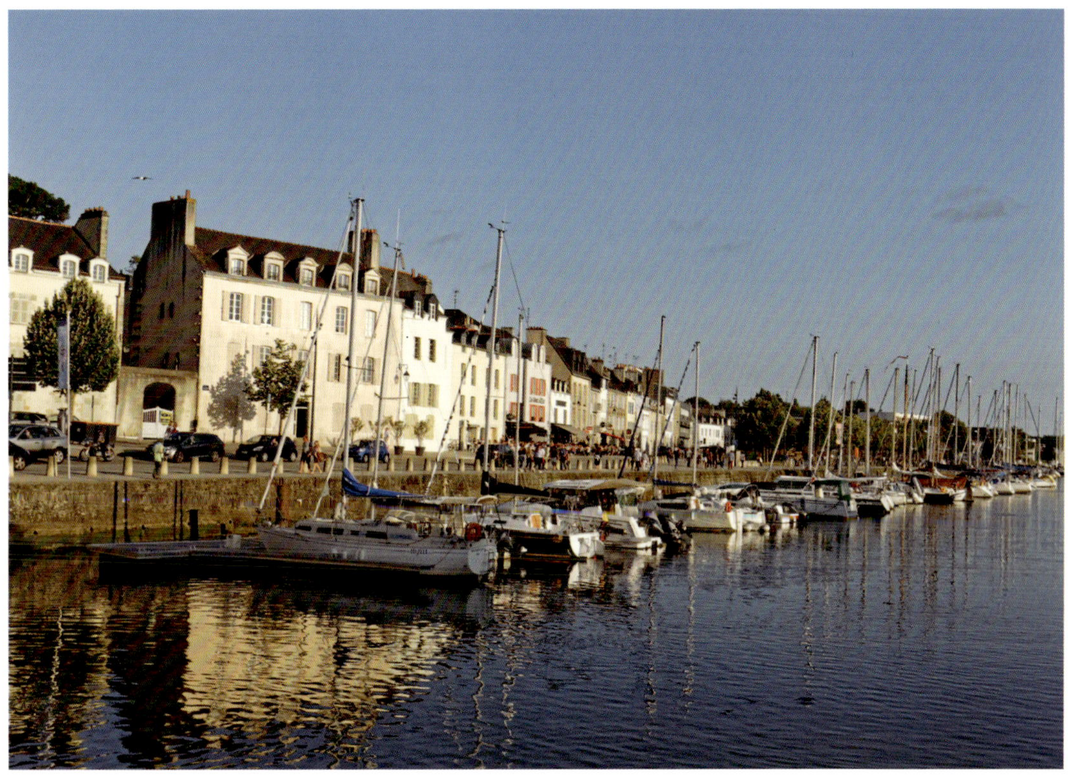

Le port de Vannes

Vannes

Vannes has many faces. The capital of the Morbihan Département impresses with its marina and its medieval city centre with a well-preserved city wall, as well as being a city of art and history.

Vannes

Capitale du Morbihan, port de plaisance, place fortifiée, cité médiévale, ville d'art et d'histoire, la ville de Vannes est plurielle.

Vannes

Vannes hat viele Gesichter. Die Hauptstadt des Départements Morbihan beeindruckt durch ihren Jachthafen, ihren mittelalterlichen Stadtkern mit einer gut erhaltenen Stadtmauer oder als Stadt der Kunst und der Geschichte.

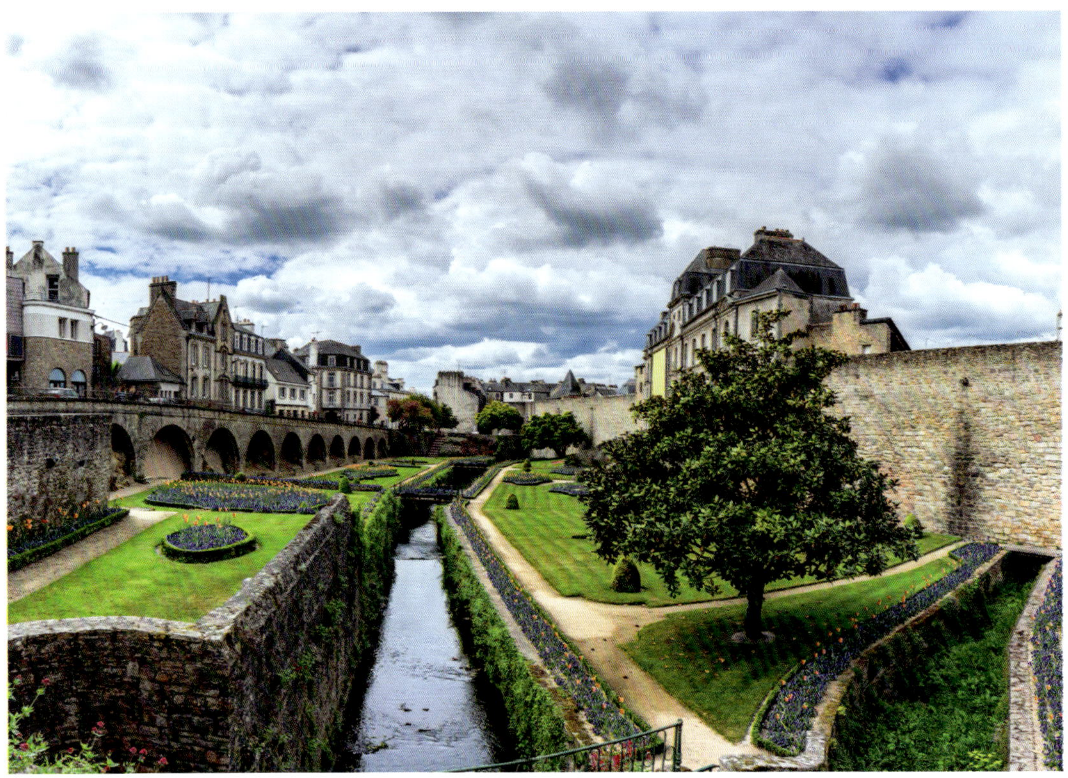

Le château et les jardins de l'Hermine, Vannes

Vannes

Vannes tiene muchas caras. La capital del departamento de Morbihan impresiona con su puerto deportivo, su centro medieval con una muralla bien conservada o como ciudad de arte e historia.

Vannes

Vannes tem muitas facetas. A capital do departamento de Morbihan impressiona quer pela sua marina de barcos de recreio, quer pelo seu centro medieval rodeado de uma muralha bem preservada, assim como cidade de arte e história.

Vannes

Vannes heeft vele gezichten. De hoofdstad van het departement Morbihan maakt indruk met zijn jachthaven en het middeleeuwse stadshart met een goed behouden stadsmuur of als stad van kunst en geschiedenis.

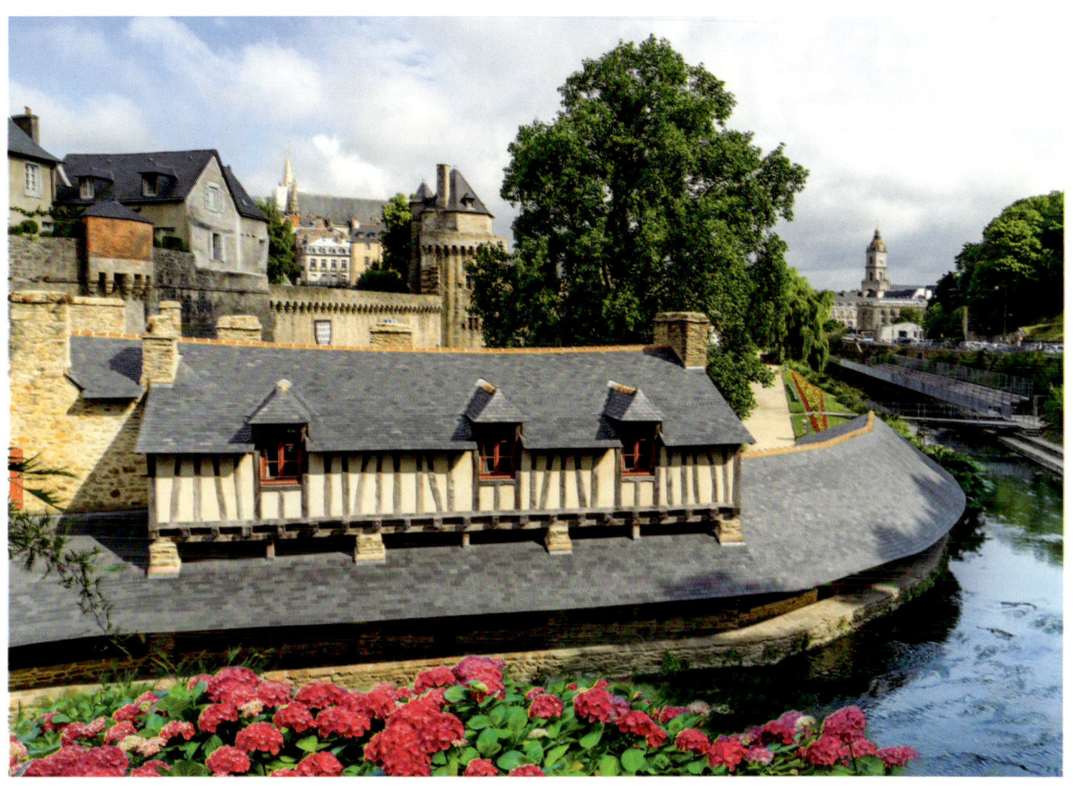

Le fleuve Marle, la « rivière de Vannes »

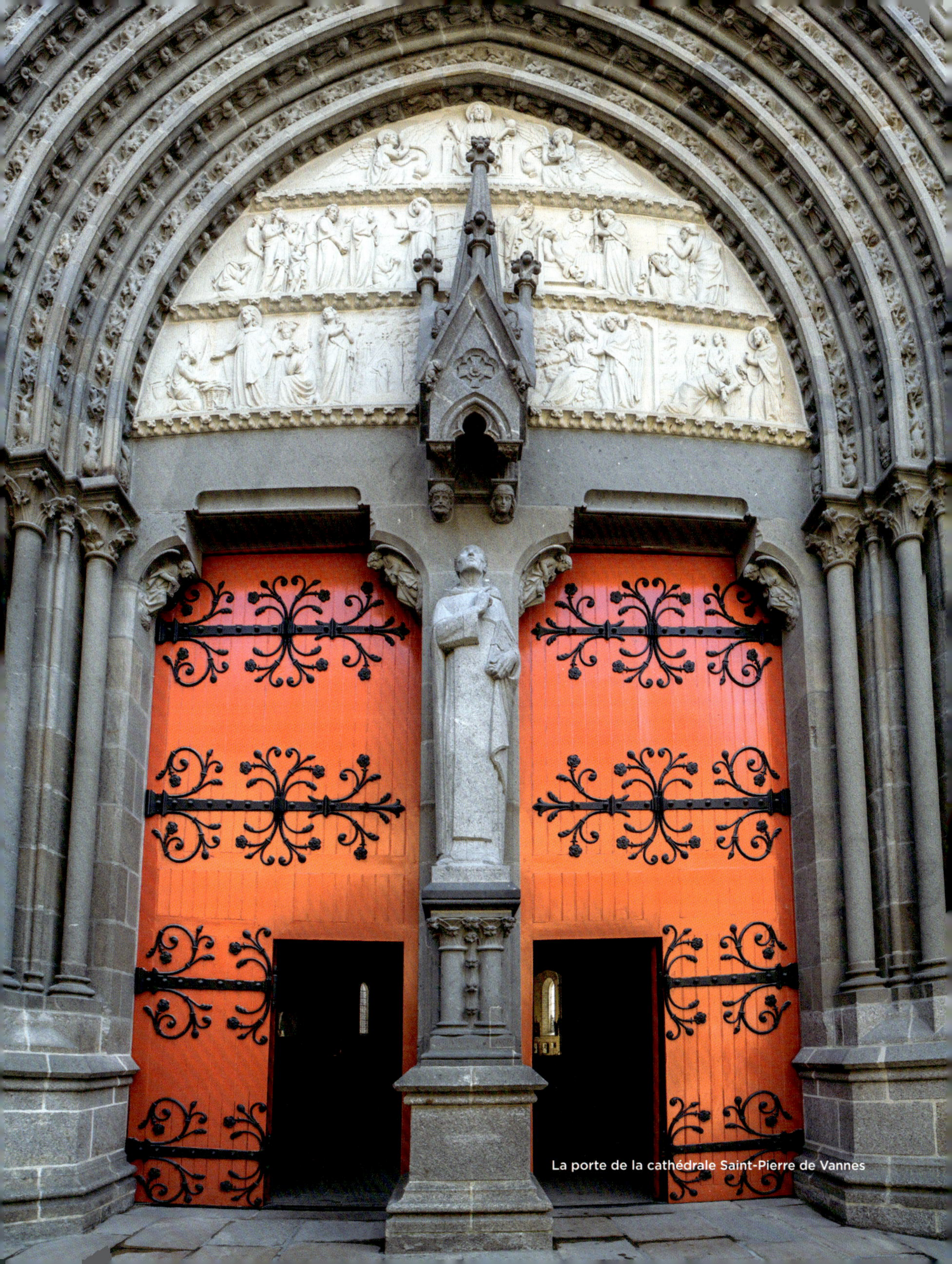

La porte de la cathédrale Saint-Pierre de Vannes

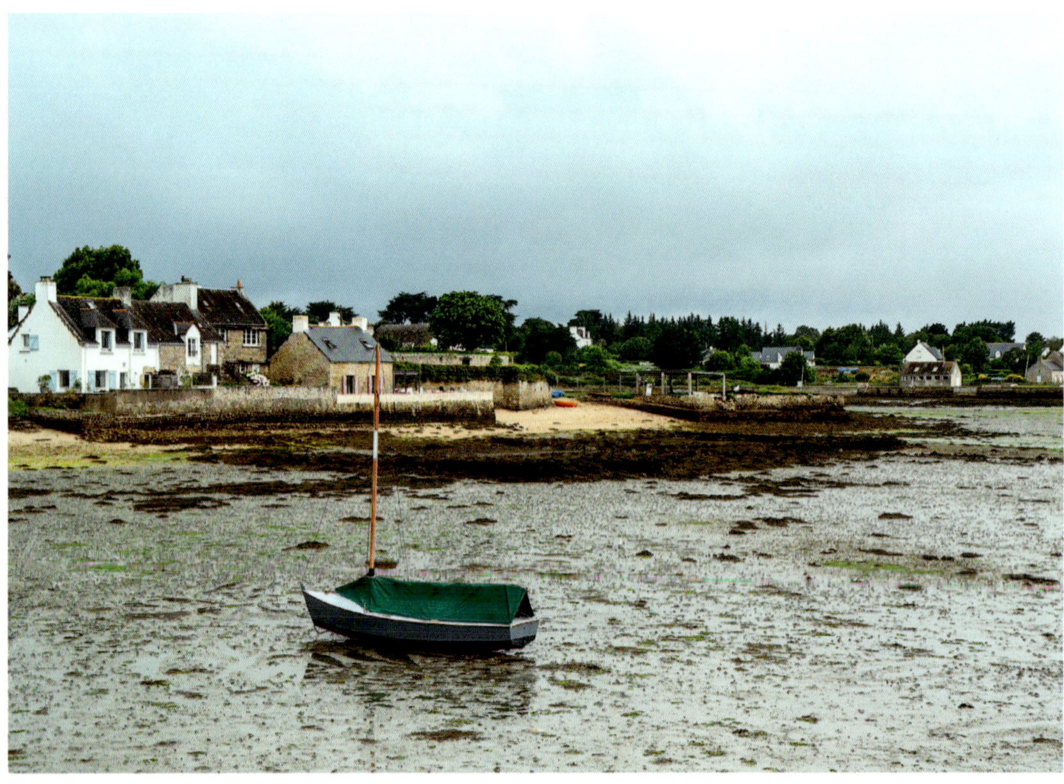

Larmor-Baden, golfe du Morbihan

The Gulf of Morbihan

The Gulf of Morbihan is an inland sea rich in islands, stretching over a length of 20 km. It is appreciated for its unique light and the peace of its nature. Its paradisiacal and untouched islands are home to a unique flora and fauna. The most famous of these is the Île-aux-Moines, also known as "The Pearl of the Gulf".

Le golfe du Morbihan

Formant comme une mer intérieure d'une longueur de 20 km et parsemée de nombreux îles et îlots, le golfe du Morbihan est une destination prisée pour la beauté de ses lumières changeantes et pour sa tranquillité. Terres d'asile de la faune et de la flore, ses îles sont des paradis sauvages. L'Île-aux-Moines, la plus connue, est appelée « la perle du golfe ».

Der Golf von Morbihan

Der Golf von Morbihan ist ein inselreiches Binnenmeer, das sich über eine Länge von 20 km erstreckt. Er wird für sein einmaliges Licht und die Ruhe der Natur geschätzt. Seine paradiesischen und unberührten Inseln beherbergen eine einzigartige Tier- und Pflanzenwelt. Die bekannteste unter ihnen ist die Île-aux-Moines, die auch «die Perle des Golfs» genannt wird.

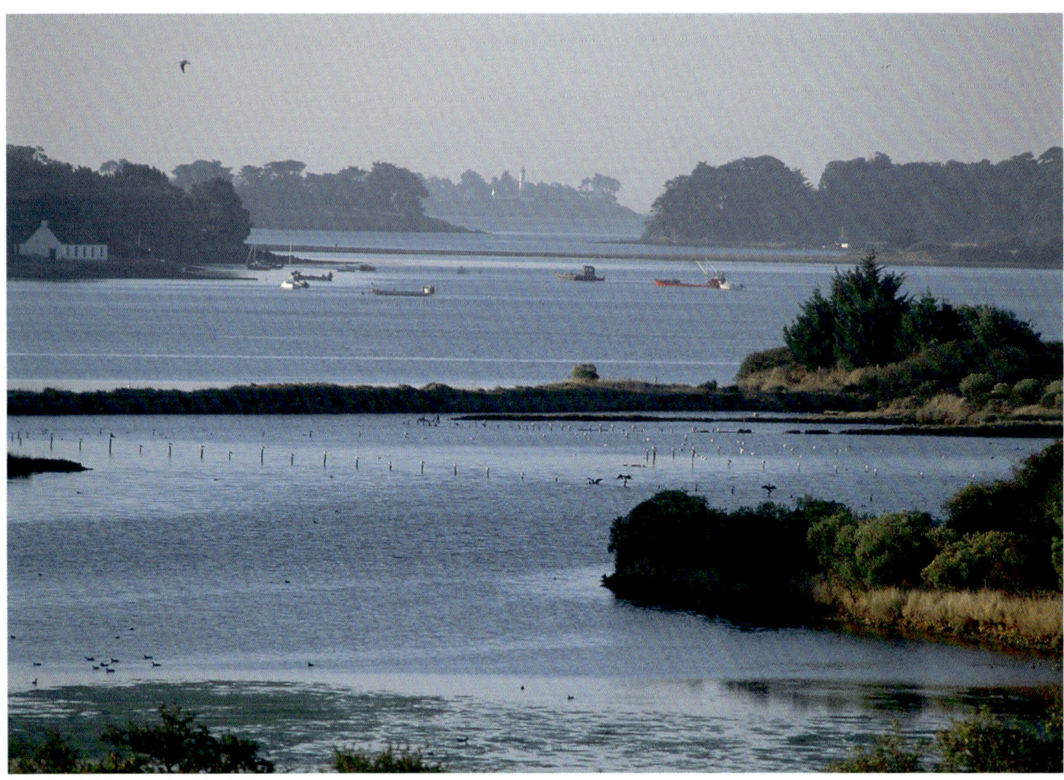

Port-Navalo, golfe du Morbihan

El golfo de Morbihan

El golfo de Morbihan es un mar interior rico en islas y se extiende a lo largo de 20 km. Es apreciado por su luz única y la paz de la naturaleza. Sus paradisíacas e intactas islas albergan una flora y una fauna únicas. La más famosa de ellas es la Île-aux-Moines, también conocida como «la perla del golf».

O Golfo de Morbihan

O Golfo de Morbihan é um mar interior com imensas ilhas e estende-se ao longo de 20 km. É apreciado pela sua luz única e pela paz da natureza. As suas ilhas paradisíacas, intactas e selvagens abrigam uma flora e fauna únicas. A mais famosa delas é a Île-aux-Moines, também conhecida como «a pérola do golfe».

De Golf van Morbihan

De Golf van Morbihan is een eilandrijke binnenzee die zich uit over een lengte van 20 km uitstrekt. Hij wordt gewaardeerd om zijn unieke licht en de rust van de natuur. De paradijselijke en ongerepte eilanden herbergen een unieke flora en fauna. Het bekendste daarvan is het Île-aux-Moines, dat ook wel 'parel van de Golf' wordt genoemd.

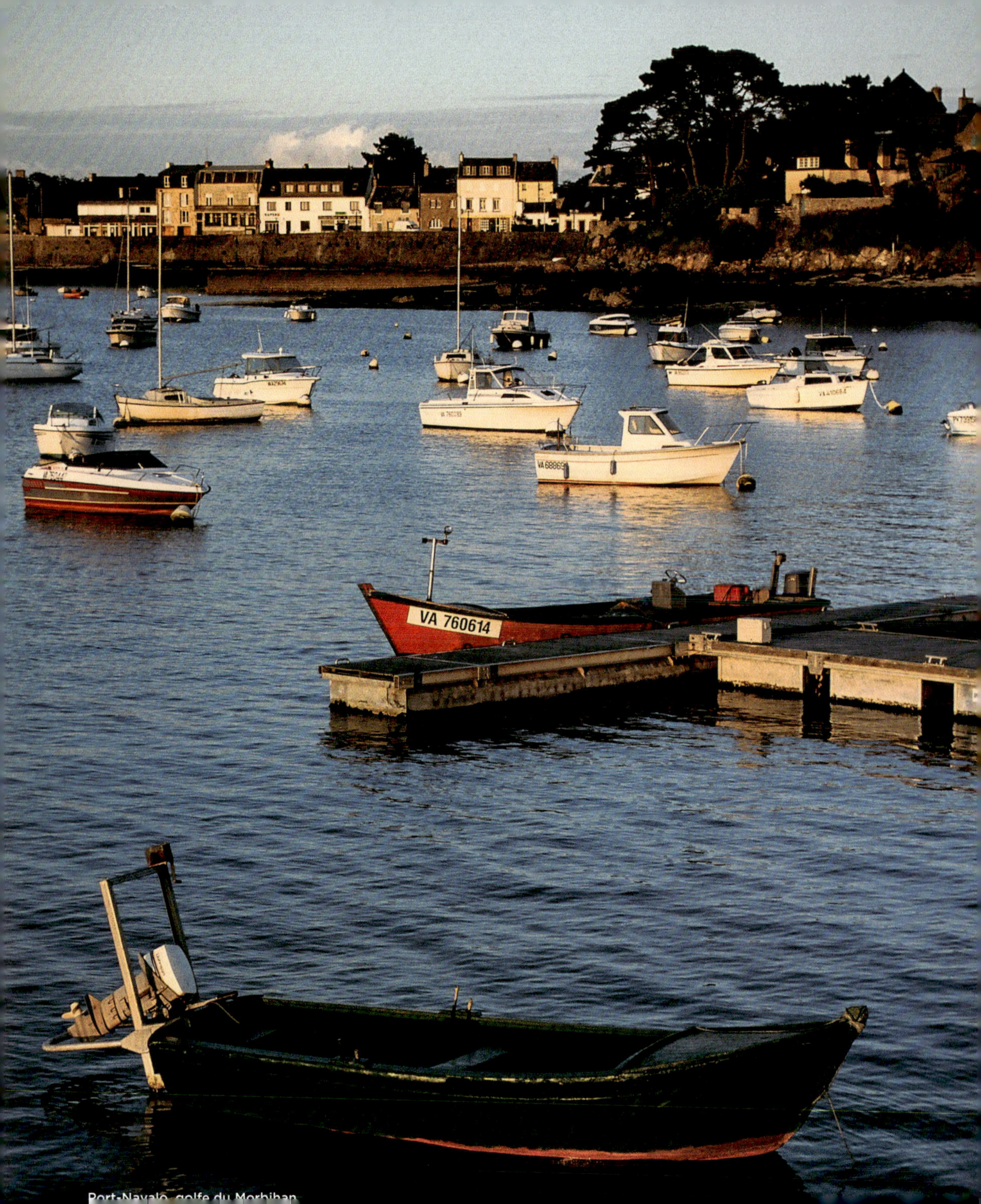

Port-Navalo, golfe du Morbihan.

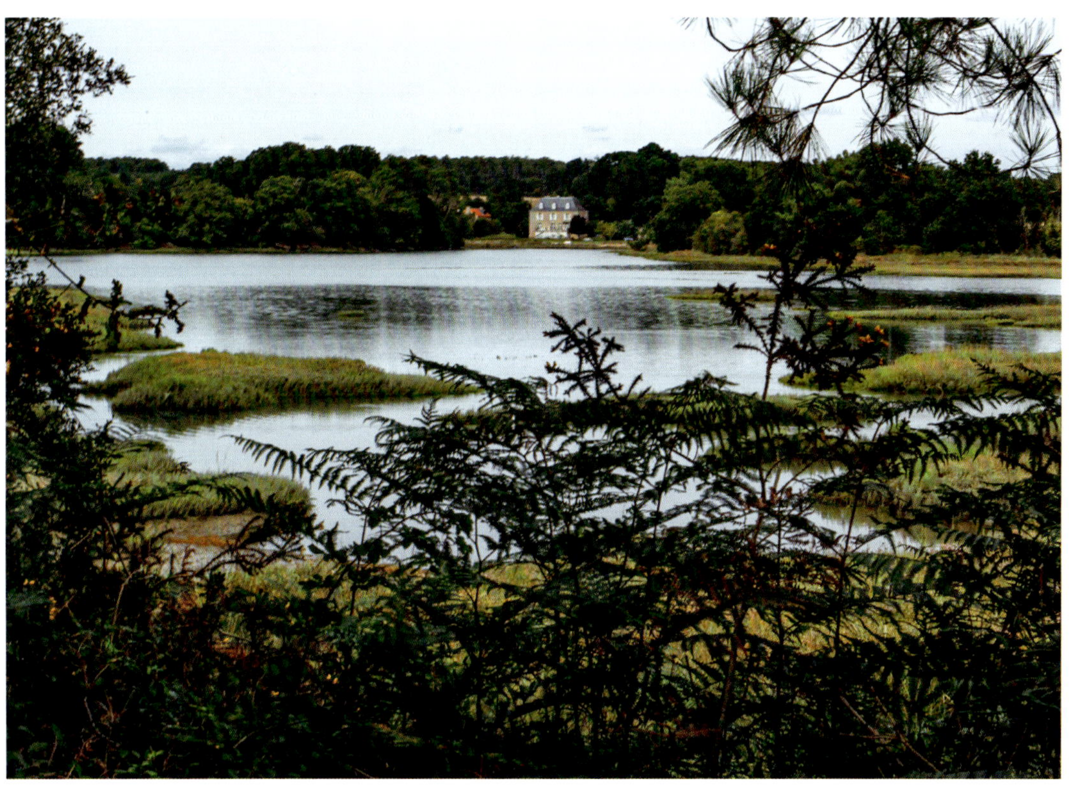

Une entrée dans le golfe du Morbihan

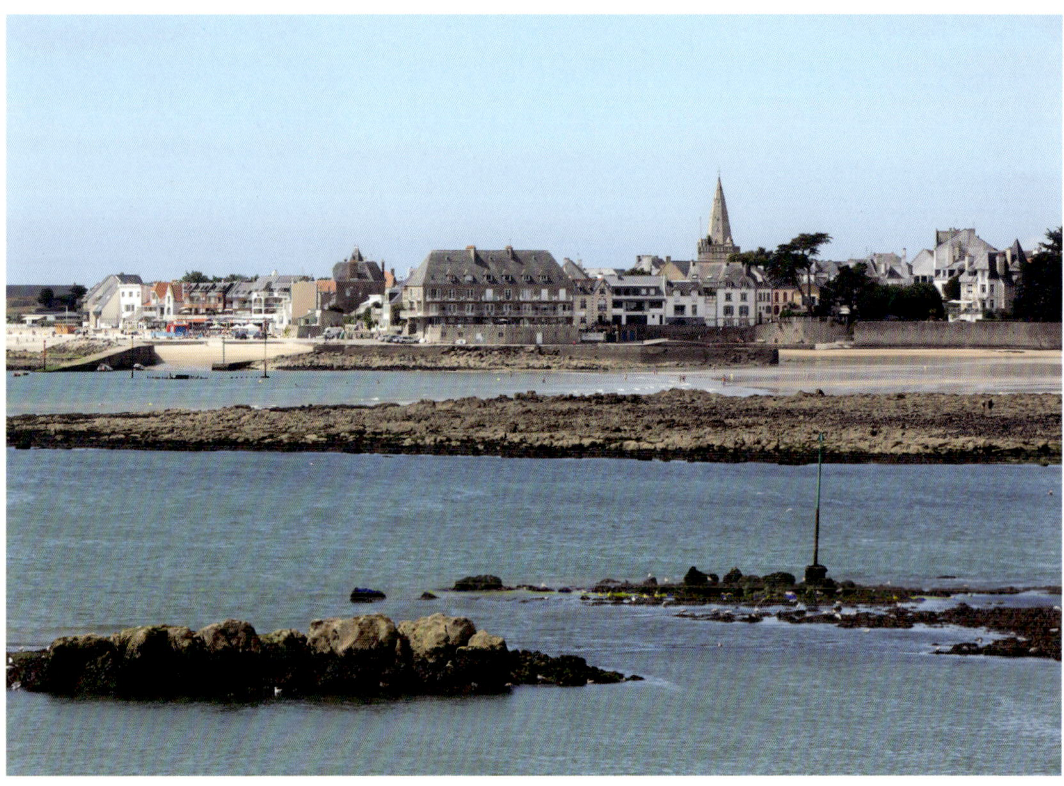

Larmor-Plage

Lorient

The bustling port city at the
roadside of Lorient is the third
largest city in Brittany and the
capital of the Morbihan
department. The annual "Festival
Interceltique de Lorient" is one of
the city's attractions. 14 km off the
coast lies the Île de Groix with its
wild nature and charming little
harbours.

Lorient

Cité portuaire active et arsenal
maritime au fond de la rade de
Lorient, la ville de Lorient est la
troisième ville bretonne. Chef-lieu
du département du Morbihan, avec
son Festival interceltique annuel,
Lorient a su affirmer son identité.
À 14 km au large : l'île de Groix,
avec sa nature sauvage et ses
charmants petits ports.

Lorient

Die geschäftige Hafenstadt an der
Reede von Lorient ist die
drittgrößte Stadt der Bretagne und
die Hauptstadt des Departements
Morbihan. Das jährlich stattfindende
„Festival Interceltique de Lorient"
ist eine der Attraktionen der Stadt.
14 km vor der Küste liegt die Île de
Groix mit ihrer wilden Natur und
ihren charmanten kleinen Häfen.

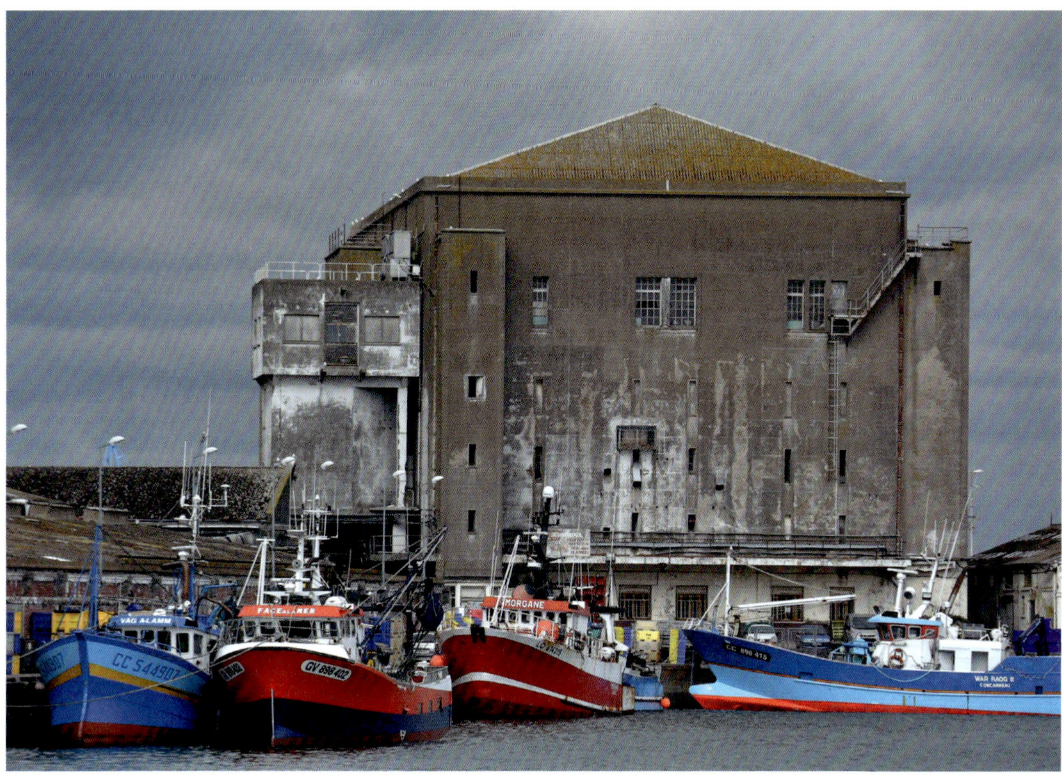

Le port de Lorient

Lorient

La bulliciosa ciudad portuaria al
borde de la carretera de Lorient es
la tercera ciudad más grande de
Bretaña y la capital del
departamento de Morbihan.
El festival anual «Festival
Interceltique de Lorient» es una
de las attracciones de la ciudad. A
14 km de la costa se encuentra la Île
de Groix, con su naturaleza salvaje
y sus pequeños y encantadores
puertos.

Lorient

A movimentada cidade portuária à
beira da estrada é a terceira maior
cidade da Bretanha e a capital do
departamento de Morbihan. O
«Festival Interceltique de Lorient»
que ocorre anualmente é uma das
atrações da cidade. A „Île de Groix",
com a sua natureza selvagem e
pequenos portos encantadores,
encontra-se a 14 km da costa.

Lorient

De bedrijvige havenstad aan de
rede van Lorient is de op twee na
grootste stad van Bretagne en de
hoofdstad van het departement
Morbihan. Het jaarlijkse 'Festival
Interceltique de Lorient' is een van
de attracties van de stad. 14 km
voor de kust ligt het Île de Groix
met zijn wilde natuur en charmante
haventjes.

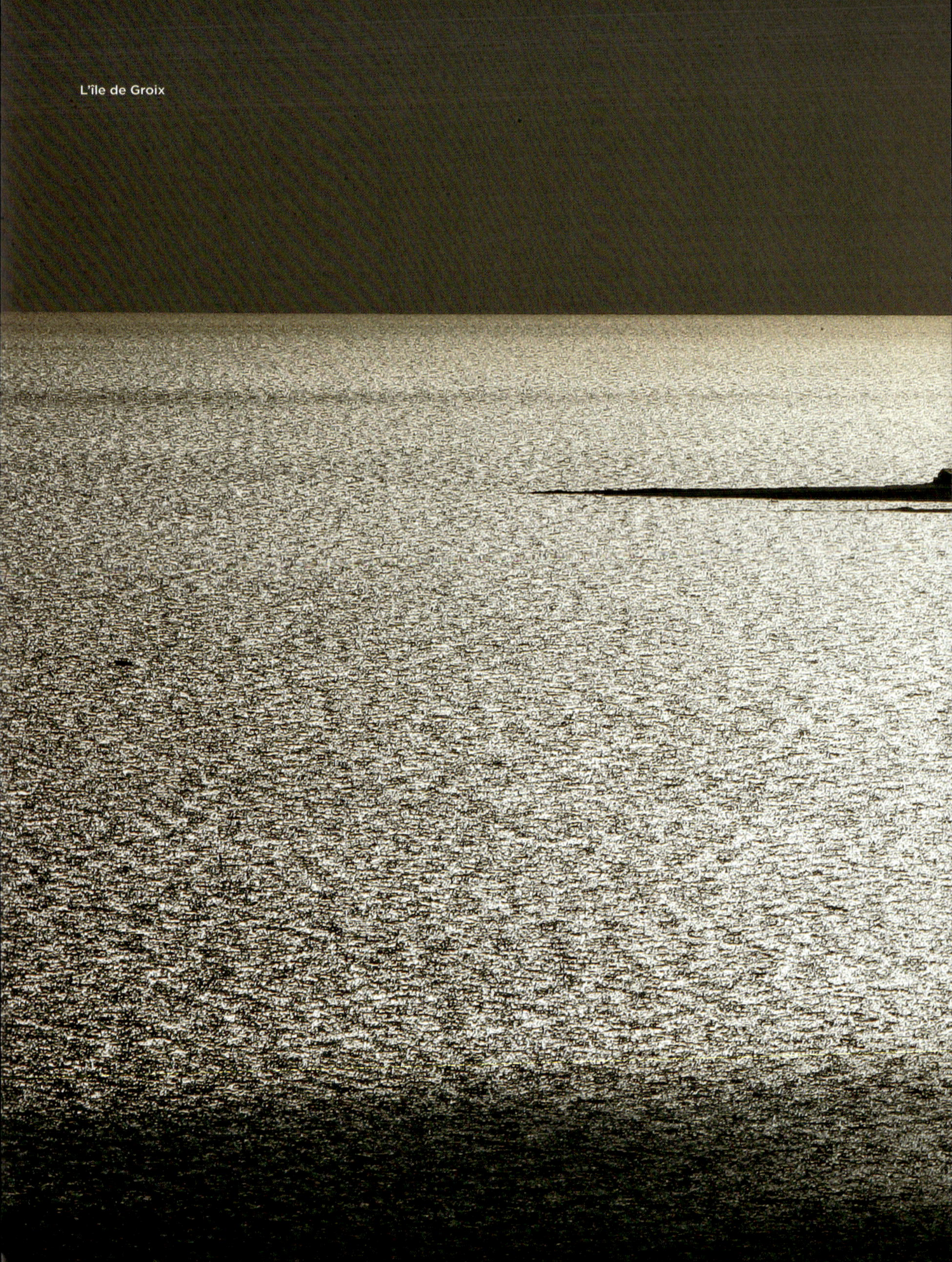

L'île de Groix

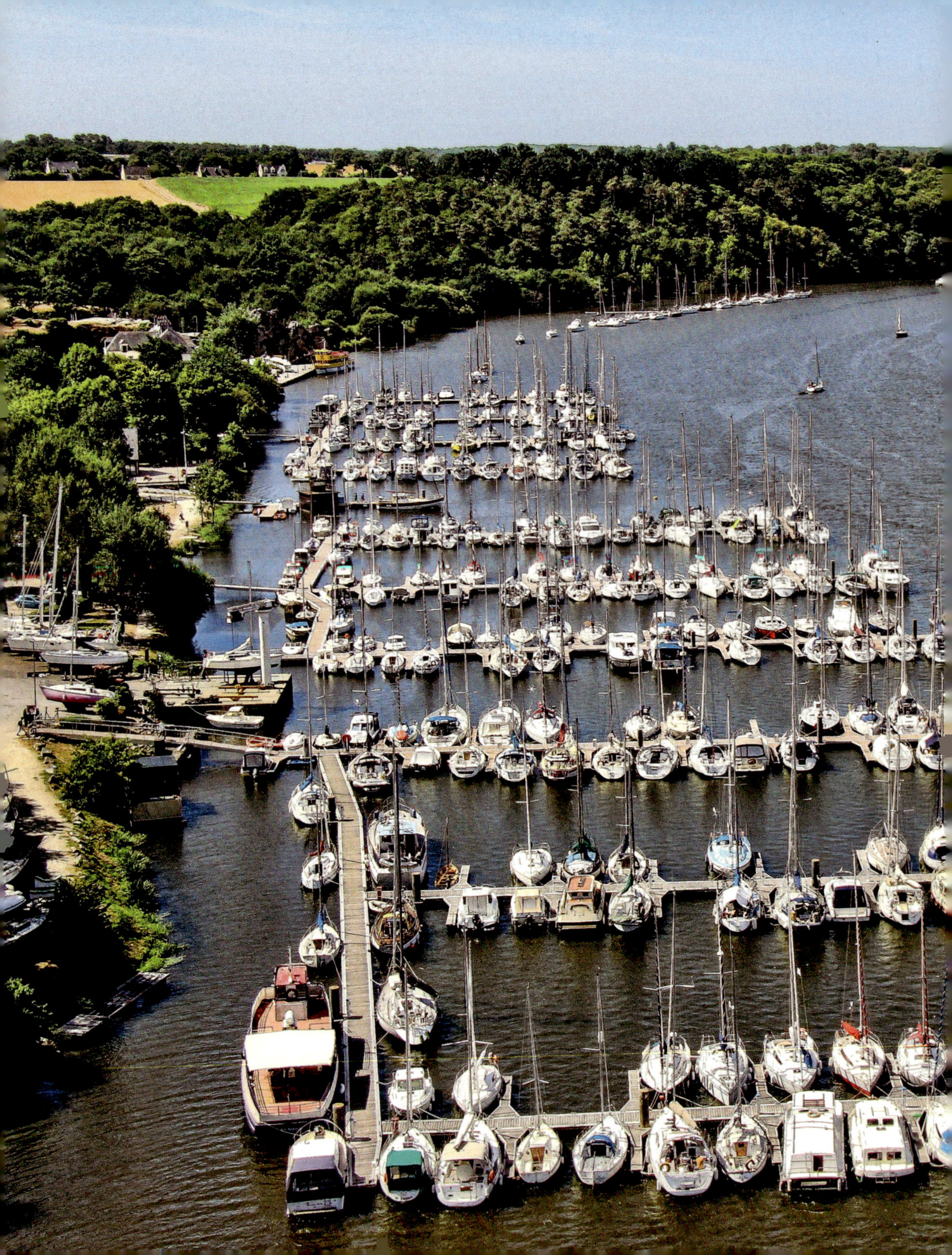

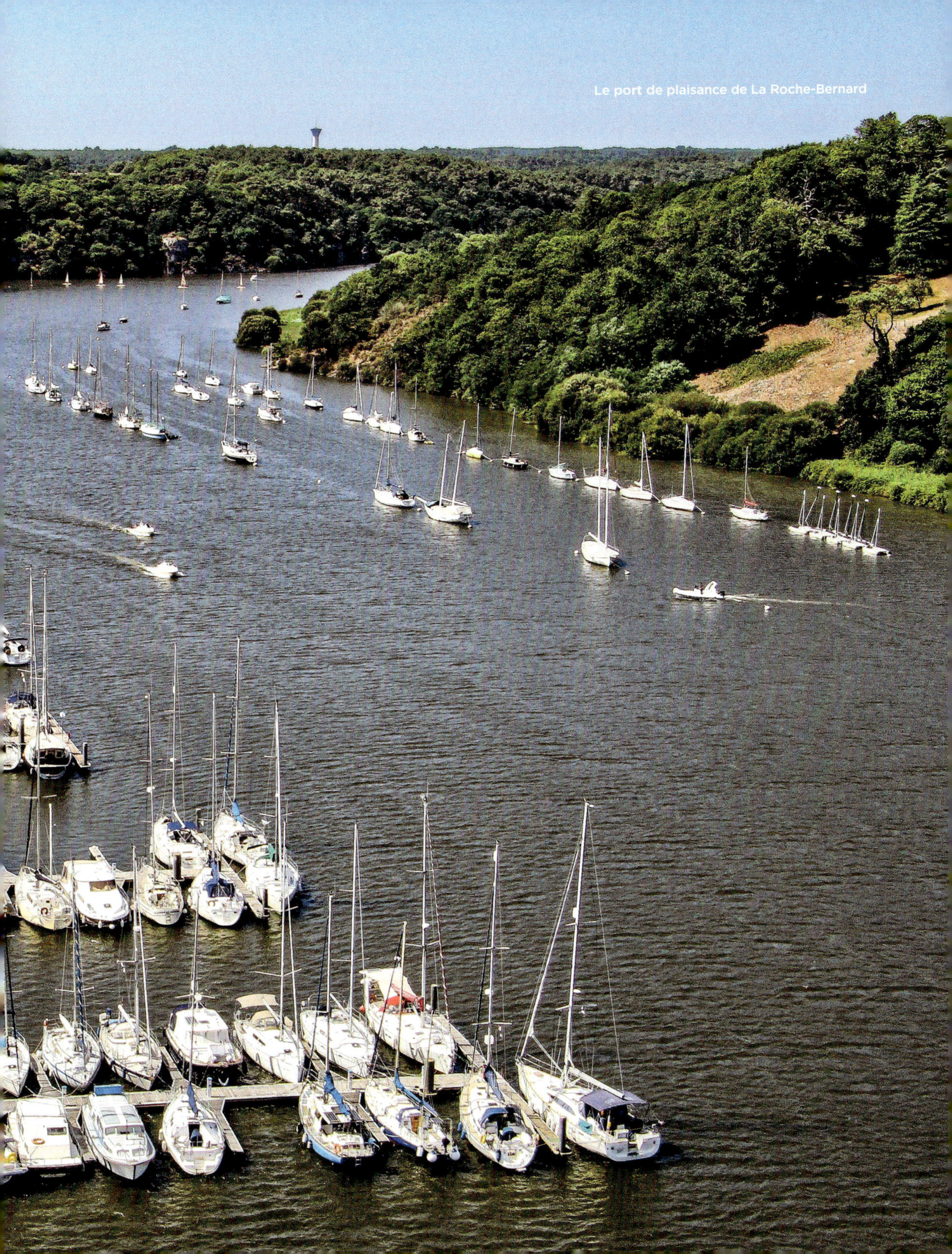

Le port de plaisance de La Roche-Bernard

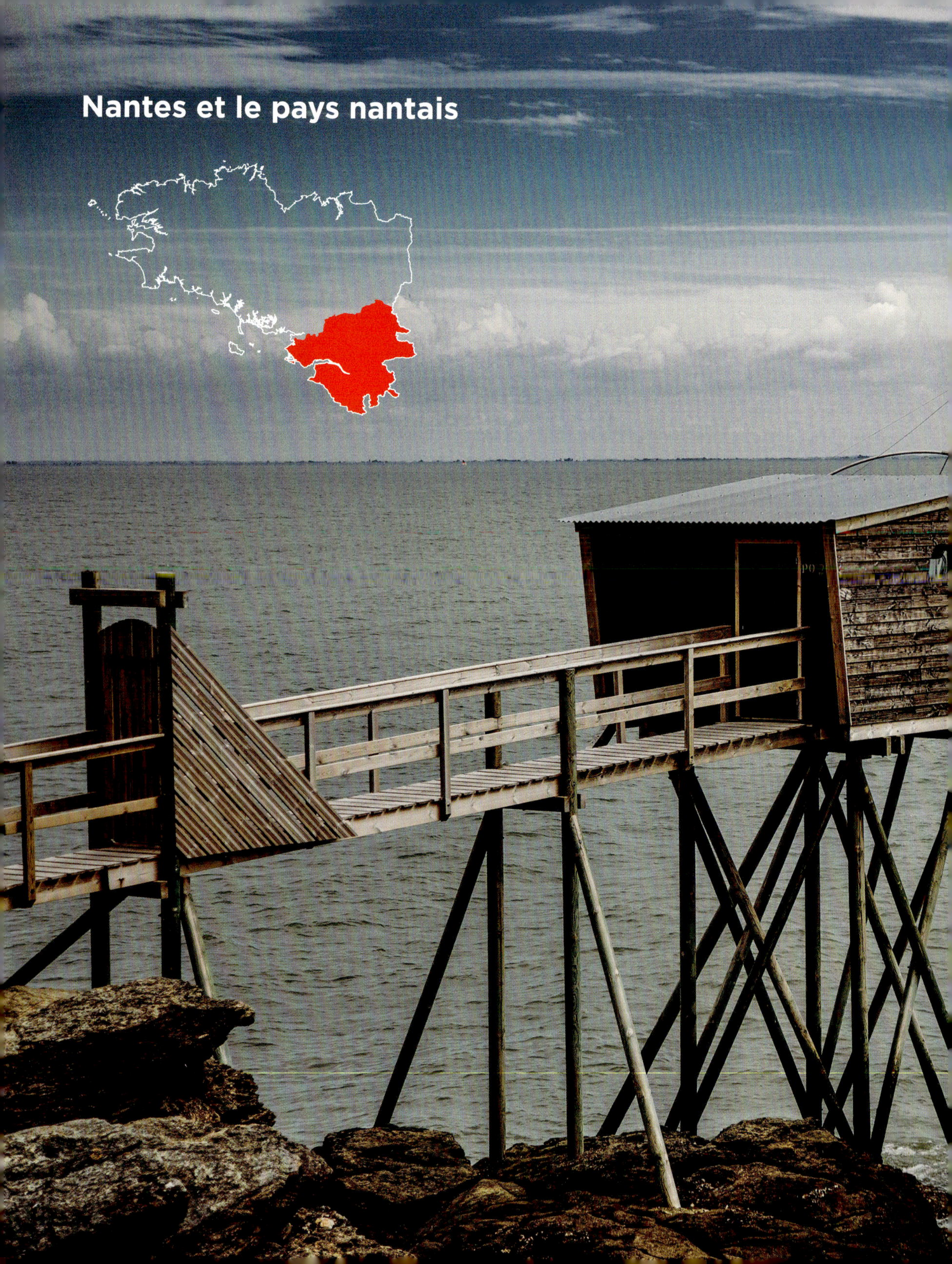

Nantes et le pays nantais

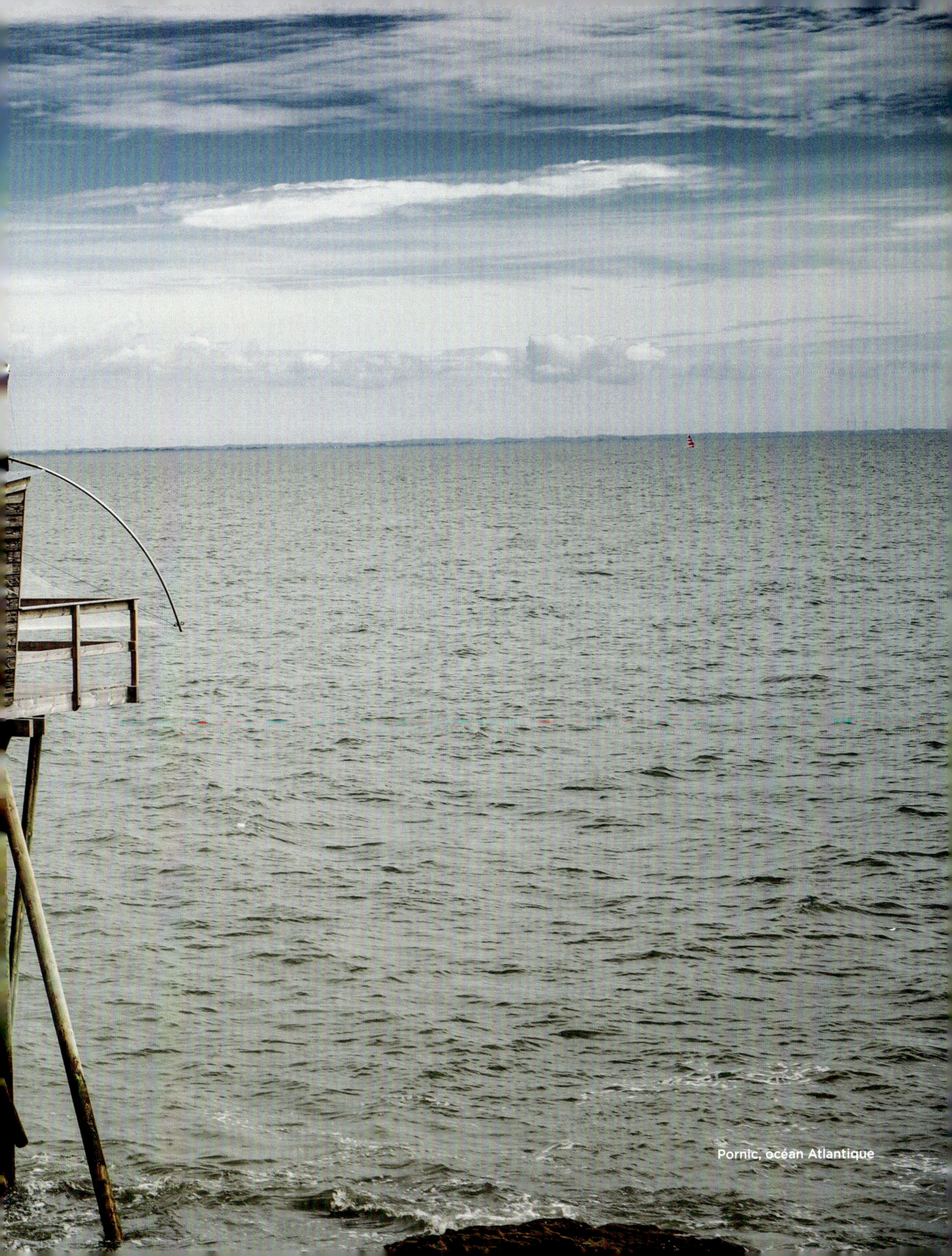
Pornic, océan Atlantique

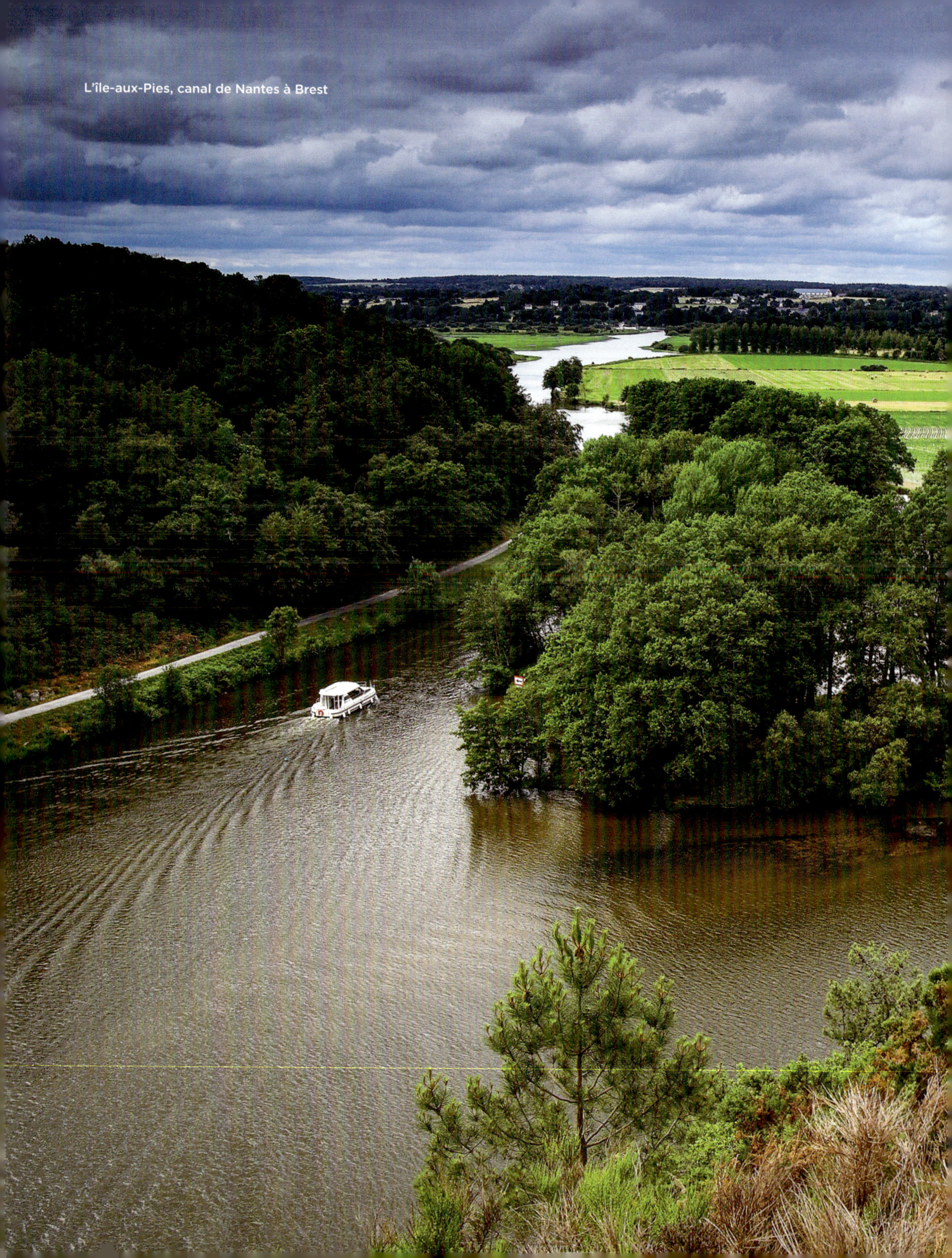
L'île-aux-Pies, canal de Nantes à Brest

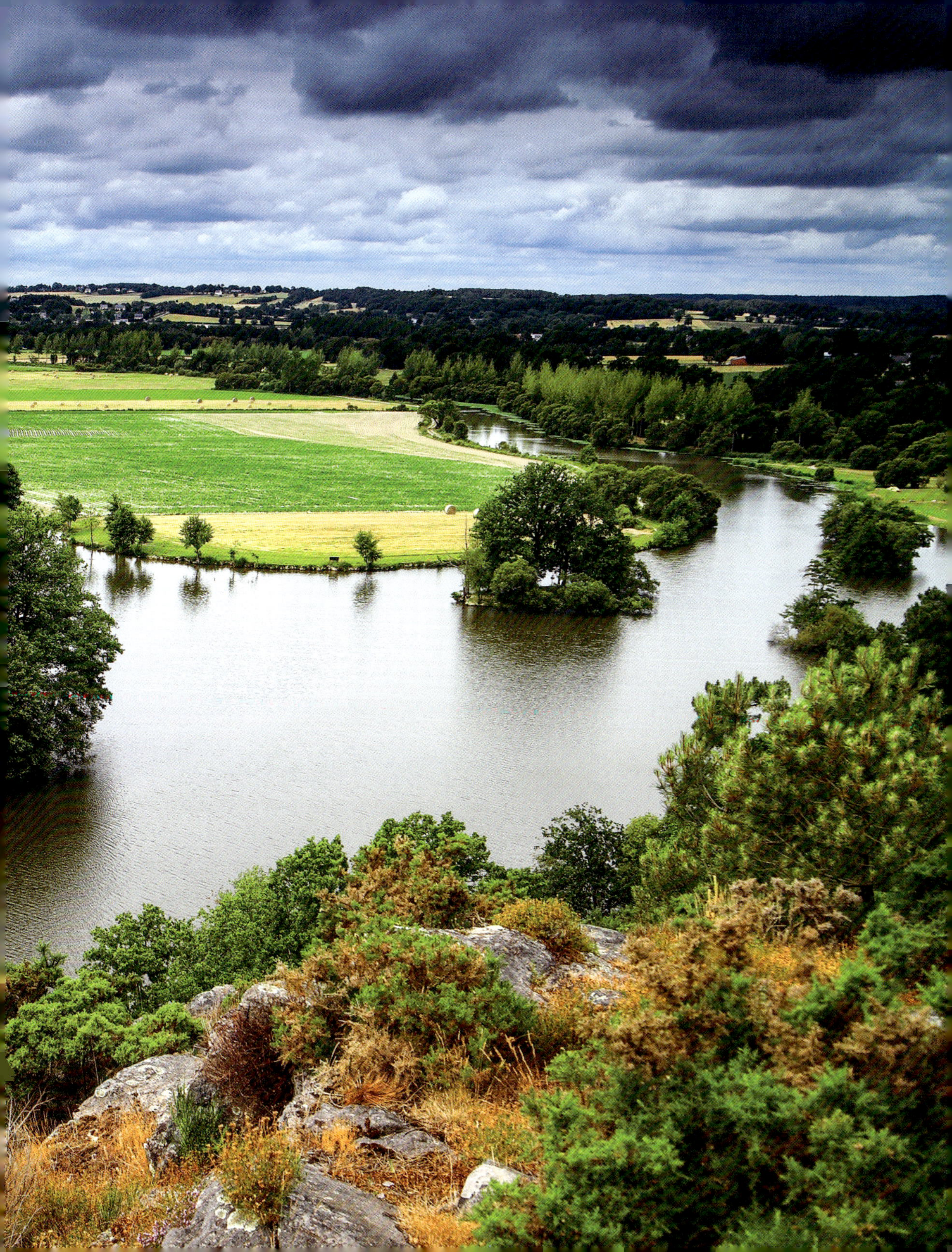

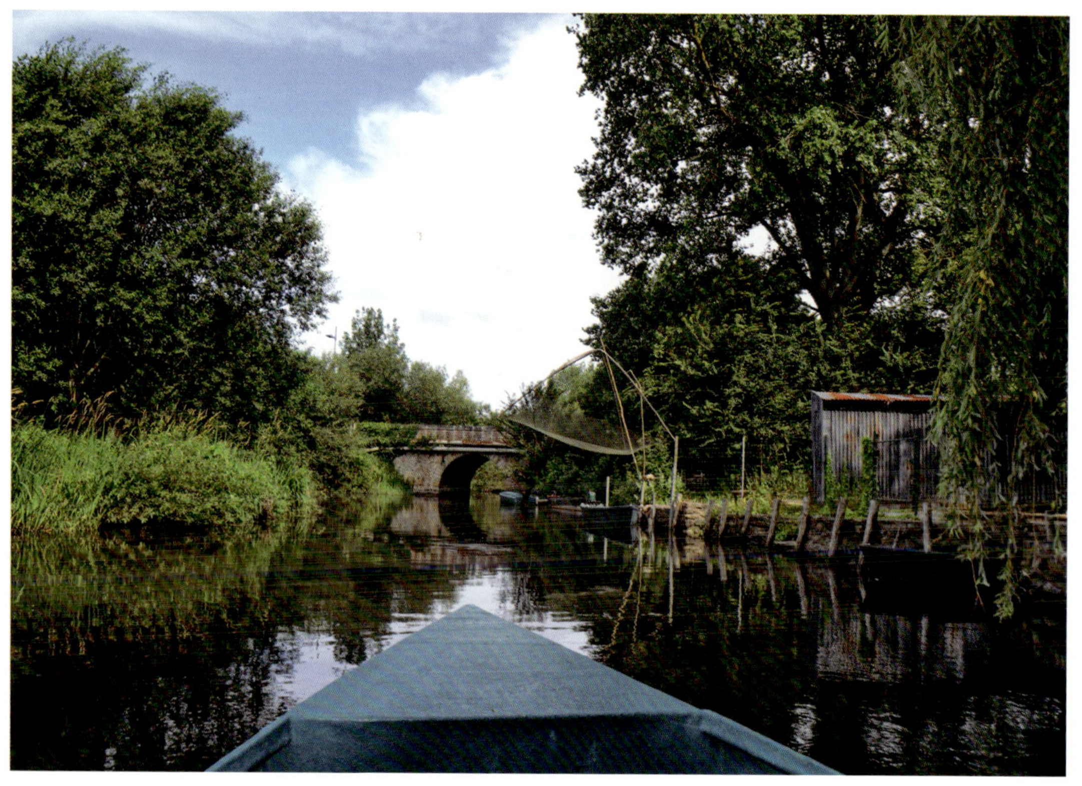

Parc de la Brière

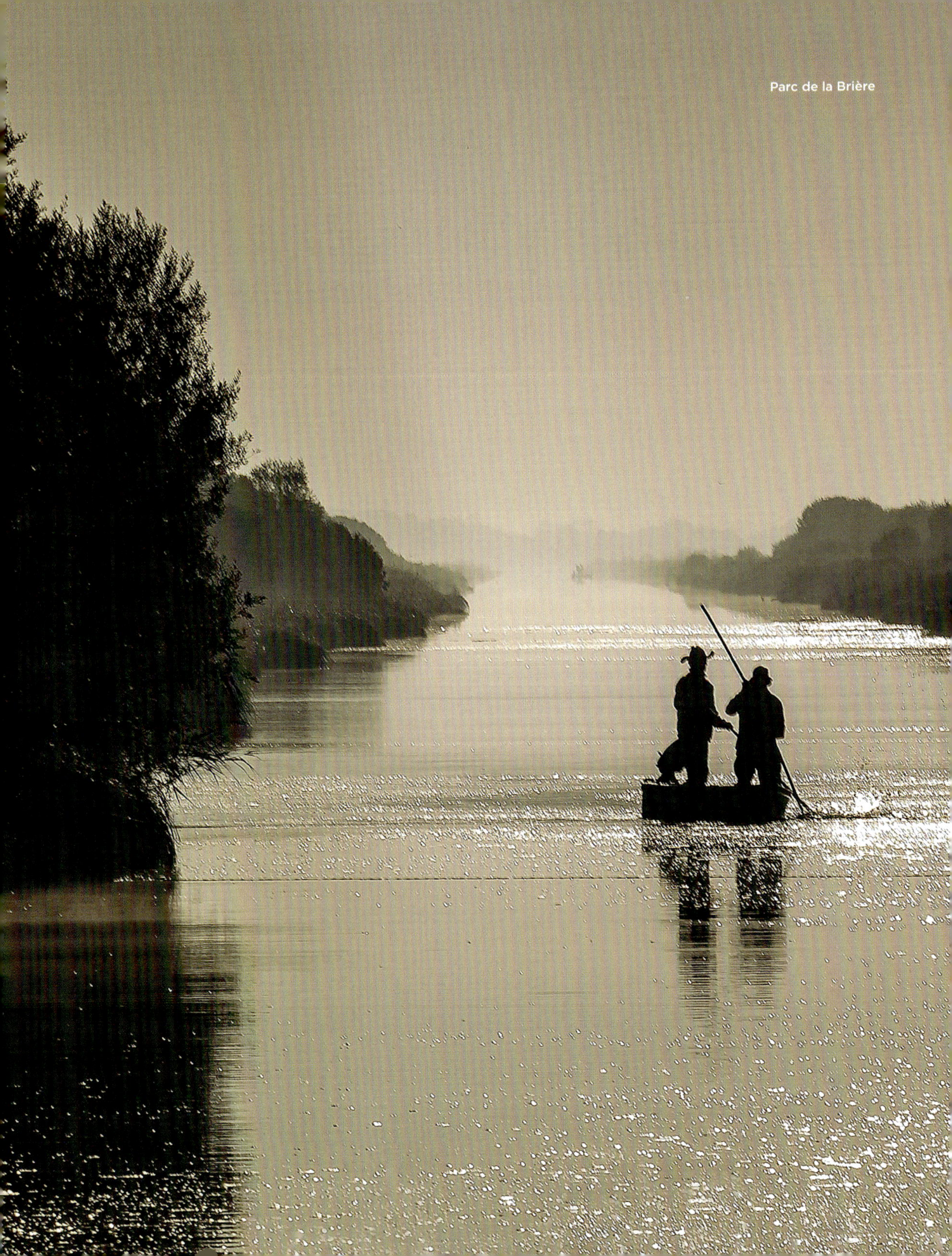
Parc de la Brière

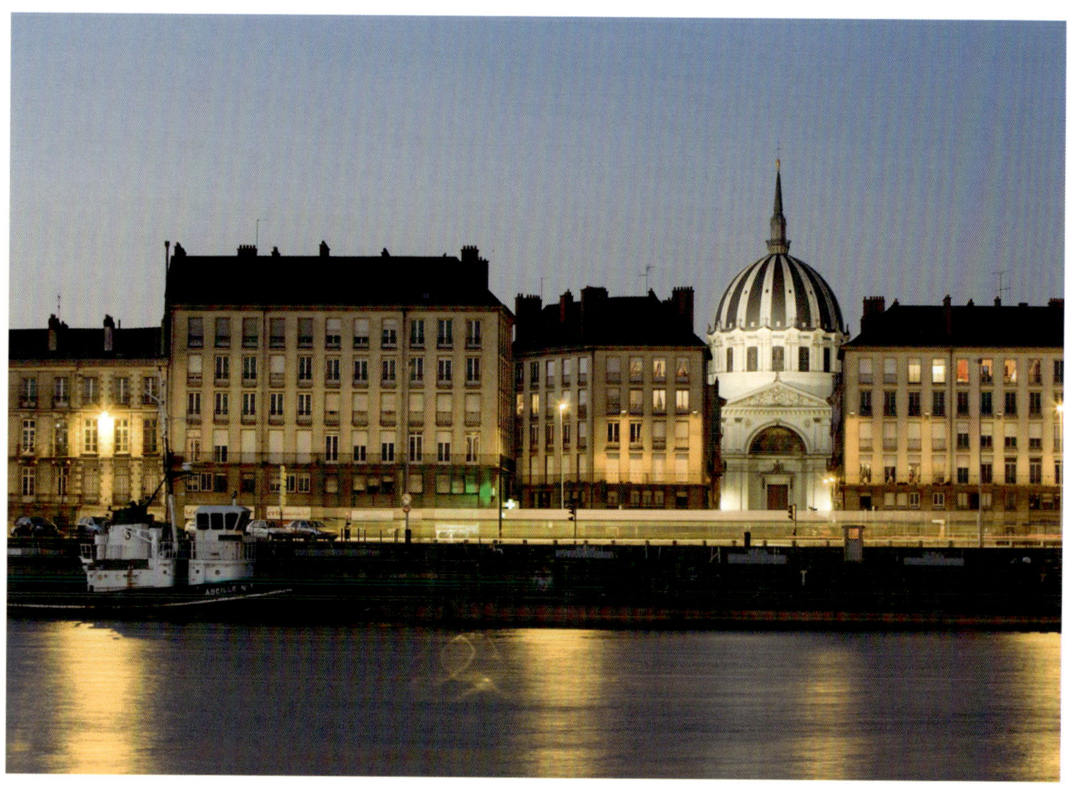

Quai de la Fosse, l'église Notre-Dame-de-Bon-Port, Nantes

Nantes

The Pays Nantais is one of the nine historic regions of Brittany. Its capital Nantes is one of the greenest cities in France: more than 100,000 trees and around 100 parks, gardens and green spaces characterise the cityscape.
Between the Loire and the sea, numerous freshwater areas form the landscape. It is crossed not only by rivers and streams, but also by canals, swamps and lakes.

Nantes

Le pays nantais est l'un des 9 pays historiques de Bretagne dont Nantes est l'une des capitales et l'une des premières villes vertes de France : plus de 100 000 arbres et une centaine de parcs, jardins et squares ponctuent le territoire.
Entre Loire et océan, cette région accueille toutes les formes d'eaux douces : fleuve, rivières, estuaire mais aussi canaux, marais et lacs.

Nantes

Das Pays Nantais ist eine der neun historischen Regionen der Bretagne. Seine Hauptstadt Nantes zählt zu den grünsten Städten Frankreichs: Mehr als 100.000 Bäume und um die 100 Parkanlagen, Gärten und Grünflächen prägen das Stadtbild.
Zwischen der Loire und dem Meer formen zahlreiche Süßwasserflächen die Landschaft. Sie wird durchschnitten von Flüssen und Bächen aber auch von Kanälen, Sümpfe und Seen.

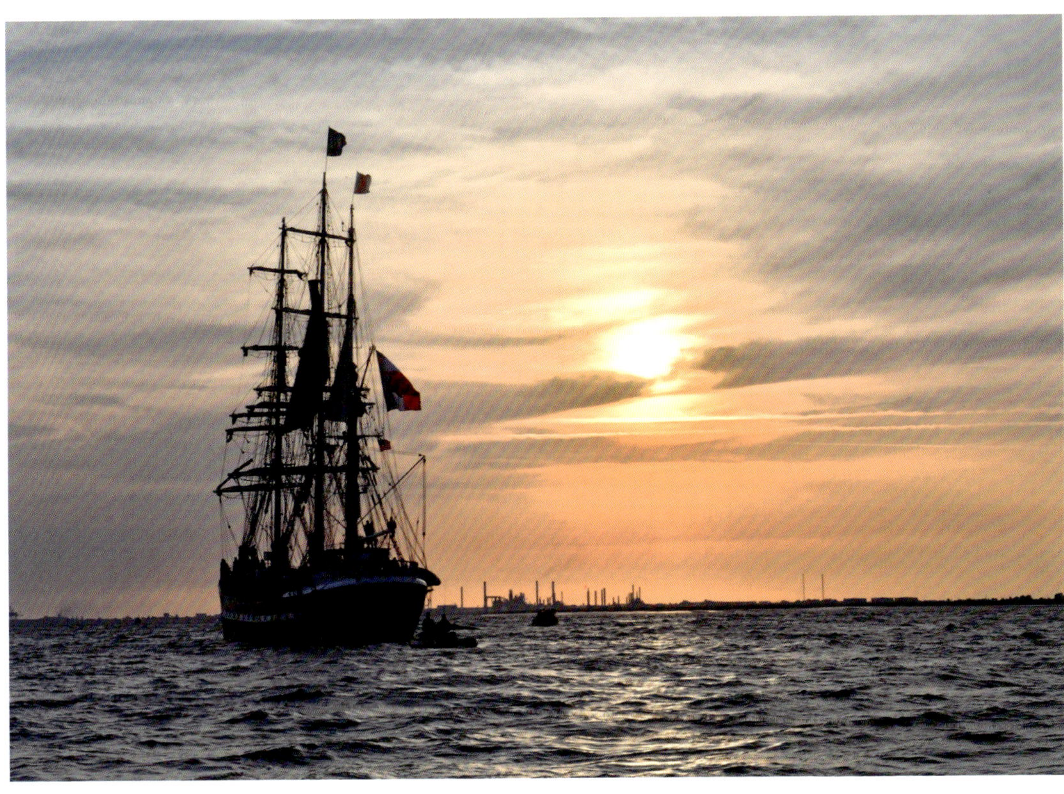

Le trois-mâts *Le Belem*, sur la Loire, Nantes

Nantes

El Pays Nantais es una de las nueve regiones históricas de Bretaña. Su capital, Nantes, es una de las ciudades más verdes de Francia: más de 100 000 árboles y alrededor de 100 parques, jardines y espacios verdes caracterizan el paisaje de la ciudad.

Entre el Loira y el mar, las numerosas zonas de agua dulce conforman el paisaje. Está atravesada por ríos y arroyos, pero también por canales, pantanos y lagos.

Nantes

O „Pays Nantais" é uma das nove regiões históricas da Bretanha. Nantes, a capital, é uma das cidades mais verdejantes da França com mais de 100.000 árvores e cerca de 100 parques, jardins e espaços verdes que caracterizam a paisagem urbana.

Entre o rio Loire e o mar existem inúmeras superfícies de água doce. A paisagem é atravessada por rios e riachos, e também por canais, pântanos e lagos.

Nantes

Het Pays Nantais is een van de negen historische regio's van Bretagne. De hoofdstad Nantes is een van de groenste steden van Frankrijk: meer dan 100.000 bomen en zo'n honderd parken, tuinen en groene ruimten bepalen het stadsbeeld.

Tussen de Loire en de zee vormen talrijke zoetwatergebieden het landschap. Het wordt doorkruist door rivieren en beken, maar ook door kanalen, moerassen en meren.

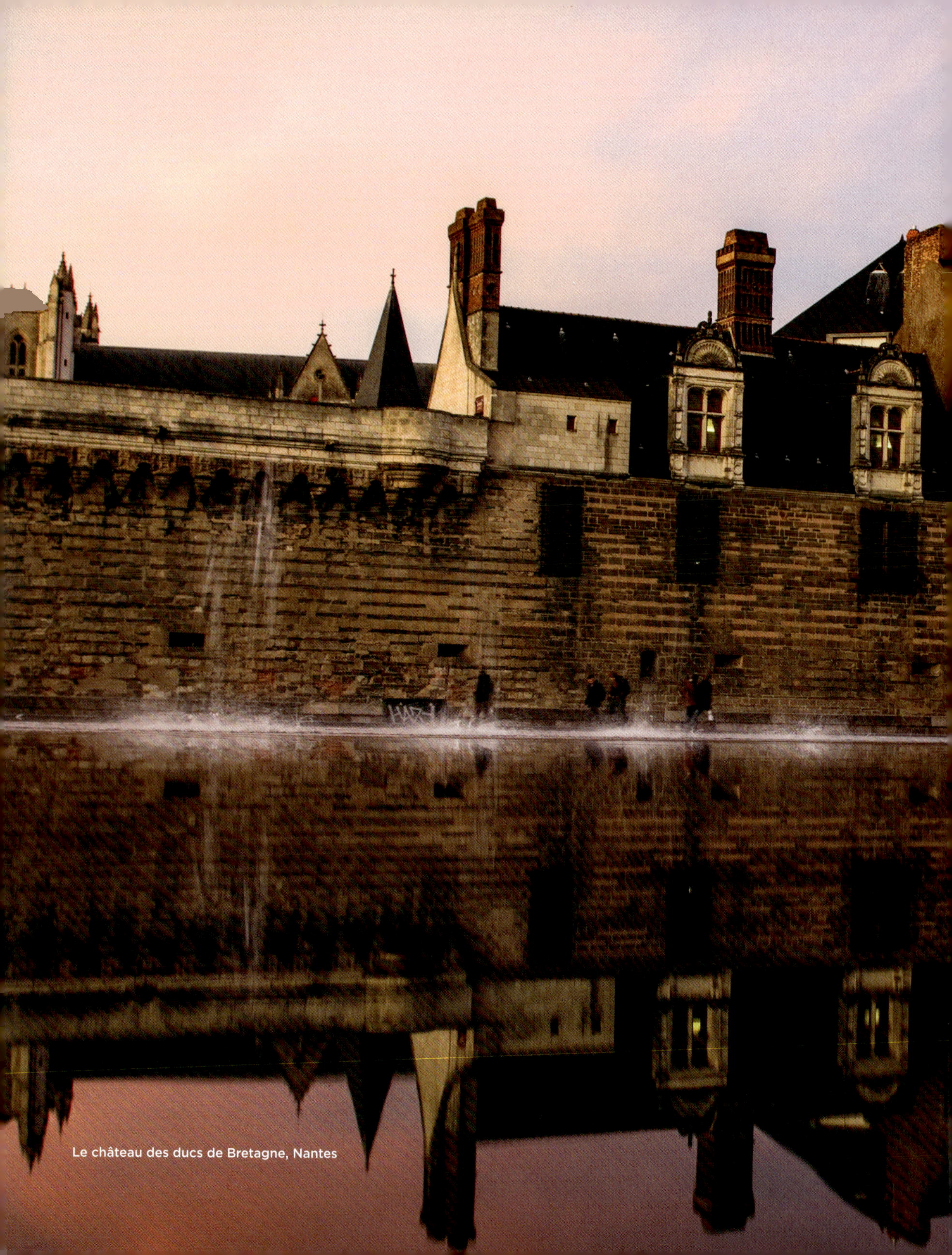

Le château des ducs de Bretagne, Nantes

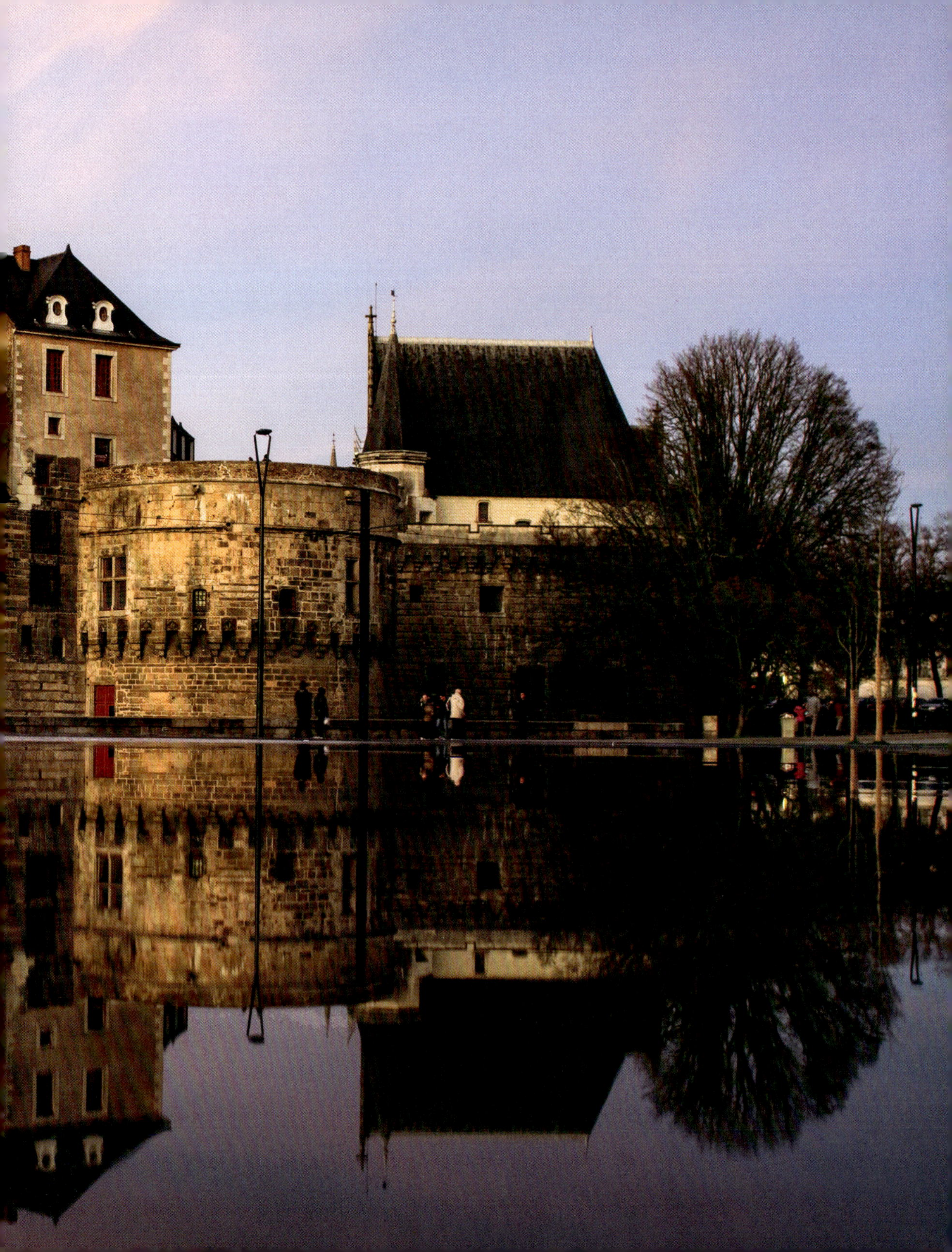

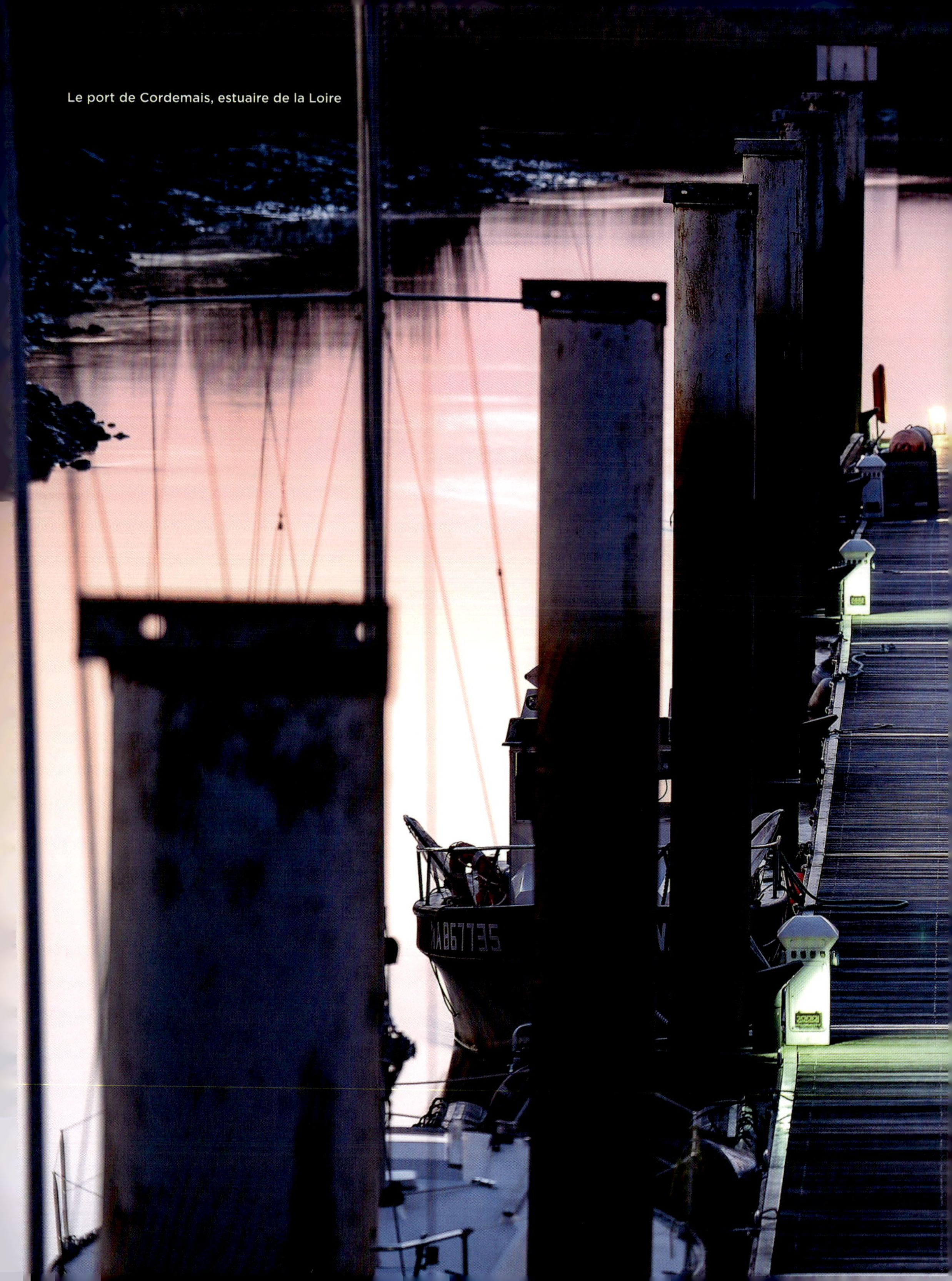

Le port de Cordemais, estuaire de la Loire

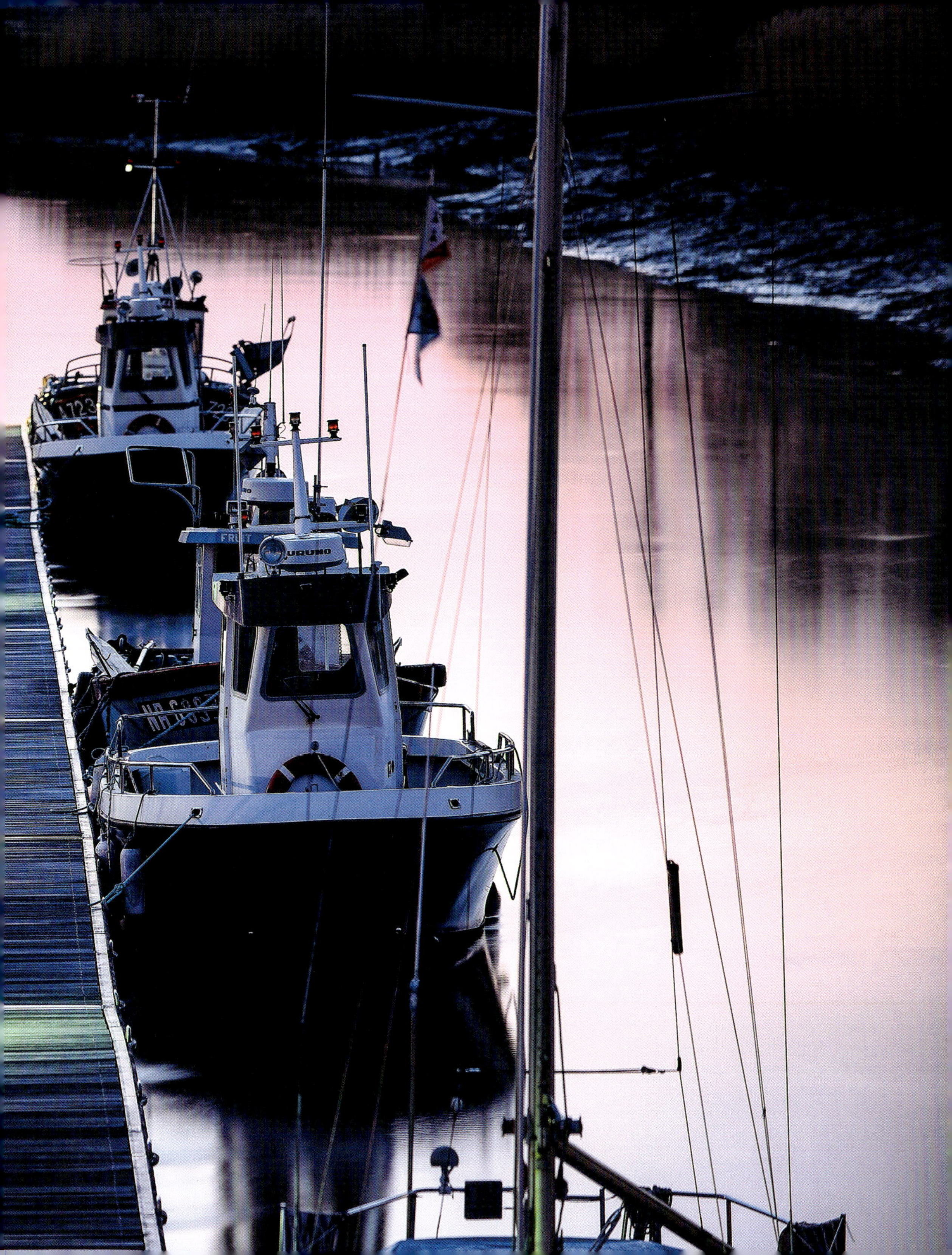

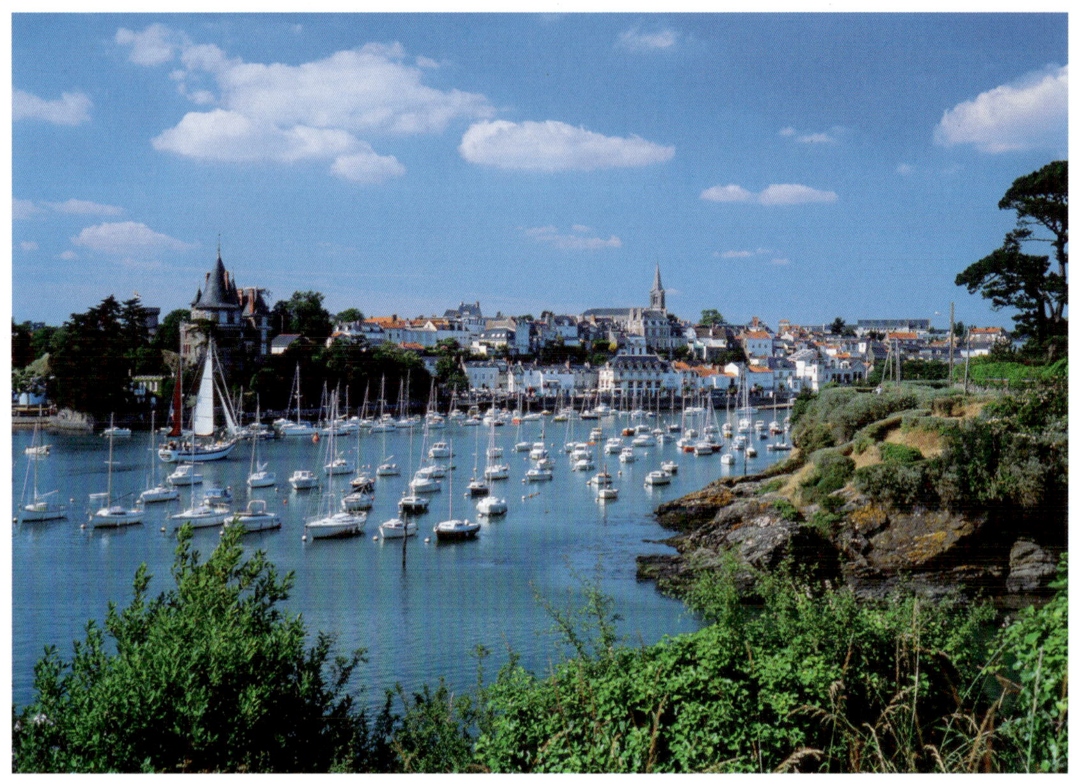

Le port de Pornic

Pornic

Pornic marks the entrance to South Brittany. The old harbour, the castle and the hiking trail along the coast make the town a beautiful stopover. This is where Brittany, the Loire and the sea meet and form a 52 km stretch of coastline lined with small coves, seaside resorts and long sandy beaches such as Saint-Brévin.

Pornic

Perle de la Côte de Jade, Pornic ouvre les portes de la Bretagne Sud avec ses grandes plages de Saint-Brevin et 52 km de littoral ponctués de criques, de plages et de petites stations balnéaires. Son vieux port, son château et son sentier côtier font de cette halte une escale de qualité au confluent de la Bretagne, de la Loire et de l'Océan.

Pornic

Pornic markiert den Eingang zur Südbretagne. Der alte Hafen, das Schloss und der Wanderweg entlang der Küste machen den Ort zu einem schönen Zwischenstopp. Hier treffen die Bretagne, die Loire und das Meer aufeinander und bilden eine 52 km langen Küstenabschnitt, der von kleinen Buchten, Badeorten und langen Sandstränden, wie bei Saint-Brévin, gesäumt ist.

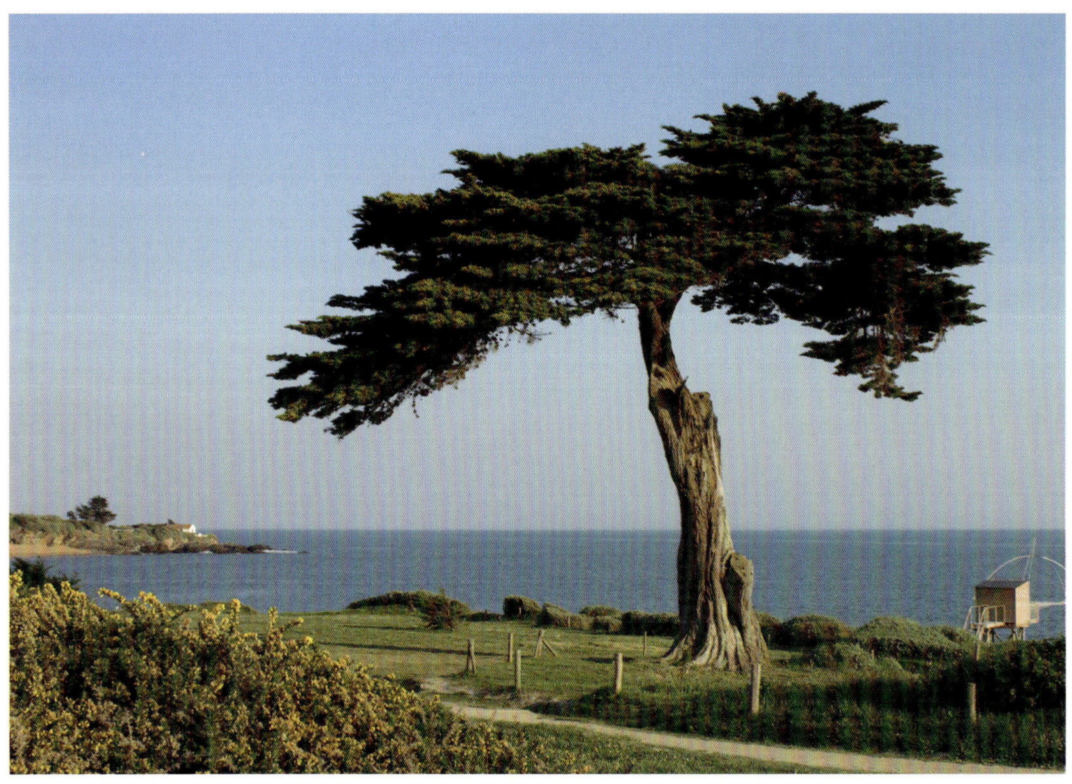

La plage du Portmain, Pornic

Pornic

Pornic marca la entrada al sur de Bretaña. El antiguo puerto, el castillo y la ruta de senderismo a lo largo de la costa hacen de este lugar una hermosa parada intermedia. Aquí es donde Bretaña, el Loira y el mar se encuentran y forman una franja costera de 52 km bordeada por pequeñas bahías, balnearios y largas playas de arena como la de Saint-Brévin.

Pornic

Pornic marca a entrada para a Bretanha do Sul. O antigo porto, o castelo e a trilha para caminhadas ao longo da costa convidam a uma paragem. É aqui que a Bretanha, o Loire e o mar se encontram e formam uma zona costeira de 52 km de extensão com pequenas enseadas, estâncias balneares e longas praias de areia como Saint-Brévin.

Pornic

Pornic markeert de ingang van Zuid-Bretagne. De oude haven, het kasteel en het wandelpad langs de kust maken de plaats tot een mooie tussenstop. Hier ontmoeten Bretagne, de Loire en de zee elkaar en vormen ze een 52 km lange kustlijn met kleine baaien, badplaatsen en lange zandstranden, zoals bij Saint-Brévin.

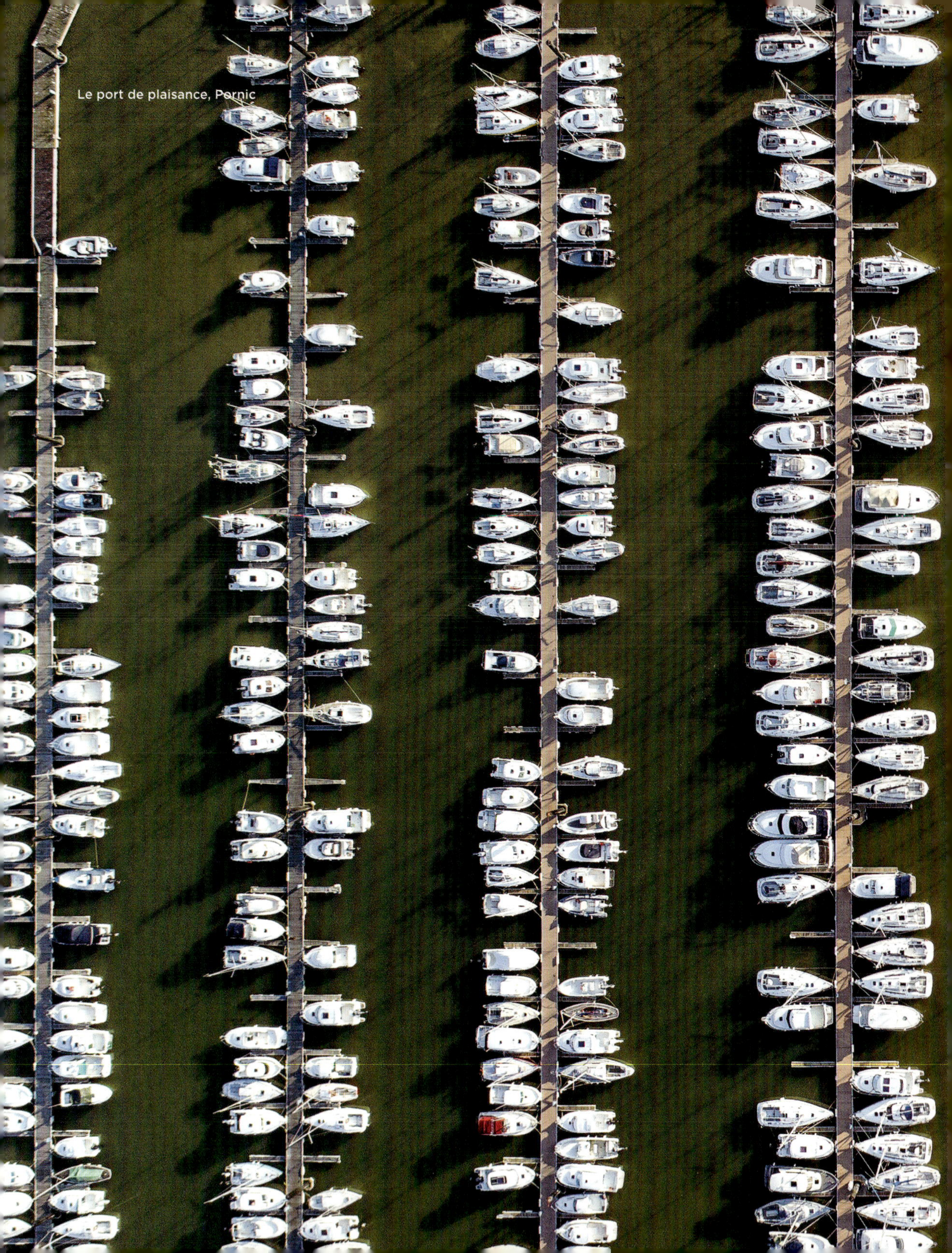

Le port de plaisance, Pornic

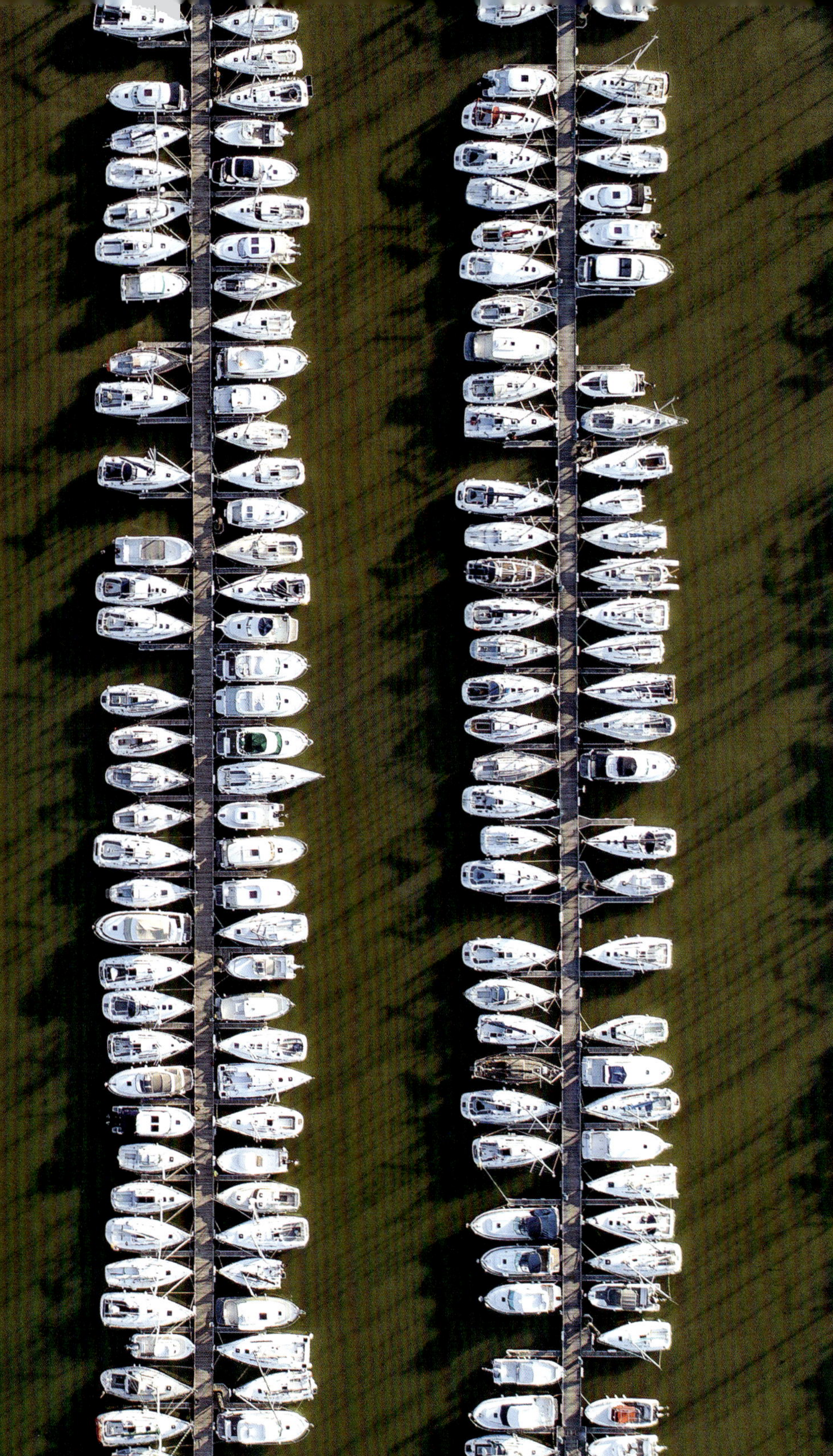

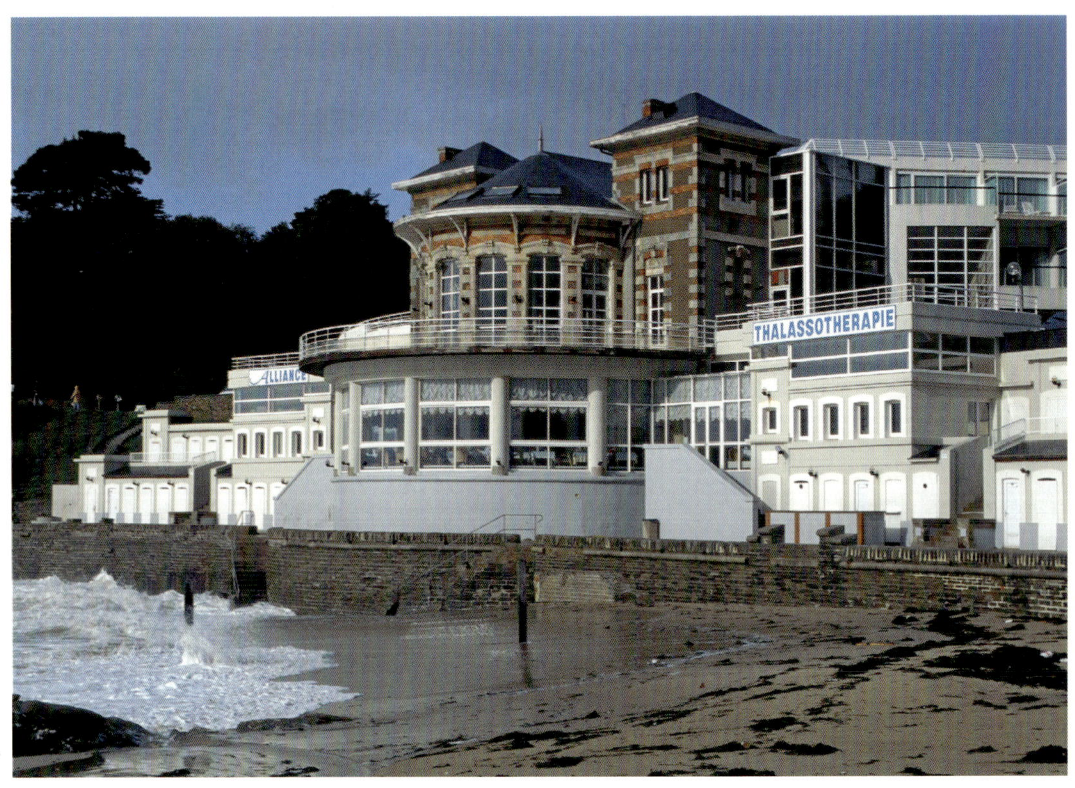

La plage de la Source, Pornic

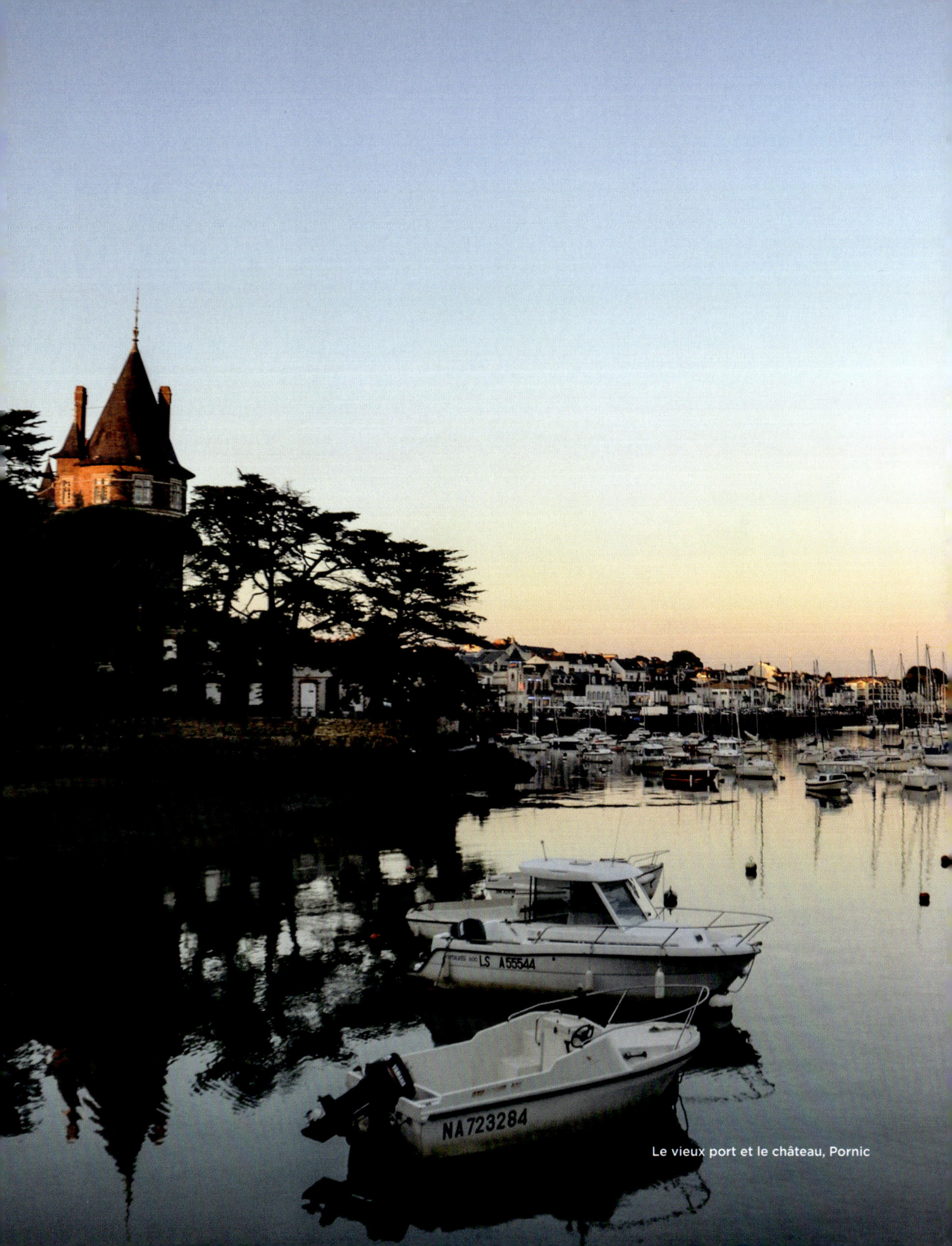

Le vieux port et le château, Pornic

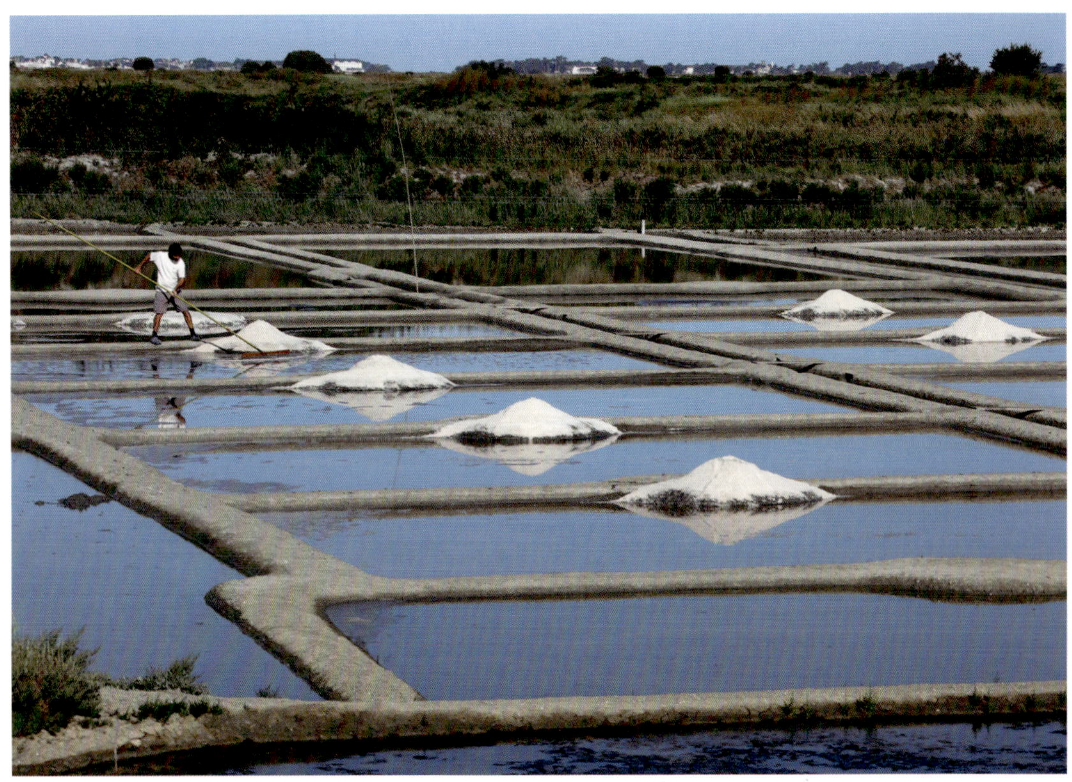

Marais salants, Guérande

The Salt Fields of Guérande

The salt fields of Guérande offer a pleasure for the eyes. A stroll will reveal an extraordinary landscape in blue, green, grey and silver tones, interspersed with the mauve of heather and the white of salt. Spread over several communities such as Guérande, Saillé or Kervalet, 10,000 tons of salt are produced here annually.

Les marais salants de Guérande

Pour le plaisir des yeux et celui de la découverte d'un paysage insolite, la promenade dans les marais salants de Guérande s'impose. Les couleurs sont exceptionnelles : bleu, vert, gris et argent auxquels s'ajoutent le mauve de la bruyère et le blanc du sel. Étendues sur plusieurs communes (Guérande, Saillé, Kervalet, etc.), 10 000 tonnes de sel sont produites chaque année.

Die Salzfelder von Guérande

Die Salzfelder von Guérande bieten einen Genuss für die Augen. Bei einem Spaziergang lässt sich eine außergewöhnliche Landschaft in blauen, grünen, grauen und silbernen Farbtönen entdecken, die vom Mauve des Heidekrautes und dem Weiß des Salzes durchsetzt ist. Verteilt auf mehrere Gemeinden, wie Guérande, Saillé oder Kervalet werden hier jährlich 10.000 Tonnen Salz produziert.

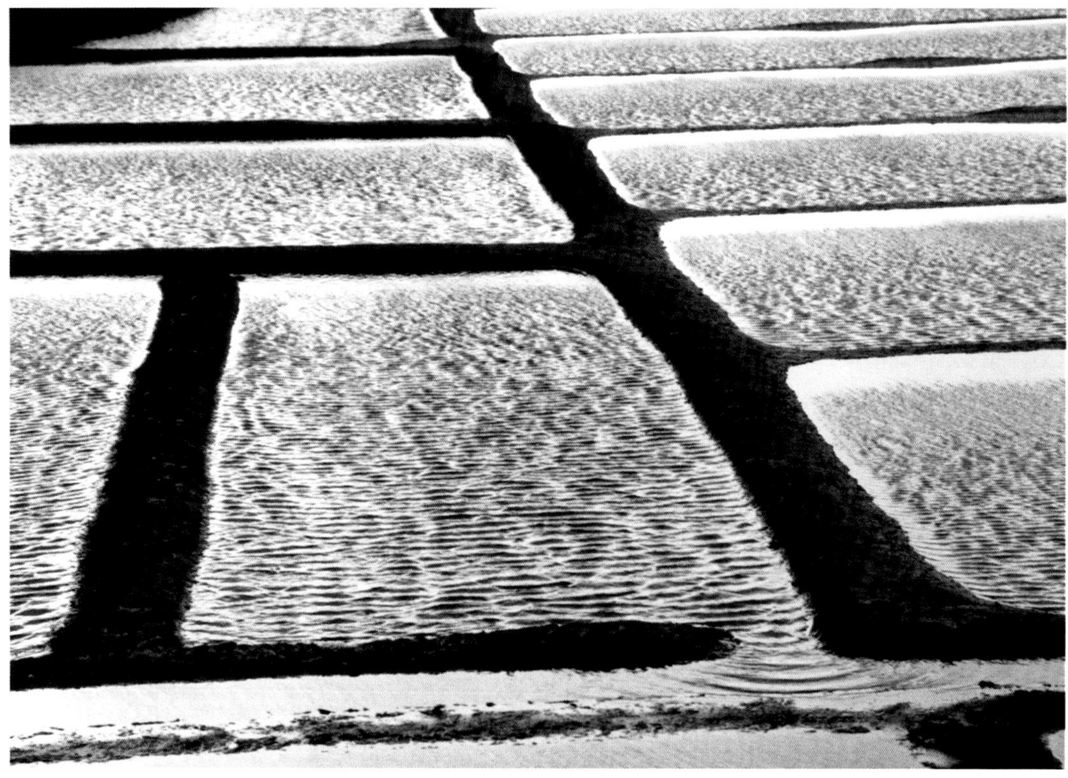

Marais salants, Guérande

Las salinas de Guérande

Las salinas de Guérande ofrecen un placer para la vista. Un paseo nos revelará un paisaje extraordinario en tonos azules, verdes, grises y plateados, intercalados con el malva de brezo y el blanco de la sal. En las salinas, repartidas en varias comunidades, como Guérande, Saillé o Kervalet, se producen 10 000 toneladas de sal al año.

As salinas de Guérande

Os campos de sal de Guérande oferecem um cenário maravilhoso. Em passeio pode-se observar uma paisagem extraordinária em tons de azul, verde, cinza e prata, intercalada com o lilás pálido da urze e o branco do sal. A produção de sal, espalhada por várias comunidades, como Guérande, Saillé ou Kervalet, atinge anualmente 10 mil toneladas.

De zoutvelden van Guérande

De zoutvelden van Guérande zijn een lust voor het oog. Tijdens een wandeling kunt u een bijzonder landschap in blauw-, groen-, grijs- en zilvertinten ontdekken, dat wordt afgewisseld door het paars van de heidestruiken en het wit van het zout. Verdeeld over meerdere gemeenschappen, zoals Guérande, Saillé en Kervalet, wordt hier jaarlijks 10.000 ton zout geproduceerd.

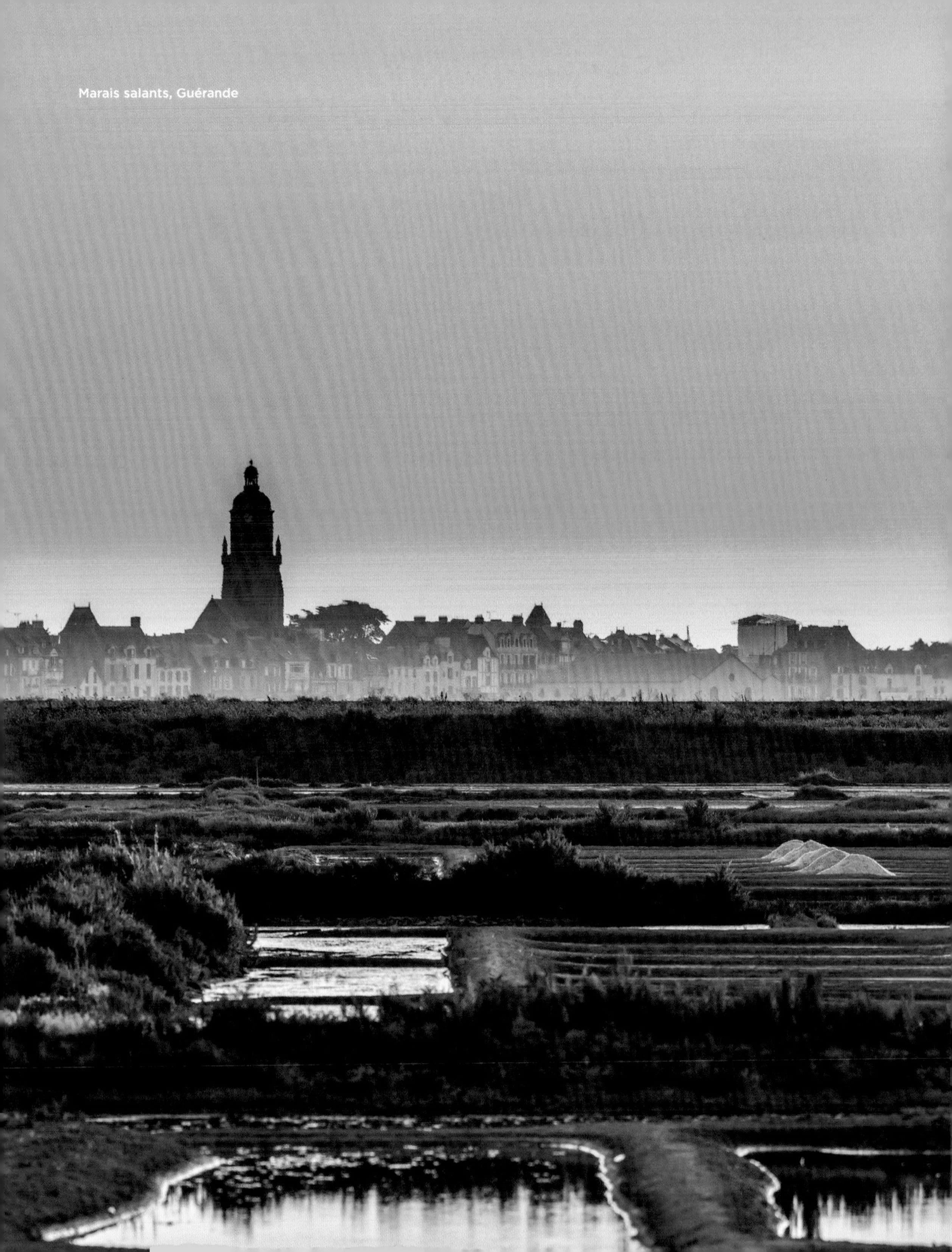

Marais salants, Guérande

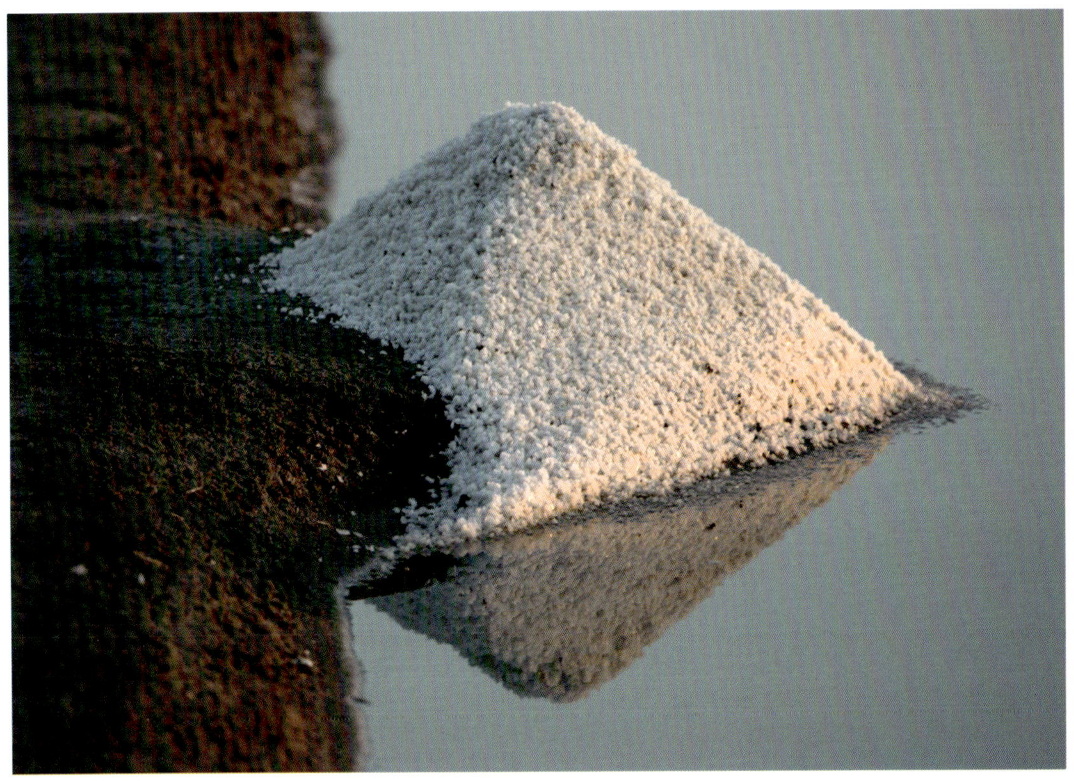
Marais salants, Guérande

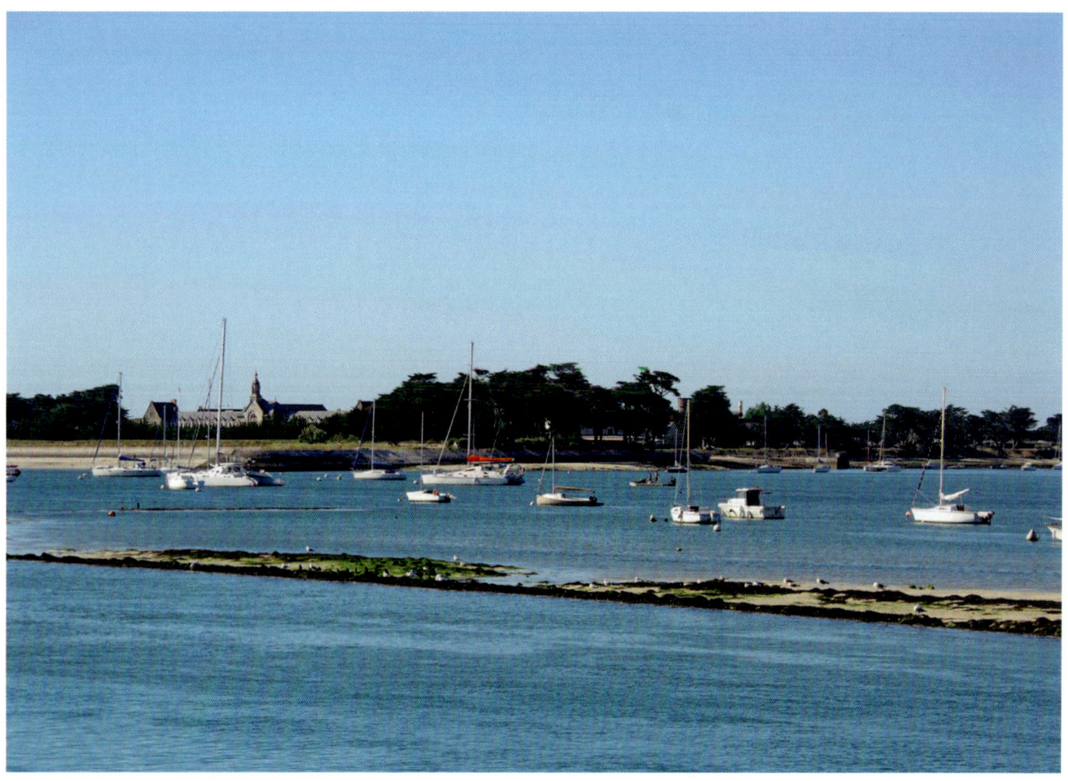

Le Croisic

Le Croisic

On the rough shore of the Guérande Peninsula lies the small fishing and yacht harbour of Le Croisic, which marks the beginning of the Breton coast. Opposite the harbour, the Pointe de Pen-Bron separates the Gulf Grand Traict from the sea, which supplies the salt fields with water.
The coastline from Port-Lin to Plage Saint-Goustan is characterised by small bays, beaches and rock formations.

Le Croisic

Installé sur la côte sauvage de la presqu'île guérandaise, Le Croisic est un petit port de pêche et de plaisance qui marque l'entrée des côtes bretonnes. Il fait face à la pointe de Pen-Bron et au Grand Traict, golfe maritime qui alimente les marais salants.
De Port-Lin à la plage de Saint-Goustan, se succèdent criques, plages et cascades de roches.

Le Croisic

Am rauen Ufer der Halbinsel Guérande liegt der kleine Fischer- und Jachthafen Le Croisic, der den Beginn der bretonischen Küste markiert. Ihm gegenüber grenzt die Pointe de Pen-Bron den Golf Grand Traict vom Meer ab, der die Salzfelder mit Wasser versorgt.
Die Küste von Port-Lin bis hin zum Plage Saint-Goustan ist geprägt durch kleine Buchten, Strände und Felsformationen.

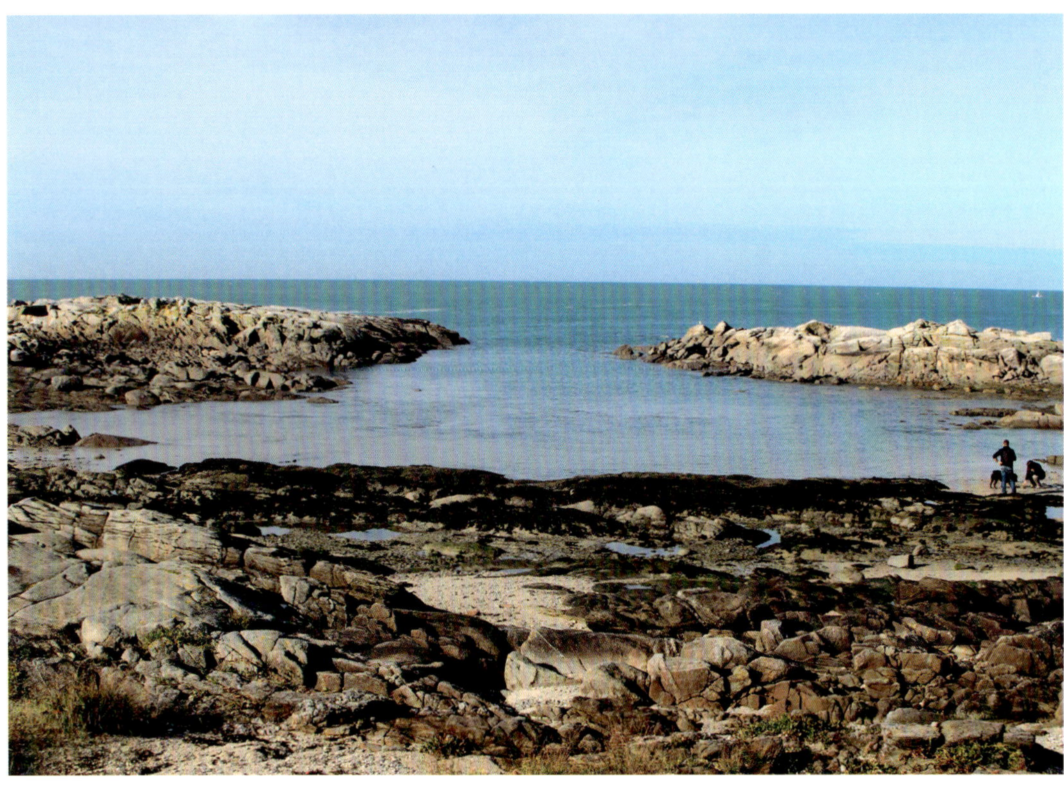

Le Croisic

Le Croisic

En la accidentada costa de la península de Guérande se encuentra el pequeño puerto pesquero y de yates Le Croisic, que marca el comienzo de la costa bretona. Frente a ella, la Pointe de Pen-Bron separa el golfo Grand Traict del mar, que abastece de agua a los campos de sal.
La costa de Port-Lin hasta la Plage Saint-Goustan se caracteriza por pequeñas bahías, playas y formaciones rocosas.

Le Croisic

Na costa agreste da península de Guérande encontra-se o pequeno porto de pesca e de recreio Le Croisic, que marca o início da costa bretã. Em frente, pode-se ver a Pointe de Pen-Bron que separa o Golf Grand Traict do mar, o qual abastece as salinas de água.
A costa que liga Port-Lin a Plage Saint-Goustan é caracterizada por pequenas baías, praias e formações rochosas.

Le Croisic

Aan de ruwe kust van het schiereiland Guérande ligt de kleine vissers- en jachthaven van Le Croisic, die het begin van de Bretonse kust markeert. Aan de overkant scheidt de Pointe de Pen-Bron de Golf Grand Traict van de zee, die de zoutvelden van water voorziet.
De kust van Port-Lin tot Plage Saint-Goustan wordt getekend door kleine baaien, stranden en rotsformaties.

KÖNEMANN

© 2019 koenemann.com GmbH
www.koenemann.com

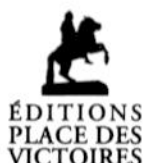

ÉDITIONS
PLACE DES
VICTOIRES

© Éditions Place des Victoires
6, rue du Mail – 75002 Paris
www.victoires.com
ISBN: 978-2-8099-1667-6
Dépôt légal: 2e trimestre 2019

Series Concept: koenemann.com GmbH

Text: Catherine Laulhère
Translations: koenemann.com GmbH
Maps: EdiCarto
Layout: Marie-Laure Miranda
Color Separation : Nord Compo

Printed in China by Shenzen Hua Xin Colour-printing & Platemaking Co., Ltd

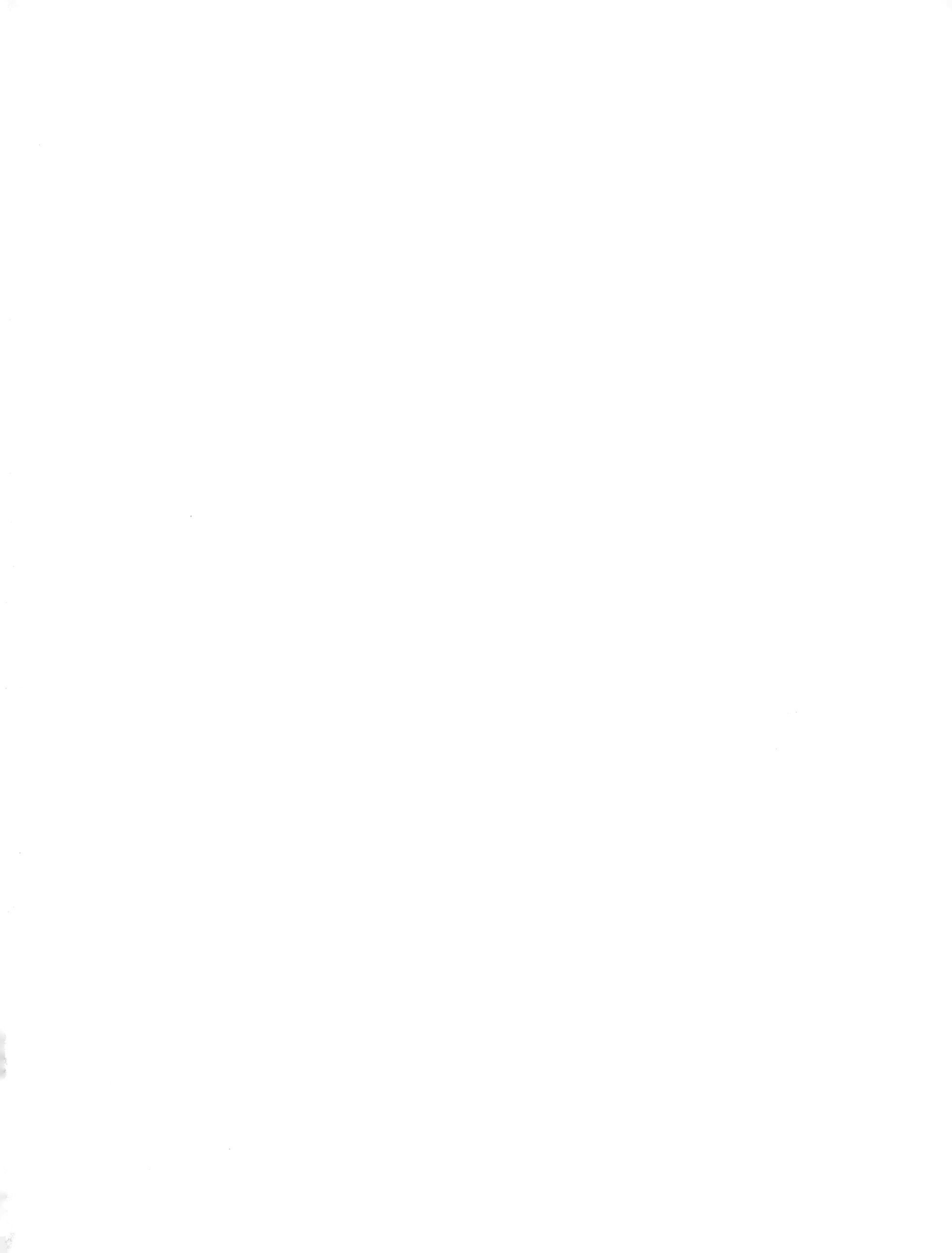